(Continued on back endsheets)

Concise Dictionary of British Literary Biography
Volume Eight

Contemporary Writers, 1960 to the Present

Concise Dictionary of British Literary Biography
Volume Eight

Contemporary Writers, 1960 to the Present

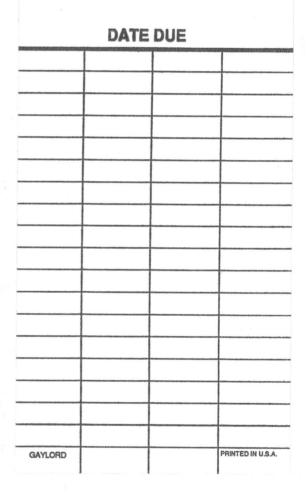

DATE DUE

GAYLORD			PRINTED IN U.S.A.

A Bruccoli Clark Layman Book
Gale Research Inc.
Detroit, London

Advisory Board for
CONCISE DICTIONARY
OF BRITISH LITERARY BIOGRAPHY

Philip Baker
Director of Curriculum
Stamford Public Schools
Stamford, Connecticut

Richard Harper
District Department Head for
Language Arts and Social Studies
Stamford, Connecticut

George Emerson
District Department Head of Media
Darien High School
Darien, Connecticut

Jack Luskay
Librarian
John Jay High School
Katonah, New York

Fay Gage
English Department Head
Darien High School
Darien, Connecticut

Margaret Montgomery
English Department Head
John Jay High School
Katonah, New York

Georgina White
English Department Head
Westhill High School
Stamford, Connecticut

Ian Willison
British Library, Retired, and
The New Cambridge Bibliography
of English Literature

Matthew J. Bruccoli and Richard Layman, *Editorial Directors*
Karen L. Rood, *Senior Editor*

Printed in the United States of America

Published simultaneously in the United Kingdom
by Gale Research International Limited
(An affiliated company of Gale Research Inc.)

The paper used in this publication meets the minimum requirements
of American National Standard for Information Sciences—Permanence
Paper for Printed Library Materials, ANSI Z39.48-1984. ∞™

ISBN 0-8103-7980-5
ISBN 0-8103-7988-0

Contents of Volume 8

Authors Included in This Series

Volume 1
Writers of the Middle Ages and Renaissance
Before 1660

Francis Bacon
Francis Beaumont & John Fletcher
Beowulf
Thomas Campion
Geoffrey Chaucer
Thomas Dekker
John Donne
John Ford
George Herbert

Ben Jonson
Sir Thomas Malory
Christopher Marlowe
Sir Walter Ralegh
William Shakespeare
Sir Philip Sidney
Edmund Spenser
Izaak Walton
John Webster

Volume 2
Writers of the Restoration and Eighteenth Century,
1660-1789

Joseph Addison
James Boswell
John Bunyan
William Congreve
Daniel Defoe
John Dryden
Henry Fielding
Oliver Goldsmith
Thomas Gray
Samuel Johnson
Andrew Marvell

John Milton
Samuel Pepys
Alexander Pope
Samuel Richardson
Richard Brinsley Sheridan
Tobias Smollett
Richard Steele
Laurence Sterne
Jonathan Swift
William Wycherley

Volume 3
Writers of the Romantic Period, 1789-1832

Volume 4
Victorian Writers, 1832-1890

Volume 5
Late Victorian and Edwardian Writers,
1890-1914

Volume 6
Modern Writers, 1914-1945

Volume 7
Writers After World War II, 1945-1960

Plan of the Work

The eight-volume *Concise Dictionary of British Literary Biography* was developed in response to requests from school and college teachers and librarians, and from small- to medium-sized public libraries, for a compilation of entries from the standard *Dictionary of Literary Biography* chosen to meet their needs and their budgets. The *DLB*, which comprises more than one hundred volumes as of the end of 1991, is moving steadily toward its goal of providing a history of literature in all languages developed through the biographies of writers. Basic as the *DLB* is, many librarians have expressed the need for a less comprehensive reference work which in other respects retains the merits of the *DLB*. The *Concise DBLB* provides this resource.

The *Concise* series was planned by an eight-member advisory board, consisting primarily of secondary-school educators, who developed a method of organization and presentation for selected *DLB* entries suitable for high-school and beginning college students. Their preliminary plan was circulated to some five thousand school librarians and English teachers, who were asked to respond to the organization of the series. Those responses were incorporated into the plan described here.

Uses for the Concise DBLB

Students are the primary audience for the *Concise DBLB*. The stated purpose of the standard *DLB* is to make our literary heritage more accessible. *Concise DBLB* has the same goal and seeks a wider audience. What the author wrote; what the facts of his or her life are; a description of his or her literary works; a discussion of the critical response to his or her works; and a bibliography of critical works to be consulted for further information: these are the elements of a *Concise DBLB* entry.

The first step in the planning process for this series, after identifying the audience, was to contemplate its uses. The advisory board acknowledged that the integrity of *Concise DBLB* as a reference book is crucial to its utility. The *Concise DBLB* adheres to the scholarly standards established by the parent series; the *Concise DBLB* is a ready-reference source of established value, providing reliable biographical and bibliographical information.

It is anticipated that this series will not be confined to uses within the library. Just as the *DLB* has been a tool for stimulating students' literary interests in the college classroom—for comparative studies of authors, for example, and, through its ample illustrations, as a means of invigorating literary study—the *Concise DBLB* is a primary resource for high-school and junior-college educators.

Organization

The advisory board further determined that entries from the standard *DLB* should be presented complete—without abridgment. The board's feeling was that the utility of the *DLB* format has been proven, and that only minimal changes should be made.

The advisory board further decided that the organization of the *Concise DBLB* should be chronological to emphasize the historical development of British literature. Each volume is devoted to a single historical period and includes the most significant literary figures from all genres who were active during that time.

The eight period volumes of the *Concise DBLB* are: *Writers of the Middle Ages and Renaissance Before 1660; Writers of the Restoration and Eighteenth Century, 1660-1789; Writers of the Romantic Period, 1789-1832; Victorian Writers, 1832-1890; Late Victorian and Edwardian Writers, 1890-1914; Modern Writers, 1914-1945; Writers After World War II, 1945-1960; Contemporary Writers, 1960-Present.*

Form of Entry

The form of entry in the *Concise DBLB* is substantially the same as in the standard series. Entries have been updated and, where necessary, corrected.

It is anticipated that users of this series will find it useful to consult the standard *DLB* for information about those writers omitted from the *Concise DBLB* whose significance to contemporary readers may have faded but whose contribution to our cultural heritage remains meaningful.

Comments about the series and suggestions for its improvement are earnestly invited.

A Note to Students

The purpose of the *Concise DBLB* is to enrich the study of British literature. Besides being inherently interesting, biographies of writers provide a basic understanding of the various ways writers react in their works to the circumstances of their lives, the events of their times, and the cultures that envelop them.

Concise DBLB entries start with the most important facts about writers: what they wrote. We strongly recommend that you also start there. The chronological listing of an author's works is an outline for the examination of his or her career achievements. The biography that follows sets the stage for the presentation of the works. Each of the author's important works and the most respected critical evaluations of them are discussed in *Concise DBLB*. If you require more information about the author or fuller critical studies of the author's works, the references section at the end of the entry will guide you.

Illustrations are an integral element of *Concise DBLB* entries. Photographs of the author are reminders that literature is the product of a writer's imagination; facsimiles of the author's working drafts are the best evidence available for understanding the act of composition—the author in the process of refining his or her work and acting as self-editor; dust jackets and advertisements demonstrate how literature comes to us through the marketplace, which sometimes serves to alter our perceptions of the works.

Literary study is a complex and immensely rewarding endeavor. Our goal is to provide you with the information you need to make that experience as rich as possible.

Acknowledgments

This book was produced by Bruccoli Clark Layman, Inc. Karen L. Rood is senior editor for the *Dictionary of Literary Biography* series. David Marshall James was the in-house editor.

Production coordinator is James W. Hipp. Projects manager is Charles D. Brower. Photography editors are Edward Scott and Timothy C. Lundy. Layout and graphics supervisor is Penney L. Haughton. Copyediting supervisor is Bill Adams. Typesetting supervisor is Kathleen M. Flanagan. Systems manager is George F. Dodge. The production staff includes Rowena Betts, Teresa Chaney, Patricia Coate, Janet Connor, Gail Crouch, Margaret McGinty Cureton, Bonita Dingle, Mary Scott Dye, Denise Edwards, Sarah A. Estes, Robert Fowler, Avril E. Gregory, Ellen McCracken, Kathy Lawler Merlette, John Myrick, Pamela D. Norton, Jean W. Ross, Laurrè Sinckler-Reeder, Thomasina Singleton, Maxine K. Smalls, Jennifer C. J. Turley, and Betsy L. Weinberg.

Walter W. Ross and Henry Cuningham did library research. They were assisted by the following librarians at the Thomas Cooper Library of the University of South Carolina: Jens Holley and the interlibrary-loan staff; reference librarians Gwen Baxter, Daniel Boice, Faye Chadwell, Jo Cottingham, Cathy Eckman, Rhonda Felder, Gary Geer, Jackie Kinder, Laurie Preston, Jean Rhyne, Carol Tobin, Virginia Weathers, and Connie Widney; circulation-department head Thomas Marcil; and acquisitions-searching supervisor David Haggard.

Concise Dictionary of British Literary Biography
Volume Eight

Contemporary Writers, 1960 to the Present

Concise Dictionary of British Literary Biography

Anthony Burgess

(25 February 1917 -)

This entry was updated by Geoffrey Aggeler (University of Utah) from his entry in
DLB 14: British Novelists Since 1960: Part One.

SELECTED BOOKS: *Time for a Tiger* (London: Heinemann, 1956);

The Enemy in the Blanket (London: Heinemann, 1958);

English Literature: A Survey for Students, as John Burgess Wilson (London: Longmans Green, 1958);

Beds in the East (London: Heinemann, 1959);

The Doctor Is Sick (London: Heinemann, 1960);

The Right to an Answer (London: Heinemann, 1960; New York: Norton, 1962);

One Hand Clapping, as Joseph Kell (London: Peter Davis, 1961); as Anthony Burgess (New York, Knopf, 1972);

Devil of a State (London: Heinemann, 1961; New York: Norton, 1962);

The Worm and the Ring (London: Heinemann, 1961);

A Clockwork Orange (London: Heinemann, 1962; New York: Norton, 1963);

The Wanting Seed (London: Heinemann, 1962; New York: Norton, 1963);

Inside Mr. Enderby, as Joseph Kell (London: Heinemann, 1963); enlarged as *Enderby*, as Anthony Burgess (New York: Norton, 1968);

Honey for the Bears (London: Heinemann, 1963; New York: Norton, 1964);

The Eve of St. Venus (London: Sedgewick & Jackson, 1964; New York: Norton, 1970);

Language Made Plain, as John Burgess Wilson (London: English Universities Press, 1964);

as Anthony Burgess (New York: Crowell, 1965);

Malayan Trilogy, as John Burgess Wilson (London: Heinemann, 1964)—includes *Time for a Tiger, The Enemy in the Blanket*, and *Beds in the East*; republished as *The Long Day Wanes: A Malayan Trilogy*, as Anthony Burgess (New York: Norton, 1965);

Nothing Like the Sun: A Story of Shakespeare's Love Life (London: Heinemann, 1964; New York: Norton, 1964);

Here Comes Everybody: An Introduction to James Joyce for the Ordinary Reader (London: Faber & Faber, 1965); republished as *Re Joyce* (New York: Norton, 1965);

A Vision of Battlements (London: Sedgewick & Jackson, 1965; New York: Norton, 1966);

Tremor of Intent (London: Heinemann, 1966; New York: Norton, 1966);

The Novel Now: A Student's Guide to Contemporary Fiction (London: Faber & Faber, 1967; New York: Norton, 1967);

Enderby Outside (London: Heinemann, 1968);

Urgent Copy: Literary Studies (London: Cape, 1968; New York: Norton, 1969);

Shakespeare (London: Cape, 1970; New York: Knopf, 1970);

MF (London: Cape, 1971; New York: Knopf, 1971);

Joysprick: An Introduction to the Language of James Joyce (London: Deutsch, 1973; New York: Harcourt Brace Jovanovich, 1975);

photograph by Mark Gerson

Napoleon Symphony (New York: Knopf, 1974);
The Clockwork Testament; Or Enderby's End (London: Hart-Davis, MacGibbon, 1974; New York: Knopf, 1975);
Beard's Roman Women (New York: McGraw-Hill, 1976);
ABBA ABBA (Boston: Little, Brown, 1977);
Ernest Hemingway & His World (New York: Scribners, 1978);
1985 (Boston: Little, Brown, 1978);
Man of Nazareth (New York: McGraw-Hill, 1979);
Earthly Powers (New York: Simon & Schuster, 1980);
The End of the World News: An Entertainment (London: Hutchinson, 1982; New York: McGraw-Hill, 1983);
On Going to Bed (London: Abbeville Press, 1982);
This Man and Music (New York: McGraw-Hill, 1983);

Enderby's Dark Lady or No End to Enderby (London: Hutchinson, 1984);
Ninety-Nine Novels: The Best in English Since 1939: A Personal Choice (London: Allison & Busby, 1984);
The Kingdom of the Wicked (London: Hutchinson, 1985);
Flame into Being: The Life and Work of D. H. Lawrence (London: Heinemann, 1985);
Cyrano de Bergerac (London: Hutchinson, 1985);
The Pianoplayers (London: Hutchinson, 1986);
Blooms of Dublin: A Musical Play Based on James Joyce's Ulysses (London: Hutchinson, 1986);
But Do Blondes Prefer Gentlemen? Homage to Qwert Yuiop, and Other Writings (London: Hutchinson, 1986; New York: McGraw-Hill, 1986);
Little Wilson and Big God: Being the First Part of the Autobiography (New York: Weidenfeld & Nicolson, 1986; London: Heinemann, 1987);
A Clockwork Orange: A Play with Music Based on His Novella of the Same Name (London: Hutchinson, 1987);
They Wrote in English (London: Hutchinson, 1988);
Any Old Iron (New York: Random House, 1989; London: Hutchinson, 1989);
The Devil's Mode: Stories (New York: Random House, 1989; London: Hutchinson, 1989);
You've Had Your Time: Being the Second Part of the Confessions of Anthony Burgess (New York: Grove Weidenfeld, 1990; London: Heinemann, 1990).

TRANSLATIONS: Michel de Saint-Pierre, *The New Aristocrats* (London: Gollancz, 1962);
Jean Pelegri, *The Olive Trees of Justice* (London: Sidgwick & Jackson, 1962);
Jean Servin, *The Man Who Robbed Poor Boxes* (London: Gollancz, 1965);
Edmund Rostand, *Cyrano de Bergerac* (New York: Knopf, 1971);
Sophocles, *Oedipus the King* (Minneapolis: University of Minnesota Press, 1972).

Widely regarded as one of the foremost contemporary fiction writers in English, Anthony Burgess began his long and prolific literary career while living in Malaya during the late 1950s. In 1949 he had written a fictional account of his wartime experiences in Gibraltar, but this did not appear until 1965 as *A Vision of Battlements*. He started writing fiction during his Malayan years "as a sort of gentlemanly hobby, because I knew there wasn't any money in it." At the time, he was an education officer with the British Colonial Service, and the fiction he was writing included realistic portrayals of actual events and personalities. Since it was regarded as indiscreet for one in his position to have such fiction published under his own name, he adopted the nom de plume "Anthony Burgess," which consists of his confirmation name and his mother's maiden name. His full name, which he seldom uses, is John Anthony Burgess Wilson.

Abundantly reflected in Burgess's fiction is his Roman Catholic background, which is part of an ancient regional and family heritage. He comes from an old Lancashire family whose Catholic heritage reaches back through centuries. Like other Catholic families, his forebears suffered severely for their faith during the penal days of the Reformation, and one of Burgess's ancestors, also named John Wilson, was martyred during the reign of Elizabeth I. Moreover, being Catholic, the family lost what land it possessed. Its later history parallels that of other steadfastly Roman Catholic Lancashire families. During the English Civil War, it "hid its quota of undistinguished Royalist leaders in Lancashire cloughs, and supported the Pretenders after 1688." Burgess renounced Catholicism at about age sixteen, but the renunciation gave him little joy. Although intellectually he was convinced that he could be a freethinker, emotionally he was very much aware of hell and damnation, and to some extent he still is.

His most persistent youthful ambition was to become a composer, and when he entered the University of Manchester, he wanted to study music. However, lacking the science background required by the music department, he had to take English language and literature instead. His personal tutor, whom he admired, was Dr. L. C. Knights, author of *Drama and Society in the Age of Jonson*, coeditor of *Scrutiny*, and one of the leading exponents of New Criticism. Through Knights, Burgess met critic F. R. Leavis and came under his influence, as well as that of I. A. Richards. He was struck by their method, which enabled one to assess a novel critically by close analysis and explication of the text.

Burgess managed to get through the required courses at Manchester without much effort, but he tended to neglect subjects other than English. The energy he failed to spend on course work he poured into editing the university magazine, the *Serpent*, and into the dramatic society. Unlike many of his contemporaries, who were involved in some form of political activity, he had no interest in politics. The university's Socialist society had no more appeal for him than its Fascist society, and he maintained, as he has maintained since about age fourteen, a stance neither radical nor conservative nor anything but "just vaguely cynical." This point of view manifests itself in his fictional conflicts between "Pelagians" and "Augustinians."

While at Manchester, he met a Welsh girl, Llewela Isherwood Jones, a distant cousin of Christopher Isherwood. Four years younger than Burgess, she was an economics honors student at the university. They were married in 1942, and the marriage lasted until her death in 1968, after many years of severe illness.

In October 1940, after taking his degree, Burgess joined the British army and was assigned to the Royal Army Medical Corps. He was then sent to join a small entertainment group as a pianist and arranger. The group, all of whose members except Burgess had been professional entertainers, gave concerts at camps and lonely batteries, relieving the boredom of soldiers who were sick of the "phoney war." Then in 1943, having been transferred to the Army Education Corps, he was sent to Gibraltar, where he remained until 1946. The story of Richard Ennis in *A Vision of Battlements* is "pretty close to my own story." Like Ennis, Burgess lectured to the troops and taught them useful skills, such as map reading and foreign languages. Unlike Ennis, however, he was involved with army intelligence in cipher work. It was a frustrating, dreary time for him. He composed a good deal of music, including a symphony and a concerto, but very little literature. Burgess's first year on Gibraltar was made especially miserable by the news that his wife was hospitalized in London with severe injuries. She had been assaulted on the street by American GIs, deserters bent on robbery, who had beaten her and caused her to abort the child she was carrying. In time Burgess overcame the consuming rage he had felt initially against all American soldiers, but his horror of the action itself, senseless male violence against a defenseless woman, remained undiminished. Clearly, this horror was the inspiration for the most shocking scene in *A Clockwork Orange* (1962), the brutal assault on the writer and his wife, as well as the woman-beating incidents in *The Right to an Answer* (1960).

After his discharge from the army in 1946, Burgess's career oscillated between music and teaching. For a time he was a pianist with a little-

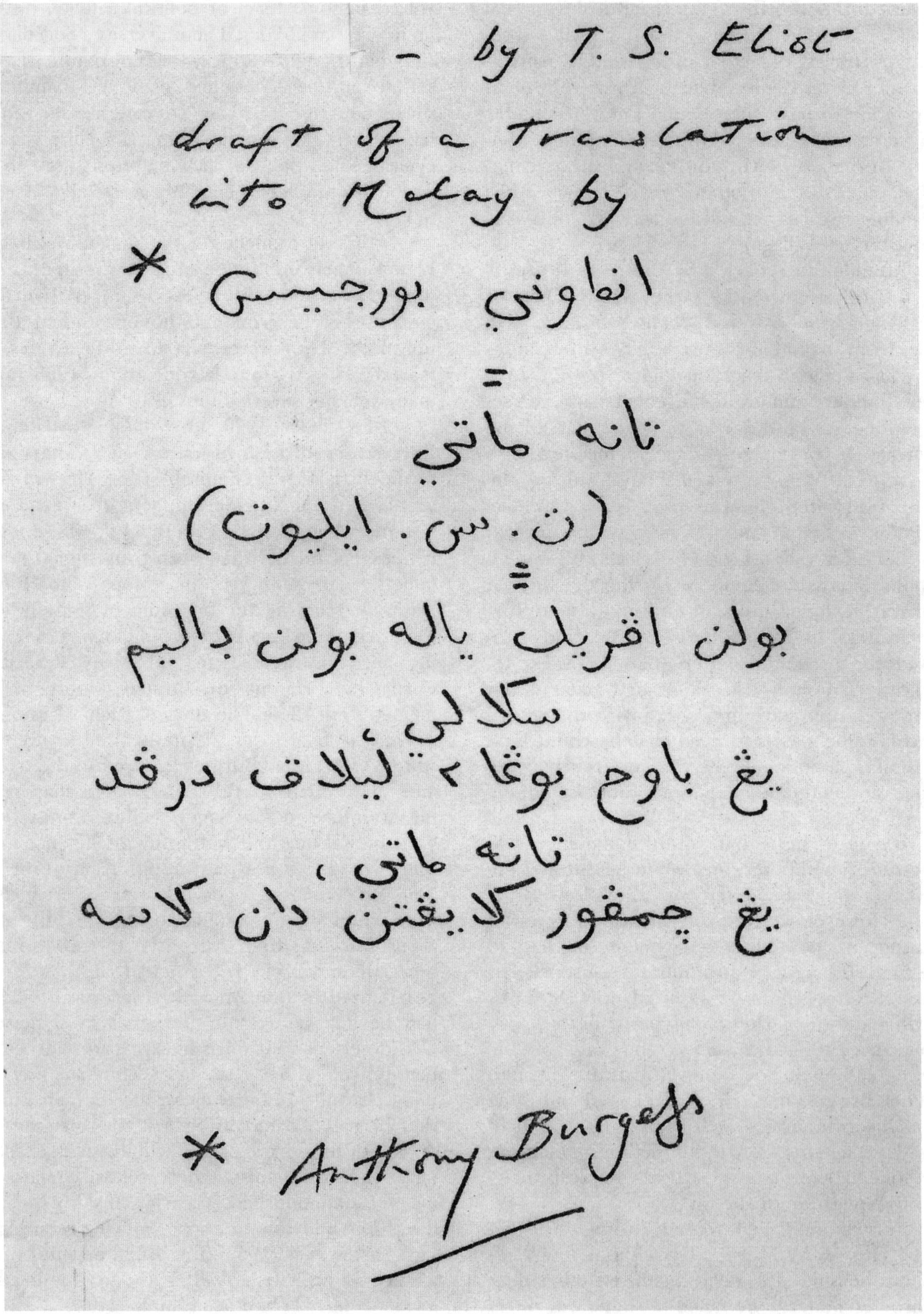

– by T. S. Eliot

draft of a translation
into Malay by

* انطاوني بورجيسي

=

تانه ماتي

(ن . س . ايليوت)

بولن اقريب ياله بولن داليم
سلالي
يغ باوح بوڠا٢ لَيلاق درقد
تانه ماتي ،
يغ چمڤور کايڠتن دان کاسه

* *Anthony Burgess*

Draft of Burgess's translation of The Waste Land *into Malay*

known jazz combo in London and did arrangements for Eddie Calvert, "the Man with the Golden Trumpet." Then he became a civilian instructor at an army college of education, a lecturer in an emergency-training college for potential teachers, and finally a senior master in a grammar school in Banbury, Oxfordshire, where he remained for four years.

The situation of grammar school teachers was, as he says, "ghastly beyond belief in those days." Negotiations were going on for a new salary scale, but nothing came of them, and Burgess's salary was so wretched that he found it "increasingly impossible to live." His dismal situation was essentially the same as that of Christopher Howarth in *The Worm and the Ring* (1961). Discouraged and desperate, he kept applying for jobs to better himself. Then one night in a drunken stupor, he "quite unconsciously" scrawled out an application for a teaching post in Malaya. He was subsequently offered a post on the staff of a public school for Malays in Kuala Kangsar, Malaya, which he accepted with little hesitation.

Burgess found Malaya a fascinating, indeed fantastic, cultural and linguistic mélange, and he was eager to record what he saw. As a musician, his first impulse was to orchestrate it, and he actually composed a symphony in which the different ethnic groups reveal themselves in snatches and strains. But the symphony was not well received, and he sought another medium. The resultant oeuvre, the *Malayan Trilogy* (1964), may be likened to a symphony or a giant canvas upon which Burgess has painted portraits representing most of the generic types he knew. He introduces Malays, Tamils, Sikhs, and Eurasians, as well as a collection of largely maladapted British colonials. The vocabulary of the novel is enriched by the addition of numerous words and expressions in Malay, Urdu, Arabic, Tamil, and Chinese. A glossary is included in the back of the book, but, as he does in *A Clockwork Orange*, Burgess weaves the strange vocabulary into the context so the meaning is readily apparent.

The trilogy—*Time for a Tiger* (1956), *The Enemy in the Blanket* (1958), and *Beds in the East* (1959)—is unified by the setting in Malaya and by the presence of Victor Crabbe, a young British schoolmaster who has come to the Far East in search of a new life. Like Richard Ennis of *A Vision of Battlements* and other Burgess protagonists, Crabbe is guilt-ridden (oppressed by the memory of a wife he accidentally drowned in an English

river), and, like many of the protagonists, he feels the inexplicable pull of a darker civilization. Crabbe's presence links the trilogy, but because the scope of the book is much broader than any individual, he is primarily a witness. Attention is focused mainly on the people he meets and their experiences, which reveal the heart of Malaya itself.

Time for a Tiger concerns the hilarious trials and adventures of a gigantic colonial police lieutenant named Nabby Adams, whose raison d'être is alcoholic drink, preferably "Tiger" beer. As his name suggests, by its closeness to Nabi Adam (Arabic for "the prophet Adam"), Nabby is a true son of Adam, for within the thematic framework of the novel he represents the condition of man. He helps introduce Crabbe to the East and reconciles him to "going forward," despite his name. Nabby has already achieved what Crabbe longs for: acceptance by, indeed absorption into, the East.

As Burgess introduces Malaya through the experiences of these and other characters, he reveals some of the reasons why the British raj must pass. Crabbe and his new wife and, to an extent, Nabby Adams gain the affection and respect of segments of the native population, but they do so at the expense of alienating the rest of the British community. Most of the British colonials are content to remain in lofty isolation from the native community. The native Malayans have little reason to love the British, but they do have reasons to be grateful to them. For one thing, the British provide protection against the Communist guerrillas who infest the jungle. Also, the British promote, albeit unwittingly, some degree of interracial harmony. The Chinese, Indians, and Malays despise each other, but the British presence gives them a unity of resentment. Unfortunately, the departure of the British will immediately liberate the old racial antagonisms. Crabbe's school is a microcosm of Malaya and a vision of its dismal future, but Crabbe is a liberal optimist, a believer in human reasonableness, and it will be a long time before he finally begins to lose hope that racial strife will yield to reason.

The problems of adjustment to a darker civilization are dealt with lightly in *Time for a Tiger*. Crabbe chooses to "let down the side" (fraternize with the natives), and Nabby Adams drowns himself in Tiger beer. In *The Enemy in the Blanket*, Burgess deals with more complex cases, shifting the scene to a different Malayan state and introducing a "very white man," an albinistic lawyer named Rupert Hardman. At the time of

Crabbe's arrival in the state to take a new teaching post, Hardman is about to become reluctantly absorbed into the Islamic culture. Hardman's experience shows how Islam might lose its enchantment for an Englishman, as it once did for Burgess himself, even if he has much to gain by embracing it. Under desperate financial pressure, Hardman decides to marry 'Che Normah, a fiery, voluptuous, and wealthy Malay widow who has been attracted by his "very white" skin, indisputable proof of his racial identity and his status as a professional man. Unfortunately for Hardman, who derives no pride from being an albino, she is also a strong-willed and orthodox Muslim. His "very white" skin and his profession are about the only vestiges of his former self she will permit him to retain.

Although Burgess does not focus exclusively on colonials in this novel—he is as much or more concerned with presenting the native community—there are other colonials who take up considerable attention and who provide a great deal of hilarity. One is Talbot, a fat, moon-faced creature who exhibits the same devotion to food that Nabby Adams has to drink. As with Nabby, most of Talbot's sexual drives seem to have been either rechanneled or replaced by the demands of other viscera. He is perpetually gorging himself, but far more nauseating than his gluttony is his lyric poetry, in which he celebrates the pleasures of the table. His wife, Ann, clings desperately to her sanity chiefly by means of affairs with other men; inevitably she and Crabbe have an affair. Ann is a small, dark-haired girl, physically resembling Crabbe's dead wife. One of the means whereby Crabbe placates his former wife's "unquiet ghost" is making love to vague images of her, such as Ann Talbot. This practice drew him earlier into an affair with a Malay divorcée, and he hopes to find his dead wife reincarnated again and again as he becomes absorbed into Malaya.

In his new academic position as head of a college, Crabbe must supervise the teaching of Malayans, Indians, Chinese, Tamils, and Eurasians. This is trying enough, but he must also contend with the vigorous hostility of some subordinates, including a not-very-bright Tamil senior master who had been bribed with the promise of the headship before Crabbe's appointment and who intrigues ceaselessly against him. The Tamil finds an unwitting ally in Hardman, who indiscreetly mentions Crabbe's undergraduate leftist activities at the English university they had both attended.

This revelation leads to the resurrection of Crabbe's Marxist juvenilia in old issues of the student magazine and their circulation in typed copies among members of the staff and community. With the Communist guerrillas still at their bloody work in the jungles, such relics of youth could be troublesome for Crabbe. But the smears of his enemy are not the worst threat. Thanks to the thievery of his Chinese cook, Crabbe has actually been feeding the guerrillas. Oddly enough, these dangerously embarrassing associations are part of an incredible chain of accidents that eventually ingratiate him with the natives. His undergraduate utopianism proves attractive to some members of the faculty who are supposed to be scandalized, and a large group of Communist guerrillas surrenders to Crabbe, considering him their benefactor. It is one of the few times in the trilogy that he is actually able to do something for Malaya. For the most part, he has no real control over events, and, all his benevolent efforts notwithstanding, he can only watch the coming of independence with helpless concern, unable to make any meaningful contribution.

The good fortune that makes Crabbe temporarily a hero of the people allows him to continue in his liberal optimism. As the novel concludes, he is preparing to take a new assignment, an important administrative post in which he hopes to accomplish something before he is replaced by a Malayan. His wife leaves him with his memories, just as Talbot's wife leaves him with his food and poetry, and Hardman makes an unlucky escape from 'Che Normah—unlucky in that the plane Hardman pilots to freedom apparently crashes.

Beds in the East, the last novel of the trilogy, begins with a description of a Malay family arising on one of the last days of British rule; it concludes with a description of a lovely Tamil girl wiping away a tear for the dead Victor Crabbe as she is pulled onto a ballroom floor. Nearly all of the novel is concerned with native Malayans, members of groups Burgess has introduced briefly in the first two books. For them it is the "dawn of freedom," an illumination of the problems of freedom. As anticipated, the only change in interracial relationships is an intensifying of mutual hostilities.

Before his death, itself partly a result of interracial hostility, Crabbe engages in benevolent activities that are little appreciated, including a daring attempt to promote interracial harmony by bringing together members of the principal ethnic groups at a cocktail party. The party is a hilarious disaster, but then a scheme potentially more effective for promoting racial amity presents itself in the form of an eighteen-year-old Chinese boy who is a bona fide musical genius. The boy is, Crabbe feels, capable of becoming Malaya's answer to Jean Sibelius and Manuel de Falla, someone capable of giving Malaya what Burgess had tried to give it, a musical monument. This benevolent scheme, like all of his others, is destined to fail, but thanks to his violent death, Crabbe is spared complete knowledge of the failure.

Throughout the trilogy Crabbe has yearned for the wife he had left dead at the bottom of an English river, and his yearning quest for her finally ends upcountry in an unbearable reunion of revelation that shatters all his illusions about his relationship with her. This is followed by a watery destruction he had shunned since her death. His disillusionment and death must inevitably arouse our pity and perhaps a degree of fear as well, since he is typical of the bulk of enlightened, well-meaning but ineffectual humanity. In presenting Crabbe's destruction, Burgess has clearly intended to evoke pitying laughter rather than tragic purgation; Crabbe and his dreams are devoured—perhaps by a crocodile or the river itself—while Malaya, in the form of a Tamil veterinarian, stands by in studied unconcern.

Although Burgess might have become a major novelist without going to Malaya and writing the trilogy, the importance of this experience in his development as a novelist was in many ways analogous to the importance of *Endymion* (1818) in John Keats's development as a poet. His success in capturing so much of Malaya's cultural variety in an extended piece of fiction seems to have been a tremendous impetus for him toward writing other fiction dealing with other worlds he either knew or imagined. He also had the encouragement of perceptive critics.

Burgess enjoyed his teaching in Malaya in spite of a tendency to clash with administrative superiors. After a quarrel with one headmaster he was assigned to Malaya's east coast as a senior lecturer in a teacher-training college. Then in 1957 Malaya gained its independence, and the future of British expatriates grew doubtful. Shortly thereafter the Malayan government generously provided each erstwhile colonial with a sum of money and then deported him. Burgess soon found another teaching post in Brunei, Borneo. Despite the favorable reception of his Malayan books, he viewed himself not primarily as a novel-

Burgess teaching at City College of New York, autumn 1972

ist, but as a professional teacher who simply wrote novels "as a kind of hobby."

In Borneo, as in Malaya, Burgess refused to join the British colonials in their isolation from the native community. His perfect command of Malay and genuine interest in the people enabled him to mix freely with them, and, at the expense of antagonizing his fellow colonial officers, he won their trust and respect. This relationship led to an invitation to lead the people's Freedom party, which he refused. Even so, rumors about his loyalty began to circulate within the British community, and he was stuck with the appellation "bolshy." The antagonism of his fellows and superiors was further augmented by an incident during a garden party in honor of Prince Philip, who was in Brunei on an official visit. As the prince wandered dutifully from group to group, he inquired casually about local conditions: "Everything all right?" All the dazzled colonials replied appropriately that indeed everything was as it should be—all, that is, except Burgess's fiery

Welsh wife, who, according to rumors, was supposed to be British socialist Aneurin Bevan's sister. She replied bluntly and insultingly that "things bloody well weren't all right," and that, moreover, the British were largely to blame. After this episode, Burgess's days in Brunei would probably have been few even without the physical breakdown that finally sent him back to England. Not long after the garden party, Burgess was giving his students a lecture on phonetics when he suddenly collapsed on the floor of the classroom. He now suspects that it was "a willed collapse out of sheer boredom and frustration." Whatever the cause, with incredible dispatch he was loaded aboard an airliner for England, where doctors at the National Hospital for Nervous Diseases diagnosed his ailment as a brain tumor. The neatness with which he was thereby eliminated as a source of official embarrassment in Borneo leads him to guess that his hasty removal had as much to do with his general intransigence and the garden-party incident as with his collapse on the classroom floor.

The political situation in Borneo was now among the least of his worries. The existence of the brain tumor had been determined primarily on the basis of a spinal tap, which revealed an excess of protein in the spinal fluid. Other excruciating tests followed. Initially, the doctors considered removing the tumor, and Burgess was apprehensive, lest "they hit my talent instead of my tumor," but they then decided that removal was impossible. Burgess was told he would probably be dead within the year, but that if he managed to live through the year, he could infer that the prognosis had been excessively pessimistic and that he would survive. His situation was extremely dismal in that he had no pension, was unable to get a job, and saw no way of providing for his prospective widow. Fortunately, they had been able to bring a bit of money with them from the Far East. His wife, Llewela, having graduated in economics from the University of Manchester, was knowledgeable in money matters, and she shrewdly invested on the stock exchange the one thousand pounds they had taken out of Malaya. The stock exchange was a free organization in those days; one could buy and sell on margins, and, in a few years, she had doubled, then quadrupled, the original sum. The initial sum enabled them to live through the year, from 1959 into 1960, that Burgess had been told would be his last. Instead of moping about in self-pitying depression, he began writing novels, chiefly to se-

cure posthumous royalties. Surprisingly, he felt more exhilarated than depressed, and his "last year on earth" was one of the most productive he has ever known. The five novels he produced— *The Doctor Is Sick* (1960), *One Hand Clapping* (1961), *The Worm and the Ring* (1961), *The Wanting Seed* (1962), and *Inside Mr. Enderby* (1963)— include some of his best work, and they were not the only things he wrote. Thus he launched himself as a professional novelist under less than favorable and quite accidental circumstances. But, as he says, "most writers who actually do become novelists do so by accident. If a man deliberately sets out to become a novelist, he usually winds up as a critic, which is, I think, something less."

His productivity astonished the critics and, paradoxically, alarmed his publisher, Heinemann. The fecundity of writers such as Charles Dickens, Anthony Trollope, and Henry James had long been forgotten in England, where there was an unfortunate trend to believe that writers of quality followed the example of E. M. Forster and produced a canon of perhaps four or five books over a period of eighty to ninety years. Fecundity, Burgess found, was looked upon as a kind of literary disease. His publisher suggested that he conceal the malady by taking another pseudonym, so that *One Hand Clapping* and *Inside Mr. Enderby* (one of his comic masterpieces) were published under the name Joseph Kell. But the two books were not widely reviewed and sold poorly, mainly because no one had ever heard of Joseph Kell. (Since then both novels have been republished profitably under the name Anthony Burgess.) A comical result of the Kell business was that Burgess was asked to review one of his own novels. The editor who sent him the book did not know that he was Joseph Kell. Appreciating what he took to be the editor's sense of humor, Burgess wrote the review—and was never again allowed to write for that journal.

As the novels came out, his health improved steadily, and he began to take various nonfiction writing chores as well. For a time he was both music critic for *Queen*—a British magazine read in the United States—and drama critic for the *Spectator*. One of the trials of this dual role was being dogged by spies assigned "to see whether I really saw an opera and a play on the same night." He also wrote television scripts, including one on Percy Bysshe Shelley and George Gordon, Lord Byron, in Switzerland and another on James Joyce. Other projects included a play written at the request of the Phoenix Theatre, London; another one for the BBC; and still another for Independent TV, as well as a new translation of Hector Berlioz's *L'Enfance du Christ* (1854). In addition he was becoming more and more in demand as a book reviewer, and his average yearly output in reviews alone was estimated by one reporter at 150,000 words. But Burgess was and is primarily a writer of fiction, and most of his boundless energy during the early 1960s went into the writing of novels. He also wrote some short fiction and, although he finds the short story a constricting form, contributed a sizable quantity of stories to the *Hudson Review, Argosy, Rutgers Review*, and other periodicals. He also contributed verse to various periodicals, including the *Transatlantic Review, Arts and Letters*, and the *New York Times*; the latter commissioned him to write a poem on the landing of Apollo 11.

He has never, however, remained rooted to his writer's chair. Always restless, he has traveled a great deal, and so far as his fiction is concerned, one of his most productive trips was a visit to Leningrad in 1961. His purpose in going "was to experience life in Leningrad without benefit of Intourist—i.e., as one of the crowd." Before the trip he spent about six weeks reviving his Russian, acquired during the war; his use of the language enabled him to gain a great deal from the experience. One of his first discoveries in Russia was that it was possible to enter the country without a passport. One simply left the ship long after everyone else, after the immigration officials had gone off duty. If one were really willing to live dangerously, one could also reap a tidy profit selling smuggled Western goods. One could smuggle a man out of the country by securing a deluxe cabin with a bathroom in which he could be hidden. Burgess actually did some of these things himself or heard about others who had succeeded in doing them. On top of all this, he found that one could get to know the secret police on a friendly basis. Late one evening these stock villains of Western spy thrillers were kind enough to take Burgess home, drunk, in one of their cars. This and other experiences finally led him to conclude that "the Russian soul is all right; it's the state that's wrong."

One of the fruits of this hair-raising "research" was *Honey for the Bears* (1963), a hilarious entertainment in which an unconsciously homosexual ("gomosexual") antiques dealer goes to Russia to sell smuggled dresses and in the process loses his wife to a lesbian. Another product was *A Clockwork Orange*, a seriously philosophical picaresque tale narrated by a demonic young hoodlum who could be either Russian or English or both. Burgess and his wife encountered some of his prototypes late one evening outside a Leningrad restaurant. As they were finishing their meal, they were startled to hear loud hammering at the door. Having been filled with the usual Western propaganda, they immediately had the terrifying thought that the hammerers were after them, the capitalist enemy. In fact, these hard-fisted young toughs, called "stilyagi," were after different prey. When the Burgesses wanted to leave the restaurant, the stilyagi courteously stepped aside, allowed them to pass, and then resumed their hammering. Burgess was struck by the Nabokovian quality of the incident, the way in which their conduct reflected the "chess mind": "Even lawless violence must follow rules and ritual." He was also struck by their resemblance to the English teddy boys of the 1950s whom they were copying, and he went home with an even sturdier conviction that "Russians are human." (When he described this incident during a recent lecture, he accidentally said "Humans are Russian," but he would not correct the slip, considering it ben trovato.)

As time passed and his "terminal year" receded, he became less worried about his own health but more about his wife's. She had never fully recovered from the injuries she received in 1943, and the years in the Far East had been hard on her. She died in 1968 of portal cirrhosis, brought on partly by alcoholism but mainly by years of vitamin deprivation in Malaya and Borneo. Although there was little Burgess could do to ease the pain of her last years, he was still burdened with a strong residue of guilt about her death, and this conflict may be reflected in one of his novels, *Beard's Roman Women* (1976).

Some months after his first wife's death, he married a lovely, dark-haired Italian *contessa*, Liliana Macellari, whom he had known for several years. She is a philologist and translator whose works include Italian translations of Thomas Pynchon's *V* (1963) and Lawrence Durrell's *Alexandria Quartet* (1962). Burgess finds the latter project "hard to forgive," not because of the quality of her translation, but because he considers the original hardly worth translating, especially into Italian, which he knows and reveres.

With their son Andrea, the Burgesses moved to Malta in 1969, where they lived, between lecture tours and a teaching stint in North Carolina, for nearly two years. They soon found that the island had little to recommend it besides its Mediterranean climate. The repressive rule exercised by a church-dominated government made life exceedingly dreary if not intolerable. Yet during his brief, unhappy residence on the island, Burgess managed to produce two books: a biography of William Shakespeare (1970) and the novel *MF* (1971), which is set in the United States and a tyrannically ruled Caribbean island called "Castita." The striking resemblance this supposedly chaste little island bears to Malta would appear to be more than coincidental.

In 1971 Burgess and his wife purchased a flat in Rome (the flat that appears in *Beard's Roman Women*) and acquired a house in the nearby lakeside town of Bracciano (the house that appears in the conclusion of *MF*). Between tours and visits abroad, they lived alternately in the two residences until 1976. Although they found the atmosphere in Rome a good deal more civilized and bearable than that of Malta, after five years they felt compelled to move again. Italy, Burgess believed, was on the verge of civil war. There was a state of general chaos, prices were rising intolerably, and shortages were becoming more than irksome. In addition there was the omnipresent danger of his son Andrea being kidnapped, since Italians tend to believe that all foreigners, especially foreign writers, are rich and capable of paying high ransoms. To escape these nuisances and threats, Burgess moved his family to Monaco.

Although Burgess has been a professional writer for many years, he still does a considerable amount of teaching. He has taught widely in the British Commonwealth and Europe as well as in the United States, and he is fairly impressed by the quality of American students "from a human point of view": "They're good and sincere, aspirant and very different from their parents. They do question everything. But it worries me that they lack basic equipment. They haven't read very widely. I don't mind their cutting themselves off from the 1930s or '40s, but I do object to their cutting themselves off from the Roman and Hebraic civilizations which made our own. It means that if one is giving a lecture on Shakespeare or Marlowe, one cannot take it for granted that they know who Niobe was, or Ulysses, or Ajax. And this is undoubtedly going to get worse in America; may indeed lead to the entire cutting off of America from the whole current of culture which gave it birth. A man like Benjamin Franklin, a great American, may become

an unintelligible figure to modern Americans. This is very frightening." He objects as well to the utilitarian view of literature held by many American students, their insistence that it is to be valued primarily in terms of the "messages" it conveys, and their concomitant tendency to regard a purely aesthetic aim as "irrelevant," "sinful," or "reactionary."

Though he enjoys university teaching, he does not see himself as an intellectual ("If I am one, I'm fighting against it all the time"). He does not want to become too much a part of the rarified, cerebral campus atmosphere in which the enwombed academic thrives. His attitudes stem largely from his view of the nature of literature and indeed reality itself. To some extent, he agrees with the Shakespeare/Burgess composite hero of *Nothing Like the Sun* (1964) that literature is "an epiphenomenon of the action of the flesh": "I don't think it's an intellectual thing. It's not made out of concepts; it's made out of percepts. People often think you're being trivial or superficial if you think it's important to describe a bottle of sauce or beer as neatly, as cleverly, as evocatively as you can. It's really more important to do that than to express an idea or concept. I believe the world of physical things is the only world that really exists, and the world of concepts is a world of trickery, for the most part. Concepts only come to life when they're expressed in things you can see, taste, feel, touch, and the like. One of the reasons I have a sneaking regard for the Catholic Church is that it turns everything into tangible percepts. There's no mystical communion with God as there is in Hinduism or Buddhism. Instead you get God in the form of a meal, which is right, which is good."

With regard to religion, Burgess still maintains a "renegade Catholic" stance that is oddly conservative in some respects. He despises liberal Catholicism, which seems to have become another religion in the process of gaining acceptance in the modern world. The ecumenical movement repels him, as do the liturgical changes and the use of the vernacular: ". . . when I say that I am a Catholic now, I mean solely that I have a Catholic background, that my emotions, my responses are Catholic, and that my intellectual convictions, such as they are, are very meager compared with the fundamental emotional convictions. Certainly, when I write, I tend to write from a Catholic point of view—either from the point of view of a believing Catholic, or a renegade Catholic, which is I think James Joyce's posi-

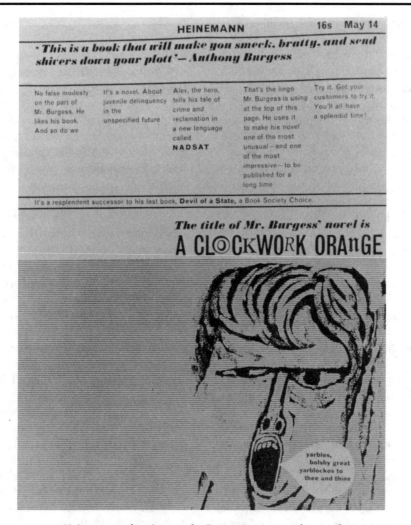

Heinemann advertisement for Burgess's most popular novel

tion. Reading *Ulysses*, you are aware of this conflict within a man who knows the Church thoroughly and yet has totally rejected it with a blasphemous kind of vigor."

To an extent, he subscribes to the Manichaean heresy, although he agrees with the church that it should be condemned as heresy. He shares the Manichaean belief that there is a perpetual conflict between two forces that dominates the affairs of the universe, and whether the forces can be accurately labeled "good" and "evil" is by no means certain. They might as reasonably be designated by terms such as "right" and "left," or "x" and "y" or even "hot" and "cold." All that is certain is that the opposed forces exist, that they are in conflict, and that earthly turmoils are relatively trivial affairs that merely "figure" the great cosmic clash. Burgess believes that the man who is aware of this conflict yet deliberately and cynically refuses to involve

himself in it is a contemptible self-server.

The five novels Burgess produced during his "terminal year" exhibit themes that he was to develop again and again—the role and situation of the artist vis-à-vis an impinging world, love and decay in the West, the quest for a darker culture, and his view of history as a perpetual oscillation or "waltz" between "Pelagian" and "Augustinian" phases.

The Pelagian-Augustinian theme is the central focus of *The Wanting Seed* (1962), Burgess's first Orwellian proleptic nightmare. The novel presents a horrifying, though richly comic, picture of life in a future world freed of the scourge of war but overpopulated beyond Thomas Malthus's most fearful imaginings. As the novel opens, it is apparent that a suffocatingly crowded England is applying what Malthus would call checks through "vice" and "improper arts." Homosexuality, castration, abortion, and infanticide are much encouraged by a desperate government. The leaders share Malthus's belief that the educated classes can be persuaded rationally while the proletariat cannot. Hence, while the state makes little attempt to sway the "proles," it seeks to influence the more "responsible" classes by education, propaganda, and social pressure. Everywhere posters blare *"It's Sapiens to be Homo."* A "Homosex Institute" offers both day and evening classes. People are able to improve their social and economic positions only if they can maintain a reputation either of "blameless sexlessness" or nonfertile sexuality. The protagonist, Tristram Foxe, misses a deserved promotion because, as a superior tells him, "A kind of aura of fertility surrounds you, Brother Foxe." Tristram has fathered a child, and, while each family is legally allowed one birth, "the best people just don't. Just don't."

But even if the "best people" can accept these inverted standards, the gods cannot. (The term "gods" is used advisedly, since Burgess's Manichaeanism is clearly evidenced in the novel.) Blights and animal diseases severely reduce the food supply. Malthus's checks through "misery" come into play in the form of famine and bloodshed. Starvation causes a total abandonment of the restraints imposed by the perverted society. People are murdered and devoured by anthropophagic "dining clubs." Frequently these cannibal feasts are followed by heterosexual orgies "in the ruddy light of the fat-spitting fires."

In a fairly short time, order is restored by a hastily created army, and it becomes apparent that the experience of cannibalism has suggested to government leaders new methods of population control. Implementation of these methods requires a re-creation of war as it had been fought long before, during the twentieth century. The objectives of the war and the character of the enemy are top secret matters, but an uninformed civilian population cheers on an equally uninformed soldiery, and only the government and civilian contractors know that the heroes are bound for a Valhalla where they will be processed for consumption. Although few people are aware of the real nature of this "warfare," there is a widely held assumption that canning makes cannibalism a relatively civilized affair. As one soldier tells Tristram Foxe, "It makes all the difference if you get it out of a tin."

The cyclical theory of history Burgess illustrates in this novel is one he had partially formu-

lated in *A Vision of Battlements.* In that novel an American officer describes how the Pelagian denial of original sin had spawned "the two big modern heresies—material progress as a sacred goal; the State as God Almighty." The former has produced "Americanism" and the latter, "the Socialist process." In *The Wanting Seed* all government history is seen to be an oscillation between Pelagian and Augustinian "phases." When a government is functioning in its Pelagian phase, or "Pelphase," it is socialistic and committed to a Wellsian liberal belief in man and his ability to achieve perfection through his own efforts. Inevitably man fails to fulfill the liberal expectation, and the ensuing "disappointment" causes a chaotic "Interphase," during which terrorist police strive to maintain order by force and brutality. Finally the government, appalled by its own excesses, lessens the brutality but continues to enforce its will on the citizenry on the assumption that man is an inherently sinful creature from whom no good may be expected. This pessimistic phase is appropriately named for the saint whose preoccupation with the problems of evil led him, like Burgess, into Manichaeanism. During "Gusphase" there is a capitalist economy but very little real freedom for the individual. What Burgess appears to be suggesting is that a Godless society that accepts Augustine's view of unregenerate human nature is apt to be a Fascist dictatorship.

In *Inside Mr. Enderby* and its sequel, *Enderby Outside* (1968), Burgess is primarily concerned with the condition of poetry and the poet in the latter half of the twentieth century. He intended *Inside Mr. Enderby* to be "a kind of trumpet blast on behalf of the besieged poet of today—the man who tries to be independent, tries to write his poetry not on the campus, but in the smallest room in the house," where he can have some privacy.

The protagonist of the Enderby novels, F. X. Enderby, is a middle-aged poet who is able to practice his art only in the monastic seclusion of his own lavatory. There, poised on the water closet, his bathtub filled with notes and rough drafts, he produces lyric poetry that is published and read with admiration by a few individuals who are still interested in poetry. His lyric gift depends to some extent on the state of prolonged adolescence he is able to maintain in his isolation. In *Inside Mr. Enderby* he emerges long enough to accept a publisher's award, which he impulsively spurns in a sudden effusion of liberal indignation, and then he returns to his water-closet study. The event has little impact on his art, but he is brought into contact with two people who are destined to exert a fatal influence on it. Vesta Bainbridge, an attractive young widow, tries to force him to mature sexually, while Rawcliffe, a ruined poet inordinately proud of the fame accruing from one short piece "in all the anthologies," jeeringly reminds him of the mortality of the lyric gift. Under these and other pressures, Enderby eventually loses his gift, and the recognition of his loss causes him to attempt suicide. The attempt leads him into the benevolent hands of psychiatrists who seek to rehabilitate him by changing his identity. The fact that the psychiatrists are succeeding as *Inside Mr. Enderby* concludes would suggest that this is one of Burgess's more melancholy comedies. (Burgess's attitude toward psychiatrists who accept the premises of behaviorist psychology may be inferred from his picaresque masterpiece, *A Clockwork Orange*, in which the psychopathic teenage protagonist triumphs gloriously over will-sapping behaviorist reformers and regains an utterly depraved self that is somehow morally superior to the well-behaved "not-self" the reformers force upon him.)

In *Enderby Outside* the behaviorists are again vanquished as Enderby regains his lyric gift and returns to the practice of poetry. Abandonment of his art has been an essential part of his rehabilitation, and his publication of a poem drives one of his psychiatrists into a rage bordering on insanity. The insanity of psychiatrists is not, however, the principal focus of the novel. Burgess is primarily concerned with the practice of poetry and its significance in the mid twentieth century, and, as in most of his novels, he provides more questions than answers.

The formidable question of what makes a poet is one that exercises Burgess in his splendid reconstruction of Shakespeare's love life, *Nothing Like the Sun*. In that novel, and in *A Vision of Battlements*, he seems to accept the Joycean verdict that, in Shakespeare's case at least, it was "overplus of Will." Shakespeare's achievement was largely the result of satyriasis. In the epilogue to *Nothing Like the Sun*, WS scornfully dismisses the spiritual pretensions of his most gifted contemporary, John Donne: "Let us have no nonsensical talk about merging and melting souls, though, binary suns, two spheres in a single orbit. There is the flesh and the flesh makes all. Literature is an epiphenomenon of the action of the flesh." Burgess, fully aware that this explanation explains little, carries the investigation much further in the Enderby books. The gift Enderby loses in *Inside*

Mr. Enderby and regains in *Enderby Outside* is an ability to write technically competent verse in a variety of traditional forms. He especially favors the sonnet, but he also essays more ambitious forms such as the Horatian ode, and in *Inside Mr. Enderby* he is involved in a long allegorical piece concerning the role of original sin in Western culture. "Uninspired" would be the wrong word to apply to Enderby's verse, for it is inspired by something. But what? He can write competent love lyrics, but he fears all women, associating them with his loathsome stepmother. Much of his poetry concerns religion, but he has long since abandoned his own religion. His art and the matter of his art really have nothing to do with one another.

The question of whether or not Enderby and others like him have what it takes to write significant poetry is left in the air in *Inside Mr. Enderby*. However, it is answered unequivocally in *Enderby Outside* by a mysterious young girl, who seems to be either Enderby's muse or her representative. She tells Enderby that he lacks courage and that "Poetry isn't a silly little hobby to be practised in the smallest room of the house." However, after this devastating indictment, she tries to rescue him for poetry, offering herself as a delectable golden avenue to the commitment he needs to make in order to achieve anything truly great. But Enderby, visualizing himself "puffing in his slack whiteness," is paralyzed with fear. The episode effectively defines his limitations: " 'Minor poet,' she said. 'We know now where we stand, don't we? Never mind. Be thankful for what you've got. Don't ask too much, that's all.' " Great poetry, then, cannot be expected from fearful little men who have "opted to live without love."

Burgess also focuses on other claimants to the title of "poet" that flourished in the 1960s. Yod Crewsy, whom Enderby is accused of assassinating, is a representative of the rock singers who received much critical acclaim at that time both as poets and as musicians. Burgess has always maintained a consistently contemptuous attitude toward their artistic pretensions, which he has expressed in various novels besides *Enderby Outside*. In *Enderby Outside* he focuses special attention on their claim to significance as poets, which even such Establishment organs as *Time* and *Life* were taking seriously. Enderby, serving as a barman in a London hotel, is horrified to hear his own verse being clumsily read by Yod Crewsy (leader of the group "Crewsy-fixers"), who has

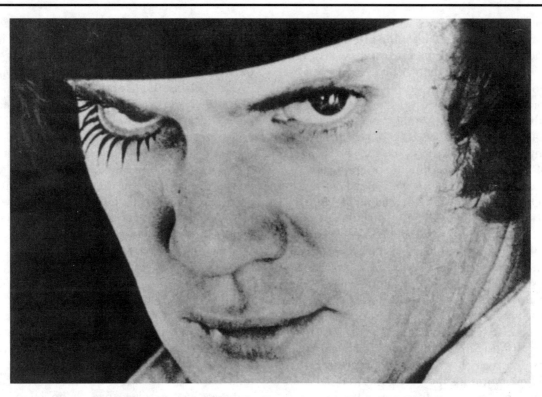

Malcolm McDowell as Alex in the film version of A Clockwork Orange

just become a fellow of the Royal Society of Litera-ture. Enderby's ex-wife, who has married the Crewsy-fixers' manager, has provided the singer with some of Enderby's old manuscripts, and these have secured for Crewsy considerable recog-nition as a poet. A large group of admiring nota-bles, including the prime minister, is assembled to celebrate the artistic triumphs of the Crewsy-fixers, and Crewsy gratifies them with a ghastly re-cital of Enderby's verse followed by a crude piece of noisy rock. The latter treat is interrupted by a shot, and Enderby suddenly finds himself framed for the shooting of Yod Crewsy.

Enderby manages to flee successfully from England to Tangier, where he comes in contact with another type of singer, the poet spawned by the so-called psychedelic revolution. He wanders into a cafe in Tangier where a group of soi-disant literati, mostly expatriate Americans, are trying to induce creativity with drugs. One of them favors Enderby with a short piece of verse addressed to "mod and rocker" on behalf of "pey-ote chiefs," "Zen roshis," and other "psychedelic guides." Enderby is unimpressed, but he is led into searching questions concerning the status of his art in the 1960s. He wonders whether per-haps these acid-inspired makers are not closer to the truth of art than he is: "Was it right that art

should mirror chaos?" He wonders whether Mar-shall McLuhan's widely accepted pronounce-ments on media and the universe have not made the whole business of putting words together in an ordered, meaningful relationship a pointless exercise. "That Canadian pundit," however, does not trouble him greatly. The sort of relationships McLuhan perceives are "too elegant . . . too much like Mallarmé or somebody. Old-fashioned too, really. Surrealist."

Burgess's point of view on these questions is hard to perceive clearly. He seems to expect as lit-tle in the way of significant verse from the chaos-obsessed and acid-inspired as he expects from rock singers or fearful little men such as Enderby. The hope for poetry, if there is any hope, seems to lie in a synthesis of the qualities and artistic points of view of these pretenders. Enderby himself possesses the most vital prerequi-sites, technical skill and saturation in the works of the masters; but he lacks courage and fears "the young and the experimental and the way-out" and the evil represented by "the black dog" in his dreams. In contrast, the rock singers and the acidheads have youth and courage but lack skill and knowledge. As they are now, Burgess im-plies, little can be expected from any of these would-be poets. In the concluding chapter, a strange persona leading a tour of schoolchildren through Tangier sneers: "They are small artists, all. Here there is a *rue* Beethoven, also an *avenida* Leonardo da Vinci, a *plaza* de Sade. But no artist here will have a square or thoroughfare named for him. They are nothing."

Burgess once rated "the whole *Enderby* book in its American form, which is the form I always wanted," as his highest achievement so far in the novel: "It's the book in which I say most, mean most to myself about the situation of the artist." For precisely these reasons, the whole Enderby book might be rated beneath some of his others, such as *Nothing Like the Sun, Tremor of Intent* (1966), and *Napoleon Symphony* (1974). The first Enderby book is a little comic masterpiece, but the sequel is flawed by didacticism and a tendency to lecture through various mouthpieces on the "role of the artist." The same flaw is apparent in other novels, most notably *MF* and *Beard's Roman Women*.

Besides *The Wanting Seed* and *Inside Mr. Enderby*, Burgess produced two other first-rate novels during his "terminal year": *The Doctor Is Sick* (1960) and *The Worm and the Ring* (1961). The latter novel is a mock-epic, or, more exactly, a mock-opera, a burlesque of Richard Wagner's *Der Ring des Nibelungen* (1874). Wagner's allegorical tale of a struggle for power between Nibelung dwarfs, giants, and gods is translated into a struggle for the control of a grammar school in a little English borough. Wotan, ruler of the gods, becomes Mr. Woolton, headmaster of the school and an old-fashioned liberal humanist. Fafner, the giant who seizes all and turns himself into a dragon, is "Dr." Gardner (Gard-drag-dragon), a cynical, academic Babbitt who has managed to ingratiate himself with members of the business community. With these back-slapping connections, the prestige of a doctorate (earned with a plagiarized dissertation), personal wealth, and a Machiavellian ruthlessness, he is bound to triumph. Woolton has no allies among the smug burghers of the town, who despise not only his weakness and inefficiency as an administrator, but also all of the humanistic values he represents. They want Gardner, and, as the novel reveals, they deserve him.

Gardner is wormlike in every respect (Anglo-Saxon *wyrm*-serpent, dragon), but he is destined to emerge triumphant, unscathed by the hero, the ruler of the gods, or anyone else—a bitter reflection that extends well beyond the arena of school politics. One of Woolton's few allies is the

protagonist, Christopher Howarth. Howarth, an ineffectual Siegfried, is a thirty-nine-year-old assistant master who teaches German and leads an ungratifying existence. In addition to feeling the conflict between Woolton and Gardner (whose dissertation is actually one of Howarth's essays), Howarth is under personal pressures. For one thing, his relationship with his wife is tense, partly because of their poverty, but mainly because of her submission to the rules of the Catholic church.

The wretchedness of Howarth's poverty, the stupid tyranny of Catholic orthodoxy, and the philistinism of the English borough are all presented with angry force. But Burgess's anger does not cause him to present any of his criticisms simplistically. If the society is drifting toward philistinism and the rule of the worm, it is not entirely because of the strength or cunning of philistine "giants." The liberal humanism of Woolton, his unshakable faith in human goodness, gives him excuses to shirk responsibility. In the face of the insidious intrigues of Gardner, which contradict Woolton's whole liberal view of human nature, he retreats into his books and makes no real attempt to defend either himself or his humanistic intellectual values on the battlefield of public opinion. Burgess's treatment of Woolton's reptilian antagonist is similarly balanced. Gardner is repulsive, more like a worm or an insect ("a quick smart daring beetle") than a man, but unlike Woolton he is capable of ruling the Valhalla of education, and he is unhampered by any illusions about human nature. An epilogue provides a depressing glimpse of the school's future under his rule, but the feeble liberalism of Woolton has failed to provide any alternative that would satisfy the community's craving for stability.

This balanced critical treatment of the extreme of rule based on liberal idealism versus the extreme of cynical autocracy agrees with Burgess's other novels. As in his dystopian books, *The Wanting Seed* and *A Clockwork Orange*, Burgess exposes the inadequacies and dangers of both as governing philosophies. At the same time he suggests that Western society is becoming increasingly incapable of accepting a sane, realistic mixture of the two philosophies that would insure the preservation of individual human dignity. That he intends this power struggle in the grammar school to have broader political implications is indicated in the thoughtful response of one of the teachers to Gardner's announcement that under the new state plan designed to insure "the realization of a genuinely democratic education" all pupil segregation will be eliminated. In reply, the teacher remarks "how the pushing of a thing to its logical limit seems to turn into its opposite . . . real democracy is anarchy, and anarchy is Hobbes's state of nature, and then we have to have a large police force to keep chaos in check, all the apparatus of totalitarianism."

The other significant novel Burgess produced during his "terminal year," *The Doctor Is Sick*, was based to some extent on his experiences in Borneo and as a patient at the National Hospital for Nervous Diseases. The protagonist, a thirty-eight-year-old philologist named Edwin Spindrift, collapses on the floor of a classroom in the Far East, is flown back to England, and is told that he must undergo brain surgery, whereupon he escapes into the night clad, like a concentration-camp inmate, in striped pajamas and undergoes a series of ordeals in London's seamier districts.

Before his escape Spindrift has been blessed with the innocence and smug pedantry that can survive only in a hermetically sealed academic atmosphere. Holder of a doctorate in linguistics awarded by the University of Pasadena for a thesis "on the semantic implications of the consonant-group 'shm' in colloquial American speech," he insists upon being addressed as "Doctor Spindrift" and is prepared to present the ocular proof of a diploma he carries inside his coat pocket. For him the important reality, perhaps the only reality, is within a purely verbal realm. He tends to elevate words above the mere phenomena denoted by them, and his resultant inability to cope effectively with the world of tangible percepts is the basic source of the troubles he is destined to experience in the course of some informal, although rigorous, postdoctoral studies.

Once outside the "safe" confines of the hospital, Spindrift goes in search of his faithless wife, Sheila; his pursuit of her becomes, among other things, a search for love, or more precisely the meaning of love. This is one of the many respects in which it parallels the quest of Leopold Bloom in *Ulysses* (1922). This novel, like some of Burgess's others, structurally parallels Joyce's masterpiece and may be regarded as one of his own treatments of Joyce's major themes. For instance, Spindrift's descent from disembodied philology into the world of tangible reality in London is like the progress of Stephen Dedalus from a world of words, in which he is an acknowledged master, to the world of Leopold Bloom. In the

third part of the Telemachia section of *Ulysses*, Stephen is walking along the seashore pondering the nature of reality and attempting to encompass the shifting, treacherous, protean world of material phenomena in language. To an extent he succeeds, and through philology he manages to achieve a partial victory over Proteus; but it is only a partial victory. He needs Bloom, for Bloom represents the world of the flesh, which Stephen has not mastered, although he has mastered words and ideas. Burgess's protagonist parallels the transition from Stephen's world to Bloom's by passing from his sphere of disembodied words, in which he is an acknowledged "doctor," to the sphere of organic and economic reality in which only the knowledge of medical doctors or technicians or worldly-wise members of the London demimonde really matters.

In terms of experiences, Spindrift and Bloom have much in common. Both have adventures and encounter obstacles that parallel, and parody, those of Odysseus. Spindrift's visit to the office of his superiors in London, for instance, like Bloom's visit to the newspaper office, seems to correspond to the sojourn of Odysseus in the cave of the wind god Aeolus. Spindrift like Odysseus, is given a gift of "wind," although he, unlike Odysseus, actually needs another gift. Both men, like Odysseus, are detained by monsters and nymphs. A masochistic monster who detains Spindrift shares with the Cyclops and the Laestrygonians an insatiable perverted appetite, and his business of dealing in stolen watches may also have analogues in the *Odyssey*. The Calypso in Spindrift's odyssey is a hardworking London prostitute who picks him up and finds him a totally unrewarding customer, except in a financial way. Like Bloom, he is questing toward a reunion with a Penelope who has been unfaithful to him, but unlike Bloom, he will not be able to revive her love.

The concluding section of *The Doctor Is Sick* is analogous to the Book of the Dead. Spindrift encounters an old schoolmate, Aristotle Thanatos, from whom he receives a great deal of sympathy and promises of assistance. With the entrance of this new "agency of the world," as he describes him, Burgess begins to introduce a new level of interpretation that may confuse a reader if one overlooks significant details and hints, perhaps the most important of which are conveyed by the name "Aristotle Thanatos." That "Thanatos" means death strengthens the suggestion that Spindrift's three days in the "underworld" have

Burgess composing music

been just that. But Aristotle Thanatos clearly represents more than death: he is both literally and symbolically a Dionysian figure. Since his last meeting with Spindrift, he has become a prosperous vintner, and he is attending a convention to promote Greek wines in England. Like Osiris, the Egyptian counterpart of Dionysus, he leads Spindrift from the underworld into a heavenly realm where he is judged and permitted to make a "Negative Confession" that he is not as wretched as he appears to be.

In introducing the mysterious Mr. Thanatos, Burgess evokes mythic treatments of death and rebirth, and connected with these regeneration motifs is an "Aristotelian" one that should not be overlooked. Spindrift, in descending from disembodied philology to a world where words are attached to things, has had to make a plunge comparable to that of Plato's true philosopher returning from the sunlit world of concepts, or forms, to the cave of percepts. The difference is that Plato's philosopher will supposedly be granted an infallible grasp of how the world of perceptible things ought to be ordered. Spindrift's career in the immaterial world of verbal forms, on the other hand, has made him simply unable to cope with the world of matter. If he is to get anything out of the world of percepts, he must completely cast off his old Platonic self and assume a new Aristotelian one. He must be ready to come to terms with the changing matter in which forms are dynamic principles. This Aristotelian motif is related to the Joycean parallels mentioned above. Stephen Dedalus, too, looks to Aristotle, the great classifier, for assistance in taming the world of matter. The motif is also related to the Book of the Dead analogue in that Spindrift's Aristotelian grasp of reality will draw him toward a state of oneness with the ever-changing universal being, the world of things "ripe for the picking."

Compared to these other products of Burgess's "terminal year," *One Hand Clapping* is a slight book, and, largely because it appeared under the pseudonym Joseph Kell, it did not receive much critical attention. Like *The Right to an Answer*, it is a first-person commentary on life in England at the time. Janet Shirley, the narrator-protagonist, is a fairly clever but ill-educated young Englishwoman, a product of what Dr. Gardner in *The Worm and the Ring* called "the realization of a genuinely democratic education." She has been required to take courses in deportment and dress sense, ballroom dancing, "and what was called Homecraft," along with some courses in English and history ineptly taught by teachers who want to be "real cool" and "with" the times.

Janet is happily married to a good-looking, upright young man named Howard, who possesses an uncommonly efficient photographic brain that is capable of assimilating incredible amounts of factual data. He can also formulate probabilities on the basis of accumulated data. Thus he is able to succeed first in winning one thousand pounds on a television quiz show and then multiplying that amount over and over again in the potentially ruinous game of horse racing. The Shirleys, having become affluent, soon discover that money does not "make for happiness, really." And like other Burgess protagonists, Howard becomes disgusted with the modern age, and he decides to express his disgust by suicide. He also tries to force his wife to join him, but she resists and kills him in self-defense with a coal hammer. She then departs for the Continent accompanied by Redvers Glass (a poet hired by Howard to celebrate their suicide in verse) and Howard's body in a pigskin trunk. She seems happy enough with her new love, free of guilt and regrets, but one gathers that the poet had better watch his step. As Glass thinks about the quality of life in modern England, he begins to indulge in morbid musings, and Janet thinks about the coal hammer she still keeps handy.

One Hand Clapping is a weak novel, but it gives an authentic picture of England in the 1960s through a young Englishwoman's mind. A reader may be startled by the callousness and ruthlessness she exhibits near the end of the novel, but eliciting this response seems to be one of Burgess's purposes. As a product of her society, Janet is so lacking in stable, meaningful values that the transition from loving wife to calculating murderess is an easy one.

Certainly the best of Burgess's early 1960s novels that focus on the decadence of modern England is *The Right to an Answer*, an account of an expatriate's experiences while visiting from the Far East, based partly on Burgess's own experiences on a visit. The narrator-protagonist, Mr. J. W. Denham, is a plump, balding, middle-aged businessman who takes what he can out of life in pleasure and novel experiences. After living in the Far East he feels alienated, but he is troubled more by the spectacle of "irresponsibility" and "instability" in "hideous, TV-haunted England." What he has seen of life in East and West has given him a Hobbesian view of human affairs. He values stability more than freedom and is convinced that "you definitely can't have both."

Although the scenes of action in *The Right to an Answer* range from England to Japan and back again—with stops in places such as Singapore, Colombo, and Aden—much of the action originates in a single drinking spot within the "rather large smug Midland city" where Denham goes to visit his retired father. This spot, the Black Swan, has a Shakespearean connection that is also its most important customer-drawing asset: the landlord himself, an extremely likable man named Ted Arden, whose connection with the family of Shakespeare's mother is proclaimed both by his name and his appearance; moreover, he has an irresistible charm that effectively transforms what is actually a dreary little pub into a place where one feels privileged to spend one's money.

Denham usually visits the Black Swan in company with his father after they have been partially lobotomized by an evening in front of the "telly." There they encounter other patrons, including some who have spent the evening in the same way and some who have spent it in more sordid fashion. The so-called suburban switch, considered by some Americans to be a peculiarly American institution, is shown to be a British sexual pastime as well. They also meet Ted Arden's three helpers, named, incredibly, Cedric, Cecil, and Selwyn. The latter character suggests an Eliot-Pound reference. One is apt to think of Ezra Pound's autobiographical poem *Hugh Selwyn Mauberley* (1920), especially if one happens to have seen the Wyndham Lewis sketch of the poet in which his spectacles are like Selwyn's "idiot's spectacles filled with light." *Hugh Selwyn Mauberley* is an indictment of modern materialism, as is another long poem Pound influenced, T. S. Eliot's *The Waste Land* (1922), in which the blind seer Tiresias appears. The major themes of these poems—the sterility and philistinism of modern culture, the loss of values and meaning accompanying a lack of belief in anything—are certainly treated in *The Right to an Answer*, and the novel demonstrates that such indictments are more valid in the age of television than they were earlier.

The brief glimpses of dreary or sordid suburban life are a prelude to the entrance of Mr. Raj, a character who provides yet another view of England from the vantage point of Far Eastern experience. He has come to England to carry out research for a thesis on "Popular Conceptions of Racial Differentiation." He tries to bridge some gaps between East and West by attempting to have an affair with a woman who has been involved in the game of wife swapping, and the results are tragic.

In many ways the story of Mr. Raj resembles the story of Othello. Like Othello, Mr. Raj is fond of self-dramatization. He has the same tendency to idealize in an unrealistic fashion a golden-haired woman he does not understand, and he is prone to fits of insane jealousy that have fatal effects. Like Othello, also, he is under the illusion that he is accepted fully by the fair-skinned society around him—only to find, during moments of stress, that those who seem to accept him are, like Brabantio, secretly repelled by his blackness. Although Mr. Raj is not created by Ted Arden, as Othello is by Shakespeare, the drama of his attempt to achieve "contact" with the West is presented largely in the theater of Ted's establishment, and it is appropriate that a man who is himself an authentic piece of Shakespeareana should provide much of the setting for an updated, tragicomic version of *Othello*.

The range of subjects treated in *The Right to an Answer*—from culture clashes to love and moral responsibility—is considerable; yet the relevance of each subject to the others is clearly evident. Denham himself, whose commentaries serve to clarify the connections, is more than a mouthpiece. He is a well-developed and delightful character, despite his essential selfishness and stuffy conservatism that conflicts with his hedonistic impulses. What repels him initially is Mr. Raj's radiant human warmth, a warmth that, by the end of the novel, he longs to acquire himself. But

what is most impressive about Denham, even more than his progress in humanity, is his wit. Even a dreary event such as a Sunday dinner at the house of his sister becomes hilarious, and his description of a voyage back to the Orient aboard a Dutch liner is a marvelous piece of comedy worthy of any anthology. *The Right to an Answer* is Burgess's funniest treatment of love and decay in the West, as well as his meatiest.

Devil of a State was a Book Society Choice when it first appeared in 1961, and, like so many of Burgess's novels, it received mixed critical response. A *New Statesman* reviewer observed that its comic devices would have been more effective "if Mr. Burgess hadn't been Scooped long ago." He and others had noted that the book seems to echo Evelyn Waugh's early satires *Scoop* (1938) and *Black Mischief* (1932). Indeed, the African setting and the sardonic detachment with which Burgess presents the chaos of life in a newly emergent state are liable to give a reader of the Waugh satires a sense of déjà vu. Burgess has acknowledged a general indebtedness to Waugh, as well as to Joyce, Laurence Sterne, and Vladimir Nabokov; but the book is essentially Burgess's own vision of life in such a state, and he likely saw the same things in the Far East that Waugh saw in Africa. Dunia, the imaginary caliphate in *Devil of a State*, is, Burgess has said, "a kind of fantasticated Zanzibar," but one senses that the real setting may be Borneo. One is tempted to toy with possible etymological connections between "Brunei" and "Dunia"; perhaps Burgess is dropping a hint that he has transferred a "brown" culture from the East Indies to Africa. Actually, *Dunia* is the Arabic word for "the world" in its Far Eastern form, but one might still view it as a Joycean etymology making Brunei and Dunia at least dream cognates.

Like Burgess's earlier novels dealing with states of transition in British colonial territories, *Devil of a State* presents a richly comic gallery of natives, Europeans, and various ethnic mixtures. Again, much attention is focused on the trials of a guilt-ridden Englishman haunted by the memory of his first wife, whom he believes is dead. But Lydgate, the fifty-year-old protagonist, has little in common with Victor Crabbe, besides guilt, bad luck, and a fondness for darker, warmer civilizations. He is an adventurer who has tried everything from importing in Nairobi to gold prospecting in Malaya. Unlike Crabbe, he has few altruistic impulses. Thoroughly selfish, he tends to use other people as means rather than ends and

Score sheet from Burgess's musical adaptation of his free-verse poem Moses

to dodge responsibilities. He had married his first wife, an older woman, for her money, only to find life with her impossible. Unable to endure her religious fanaticism, he had deserted her, and much of his wandering from place to place has been continual flight to avoid her. When he believes she is dead, he remarries, only to be divorced and remarried again.

For all his problems with women, Lydgate adjusts to Dunia more easily than most of the other Europeans in the novel. Among the more sympathetically drawn and pathetic characters is the Honorable Mr. Tomlin, United Nations adviser, a competent, conscientious veteran of the British colonial service. One can see in the general presentation of British administrators in this novel a bit more sympathy than was shown in the *Malayan Trilogy*. Burgess, a former colonial officer, may have become fed up with the abuse heaped on the British by those who had gained from them as much as, or more than, they had lost.

Overall, however, this novel is more comic than bitter, and some of the funniest effects are provided by an Italian, Nando Tasca, and his son, Paolo, who have been brought to Dunia to complete the marblework on a new mosque. Their relationship is as utterly without either filial or paternal devotion as one could imagine. The son feels wronged by the father, the father by the son, and each looks forward to a day of retribution. The son falls under the influence of native revolutionaries who see in him a potentially moving symbol of the plight of the downtrodden native working classes under "the oppression of paternal white rule." They elevate him to glory, and one suspects that Burgess's depiction of them was heavily influenced by his own experiences with revolutionaries in Borneo, including the invitation to lead their Freedom party. (Such conjectures about the relevance of his experiences in Borneo are based on the predominance of Asians in the novel and the fact that most of Burgess's fiction is based on his own experience.)

The novel's protagonist, Lydgate, like backward-looking Victor Crabbe in the *Malayan Trilogy*, progresses toward a terrible reckoning with his past, and his progress, like Crabbe's, is set against the chaotic movement of a former British colony toward independence. But while it is possible to become involved with Crabbe and the Malaya he loves, in *Devil of a State*, Burgess does not permit involvement with Lydgate and Dunia. He compels instead sardonic detachment from the horribly comic spectacle of irresponsibility

and its fruits both on the individual and on the state level. The book is both farce and parable. Like the satire of Jonathan Swift, it points in many directions and sustains its irony throughout.

In 1962 what was to become Burgess's most widely read novel, *A Clockwork Orange*, was published. (Even before Stanley Kubrick filmed it in 1971, it was his most popular novel, a fact that does not greatly please Burgess, who values some of his other works more.) Like *The Wanting Seed*, *A Clockwork Orange* is a proleptic nightmare with antiutopian implications. Although it can be read as an answer to and a rejection of the main ideas of the psychologist B. F. Skinner, Burgess was less directly influenced by Skinner's ideas in particular than by accounts he had read of behaviorist methods of reforming criminals that were being used in American prisons, with the avowed purpose of limiting the subjects' freedom of choice to what society called "goodness." This effort struck Burgess as "most sinful," and his novel is, among other things, an attempt to clarify the issues involved in the use of such methods.

The setting of *A Clockwork Orange* is a city somewhere in either Western Europe or North America where a civilization has evolved out of a fusion of the dominant cultures east and west of the Iron Curtain. This cultural merger seems partly the result of successful cooperative efforts in the conquest of space, efforts that have promoted a preoccupation with outer space and a concomitant indifference to exclusively terrestrial affairs, such as a maintenance of law and order in the cities. A reader is apt to assume that Burgess was thinking of the United States when he envisioned this situation of the future. In fact, he was more influenced by what he had seen during his visit to Leningrad in 1961. At that time Russia was leading in the space race, and the gangs of young thugs, or stilyagi, were becoming a serious nuisance in Russian cities. At the same time, London police were having their troubles with the teddy boys. Having seen both the stilyagi and the teddy boys in action, Burgess was moved by a renewed sense of the oneness of humanity, and the murderous teenaged hooligans who are the main characters in *A Clockwork Orange* are composite creations. Alex, the fifteen-year-old narrator-protagonist, could be either an Alexander or an Alexei. The names of his three comrades, Dim, Pete, and Georgie, are similarly ambiguous, suggesting both Russian and English given names.

A reader may completely miss these and other hints, but what one cannot overlook is the effect of the cultural fusion on the teenage underworld patois in which the story is narrated. The language, Burgess's invention, is called *nadsat*, which is a transliteration of a Russian suffix equivalent to the English suffix *-teen*, as in *fifteen*. Most, but by no means all, of the words nadsat comprises are Russian, and Burgess has altered some of them in ways that one might reasonably expect them to be altered in the mouths of English-speaking teenagers. For instance, the word *horrorshow* is a favorite adjective of nadsat speakers meaning everything from "good" to "splendid." The word sounds like a clever invention by an observer of teenagers who is aware of their fondness for films such as *I Was a Teen-age Werewolf* (1957) and *Frankenstein Meets the Wolf Man* (1943). Actually, it is an imagined development from *kharsho*, a Russian adjective meaning "good" or "well."

Many of the non-Russian words in nadsat are derived from British slang. For example, a member of the city's finest, the ineffectual safeguards of law and order, is referred to as a "rozz," a word derived from the English slang term *rozzer*, meaning "policeman." The American edition of the novel has a glossary, prepared without Burgess's consultation, which is not entirely accurate either in its translation of nadsat words or in the information it gives concerning their origins. Actually, after a few pages of the novel, a reader of even moderate sensitivity should not need a glossary and will do well to refrain from consulting this one, whose translations, even when they are accurate, may substitute terms that lack the rich onomatopoeic suggestiveness of Burgess's language.

The novel is more than a linguistic tour de force. It is also one of the most devastating pieces of multipronged social satire in recent fiction, and, like *The Wanting Seed*, it passes the test of "relevance." The protagonist, Alex, is one of the most appallingly vicious creations in recent fiction. Although his name suggests his composite Russian-English identity, it is ambiguous in other ways as well. The fusion of the negative prefix *a* with the word *lex* suggests simultaneously an absence of law and a lack of words. The idea of lawlessness is readily apparent in Alex's behavior, but the idea of wordlessness is subtler and harder to grasp, for Alex seems to have a great many words at his command, whether he happens to be snarling at his "droogs" in nadsat or respectfully addressing his elders in Russianless English. He is articulate but "wordless" in that he apprehends life directly, without the mediation of words. Unlike the characters who seek to control him and the rest of the society, he makes no attempt to explain or justify his actions through abstract ideals or goals such as "liberty" or "stability." Nor does he attempt to define any role for himself within a large social process. Instead, he simply experiences life directly, sensuously, and, while he is free, joyously. Indeed, his guiltless joy in violence of every kind—from the destruction or theft of objects to practically every form of sexual and nonsexual assault—suggests, however incongruously, innocence to the reader. Alex also has a fine ear for European classical music, especially the works of Ludwig van Beethoven and Wolfgang Amadeus Mozart, and although such widely differing tastes within one savage youngster might (again) seem incongruous, they are in fact complementary. Knowing his own passions, Alex is highly amused by an article he reads in which some would-be reformer argues that "Modern Youth" might become more "civilized" if "A Lively Appreciation Of The Arts," especially music and poetry, were encouraged.

The first third of the novel is taken up with Alex's joyful satiation of all his appetites; and as rape and murder follow assault, robbery, and vandalism, the spectacle of pleasure in violence overwhelms. While it might be argued that psychopathic delight could not be experienced by a sane person, there is no implication in the novel that Alex is anything but sane—sane and free to choose what delights him. Since his choices are invariably destructive or harmful, it appears that society's right to deprive him of his freedom, if not his life, can hardly be disputed. What the novel does dispute is society's right to make Alex less than a human being by depriving him of the ability to choose a harmful course of action.

Partly as a result of his own vicious activities and partly as a result of struggles between Pelagian and Augustinian factions in government, Alex is destined to experience life as a well-conditioned "good citizen." (Although the labels "Pelagian" and "Augustinian" are not used, it is not difficult to recognize these factions by their policies.) The Pelagian-controlled government that is in power as the novel opens is responsible by its laxness for the enormous amount of crime that occurs. When Alex is finally caught, while attempting to escape from a burglary involving a fatal assault on an old woman, it is mainly because his gang has betrayed him and facilitated the capture. He is sentenced to fourteen years in prison, and while there he will feel the effects of a major change in government policy.

The failure of liberal methods of government generates the usual "DISAPPOINTMENT" and the concomitant yearning for Augustinian alternatives. Realizing that the terrorized electorate cares little about "the tradition of liberty" and is actually willing to "sell liberty for a quieter life," the government seeks to impose order by the most efficient means available. Unlike the Augustinian-controlled government in *The Wanting Seed*, this body does not resort to mass murder. Instead, it relies upon the genius of modern behavioral technology, specifically the branch of it that aims at the total control of human will. When Alex brings attention to himself by murdering a fellow inmate, he is selected as a "trailblazer" to be "transformed out of all recognition."

The purpose of Alex's transformation is to eliminate his capacity to choose socially deleterious courses of action. Psychological engineers force upon him what B. F. Skinner might call "the inclination to behave." Strapped in a chair, he is forced to watch films of incredible brutality, some of them contrived and others actual documentaries of Japanese and Nazi atrocities during World War II. In the past, violence has given him only the most pleasurable sensations; now, he is suddenly overcome by the most unbearable nausea and headaches. After suffering these agonizing sessions, he finds that the nausea has been induced not by the films but by injections given beforehand. Thus his body is being taught to associate the sight, or even the thought, of violence with unpleasant sensations. His responses and, as it were, his moral progress are measured by electronic devices wired to his body. Quite by accident, his body is conditioned to associate not only violence but also his beloved classical music with nausea. The last movement of Beethoven's Fifth Symphony (1807) accompanies a documentary on the Nazis, and the connection of the two with bodily misery is firmly fixed.

Having gratified his rehabilitation engineers with proof that he is a "true Christian," Alex is free to enter society again—if not as a useful citizen, at least as a harmless one—as living proof that the government is doing something to remedy social ills and therefore merits reelection. He is not only harmless but helpless as well. Shortly after his release he is the victim of a ludicrous,

vengeful beating by one of his most helpless former victims, an old man assisted by some of his ancient cronies. Unable to endure even the violent feeling needed to fight his way clear, he is "rescued" by three policemen. The fact that one of his rescuers is a former member of his own gang and another a former leader of a rival gang suggests that the society is experiencing a transitional "Interphase" as it progresses into its Augustinian phase. These young thugs, like the "greyboys" in *The Wanting Seed*, have been recruited into the police force apparently on the theory that their criminal desires can be expressed usefully in the maintenance of order on the streets. Again, it is tempting to suppose that Burgess was influenced by conditions in some American cities where, as he has remarked, the police seem to represent little more than "a kind of *alternative* criminal body."

Alex, having been beaten by his rescuers, drags himself to a little cottage that was the scene of the most savage atrocity he and his droogs had carried out before his imprisonment. One of his victims, a writer named F. Alexander, still lives there. The writer's political and philosophical ideals incline toward Pelagian liberalism, and he has remained, in spite of his experience as a victim of human depravity, committed to the belief that man is "a creature of growth and capable of sweetness." Because of this view, he remains unalterably opposed to the use of "debilitating and will-sapping techniques of conditioning" in criminal reform. To some extent, he is an autobiographical creation. Like Burgess, he has written a book entitled *A Clockwork Orange* with the purpose of illuminating the dangers of allowing such methods. The fact that he has had the sincerity of his beliefs about criminal reform tested by the personal experience of senseless criminal brutality is something else he shares with Burgess. Recall that during the war, while Burgess was stationed in Gibraltar, his pregnant wife was assaulted on a London street and suffered a miscarriage as a result. But here the resemblance ends. Although Burgess believes man is capable of sweetness and should not be turned into a piece of clockwork, he is no Pelagian, and his book, unlike F. Alexander's, is no lyrical effusion of revolutionary idealism.

Although F. Alexander and his associates seem motivated by the loftiest of liberal ideas, they are incapable of seeing Alex as anything but a propaganda device. To them Alex is not an unfortunate human being to be assisted, but "a martyr to the cause of Liberty" who can serve "the Future and our Cause." When F. Alexander begins to suspect that Alex is one of the attackers who invaded his home, he and his associates decide that Alex will be more effective as a dead "witness" against the government than as a living one. Utilizing the responses implanted in him by the government psychologists, they attempt to drive him to suicide, and they nearly succeed. Thus Burgess effectively underlines what Pelagian idealism shares with Augustinian cynicism. The Pelagian preoccupation with the tradition of liberty and the dignity of man, like the Augustinian preoccupation with stability, will make any sacrifice for "the Good of Man" worthwhile, including the destruction of Man himself.

The government receives ample amounts of embarrassing publicity concerning Alex's attempted suicide, but somehow survives. One day Alex awakens to find himself fully as vicious as before his treatment. More psychological engineers, using "deep hypnopaedia or some such slovo," have restored his moral nature, his "self," and his concomitant appetites for Beethoven and throat cutting. In this "depraved" condition, he cannot further embarrass the Augustinian government.

At this point the American edition of *A Clockwork Orange* ends, and Stanley Kubrick, following the American edition, ends his film. In its earlier British editions, however, the novel has one additional chapter that makes a considerable difference in how one may interpret it. This chapter, like the chapters that begin the novel's three main parts, opens with the question, "What's it going to be then, eh?" The reader has been led to believe that, aside from imprisonment or hanging, the two conditions presented are the only possible alternatives for Alex. The omitted chapter, however, reveals yet another alternative: Alex is shown becoming weary of violence. Having met one of his old comrades who has married and settled down, he realizes that this is what he wants for himself. He wants to marry and have a son, whom he will try to teach to avoid his own mistakes, though he knows he will not succeed.

Burgess's American publisher insisted on omitting this chapter so that the book would end "on a tough and violent note," and Burgess agrees that the omission was in some ways an improvement. The missing chapter in effect suggests that individuals are capable of growing and learning through suffering and error. It further suggests that suffering, fallen human beings— not behavioral technology or the revolutionary

schemes of idealists—bring "goodness" into the world.

Between 1962 and the end of 1980 Burgess produced fifteen novels. Some of these, such as *The Eve of St. Venus* (1964), *The Clockwork Testament* (1974), *Beard's Roman Women*, and *ABBA ABBA* (1977), are rather slight books. The most significant are *Nothing Like the Sun: A Story of Shakespeare's Love Life*, *Tremor of Intent*, *Enderby Outside*, *MF*, *Napoleon Symphony*, and *Earthly Powers* (1980).

One of Burgess's most remarkable achievements in the novel is *Nothing Like the Sun*, a book that, unfortunately, did not receive its due from critics at the time of its appearance in the year of the Shakespeare quadricentennial. Its setting is a classroom somewhere in Malaya or Borneo; the narrator, as Burgess states in a prologue, is "Mr. Burgess," who has just been "given the sack" by his headmaster, and it is time to bid his students farewell. His farewell speech, a last lecture, will be primarily for the benefit of those "who complained that Shakespeare had nothing to give to the East." It is a long discourse, but he is well fortified with a potent Chinese rice spirit called *samsu*, a parting gift from his students. The *samsu* and his considerable knowledge of Shakespeare enable him to transport himself and his class back into sixteenth-century England. In a sense, however, he also brings Shakespeare forward into the twentieth century through identification with himself. As his lecture progresses, accompanied by much *samsu* swigging, the identification becomes stronger and stronger until finally, in the epilogue, we are able to hear the voice of a Shakespeare-Burgess composite hero.

The lecture begins with a vision of an adolescent Master Shakespeare at home in Stratford. As a youth he dreams of a "goddess," a dark golden lady who is his muse, his ideal of beauty, and his forbidden fruit. He finds her literally embodied in various dark-complexioned country maidens, and occasionally she inspires verse. Next we see "WS the married man," who has been trapped into marriage with a fair-complexioned lady, Anne Hathaway. Burgess's characterization of her reveals how she might have served as a model for Regan in *King Lear*, Lady Ann in *Richard III*, and Gertrude in *Hamlet*.

A position as a Latin tutor enables WS to escape for a time from Anne and the glove-making trade, and this experience gives birth to Shakespearean comedy in *The Comedy of Errors*, which is based on a Latin play, Plautus's *Menaechmi*. A careless bit of pederasty ends his teaching career, but the play enables WS to join a touring company of players with a completed script in hand. Soon he is with Philip Henslowe's company, and events occur that are destined to influence his art. Perhaps the most momentous is his meeting with Harry Wriothesley, third Earl of Southampton, who is to become "Mr. W.H." of the sonnets. Like the poet himself, Harry is sexually ambiguous, and when he seems to favor other effeminate young lords and a rival poet named Chapman, WS is wracked by jealousy.

As he rises to prominence as both playwright and poet, WS is drawn on by occasional glimpses of his goddess. No longer an unsophisticated country boy, he does not see her embodied in every dark-haired wench, but when he catches a glimpse of Fatimah, more commonly known as Lucy Negro, a brown-gold girl from the East Indies, the old yearning to know his goddess fully in the flesh overwhelms him again. His conquest of this dark lady is a long and arduous process, but he finally succeeds and finds himself in a state of desperate sexual bondage.

His deliverance from this enchantment is painful and disillusioning. His two "angels" (as he describes them in Sonnet 144) meet each other, and, knowing the lady's courtly ambitions and Wriothesley's voluptuous nature, he must before long "guess one angel in another's hell." Eventually he is reconciled with Wriothesley, but then his refusal to join the young man in supporting the Essex revolt causes another break, which is permanent. Eventually, too, he is reconciled with the dark lady, whose relationship with Wriothesley has been terminated by a pregnancy for which WS is probably responsible. The golden son she bears is to be raised as a gentleman and sent to her homeland in the Far East, and the poet is exhilarated by the thought that "his blood would, after all, flow to the East." Unfortunately, she also bears within her "hell" the fatal spirochete, a gift of Mr. W.H., which will have a profound influence on the development of Shakespeare's art.

With the poet's discovery that he is syphilitic, Mr. Burgess is near the end of both his lecture and the *samsu*. In the epilogue, the voice of the poet merges completely with that of the writer-lecturer, and, although the latter is not himself syphilitic, he describes how the disease molded "his" art even as it ravaged his body. Burgess has observed that students of serious literature may owe as much to the spirochete as they do to the tubercle bacillus. Tuberculosis and syphilis would

seem to be the most "creative" diseases, and it is significant that John Keats, who had "an especially good hand," had both, Mr. Burgess says. The list of syphilitic poets is long, including such widely differing talents as Charles-Pierre Baudelaire and Edward Lear, and to this list Burgess would add the greatest name of all. His reasons are based chiefly upon close study of the poet's later works and the actual experience, while he was serving with the Royal Army Medical Corps, of seeing genius flower in individuals suffering the last stages of the disease.

This is not to suggest that Burgess simply used his imagination in lieu of doing his homework. His knowledge of the late Tudor period and its well-documented events is considerable, and by his deft use of allusion and descriptive detail, as well as his imitation of Elizabethan idiom, he gives us an extremely convincing picture of the vigor, violence, filth, and color of Elizabethan town and country life.

In 1966 Burgess, having already experimented successfully with a wide variety of subgenres of the novel—mock-epic, historical romance, picaresque, proleptic satire—turned his hand to a type that seems to be, by its very nature and purpose, fatally constricting to a writer with Burgess's philosophical and artistic concerns. *Tremor of Intent* is a spy thriller, and upon the well-worn framework of Ian Fleming's James Bond formula Burgess has fleshed out and molded a tale of intrigue that must fire the senses of even the most Bond-weary aficionado of the spy thriller. The typical Bond feats of appetite are duplicated and surpassed, sometimes to a ridiculous extent. The protagonist, Denis Hillier, has bedroom adventures that make Bond's conquests seem as crude and unfulfilling as an adolescent's evening affair with an issue of *Playboy*. His gastronomic awareness is such that Bond is by comparison an epicurean tyro. In addition, Hillier possesses a mind that is good for something besides devising booby traps and playing games with supervillains.

Hillier is one of Burgess's Augustinians, a believer in original sin and a pessimist about human nature, and the novel focuses on the course of his spiritual progress as he tries to carry out a final mission for Her Majesty's Secret Service. He must sneak into Russia in disguise and kidnap a British scientist who has defected. The scientist, Dr. Edwin Roper, is an old friend.

In the course of attempting the kidnap, he encounters an obese supervillain by the name of

Theodorescu, who exemplifies the state of self-serving "neutrality" that Burgess regards as the most contemptible and evil moral attitude a human being can assume. He agrees with Dante that such human beings are unworthy of the dignity of damnation. His protagonist, Hillier, discovers that the world is full of such "neutrals," and his mission for his government, which is dominated by bureaucratic neutrals, becomes a search for a way to make a meaningful commitment of himself against evil in the modern world. He is assisted in his spiritual progress by two women, who represent stages in a Dantesque progress through Hell into Heaven. One of them, an Indian woman named Miss Devi, is herself a "hell," in the Elizabethan sense of a locus of sexual excitement. The other, a young girl named Clara, becomes for him a Beatrice figure. Eventually, Hillier finds his way back into the Catholic church, which he had left as a youth because of its puritanical view of the flesh. Only the church can satisfy his craving for commitment in the great conflict between the forces of "God and Notgod" that dominates the universe. Like other Burgess protagonists, he has become a Manichee.

Burgess has accomplished something amazing in *Tremor of Intent*. He presents violence and a variety of sensual experience with an evocative linguistic verve that must dazzle even the most jaded sensibility. At the same time, he makes some provocative eschatological statements and conjectures. This in itself is amazing because the spy thriller by its very nature tends to avoid eschatology. In the hands of a less competent novelist, any involved religious or philosophical questions would be a fatally distracting burden; but *Tremor of Intent* is such a brilliantly integrated package that somehow we pass easily from an irresistible, corrupting, and vicarious involvement in gastronomy, fornication, and bloodshed to involved questions of ethics and eschatology and back again.

In some of his novels, notably *The Wanting Seed, The Eve of St. Venus, The Worm and the Ring*, and the Enderby novels, Burgess builds deliberately upon mythic frames and, like his master Joyce, even reveals some mythopoeic tendencies. Many of Burgess's characters are ironically modified archetypes who undergo archetypal experiences or ironic parodies of such experience. However, none of these novels fits wholly within a mythic frame, presumably because Burgess found archetypes too confining for his purposes. In his novel *MF*, however, he found a framework large enough to accommodate his total artistic de-

sign. He fused incest myths—Algonquin Indian and Greek—and gave them new meaning as a devastating satiric indictment of contemporary Western cultural values that goes well beyond the criticisms leveled in the Enderby novels.

The novel's title, *MF*, derives in part from the initials of the narrator-protagonist, Miles Faber. It also stands for "male/female," a valid human classification that the book implicitly contrasts with various false taxonomies, and it has another reference to the all-encompassing theme of incest, especially when certain racial factors, bases of false taxonomies, are revealed in the conclusion. While the obscenity *motherfucker* has a wide range of usages in the North American black idiom, Burgess reveals that the range can be widened further to encompass all the maladies currently afflicting Western culture.

The novel consists mainly of Faber's recollections of youthful experiences. As a young man he had been gifted with an Oedipean skill as a riddle solver. This talent emphasizes his role as an archetypal MF, and it becomes more and more important as the mythic design of the novel unfolds. Like "that poor Greek kid" who had been crippled and left to die, he is propelled unwittingly but inexorably toward a solution to the riddle of his own origins and destiny. The gods have managed to place him under the influence of a professor who introduces him to the works of one Sib Legeru, a poet and painter who had lived, created, and died in almost total obscurity on the Caribbean island of Castita. The samples he has seen of Legeru's work lead Faber to hope that the main corpus will reveal the "freedom" he passionately yearns to see expressed in art—"beyond structure and cohesion . . . words and colors totally free because totally meaningless." To be vouchsafed this vision, he must make a pilgrimage to the island and seek out a museum where Legeru's works have been decently interred.

In the course of relating the story of this pilgrimage and the events that take place on the island of Castita, Faber reveals the connections between riddling and incest. In developing this theme, Burgess was heavily influenced by Claude Lévi-Strauss's essay *The Scope of Anthropology* (1967), which discusses the parallels between American Indian myths involving incest and the story of Oedipus. Riddling and incest, Lévi-Strauss argues, have become associated in myth because they are both frustrations of natural expectation. Just as the answer to a riddle succeeds against all expectation in getting back to the question, so the parties in an incestuous union—mother and son, brother and sister, or whoever—are brought together despite any design that would keep them apart.

Burgess uses the Algonquin-Greek mythic framework to encompass much of Western culture and especially those branches that seemed to be flowering in North America during the late 1960s. Clearly, Burgess's American experiences, perhaps as much as his reading of Lévi-Strauss, had a great deal to do with generating his vision of incest. According to Miles Faber's grandfather (who may or may not be expressing Burgess's own point of view), incest "in its widest sense" signifies "the breakdown of order, the collapse of communication, the irresponsible cultivation of chaos." This same character, who had a Tiresian vision of the world's corruption as a result of a long lifetime's immersion in it, observes that the totally free (because totally meaningless) "works of Sib Legeru exhibit the nastiest aspects of incest. . . . In them are combined an absence of meaning and a sniggering boyscout codishness. It is man's job to impose order on the universe, not to yearn for Chapter Zero of the Book of Genesis. . . . Art takes the raw material of the world about us and attempts to shape it into signification. Antiart takes that same material and seeks insignification." For several reasons one may suspect that these are Burgess's sentiments. For one thing, they echo sentiments expressed by the semi-autobiographical Shakespeare (WS) in *Nothing Like the Sun*. In refusing to support Essex's revolt, WS explains that "the only self-evident duty is to that image of order we all carry in our brains," and this duty has a special meaning for the artist: "To emboss a stamp of order on time's flux is an impossibility I must try to make possible through my art, such as it is." Recall also the opposition between the honest, technically competent poetry of Mr. Enderby and the utterly chaotic, meaningless drivel of the chaos- and acid-inspired makers who scorn him.

The focus of *MF* is actually much broader than art. The whole pattern of Western culture, as Burgess sees it, is incestuous. Race consciousness in particular, which has in no way diminished in recent years, is symptomatic of an incestuous pull. In Burgess's view, "the time has come for the big miscegenation." He had ridiculed white racial consciousness in some of his earlier novels, including the *Malayan Trilogy* and *A Vision of Battlements*. In *MF* he focuses on what he regards as the equally absurd and incestuous black

preoccupation with race. Some months before he began writing *MF*, he observed "that it's about time the blacks got over this business of incest, of saying they're beautiful and they're black, they're going to conquer, they're going to prevail." In *MF*, he attempts to jolt his readers out of their race consciousness by allowing them to finish the entire novel before he reveals a racial factor that most writers would feel compelled to clarify on their first page. And one of the "alembicated morals" he offers the reader is "that my race, or your race must start thinking in terms of the human totality and cease weaving its own fancied achievements or miseries into a banner. Black is beauty, yes, BUT ONLY WITH ANNA SEWELL PRODUCTS."

Burgess has invited the recognition of the incestuous pattern on the racial plane as it mirrors the incestuous yearning in art or, rather, anti-art. The two are related in that they both reveal a colossal willed ignorance and laziness on the part of Western man. Just as it is a good deal easier to shirk the burdens of true art in the name of "freedom," so it is easier to allow oneself to be defined and confined by a racial identity so that the search for truths that concern "the human totality," truly a "man's job," can be put off. Both the "freedom" of the artist who incestuously allows his own masturbatory "codishness" to create for him and the "identity" of the black or white racial chauvinist are pernicious illusions that the artist, perhaps more than anyone else, is bound to expose.

Burgess's next important novel after *MF* was an attempt to fuse his two major interests, the novel and music. *Napoleon Symphony* presents the life of Napoleon Bonaparte, from his marriage to Josephine until his death, in the "shape" of Beethoven's *Eroica* Symphony (1803). On the title page of his score, Beethoven had written "Sinfonia grande intitolata Bonaparte" (Grand Symphony entitled Bonaparte). Burgess has deliberately matched the proportions of four "movements" within the novel to each of the four movements within the symphony. He began the project by playing the symphony on a phonograph and timing the movements. He then worked out a proportionate correspondence of pages to seconds of playing time. He worked with the score of the *Eroica* in front of him, making sections within his prose movements match sections within the *Eroica*; thus a passage of so many pages corresponds to a passage of so many bars. Beyond this, he sought to incorporate the actual parameters of the symphony, the same moods and tempi and dynamics. The project probably would not have astonished Beethoven, for, as Burgess observed while he was in the process of writing *Napoleon Symphony*: "Beethoven himself was a more literary composer than many people imagine. He was a great reader of Plutarch's *Lives*, which of course always deal with two parallel lives. And he seems to have done something like this in the *Eroica*, though we have no external evidence to prove it. It has seemed to many musicologists that the first two movements of the *Eroica* deal with a sort of Napoleonic man. We see him in action, then we hear his funeral oration, and after that we get away from the modern leader and back to the mythical. The scherzo and the finale of the *Eroica* both seem to deal with Prometheus. In the last movement Beethoven puts all his cards on the table because it is a series of variations on a theme taken from his own ballet music about Prometheus and his creatures." This left Burgess with the task of writing a set of variations on a Promethean theme. After his death on St. Helena, Burgess's Napoleon turns into a Promethean character in the last two "movements" of the novel, and there is a posthumous resurgence of the triumphant mood of the earlier movements, with Napoleon being crowned for having, despite all obstacles, at least partly fulfilled his dream of a united Europe.

Reading *Napoleon Symphony* is a pleasure despite the complexity of its form. Napoleon emerges as a human being in a way he has seldom been allowed to emerge from lengthy historical tomes or even other works of historical fiction. Like Coriolanus, he is simultaneously tragic and ridiculous, a grand comic creation demanding sympathy as well as laughter. He is seen from within engaged in spectacular rationalization and romantic self-delusion, and from without through the eyes of the lesser creatures who follow his fortunes—cynical political observers in Paris, wretched foot soldiers in Egypt and elsewhere, and his faithless empress. The disastrous effects of his Promethean efforts are in no way softened, but there is sympathy for the dreams inspiring the efforts.

Napoleon Symphony was followed by *The Clockwork Testament*, which outraged many New Yorkers, and two novellas, *Beard's Roman Women* and *ABBA ABBA*. The latter two works represent, Burgess says, "a sort of farewell-to-Rome phase." In *Beard's Roman Women* he draws upon his experiences as a scriptwriter and, as he does in *The Clock-*

work Testament, puts cinematic art in its proper place, well below literature, in the hierarchy of artistic achievement. *ABBA ABBA* is primarily a collection of sonnets by the blasphemous dialect poet Giuseppe Gioacchino Belli (1791-1863), which Burgess translated, maintaining the Petrarchan rhyme scheme, *abba abba cdc cdc*. The collection, seventy-two of Belli's nearly three thousand poems, is introduced by a brief novella about John Keats's death in Rome and his possible meeting there with Belli in 1820 or 1821. Another poetic exercise for Burgess, written at about the same time as *ABBA ABBA*, is a long original poem in free verse entitled *Moses*. As he explains, the poem was actually the "source" of the script for the television epic *Moses the Lawgiver*, starring Burt Lancaster, which in turn became a movie for theatrical release (titled *Moses*, 1975): "I was trying to get a rhythm and a dialogue style, and verse-writing helped." The *Moses* epic was part of what Burgess calls his "TV tetralogy," which also includes specials on Shakespeare and Michelangelo and the widely acclaimed *Jesus of Nazareth*. This latter script became a novel, *Man of Nazareth* (1979), in which Jesus is portrayed as a man among men, married and widowed, a miracle worker fulfilling the scriptural prophecies but also living a fully human life. Like the original script, the novel is generally faithful to the Gospels, but there are some imaginative interpolations. Joseph's quiet acceptance of Mary's pregnancy is explained by his impotence. The wedding at Cana was Jesus' own, to a young woman who died several years later. Salome, driven by remorse over the death of John the Baptist, becomes a follower of Jesus. The book also contains useful information for the general reader regarding local customs, history, and Roman politics.

As a result of the highly favorable reception of his television productions, Burgess was asked to write scripts for several others, including a six-hour television epic on "Vinegar Joe" Stilwell, who hated the British; a Persian film on Cyrus the Great; and a disaster epic for Richard Zanuck and David Brown of Universal, "ultimate, really, since it's about the end of the world." Like *Jesus of Nazareth*, this script became a novel, *The End of the World News: An Entertainment* (1982).

The End of the World News is actually three stories in one: a fictionalized account of the dying Sigmund Freud being exiled from Vienna, a libretto for a musical about Leon Trotsky in New York in 1917, and the ultimate disaster that gives the entertainment its title. The inspiration for this work was a photograph, "widely published in European picture magazines in the last year of President Carter's tenure . . . of himself and his lady viewing simultaneously three television programmes."

The same year that he produced this entertainment, Burgess also published a witty little book, *On Going to Bed*. In it he includes some history, some anecdotes, and an explanation of why he personally prefers to sleep on a mattress on the floor: "I am a great faller out of beds . . . a mattress also allows you to spread your possessions around the bed, within easy reach."

Burgess remains, however, primarily a novelist, and in December 1980 he had published what many regard as his masterpiece, *Earthly Powers*. It is a long book, about the length of *Ulysses*, and it took Burgess nearly a decade to complete it. The novel's original title was "The Affairs of Men." Then it became "The Prince of the Powers of the Air" and finally *Earthly Powers*. The second title was taken from Thomas Hobbes's description of Satan and his kingdom in part 4 of *Leviathan* (1651).

The protagonist, Don Carlo Campanatti, is modeled on the late Pope John XXIII, a pontiff whom Burgess neither revered nor admired. He has referred to him as a "Pelagian heretic" and an "emissary of the devil" who caused the church enormous damage by raising unrealistic hopes that there would be radical doctrinal changes to accommodate the pressures of twentieth-century life. His character Don Carlo is a Faustian figure who made a bargain with the devil in return for the earthly powers of the papacy.

Perception of Don Carlo is dependent upon another protagonist, Kenneth M. Toomey, an eighty-one-year-old homosexual novelist-playwright modeled deliberately on W. Somerset Maugham. The ubiquitous references to Maugham and the obvious parallels between Toomey's career and Maugham's make the identification virtually explicit. Toomey has throughout his long life acted in accord with his nature and his occupation as a writer. Where they have brought him is clearly revealed in what he himself calls the novel's *"arresting opening"*: "It was the afternoon of my eighty-first birthday, and I was in bed with my catamite when Ali announced that the archbishop had come to see me." Especially suggestive in this first sentence is the word catamite, evoking as it does an image of refined decadence and pagan luxury in a quasi-Olympian

setting. Generally acknowledged "greatness" as a writer has eluded Toomey, but he has achieved a kind of Olympian eminence of fame and wealth and the freedom of fleshly indulgence that goes with wealth. The Ganymede (a Greek name from which the Latin word *catamite* derives), however, is no downy-chinned little Greek boy, but a fat, sadistic drunkard named Geoffrey Enright, whom Toomey keeps and who may be modeled on one of Maugham's secretary-companions. Burgess demonstrates that the freedom of fleshly indulgence is also the bondage. Enright is only one in a line of lovers who have made Toomey pay for their favors with more than money. To escape the pain of loneliness he has had to endure repeated humiliation, spite, and treachery.

As with so many of Burgess's novels, the Pelagian versus Augustinian theme is central to *Earthly Powers*. He introduces it subtly in several places in the novel by means of a fragment from Catullus: "*Solitam . . . Minotauro . . . pro caris corpus.*" In other Burgess novels, notably *The Worm and the Ring* and *Inside Mr. Enderby*, the Minotaur is described as a Greek mythic analogue of original sin, and Theseus (who killed the monster) is analogous to the heretic Pelagius, who denied original sin and asserted that man was capable of achieving perfection without the aid of divine grace. Enderby is in the process of writing a long poem about Theseus and the Minotaur, the argument of which is "Without Original Sin there is no civilization."

Earthly Powers is mainly about the monsters that abide within the labyrinth of the human soul. That there are such monsters is something Toomey and Don Carlo both believe. For Toomey, one of Burgess's "Augustinians," the monsters are the forms of badness that are part of fallen human nature. His personal monster is his homosexual nature, which he has managed to overcome only once, through the experience of a nonphysical love for another man that in effect drove out all desire. The death of this man, which is the result of diabolical machinations, in effect deprives Toomey of a grace bearer, indeed the only source of grace in his life, leaving him prey to the monster of his own nature and the monstrous relationships his nature demands. For Don Carlo, on the other hand, the monsters within are all intruders who have come from the kingdom of darkness. Since man is God's creation, he is perfect. Evil is wholly from the devil, who taught man how to be evil and is still teaching him. God permits this because he will in no way abridge human freedom. Man is free to reverse the consequences of the Fall: "the return to perfection is possible." These beliefs shape Carlo's theology and his career. Toomey emphasizes and reemphasizes their importance in Carlo's thinking. Initially, they lead him into prominence in the field of exorcism, and Toomey sees him in action against devils in Malaya and the devils inhabiting Italian mobsters in Chicago. Wherever the devil is at work, it seems, he may expect to encounter Carlo.

While Carlo sees himself as Satan's enemy and a champion of mankind against the powers of darkness, it is suggested early in the novel that he is vulnerable to these same powers, and one must be attentive to these suggestions if one is to accept some of the later developments in the novel as plausible. The genuinely heretical nature of Carlo's beliefs in human perfectibility is made clear in a treatise he writes that includes, among other things, a defense of Pelagius.

Burgess effectively juxtaposes Carlo's and Toomey's views and explanations of various evils in the twentieth century, and he suggests that both views are to some extent partially correct, but both are also significantly limited. Toomey would attribute such triumphs of evil as nazism wholly to innate human depravity, while Carlo would credit them wholly to the devil. Burgess's depiction of events suggests, however, that there is an interaction, a cooperation between the demons that are a part of man's nature and the devil himself. Failure to recognize the existence of both may lead to dreadful consequences.

Earthly Powers has been generally praised by critics, and it was a Book of the Month Club choice. Enormous in scope, encompassing much of twentieth-century social, literary, and political history, it inevitably has some flaws: parts of the book are wearisome, and the language is occasionally pedantic. These flaws are, however, minor and unavoidable in a work so large and ambitious. Overall it is a magnificent performance.

Another novel, *1985* (1978), was less well-received by critics than *Earthly Powers*. Originally conceived as an introduction to George Orwell, it begins with a 106-page dialogue-discussion of *1984* that suggests, among other things, that Orwell's vision of England in 1984 was shaped essentially by his vision of England in 1948. The remaining 166 pages present Burgess's own proleptic vision, one that differs markedly from those of *A Clockwork Orange* and *The Wanting Seed*, as well as that of *1984*. One of Burgess's more sympa-

thetic critics has argued convincingly that this latter section of *1985*, Burgess's fiction, is intended as an ironic counterpoint to *1984*, one that presents a near future that is "harrowing but not horrific." The England of Burgess's *1985* has left behind any belief in moral absolutes, is populated almost entirely by small people who are moral neutrals. What makes it such a bad place is the all-pervasive dullness that is the end result of social impulses carried too far, thus leveling intelligence, taste, and knowledge.

A nonfiction work that should interest students of Burgess's fiction is *This Man and Music* (1983). Burgess still composes music, and in this book he takes the reader step-by-step through the writing of his Symphony No. 3 in C. He goes on to discuss the relationship between music and life, the language of music, and music in literature, focusing mainly on the work of Gerard Manley Hopkins and James Joyce. Then he concludes with an illuminating discussion of the musical motifs in *MF* and *Napoleon Symphony*. While several critics have discussed the relationship between the latter novel and the *Eroica*, the musical elements in *MF* have been generally overlooked.

Readers who were distressed by the death of the poet Enderby in *The Clockwork Testament* were "placated" ten years later by his reappearance in *Enderby's Dark Lady or No End to Enderby* (1984). The novel begins and ends with Elizabethan fantasy scenes involving Shakespeare and several of his fellow dramatists, but most of it focuses on Enderby. Very much alive, Enderby returns again to America, hired by a theater company in Indiana to write the libretto for a musical about the life of Shakespeare. The Dark Lady in the cast, a "numinous" black singer named April Elgar, rescues him from artistic paralysis, and he himself plays Shakespeare in what turns out to be a disastrous production. He also masquerades as a preacher and delivers an improvised sermon to a black congregation in North Carolina. As in *Enderby*, the poet finds himself unable to enjoy his muse both sexually and artistically.

In a prefatory note, Burgess explains how the inspiration for the Enderby novels came to him in Borneo in 1959, when, "delirious with sand-fly fever, I opened the door of the bathroom in my bungalow and was not altogether surprised to see a middle-aged man seated on the toilet writing what appeared to be poetry. The febrile vision lasted less than a second, but the impossible personage stayed with me and demanded the writing of a novel about him." He goes on to leave open the possibility of still another Enderby novel, saying that Enderby exists for him and "may probably go on existing."

Burgess's next novel, *The Kingdom of the Wicked*, appeared the following year. A historical novel, it draws primarily from the classical historians, especially Tacitus, Suetonius, and Josephus, and the Acts of the Apostles. Like *Earthly Powers*, another study of Christianity and evil, it is enormous in scope, placing the apostles and the founding of Christianity within a context of events that includes the razing of the Temple, the conquest of Britain, the burning of Rome, and the destruction of Pompeii. Again, as in *Man of Nazareth*, there are imaginative interpolations, some of them highly comic, including an account of how the doctrine of the Trinity evolved in twenty seconds while the disciples were napping on Pentecost.

In 1986 Burgess published the first volume of his autobiography, *Little Wilson and Big God*. The second volume, *You've Had Your Time: Being the Second Part of the Confessions of Anthony Burgess*, appeared in 1990. The first volume is an account of his first forty-two years, concluding with his being told that he has an inoperable cerebral tumor. He did not believe the prognosis, but, granting that it might be true, he was exhilarated by the prospect of "something I had never had before: a whole year to live." Having remarked to his wife that she'll "need money" as a widow, he turned to his typewriter: " 'I'd better start,' I said. And I did."

This was of course the turning point of his life, when he launched himself as a professional novelist. Everything that led up to this "start" is presented with startling frankness and apparently a total lack of self-concealment. He describes his adolescent struggles between his conscience and sex, in which the latter was generally victorious. Marriage to his first wife did not end these conflicts. She believed in "free love" and had a fondness for liquor, and he came to share these proclivities.

His wartime experiences in Gibraltar, which became *A Vision of Battlements*, and his years as a teacher in England and the Far East, which gave him material for the *Malayan Trilogy* and other early novels, are chronicled, providing material for students of his fiction not available in any of the biographies. Of interest to more general readers are the entertaining digressions upon various topics—Malayan expressions for a variety of sexual acts, and recipes for old-fashioned Lancashire dishes, among others. He also describes the enormous impact of discovering new languages in the Far East: "The Malay Language, and later the Chinese, changed not just my attitude to communication in general but the whole shape of my mind."

The same year that *Little Wilson and Big God* appeared, Burgess published *The Pianoplayers*, a novel based in part on his father's career as a pub and cinema pianist. The narrator, Ellen Henshaw, recalls how her father, a piano player in silent-movie houses, tried to cope financially with the arrival of the talkies. He attempts a thirty-day nonstop piano marathon, playing an incredible string of selections that ranges from Beethoven and George Frideric Handel to pop songs, along with improvised pieces. He is given two hour-long breaks at midnight and lunchtime but not allowed to leave the piano for any other purpose, even having to relieve himself through a rubber tube connected to a gasoline can. Well before he completes his marathon, the old man is totally exhausted and dies of cardiac failure. The remainder of this entertaining novel is Ellen's account of how she progressed from a teenage prostitute to headmistress of The London School of Love, where wealthy gentlemen are taught to play a woman's body like a musical instrument.

This is not the first novel in which Burgess has assumed the narrative voice of a lower-class Englishwoman. *One Hand Clapping* is narrated by a clever working-class girl, Janet Shirley, but *The Pianoplayers* is a much better book, partly because the main characters are so much more alive and engaging, but mainly because of Burgess's skillful use of Ellen's "Uneducated English" to achieve some delightfully outrageous comic effects throughout, and the brilliant integration of musical motifs.

In 1989 Burgess published two more books of fiction: *Any Old Iron*, a novel, and *The Devil's Mode*, a collection of stories. The latter work includes a novella about Attila the Hun and eight short stories. Attila is presented as the brutal conqueror every schoolchild meets in history books, but he also reveals a surprising anxiety about how he will be remembered by posterity. Especially notable among the stories is one dealing with an imagined meeting between Miguel de Cervantes and Shakespeare in Spain; a retelling of Richard Strauss's comic opera *Der Rosenkavalier* (libretto by Hugo von Hofmannsthal, 1911); and a new Sherlock Holmes tale pompously narrated by Dr. John Watson. In all of these pieces, Burgess exhibits his characteristic fondness for literary and historical allusions and his knowledge of language and music. His erudition and tendency to be didactic are balanced by his playfulness and wit. Perhaps the best critical summation of this collection is that of John Melmoth in the *Times Literary Supplement*: ". . . *The Devil's Mode* is chipper, extravagant, eclectic and logophiliac."

Any Old Iron is, like *The Kingdom of the Wicked* and *Earthly Powers*, epic in scope. Its title refers to a sword, thought to have belonged to Attila and subsequently to King Arthur, that prompts the main characters, members of a Welsh-Russian and Jewish-French family, to undertake various hazardous activities in connection with the major events of the twentieth century—the two world wars, the Russian Revolution, and the Spanish civil war, among others. There is a great deal of human suffering, but the tragic elements are skillfully blended with comedy to generate in the reader the same sort of complex response that one has watching, say, Henrik Ibsen's *The Wild Duck* (1884) or Gloucester's attempted suicide in Shakespeare's *King Lear* (circa 1605-1606). If one had to reduce *Any Old Iron* to a statement or theme, it would probably be that mankind must learn to love and forgive and overcome ethnic barriers if peace is to be achieved. This was the "message" of earlier Burgess novels, from the *Malayan Trilogy* to *MF*, but Burgess's presentation of it has lost neither freshness nor vitality.

Burgess's stature as one of the major British novelists of the century was recognized by critics at least two decades before these latest works appeared, and his most recent novels have not diminished his importance as a force in English fiction. It should also be noted that he has produced a considerable body of criticism. He still contributes reviews of new novels, and he has written book-length studies of various writers intended to be helpful to and increase the critical appreciation of what he calls the "average reader." The earliest of these was a useful overview of British literature entitled *English Literature: A Survey for Students* (1958). His other early critical work included several studies on the fiction of James Joyce. *Re Joyce* (1965) focuses on *Dubliners*, *Ulysses*, and *Finnegans Wake*. *A Shorter Finnegans Wake* (1965) is an abridgement with linking commentaries designed to guide the reader through the complete novel, and *Joysprick* (1973) is an introduction to Joyce's language. *Shakespeare* (1970) is an entertaining biography, full of fanciful conjec-

ture, and useful to the beginning student. *Language Made Plain* (1964) is an introduction to linguistics that persuasively encourages readers to become involved in the matter of language and in languages other than their own. *Urgent Copy* (1968), a collection of essays and reviews on various topics, mostly literary, contains an essay on Claude Lévi-Strauss that is of considerable interest to readers of Burgess's *MF*. *The Novel Now* (1967) is a survey of the contemporary novel in various languages. Burgess intended to update it to include "more Americans," and this he has partially done in *Ninety-Nine Novels: The Best in English Since 1939* (1984). *Ernest Hemingway & His World* (1978) is a critical biography, as is *Flame into Being: The Life and Work of D. H. Lawrence* (1985). Burgess is a perceptive, sympathetic critic of the works of other writers, and students of his fiction will find that he frequently illuminates his own work in the process of discussing the fiction of others.

Bibliographies:
Beverly R. David, "Anthony Burgess: A Checklist (1956-1971)," *Twentieth Century Literature*, 19 (July 1973): 181-188;

Carlton Holte, "Additions to 'Anthony Burgess: A Checklist (1956-1971),' " *Twentieth Century Literature*, 20 (January 1974): 44-52;

Paul Boytinck, *Anthony Burgess: An Enumerative Bibliography with Selected Annotations*, second edition, with foreword by Burgess (Norwood, Pa.: Norwood Editions, 1977);

Jeutonne Brewer, *Anthony Burgess: A Bibliography*, with foreword by Burgess (Metuchen, N.J. & London: Scarecrow Press, 1980).

References:
Geoffrey Aggeler, *Anthony Burgess: The Artist as Novelist* (University, Ala.: University of Alabama Press, 1979);

Aggeler, ed., *Critical Essays on Anthony Burgess* (Boston: G. K. Hall, 1986);

Harold Bloom, ed., *Anthony Burgess* (New York: Chelsea House, 1987);

Samuel Coale, *Anthony Burgess* (New York: Ungar, 1982);

A. A. DeVitis, *Anthony Burgess* (New York: Twayne, 1972);

Carol M. Dix, *Anthony Burgess* (London: Longman, 1971);

Richard Matthews, *The Clockwork Universe of Anthony Burgess* (San Bernardino, Cal.: Borego Press, 1978);

Modern Fiction Studies, special Burgess issue, 27 (Autumn 1981);
Robert K. Morris, *The Consolations of Ambiguity: An Essay on the Novels of Anthony Burgess* (Columbia: University of Missouri Press, 1971).

Papers:
Most of Burgess's papers are collected at the Mills Memorial Library, McMaster University, Hamilton, Ontario.

Len Deighton

(18 February 1929 -   )

This entry was updated by Gina Macdonald (Loyola University in New Orleans) from her entry in
DLB 87: British Mystery and Thriller Writers Since 1940: First Series.

BOOKS: *The Ipcress File* (London: Hodder & Stoughton, 1962; New York: Simon & Schuster, 1963);

Horse under Water (London: Cape, 1963; New York: Putnam's, 1968);

Funeral in Berlin (London: Cape, 1964; New York: Putnam's, 1965);

Action Cook Book: Len Deighton's Guide to Eating (London: Cape, 1965); republished as *Cook-strip Cook Book* (New York: Geis, 1966);

Où est le garlic; or Len Deighton's French Cook Book (London: Penguin, 1965); revised as *Où est le garlic; or French Cooking in 50 Lessons* (New York: Harper & Row, 1977); revised and enlarged as *Basic French Cooking* (London: Cape, 1979);

Billion-Dollar Brain (New York: Putnam's, 1966; London: Cape, 1966);

An Expensive Place to Die (London: Cape, 1967; New York: Putnam's, 1967);

Len Deighton's London Dossier, with contributions by Adrian Bailey and others (London: Cape/ Penguin, 1967);

Len Deighton's Continental Dossier: A Collection of Cultural, Culinary, Historical, Spooky, Grim and Preposterous Fact, compiled by Victor Pettitt and Margaret Pettitt (London: Joseph, 1968);

Only When I Larf (London: Joseph, 1968); republished as *Only When I Laugh* (New York: Mysterious Press, 1987);

Bomber: The Anatomy of a Holocaust (London:

Cape, 1970; New York: Harper & Row, 1970);

Declarations of War (London: Cape, 1971); republished as *Eleven Declarations of War* (New York: Harcourt Brace Jovanovich, 1975);

Close-up (London: Cape, 1972; New York: Atheneum, 1972);

Spy Story (London: Cape, 1974; New York: Harcourt Brace Jovanovich, 1974);

Yesterday's Spy (London: Cape, 1975; New York: Harcourt Brace Jovanovich, 1975);

Twinkle, Twinkle, Little Spy (London: Cape, 1976); republished as *Catch a Falling Spy* (New York: Harcourt Brace Jovanovich, 1976);

Fighter: The True Story of the Battle of Britain (London: Cape, 1977; New York: Knopf, 1978);

Airshipwreck, by Deighton and Arnold Schwartzman (London: Cape, 1978; New York: Holt, Rinehart & Winston, 1979);

SS-GB: Nazi-Occupied Britain, 1941 (London: Cape, 1978; New York: Knopf, 1979);

Blitzkrieg: From the Rise of Hitler to the Fall of Dunkirk (London: Cape, 1979; New York: Knopf, 1980);

Battle of Britain (London: Cape, 1980; New York: Coward, McCann & Geoghegan, 1980);

The Orient Flight: L. Z. 127-Graf Zeppelin, by Deighton, as Cyril Deighton, and Fred F. Blau (Maryland: Germany Philatelic Society, 1980);

Len Deighton, circa 1984 (photograph by Paul Kavanagh)

XPD (London: Hutchinson, 1981; New York: Knopf, 1981);

The Egypt Flight: L. Z. 127-Graf Zeppelin, by Deighton, as Cyril Deighton, and Blau (Maryland: Germany Philatelic Society, 1981);

Goodbye, Mickey Mouse (London: Hutchinson, 1982; New York: Knopf, 1982);

Berlin Game (London: Hutchinson, 1983; New York: Knopf, 1984);

Mexico Set (London: Hutchinson, 1984; New York: Knopf, 1985);

London Match (London: Hutchinson, 1985; New York: Knopf, 1986);

Game, Set & Match—comprises *Berlin Game, Mexico Set*, and *London Match* (London: Hutchinson, 1986);

Winter: A Berlin Family 1899-1945 (London: Hutchinson, 1987; New York: Knopf, 1987);

Spy Hook (London: Hutchinson, 1988; New York: Knopf, 1988);

Spy Line (London: Hutchinson, 1989; New York: Knopf, 1989);

Spy Sinker (London: Hutchinson, 1990; New York: Knopf, 1990);

ABC of French Food (New York: Bantam, 1990);

Hook, Line and Sinker—comprises *Spy Hook, Spy Line*, and *Spy Sinker* (London: Century, 1991).

MOTION PICTURES: *Only When I Larf*, screenplay by Deighton, Paramount, 1968;

Oh! What a Lovely War, screenplay by Deighton, Paramount/Accord, 1969.

TELEVISION: *Long Past Glory*, ABC, 17 November 1963.

OTHER: *Drinks-man-ship: Town's Album of Fine Wines and High Spirits*, edited by Deighton (London: Haymarket, 1964);

The Assassination of President Kennedy, edited by Deighton, Howard Loxton, and Michael Rand (London: Cape, 1967);

How to Be a Pregnant Father, edited by Deighton and Peter Mayle (London: Stuart, 1977);

Tactical Genius in Battle, edited by Deighton and Simon Goodenough (London: Paidon, 1979);

The Long Engagement: Memoirs of a Cold War Legend, by John Peet, introduction by Deighton (Trafalgar Square, London: Fourth Estate, 1990).

SELECTED PERIODICAL PUBLICATION—
UNCOLLECTED: "Even on Christmas Day," in "How I Write My Books," compiled by H. R. F. Keating, *Writer's Digest*, 63 (October 1983): 26-27.

Len Deighton is a celebrated spy-thriller writer and military historian whose fiction is innovative and convincing. His novels are well crafted and entertaining. He has been called "the Flaubert of contemporary thriller writers" (Michael Howard, *Times Literary Supplement*, 15 September 1978) because of his carefully detailed and complicated backgrounds, his intriguing digressions, and his layered levels of perception. His works are consistently popular, and yet critical response to them has been oddly mixed, ranging from high praise to deep contempt with little middle ground, perhaps because of his comic departures from the standard patterns of the genre and his unwillingness to opt for either the fully serious or the fully popular. Graham Greene, W. Somerset Maugham, and Dashiell Hammett have been named his mentors and Ian Fleming's James Bond the reverse of his reluctant and not-so-debonair heroes. His works have always been characterized by a painstaking attention to detail, both technical and otherwise; a concern with the illusions that obscure reality; and the depiction of the double-and-triple crosses of espionage. Consistent in them is a disdain for the pretensions and snobbery of "old boy" networks, Oxford and Cambridge graduates, and upper-class English society in general. Deighton's works critically and closely examine the ethics and morality of the shadowy world of espionage. At the same time they investigate—with humor and forgiveness—the nature of man, the experiences, the values, the loyalties, and the betrayals that make him what he is. Deighton has a sound understanding of human behavior. His characters are usually well rounded, his plots intricately developed though elliptic and challenging, and his concerns sophisticated and humanistic. His most recent works are stylistically much better than his first.

Leonard Cyril Deighton was born in Marylebone, London, England, on 18 February 1929, of Anglo-Irish parentage. His father was a chauffeur, and his mother was the cook of Campbell Dodgson, the keeper of prints and drawings at the British Museum. Deighton attended Marylebone Grammar School, playing hooky to attend plays and visit museums whenever possible. During World War II he dropped out of school to act as a messenger for his father's first-aid post. At seventeen he was conscripted into the Royal Air Force, serving two years as a photographer. While working for the Special Investigation Branch, he developed interests that eventually led to his becoming an expert with rifle and pistol, an experienced frogman, a pilot (though not a legally qualified one), and an authority on weaponry and aircraft. Upon being demobilized he took a veteran's grant to study for three years at St. Martin's School of Art, London, and later he entered the Royal College of Art, from which he was graduated in 1953 as a commercial artist. He has been an illustrator for advertising agencies in London and New York. Always curious and willing to try out new areas, Deighton has held quite diverse jobs, including railway lengthman, assistant pastry cook (Royal Festival Hall, 1951), manager of a gown factory (Aldgate), waiter (Piccadilly), teacher (Brittany), coproprietor of a glossy magazine, magazine artist, travel editor for *Playboy* magazine, news photographer, B.O.A.C. steward (1955 to 1956), syndicated cooking columnist, founder of a London literary agency, scriptwriter, and motion picture producer. He married Shirley Thompson (an illustrator) in 1960. He has resided longest in London, though he spends several months of each year at a residence north of Los Angeles and has an isolated farm near the mountains of Mourne in Ireland.

Inevitably, Deighton's experiences are reflected in his novels. While a producer he developed an affinity for the cinematic style that characterizes his novels. As B.O.A.C. steward he traveled widely, from Hong Kong to Cairo, employing his layovers to explore new places and to read extensively. Even his knowledge of Communist countries and their bureaucracy derives from personal experience. According to Hugh Moffet in an interview for *Life* (25 March 1966), Deighton was at one time "hauled into police barracks in Czechoslovakia when he neglected to renew his visa." Another time, in Riga, Latvia, when he was unable to find a map of the city, he drew one—risking the possibility of search and seizure. He has personal knowledge of such diverse locales as Havana, Casablanca, Tokyo, Berlin, Cuernavaca, and Anchorage. He knows gold smugglers in Bangkok and counts as friend a military attaché from behind the old Iron Curtain. He has experienced a hurricane in New York and a typhoon in Tokyo, claims to have hunted alligators in the New York sewers, and to have been taken into custody in old East Berlin. He has watched blue movies in pre-Castro Cuba and accompanied Los Angeles cops as they kicked their way into a narcotics dealer's apartment. Deighton has fallen into Hong Kong harbor and been a crew member on a burning airliner.

Deighton is self-deprecating about his work. He told Moffet in the *Life* interview that he only began writing "for a giggle" while traveling with his wife in France in 1960 and wrote much of *The Ipcress File* (1962), his first novel, while on that vacation. A chance conversation with Jonathan Clowes, a literary agent, at a cocktail party sometime later led him to submit the manuscript to publishers. In an interview with Edwin McDowell in the *New York Times Book Review* (21 June 1981) he claimed he began by writing spy books because he did not know enough about police procedure to write detective fiction: "So I wrote my first books the way people would write science fiction, because they gave me much more latitude to invent situations." In a *Tatler* interview (4 November 1964) he expressed an "interest in narration and in the pattern of events" that lead to "a good, bold pattern, a geometric shape" but disclaimed any real ability as a writer. In a *Writer's Digest* article about his method of composition (October 1983) he deplored his lack of formal training, claiming to have "evolved a muddled sort of system by trial and error." He has said he prefers "the initial dynamic vulgarity" to any pretensions to art, though his latest works have been both polished and literary. Although many of his novels have made the best-seller lists in England and America, Deighton has asserted he is more interested in "a strong rapport from a small number" than in widespread notoriety. His method is careful, meticulous, "characterized by an agonizing reappraisal of everything" he writes and a difficult discarding of "thousands and thousands of words."

His writing builds on personal experience, travel, and interviews with experts, supplemented by painstaking research. For *Fighter: The True Story of the Battle of Britain* (1977) and *Blitzkrieg: From the Rise of Hitler to the Fall of Dunkirk* (1979), he visited the place where the German spearheads crossed the Meuse River, so as to be able to match the current season with that of the actual event. For *Horse under Water* (1963) he practiced scuba diving, and for *Billion-Dollar Brain*

(1966) he learned to pilot helicopters and even flew with the U.S. Air Force on a simulated dropping of an atomic bomb off the coast of Britain. To assure historical accuracy he finds the people involved in real situations and either interviews them or corresponds with them. He keeps a notebook of observations, conversations, and images; draws maps and sketches as guidelines for description; and forces himself to write seven days a week, even on Christmas. Each novel usually requires six to eight drafts and continuous, year-round work. Often he has several projects in progress and has never completed a book in less than five years.

An important project might take as long as nine years. *Declarations of War* (1971; published in the United States as *Eleven Declarations of War*, 1975), a quickly written book, resulted from family conditions (living in hotels and temporary accommodations while house hunting) that made a longer work impossible. *Bomber* (1970), in contrast, involved a monumental effort both of research and travel, gathering maps, charts, movies, and recordings of interviews; taking about "half a million words" in notes, all color-coded in loose-leaf notebooks by topic and planned final use; and keeping straight the many characters who were physically and psychologically similar because of the nature of their work and the fact that they all had to reflect the vocabulary, background, and mental attitudes of 1943. For a book (which has never been completed) about how the fighter pilots of the air war in Vietnam compared with those of previous wars, Deighton spent weeks at air bases in England and Germany. His dedication to his craft has involved experimentation and a willingness to take chances with new approaches, ones that do not always work but that further his understanding. As Pete Elstob points out in *Books and Bookmen* (December 1971), he develops with each new book, trying "for more subtlety, for more convincing, more substantial characters."

Deighton makes use of all his experiences in his fiction. Typical is the way he builds on his expertise as a cook and as a writer of cookbooks detailing the secrets of French cuisine, an expertise possibly cultivated by his mother. In *The Ipcress File* the protagonist prides himself on being a connoisseur of fine foods, discussing the merits of fresh mushrooms over canned; carefully selecting Normandy butter, garlic sausages, fresh salmon, and *pommes allumettes*; and savoring vichys-

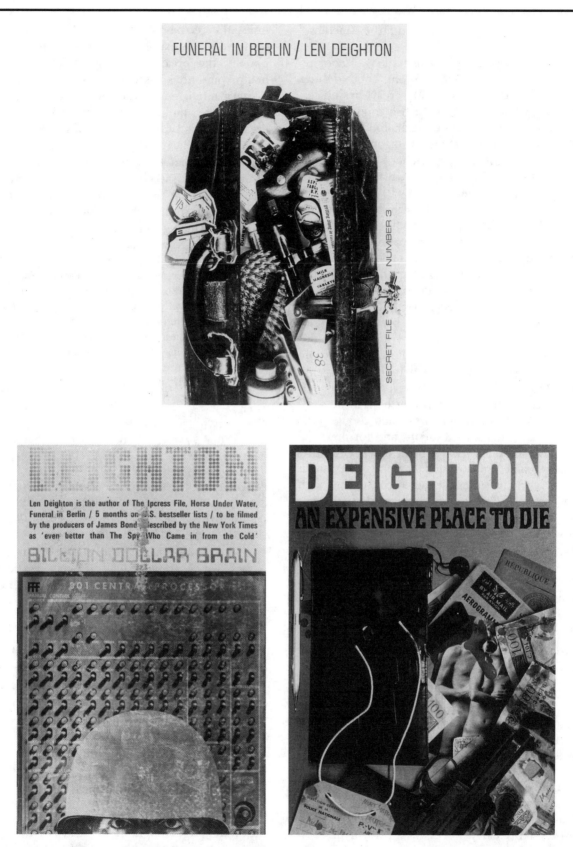

Dust jackets for the first British editions of three of Deighton's early spy thrillers that share the same unnamed agent-narrator

soise rich with fresh cream and the "mellow," "earthy" flavor of leek.

In his trilogy *Berlin Game* (1983), *Mexico Set* (1984), and *London Match* (1985), food defines the man and the culture, and reveals prejudices, values, and temperaments. British food is played off against French food, German food, and Russian food. In *Mexico Set* the protagonist, Bernard Samson, a cynical, experienced professional agent with fixed loyalties, is in marked contrast to his immediate superior, Dicky Cruyer, an amateurish dilettante who dabbles and samples culture with no real depth of feeling. The difference in their personalities and abilities is summed up in their reaction to Mexican food. Samson is knowledgeable and culturally oriented but knows what he likes and cautiously sticks to it. "I have a very limited capacity for the primitive permutations of tortillas, bean mush, and chilis that numb the palate and sear the insides from Dallas to Cape Horn," he quips, and he claims to "never really trust drinking water anywhere but Scotland, and I've never been to Scotland." Cruyer, in contrast, prides himself on sampling market food, trying *surtido* and *carnitas* with various *salsas*, marinated cactus, and tortillas, lecturing on their virtues as the more culturally knowledgeable Samson quietly points out that it is pork ear and intestine he is consuming with such gusto. As Cruyer, with cultivated condescension, pedantically explains the differences in chilis, while mistaking "cayenne for one of the very mild *aji* chilis, from the eastern provinces," Samson silently watches and relishes Cruyer's reactions to the fiery pepper. Samson can merge with an alien population, lose himself in the crowd, and, because of his sensitivity and caution, survive. Cruyer alienates the locals, rushes headlong into disaster, and does not have a clue to the subtleties around him.

Deighton's novels are crammed full of minutiae—technical data, statistics, and references to documents, training manuals, and memos—that lend authenticity and realism to his descriptions and leave the reader feeling he has learned something about an area of expertise. His control of the specialized jargon of spying, flying, and computer operations is impressive and convincing. The need to incorporate interesting tidbits gathered while researching his books finds release in his early works in the form of footnotes explaining the current jargon of espionage, and appendices on such diverse topics as Soviet military districts, privately owned intelligence units, the recipe for a powerful cocktail, advice on handling unfamiliar pistols and tapping telephones, the prices currently fetched by Indian hemp, poisonous insecticides, the Abwehr (Nazi military intelligence), the Official Secrets Act of 1911, Soviet and French security systems, and the composition of neutron bombs.

His scholarly apparatus can become a vice when it dominates the main text at the expense of plot, theme, and characterization. *Bomber*, powerful though it is, exemplifies this problem. Throughout it are banal conversations, stilted and unconvincing because they function only to detail masses of information:

> "I've never seen a LaG3, but its newest variant is the La5FN. It's got fuel injection, a 1,650-h.p. motor, and the exhaust gases—carbon dioxide and nitrogen—are passed into the fuel tanks as a precaution against incendiary bullet hits. It's got two cannons with supplementary rockets. . . . It's a good plane."
>
> "How fast?" asked Kokke.
>
> "I got nearly 400 m.p.h. out of it at 15,000 feet."
>
> "That's fast," said Beer.
>
> "But what can it do at higher altitudes?" asked Kokke.

Paul West believes Deighton loads his books with data "not to create plausibility, but because he seems to like data for data's sake" (*Book World*, 27 September 1970). He finds Deighton's obsession with digressive detail "infuriating" and "stultifying." For example, Deighton tells readers of *Bomber* that the price of training a Lancaster crew would be enough to send them all to Oxford or Cambridge for three years and that the cost of maintaining a single bomber totaled 120,000 pounds in 1941, though of course a central point throughout *Bomber* is the wastefulness of war. T. J. Binyon in the *Times Literary Supplement* (13 March 1981) is disturbed by what he calls "the redundant adverbial and adjectival clutter" that sacrifices literary quality for documentation.

Deighton certainly makes no claim to being a stylist; he used metaphors and literary allusions sparingly in his first efforts and rarely strove for the poetic touch. His prose, however, has always been serviceable. One difficulty may be that critics often judge Deighton in terms of the traditions of the genre when in fact most often he works against the genre, using it, parodying it, transforming it to suit his own purposes.

Deighton, circa 1967

Mexico Set illustrates the way Deighton works in information he wants to share with the reader, while integrating it into the progression of his novel. In it Samson's friend, Werner Volkmann, delivers a brief dissertation on why Mexico is ripe for revolution: " 'Look around; two-thirds of the Mexican population—about fifty million people—are living at starvation level. You've seen the *campesinos* struggling to grow crops in volcanic ash or rock, and bring to market half a dozen onions or some such pathetic little crop. You've seen them scratching a living here in the city in slums as bad as anywhere in the world. Four out of ten Mexicans never drink milk, two out of ten never eat meat, eggs, or bread. But the Mexican government subsidizes Coca-Cola sales. The official explanation is that Coca-Cola is nutritious.' Werner drank some of the disgusting coffee. 'And now that the IMF have forced Mexico to devalue the peso, big U.S. companies—such as Xerox and Sheraton—can build factories and hotels here at rock-bottom prices, but sell to hard-currency customers. Inflation goes up. Unemployment figures go up. Taxes go up. Prices go up. But wages go down. How would you like it if you were Mexico?' " Such details obviously give Deighton an opportunity to express a moral outrage he personally feels, and, within the context of *Mexico Set*, they function to make the point that the KGB agent the British all assume has subversive intelligence business in Mexico has

obviously not been briefed by his diplomatic service; the inevitable conclusion is that he is there for some other purpose than what London assumes.

The Ipcress File combines humor and suspense in a taut story of betrayal and survival, establishing a pattern and a sensibility that has remained Deighton's hallmark throughout his literary career. It depicts a deceptive world of antagonism and secret hatreds sugared over with the polite and ambiguous catchphrases of upper-class social manners. Deighton's world of espionage is one of bureaucrats and civil servants, competing for power and prestige, deceiving and betraying one another, and institutionalizing incompetence. It is a world of "old boy" networks in which rank and class, attendance at the right schools, and use of the right accent count for more than intelligence, competence, or loyalty. The result is a collection of self-centered dilettantes—lisping homosexuals, senile eccentrics, bumbling idiots—engaged in ambitious interdepartmental games that lead to serious betrayals. There is trickery and deceit on every hand, and loyalties and values are readily subverted by power and money. The interoffice intrigues are often as complex as those dealing with the enemy abroad.

The nameless protagonist of *The Ipcress File*, so effectively played by Michael Caine in the 1965 Universal Pictures production (in which the character was given the name Harry Palmer), is a cunning, versatile, adaptable rebel, one convinced of his skills and arrogant enough to treat his superiors with a measure of roguish disrespect. He is a cynical, competent professional. Anthony Boucher finds him "completely of the 1960's" (*New York Times Book Review*, 10 November 1963). Robert Spector (*Book Week*, 17 November 1963) calls him a modern "picaro" through whom Deighton satirizes and parodies "modern espionage agencies" and "the fictional techniques of Ambler, Fleming, and Greene." The nameless agent-narrator is the mainstay of Deighton's early works, appearing in *Horse under Water, Funeral in Berlin* (1964), *Billion-Dollar Brain*, and *An Expensive Place to Die* (1967), among others, his aliases shifting with time and place. He is a loner, an outsider with only one or two friends (who are usually not fully reliable), a man beset by danger and intrigue on all sides, from enemy and colleague alike. If the KGB does not entrap him, then the incompetence, malevolence, or perverse ideology of an ally might well achieve the same effect. In *The Ipcress File* he asks, "what chance did I stand between the Communists on one side and the Establishment on the other—they were both outthinking me at every move." In *Funeral in Berlin* a quote from Albert Einstein sums up the dilemma of Deighton's heroes: "If I am right the Germans will say I was a German and the French will say I was a Jew; if I am wrong the Germans will say I was a Jew and the French will say I was a German."

Unlike the suave, debonair, upper-class superagent created by Ian Fleming, Deighton's hero is street-tough, self-educated, and independent, a man of irreverent quips and surprising strengths. He is impudent and fallible but a survivor, highly skilled and highly trained. Like Deighton he lacks a classical education but is worldly, brash, and insolent. He has a cheeky working-class rudeness and uses his superior knowledge of gourmet food, locale, and language to goad his superiors. He knows how to do his job far more competently than those around him, which also irritates his supervisors. Thus, he wages the class battle with wit and charm, and the ideological battle between the superpowers with deep-rooted moral and physical resources. Unyielding professionalism and personal integrity help him survive the deception and the treachery that are the essence of his world. When Ross tests "Harry's" reliability by pre-

tending to offer him stolen information, "Harry" is insulted:

> You're prepared to sell information. But you won't sell it to anyone who really wants it, like the Russians or the Chinese, 'cos that would be unsporting, like pinching knives and forks from the mess. So you look around for someone on your side but without your genteel education, without your feeling for social niceties about who it's nice to sell information to. . . . You've got the nerve to sell something that doesn't belong to you to someone you don't like. . . .

He chokes on his Tio Pepe, and returns to his assignment; "even if I don't get the Minister's certificate of Good Housekeeping doing it," he shouts as he rushes away. Ultimately, in Deighton's work there is the sense that there is no national honor, only the personal honor of a few individuals who dare to stand up against the faceless majority of self-seeking hypocrites who run the spy agencies on both sides of the Iron Curtain.

His protagonist, to some extent, reflects Deighton's interest in Dashiell Hammett. Deighton has him read and quote from Hammett. In fact, the first-person narrator of Deighton's early works tells his story with patterns like those Hammett uses in *The Continental Op* (1945): a series of seemingly disconnected episodes, vividly related and packed with action. The unified pattern is only visible in its entirety at the end of the game (discussed in "Cloak without Dagger," *Times Literary Supplement*, 8 February 1963). This approach has irritated critics who decry the loose, episodic sequences as baffling, enigmatic obfuscation, but beneath the seeming chaos there is almost always a brilliantly executed design.

In Deighton's early works the protagonist is a young man, new to the espionage game, a pawn in the hands of his superiors as well as a pawn of competing agencies. In his later works the protagonist is middle-aged, entering his forties and experiencing the disillusionment inevitable from thwarted ambition, constant betrayal, and a knowledge that incompetent amateurs are still playing games with his life and the lives of those around him. He is a man who has more in common with a middle-aged KGB agent than with his own people, a man for whom seeing through illusion has become so much a way of life that he instinctively mistrusts his own prejudices and reexamines his most cherished allies with the realistic knowledge that ultimately one's closest companions remain to some degree strang-

Dust jacket for the first American edition of Deighton's 1982 novel, set in England during World War II

ers, and that the patterns of an incompetent are more to be trusted as predictable and manageable than those of an intelligent equal who can catch one by surprise. In *Mexico Set* the high-ranking amateurs, both British and Russian, turn a standard exercise in defection into a near-disaster, and the two professionals from London Central and the KGB share disdain at that unprofessional behavior and admire their mutual caution:

> "I had no intention of going up there all on my own. The blinds were down; narrow stairs, crowded bar. It didn't look healthy. What happened?"
> "Nothing much," I said. "Moskvin's a deskman, isn't he?"
> "Yes," said Stinnes. "And I hate deskmen."
> "So do I," I said feelingly. "They're bloody dangerous."

In *London Match* a section head framed by the KGB turns to Samson for assistance, though the two have always been at odds, and explains his trust in terms much like those expressed by

the surviving head agent at the end of *The Ipcress File*: "You're an egomaniac. You're cynical and intractable. You're the only son of a bitch in that Department who'd take the rest of them on single-handed." As expected, Samson has in mind a clear-cut plan that will expose the KGB scheme, prove his and his associates' innocence, and remedy certain of his personal problems as well. Throughout these works the protagonist remains morally superior to those around him, not because he is any less self-interested, but because he has no illusions about himself and does not disguise his personal motives behind the stodgy and hypocritical guise of principle, ideology, or patriotism. He is loyal to his friends, his family, and himself. At the end of *London Match* he concocts a sophisticated scenario that will save London Central great embarrassment, thwart a devious KGB plot that has already greatly upset the structure and balance of his agency, and vindicate his superior, who has been erroneously labeled a mole by ambitious fellow intelligence officers. Those who know Samson's record assume his real motive is to rescue a childhood friend who has long assisted him unofficially on various assignments. Those privy to his secrets, in turn, know that his most pressing motivation is to make sure Fiona Samson, his wife and nemesis, understands she dare not ever take their children from him. This is not to say that he no longer believes preventing tyrannical regimes from overpowering individuals is important; he is simply distrustful of all government bureaucracy.

The Ipcress File was an immediate commercial success, praised by critics, serialized in the London Evening Standard, and declared a best-seller in England, France, and the United States. According to Current Biography Yearbook 1984 its sales "topped 2.5 million" in a mere three years. It concerns the mass abduction of British biochemists (eight in six weeks) by a free-lance dealer in information, code-named Jay, who supposedly masterminded the successful escapes from England of Guy Burgess and Donald Maclean. The story begins with surveillance in a Soho coffeehouse, moves on to a rescue in Beirut and a nuclear test on a Pacific atoll, and ends with a brainwashing in an unknown locale. As it does so it exposes the weaknesses of the CIA, Scotland Yard, and MI 5, among others. The hero works for an organization called WOOC(P) and claims to be "in a very confusing business." Boucher concludes that the "spasmodic pointlessness" of much of the action is "part of Deighton's picture of what espionage is really like" (New York Times Book Review, 10 November 1963).

Horse under Water, about attempts to salvage Nazi-forged currency from a German submarine sunk off the coast of Portugal, is one of Deighton's weaker efforts and was not considered worth reprinting until after the success of his other works. The protagonist from The Ipcress File, at an earlier stage in his career, finds himself caught up in deep-sea diving, blackmail, and the heroin traffic (the "horse" of the title), topics to which Deighton devotes whole chapters. As usual there are plots within plots, a plethora of details, and, as Boucher calls it, "the crisp, precise indirection of Deighton's prose" (New York Times Book Review, 14 January 1968). Richard Boeth (Book World, 4 February 1968) finds the character of "cartoon" quality and the plot merely a series of "elaborate charades," and Richard Schickel (Book Week, 1 May 1966) finds the novel lacking in "literary craft." Nonetheless, there is a subtle tension that unifies and propels the action, and the complexities of the plot do not unravel until almost the final page. At the close of the book all

that is left the hero is to seek consolation in the arms of an admiral's daughter.

On the New York Times best-seller list for twenty weeks, Deighton's third novel, Funeral in Berlin, was filmed by Paramount in 1966, again starring Caine. The book sold more than forty thousand hardcover copies by its second year in print. Called by Sergeant Cuff a "sure-footed, and thoroughly adult espionage number" (Saturday Review, 30 January 1965) and by Boucher "a ferociously cool fable of the current struggle between East and West" with "a plot very nearly as complex and nicely calculated as that of 'The Spy Who Came in From the Cold'" (New York Times Book Review, 17 January 1965), Funeral in Berlin tells of a Russian scientist supposedly smuggled out of East Berlin in a coffin with the aid of Col. Alexeyevitch Stok, a sympathetic, clever, but not too trustworthy Russian master spy. It moves from London to Prague and from the Franco-Spanish border to Berlin—the prototype of the cold war, a dangerous, divided city where multiple sets of spies watch "the watchers and the watched." The seemingly haphazard plotting, unified by obscure chess-game images, comes together at the end, and the elusive conversations ultimately lead to intriguing revelations. There are gruesome deaths, including a traitor stabbed in the back by a display case of drills and another consumed by his own Molotov cocktail amid celebratory fireworks. The protagonist-narrator, code-named Kadavar, is skewered in the palm with a shish kebab stick and seduced by a redheaded Israeli spy named Samatha Steel. It is the world of "the expendable hero" in which one must make "plans upon the basis of everyone being untrustworthy."

Billion-Dollar Brain, filmed by United Artists in 1967 and once again starring Caine, went into its fifth printing in the United States in 1966, its first year in publication. Julian Symons in his Mortal Consequences: A History—From the Detective Story to the Crime Novel (1972) says of Deighton in Billion-Dollar Brain that "there is something almost lyrical about his re-creation of the dangerous and transitory lives of agents, as well as something sharp and knowing." Symons describes Billion-Dollar Brain as having a plot "as intricate as the lock of a good safe," and he praises the "characterization of the clownish double agent Harvey Newbigin," the "wonderfully vivid picture of the shooting of Harvey in the snow outside the Russian Train," and the "evocation of General Midwinter's dotty neo-Fascist organization in Texas."

Dust jacket for the 1984 first American edition of the first volume of the trilogy that also includes Mexico Set *and* London Match

The story's action occurs worldwide: London, Helsinki, Leningrad, Riga, New York, and San Antonio. General Midwinter, a reactionary Texan, and his sexy Scandinavian agent, Signe Laine, recruit the unnamed protagonist into Facts for Freedom, their huge, private, international espionage organization at whose heart is the horrifying menace, a giant computer, the "billion-dollar brain" of the title. The organization is dangerous to all governments, and its head, Midwinter, is maniacal in word and deed and Napoleonic in ambition. The story features the bumbling George Dawlish, the unnamed cynical British protagonist, his pragmatic friend Colonel Stok, and the neurotic, driven American agent, Newbigin, "an unstable man in a high-pressure world." The hero becomes more and more disillusioned with space-age machinery, fearing that "it's only a matter of time before machines are pressing buttons to call people." He joins with KGB Colonel Stok in his

musings on the similarities of their worlds. Christianity and Marxism both postulate a life of hard work rewarded by a paradise either for the individual or the future; both fear a loss of faith, the "abandoning of principle for the sake of policy"; and both seek "an economic miracle." Stok sums up their situation:

> You must imagine, English, that there are two mighty armies advancing toward each other across a vast desolate place. They have no orders, nor does either suspect that the other is there. You understand how armies move—one man a long way out in front has a pair of binoculars, a submachine gun and a radiation counter. Behind him comes the armor and then the motors and the medical men and finally dentists and generals and the caviar. So the very first fingertips of those armies will be two not very clever men who, when they meet, will have to decide very quickly whether to extend a hand or pull a trigger. According to what they do, either the armies will that night share an encampment, exchange stories and vodka, dance and tell lies; or those armies will be tearing each other to shreds in the most efficient way that man can devise. We are the fingertips.

The protagonist calls Stok "an incurable romantic," but it is clear from the context that the description is accurate. This is a story of those "fingertips" meeting with very disastrous potential. There are surprise targets in a shooting gallery, a murder in bed with a hat pin, and cat-and-mouse games on every side, but ultimately both sides lose out. At the end the hero concludes that the case will never be over, that "it's like a laboratory experiment where some poor bloody mouse is infected and everything is normal for one hundred generations and then they start bearing offspring with two heads." Thinking of the story's action, he concludes that the usual "path to hell" for agents is not betrayal for the sake of an ideal, but in response to immediate problems:

> They do the things they do because they want a new car or they fear they'll be fired or because they love a teen-age girl or hate their wife, or just because they want to get away from it all. There was no sharp motive. There never is, I should have known that, just a ragged mess of opportunism, ambition and good intentions that go wrong.

An Expensive Place to Die, with a title derived from a quote by Oscar Wilde about the cost of dying in Paris, has been praised for its tight construction, crisp prose, fast action, and vivid scenes. It continues Deighton's focus on dangerous and misleading cold-war games. Jack Nessel (*Book Week*, 7 May 1967) places it "somewhere between Fleming's bizarre exaggeration and le Carré's gray understatement." In it a CIA operation to leak information on nuclear fallout to the Chinese, coupled with plans to explode a Chinese hydrogen bomb, could produce a catastrophe that the nameless protagonist is made personally responsible for preventing. Deighton explores the seamy underside of Paris with its hallucinogenic drugs, its institute for sex research, and its rejects, perverts, and social misfits: "Paris is a woman with too much alcohol in her veins. She talks a little too loud and thinks she is young and gay. But she has smiled too often at strange men and the words 'I love you' trip too easily from her tongue. The ensemble is chic and the paint is generously applied but look closely and you'll see the cracks showing though." There is blackmail, murder, and an especially gory climax. The wary protagonist must deal with a melancholy French police-inspector from the Sureté Nationale with octopuslike contacts and a too knowing habit of analysis, a sadistic Chinese agent who recites poetry, a talented but destructive Englishman, a fascinating woman who is playing both ends against the middle, and Monsieur Datt, "a puppet master" who operates a brothel on Paris's Avenue Foch. He sells information on his influential clients to the highest bidder and identifies "thuggery with capitalism." The protagonist is interrogated while under the influence of LSD and suffers muscular pain induced by acupuncture but somehow manages to come through unscathed, though those around him are not so lucky.

Deighton's sixth novel, *Only When I Larf* (1968; published in the United States as *Only When I Laugh*, 1987), filmed by Paramount (1968) and starring David Hemmings, Richard Attenborough, and Alexandra Stewart, is a comedy thriller about three confidence tricksters—Bob Appleyard, Silas Lowther, and Liz Mason—exploring exotic territory for the pleasure of a good con. A ménage à trois binds the three as they operate with skill and style to gain thousands of dollars, until their final falling-out. The point of view shifts from one to the other, with each at some point assuming the narrative "I."

Bomber, subtitled *The Anatomy of a Holocaust*, is a powerful and moving account of the devasta-

Dust jacket for the first British edition of Deighton's 1987 novel

tion, destruction, tragedy, capriciousness, and irreversible vicissitudes of war. Edward Weeks (*Atlantic Monthly*, December 1970) rightly sums up the book's theme: "the devastation of machines and the decent powerless to bring them to a halt." John Sutherland (*London Review of Books*, 19 March 1981) asserts it is "probably the best and certainly the most accurate popular novel about the Second World War in the air." Michael Howard (*Times Literary Supplement*, 25 September 1970) labels it a "dispassionate record of horror," admirable in moral purpose and in technical detail, research, and reconstruction, though a bit ponderous and occasionally tedious. Paul West (*Book World*, 27 September 1970) praises it as "first-rate imaginative reporting . . . done with obsessive care" to "convey as well as anything written by an Englishman what it feels like to fly, to crash, to bomb, to be bombed, to be conscious that you are experiencing the first of your last sixty seconds of life as you fall without parachute."

The format is an alternating pastiche of action and perspective from both sides of a fictional World War II bombing raid directed at the heavy industry of the Ruhr valley but by error centered on the quiet town of Altgarten, Germany, 31 June 1943. The novel sympathetically renders the worries and suffering of human beings on both sides of the struggle: British Lancaster bombardiers, German night fighters and aircraft crews, support forces at Little Warley and at Kroonsdijk, and, most significantly, the townspeople of Altgarten. It captures their fears, their prejudices, their innocence, and their guilt and transforms into human terms the impersonal terrors of war. It also provides an ironic tension as the scene moves from a Spitfire reconnaissance team to a historical discussion of a thirteenth-century village, from preparations for a bombing raid to discussions of lovely sunsets, from an unexpected revelation of love to six hundred pounds of explosives annihilating the would-be lovers.

Endorsing the book's theme, the father of one of the British crew members, a Mr. Cohen, notes that "There is a common mistake made by historians: to review the past as a series of errors leading to the perfect condition that is the present time"; what Deighton so graphically illustrates is that for the errors of war there is no remedy because only by the prevention of war can devastation be prevented. *Bomber* ends with a field report: "It doesn't look like anywhere. It doesn't look like anywhere," and the official military sentencing of the German and British scapegoats. Ultimately, Deighton's depiction of a village transformed by war is so realistic and so horrifying that even the most rabid of anti-Germans cannot help but feel compassion. It shows havoc wreaked on a world that, as one of his characters points out, "it's taken . . . old men so long to put together." Quoted on the dust jacket, William McPherson criticizes the novel as "overlong, overpopulated and underedited," but "despite its gross faults the final impact of *Bomber* stuns. I have never been in a war but having just read *Bomber* I felt shell shocked and battle-fatigued, and I was moved beyond tears."

Close-up (1972) departs from Deighton's established repertoire to focus on the Hollywood film industry, portraying the life and associates of British movie star Marshall Stone as his ex-wife's husband, Peter Anson, writes Stone's biogra-

phy. The *Times Literary Supplement* (16 June 1972) reviewer finds Deighton doing what he does best, "reporting, lucidly, and readably, on what his imagination sees," in this case "a business so obsessed with surfaces he can exploit his eye for what one might (reluctantly) call the 'furniture' of the world." In his *Writer's Digest* article Deighton called *Close-up* one of the best books he had ever written, perhaps because "it was a safety valve," something he did "instead of murdering certain people." Douglas Dunn of the *New Statesman* (2 June 1972) called the novel "an earnest demolition job . . . an old-fashioned expose" that "leaves no stone unturned" as it grinds "down every falsity of an industry obsessed with itself." Deighton captures the essence of the motion picture industry: the narcissism, the insecurity, the cynicism, the hypocrisy, the back-stabbing, the pandering to youth and to profit, all beneath a gaudy and hyperactive exterior. Its cast of characters includes a movie mogul who enjoys playing with people's lives; a legendary agent out for his percentages; a blackmailing producer; and a leading man who demands a million dollars for each picture, fawning admiration, and satisfaction of his every whim and desire—a world of predators and victims. As the biographer proceeds about his work, he uncovers scandals and a world of cutthroat competition where ratings are rigged and people are bought and sold as easily as books and films.

In *Spy Story* (1974) Deighton returns to the spy format, telling of British secret agent Peter Armstrong, recently hired by a joint Anglo-American naval warfare committee to aid a defecting Russian admiral, a task that necessitates worldwide travel and, at one point, participation in a "hair-raising" nuclear submarine battle beneath the Arctic ice pack. Despite Pearl Bell's denunciation of the work as "an impenetrable lemon" (*New Leader*, 19 January 1976), the *Times Literary Supplement* (3 May 1974) reviewer called *Spy Story* "a vintage Len Deighton thriller" with "an overall impression of richness," "too laconic for an old-fashioned cliffhanger" but embodying "a sort of dispassionate cerebral excitement which, like the polar ice itself, is nine-tenths submerged and all the more menacing for that." Roderick MacLeish of the *Washington Post Book World* (17 September 1974) praised its atmospherics, noting particularly "the bone-buckling cold and interminable rain of the Highlands . . . [and] the hushed, lifeless world of ice, emptiness and stars that looks as if they would break from the sky while submarines, with the power to incinerate the world, play tag miles below." The story revolves around the insanity of a NATO think tank located in north London, one plotting global strategy on computers, in this case war games in the Arctic. A cocky, sardonic U.S. Marine Corps colonel named Schlegel chooses Deighton's unnamed narrator as his personal assistant, as he puts into play the strategies played out by the computer. The hero, Patrick Armstrong, is a typical Deighton protagonist, another reluctant spy, at odds with the world of unintelligent intelligence, a bit despairing, cynically detached and disenchanted, fumbling but decent—a survivor. The game begins at a Scottish loch where nuclear submarines are stationed and ends aboard one such sub, beneath the polar ice cap. In between, Armstrong finds his flat and himself duplicated down to the last detail, and he is propelled into an East-West power play that involves Colonel Stok. He is sent on a trek across the arctic ice pack, suffering from snow blindness and concussion, and carrying on his back his injured, dying companion— all because of a computer's theoretical concern with German reunification. The novel was filmed in Great Britain in 1976.

Yesterday's Spy (1975) moves from the French Riviera to Bonn and south again in a fast-paced story of the complex deceptions of espionage. The protagonist, Charlie, is sent after an old friend who saved his life in the war: Steve Champion, a retired British agent with a distinguished record with the French Resistance but now suspected of a double game involving atomic shells, a game dangerous to Eygpt and thereby to Britain. To rewin Champion's trust and prompt him to betray his position, Charlie pretends to be ousted from his agency in disgrace and left desperate and bitter. The protagonist must face the discovery that the past is not what it seems and that an old friend is just as much a stranger as the unknown man on the street—and perhaps more dangerous. The final confrontation takes place in a mine shaft beneath a chemical plant, with bullets ricocheting "like a drunken steel band at Mardi Gras." Robin Winks in the *New Republic* (13 December 1975) finds the novel "a story written to the attitudes, the manners, the very style of the 1960s in which he won his audience" so that "it is Deighton who is truly Yesterday's Spy."

Twinkle, Twinkle, Little Spy (1976; published in the United States as *Catch a Falling Spy*) also involves a defection, this time of a Soviet scientist, a flying-saucer fanatic and a developer of a new maser. He is aided both by an American, CIA major Michael Mann, and a nameless British agent, but this time the abrasive CIA agent is the protagonist, and the operation is American, not British. This change in focus reduces to some extent the effectiveness of the tale, for, despite the fact that the English might well consider Deighton's work American in nature, his treatment of Americans is almost always slightly askew, a little overdone and never on target. Nonetheless, the focus on political stupidity and duplicity is typically Deighton. The action catapults from New York to France, back to America again, and finally to a clandestine communications-satellite tracking station in the Algerian Sahara. The story contains red herrings, a baroque plot, and multiple potential villains, from a disgraced CIA agent to a reactionary American tycoon. There are karate chops, explosions, hijacking, a lesbian relationship (London controlled), and the murder of a U.S. senator, and readers are left with the discouraging impression that everyone is using everyone else.

SS-GB: Nazi-Occupied Britain, 1941 (1978), a Book-of-the-Month Club alternate selection, speculates in a convincing way about what might have happened had Britain lost World War II. Set in London in November 1941, it draws on Deighton's wide-ranging knowledge of military history, and it is crammed with details about the German army, London geography, the SS, and British art treasures. It describes England enthralled, King George VI a prisoner in the Tower of London, Scotland Yard controlled by an SS-Gruppenfuhrern, and the Germany army and the SS torn by rivalries so fierce that sabotage as a means to power and authority is inevitable. P. S. Prescott (*Newsweek*, 19 February 1979) calls *SS-GB* "A superlative muddle which might have become chaotic," but which, thanks to Deighton's competence, "compels belief," while Michael Howard (*Times Literary Supplement*, 15 September 1978) admires its "counter-factual situation" yet deplores its "unnecessarily ... confused" plot. Most of Deighton's novels, this one included, tend to be more concerned with ideas and action than with characterization, a fact that is perhaps the root of the critical controversy surrounding much of his efforts. Inevitably, the portrait of German interservice rivalries (Gestapo, Wehrmacht, SD, Abwehr, SS, Geheime Feldpolizei) and the details about military protocol, insignia, uniforms, and policies are so lovingly recorded, so credibly conceived (as are the imaginative and speculative touches about a conquered England in which German army bands play "Greensleeves," cathedral ruins attract American visitors, and a fast-trade in devalued antiques keeps Wehrmacht personnel spending) that the fictive plot, which should be the center of reader interest, seems a minor concern.

Capt. Jamie Farebrother and Lt. Z. M. "Mickey" Morse, American pilots fighting in World War II Europe in *Goodbye, Mickey Mouse* (1982), alternate between arresting and realistic aerial combat and love scenes with two English women, Victoria Cooper and Vera Hardcastle, respectively. In this novel Deighton departs from the witty byplay and moral vision of his earlier works to attempt, as Peter Andrews of the *New York Times Book Review* puts it (14 November 1982), "a straightforward commercial novel" about a meddlesome general and his effect on the lives and loves of his subordinates. Critical opinion is greatly divided over this book, with most rejecting the dialogue as stilted, the characters as two-dimensional, and the plot as lumbering and incoherent, but a few finding the love scenes as skillfully handled as the combat scenes and the work overall effective entertainment.

In *XPD* (1981) a compromising and potentially destructive World War II document has for forty years been stamped XPD, meaning expedient demise (sanctioned murder), to ensure total secrecy. Part of a Nazi treasure hoard confiscated by American GIs, it exposes a clandestine face-to-face meeting between Winston Churchill and Adolf Hitler in a Belgian bunker in June 1940 to discuss the possible surrender of England. Once stolen, the document sets in motion a ruthless and desperate battle between secret agents from Great Britain, the United States, Germany, and Russia. However, unlike the historical invention of *SS-GB*, here Deighton weighs down his novel with heavy-handed documentation to suggest that the postulated meeting did in fact take place. He argues that, if the facts were admitted and Churchill thereby discredited for considering surrender—yielding land and sea to Germany and giving vast reparations—"it would mean the end of the Tory party," world outrage against Britain, and the collapse of the pound sterling, conclusions *Times Literary Supplement* reviewer T. J. Binyon (13 March 1981) finds difficult to accept. John Sutherland finds *XPD* building on many of Frederick Forsyth's techniques, including "the rapidly changed international setting, the dead-pan reportage style, the cut-out charac-

Dust jacket for the first British edition of Deighton's 1988 thriller, the first volume of his second trilogy featuring secret agent Bernard Samson

ters, the stress on insider's knowledge and terminology, familiar to the author, alien to the average reader" and admiration for the "front-line men" (*London Review of Books*, 19 March - 1 April 1981). Despite vicious critical attack, *XPD* was a Literary Guild alternate selection whose first printing ran to sixty-five thousand copies and which became a best-seller in both England and America.

Deighton's two trilogies, *Game, Set & Match* (1986), and *Hook, Line and Sinker* (1991), reflect the changes in his approach. Still oblique and ironic, with a sense of humor and disillusionment and a sensitivity to "manners," his writing has become more serious, more credible, more fully developed, and even more adept at innuendo than his earlier work. There are more metaphors and more allusions. Bernard Samson cites *Hamlet* and makes Oscar Wilde-like assertions. For example, in *London Match* he says, "The tragedy of marriage is that while all women marry thinking that their man will change, all men marry believing their wife will never change. Both are invariably disappointed." "What rot," remarks his listener. Both sets of novels share overlapping characters that readers come to know in greater depth as the two series progress and as they see them in changing circumstances and from different perspectives—an intricate record of cold-war games, moves and countermoves in which individuals play out intricately conceived strategies at great cost to family, friends, and foes.

Readers learn, as do the characters themselves, that initial impressions may be deceptive but that beneath the cover-ups and the social games is an essence of the person that to some degree can be known and that can form a basis for predicting behavior or attitudes with some degree of success. Samson's immediate supervisor, Dicky Cruyer, for example, may change styles and fads, but he remains lazy, incompetent, and self-convinced. Whatever he says will be glib, a neat theory, but totally superficial and totally at odds with reality, for he is insensitive to people, place, and atmosphere; revels in a geopolitical drama that calls "for maps and colored diagrams"; and seems more often "a clown" than "the cool sophisticate that was his own image of himself." He achieves competence only in his methodology for rising on the political ladder of the "old boy" network by undercutting his personal opposition—he keeps little cards with short résumés of what he estimates to be his acquaintances' and contacts' wealth, power, and influence.

In *Berlin Game* a leakage of sensitive intelligence information suggests the presence of a high level KGB mole who threatens the continued success of an undercover intelligence-gathering operation and its key intelligence source, Dr. Walter Von Munte, code-named Brahms Four. Munte is a highly placed official in the Deutsche Notenbank, in on the money exchanges between East and West but now frightened by a secret control change and personal knowledge of a traitor who could destroy him. The protagonist, Samson, is an honorable, competent professional surrounded by opportunistic upper-class "twits." One of these may be having an affair with his luscious, wealthy, aristocratic wife, Fiona, who is a fellow agent adept at computer operations. Samson grew up in Berlin, which he considers home, and has a set of close allies from his childhood days

whom he trusts and values far more deeply than he does any of his British associates. His friends include Werner Volkmann, a competent Berliner with tough, self-made rules and a yen for espionage, one who "instinctively sees things in people that you and I have to learn about," but who is on the outs with British intelligence. Another friend is Tante Lisl, a brave old woman whose hotel once hid a Jewish family (Werner's) from the Nazis for the whole of the war. Samson is in his forties, obsessed with aging and feeling too tired and too well known to attempt undercover intelligence work. But he is the only one in his department with a jaundiced enough view of human nature to be able to ferret out the traitor. More importantly he is the only one Munte trusts to bring him across the Berlin Wall. Twenty years before Munte had saved his life ("I owe him . . . I know that and so does he. That's why he'll trust me in a way he'll trust no one else. He knows I owe him").

Frederick Busch in the *Chicago Tribune* (18 December 1983) names *Berlin Game* among Deighton's best efforts, the writing "pungent," the characters "persuasive," the information "authentic feeling," and the social perceptions "right." Julian Symons in a *Times Literary Supplement* review (21 October 1983) calls it "a masterly performance," though critical opinion in general has been unjustifiably lukewarm, perhaps because one needs to read the six works together to appreciate the subtlety and complexity of Deighton's achievement. The plot turns on intricate psychological maneuverings, sexual misalliances, an allusion to Nikolay Gogol's *The Inspector General* (1836), and a handwritten report that betrays identity.

Mexico Set begins with Werner and his wife, on vacation in Mexico, spotting a known KGB agent, and with Samson being sent to follow up. Under suspicion because of Fiona's defection, Samson must prove his loyalty by doing the seemingly impossible—persuading a successful KGB agent, Maj. Erich Stinnes, to "enroll," a specialized term Samson says "could mean a lot of things, from persuaded to defect to knocked on the head and rolled in a carpet." The agency's reasoning is that Stinnes, whose real name is Nikolai Sadoff, is the only one who can tell them who is reliable and who is not and which operations have been successful and which have been failures. Samson moves from Mexico to London, Paris, Berlin, and the East-West border, making apt observations about culture and place. He is aided by

Deighton, circa 1988 (photograph by Mark Gerson)

Werner and obstructed by Werner's young, beautiful, unfaithful, money-hungry wife, Zena, as well as by the distrustful amateurs of his own department who fear the Russian will expose their past mistakes. In fact, the internecine office warfare and the machinations for manipulating the senile director-general almost give the game to the Russians; and Samson, insubordinate with just cause, finds himself continually placed in incriminating positions, his strategy undermined, his scenarios interfered with disastrously. At the very end of the novel, however, his competence, professionalism, and an understanding of the weaknesses of his support and the strengths of his opposition allow him to perform his directive and thereby to clear his name to some extent. Samson seems to win this set.

London Match, the final set before a new match begins, completes the first trilogy about loyalty and deception and the politics of espionage, and exposes what seems to be the final twists in the game of wits between Samson, Fiona, and the KGB. The *New York Daily News* calls it a "stylish, complex story, told at disarmingly slow speed"; Hans Knight of the *Philadelphia Inquirer* finds Deighton anticipating real events in his fiction with "uncanny" accuracy; and John Barkham of *John Barkham Reviews* praises Deighton for his "superior characterization" and for "a degree of sophistication rarely found in such thrillers." As

the KGB defector from *Mexico Set* is debriefed and his information checked against other sources, detail after detail suggest that there is a second KGB agent still active in London Central. The bureau suspects Samson, the loving husband of a defector, but is willing to accept another scapegoat if the circumstantial evidence will fit. Only Samson himself, depending on old friends and old alliances instead of his own department, figures out the multiple-crosses played by the KGB. He ferrets out planted misinformation and arranged "deaths," sees through the hypocrisies of his associates, and unravels the complex scheme to turn London against its own. His children are threatened and his old associates murdered, but he manages, amid all this, to begin a new romance of enduring quality and to field a backhand that ends the game—for the moment. Samson sums up at the end:

> The willingness to break rules now and again is what distinguishes free men from robots. And we spiked their guns, Werner. Forget game, set, and match. We're not playing tennis; it's a rougher game than that, with more chances to cheat. We bluffed them; we bid a grand slam, with a hand full of deuces and jokers, and we fooled them ... Okay, there are wounds, and there will be scars, but it's not game, set, and match to Fiona. It's not game, set, and match to anyone. It never is.

A 1989 television production, *Game, Set, Match,* does a credible job of capturing the essence of the books in twelve episodes.

Before continuing his saga of the Samson/Fiona betrayals, Deighton produced *Winter: A Berlin Family 1899-1945* (1987), his most disturbing, most serious, most compelling work to date. It is a study of the authoritarianism, the patriotism, and the religious and economic fervor that were both the strengths and the weaknesses of wartime Germans. To answer the question of how German citizens could accept and participate in Nazi atrocities, Deighton follows the rise and fall of a German-Austrian family from the days of the kaisers to the fall of Berlin and the Allied occupation. The elder Winter, with his Jewish mistress in Vienna and his American wife in Berlin, expands his growing banking empire by investing in zeppelins before World War I, thereby assisting in the step-by-step buildup of the German war machine. His sheltered sons, Peter and Pauli, attend proper military academies and move into elite and competing branches of the army, one flying spy missions over England aboard his father's new craft and the other trapped in the no-man's-land of trench warfare. In the Weimar years Peter stands firm for the standards of old Germany, while his brother is drawn deeper into the vortex that would become Hitler, anti-Semitism, the SS, and blitzkrieg.

Fritz Esser, an ignorant and rowdy peasant youth who saves the two Winter boys from drowning, exploits Pauli's gratitude to rise quickly in politics, first on the left, then on the right. He becomes one of Hitler's intimates, assigned to handle the dirty work of the regime. Peter's and Pauli's American mother closes her eyes to the steady changes occurring around her until it is too late. Their father continues to amass wealth by investing in aircraft production. Pauli himself, his hands physically untouched by blood, is nonetheless responsible for many of the horrors perpetuated by the Nazi party, for it is his advice that reveals legal loopholes that allow confiscation of Jewish property, internment, and deportation, and his suggestions that help produce the terrifying efficiency of the camps. Deighton makes the reader understand and even sympathize with Pauli, who denies the consequences of his acts and continues a bourgeois life-style without feeling guilt or self-incrimination. The author also illuminates the conflict between duty and honor of the traditionalist Peter, who must survive in a world in which honor takes second place.

In one ghastly sequence Pauli saves his Jewish sister-in-law by unknowingly placing in her stead (in a cattle car headed for the death camps) his illegitimate Jewish half brother from his father's Viennese romance. Later, when that same sister-in-law dies, Peter grudgingly joins the American forces to help them bring down the country that has been his life's joy but that has destroyed what he held most dear. Most novels about World War II make the American and British liberators heroes, but Deighton, providing a German perspective, makes them seem fanatical and abrasive. After the war, as the brothers meet in a bitter life-and-death struggle at the Nuremberg trials, both must confront the realities of what they were and what they have become. This final sibling confrontation takes readers deep inside the German mind to the extent that Deighton must indicate that the opinions expressed by his characters are not necessarily his own. The ultimate question raised by the novel is whether anyone could completely honor his values if placed in the same situation as Peter or Pauli.

Spy Hook (1988), the first in Deighton's second espionage trilogy, *Hook, Line and Sinker*, returns to the British Secret Service agent who untangled the maze of *Game, Set & Match*: the cool, cynical, would-be detached Bernard Samson. For so long the London Central "dogsbody who got the jobs that no one else wanted," Samson now possesses dangerous and confounding information about a huge in-Service financial scam. This information leads him to move secretly back and forth from London to Washington, D.C., from a heavily guarded California estate, to the south of France, East and West Germany, and the home of the Secret Service's Berlin Resident. The old crew (Bret Rennselaer, Dicky Cruyer, Frank Harrington, Lisl Hennig, and Werner Volkmann) are playing out their private games once more, as is Ingrid Winter, a relative of the Berlin Winters of Deighton's *Winter*. Fiona Samson, now a KGB colonel, is also intricately involved in action that leaves one puzzling over new twists and turns in an ever more complicated sequence.

While Samson's associates begin to suspect him of paranoia, he begins to understand that, though he has "enough enemies without looking for more," some of his closest associates may be involved in the most damaging security breach yet. Sir Henry Clevemore describes the world as an onion, with each layer fitted closely upon its neighbor, but each layer "separate and independent: terra incognita," while Bret Rennselaer advises Samson to make quite sure he knows what is at stake. However, the real stakes do not become clear until after the baited hook has been taken and it is too late to heed Frank Harrington's warning that Samson could be signing his wife's death warrant, whether what he says about the funding for her defection is true or false. While trying to prove he is not a Soviet mole and attempting to ferret out a high-level conspiracy, on a more mundane level Samson must worry about endless household problems, from caring for his children to pacifying his youthful mistress. *Spy Hook*, dealing with places and characters the author knows intimately, gives the reader Deighton at top form: the book is riveting, suspenseful, masterful.

Spy Hook ends with Samson angry at his loss of civil liberties and at accusations of treachery, but hooked on solving a mystery that has put him on the run. It leaves the reader hooked as well, with many questions and multiple, contradictory possibilities. *Spy Line* (1989) toys with the reader just as London Central toys with Samson. It begins with Samson down and out, hiding in

Berlin, and convinced he has played into London's hands by creating a self-imposed prison at no cost to the authorities. He muses on the grayness of life in Eastern Europe, with communism faded and everyone muddling along, "complying but not believing," but he is equally disturbed by the "over-" people of the West: "overanxious, overweight, overbearing, overeducated, overrated, overweening, overachieving, overselling, overspending, and overproducing." When he is finally invited to return to London with all charges dropped, he finds himself once again the center of a complex and perilous Secret Service subterfuge that involves the CIA, his father's relationship with the Winter family, his new girlfriend Gloria's Uncle Dodo, and, inevitably, his defected wife, Fiona. Sent on assignment to Vienna, Samson discovers truths that leave him feeling "swindled"—"systematically deceived for years and years" in the name of patriotism. Later, on a rescue mission in East Berlin, he finds himself once again set up, his sister-in-law deliberately killed, himself part of a cover-up involving Fiona's return to the West, and "no stars, no glimmer of moonlight," only darkness.

Spy Sinker (1990) concludes the two trilogies and provides a final summing up and reinterpretation of events, but from a new perspective: that of Fiona—wife, mother, defector, double agent. She is bright and tough, but worn by the pressure of living so many lies. Groomed from university days as a double agent, she is part of a grand establishment scheme to facilitate the westward defection of East German professionals, undermine the East German economic structure, and dismantle the Berlin Wall. This final work in the series is a plodding, unsuspenseful scenario, with few action scenes except at the beginning and end. Fiona is a cold, remote, less convincing personality than Samson, despite Deighton's attempts to humanize her fears. The final explanations are plausible but passionless within a fictive mode.

Ultimately, however, the two trilogies are an effective unit, though the first trilogy is clearly the better written and the more engaging. The cosmopolitan, cynical Samson learns that the world is even more complex and yet simpler than even he thought, and that no twist or double-twist is too tortuous for reality. He has been a pawn in an international game from his early days of courtship. His and the reader's lesson is that of *Hamlet*—the illusory nature of reality, the deceptive nature of appearances, the potential for betrayal everywhere. Amid multiple possibilities how does

one settle on one truth? Is Samson's reality merely a distorted reflection of Fiona's, or is Fiona's reality the distortion? Yet again like *Hamlet*, the reality exists—difficult to determine, nearly impossible to confirm, beset by deceptions, lies, and misdirections. Deighton's two trilogies are a tour de force, an ambitious and extended exploration of disillusionment, betrayal, loyalty, and angst.

Deighton's short stories, *Declarations of War*, read like genuine fragments of history, realistic stories of the experiences and dramatic confrontations of soldiers, whether in South American revolutions, world wars, the Vietnam War, the American Civil War, or potential colonial uprisings. They are tightly plotted, dramatic tales with moral twists aimed at making readers reconsider their perceptions and their judgments, at making them accept, as does Deighton, the humanity of the soldier but reject the inhumanity of the war in which he is engaged. "Winter's Morning," for example, captures the beauty and the dangers of a dawn patrol as recounted by a World War I flying ace, Major Winter, who downs two enemy planes but at the cost of his youthful flight assistant; the major wins the reader's sympathy and only at the story's close reveals his German identity. In another story a munitions salesman to a South American country in the thralls of revolution so successfully demonstrates his wares that he escapes imprisonment and winds up a general. In other of these stories a general's losing a paper war means a real loss of command, a young British World War I pilot rushes home (across the English Channel) for his birthday, a colonel and a corporal (now civilians) recall a night spent trapped in a farmhouse by German tanks, and a British flight officer denied a medical leave becomes a hero in order to gall the hard-nosed, noncombat doctor who refused him. Whatever the situation, these stories succinctly and effectively capture the sentiments and interaction of men at war. Peter Elstob in *Books and Bookmen* (December 1971) ranks these stories with those of Stephen Crane in their haunting and realistic depiction of men in battle.

Deighton's nonfiction treats particulars of World War II with the same attention to detail and accuracy and the same expertise as does his fiction. Based on meticulous research and personal interviews, *Fighter: The True Story of the Battle of Britain* is a careful, incisive, and gripping account of the planes, personalities, inventions, and strategies that decisively changed the war. It is impressive in its technical discussion of the history and development of the aircraft used by England and by Germany, and in its detailed and specific analysis of aircraft strength and limitation. It is also impressive in its sensitivity to the organizational structures and to the personality conflicts and motivations behind the scenes, as well as to national and individual psychology that affected strategy and day-to-day results. Its dramatic rendering of fighter action and its balanced analysis of both German and English perspectives earned praise from both sides of the Channel.

Blitzkrieg is more rambling and anecdotal and as a result less effective than *Fighter*. Building on some new sources, Deighton traces the idea, planning, and realization of blitzkrieg, recounting the how and why of the German victory of 1940, particularly focusing on the influence of industrial change on the German war machine and the interaction of technology and personality. D. E. Showalter in *Library Journal* (15 May 1980) found it oversimplified and lacking synthesis, but John Keegan in *New Statesman* (14 September 1979) praised it for "some gems of research and some arresting conclusions." Deighton argues that the attack on Poland in September 1939 was too conventional to be really called a blitzkrieg. He outlines the development of military communications, tanks, and air power; praises the German military emphasis on individual initiative; and concludes that German failure to annihilate the British troops at Dunkirk was a "fatal flaw" that limited German chances for final success. *Airshipwreck* (1978) plainly and graphically through text and photographs gives a brief record of the natural and man-made hazards faced by lighter-than-air dirigibles and the heroism of their crews when faced with calamity. Extensively researched, it is a tribute to the perseverance and ingenuity of those dedicated aviation experimenters.

Throughout Deighton's canon there is an attempt to make readers see events from a new perspective, to present opposing ideologies, and to debunk sacred cows. This is clear from the way Churchill in particular receives the brunt of his attack. In *SS-GB*, Churchill is in part responsible for the German success and is shot early in the book; in *XPD* he behaves more like a whipped dog than a tenacious bulldog, submitting to Hitler's every demand, betraying tradition and honor. Deighton's attempt to disorient and suggest new perspectives is also clear from the sympathetic portraits of some Germans and Russians,

who are humanized and who, for all their faults, are at times more admirable than the English or Americans for whom readers would traditionally root. The Russian KGB officer in *Funeral in Berlin* (and several other Deighton novels), Colonel Stok, is a likable, jaded professional who finds irritating the naïveté, prejudice, and mindlessness of his associates, particularly the Stalinists. He tells amusing jokes that mock his own system, and only he and his British counterpart, the protagonist, are really able to determine what is going on. In fact, the protagonist finds Stok's outwitting Western intelligence amusing and says, "Stok and I are in the same business—we understand each other only too well." Samson finds the same affinity with his opposite number, Stinnes. While the enemy at times proves as upright as the protagonist, there is often disdain for commanding officers in Deighton's work. Samson's tirades are directed as much against the public-school aristocrats, who learned to enjoy physical discomfort but who depend for self-identity on "some grand illusory image" they have of themselves, or who arrogantly consider personal satisfaction of greater importance than country or duty, as against the duplicitous Soviet opposition.

One might, with time, forget Len Deighton's plot, the details that created the suspense, the host of characters, and even the main point of an individual work, but what stays with the reader is a vivid image of Berlin and clandestine East-West relationships, of the Deighton protagonist: his wit, his irreverence, his competence, his disillusionment. One also remembers the attitudes central to Deighton's canon: a disdain for self-serving, amateurish games of the top-level "authorities," admiration for the competence and humanity of the men of the rank and file, a horror of war and the machinery of war, a sense of the basic humanity of men on both sides of the political barriers, and a deep-seated awareness that all is never what it seems and that one must look closely and think carefully with the mind, not the heart, to find the reality behind the illusion—and even then still be wrong.

Interviews:
"Interview: Len Deighton," *Tatler* (4 November 1964);

Hugh Moffet, "Hot Spy Writer on the Lam," *Life*, 60 (25 March 1966): 84-86;

Edwin McDowell, "Behind the Best Sellers," *New York Times Book Review*, 21 June 1981, p. 34.

References:

Fred Erisman, "Romantic Reality in the Spy Stories of Len Deighton," *Armchair Detective*, 10 (April 1977): 101-105;

Constantine Fitzgibbon, "Len Deighton's Cold New View," *Spectator*, 228 (8 April 1972): 546;

H. R. F. Keating, *Whodunit?: A Guide to Crime, Suspense and Spy Fiction* (New York: Van Nostrand, 1982);

"Men Who Throw Cold Water on Hot Spies," *Vogue* (July 1965): 94-95;

Edward Milward-Oliver, *The Len Deighton Companion* (London: Grafton, 1987);

Lars Ole Sauerberg, *Secret Agents in Fiction: Ian Fleming, John le Carré and Len Deighton* (New York: St. Martin's Press, 1984);

Julian Symons, *Mortal Consequences*: *A History— From the Detective Story to the Crime Novel* (New York: Harper, 1972).

Shelagh Delaney

(25 November 1939 -   )

This entry was updated by Susan Whitehead from her entry in
DLB 13: British Dramatists Since World War II: Part One.

BOOKS: *A Taste of Honey* (London: Methuen, 1959; New York: Grove, 1959);

The Lion in Love (London: Methuen, 1961; New York: Grove, 1961);

Sweetly Sings the Donkey (New York: Putnam's, 1963; London: Methuen, 1964).

PLAY PRODUCTIONS: *A Taste of Honey*, Stratford, London, Theatre Royal, 27 May 1958; London, Wyndham's Theatre, 10 February 1959 (transferred 8 June 1959 to Criterion Theatre); New York, Lyceum Theatre, 4 October 1960, 376 [performances];

The Lion in Love, Coventry, Belgrade Theatre, 5 September 1960; London, Royal Court Theatre, 29 December 1960; New York, One Sheridan Square, 25 April 1963, 6.

MOTION PICTURES: *A Taste of Honey*, screenplay by Delaney and Tony Richardson, Woodfall Films, 1962;

Charlie Bubbles, screenplay by Delaney, Memorial Enterprises/Universal Films, 1968;

Dance With a Stranger, screenplay by Delaney, First Film-Goldcrest, 1985.

After seeing the first production of Shelagh Delaney's *A Taste of Honey* in May 1958, Lindsay Anderson said of the play in *Encore*: "To talk as we do about new working-class audiences, about plays that will interpret the common experiences of today—all this is one thing and a good thing too. But how much better even, how much more exciting, to find such theatre suddenly here, suddenly sprung up under our feet!" He went on to call *A Taste of Honey* "A work of complete, exhilarating originality," which "has all the strength and none of the weaknesses of a pronounced, authentic local accent," and proclaimed it "a real escape from the middle-brow, middle-class vacuum of the West End." His view was shared by many critics, and although Delaney's second and only other stage play was later pronounced a flop, it was generally accepted that this tall, poised Salford girl, scarcely out of her teens, brought to the English theater a badly needed influx of new ideas from the provinces.

Of Irish heritage, Shelagh Delaney is the daughter of Elsie Delaney and Joseph Delaney, a bus inspector. She was born and brought up in the industrial town of Salford, Lancashire. Her father, who died a few months after the first per-

Shelagh Delaney

formance of *A Taste of Honey*, is remembered by Delaney as a great reader and storyteller. Delaney's formal education was patchy: she attended three primary schools, apparently enjoying the change from one to another; after failing the eleven-plus examination to qualify for grammar school, she moved on to Broughton Secondary School. However, she proved a late developer and finally transferred to the local grammar school, where she had a record of fair achievement. In spite of this move, she seems to have lost any academic ambition she may have had and left school at seventeen for a succession of jobs, which included working as a shop assistant, milk-depot clerk, and usherette.

Even so, Delaney's school experience had left her with confidence in her literary ability, and, between "enjoying myself, going out dancing," she began work on *A Taste of Honey* as a novel. At eighteen she was already considering transforming her work-in-progress into a play when she saw Margaret Leighton in Terence Rattigan's *Variation on a Theme*. She told one inter-

viewer: "It seemed a sort of parade ground for the star.... I think Miss Margaret Leighton is a great actress and I felt she was wasting her time. I just went home and started work." *A Taste of Honey* was written in a fortnight, while Delaney was taking time off from her latest job as a photographer's assistant in the research department of a large firm. The young author sent her script to Joan Littlewood's Theatre Workshop in London's East End for criticism, and two weeks later the play went into rehearsal.

In *A Taste of Honey* two women—Helen, a "semi-whore," and her worldly-wise schoolgirl daughter Jo—move into the latest in a series of cheerless rented rooms. Helen has taken up with a faded roué, Peter, who promises marriage and whisks her away in the first act. Jo, left alone, spends Christmas with a black sailor from Cardiff. In the second act, he has disappeared, presumably gone back to the navy, and Jo, expecting his baby, has taken a job and is living alone in the flat. Geof, a homosexual art student, moves in, and the pair become mutually dependent on

Stage design for the first New York production of A Taste of Honey

each other until Helen, returning after a row with her boyfriend, bustles back to her carelessly discarded maternal role and shoos Geof away. In summary, the plot sounds unwholesome and uninteresting, yet the play itself is a tart, humorous, sensitive study alive with pungent Lancashire dialogue. Delaney reveals an impeccable ear for contemporary speech and the language of her native Salford as well as a gift for re-creating what she has heard in warm and natural dialogue. She also demonstrates an acute eye for character and local mores and a generous measure of confidence, tact, and theatrical sense.

John Russell Taylor, who has compared Delaney's original manuscript with the version finally produced and published, notes that all these virtues are the playwright's own, but the whole play is the better for the imprint of its first director, Joan Littlewood, whose method was to develop an original playscript through improvisation, adaptation, and elaboration. It was probably sheer coincidence that led Delaney to send her script to Stratford: she remembers reading a newspaper report of conflict between Theatre Workshop and the lord chamberlain, and she also may have known of Theatre Workshop's origins with a group of radicals in nearby Manchester. But the decision was a lucky one: Littlewood's group

eradicated several major weaknesses in the work without destroying the play's special character. The dialogue was pruned and tightened, and some Brechtian and music-hall devices brought out elements of popular theater already present in the play. The "larger-than-life" presentation characteristic of the play's director proved ideal for *A Taste of Honey* and served to heighten its strangely delicate atmosphere where, in the midst of squalid realism, the action seems almost a dream spun by the adolescent Jo, through whose eyes the audience sees events unfold. But, according to Taylor, the play as we know it was largely present in the original typescript and the central character of Jo already fully formed and delightfully recognizable.

While some critics denied Delaney any credit for her play's success, attributing it instead to the Littlewood touch alone, others went too far in the opposite direction, extolling the young playwright for achievements that must have been largely unintentional—her creation of a distinctly English accent, entirely free from American and Continental influence, and her appreciation of the fresh subject matter to be found in the lives of ordinary working people. For, along with popular culture, Delaney had absorbed the speech patterns and essential character of her hometown

Angela Lansbury and Joan Plowright in the first New York production of A Taste of Honey

and had discovered her ready-made subject area at just the right time—when the English theater, after many years of genteel drawing-room pieces by gentlemen playwrights, was undergoing a class revolution. Moreover, it would have been strange if Delaney, imperfectly educated and still in her teens, had shown in her first work the influences of foreign dramatists. But it would be wrong to suggest that she was totally screened from theatrical experience—she remembers seeing her first play, *Othello*, in a school production and was encouraged by a perceptive teacher at Broughton Secondary, who recognized her literary ability: Delaney remembers that this woman understood what she wrote, "and she didn't harp so much as others on rigid English. I write as people talk. . . . I had strong ideas about what I wanted to see in the theatre. We used to object to plays where factory workers come cap in hand and call the boss 'Sir.' Usually North Country people are shown as gormless, whereas in actual fact they are very alive and cynical." Apart from touring companies and school productions there were the cinema and pantomime. Her absorption of popular traditions dating back to the music hall proved one of the most exciting new aspects of *A Taste of Honey*,

in which actors break down the theatrical illusion by addressing the audience directly, keep up a steady patter of insult jokes, and frequently break into song or a form of comic routine—all stage devices yet all in character, since Helen has sung and played in a pub, Jo thinks of taking up the same line, and Peter has cast himself as the life and soul of the party.

The play won several awards, including the Charles Henry Foyle Award for best new drama of 1958 and the New York Drama Critics Circle Award for best foreign play of 1961. Delaney received an Arts Council bursary in 1959. After the huge success of *A Taste of Honey*, critics waited eagerly to see what Delaney would produce next—some, no doubt, anxious to denounce her first play as beginner's luck, no more indeed than "the best play ever written by a 19 year old photographer's assistant." In fact, her next work, *The Lion in Love* (1960), was a commercial and critical failure, although in it Delaney took up many of the themes of *A Taste of Honey* and developed them with greater maturity. First produced in Coventry by Wolf Mankowitz, this play did not receive the Theatre Workshop treatment, although Littlewood's influence on director and playwright alike was evident in its music-hall inheritance—the constant flow of movement across the stage, the dances, the conscious joking, and the loose style. But this effect contributed to the play's general lack of purpose and only served to underline Delaney's failure to resolve her various themes into a focal point of dramatic interest. Like *A Taste of Honey*, the play deals simply with the lives of a few people subsisting on the edges of urban society, but it lacks the charm and briskness that enabled the earlier play to succeed. Moreover, the drama is often too uncomfortably like life—slightly boring, humdrum, and lacking a sense of beginning and end.

The Lion in Love deals with a loosely assembled family dependent for its income on selling tawdry wares from a peddler's tray. The action is framed by the son Banner's casual arrival after two years' absence and his equally casual departure for Australia. Meanwhile, his sister Peg meets and may go to London with a Glaswegian dress designer, but it is a symptom of the play's general dramatic shapelessness that neither brother nor sister is an adequately developed character. In fact, the central position in *The Lion in Love* is taken by their parents, the long-suffering Frank and his alcoholic wife, Kit. Throughout the play Frank struggles to escape his worn-out marriage but finally lacks the conviction to break away and join his mistress. Oddly, it is his wife, continually in court on charges of drunken and disorderly behavior, who emerges as the more sympathetic character, and her live-for-today philosophy finally dominates the play:

> KIT: I can't be bothered with things that might happen. I'll face 'em when they comes and not before. Now lend me some money and I'll get going—
>
> FRANK: It's as easy as that, isn't it?
>
> KIT: Look, Frank, don't expect me to start thinking twenty years ahead of myself because I'm not going to do it. It's a waste of time. It does no good at all, and if you won't lend me half a dollar I'll just have to go and find someone who will, won't I?

By creating two successful adult characters in the husband and wife, Delaney proved that she was capable of more than the re-creation of a young girl's dream. *The Lion in Love* bears witness to Delaney's development as a writer; it is more dramatically complex than *A Taste of Honey* and has a larger cast and more diffuse action. Her gift for dialogue reveals itself in flashes, but she seems to have lost her instinct for selecting from everyday conversation in order to re-create speech for the stage—here the audience is often presented with banal dialogue dulled by clichés.

After *The Lion in Love*, many critics wrote *A Taste of Honey* off as a freak success and expected no more from Delaney. Others, however, among them Kenneth Tynan and John Russell Taylor, saw in the second play a promise of greater things to come. But although Delaney has continued to support herself through writing, she has produced nothing more for the stage. Delaney has pointedly withdrawn from public scrutiny since *The Lion in Love*. She exercises her creative impulse through radio plays and film scripts. Her screenplays include an adaptation, with Tony Richardson, of *A Taste of Honey* (1962), *Charlie Bubbles* (1968), and *Dance With a Stranger* (1985), which concerns Ruth Ellis, the last woman to be hanged in England. *Sweetly Sings the Donkey* (1963) is a collection of her partially fictionalized autobiographical reminiscences.

Because she rode in on the wave of new drama that hit London in the 1950s, Delaney can hardly escape comparison with John Osborne and his angry young contemporaries. Like the other young playwrights, she dealt with seamy reality; her characters spoke the slangy, colorful speech of their class and time; and she included, with complete acceptance, a Negro and a homosexual in the dramatis personae of her first play. It was not only her plays that tended to ally her with the new realism—she was active in the movement for nuclear disarmament, and in 1961 she was arrested, along with Osborne and actress Vanessa Redgrave, at a Committee of 100 demonstration. On the other hand, a program note for *A Taste of Honey* maintained she was different from the other new dramatists because she knew what to be angry about. But anger of any kind is not an emotion that underlies her writing. Instead, Delaney has created characters such as Helen and Jo, Kit and Peg, who, while struggling against each other, ultimately accept their lives. There is plenty to complain about in their world, and both plays implicitly condemn social problems such as poor housing and lack of opportunity. But despite flashes of rebellion her characters accept their lot in life without rancor and sometimes with a kind of unquenchable optimism. Even Frank seems oppressed by a sense of circumstance and twice fails to leave his wife. Delaney seems to write from an urge to communicate direct experience rather than from any sociopolitical standpoint. Nevertheless, it was as part of the general dramatic upheaval signaled by the arrival of the "angry young men" that Delaney had her importance, and it is there that we must ultimately place her.

References:

Lindsay Anderson, "*A Taste of Honey*," *Encore*, 5 (July-August 1958): 42-43;

W. A. Armstrong, ed., *Experimental Drama* (London: Bell, 1963), pp. 186-203;

Laurence Kitchin, *Mid-Century Drama* (London: Faber & Faber, 1960), pp. 175-177;

Colin MacInnes, "A Taste of Reality," *Encounter*, 12 (April 1959): 70-71;

Jacques Noel, "Some Aspects of Shelagh Delaney's Use of Language in *A Taste of Honey*," *Revue des Langues Vivantes*, 26, no. 4 (1960): 284-290;

Arthur K. Oberg, "*A Taste of Honey* and the Popular Play," *Wisconsin Studies in Contemporary Literature*, 7 (Summer 1966): 160-167;

John Russell Taylor, *Anger and After: A Guide to the New British Drama* (London: Methuen, 1962), pp. 109-118;

George Wellwarth, *The Theatre of Protest and Paradox* (London: McGibbon & Kee, 1965), pp. 250-253.

Margaret Drabble

(5 June 1939 -   )

This entry was written by Barbara C. Millard (La Salle College) for
DLB 14: British Novelists Since 1960: Part One.

BOOKS: *A Summer Bird-Cage* (London: Weidenfeld & Nicolson, 1963; New York: Morrow, 1964);

The Garrick Year (London: Weidenfeld & Nicolson, 1964; New York: Morrow, 1965);

The Millstone (London: Weidenfeld & Nicolson, 1965; New York: Morrow, 1966); republished as *Thank You All Very Much* (New York: New American Library, 1969);

Wordsworth (London: Evans Bros., 1966; New York: Arco Literary Critiques, 1969);

Jerusalem the Golden (London: Weidenfeld & Nicolson, 1967; New York: Morrow, 1967);

The Waterfall (London: Weidenfeld & Nicolson, 1969; New York: Knopf, 1969);

The Needle's Eye (London: Weidenfeld & Nicolson, 1972; New York: Knopf, 1972);

Virginia Woolf: A Personal Debt (London: Aloe Editions, 1973);

Arnold Bennett: A Biography (London: Weidenfeld & Nicolson, 1974; New York: Knopf, 1974);

The Realms of Gold (London: Weidenfeld & Nicolson, 1975; New York: Knopf, 1975);

The Ice Age (London: Weidenfeld & Nicolson, 1977; New York: Knopf, 1977);

For Queen and Country: Britain in the Victorian Age (London: Deutsch, 1978; New York: Seabury Press, 1979);

A Writer's Britain: Landscape in Literature, text by Drabble and photographs by Jorge Lewinsky (London: Thames & Hudson, 1979; New York: Knopf, 1979);

The Middle Ground (London: Weidenfeld & Nicolson, 1980; New York: Knopf, 1980);

The Radiant Way (London: Weidenfeld & Nicolson / New York: Knopf, 1987);

Stratford Revisited (Halford, Shipston-on-Stour, Warwickshire: Celandine Press, 1989);

A Natural Curiosity (Toronto: McClelland & Stewart, 1989; New York: Penguin, 1990);

Safe As Houses (London: Chatto & Windus, 1990);

The Gates of Ivory (Toronto: McClelland & Stewart / New York: Viking, 1991).

PLAY PRODUCTION: *Bird of Paradise*, London, 1969.

MOTION PICTURE: *Thank You All Very Much*, screenplay by Drabble, Columbia Pictures, 1969; as *A Touch of Love*, Palomar Pictures, London, 18 August 1969.

Margaret Drabble (photograph by Fay Godwin)

TELEVISION: *Laura*, Granada Television, 1964.

OTHER: "The Reunion," in *Winter's Tales 14*, edited by Kevin Crossley-Holland (London: Macmillan, 1968);

"The Gifts of War," in *Winter's Tales 16*, edited by A. D. Maclean (London: Macmillan, 1970);

London Consequences, edited by Drabble and A. S. Byatt (London: Greater Arts Association, 1972);

Jane Austen, *Lady Susan, The Watsons, Sanditon*, edited, with an introduction, by Drabble (London: Penguin, 1975);

New Stories 1, edited by Drabble and Charles Osborne (London: Arts Council of Great Britain, 1976);

"Hardy and the Natural World," in *The Genius of Thomas Hardy*, edited by Drabble (London: Weidenfeld & Nicolson, 1976; New York: Knopf, 1976), pp. 162-169;

The Oxford Companion to English Literature, edited by Drabble (Oxford & New York: Oxford University Press, 1985);

The Concise Oxford Companion to English Literature, edited by Drabble and Jenny Stringer (Oxford & New York: Oxford University Press, 1987).

SELECTED PERIODICAL PUBLICATIONS— UNCOLLECTED:

FICTION

"Hassan's Tower," *Nova* (June 1966): 100ff.;

"Voyage to Cytherea," *Mademoiselle*, 66 (December 1967): 98-99, 148-150;

"Faithful Lovers," *Saturday Evening Post*, 241 (April 1968): 62-65;

"A Pyrrhic Victory," *Nova* (July 1968): 80ff.;

"Crossing the Alps," *Mademoiselle*, 72 (February 1971): 154-155;

"Success Story," *Ms.*, 3 (December 1974): 52-55;

"Homework," *Ontario Review*, 7 (1977-1978): 7-13.

NONFICTION

"Margaret Drabble Talking about Discipline,"

Guardian, 10 January 1966, p. 6;

"The Fearful Flame of Arnold Bennett," *Observer* (London), 11 May 1967, pp. 12-14;

"The Sexual Revolution," *Guardian* (Manchester), 11 October 1967, p. 8;

"Women," *Listener*, 4 April 1968, pp. 425-426;

"Stepping into Debt," *Guardian*, 12 August 1968, p. 7;

"Denying the Natural," *Listener* (London), 5 December 1968, pp. 750-751;

"Wordsworth: So Honourably Born," *Times* (London), 14 December 1968, p. 17;

"Money as a Subject for the Novelist," *Times Literary Supplement*, 24 July 1969, pp. 792-793;

"A Shocking Report," *Author*, 80 (Winter 1969): 169-171;

"A Myth to Stump the Experts," *New Statesman*, 26 March 1971, p. 435;

"Perfect Ending," *Listener*, 1 April 1971, pp. 420-421;

"Doris Lessing: Cassandra in a World Under Siege," *Ramparts*, 10 (February 1972): 50-54;

"How Not To Be Afraid of Virginia Woolf," *Ms.*, 1 (November 1972): 68ff.;

"A Woman Writer," *Books*, 11 (Spring 1973): 4-6;

"Lawrence's Aphrodite: The Life of Frieda van Richthofen," *Encounter*, 41 (August 1973): 77-79;

"The Writer as Recluse: The Theme of Solitude in the Works of the Brontës," *Brontë Society Transactions*, 16 (1974): 259-269;

"T.V.," *Ms.*, 4 (February 1976): 32;

"Travels of a Housewife," *Spectator*, 21 February 1976, p. 20;

"Jane Fonda: Her Own Woman at Last," *Ms.*, 6 (October 1977): 51-53;

"Elders and Betters?," *Observer*, 9 October 1977, p. 13;

"A Woman's Life," *New Statesman*, 3 November 1978, pp. 585-586;

"Rape and Reason," *Observer*, 10 December 1978, p. 9;

"No Idle Rentier: Angus Wilson and the Nourished Literary Imagination," *Studies in the Literary Imagination*, 13 (Spring 1980): 119-129.

Margaret Drabble's rise as one of the most important and well-known British novelists writing today has been steady and sure. She has received serious attention in Great Britain since the appearance of her first novel, and since the publication of *The Needle's Eye* (1972) she has established an impressive reputation in America as well. Behind her is a solid body of work including several volumes of criticism and biography, television and film scripts, and many pieces of short fiction and journalism, in addition to the novels that have brought her both popularity and critical acclaim. She is a traditionalist in form and a pioneer in subject. From her first novel, written immediately after graduation from Cambridge, Drabble has recorded the conflicting sensibilities of the "new," educated woman seeking her place in the modern world. Her heroines are self-aware, articulate, intelligent, career-concerned; they are also wives and mothers caring for and redeemed by their children, while desirous of emotional, moral, and economic autonomy.

Drabble's fiction has grown in scope, richness, and sophistication, as have her female protagonists. Her angle of vision has shifted from the psychological interiors of single female characters to omniscient panoramas of men and women struggling with the ambiguities of life in contemporary Britain. As Elaine Showalter has observed, Drabble's early concern with self-analysis and female realism has combined with twentieth-century sociological and political issues. While her literary credo deliberately reflects her admiration for the "Great Tradition" of the British novel, her particular contribution to the novel emerges from her experience of the human situation and her reflection on it. "I try to confront the problems that confront me ... but I now find myself increasingly interested by and able to tackle more general subjects," she has said. "I think literature is one of the ways of mapping out territories and problems. I'm trying to find out where we are going." Consequently, Drabble has explored the individual's search for identity; the particular self-awareness of womanhood; the individual's relationship with his own and his country's past; the interaction of fate, chance, and character; and the guilt and anxieties of the liberal conscience. In her role as chronicler of contemporary Britain, Drabble aims in her fiction for the amplitude, centrality, and autonomy of the major novelist.

The second of four children, Margaret Drabble was born in Sheffield, Yorkshire, on 5 June 1939 to Kathleen Bloor and John Frederick Drabble. Drabble's strong ties to the region of her birth are reflected in some of her works. Her family tradition claims kinship with Arnold Bennett, and Drabble identifies with him in her roots: "We had the same kind of Methodist upbringing ... a rather repressive, dull family background like that of my grandparents." Her parents, however, broke from family roots by attending university and separating themselves from strong religious practice. Although her immediate family often changed houses, Drabble always regarded her grandparents' cottage as home. Growing up in an intellectual, middle-class, liberal household, she absorbed a small amount of puritan guilt and a large amount of the work ethic, which she believes is "good for the soul." Her family is both industrious and illustrious. Her father, also an author, was a barrister and then a circuit judge until he retired in 1973; her only brother is also a barrister. Before and after child-rearing, her mother taught English; her younger sister is an art historian, and her older sister, Antonia, is a novelist of considerable reputation who writes under the name A. S. Byatt.

Despite the context of a large family, Drabble describes her childhood as lonely. Often ill, she saw herself as a "Maggie Tulliver": "I had a bad chest and was always rather feeble—hated games. I certainly did not feel I was part of the mainstream." She spent her time alone writing, reading, and "just being secretive." Her early love of literature became an affair of constant duration. She read books about Boudicca and, like Rose Vassiliou in *The Needle's Eye*, was profoundly affected at an early age by John Bunyan's *Pilgrim's Progress*. Like the Brontë family, the Drabble children composed magazines, stories, and plays together.

Drabble was educated at an old Quaker boarding school, the Mount School, where she made many friends and became more socially oriented. Like her father and her older sister, she went on to Cambridge with a major scholarship. She read English literature at Newnham College, and "enjoyed it so much," she says, "that I really think it took me a long time to get over it." While at the university, she stopped writing stories in her head and started acting, with some success, because "it was so much more sociable." When she did write anything at Cambridge, she kept it to herself because she found the critical atmosphere "forbidding and difficult." Drabble still challenges a critical standard so high that it discourages the young writer who cannot know at eighteen whether he will be "a minor writer or a major writer."

In 1960 Drabble took a B.A. degree with first-class honors, and she might have stayed on as a lecturer if she had not wanted to be an actress. She married Clive Swift the week after she left Cambridge and went with him to work with the Royal Shakespeare Company, understudying Vanessa Redgrave and doing occasional walk-ons. Drabble describes her life at this point as without an objective, consisting of "jumping over obstacles: marriage, having babies." Bored with such small roles as a fairy in *A Midsummer Night's Dream* and expecting her first baby, she began writing her first novel, *A Summer Bird-Cage* (1963), to fill the time and disprove the theory that "one kind of creativity displaces another." Other causes contributed to the start of her career as a novelist. She was encouraged in her choice of genre by her perception that writing novels was an open-ended profession in which English women had a strong tradition. She was also encouraged by recent British and American fiction to write something "human and contemporary." Finally, Simone de Beauvoir's *The Second Sex* (1949) presented her with material personally important to her. "It was material that nobody had used and I could use," she told Peter Firchow in 1972, "and nobody had ever used as far as I could see as I would use it." Drabble still sees this as an exciting time for women to be writing, since the writer—like her characters—has to find her own path among the profusion of choices.

Drabble began *A Summer Bird-Cage* in Stratford-upon-Avon during the first year of her marriage. She describes with characteristic candor the process of learning to write by doing: "I just wrote, day after day, like a very long letter, with no conscious sense of form or plot at all." A better novel than such a description would indicate, *A Summer Bird-Cage* reflects the experiences of Drabble and her contemporaries upon leaving the university, unemployed and without focus. The title comes from John Webster's observation: " 'tis just like a summer bird cage in a garden, the birds that are without despair to get in, and the birds that are within despair and are in consumption for fear they shall never get out." As the bird outside in her black and drab-green clothes, Sarah Bennett is fresh from a first at Oxford and a summer interlude as a tutor in Paris. With her "shiny, useless new degree," she returns to England for the wedding of her beautiful older sister, Louise. The first-person narration is primarily a record of Sarah's attempt to find the direction of her life. She drifts into a BBC job "filing things" and ponders the mystery of her sister's motive for her marriage to the snobbish, obsessive writer Stephen Halifax.

The real thematic center of the novel, however, is the relationship between the two sisters, which involves competition, jealousy, self-definition, the failure of love, and Sarah's fear of subsiding into nothingness. Sarah looks to the soaring, white and lavender Louise to teach her success, but she must find her own way out of the social dislocation and lack of commitment she feels. Contemptuous of her sister's marriage for money and convenience, Sarah rejects the other roles modeled by foil characters, including the high-powered Simone, who lives a "wholly willed, a wholly undetermined life," but who is finally sexless. Sarah wants the best of worlds: "I should like to bear leaves and flowers and fruit, I should like the whole world . . . oh, I should indeed." She begins her quest by liberating herself from her study-bound conceptions of human nature in the appropriate arena of London. Ultimately, Louise's revelation of her extramarital affair and Sarah's confrontation with her sister result in a new intimacy between them and a firmer sense of self for Sarah.

Drabble's style is witty and urbane, her narrative salted with the literary allusions and bons mots of the graduate narrator. More indicative of Drabble's later technique is her use of literary and folk myths of female relationship to provide an archetypal structure for the novel. Despite the book's thematic strength and vigorous imagery, Drabble's apprenticeship is evident in the self-consciousness of the narrator's voice. The introduction of characters and events is sometimes plodding, the minor characters are caricatured, and Drabble's authorial tongue-in-cheek style sometimes intrudes in what she calls a "female love-love story." Although the book was not a commercial success, Drabble found the critical response enthusiastic and encouraging. Reviewers immediately appreciated the novel's panache, its ability to capture the tone of contemporary life, the author's good humor, and her acknowledgment of her limits in the narrative form.

Drabble wrote her second novel in her dressing room at Stratford. Expecting her second child and discouraged with her acting career, she wrote *The Garrick Year* (1964) rapidly, expressing her situation and surmounting it simultaneously: "I know that partly I was writing these books in order to assert myself against the environment which I felt was hostile and unbelievably boring." Actually, Drabble was understudying the role of Imogen in *Cymbeline* and doing a walk-on in *The Taming of the Shrew*. The central episode in the

novel mirrors her concern about children drowning literally and women drowning figuratively in the Avon.

Emma Evans, the narrator—a former model ("all bones, no blood") and a young mother with a predilection for physical facts—is rescued from an extramarital affair by her daughter's nearly drowning. Frustrated and resentful, Emma had sacrificed a job as a BBC announcer to follow her egotistical and unfaithful actor-husband to a provincial theater festival. In retrospect, Emma sees the year as a turning point in her problematic marriage and in her search for self-purpose. Asking if there is life after motherhood, the novel portrays Emma's coy hide-and-seek affair with the "glossy" director Wyndham Ferrar, her idyllic return visit to an aunt's cottage, a timely car accident, and the drowning scene with its mutual rescue. The long-delayed consummation of her intrigue is a disturbingly sterile experience that does little to reinforce her sense of identity. While recuperating from her collisions with the automobile and with Ferrar, Emma recognizes both her strength and her mistake in "trying to relapse into self-pity" or romantic self-centered indulgence. In fighting against domestic chaos, she has almost capitulated to her "dangerous nature." Having survived, she vows to protect others (especially her children) from herself. Saving her daughter, Flora, convinces her that the domestic imperative is her lifeline, at least for the present, even if she cannot "patrol the bank" for the rest of her life. If the children root her in the earth of her unsatisfactory marriage, they also keep her from sinking in the river of despond. This solution is not only temporary, but also far from ideal: "Time and maternity can so force and violate a personality that it can hardly remember what it was." Emma insists on confronting the truth unflinchingly, if quietly, and Drabble's concluding emblematic image clarifies how destructive Emma's choice of motherhood over sexuality and self-definition can be. During a day in the countryside with her family, Emma sees a snake clutching at the belly of a sheep, but maintains wryly that "one just has to keep on and to pretend for the sake of the children not to notice. Otherwise one might just as well stay at home."

Although criticized for thin plot and some superficial characterization, the novel drew praise for its delicacy of nuance and the psychological portrait of its protagonist. The pertinence of Emma's conflict was especially recognized by feminist critics. Virginia K. Beards commented: "As a portrait of the frigid-seductive woman with a muddled concept of both male and female sexual rights, the novel is wise and complete." Both *A Summer Bird-Cage* and *The Garrick Year* are primarily character studies in which the protagonists resolve their uncertainty about the future to some extent, but fall short of real autonomy. Since *The Garrick Year*, Drabble's novels have become more dense psychologically and more involved with exploring the implications of the characters' socioeconomic pasts. Drabble attributes some of this growth in scope to her experience with motherhood: "Having children gives you access to an enormous common store of otherness about other people."

During her third pregnancy, Drabble wrote her third book, *The Millstone* (1965). At this point, having produced three of each in five years, she saw clearly that children and books could be managed together, but that an acting career could not fit in. She was also involved in some radio and television work (which included the 1964 television play *Laura*). Abandoning acting and working at night after her children were asleep, Drabble completed *The Millstone*. A moral fable, the book takes its title from Matthew's Gospel (18:6) and suggests that the child born out of wedlock to the heroine, Rosamund Stacey, is both a millstone and a salvation. Drabble later wrote a film script based on the novel, which bears the title *Thank You All Very Much*, a line from the film. Consequently, a later edition (1969) of the book is so titled. Since its emergence in a casebook edition (1970), *The Millstone* has been one of Drabble's most popular books.

Rosamund Stacey, like her predecessors, is young, attractive, intelligent, and possesses a "strange mixture of confidence and cowardice." The offspring of socialist, middle-class parents, she is a virgin at twenty-five who lives in her parents' comfortable flat while writing a doctoral thesis on the Elizabethan poets. Considering her limited sexual activity "misguided" in this age and deploring a figurative scarlet letter on her bosom that stands for Abstinence, Rosamund succumbs to a BBC announcer whose reticence and detachment resemble her own. This one "pointless" encounter leaves Rosamund pregnant. When her attempts to abort fail, she decides to have the baby without informing George, the father, or her parents. Her experiences with gestation and the National Health Service teach Rosamund what many hours at the British Museum did not: "the

human limit" of her female body, her common bond with the poor women at the clinic, and her susceptibility to forces "not totally explicable." Similarly, her baby, named for the feminist Octavia Hill, teaches her what the sonneteers could not—the trauma and necessary selfishness of love.

Rosamund's education in the quality of life does not hinder her academic project, but it does necessitate a compromise of her independence and privacy. When she takes in a roommate for financial help, she becomes the subject of her lodger's novel; and it is no meaningless accident that Octavia chews up this manuscript. The literary allusions that spring to Rosamund's lips throughout the first-person narration may give meaning to the facts of life as she discovers them, but Octavia is a paradox that all her erudition will not resolve. The baby exposes her and saves her at the same time. When Rosamund finally encounters George at the end of the novel, Drabble thwarts any expectation of a conventional ending. George's indifference on viewing the baby he unknowingly fathered convinces Rosamund that she has grown beyond his numbness. He is the image of what she would have been, but for the grace of motherhood. George remains a shadowy character throughout the novel because Rosamund sees him only with the "half-knowledge" of adult affection rather than with the certainty of parental love that imparts luminescence to Octavia. Since childbirth does not ultimately interfere with the completion of Rosamund's thesis or her later academic career, she finds in Elizabethan poetry the analogue by which to assess the condition of the modern woman. This Rosamund's "complaint" is, therefore, an ironic reversal of the heroine's in Samuel Daniel's poem (1592). Though his Rosamund is punished with death for her sexual transgression, Drabble's heroine finds that the accident of her sexual act and her fate to bear children liberate her from a sterile solipsism and an emotional paralysis. However, while her maternal love may be pure, her cold and unethical treatment of George indicates that her "salvation" is not complete.

Critics have noted the moral ambiguities of this novel, its psychological subtlety and its more sophisticated narrative skill. The subject and theme of *The Millstone* drew much attention, especially from feminists, and led to Drabble's identification as "the novelist of maternity." If some reviewers dismissed these issues as insignificant, they admired her wit and were impressed by the Jamesian nuance of her style. Commenting that

Drabble's "deliberate unpretentiousness" led her to concentrate on the ordinary and "hide her lights in rough homespun," Peter E. Firchow characterized her writing as unmistakably distinctive. *The Millstone* continues to be a commercial success, but after its publication Drabble was still unsure that she could be financially independent as a writer. She characterizes her life at this time as bourgeois and domestic and her writing as both limited and enriched by her familial obligations. Shortly after *The Millstone*, she produced her first critical book (1966), a monograph on William Wordsworth, whose heightened sense of the ordinary life and the beneficence of children echoes in the themes of *The Millstone* and her later novels.

In December 1966 Drabble received the John Llewelyn Rhys Memorial Award, a travel grant that enabled her to take her children to Paris for six months, where she finished *Jerusalem the Golden*. Published in 1967, this novel unites a more elaborate structure with more intense personal feeling in the narrative. Unlike her detached predecessors, Clara Maugham is intense, insecure, greedy, upwardly mobile—and a young woman already heavily burdened with her past. The author describes Clara's tension as a cross between Drabble's and her mother's reactions to their family history, yet Drabble personally finds Clara to be the toughest, most unsympathetic of her characters. A third-person narration explains immediately that Clara's personal unease began with her name and continued with her family and intelligence. Clara's love-starved childhood with a vicious, puritanical mother has left her desperate to escape from her stifling house and narrow midland town and find a glittering life. Carefully selected boyfriends and a class trip to Paris provide her with moments of glamour until she breaks away by means of a university scholarship.

However, Clara's personality is inhibited from expressing itself in any outward way. But she is amazed at the fortuitous aspect of her meeting Clelia Denham. Through Clelia, whom Clara finds a more fascinating alter ego than the reader does, Clara gains admission to the decadent, middle-class opulence of the Denham household. If Clara's family is hopeless and its members mutually repellent, the brilliant Denhams are full of promise, mutually attractive, and dependent. They embody Clara's fantasy of an alternative social and economic realm, the Jerusalem of the title: "a terrestrial paradise, where beautiful people in beautiful houses spoke of beautiful things." Clara's inevitable affair with the romantic but married Gabriel Denham has spontaneity and passion, but is clearly motivated by his elegance, good looks, and money. Moreover, the affair introduces Clara to the chic circles of London and Paris where she discovers the perimeters of her personal strength and independence.

Returning alone to Northam after a rift with Gabriel, Clara weathers the recrimination of a deathbed scene with her mother and accepts the impossibility of reconciliation. Browsing through her mother's girlhood journal, Clara belatedly discovers the truth of her mother's aspirations, the degree of hopelessness in her adult life, and her own "true descent" from her mother. Clara, however, is able to separate herself from her mother's death, and, confident of her survival and success, she is all the more determined to realign herself in a starry conjunction with Clelia and Gabriel.

Once again Drabble conveys moral ambiguity through metaphor. Clara's fable of the two weeds suggests that superficially she may resemble the glorious flowering plant, but that as a result of her tough tactics for survival she may finally emerge as the low, brown one. Despite determination, Clara is as isolated as her family—and Drabble's other heroines—in a world of her own hypersensitive perceptions. Although her sense of profound despair at the pull of hereditary fate strikes familiar and sympathetic chords, her personality frequently alienates the reader. Her notion of love is inextricably woven with her admiration of class and money; her sexuality is inevitably exploitive. One is ambivalent as to whether her new pattern of life is too costly, too cold. Just how well Clara succeeds in escaping her grim history is also uncertain.

Although noting the "mandarin" coolness of Drabble's style, British reviewers saw *Jerusalem the Golden* as living up to the promise of her earlier works. The particularity of her subject generally met with greater enthusiasm in Great Britain than in America. A reviewer for the *New York Times* quibbled with both characterization and plot but appreciated the novel's "promising depths." Noting that Drabble asserts rather than depicts, another critic found her heroines, especially Clara, annoyingly self-satisfied. Despite the harsher judgments, Drabble's work was beginning to command wider and more serious attention in the United States.

With the publication of *Jerusalem the Golden*, Drabble began to realize her goal of a financially independent career. While her husband continued to tour in the theater, she settled with her three children into a home in Hampstead, a handsome red-brick house that backs onto the "Keats" house. In 1968 she received the James Tait Black Memorial Book Prize. Confident that her writing career was established and that her books "were bound to get printed," Drabble began a regimen and moved her writing to daylight hours. With her children in school, she was able to take an office in Bloomsbury where she could escape interruptions. She writes in the mornings, rarely for more than three hours at a stretch. She composes easily, she says: "If a book is going reasonably well, I write terribly fast. And I don't rewrite very much either.... I think that this is because I've always been short of time. I've always been saving up the time to work so that by the time I actually get to the typewriter ... it's all there waiting."

A devoted mother, Drabble has so closely harmonized her professional life and her domestic life that she has steadily been able to increase her professional commitments. If necessary, she manages "by cutting out a lot of things that other people find necessary, like social life." As a result, the time between 1968 and 1969 was productive for Drabble and brought her often into the public eye. She began lecturing to adults in evening classes at the University of London. The film *Isadora* (for which Drabble wrote the dialogue) was released, as was the film version of *The Millstone* (as *A Touch of Love* in England), and her play *Bird of Paradise* opened in London. Thus, she became a radio and television personality, and her fifth novel, *The Waterfall* (1969), was published to a waiting audience.

As an outgrowth of Drabble's writing about Wordsworth and his vision of a "flood" of love, *The Waterfall* depicts a woman paradoxically saved and destroyed by her discovery of sexual love. The paradox is related to those in earlier novels in which the agents are children. In *The Waterfall*, Jane's baby is only tangential to her mother's rebirth. The novel's title ostensibly refers both to the watery vision of the Goredale Scar and to a card trick whereby cascading cards are a metaphor for orgasm in coitus. Drabble uses the sublime waterfall in the scar to represent the reality of true romantic passion between Jane Grey and her lover (and cousin's husband), James Otford: "It is impressive not through size, as I had perhaps expected, but through form: a lovely or-

ganic balance of shapes and curves, a wildness contained within a bodily limit."

As the novel opens, Jane Grey is suspended in frigidity, immobile. Her husband gone, her second child due, she has relinquished control of her life in an effort to absolve herself of responsibility: "If I were drowning, I couldn't reach out a hand to save myself, so unwilling am I to set myself up against fate." Embracing fate more passionately than prior Drabble women, Jane stops all effort to maintain her home or herself; she informs neither her husband of the child's birth nor her parents of her husband's desertion. Deliverance from her "dry integrity" comes with the delivery of her baby and her seduction of James during her convalescence in a warm, womblike bedroom.

The duality of female existence structures the novel. Deliberately commenting on the continuity of female doom and moral conflict as registered in the tradition of the novel, Drabble's heroine exclaims: "These fictional heroines, how they haunt me. Maggie Tulliver had a cousin called Lucy, as I have, and like me she fell in love with her cousin's man. She drifted off down the river with him, abandoning herself to the water.... In this age what is to be done? We drown in the first chapter." Drabble's layered fiction presents a hierarchy of female creative form. It begins with the gestation and delivery of her child Bianca Grey, moves from Jane's poetry to the double-point-of-view narration of her affair, and culminates in the all-encompassing control of Drabble's irony. The reader must participate in this fiction by integrating Jane's "schizophrenic" point of view: her objective, controlled third-person description of her life and her first-person impassioned account of her feelings about her experience. While the third-person narrative is a contemporary story, the first-person voice is at once a more honest expression and a neurotic parody of Victorian sensibility. "Lies, lies, it's all lies. A pack of lies," the narrator says of the third-person narrative. "I've even told lies of fact, which I had meant not to do.... Reader, I loved him: as Charlotte Brontë said."

When Drabble's Victorian-named heroines find themselves in uncharted waters, they often fall back on literary precedent. Jane especially reflects this thesis that art can teach us about life when she argues with Jane Austen's solutions: "Emma got what she deserved in marrying Mr. Knightley. What can it have been like, in bed with Mr. Knightley? Sorrow awaited that woman." Denying that the book is experimental, Drabble accounts for her split-point-of-view technique as indigenous to her material, the dualism of Jane's experience: "I wrote the first chunk in the third person and found it impossible to continue with, because it did not seem to me to tell anything like the whole story. . . . I thought the only way to do it was to make Jane say it." Drabble's controlling device for this narrative structure is the network of images and symbols mostly derived, like the water imagery, from Romantic poetry and Victorian novels. If Drabble's structure presents the dualism of reality and fiction, of character and author, Jane's divided vision presents the novel's theme: death in love, virtue in guilt, and pleasure in pain. After a car accident alerts Lucy to her husband's affair, Jane must decide on an ending for the story: James's death, his impotence, or her relinquishment. Preferring to "suffer," Jane opts finally for a continuation of the affair that began with Bianca's birth and culminates in the price a modern woman must pay, the threat of thrombosis from the pill or neurosis: "one can take one's pick."

The Waterfall has become Drabble's most controversial book. She wryly calls it "a wicked book" that brought serious attack from those "who say that you should not put into people's heads the idea that one can be saved from fairly pathological conditions by loving a man." Critical response to The Waterfall tended generally to divide along lines of sexual politics. Several male critics expressed concern that Drabble was becoming "more of a woman novelist" with an obsessive quality to her style, "particularly when characters are going through the motions of love." Noting as well the domestic character of her journalism, Bernard Bergonzi saw both Jerusalem the Golden and The Waterfall as close to "woman magazine fiction." However, other (notably female) critics came to view The Waterfall as an intriguing sequel to the spectrum of liberationist issues in Drabble's first four novels. Ellen C. Rose has asserted that The Waterfall is the most female of Drabble's novels because it is the most nearly androgynous. In it, Rose says, Drabble has discovered female nature to be divided between male and female form "which amalgamates feminine fluidity and masculine shapeliness."

The critical debate as to the feminism or femininity of her work has prompted Drabble to declare the autonomy of her art. Denying that her books are "about feminism," she specifies that her concerns are privilege, justice, salvation, equal-

Dust jacket for Drabble's favorite among her novels, which established her as a major writer

ity, and egalitarianism. Justice for women is for her not a subject, but a tenet so basic that it "is part of a whole." From the beginning, Drabble has written independently of outside, even editorial, influence. Although she writes many articles and reviews for income, she has not been concerned about the commercial success of her novels, her most serious work. After the publication of The Waterfall, however, she began to respond to the pressure of analytic criticism. Charges that her heroines were of a similar, autobiographical pattern have made her "cagey" in responding to queries about her life, although she acknowledges that she uses incidents from her experience and that the truth of her characters' emotional response derives from her identification with them to a certain extent. She avoids reading reviews while she is writing, but, an astute critic herself, she has found constructive criticism helpful.

The Needle's Eye, a pivotal novel in Drabble's career, seems to have been encouraged by comments such as those of William Trevor, who in the *New Statesman* urged her to expand her range. She also credits Doris Lessing with having influenced her development of technique. Politically, philosophically, and technically more complex than her previous fiction, *The Needle's Eye* seems to reflect Drabble's increased involvement with public activities, such as her literary tours for the British Arts Council and her research on Arnold Bennett. Preferring the social sympathy of Bennett to the elitism of Jane Austen or Henry James, Drabble set about blending the humanity of the former with the sensibility of the latter in her novel of contemporary British manners.

When the *Guardian* asked her to write an article on child custody cases for the women's page, Drabble conducted extensive research on the subject. Instead of the article, she wrote *The Needle's Eye*. According to Drabble, her favorite novel not only introduces her first fully developed male character as narrator, but it also tests for her a certain life-style in Rose Vassiliou's eccentric and passionate rejection of wealth and middle-class status. Whether she plays "lady of the manor" in the shabby neighborhood she forces herself to embrace or experiences true religious and philosophical integrity is an interpretive question not easily resolved. One admiring but skeptical perspective on Rose's self-imposed martyrdom is provided by the attorney Simon Camish. Drabble skillfully balances the two points of view within a complex temporal structure. Rose's chosen life "in the depths" suggests Wordsworth's philosophy of plain living and high thinking, but also reverberates with the neurosis and guilt of John Bunyan.

A lonely, self-effacing child, Rose Virtue Bryanston was warned of her spiritual danger by Bunyan's Pilgrim and her nurse, Noreen, who was given to intoning such biblical texts as that of the camel and the eye of a needle. Rose's adult life is propelled by the Pilgrim's own question: "What must I do to be saved?" Meditating on the hopelessness of his marriage and disinterested personality, Simon meets Rose at a trendy dinner party and drives her home. Fascinated by her vitality and unpretentiousness, he becomes involved in her legal and personal affairs. As he immerses himself in the sensational newspaper accounts of

Rose's past—including her defiant marriage to a poor Greek, her legal battles with her parents, and her nasty divorce case—Simon must confront his own motives for marrying a wealthy but superficial woman. His working-class history makes him sympathetic to Rose's scruples about money, and, like her, he operates from a sense of duty and decency. He gradually takes refuge in the warmth and authenticity of her home and advises her on her husband Christopher's custody suit for the children.

Their platonic, domestic love and Christopher's desperation bring the action to its climax in a series of scenes reminiscent of a Noel Coward comedy: a police-and-lawyers race, a rendezvous in the garden of the Bryanstons' country house, a confrontation in the drawing room, and a picnic for all parties on the beach. Unable to deny Christopher his children and unable to give up the grace they impart, Rose can only yield to the dilemma. Her self-sacrifice in readmitting Christopher and giving up Simon is an act of puritan desperation, a "leap off the ladder even blindfold into eternity, sink or swim, come heaven come hell." As part of the frustration of all Rose's choices, even her run-down neighborhood becomes fashionable and redeveloped. Thwarted in the design of her life (her husband keeps making money; Rose must inherit more), she strives to remain the ordinary person she believes nature intended her to be. She continues to defy the fatal accident of wealth, but clearly, at the end of the novel, her "living death" with Christopher cannot last. The "dry light of arid charity" and duty to her former husband is as questionable a virtue as her haphazard donation of her fortune to a revolutionary African regime.

Although *The Needle's Eye* has been seen as a defeatist novel because of Rose's impasse, its main thematic thrust is Simon's agonizing Shakespearean question: why should man have such exquisite perception of justice, equality, and the eternal, when he is possessed of "just enough lumination . . . to suffer for failure and too little spirit to live in the light, too little strength to reach the light." Drabble, however, insists that she intended the novel to be optimistic in its portrayal of people struggling to live as best they can in a difficult situation. For its moral intensity *The Needle's Eye* was almost universally praised as a mature and impressive expression of Drabble's talent. Joyce Carol Oates commented that Drabble, like Rose Vassiliou, had made "an extraordinary leap forward" in this intelligent and densely textured novel: "Drabble is not a writer who reflects the helplessness of the stereotyped 'sick society,' but one who has taken upon herself the task . . . of attempting the active, vital, energetic, mysterious recreation of a set of values by which human beings can live." In the general praise, some commentary took exception to the ratio of interior monologue to plot and questioned the plausibility and coincidence of events. The consensus, however, was that *The Needle's Eye* established Drabble as a major writer. The novel was especially appreciated in the United States and drew the attention of academics to Drabble's work. Articles on her books proliferated in scholarly journals, and the American Academy of Arts and Letters awarded her the E. M. Forster Award in 1973. Subsequently, all of her novels have been in print in both Great Britain and the United States, and most have been translated into several languages.

Also published in 1972 was *London Consequences*, the collaboration of several young writers, which Drabble edited with her sister, A. S. Byatt. Although the early works of the sisters portray sibling rivalries, both writers have discouraged the comparative articles (and their hints of competitive friction between the women) that have appeared in London tabloids. Despite her reticence on the subject, Margaret's relationship with Antonia appears to be personally important if professionally complex.

Separated from her husband and eventually divorced in 1975, Drabble did not produce another novel for three years after *The Needle's Eye*. Writing nonfiction steadily during this interval, she had her literary biography of Arnold Bennett published in 1974. Drabble intended, in doing this project, to stimulate a reappraisal of Bennett's work, but a by-product of her research was a reexamination of her own provincial origins and a deeper commitment to social realism in her fiction. She looked more intently to the public domain for material for her novels. Newspapers still provide her with stories she can connect to the personal tragedies of people she knows. To assure accuracy, she researches extensively and conducts interviews with those involved in the sphere of her interest.

Inspired by stories "about old ladies dying alone in cottages," especially one starved woman who had eaten the family Bible, Drabble began *The Realms of Gold* (1975), a novel that employs archaeology as a controlling metaphor for the fragments of contemporary families. In addition to reading and interviewing archaeologists, she took part in an archaeological expedition to gather background for the novel. *The Realms of Gold*, which contends with *The Needle's Eye* as Drabble's best novel, is actually a work about the survival of human community. Her return to Yorkshire while working on the Bennett biography suggested her story of a family plagued through three generations with "hereditary depressions." Speaking with an interviewer before she finished the novel, Drabble commented: "It would fit in very nicely with my interest in predestination and fate and whether you can escape your destiny— whether it's right to escape it by taking drugs or just being happy in other ways; whether it will get you in the end anyway." Certainly many of the novel's physical details derive from the landscapes of her childhood—the cottages, the ditch, even the newts.

All of the primary characters in *The Realms of Gold*, except Frances Wingate's lover, are related by blood, and all are afflicted in some way with the Ollerenshaw family's "Midlands sickness." The various ways in which the characters cope with this depressive tendency make up most of the story. Frances Wingate, the novel's protagonist, is far removed from Drabble's earlier, agoraphobic women. Feminist issues are not a problem for Frances, a golden girl who has emerged unscathed from a dissolved marriage. Despite occasional bouts with the family malaise, Frances successfully pursues her career as an archaeologist, rears four children, and wins the devotion of her lover. Her mobility, freedom, financial independence, and professional security are offset dramatically by the foil characterization of her cousin Janet, the more familiar Drabble housewife, incarcerated in a "tiled hygienic box" with a nasty husband and a teething baby. Nevertheless, while freed from the more personal female problems, Frances must face the stress of the Ollerenshaw neurosis and that of the larger human community: boredom, a sense of the futility of endeavor, isolation, and, occasionally, an overwhelming sense of spiritual desolation. Her suicidal nephew fuels her more despairing vision by asking her to convince him that life has meaning: "How can you possibly imagine," he taunts, "that the things you do are worth doing?"

An expert in reconstructing the era of the ancient Phoenicians, Frances struggles to discover her past and come to terms with her family's Darwinian climb up the beanstalk of economic and educational opportunity. Her perspectives are tempered by those of her historian lover, Karel, and

Margaret Drabble, early 1970s (photograph by Mark Gerson)

her geologist cousin, David. She understands such scientific endeavors as theirs and hers to be "a fruitless attempt to prove the possibility of the future through the past. . . . We seek golden worlds from which we are banished, they recede infinitely for there never was a golden world, there was never anything but toil and subsistence, cruelty and dullness." Only when her reclusive great-aunt dies grotesquely from starvation does Frances begin to find some answers. Huddled in her aunt's overgrown and womblike cottage, Frances comprehends the simple dignity and integrity in the elemental human struggle for survival. Her moment of grace is alternately replenished and diminished by the return of her lover and the deaths of her nephew and his baby. Unlike his Aunt Frances, Stephen is convinced by the old lady's death of the indignity of life and chooses the "pure triumph" of suicide. For lack of any other "revelation," Frances eventually accepts death and love as the only inexplicable absolutes. Oriented by her relationships of the heart and "wedded" to culture, process, and human effort, she accepts Stephen's death as a sacrificial act intended to save all of the Ol-

lerenshaws from their sad inheritance. The novel concludes with tears for the dead and joy for the survivors, including marriages, middle-age adjustments, and renewed family ties.

Perhaps in response to criticism about her other heroines' fates, Drabble invites the reader to "invent a more suitable ending if you can." She further knits her several points of view together by means of a network of symbols, images (especially archaeological), and parallel or juxtaposed scenes like Janet's and Frances's separate visits to their great-aunt's May Cottage. She balances the images of a golden existence, which sustain Frances, Karel, and David, with the apocalyptic visions of the abyss into which Stephen, Frances's sister Alice, and great-aunt Con leap. The novel is textured with descriptions of natural phenomena—muddy ditches, glaring sun, desert sands—and threaded with the labyrinths of human intellection. Both the interior and exterior landscapes have their "black holes" and precious lodes.

Although *The Realms of Gold* was praised for such detail, some critics questioned its efficacy. A *Spectator* review quipped that Drabble "sometimes dabbles in the still water of tedium" and indulges in a "misplaced seriousness" in some sections of this lengthy novel. The high level of coincidence and fairy-tale resolutions have been challenged as well. Yet the extension of Drabble's imaginative sympathy in this novel "exposed the narrowness of ours," according to critic Patricia Sharpe, who finds the improbabilities appropriate to the "drama of discovery" reflective of the John Keats sonnet from which the title comes. And Roger H. Sale, who had previously charged Drabble with a willingness "to settle for superb parts and inferior wholes," declared that the title was the true name for the quality of this fiction. For him, the joy at the end "overwhelms disbelief."

Drabble's narrative technique in this novel successfully presents a triptych of discovery through the three cousins' points of view. Compared to her previous novels, *The Realms of Gold* contains a looser plot, a more complex temporal structure, and daring shifts in narrative style. Drabble deliberately uses a humorously self-conscious authorial voice whose omniscience, she slyly admits, "has its limits." While examining the multiplicity of the characters' responses to the same issues, this voice often archly baits the reader about his response: "And that is enough for the moment of Janet Bird. More than enough, you might reasonably think, for her life is slow, even slower than its description, and her dinner party seemed to go on too long to her, as it did to you." Such tone indicates Drabble's self-assurance in this novel, which reviews some of her earliest themes—fate, luck, sexual relations, identity—on its way to presenting new, more profound concerns. The ambiguity expressed in the resolutions of her other novels finds a definitive shape in this one as a truth unearthed by Frances both in the desert and in her heart: there is no finished truth, no definitive past, no inevitable future. The hope and terror of such a perception have provided the focus of her next two novels.

However much the subject of critical debate, Drabble's themes and her stylistics have inspired a rash of "pseudo-Drabblerians," according to the Society of Authors. Drabble continued to write for such periodicals as *Spectator, Guardian, Punch, Ms.,* and *Saturday Review.* In 1976 the University of Sheffield presented her with the honorary degree doctor of letters. As her involvement with committees of cultural and social organizations increased, so did her interest in the public characters and private quality of British life. In her next novel, *The Ice Age* (1977), Drabble continued to reduce plot and emphasize the characters' contemplation of their past and present situations, but she alternated soliloquies with detailed vignettes of the contemporary British scene. She has said that the impetus for *The Ice Age* was Oliver Marriott's *The Property Boom* (1967), which details the fortunes people made by speculating in real estate and property development in the 1950s and 1960s. A visit to redeveloped Sheffield while researching the Bennett biography convinced Drabble that the issue was a complex and intriguing one. The title of the novel refers both to the disastrous economic freeze of the 1970s and to the spiritual wastes of modern life. Consequently, *The Ice Age* has a fair measure of the naturalistic pessimism glimpsed in *The Realms of Gold.*

The novel's central metaphor suggests that the individual character's malaise is part of a larger crisis created by the drastic, enormous changes in the nature and quality of life in the past hundred years. Particularly, the moral and financial decline of several characters seems to parallel that of Britain, a "shabby, mangy old lion now." Like the northern wastes and dumping sites they have created, Drabble's land speculators are now bankrupt, "living in the ruins of their own grandiose excesses." Designed as a more universal portrait of modern times, the

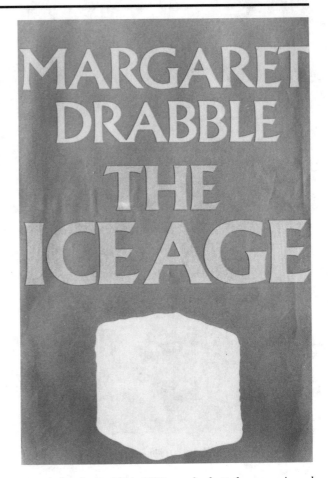

Dust jacket for Drabble's 1977 novel, about the economic and spiritual freeze of the 1970s

novel includes almost every imaginable social theme: ecology; television; the failure of the upper class and the liberal arts; dissolution of traditional forms; the dissipation, self-centeredness, and aggression of youth; the sexual promiscuity of everyone; the plight of the elderly; prison conditions; the Americanization of the world; inflation; oil and energy conservation; Arabian acquisition in Britain; terrorism; and the IRA. Behind the topical issues lurks the central problem of a paralyzed, disillusioned middle class and its loss of ethos: "a huge icy fit, with large cold fingers, was squeezing and chilling the people of Britain, that great and puissant nation, slowing down their blood, locking them into immobility, fixing them in a solid stasis, like fish in a frozen river."

"Fed up with women—slightly," Drabble chose a male character as the primary focus of her omniscient narrative. A middle-class, thirty-eight-year-old Oxford graduate, Anthony Keating abandons a comfortable but static career in television production to go out of his depth in a partnership with two shrewd and manipulative land developers. While riding the crest of the development boom Anthony "was a modern man, an operator, at one with the spirit of the age." As the novel opens, however, Anthony is retired in his heavily mortgaged country home, recuperating from a heart attack and awaiting financial ruin and persecution for his part in a recent development scheme. Since Anthony must eschew the ordinary panaceas of his culture—food, alcohol, and sex—he is defenseless against the ennui that has stalked him as it has Drabble's other protagonists, a "profound, disabling, terrifying boredom." Amicably divorced, Anthony has had a long-running if limping affair with a woman who has abandoned her acting career to care for a child afflicted with cerebral palsy. Obsessive in her devotion to Molly, Alison Murray incurs the resentment of her other daughter, sullen teenaged Jane. The novel shifts narrative focus from Anthony's meditations in his garden to draw parallels with Alison's fruitless vigil in a Communist-bloc country where Jane awaits trial for dangerous driving. The Alison-Anthony separation is placed in counterpoint with that of Len Wincobank, an entrepreneur in prison for fraud, and his mistress, Maureen Kirby. As Drabble had observed about Jane's dinner party in *The Realms of Gold*, art mirrors life. Alison's futile wait in Wallacia, Anthony's boredom at Rook House, Len's tedium in prison, and Maureen's frustration without him are all projected by the absence of plot in part 1, which surveys one day in the lives of the characters and their several pasts through lengthy flashback and exposition.

Thereafter the novel has little action. The energetic and ruthless characters, such as Len Wincobank and Giles Peters, continue to scheme and deplete themselves. The survivors—Maureen Kirby and her new lover, architect Derek Ashby—move steadily upward, cutting competently through the ice to self-satisfaction and a brave new world of their own making. The victims—Molly, Max (murdered by a terrorist bomb), and Maureen's displaced aunt—are silent. The lost and seeking, Anthony and Alison, learn to accept failure in child-rearing and real estate and find only their own mortality. Alison returns alone to England, only to learn that her loss is total, that she is no longer indispensable to Molly. Having found her identity in both her beauty and her devotion to Molly for one half of her life, she faces the mid-life crisis of Drabble's other recent heroines and sees no basis for the second half. Worse,

the surrealistic images of London offer no rescue to her failed imagination. Reunited with Anthony at Rook House, Alison watches him dwindle to triviality and wonders, "what next, what next, what next?" Convinced that "ill-thoughts" and poor choices bring our fate, Alison believes she bears the terrible weight of a retribution that reflects the chaos of the economic-social sphere. Her generation had its certainties when young, but they have since "fragmented and dissolved into uncertainty." After such knowledge as theirs, Drabble asks, what action?

Her answer to this thematic question has elicited conflicting responses. Anthony survives his financial crisis only to fall victim to his own quixotic impulse. As a result of the sermons he found in his stony garden, he rushes off to rescue Jane and, incidentally, to spy for Whitehall. He reaffirms the old beliefs with grim determination and succeeds in rescuing Jane despite his contempt for her callousness. After an unconvincing arrest episode, Anthony becomes a contemplative in prison, gets "high on suffering," and is spiritually reborn. Unlike *The Realms of Gold*, *The Ice Age* presents no alternative to the dreadful revelation experienced by its female protagonist. There is no fairy-tale ending for Alison: "Her life is beyond imagining. It will not be imagined. Britain will recover, but not Alison Murray."

The Ice Age begins with patriotic exhortations by Milton and Wordsworth, and the rest of the novel is spotted with allusions to Shakespeare's island jewel and Milton's puissant giant. The promise is that England will recover even if she has replaced the cathedral spire with the gasometer as her inspiration. The sun that thaws the ice age is literally a golden one, and the discovery of oil in the North Sea may produce "a senile Britain, casting out its ghosts. Or a go-ahead Britain, with old rig men toasting their mistress in champagne in the pubs of Aberdeen." Drabble's ambivalence toward such renewal is conveyed by style as well as by image. Double negatives such as "without implausibility" or "hot unattractive" set the tone, as does an ironic authorial voice. Expanding a tactic initiated in *The Needle's Eye* and developed in *The Realms of Gold*, Drabble speaks to the reader about her art: "It ought now to be necessary to imagine a future for Anthony Keating. There is no need to worry about the other characters, for the present." The characters alternate between choice and an existence determined as often by that authorial voice as by accident of plot.

Valerie Grosvenor Myer's assertion that Drabble's early novels contain a dominant judgmental vein has been disputed by other critics. However, puritan fatalism becomes a dominant tone in *The Ice Age*, not only in Alison's determined view, but also in the authorial voice: "Evelyn Ashby, who has not been allowed to appear, will not remarry; she will grow eccentric and solitary, and refuse to see her own children." Such comments prompted James Gindin, who admired much in the novel, to observe that Drabble's shift in perspective has placed many of her characters in double jeopardy, up against the rock of fate and the "hard edge" of the author's disapproval. Since the author creates a "determined immobility" for the characters, he argues, she punishes Alison unfairly and makes the possibility of a "recovery" for anyone other than Anthony a matter of fantasy. While acknowledging Drabble's superior talent, Granville Barker also found her characters in this novel singularly unattractive and "masochistic." Moreover, he considers her style too journalistic and insists that, by concentrating on exploiters rather than their victims, she "sacrifices the essential dramatic and moral validity of her subject." Nevertheless, her more aggressive style has won the applause of critics such as Maureen Howard, who finds event and character convincing because they are given "full thematic and emotional support." As is the case with such large and ambitious novels, *The Ice Age* received few unmixed reviews, but won general notice as an important work. *The Ice Age* takes the shape of a nineteenth-century novel and draws from its traditions: elaborate structure, expansive focus, coincidence, a definitive social context, interlocking lives, and meaningful resolution. In her authoritative stance, Drabble admits to technique and the self-consciousness of her art in a way that imparts vigor to the form. With its panoramic view of British society and its multiplicity of character and theme, *The Ice Age* is one of her most ambitious novels so far, but in the particularity of its issues, it may also become one of her most dated.

Drabble had intended her next book to be "a public health drama" about the immunization program of the national health-care system, but she "threw it away" in preference for *A Writer's Britain* (1979), a book on literary landscapes. In her novels London settings have a specific presence and are portrayed with exquisite attention to detail: inhuman traffic circles, fortresslike office buildings, a vacant lot with chickens roosting in a chair, a littered tube station. Her attention to countryside herb and flower rivals that of Thomas Hardy. Descriptions of the microscopic life in a ditch, of wild and formal gardens, have the power of incantation. Understandably, Drabble was "over-excited" about this book, and her contribution (along with the many handsome photographs by Jorge Lewinsky) illustrates her conviction that physical setting is a large part of the determined aspect of a character's personality and life.

Commenting on her movement from private to public concerns in her novels, Drabble has said that, having come to terms with her own interior life, she no longer felt the need to write about it. Instead, she is "very interested in the way society works." Yet *The Middle Ground* (1980) returns to issues germane to her circumstances and combines them with several of the larger social problems depicted in *The Ice Age*: the alarming fluctuations of youth, the economy, social injustice, and foreign immigration. Drabble also returns to the female narrator. Like Frances Wingate, Kate Armstrong is a vigorous, sexy, slightly bohemian, divorced woman; like Alison Murray, she stands at the edge of her children's independence and feels the loss of definition; like Anthony Keating, she is bored with her career as a journalist writing about women's matters.

Drabble has said that Kate "could be an analogy for the novelist who is fed up with the feminist critics." Her character has reached the stage where she is "fed up with the narrow little ditch that she's got herself stuck in," and worst of all, she is "bored with herself." At the crossroads of her life, Kate wonders where to go next. Toward the novel's end, she goes back to her hometown to trace the subsequent lives of her childhood friends. Ostensibly, she is working on a television documentary on women (again), but in actuality she is looking for herself. The daughter of a sewer worker, Kate is self-educated and self-made. She is limited not as a woman but, like most people, as a person with few talents. In the process of her evolution she has traded sexual guilt for feminist guilt, feminist guilt for ennui.

Drabble's comment about the book, that "nothing really happens in it at all," accurately describes the novel's Woolfian temper. People drift in and out of Kate's house: miscellaneous friends of her teenaged children, punks, and musicians "crash" there; an old sot and former mentor gets sick on the floor; an Iraqi student seeks refuge from political trouble; and a close friend and fel-

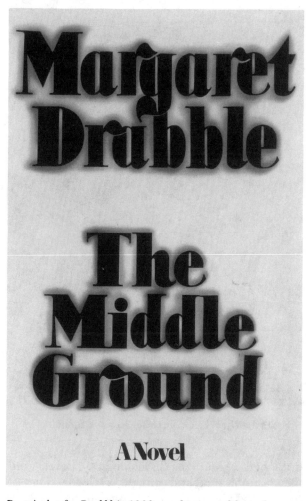

Dust jacket for Drabble's 1980 novel, narrated by a character who "could be an analogy for the novelist who is fed up with the feminist critics"

low journalist, Hugo Mainwairing, finds the impetus there to resume his career as a foreign correspondent. The narrative consists mostly of the characters' retrospection. Things that have happened in the past are reviewed in detail: Kate's marriage to a bohemian artist "done in" by her capability; her abortion; the hate mail sent to her anonymously by her brother; her affair with her best friend's insensitive and egotistical husband; the friend's problems with her adolescent children and her cases as a social worker. Even the attack on the friend, Evelyn Stennett, by the husband of one of her clients is revealed after the fact.

Characters from Drabble's other novels reappear. Gabriel Denham has survived *Jerusalem the Golden* as a television producer and a potentially romantic lead in *The Middle Ground*, and Kate has invited Rosamund Stacey of *The Millstone* to her party. Drabble may be building a saga, but she is

surely suggesting the closed circuit of London chic. There are snappy set pieces, including Kate's contemplation of underwear advertisements on billboards and the phenomenon of planned, "edenic" suburban communities. Portentous occurrences of animal and bird deaths continue an ominous motif begun in *The Ice Age*. The book concludes with a "Mrs. Dalloway-type party" and with what Drabble calls a note of "guarded optimism." Before the party, Kate enjoys her first automobile ride with her nineteen-year-old son as driver. This ride, her son's adult demeanor, a bouquet of flowers, and the prospect of intrigue at the party suddenly combine to buoy Kate with hope. Her life, after all, has the potential of a soap opera: "Will Stuart be civil to Ted; will Ted make a pass at Rosamund Stacey?. . . Anything is possible, it is all undecided. Everything or nothing. . . . Something will happen." A child calls her downstairs to reality; the doorbell rings, signaling possibility; the telephone rings, reestablishing contact with the outside world; and Kate "rises" to embrace life.

Once again Drabble asserts the miracle of children and the real spiritual benefit to rearing them. Kate's children have their abominable stages but return, like Mark, the eldest, capable and caring. The necessity of caring within reason has been a steady chord in Drabble's composition, played in counterpoint to the paradoxical theme of the inevitable failure of male-female love relationships. The paradoxical mode characterizes Kate's mid-life experience. Whereas earlier novels embody opposing perspectives in a pair of female characters, such as Louise and Sarah in *A Summer Bird-Cage*, *The Middle Ground* presents a divided self in Kate, the image of middle age. She is set in her convictions about the quality of life (she knows what she wants, as distinct from earlier heroines who knew only what they did not want), but she is full of questions and doubts about its meaning now. The division is, in one way, a conflict of past and present: "Those two selves, that prattling chattering journalist in Kentish town, with her smart views and expensive boots and trendy house . . . and the child in its skimpy cotton dress, lonely, cast out, cut off— what had they in common?" She is "settled-in," tired, jaded, but also unsettled. Things in the outer world seem to be in total flux; in the inner world all is moribund. Only Kate's resilient personality glues her together at the end. Fittingly, she rises to a social occasion, accepting the challenge of facing "everything or nothing."

Drabble's theme has its logic in the development of her work, but it inspires a style that suffers from imitative fallacy. *The Middle Ground* often exhibits, to use one reviewer's phrase, "narrative paralysis." In describing Kate's situation, Drabble characterizes the novel. Her plot, like Kate's middle years, "stretches back too densely. . . . No wonder a pattern is slow to emerge from such trivia, from such serious but hidden connections. Everything has too much history." Similarly, Kate goes to a play by and with famous people, only to be bored stiff because "Nothing happened at all. The characters talked and talked." For every opinion Drabble's cast members express, they offer a counteropinion; for every question they pose, they continue with a catalogue of qualifying or opposing questions: "Oh dear, oh dear, thought Kate . . . the trouble is, anything *could* mean anything. Or its opposite." Presenting paragraph after paragraph of such speculation, the novel is an epic quandary and thwarts every expectation of revelation from beginning to end.

The novel has its admirers, who consider Drabble at the top of her form in expressing Kate's "articulate doubt." A *New Statesman* review totally disagrees, observing that "assertion is about all we ever get." Drabble's authorial voice still addresses the reader, but the tone has changed, and it has dropped its ironic stance toward the characters' self-indulgences. Perhaps Hugo Mainwairing's comment about his own writing explains Drabble's intention in this novel: "Now that . . . is really bad writing despite the fact that I mean every word of it. . . . The more I try to tell the truth, the worse I write. But surely, at my age, I ought to have the courage to write badly? What do I fear to lose?" Drabble refers to her book as a "document" and reminds us that if we see Hugo as "a depressing spectacle," that is our choice. Drabble anticipated that *The Middle Ground* might be regarded "as a true feminist tract" or as "a complete failure," and said she did not care: "The truth is more important than ideology." For all its faults, *The Middle Ground* is an honest book. One hopes with a *Spectator* reviewer that, the "crisis of confidence" passed, Kate's reasserted hope may be the author's as well. *The Gates of Ivory* (1991) continues the lives of characters Liz Headleand, Alix Bowen, and Esther Breuer, heroines of Drabble's previous novels *The Radiant Way* (1987) and *A Natural Curiosity* (1989). Characters from *The Needle's Eye* also appear, but "they have wandered into this story from the old-

Margaret Drabble, 1982 (photograph by Mark Gerson)

fashioned, Freudian, psychological novel, and they cannot mix and mingle." In *The Gates of Ivory*, Drabble eschews a conventional plot in favor of a compelling scrutiny of her ongoing characters.

Beset by the claims of popularity and critical regard, Drabble has learned to become even more chary of her time, more careful in her commitments, more protective of her privacy. Generally appearing unruffled, she is much sought after for interviews, appearances, and reviews. She made her first trip to the United States in the summer of 1974, financing her journey with funds received from a grant from the American Academy of Arts and Letters. In the fall of 1980, at a Buckingham Palace ceremony, the Queen Mother dubbed Margaret Drabble a Dame Commander of the British Empire. Possessing immense creative energy, Drabble does not regard herself as remarkable, but—in keeping with her themes—"ordinary," fated, and lucky. By her own admission, her novels reflect her progress from graduate and actress, through housewife and mother, to novelist and critic. Like her characters who escape self-absorption by establishing links with their communities, Drabble has increased her public involvement, sitting on committees because she believes she should. She maintains, however, that what she does for pleasure, money, or society will always be secondary to her commitment to writing serious novels. When not writing or serving, she is reading: "I find out about living and about the values of living—and a lot of my beliefs in life and my feelings about people and what to do—from reading novels." Bent on developing her craft, but eschewing modern experimentation, she still studies the classics of Western literature to learn what can be done with the medium of the novel. "I'd rather be at the end of a dying tradition which I admire," she said in 1967, "than at the beginning of a tradition which I deplore." In 1982 Drabble married the biographer Michael Holroyd.

Drabble began testing the parameters of human life through a feminist consciousness. Her discoveries led to the creation of male and female characters who perceive yet wryly question their circumspection in their domestic and social spheres. Believing that striving, not happiness, is important to human fulfillment, Drabble sets her characters to moral choice in today's society. Like Hardy, about whom she has written, she locates her fatalism in both the human condition and the nature of society. In her novels she perpetually seeks to define the relationship between accident and plan. Her attention to detail and nuance has led to her identification as a novelist of manners, and therefore to comparisons with Jane Austen and Henry James. Noting her focus on female discovery and aestheticism, critics have also aligned her with George Eliot, Virginia Woolf, and Doris Lessing. Drabble's art bears comparison as well with those classic and contemporary novelists she admires: Angus Wilson, Iris Murdoch, the Brontës, Arnold Bennett, and Saul Bellow. But finally, Drabble's voice is her own. She is a lucid, intelligent writer whose wry humor, incisive wit, technical skill, and sensitivity to the minutiae of events have become the hallmarks of her style. A novelist on whom nothing is lost, Drabble is articulate about what she is attempting in her novels, yet she refuses to define any single meaning. As she avoids strong closure in the novels, so she rejects solutions. The ambivalence with which her characters meet their fates, the dualism of their perceptions, and the ambiguity of the narrative tone all reflect Drabble's variousness and her vision of the novel: "There is no answer to a novel. A novel is like a person's life. It's full of complexities and therefore any explanation is unsatis-

factory. It's the constant flux, the going to and fro between various emotions that makes fiction interesting to me." Drabble's work has steadily achieved maturity; many critics and readers expect that in its maturity it will achieve greatness. One might say of her novels what she has said of Arnold Bennett's, that they deal with material never encountered in fiction but only in life.

Interviews:

Bolivar Le Franc, "An Interest in Guilt: Margaret Drabble," *Books and Bookmen*, 14 (September 1969): 20-21;

Terry Coleman, "A Biographer Waylaid by Novels," *Guardian* (Manchester), 15 April 1972, p. 23;

Nancy S. Hardin, "An Interview with Margaret Drabble," *Contemporary Literature*, 14 (Summer 1973): 273-295;

Joseph McCulloch, "Dialogue with Margaret Drabble," in his *Under Bow Bells: Dialogues with Joseph McCulloch* (London: Sheldon Press, 1974), pp. 125-132;

Nancy Poland, "Margaret Drabble: 'There Must Be a Lot of People Like Me,'" *Midwest Quarterly*, 16 (April 1975): 255-267;

Peter Firchow, ed., *The Writer's Place: Interviews on the Literary Situation in Contemporary Britain* (Minneapolis: University of Minnesota Press, 1975), pp. 102-121;

Barbara Milton, "Art of Fiction LXX," *Paris Review*, 74 (Fall 1978): 40-65;

Iris Rozencwajg, "Interview with Margaret Drabble," *Women's Studies*, 6 (1979): 335-347;

Dee Preussner, "Talking with Margaret Drabble," *Modern Fiction Studies*, 25 (1980): 563-577;

Diana Cooper-Clark, "Margaret Drabble: Cautious Feminist," *Atlantic Monthly*, 246 (November 1980): 69-75.

Bibliography:

Joan Garret Packer, *Margaret Drabble: An Annotated Bibliography* (New York: Garland, 1988).

Biographies:

Joanne V. Creighton, *Margaret Drabble* (London & New York: Methuen, 1985);

Lynn Veach Sadler, *Margaret Drabble* (Boston: Twayne, 1986).

References:

Virginia K. Beards, "Margaret Drabble: Novels of a Cautious Feminist," *Critique*, 15 (1973): 35-46;

Colin Butler, "Margaret Drabble: The Millstone and Wordsworth," *English Studies*, 59 (August 1978): 353-360;

Cynthia Davis, "Unfolding Form: Narrative Approach and Theme in *The Realms of Gold*," *Modern Language Quarterly*, 40 (1979): 390-402;

Lee Edwards, "*Jerusalem the Golden*: A Fable for Our Times," *Women's Studies*, 6 (1979): 321-335;

Peter E. Firchow, "Rosamund's Complaint: Margaret Drabble's *The Millstone*," in *Old Lines, New Forces: Essays on the Contemporary British Novel, 1960-70*, edited by Robert K. Morris (Rutherford, N.J.: Fairleigh Dickinson Press, 1976), pp. 93-108;

E. Fox-Genovese, "Ambiguities of Female Identity: A Reading of the Novels of Margaret Drabble," *Partisan Review*, 46 (1979): 234-248;

John Hannay, *The Intertextuality of Fate: A Study of Margaret Drabble* (Columbia: University of Missouri Press, 1986);

Nancy S. Hardin, "Drabble's *The Millstone*: A Fable for Our Times," *Critique*, 15 (1973): 22-34;

Mary M. Lay, "Temporal Ordering in the Fiction of Margaret Drabble," *Critique*, 21 (1979): 73-84;

Marion V. Libby, "Fate and Feminism in the Novels of Margaret Drabble," *Contemporary Literature*, 16 (Spring 1975): 175-192;

Joan Manheimer, "Margaret Drabble and the Journey to the Self," *Studies in the Literary Imagination*, 11 (1978): 127-143;

Mary Hurley Moran, *Margaret Drabble: Existing Within Structures* (Carbondale: Southern Illinois University Press, 1983);

Valerie Grosvenor Myer, *Margaret Drabble: Puritanism and Permissiveness* (London: Vision Press, 1974; New York: Barnes & Noble, 1974);

Ellen C. Rose, "Feminine Endings—and Beginnings: Margaret Drabble's *The Waterfall*," *Contemporary Literature*, 21 (February 1980): 81-99;

Rose, *The Novels of Margaret Drabble: Equivocal Figures* (London: Macmillan, 1980);

Rose, "Surviving the Future," *Critique*, 15 (1973): 5-21;

Rose, ed., *Critical Essays on Margaret Drabble* (Boston: G. K. Hall, 1985);

Susanna Roxman, *Guilt and Glory: Studies in Margaret Drabble's Novels, 1963-1980* (Stockholm: Almqvist & Wiksell, 1984);

Roger H. Sale, "Williams, Weesner, and Drabble," in his *On Not Being Good Enough: Writings of a Working Critic* (London: Oxford University Press, 1979), pp. 42-53;

Patricia Sharpe, "On First Looking into 'The Realms of Gold,'" *Michigan Quarterly Review* (Spring 1977): 225-231;

Susan Spitzer, "Fantasy and Femaleness in Margaret Drabble's *The Millstone*," *Novel*, 11 (Spring 1978): 227-245.

John Fowles

(31 March 1926 -   )

This entry was written by Ellen Pifer (University of Delaware) for
DLB 14: British Novelists Since 1960: Part One.

BOOKS: *The Collector* (Boston: Little, Brown, 1963; London: Cape, 1963);

The Aristos: A Self-Portrait in Ideas (Boston: Little, Brown, 1964; London: Cape, 1965; revised edition, London: Cape, 1968; Boston: Little, Brown, 1970);

The Magus (Boston: Little, Brown, 1965; London: Cape, 1966; revised edition, Boston: Little, Brown, 1977; London: Cape, 1977);

The French Lieutenant's Woman (Boston: Little, Brown, 1969; London: Cape, 1969);

Poems (New York: Ecco Press, 1973; Toronto: Macmillan, 1973);

The Ebony Tower (Boston: Little, Brown, 1974; London: Cape, 1974);

Shipwreck, text by Fowles and photographs by the Gibsons of Scilly (London: Cape, 1974; Boston: Little, Brown, 1975);

Daniel Martin (Boston: Little, Brown, 1977; London: Cape, 1977);

Islands, text by Fowles and photographs by Fay Godwin (Boston: Little, Brown, 1978; London: Cape, 1978);

The Tree, text by Fowles and photographs by Frank Horvat (Boston: Little, Brown, 1979; London: Aurum Press, 1979);

The Enigma of Stonehenge, text by Fowles and photographs by Barry Brukoff (New York: Summit Books, 1980; London: Cape, 1980);

Mantissa (London: Cape, 1982; Boston: Little, Brown, 1982);

A Short History of Lyme Regis (Boston: Little, Brown, 1982);

A Maggot (London: Cape, 1985; Boston: Little, Brown, 1985);

Lyme Regis Camera (Boston: Little, Brown, 1990).

MOTION PICTURES: *The Collector*, screenplay by Fowles, Stanley Mann, and John Kohn, Columbia, 1965;

The Magus, screenplay by Fowles, 20th Century-Fox, 1968.

photograph by Jacob Sutton

OTHER: "Notes on an Unfinished Novel," in *Afterwords: Novelists on Their Novels*, edited by Thomas McCormack (New York: Harper & Row, 1969), pp. 160-175;

Sabine Baring-Gould, *Mehalah: A Story of the Salt Marshes*, introduction, glossary, and appendix by Fowles (London: Chatto & Windus, 1969);

Henri Alain-Fournier, *The Wanderer*, afterword by Fowles (New York: New American Library, 1971);

Sir Arthur Conan Doyle, *The Hound of the Bas-kervilles*, foreword and afterword by Fowles (London: John Murray & Jonathan Cape, 1974);

Charles Perrault, *Cinderella*, translated by Fowles (London: Cape, 1974; Boston: Little, Brown, 1976);

Piers Brendon, *Hawker of Morwenstow: Portrait of a Victorian Eccentric*, foreword by Fowles (London: Cape, 1975);

Claire de Durfort, *Ourika*, translated, with introduction and epilogue, by Fowles (Austin, Tex.: W. Thomas Taylor, 1977);

"Hardy and the Hag," in *Thomas Hardy After Fifty Years*, edited by Lance St. John Butler (London: Macmillan, 1977), pp. 28-42;

"The Man and the Island," in *Steep Holm—A Case History in the Study of Evolution* (London: Kenneth Allsop Memorial Trust, 1978), pp. 14-22;

Marie de France, *The Lais of Marie de France*, foreword by Fowles (New York: Dutton, 1978);

Harold Pinter, *The French Lieutenant's Woman: A Screenplay*, foreword by Fowles (Boston: Little, Brown, 1981).

SELECTED PERIODICAL PUBLICATIONS—
UNCOLLECTED: "I Write Therefore I Am," *Evergreen Review*, 8 (August-September 1964): 16-17, 89-90;

"On Being English but Not British," *Texas Quarterly*, 7 (Autumn 1964): 154-162;

"My Recollections of Kafka," *Mosaic*, 3 (Summer 1970): 31-41;

"Is the Novel Dead?," *Books*, 1 (Autumn 1970): 2-5;

"Weeds, Bugs, Americans," *Sports Illustrated*, 33 (21 December 1970): 84ff.;

"*The Magus* Revisited," *Times* (London), 28 May 1977, p. 7; republished as "Why I Rewrote *The Magus*," *Saturday Review*, 5 (18 February 1978): 25-30;

"Seeing Nature Whole," *Harper's*, 259 (November 1979): 49-68;

"Book to Movie: *The French Lieutenant's Woman*," *Vogue* (November 1981): 266, 269, 271.

A novelist who writes for a living, says author John Fowles, is an altogether different creature from one whose art *is* his life. The latter, a "dynamic artist," seeks "to form new images and new methods of describing his world," while his less adventurous cousin, the "static artist," uses the traditional techniques of his craft to ensure the current "market value" of his work. As a novelist, Fowles has managed to succeed in both categories. He has earned international prominence not only as an innovator seeking new methods of describing contemporary reality, but also as the author of works of fiction that have ranked high on best-seller lists in the United States and abroad. In 1972 Fowles's first three novels had sold more than four million copies in paperback reprints alone. Three of these—*The Collector* (1963), *The Magus* (1965), and *The French Lieutenant's Woman* (1969)—have been made into motion pictures. Fowles's success in the marketplace derives from his great skill as a storyteller. His fiction is rich in narrative suspense, romantic conflict, and erotic drama. Remarkably, he manages to sustain such effects at the same time that, as an experimental writer testing conventional assumptions about reality, he examines and parodies the traditional devices of storytelling. Less known to the reading public are his published works of poetry and philosophy. Along with his many essays, articles, reviews, and translations, they reflect their author's wide range of intellectual interests. Erudite in several fields of art and science, Fowles has written on subjects as diverse as medieval French literature, natural history, and biological evolution. He is one of the few writers today who commands the attention of both a mass audience and the literary scholar and critic.

Born 31 March 1926 in a small suburb of London, Fowles describes his hometown as "dominated by conformism—the pursuit of respectability." A fierce individualist, he attributes his dislike of groups, of "mankind *en masse*," to the oppressive social pressures of his childhood. Fowles learned, however, to cope with these pressures by developing, in his words, "a facility with masks." This ability "to pretend to be what I am not" helped him to win popularity as a student leader at Bedford School, a suburban London preparatory school he attended between the ages of fourteen and eighteen. Fowles attributes his facility with masks to being English, to the way Englishmen "very rarely say what they actually think. That could derive from Puritanism—hiding emotions and wearing a public mask. I suffer from it like everyone of my type and background. I've played the game all my life." Many of the protagonists in Fowles's fiction share their author's facility with masks, and their success at masking their real feelings often proves a hindrance to their internal development.

During the years that Fowles was at Bedford School, excelling in scholarship and sports, World War II was at its height. At one point his family was forced to evacuate their home in order to escape German air raids, and Fowles left Bedford for a term to join them in Devonshire. Here, in the unspoiled southwestern countryside of England, he first encountered the "mystery and beauty" of nature—whose powerful attraction is evident in his fiction, philosophy, and lifelong avocation as an amateur naturalist. After preparatory school, Fowles served two years compulsory military service as a lieutenant in the Royal Marines, attending the University of Edinburgh for six months as part of this training. The war ended just at the time his military training did, so he never saw combat duty. Instead, he entered New College, Oxford, to read French and German languages and literature. His study of French, especially, has had a lasting influence on his intellectual and literary development.

When Fowles was at Oxford, the French existentialist writers Albert Camus and Jean-Paul Sartre were being widely read and discussed. Fowles and his friends eagerly took up their ideas and imitated their philosophical stance, although he now points out that there was more fashion than substance to his understanding of existentialism at that time. All the same, much of Fowles's fiction reflects the existentialist's preoccupation with individual freedom and choice. The postwar existentialists were not the only French writers to have an abiding effect on Fowles's literary imagination. Of his other reading at Oxford, he says: "I was to discover later that one field of Old French literature refused to subside into the oblivion I wished on the whole period once I had taken Finals. This field—'forest' would be more appropriate—was that of the Celtic romance." Fowles believes that the origin of modern fiction, of "the novel and all its children," can be traced to Celtic lore and its influence on medieval French tales of chivalry and courtly love. Many years after his graduation from Oxford, he paid tribute to his Celtic and French precursors. In a collection of his own stories called *The Ebony Tower* (1974), he included a translation of Marie de France's twelfth-century French romance, *Eliduc*. In reading *Eliduc*, he says, the contemporary writer "is watching his own birth."

After graduation from Oxford, Fowles left England for Europe, teaching English first at the University of Poitiers in France and then at Anargyrios College, a boarding school for boys on the Greek island of Spetsai. On this island he rediscovered the enchantments of nature in a dazzling Mediterranean guise. The purity of the Greek landscape—the starkness of sea, sky, and stone—inspired his first sustained attempts at writing. Fowles did not think seriously about becoming a writer until he was in his early twenties. Then a "burning need to translate a French poem by [Pierre de] Ronsard" overcame his repression of writing. Fowles attributes this repression to "that stark, puritanical view of all art that haunts England, [the sense] that there is something shameful about expressing yourself." Although Fowles had done some writing while teaching school in France, his efforts intensified considerably in Greece. The two years he spent there, in 1951-1952, proved a formative influence on both his artistic and his personal life.

On the island of Spetsai, Fowles met Elizabeth Whitton, the woman he married three years later in England, after her divorce from her first husband. It was on Spetsai, too, that he wrote poems that later made up one section of his published volume of poetry. The Greek landscape had a direct influence on Fowles's first attempts to write fiction as well. In *The Magus*, a novel he began writing shortly after leaving Greece in 1952, the fictive island of Phraxos is directly modeled after Spetsai. Years later, Fowles described the powerful hold that the island landscape of Greece had on his literary imagination: "Its [Spetsai's] pine forest silences were uncanny, unlike those I have experienced anywhere else; like an eternal blank page waiting for a note or a word. They gave the curious sense of timelessness and of incipient myth. . . . I am hard put to convey the importance of this experience for me as a writer. It imbued and marked me far more profoundly than any of my more social and physical memories of the place. I already knew I was a permanent exile from many aspects of English society, but a novelist has to enter deeper exiles still."

This image of the writer as exile—one who lives in isolation and periodically voyages to regions unknown—persists both in Fowles's fiction and in his personal life. Since 1966 he has lived in the small coastal town of Lyme Regis, in Dorset County, on the southwestern tip of England. Hours away from the nearest city, Fowles frankly regards living in Lyme Regis "as a kind of exile." He says: "I have very little social contact with anybody; they mainly hold right-wing political views that have nothing to do with my own.

The old idea of exile for an English writer was to go to the Mediterranean. To do what Durrell has done, or Lawrence did. For me, the best place to be in exile, in a strange kind of way, is in a town like this, in England. That's because novelists have to live in some sort of exile. I also believe that—more than other kinds of writers—they have to keep in touch with their native culture . . . linguistically, psychologically and in many other ways. If it sounds paradoxical, it feels paradoxical. I've opted out of the one country I mustn't leave. I live in England but partly in the way one might live abroad." With this paradoxical form of self-imposed exile, Fowles has apparently freed himself from the social and psychological restrictions of British middle-class life, which he has always hated, while at the same time remaining in close contact with the English landscape and language he has always loved.

At the end of 1952, Fowles left Greece and returned to England, where he taught for the next decade at various schools in and around London. He was also working on the first draft of *The Magus*, while experiencing an acute sense of loss at having left Greece. "It was agony," he says. "I thought I'd never get over having left." Yet in retrospect Fowles is glad of having left, believing it necessary to his development as a writer. "I had not then realized that loss is essential for the novelist, immensely fertile for his books, however painful to his private being." Although he has settled permanently in England, having never returned to Spetsai, he continues to feel spiritually rooted in three countries rather than one: France, England, and Greece. His personal ties to the landscape of Greece and to the literature of France— as well as to the language, landscape, and literature of England—may help to explain Fowles's sense of living "in exile" within Britain, socially and politically. Both the themes and the settings of his fiction reflect his abiding sense of being "much more European than British."

On 2 April 1954 Fowles married Elizabeth Whitton and became stepfather to his wife's three-year-old daughter, Anna, by her previous marriage. For the next ten years the family lived in Hampstead, London. Here Fowles's teaching career continued to offer him exposure to a variety of social environments. He spent a year teaching English at an adult education institution, Ashridge College, where he "took strongly to the trade union and socialist side; and I haven't seen reason to change my mind since." With the success of *The Collector*, his first published novel, he re-

tired from the teaching profession, having last served as the head of the English department at St. Godric's College in Hampstead. Several years later he and his wife moved to Lyme Regis. They settled at first in an isolated old farmhouse on Ware Commons, a mile to the west of the town. Eventually finding the solitude too unbroken, the Fowleses moved into Lyme Regis in 1968. The pleasant old house they now occupy overlooks a garden enclosed by trees, sheltered from the sight of any other house in the environs. Fowles spends most of his time writing and rambling through his two-acre garden and along the Dorset coast, where he pursues his studies as a naturalist. He is also honorary curator of the little museum in Lyme Regis and has spent a lot of time researching the town's history. He says that his study of local history has begun to supplant that of natural history; but Fowles regards the two activities as "faces of the one coin."

Even as a boy Fowles was fascinated by nature. In Devonshire he developed a love not only for natural beauty but for natural history. During the summer holidays from Bedford School, he shot, fished, and collected butterflies. But an increasing intimacy with nature led him to reject predatory sport for efforts, instead, to save nature preserves and threatened species. Fowles once told an interviewer, "I loathe guns and people who collect living things. This is the only thing that really makes me angry nowadays, I'm afraid—the abuse of nature." Among other things *The Collector* is the social and psychological analysis of a character who collects not merely "living things" but other human beings.

The Collector was not Fowles's first effort at writing fiction. By 1963, when this novel appeared in print, he had been writing for more than ten years and had produced seven or eight other manuscripts—most particularly *The Magus*, which was not published until 1965. *The Collector* was the first book Fowles sent to the publishers, because in his view it was the first manuscript he had completed satisfactorily. The others were "too large," and he found he lacked the technical mastery to bring them off. Set in London and its environs, *The Collector* is based on a central dramatic incident: the kidnapping of a young woman by a total stranger. Frederick Clegg, a nondescript clerk who works in a government office, kidnaps a twenty-year-old art student, Miranda Grey, as she is walking home from a movie. Although Miranda's family lives across the street from the town hall annex where Clegg works, their world is remote from his. Miranda enjoys all the privileges of an upper-middle-class background and education. She is talented, beautiful, and surrounded by friends and admirers. Clegg is the son of lower-class parents whose marriage ended in disaster even before Clegg was orphaned at the age of two. Clegg is an introvert who suffers an acute sense of social and sexual inferiority. He spends most of his leisure time collecting butterflies, and he is attracted to Miranda as an amateur lepidopterist is drawn to a rare and beautiful specimen. Secretly he begins to follow her activities, suffering pangs of resentment as he observes her casually going out with other young men. He also indulges in romantic daydreams, picturing a cozy life with Miranda in a "beautiful modern home." His fantasies remain only that until, one day, he wins a huge sum of money—the equivalent in the early 1960s of two hundred thousand dollars—at the football pools, which he has routinely played for years.

Finding himself suddenly graced with "time and money," Clegg begins making plans to realize what before had been only a daydream. As he meticulously devises a plan by which to ensnare Miranda, he is not even sure that he will carry it out. Even after he buys an old cottage in the country, with a set of rooms hidden in the cellar, he does not fully admit his plan to himself. But the line between fantasy and reality is gradually crossed. Clegg furnishes a cellar room, stocks it with books and clothes he thinks Miranda will like, and finally brings her, chloroformed and gagged, to live in captivity.

The first half of the novel consists of Clegg's account of his relationship with Miranda. It is soon apparent that what he calls his "love" for the girl is really his desire to own her, to possess her not sexually but as one would acquire a beautiful object or butterfly. *The Collector* introduces a theme to which Fowles returns in his later works: how the obsession with "having" has overtaken modern industrial society. Clegg's actions dramatize the confusion inherent in contemporary values—society's failure to distinguish the urge for control from the liberating power of love. Clegg's confusion intensifies when, after he captures Miranda, the real and proximate human being proves very different from the remote and unchanging image he has worshiped at a distance. Miranda's verbal assaults, abrupt shifts of mood, and probing wit unsettle and bewilder her captor. At times driven to retreat altogether from her volatile presence, Clegg consoles himself

with photographs he has secretly taken of the drugged and sleeping girl. As he says, "I used to look at them sometimes. I could take my time with them. They didn't talk back at me."

Following Clegg's narration, the second half of the novel launches a subsequent account of the same events, this time from Miranda's perspective. In her diary Miranda secretly records her responses to what has happened, along with an account of the thoughts and memories that occupy her in her cell. Now the reader gains a vivid sense of the stifling tedium and oppression of her daily life in captivity—the misery of confinement that ends only with her death. From Miranda's viewpoint Clegg's attempts to make his prisoner "comfortable" appear even more absurd. Gifts of perfume and chocolate can hardly compensate for her loss of freedom—for fresh air, sunlight, the sheer delight of unhampered being. Yet to this experience of freedom, precious and inalienable, Clegg remains persistently blind. As Miranda begins to observe and analyze her captor, she recognizes that he is the true prisoner. Trapped in an airless and dead existence, Clegg is mortally afraid of feeling, of human contact, of what is alive in himself and in others. Miranda records the discovered paradox in her diary: "He's the one in prison; in his own hateful narrow present world."

As Miranda vainly struggles to win her freedom, she begins to perceive Clegg's power over her as embodying "the hateful tyranny of weak people." Those who are themselves imprisoned by fear, ignorance, and resentment will naturally seek to repress and confine others, just as those who have a deadened perception of reality will tend to regard other people as objects. In his subsequent novels, Fowles's protagonists confront situations in some way analogous to Miranda's. Though not literally prisoners, as she is, they nevertheless struggle to assert their freedom and independence against the tyranny of the weak, ordinary, conventional—and most especially, against what, in their own psyches, is enslaved by fear or convention.

Hoping to convince Clegg to release her, Miranda strives to make him understand that she is a living human being, not a specimen he can keep in his private collection. Although totally in his power—Clegg prepares her food, buys her what she needs, determines whether she may be allowed a five-minute walk in the night air—Miranda nevertheless asserts her natural as well as her social superiority in their relationship. She calls him her Caliban (though he tells her his name is Ferdinand) because she regards him as more brute than human. Similar allusions to *The Tempest* recur throughout the novel, but the atmosphere of grim realism starkly contrasts with William Shakespeare's romance. Miranda needles Clegg with questions he cannot answer, scorns his lack of taste in art and books, and even tries to educate him morally and intellectually. To her, Clegg represents the vulgar and unenlightened world of mass taste and education. He is one of "the Many," while she is struggling to develop the civilized and liberated values of "the Few."

The social dimensions of this conflict between Miranda and Clegg, the Few and the Many, were immediately recognized by critics and reviewers of the novel, some of whom charged Fowles with elitism and even cryptofascism. Responding to what he considered a misunderstanding, Fowles attempted to explain his intent. "My purpose in *The Collector*," he wrote in 1968, "was to attempt to analyse, through a parable, some of the results" of the historical confrontation "between the Few and the Many, between 'Them' and 'Us.'" He continues: "Clegg, the kidnapper, commited the evil; but I tried to show that his evil was largely, perhaps wholly, the result of a bad education, a mean environment, being orphaned; all factors over which he had no control. In short, I tried to establish the virtual innocence of the Many. Miranda, the girl he imprisoned, had very little more control than Clegg over what she was: she had well-to-do parents, good educational opportunity, inherited aptitude and intelligence. That does not mean she was perfect. Far from it—she was arrogant in her ideas, a prig, a liberal-humanist snob, like so many university students. Yet if she had not died she might have become . . . the kind of being humanity so desperately needs." Fowles believes that society—the inequities of environment and social class—is largely responsible for the evils men commit against the system. In his next published book, *The Aristos* (1964), he states that "one cause of all crime is maleducation."

The author's expressed belief in the essential innocence of a man like Clegg may come as a surprise to readers of *The Collector*. It is questionable whether the novel really achieves this intended effect. The reader is naturally horrified as Clegg passively observes Miranda's slow death from pneumonia, which she contracts from the damp and unhealthy air of the cell. Clegg cannot

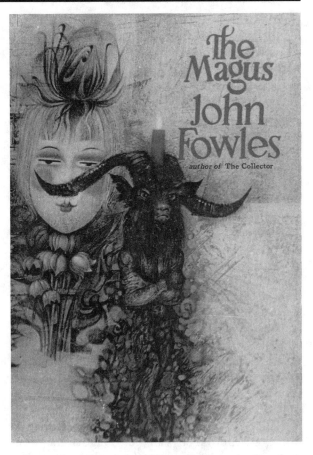

Dust jacket for Fowles's 1964 novel, an examination of a modern Prospero's "godgame"

bring himself to take her to a doctor, preferring to watch her die rather than to grant her freedom. At the end of the novel, soon after he buries Miranda's body under a tree, Clegg begins to follow the movements of a young woman in a nearby village who strikingly resembles Miranda. The future is grimly predictable. Considering Fowles's comments about the Few and the Many, are we to assume that Clegg would have been a good and productive citizen if he had been given a few of the benefits and privileges enjoyed by Miranda? The intended social parable may be lost on many readers, because the immediate effects of Clegg's actions tend to overwhelm any thoughtful consideration of their alleged social cause. The symptomatic expression of Clegg's fixation seems a more fit subject for clinical diagnosis than for social analysis. One tends to regard him as a psychotic, a pathetic madman, not as a product of social and historical forces. The Many are obviously victims of tremendous inequities in the social system; but while these conditions create unjustifiable human suffering and waste, they can hardly be said—by themselves—to produce mad-men. Fowles may have intended that the reader perceive Clegg's deadened sensibility as an extreme product of the deceptively ordinary conditions of existence—rather as Samuel Beckett and Harold Pinter ask us to see. Miranda observes that Clegg is "so ordinary that he's extraordinary." She recognizes that he is "a victim of a miserable . . . suburban world and a miserable social class"; and she identifies Clegg with "the blindness, deadness," "apathy," and "sheer jealous malice of the great bulk of England." When Miranda violently smashes the china ducks sitting on Clegg's mantelpiece, the reader knows she is expressing her hatred for the stifling banality of conventional taste and wisdom. Yet perhaps because this novel is rendered with such realistic detail, because the ordinary world is evoked in all its familiarity, Clegg appears too abnormal, too mentally disturbed to function as a convincing emblem of the "deadweight" of ordinary English life.

The Collector surprised Fowles with its commercial success. Even before the book was published, he had earned several thousand pounds from the sale of paperback, translation, and film rights. The novel was eventually translated into twelve languages, and a commercially successful motion picture—directed by William Wyler and starring Terence Stamp and Samantha Eggar—was released by Columbia Pictures in 1965. For someone who, until the age of thirty-five, could not at times afford a pack of cigarettes, such financial success must have proved a heady experience. Since then, Fowles has sold many more books and paperback, translation, and film rights. Yet what he says he enjoys most about being so well off is not the power to buy, but the freedom to live independently and do with his time what he chooses. Money appears, in fact, to have freed Fowles from *wanting* things: "I'm rich in a minor financial way," he says, "rich enough never to buy new clothes, never to want to go abroad, rich enough not to like spending money any more. I'm also rich in having many interests. I always have a backlog of books to read, there's the garden, nature, walking. . . ."

Taking advantage of the freedom success brings, Fowles made his next publication a book that was certain *not* to be a best-seller. A year after *The Collector* appeared, Fowles produced a work of informal philosophy, presented as a series of notes resembling Blaise Pascal's *Pensées* (1670) or Friedrich Nietzsche's more aphoristic writings. As the subtitle to the original edition indicates, *The Aristos: A Self-Portrait in Ideas* is the personal expression of the author's views on a wide range of subjects. "The notion I had," Fowles explains, "was that if you put down all the ideas you hold, it would amount to a kind of painter's frank self-portrait." He admits that *The Aristos* was in part a reaction to the commercial success of *The Collector*: "I didn't want to get docketed as a good story teller or as a thriller writer. *The Collector* . . . was widely reviewed in England as a thriller, it didn't even make the serious novel columns. Which is why I'm certainly tender towards the American critical scene. They at least realized it was simply borrowing something from the thriller form, but that, of course, the deeper intentions were quite different."

Four years after its initial publication, Fowles described the opposition *The Aristos* met even before it appeared in print: "I was told that it would do my 'image' no good; and I am sure that my belief that a favourable 'image' is conceivably not of any great human—or literary—significance would have counted for very little if I had not had a best-selling novel behind me. I used that 'success' to issue this 'failure.' " Fowles's disdain for the writer's so-called image suggests the irony of his situation, that of a "dynamic artist" seeking to work within the limits of a system dominated by the values of the marketplace. By making use of his commercial success to bring forth his "failure," he demonstrates his commitment to the moral and philosophical convictions set forth in *The Aristos*.

Presenting Fowles's views on such diverse subjects as human nature, evolution, art, society, religion, and politics, *The Aristos* provides a fruitful introduction to the major themes of his fiction. His main concern in this book is, as he says, "to preserve the freedom of the individual against all those pressures-to-conform that threaten our century." Like the existentialist philosophers to whom he pays tribute in *The Aristos*, Fowles is urgently concerned with the question of human freedom and the value of independent existence and action. The Greek word *aristos* means, as he explains, "best or most excellent of its kind," and "the Aristos" is Fowles's description of the individual most ideally suited to will and enact excellence under the conditions of existence as he perceives them. He takes the word and concept of the Aristos from Heracleitus, a pre-Socratic Greek philosopher whose thought has come down to us in the form of a few surviving fragments. Fowles also owes to Heracleitus his perception of the two opposing forces or principles at work in the universe: "the Law, or organizing principle, and the Chaos, or disintegrating one." The opposition of these two forces is what constitutes "the War" of existence, the tension between polar forces in which all forms of matter, including human beings, exist. Conflict and hazard, the operation of blind chance, are the inescapable grounds of existence.

Like Sartre, Camus, and other existentialist precursors, Fowles seeks a philosophical basis for human choice, value, and action in a universe that is not, so far as can be known, guided by a supernatural agent or power. Fowles's existential man inhabits a precarious universe that is constantly evolving but has no ultimate purpose. "All that is has survived where it might not have survived," says Fowles. Not only are the welfare and survival of human beings contingencies, but the very world we inhabit—this globe, those planets, our sun—is an accident, a contingent world that happened to "survive where it might not have." Such a world—and its survival—has purpose only to us, because human beings have the conscious desire to see it survive, along with our race. Fowles wrests the responsibility for survival out of the hands of a putative god and places the burden squarely on the shoulders of human beings. Dispensing with myths of a golden age, whether the lost Garden of Eden or future utopias, man must confront and embrace the hazardous (in both senses of the term) conditions of existence, for they constitute his freedom. This freedom, like everything else, is relative because all people are limited—as Miranda is in *The Collector*—by circumstances and forces over which they have little or no control. Yet by asserting our freedom to will, choose, and act within such limits, we can constrain the blind power of chance in our lives or, conversely, seize the opportunities cast up to us by chance. By struggling to establish some measure of justice and equality in society, moreover, human beings may inhibit the harsher effects of social and biological inequities.

The Aristos is, in Fowles's view, the ideal man to contend with the hazardous conditions of existence, because he does not blind himself to the existential situation into which he was born. He "accepts the necessity of his suffering, his isolation, and his absolute death. But he does not accept that the War cannot be controlled and limited" for the benefit of himself and others. True to his recognition of the contingencies of existence, Fowles points out that the Aristos is an

ideal model, not a real person. He is a goal, a potential toward which anyone may strive and which in some cases he may realize. "The Aristos is never always."

In 1968 Fowles had a revised edition of *The Aristos* published, stating in his preface that he hoped to clarify both the style and the organization of his ideas. In so doing, he cut much of the original material, restructured and occasionally retitled whole sections, and introduced new material that provides helpful transitions and more ample context for the development of particular ideas. Despite these noteworthy improvements, *The Aristos* is still not a wholly convincing work. Fowles admits that his manner of presentation is "dogmatic" rather than persuasive. He aims not to plead a case but, by "baldly" stating what he thinks, to provoke the reader into articulating his own ideas. Yet "bald" statements seem insufficient when the reader is faced with metaphysical questions concerning the origins of the universe and the nature of human consciousness. The loosely linked notes and paragraphs that *The Aristos* comprises frequently seem an inadequate mode of discourse for such complex subjects. Moreover, the dogmatic nature of some of Fowles's assertions tends to contradict his avowed belief in the essential mystery of being. The "why" of existence and of the universe, he says, will never be solved by science or art. But his attitude toward "old religions and philosophies" is often condescending. He speaks of them as "refuges, kind to man in a world that his ignorance of science and technology made unkind." Fowles's assumption that the great religions and philosophies of former ages were merely a refuge from mystery—not a means of engaging it— seems an oversimplification, a manifestation of the "scientized" thinking he argues against later in the book. In the words of critic Walter Allen, *The Aristos* "falls short of what it promises . . . but at least it can be taken as an indication of [Fowles's] ambition." And ambition, Allen adds, "is probably the first thing that strikes one about Fowles's second novel, *The Magus*."

In 1964, the year *The Aristos* was published, Fowles resumed work on *The Magus*, which he had begun writing twelve years before. Over a span of a quarter century, he worked and reworked this book, so that it became inextricably bound up with his life. Having begun the novel shortly after leaving Greece in 1952, Fowles completed the first draft in London in 1953; then he dropped the project for new ones. Yet for the next ten years he returned to the novel from time to time, revising and rewriting various versions. In 1964, he collated and rewrote all previous drafts, and in 1965 the novel was published. As soon as the first edition appeared in print, Fowles knew he was dissatisfied, later remarking that the novel remained the "notebook of an exploration, often erring and misconceived." In interviews over the next several years, he candidly stated that he did not regard the work a success. Finally, in 1977, twenty-five years after it was begun, *The Magus* reappeared in a thorough revision, with stylistic or structural changes occurring on nearly every page of the new edition.

The novel's protagonist, Englishman Nicholas Urfe, is, like Miranda Grey in *The Collector*, a bright, well-educated person in his twenties. Having graduated, like Fowles himself, from Oxford University, Nicholas—for lack of a better idea of what to do with himself—accepts a job teaching English at a private boarding school for boys on a Greek island. As Fowles says in his introduction to the revised edition of the novel, he modeled the fictive island of Phraxos after Spetsai. But the school on Spetsai, Anargyrios College, where Fowles taught from 1951 to 1952, is apparently not the model for the Lord Byron School, where Fowles sends his character Nicholas to teach. Although quickly bored with his job at this school, Nicholas remains enchanted with the gleaming Mediterranean landscape. The azure sea and sky give him the sense of inhabiting a pristine universe, an Eden untouched by human suffering or fear. Walking along the edge of a deserted beach, Nicholas feels like "the very first man that had ever stood on it, that had ever had eyes, that had ever existed, the very first man." But Nicholas is soon stripped of this illusion—the first in a series of illusions from which he will be separated. He meets Maurice Conchis, the wealthy owner of a villa overlooking this Eden. What Conchis says to him about Greece proves a more accurate description of the world Nicholas has entered: "Greece," Conchis says, "is like a mirror. It makes you suffer. Then you learn."

A cultivated European of Greek and English extraction, Conchis is a man of many and exceptional talents. Both scientist and artist, he has mastered disciplines as various as medicine, music, psychology, and the dramatic arts. What strikes Nicholas upon first meeting him is Conchis's extraordinary vitality: "He had a bizarre family resemblance to Picasso: saurian as well as simian; decades of living in the sun, the quintessential Mediterranean man, who had discarded everything that lay between him and his vitality." Among the things Conchis has discarded are those conventional patterns of thought and behavior that mark an individual as belonging to a particular nation or class. Conchis, like Pablo Picasso—or Prospero, to whom Nicholas later compares him—presides over a world of his own making, a world summoned into being by his creative energies and dominated by his will.

Like Prospero in Shakespeare's *The Tempest*, Conchis is a master of illusion. The "Magus," or magician, of the novel's title, he dominates an island that, like Prospero's, is a stage for dramatic spectacles and masques that bring revelation to their audience. Conchis's audience does not merely observe but participates in the dramatic action, which takes the form of a psychodrama. Nicholas soon becomes involved as actor-audience to the drama, and his spontaneous reactions contribute to the way it develops. What occurs between Nicholas and the Magus is, in Fowles's words, a kind of "godgame"; Conchis "exhibits a series of masks representing human notions of God, from the supernatural to the jargon-ridden scientific." By staging "a series of human illusions about something that does not exist in fact, absolute knowledge and absolute power," Conchis provokes Nicholas into confronting the essential mystery and hazard of existence. Conchis's motives for devoting his personal fortune and energies to such an elaborate enterprise are never fully explained in the novel. It is suggested, however, that the "godgame" is the result of a lifetime's study of human nature and the pursuit of a valid philosophy. Reflecting Fowles's existential vision in *The Aristos*, Conchis's philosophy is not a formal theory that can be systematically presented. The participant in the godgame discovers, through a series of concrete actions rather than a system of abstract logic, his capacity for free choice and action.

As Fowles suggests through numerous allusions to *The Tempest*, Homer's *Odyssey*, and medieval romance, the quest on which Nicholas embarks has romantic and mythic parallels. The island of Phraxos resembles that unknown otherworld to which the hero of ancient myth journeys in search of adventure and, ultimately, his true self. Fowles's final purposes are, however, those of the novelist, not the romancer. Nicholas is in no way an idealized hero, and the larger context for his adventure is the specific social-historical condition of modern industrial society.

Nicholas belongs to Fowles's own generation, coming of age immediately after World War II. According to Fowles, these college-educated young men grew up privileged, bored, and burdened with a sense of personal defeat and social exhaustion. Accepting few traditional beliefs or inherited values, Nicholas, like so many of his peers, feels incapable of sustaining a commitment to any person or ideal that might shape the course of his life.

In one sense, Nicholas is both Miranda Grey and Frederick Clegg. He shares with Miranda an interest in art and literature; and, like her, he desires to rise above the unexamined life of "the Many," to define himself apart from the stultifying conventions of respectable middle-class life. Yet Nicholas remains detached from life, an outsider looking in. Not mentally ill, as Clegg is, or afraid of human contact (he has already had many sexual affairs), he is reluctant, all the same, to give full range to his feelings. In *The Collector*, Miranda deplores Clegg's inhuman detachment from feeling. The "only thing that really matters," she writes, "is feeling and living what you believe—so long as it's something more than belief in your own comfort." Unlike Miranda, Nicholas has neither found what he believes in nor actively begun to seek it. As though subconsciously recognizing that feeling is the catalyst to both belief and action, Nicholas treats his emotional relationships with studied, even determined casualness. His impulse is not to "collect" women, but to use and dispose of them before he should have to commit himself to a lasting relationship. In some ways the result is the same, however; for Nicholas, like Clegg, purposely detaches himself from the object of his affections. In London, before leaving for his teaching post in Greece, Nicholas meets, and briefly lives with, a young Australian, Alison Kelly, whose affection for him is warm and spontaneous. But while he is sexually and emotionally drawn to Alison, he refuses fully to admit, or to allow to flourish, his feelings for her. To others and at times to himself, he pretends that Alison is a mere convenience. When an old friend from his Oxford days runs into them, privately commenting to Nicholas that Alison is attractive, Nicholas feigns cool indifference. She is, he condescendingly remarks, "cheaper than central heating."

Behind Nicholas's cold and cruel remark lies a host of implications that Fowles directly addresses in *The Aristos*. There he describes the values of contemporary industrial society as based almost exclusively on the marketplace. Members of a marketplace or "agora" society tend "to turn all experiences and relationships into objects; objects that can be assessed on the same scale of values as washing machines and central heating, that is, by the comparative cheapness of the utility and pleasurability to be derived from them." Fowles criticizes the industrial societies for their tendency to reify experience, nature, and human beings, treating them as objects, or products, of consumption. Just as the relationship between Miranda and Clegg reflects the tensions existing within contemporary British society, so does Nicholas's dishonesty toward Alison reflect a profound social malaise. Nicholas is a representative not only of his particular class, generation, and nation, but also of the distorted values of the marketplace society now dominating Western culture.

Yet while he exhibits the confused values of his society, Nicholas is more than a product of social forces. Confused as to his real identity, he seeks to change this condition. The promise of discovering a new mode of existence draws him deeply into Conchis's drama. He experiences "an awareness of a new kind of potentiality," sensing that the "mess" of his life—"the selfishness and false turnings"—could "become a source of construction rather than a source of chaos." To Nicholas, the entry into Conchis's labyrinth feels "like a step forward—and upward." Even this initial sense of progress, of getting somewhere, will later prove to be one more in the "series of illusions" that Conchis will shatter. As he seeks the answers to riddles posed by the dramatic scenarios orchestrated by Conchis and enacted by his company of actors, Nicholas discovers behind each question not an answer but another question, or a series of questions; and, mirrorlike, they all seem to double back on the seeker. Nicholas will not be granted, by the "god" of this game, any ultimate answers to his questions.

The twists and turns of the godgame, the false leads and dead ends into which Nicholas is led, are a dramatization of the essential mystery of existence. Existential uncertainty is, for Fowles, the ground of being; in that uncertainty man affirms not the answers to his questions but his freedom to seek them. As Conchis erects one version of reality after another like a series of stage sets, each collapsing as successive fictions dissolve before new versions of reality, Nicholas persists in seeking explanations for the drama itself. He wants to know whether each dramatic action has a basis in fact. He wants to find "the reality behind all the mystery." Gradually, however, he begins to recognize that the source, or truth, of the fictions is not the point. What is important is the culmination of the dramatic action—the way his own response becomes critical to the outcome. Not until the godgame on Phraxos draws to a climax does Nicholas suddenly perceive the point to which "all Conchis' maneuverings . . . all the charades, the psychical, the theatrical, the sexual, the psychological" have brought him: to this moment of "absolute freedom of choice." Much earlier in the novel, Conchis has told Nicholas that "there comes a time in each life, like a point of fulcrum," which is a moment thrown up by pure chance or hazard. The moment is pivotal to one's life because the choices one makes at this time affect "what you are and always will be." The truth of the godgame lies in the fiction itself, in bringing the participant to a "point of fulcrum" and self-revelation.

The labyrinthine complexity of *The Magus*—the mazes of the godgame, the multiple identities of its dramatis personae, the ambiguous nature of each version of "reality" devised by Conchis—disturbed many critics and reviewers when the novel first appeared. Yet the complexity of its form, so unlike the tightly compressed action of *The Collector*, is complemented by a greater complexity of characterization. In the earlier novel, the conflict between psychological polarities—between the Few and the Many, freedom and repression, love and possession, individuality and conformity—was played out, rather too neatly and with somewhat melodramatic effect, between Miranda on the one side and Clegg on the other. In *The Magus* that conflict does not take place between polarized characters but *within* Nicholas himself. Thus, despite the latter novel's somewhat cluttered form and frequently mystifying effects, *The Magus* is a more convincing dramatization of Fowles's vision of human existence. For if, as Fowles believes, existence is conflict, then surely the primary battleground for this ongoing struggle between opposing forces is not merely external reality but the human heart and mind.

In part 3 of *The Magus*, Nicholas leaves Phraxos and returns to England. As one critic, Barry Olshen, has noted, Nicholas's journey from England to Greece and back is patterned after "the traditional quest story, involving a voyage to a distant land, the achievement of a mission or the acquisition of special knowledge, and the return home." Having acquired a degree of self-knowledge, Nicholas returns to London to con-

front Alison and resolve their relationship. But Nicholas is not the only one who has been changed by his journey; Alison, too, is not the same. Nicholas learns that she has secretly taken part in the godgame, and in London he discovers that the game is not over. Although the presiding figure of Maurice Conchis disappears, he is replaced by an equally extraordinary being, Lily de Seitas. Mrs. de Seitas, an old friend of Conchis and a veteran of the godgame, turns out to be the mother of two young women, Rose and Lily, who played major roles in the game on Phraxos. It is the younger daughter, Lily, with whom Nicholas has recently believed himself to be in love— only to have that illusion rudely shattered as well. In London, Mrs. de Seitas is the one who knows where Alison Kelly is and what terms Nicholas may have to fulfill in order to see her. Once again ordinary reality is temporarily suspended, and the actors in this new phase of the drama take on luminous significance as timeless figures of myth. In one of Nicholas's meetings with Mrs. de Seitas, she sits before him in a "corn-gold chair," appearing "like Demeter, Ceres, a goddess on her throne; not simply a clever woman of nearly fifty in 1953." The personal magnetism and power that make Conchis loom like Prospero on his island also emanate from Lily de Seitas. As Nicholas discovers, she and the other actors have all been through the harrowing spiritual journey on which he himself is embarked. This experience, as a seeker in the godgame, is what has given each of them such impressive vitality and courage. Like Conchis, Mrs. de Seitas seems to have "discarded everything that lay between [her] and [her] vitality." She and Conchis are those rare individuals (and Nicholas may one day join them) who embrace their freedom, reject the values of the marketplace, and recognize the Aristos—the ideal individual—as their true model.

At the end of the novel Nicholas and Alison finally encounter each other, but their relationship remains unresolved. They are, as Nicholas realizes, at a "point of fulcrum," an experience of potential freedom that is the goal of the godgame. Here Fowles chooses to leave them, saying only that what happens to Nicholas and Alison after this "is another mystery." The apparent finality of endings is also an illusion. Like Conchis, the Magus, Fowles believes that mankind "needs the existence of mysteries. Not their solution." For mystery "pours energy into whoever seeks the answer to it." As a novelist Fowles seeks to provide his readers with that energy, too, bringing them to their "point of fulcrum." At the end the reader recognizes, if he has not already, that Fowles's novel is a godgame; the game's "two elements," "the one didactic, the other aesthetic," form a paradigm of the novel's own.

For the sake of the game, Conchis tells Nicholas, one must "pretend to believe." As a participant in the game between reader and author, the reader likewise obliges, pretending to believe in the staged illusions of the novelist until, in the last pages of the book, the author breaks the spell of his magic making and announces that we, like his "anti-hero," are also "at a crossroads, in a dilemma." "We too are waiting in our solitary rooms where the telephone never rings, waiting for this girl, this truth . . . this reality." The novel, like the godgame, is a metaphor for existence. What Fowles "teaches" in *The Magus* is not a particular set of truths or solutions, but the unique responsibility of each individual to seek his own. In the foreword to the revised edition of the novel, Fowles emphasizes his reader's "freedom of choice," saying: "If *The Magus* has any 'real significance,' it is no more than that of the Rorschach test in psychology. Its meaning is whatever reaction it provokes in the reader, and so far as I am concerned there is no given 'right' reaction."

Though not as great a commercial or critical success as *The Collector*, *The Magus* won, in Ian Watt's phrase, "a special following among the under twenty-fives." Its popularity with the young may be explained by its being, in Fowles's own words, "a novel of adolescence written by a retarded adolescent." Though he finds this quality to be his novel's weakness, Fowles defends the novelist's right to "regress" in this manner. "The rest of the world can censor or bury their private past. We [artists] cannot, and so have to remain partly green till the day we die . . . callow-green in the hope of becoming fertile-green."

Although Fowles was dissatisfied with *The Magus* almost as soon as it was published, the novel aroused sufficient public attention to warrant a film version. Fowles wrote the screenplay, and he also spent some weeks on location, on the island of Majorca. Although he wrote the script, Fowles says he had little authority over the final product. It had to be altered to suit the director, and then "the producers wanted changes, the Zanucks had their ideas." To this "nonsense" was added "the wrong director" and bad casting. The resulting film, in Fowles's words, was "a disaster."

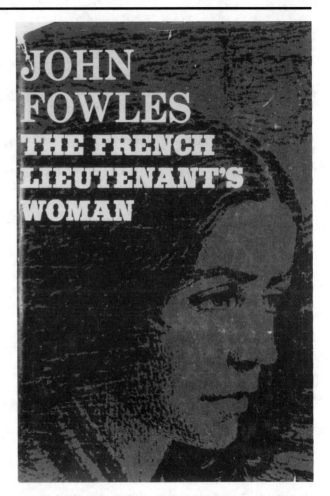

Dust jacket for Fowles's 1969 "Victorian" novel, which imitates the conventions and assumptions of that form

Directed by Guy Green, it starred Anthony Quinn as Conchis and Michael Caine as Nicholas Urfe, with Candice Bergen and Anna Karina heading the female cast. While he regards the film made from his first novel, *The Collector*, as "just passable," he ranks *The Magus* and *Justine* (the movie made from Lawrence Durrell's novel) as "the two worst films of the Sixties." Ironically, Fowles speaks the first line of this motion picture "disaster." Because the director persuaded him, on the spur of the moment, "to do a Hitchcock-style walk-on," as critic Robert Huffaker puts it, the novelist appears in the first scene of the film. He plays a Greek sailor who "casts a line ashore, turns to actor Michael Caine, and announces, 'Phraxos.'" Even this spontaneous attempt at a private joke contributed another mistake to the ill-fated film. As Fowles explains, "only Greek priests wear beards," so the appearance of Fowles as a bearded Greek sailor "set an inauthentic note from the beginning."

Despite, or perhaps because of, the failures associated with the first version of *The Magus*, Fowles decided, more than a decade later, to revise this "endlessly tortured and recast cripple" one more time. In 1977 he had the new version published, explaining his intentions in the foreword. In rewriting the novel one final time, Fowles did not attempt to answer "the many justified criticisms of excess, over-complexity, artificiality and the rest that the book received from the more sternly adult reviewers on its first appearance." *The Magus* would have to remain a novel of adolescence, one that was, "in every way except that of mere publishing date," a "first novel." In what way, one might ask, did Fowles attempt to improve his young man's book, if not in conception? The answer apparently lies in the mature writer's sense of responsibility to his craft and medium. Fowles wanted to rescue this novel from a clumsiness of style and structure he regarded as criminal. Explaining why he rewrote *The Magus*, he says: "I do not believe that the intention matters more than the craft, idea more than language; and I do believe that almost all major human evils in our world come from betrayal of the word at a very humble level. In short, I have always felt with *The Magus* like an insufficiently arrested murderer." The novelist thus "paid" for his literary "crime" by rewriting phrases and paragraphs on almost every page of the novel and by recasting whole sequences of action and dialogue. He also corrected "a past failure of nerve" by strengthening the "erotic element" in two pivotal scenes. The effect is a noteworthy improvement not only in the novel's formal qualities but in thematic clarity as well. Many of the novel's themes, rather obscurely buried in the original text, are more lucidly rendered in the subsequent revision. The analogy between the strategies of the godgame and those of the novelist is, for example, more fruitfully developed in the revised edition.

Nicholas's emotional and moral blindness also receives more emphatic treatment in the new version, as Fowles supplies him more opportunities to act like a cad. Nicholas more openly disavows his relationship with Alison, for instance, clearly betraying past affection as well as present loyalties. Brought to a harsher confrontation with the worst in himself, Nicholas more clearly perceives his own selfishness. Like Pip in *Great Expectations* (1861)—the Dickens novel Fowles most admires and the one that, by his own admission, influenced the writing of *The Magus*—Nicholas

sternly judges his past behavior. But the rigor of his self-condemnation is also shown, as in Pip's case, to be a sign of moral growth. The new ending that Fowles wrote for the revised edition hints at a greater likelihood for reunion between Nicholas and Alison; yet the final scene is more open-ended. Nicholas demands that Alison choose, and choose now, whether they are to remain together. He then waits for her answer; and in this "frozen present tense" the author leaves his characters, and the reader, "suspended."

This withholding of any fixed solution, or resolution, to the story has troubled many of Fowles's readers, prompting some of them to write him angry letters demanding that he tell the reader what does in fact happen to his characters. Yet Fowles's purpose in sustaining ambiguity is not to shirk his responsibilities as a novelist, but to redefine them. In his next novel, *The French Lieutenant's Woman*, published in 1969, he overtly tells the reader that he does not exercise absolute authority over his characters. For him the novelist's traditional role as "omniscient god" is outmoded and untenable. Victorian novelists adopted this stance because they sought to model themselves after God himself, the all-knowing Creator of the universe. But Fowles, a twentieth-century existentialist, rejects the notion of a universal Creator; and in *The French Lieutenant's Woman* he announces his abdication from the throne of literary omniscience. He drives home the point by writing a convincing version of a "Victorian" novel—one that captures with detailed fidelity the manners and milieu of the time—but a Victorian novel that conspicuously lacks the assuring presence of an omniscient author. Thus, eighty pages into the novel, the narrator declares that his character Sarah Woodruff remains a mystery even to him. He confesses that his apparent omniscience is only a guise, an aspect of the literary game: "This story I am telling is all imagination," he says. "If I have pretended until now to know my characters' minds and innermost thoughts, it is because I am writing in . . . a convention universally accepted at the time of my story: that the novelist stands next to God. He may not know all, yet he tries to pretend that he does." A remarkable evocation of the historical and social matrix of the Victorian age, *The French Lieutenant's Woman* is also a parody of the conventions, and underlying assumptions, that operate within the Victorian novel.

While Fowles's narrator draws attention to the contrasts in habits and ideas that exist between Victorian times and our own, he also reminds us that the Victorians' apparently stable and unchanging world was, in 1867, about to vanish forever. In this year Karl Marx published the first volume of *Das Kapital*; Charles Darwin's *Origin of Species* had already appeared in 1859. These eminent Victorians, steadily and without any violent action, helped to shatter the age in which they lived—its faith, morality, confidence. The shocks to the system that lie ahead—though unsuspected by Fowles's characters, who are naturally caught up in the present—are well known to Fowles's readers. This contemporary perspective imbues the historical elements of the novel with poignant irony. An example appears in the narrator's description of Ernestina Freeman, the pretty and pampered young lady engaged to the novelist's protagonist, Charles Smithson. Ernestina's doting parents worry unnecessarily about their precious daughter's supposedly frail health. To these Victorian parents a genteel young lady is by definition fragile and must be treated like a porcelain doll. The narrator (sounding suspiciously omniscient) then provides the reader with some salient information to counter the assumptions of Ernestina's fond parents: "Had they but been able to see into the future! For Ernestina was to outlive all her generation. She was born in 1846. And she died on the day that Hitler invaded Poland." That Ernestina will live into an age when healthy young ladies are not treated like invalids is only the mildest indication of the forces of change about to unleash themselves on her world. For now, in the year 1867, Ernestina is a complacent, unsuspecting member of her class and generation. Her habits of thought and action are a straightforward reflection of the predominant attitudes of her day.

Fowles's parodic exposure of Victorian conventions serves as a springboard for testing not only literary devices but also cultural values and assumptions—those of the Victorian age and the present as well. The critical examination of one historical period against the background of another transforms this apparently historical novel into a truly experimental one. In a memorandum Fowles wrote to himself while working on *The French Lieutenant's Woman*, he says: "Remember the etymology of the word [novel]. A novel is something new. It must have relevance to the writer's now—so don't ever pretend you live in 1867; or make sure the reader knows it's a pretence."

Both the experimental nature of this novel and its display of erudition—crammed as it is with scholarly information on Victorian mores, politics, art, medicine, science—could hardly have prepared one for the extraordinary popular success that greeted its publication.

For many months a best-seller in the United States, the novel also received enthusiastic reviews from distinguished critics such as Ian Watt, who said in the *New York Times Book Review* that Fowles's "immensely interesting, attractive and human" third novel is "both richly English and convincingly existential." Though less enthusiastically received in Britain, as has steadily been the case for Fowles's work, *The French Lieutenant's Woman* was more warmly received there than his previous novels. In 1969 the International Association of Poets, Playwrights, Editors, Essayists, and Novelists gave Fowles its Silver Pen Award for *The French Lieutenant's Woman*, which also won the W. H. Smith and Son Literary Award in 1970. In September 1981 a filmed version of the novel was released, receiving wide public attention. The film's screenplay was written by the distinguished British playwright Harold Pinter, and its cast featured Meryl Streep as Sarah and Jeremy Irons as Charles.

Fowles himself was surprised by the critical and commercial success of this novel, whose conception had imposed itself on him while he was halfway through another. One predawn autumn morning in 1966, a vision of a woman standing on a deserted quay (one much resembling Lyme Regis harbor, which can be seen from Fowles's garden) came to him while he was still half-asleep. The woman was dressed in black and stood, with her back turned, gazing at the distant horizon. Readers of the novel will immediately recognize the figure as Sarah Woodruff, the "French lieutenant's woman." Chapter 1 of the novel ends with a description of Sarah, in black, standing "motionless, staring, staring out to sea . . . like a living memorial to the drowned, a figure from myth. . . ." According to Fowles, these "mythopoeic 'stills'" often float into his mind. He ignores them at first, waiting to see if they are of the persistent variety that opens "the door into a new world"—the new world, that is, of a new novel. Fowles ignored the image, but it duly persisted, the woman always appearing with her back turned. That turned back, Fowles began to perceive, signaled a rejection of the age in which she lived, and Fowles already knew that the figure was Victorian. Ultimately the figure in black recurred with such power that it made Fowles's previously planned work seem a bothersome intrusion on a deeper and more compelling task. He had fallen in love with the French lieutenant's woman, and he set to work on the first draft of the book.

Unlike Ernestina Freeman in every way, Sarah Woodruff is, in both senses, the other woman in this novel. Mystifying everyone, including the author, Sarah rejects the values of her age, refusing to live by its conventions. She is an outsider, a nineteenth-century character with a distinctly twentieth-century cast of mind. The daughter of a tenant farmer, she has been sent to boarding school and thus educated beyond her station. Sarah also possesses a strong will, independent mind, and passionate heart—qualities that were hardly viewed as desirable in a young Victorian lady. By nature, temperament, and social circumstance, Sarah breaks the mold of respectable Victorian womanhood.

Between these two women and the opposing values they represent, Charles Smithson, an intelligent though aimless Victorian gentleman in his early thirties, is driven to choose. Already engaged to Ernestina Freeman when he first encounters Sarah, Charles is at once fascinated and a little frightened by Sarah's striking presence. Rumors that she has been seduced and abandoned by a French lieutenant are adrift in the quiet little town of Lyme Regis, where the novel is set. On this lonely coast Charles first sees Sarah, in chapter 1, staring tragically out to sea. Her isolation from respectable society and her "untamed" nature seem to require that Charles encounter Sarah in the wilds of nature rather than in a well-furnished drawing room. Their relationship thus develops outside the constraining walls, symbolic as well as literal, of Victorian society.

As this relationship (and the novel's plot) progresses, the "mystery" of Sarah's nature is not solved but augmented. She eventually tells Charles a different version of the tale concerning the French lieutenant, but she verifies the rumors of her seduction and abandonment. Not until much later, after a great internal struggle on Charles's part to resist her mysterious power over him, does he discover that Sarah's version of the story is also a fiction. She was not seduced by the French lieutenant at all. It is Charles, in fact, who deflowers her, never suspecting that she is still a virgin. Far from being seduced, however, Sarah orchestrates the events that lead to her brief tryst with Charles. And he, now in love

with Sarah, finds it impossible to go through with his engagement to Ernestina.

Like Conchis, the Magus, Sarah Woodruff lives outside the bounds of social and moral conventions. And while she is drawn to Charles—and even, apparently, loves him—she desires not to make him happy, but to be free. This fierce desire for personal freedom is something that attracts Charles, though he does not understand it. He begins to discover the meaning of personal freedom through this relationship with Sarah. She is the mystery that gives him energy to seek answers; she is the catalyst for the discovery of his potential freedom. This slow and painful process takes place over a period of twenty months, beginning shortly after Sarah vanishes, upsetting all of Charles's romantic expectations. Utterly alone and hopelessly confused, Charles is determined to find Sarah, vowing that "if he searched for the rest of his life, he would find her." On a train speeding toward London, Charles, having chosen an empty compartment, is abruptly joined by a bearded stranger, who sits down and eventually begins to stare at him with "cannibalistic" intensity. Here the author of this deceptively Victorian novel is making a brief theatrical appearance, in the nineteenth-century guise of a magisterial graybeard in a frock coat. Although his "prophet-bearded" persona gazes at Charles like an "omnipotent god," Fowles's narrator denies authorial omniscience. "What Charles wants," he admits, "is clear," but what Sarah, his more inscrutable character, wants "is not so clear; and I am not at all sure where she is at the moment." Appearances—even those of an author in his own novel—can be deceiving.

This playful introduction and ultimate debunking of the author's Victorian persona is a device by which Fowles reminds his readers, once again, that they are not engaged in a Victorian novel. The fact is, the present world of the author and the reader is at a century's remove from the Victorian era; and the enforced awareness of such temporal distance only augments the contemporary reader's sense of disjunction between the world—of any era—and its fictional representation. The contemporary writer cannot adopt the confident posture of omniscience so favored by his Victorian predecessors, because belief in omniscience, like God, is now dead. Fowles's narrator dramatizes his abdication, or fall, from omniscience by saying that his characters must be granted their freedom. Refusing "to fix the fight" and determine their fate, the author will present, instead, two alternative endings to the story. Now his bearded persona, whose aura of imposing authority has already begun to fade (he later reappears as a dandified impresario), flips a coin to decide which of the two endings will be given the position of "last" chapter. The narrator regrets that in the novel's sequential narrative two versions of the ending cannot be presented simultaneously. He laments that the second ending inevitably "will seem, so strong is the tyranny of the last chapter, the final, the 'real' version." And this is exactly what happens in *The French Lieutenant's Woman*, though whether the novelist actually regards it as unfortunate is another question.

The author's expressed determination to grant freedom to his characters is an argument with which the reader may sympathize but can hardly accept in a literal sense. Nor did Fowles intend that his provocative statements be taken literally. He has described, in an interview, what he feels to be the freedom of his characters. It is the "bizarre experience" of having his inventions, at some point in the process of writing, suddenly "start up on their own." Then, Fowles says, he has the strange feeling that these characters "know the line they ought to be saying" and that he must grope "around in the dark to find it." "Of course in reality," he adds, "the writer has the final say. And on the final draft you have to let the characters know it. Very often by then you know them so well that you are like a really skilled puppetmaster. You can make them do anything, almost. You have to guard against that. You have to say to yourself, this is just an assemblage of words and I can take my scissors and cut it where I want. In other words, you're cutting words, not some real person's skin and flesh." The novelist, as Fowles sees him, navigates a sometimes treacherous course between the insistent reality of his "new world" and the formal strictures of artistic creation. In *The French Lieutenant's Woman* he repeatedly draws attention to the paradox of literary creation, of having his characters take life in the imagination even while they are confined to the pages of a written text. This self-consciousness about the processes of art is a hallmark of much twentieth-century fiction. As a writer Fowles is as conscious of the limits on the life of a character as he is of the limits of his own omniscience. The freedom of an author's characters is metaphorical rather than literal, as is the reality embodied in his fiction.

The choices Fowles leaves to both his characters and the reader, in the form of open or alternative endings, reflect his existential preoccupation with human freedom. "How you achieve freedom," he told an interviewer, "obsesses me. All my books are about that. The question is, is there really free will? Can we choose freely? Can we act freely? Can we choose? How do we do it?" One of the ways we do it, Fowles appears to suggest, is through the process of literary creation. For the writer, "the novel is an astounding freedom to choose." With every word, every page, one makes a multitude of choices. Literary composition is thus bound up with the most essential principles of human life; and the novel, for Fowles, is a metaphor for the potential freedoms of that life. The novel will last, he says, "as long as artists want to be free to choose. I think that will be a very long time. As long as man."

By affirming his characters' freedom, Fowles also reminds his readers of their own. The reader, like the writer, is faced with choices; obviously, however, the choices he or she makes are inextricably bound up with the author's, which have already been made. Art, like life, has its deterministic principle; true freedom, Fowles affirms, "can never be absolute." Any choice the reader makes will be influenced or guided by the artistic choices the author makes—as, for example, when he provides two endings to the same novel. In *The French Lieutenant's Woman*, it is clear, the second ending proves more convincing because the artistry is more complete. This is the "tyranny" not only of the "last chapter," but of art itself. The author's persona may have flipped a coin in the railway compartment, but the real author, stationed in the wings, is arranging the sequence of endings just as he wants them. True, the novel's first ending is more emotionally satisfying, because the lovers are reunited after Sarah has "tested" Charles, but the reader, no matter how sentimentally inclined, cannot ignore the greater impact of the second ending even though Sarah here rejects Charles. In the second ending Charles does not discover that Sarah has given birth to his child. The scene does not end with Sarah's head modestly inclined on Charles's breast, in the manner of so many literary reconciliations of that era. It is as though Fowles were giving us a taste of old-fashioned assurances in the first ending in order to brace us for the harsh and lonely realities of the second. Only here, bereft of Sarah, past hope and expectations, does Charles discover "an atom of faith in himself, a

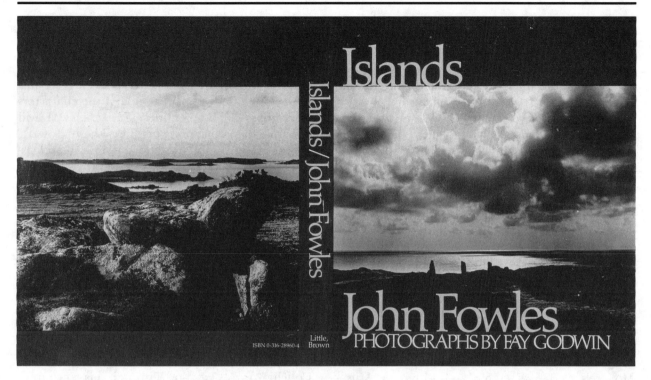

Dust jacket for Fowles's consideration of real and metaphorical islands, accompanied by Fay Godwin's photographs of the Scilly Islands

true uniqueness, on which to build." The second ending, and the final chapter, of Fowles's novel closes with a line from Matthew Arnold's poem "To Marguerite," which the narrator avows is "perhaps the noblest short poem of the whole Victorian era." Although the poem is Victorian, the image it offers of solitary human existence is an eloquent expression of Fowles's twentieth-century vision: men and women struggle alone, isolated one from the other like islands in the great "unplumb'd, salt, estranging sea." This vision, rather than the blessings of good fortune, Charles Smithson embraces in the second and final ending to the novel.

From the self-conscious artifice of *The French Lieutenant's Woman*, Fowles turned with admitted relief to his next project, a collection of poetry he had begun writing in 1951. This volume, simply entitled *Poems*, was published in 1973; it contains poems dating from 1951 through 1972. The personal immediacy of these poems, written in a compressed, even terse style, presents a striking contrast to the richly inventive language and structure of his major novels. Fowles says he regards poetry as a more honest reflection of the self, because the poet speaks directly from his thoughts and feelings. By contrast, the novel is "first cousin to a lie. This uneasy consciousness

of lying is why in the great majority of novels the novelist apes reality so assiduously; it is why giving the game away—making the lie, the fictitiousness of the process, explicit in the text—has become such a feature of the contemporary novel. Committed to invention . . . the novelist wants either to sound 'true' or to come clean." This impulse "to come clean" obviously manifests itself in *The French Lieutenant's Woman*, as Fowles's narrative persona self-consciously focuses attention on literary artifice and declares that "all is fiction." The novelist's clever and playful persona is a far cry from the quiet self whose voice we hear in *Poems*. In "Suburban Childhood," he describes a familiar world where "downstairs / the wireless droned immortally / important Sunday hymns." In the poem "In Chalkwell Park" the poet takes a walk with his aging father, quietly hoping that death will not take him soon. Despite the difference in tone and voice, many of the poems echo themes more amply treated in Fowles's novels. The poem "Crusoe," for example, treats the theme of the quest that underlies much of Fowles's fiction. Defoe's Robinson Crusoe is a symbol of the lonely voyager. People are "Crusoes, all of us. Stranded / On solitary grains of land." The image recalls the line from Arnold's "To Marguerite," with which *The French Lieutenant's Wom-*

an concludes. Cast into the "unplumb'd, salt, estranging sea" of life, each man is an island.

The Ebony Tower, a collection of stories published in 1974, represents a further departure for Fowles from the extended form of the novel, a far more impressive departure than his poetry. It also reflects his continuing fascination with the literature and landscape of France, a fascination that began during his college years. Although Fowles does little traveling these days, when he does leave England he usually visits the French countryside, which provides the setting for several of these stories. Moreover, Fowles includes among the original stories in this collection his translation of a twelfth-century French romance, *Eliduc*, by Marie de France. The love of French literature that Fowles developed during his Oxford years is evident in the translations and adaptations he has written since. In 1974 his adapted translation of Charles Perrault's seventeenth-century fairy tale *Cinderella* appeared. In 1977 he translated two classics of the French theater, Moliere's *Dom Juan* (1665) and Alfred de Musset's *Lorenzaccio* (1834) for London's National Theatre. His translation of Claire de Durfort's early-nineteenth-century novella *Ourika*, about a young Senegalese girl brought to France as a child and raised among Europeans, was published in 1977. In his foreword to this translation Fowles admits that "the African figure of Ourika herself," a social outcast, must have subliminally inspired his depiction of Sarah Woodruff in *The French Lieutenant's Woman*. "The case history of an outsider," *Ourika* "touches on one of the deepest chords in all art, the despair of ever attaining freedom in a determined and determining environment."

In "A Personal Note" appended to one of the stories in *The Ebony Tower*, Fowles explains that the working title of this collection was "Variations," "by which I meant to suggest variations both on certain themes in previous books of mine and in methods of narrative presentation." Each of the stories is also a kind of variation on a mood, setting, or theme found in Marie de France's *Eliduc*. By including his prose translation of this romance among the original stories collected in this volume, Fowles encourages his readers to look for thematic correspondences and common motifs. He thus continues to provoke the reader's interest in the literary process as well as in the product. Fowles asks that his readers be as attentive to the way characters and events are portrayed as they are to the events themselves. Each of these stories is in some way about art, visual or

literary; and at the same time it self-consciously reflects, or exposes, the process of its aesthetic creation. The author plants various self-conscious devices, announcing that "all is fiction," throughout. In the title story, also the longest—just under one hundred pages—one of the characters is reading a book entitled *The Magus*. David Wiliams, the protagonist of "The Ebony Tower," has never heard of the book, however, and assumes it is about astrology and "all that nonsense." The irony, shared by the author and reader alone, is that David Williams is about to undergo the kind of personal ordeal, or test, that Nicholas Urfe in *The Magus* faces at each stage of the godgame.

An abstract painter who also writes and lectures on contemporary art, David Williams travels to France to interview a famous British expatriate, the seventy-year-old painter Henry Breasley. Breasley, who lives with two young female companions in a secluded old manor house in Brittany, possesses the vitality that reminds one of Maurice Conchis or of Picasso. Through his encounter with Breasley—and with one of the young women living at the manor, a promising young painter—David finds the orderly "solutions" of his life suddenly thrown into question. Feeling a vital attraction to the young woman, David takes a fresh look at his comfortable, arid marriage. At Breasley's provocation, he begins to question the enterprise of abstract painting as well. (Fowles, whose stepdaughter, Anna, and her husband are both art teachers, says that their problems as art students helped him to understand the general problems of modern art as well as literature. He has, therefore, tacitly dedicated this story to them.) Breasley tells David that abstract painting exists in an "ebony tower," his designation for the obfuscating tendencies of contemporary art. A modern variant of traditional "ivory tower" idealism, the ebony tower signifies the contemporary artist's retreat from reality. Obscurity and cool detachment mask his fear of self-exposure and his failure to engage with life's vital mysteries. David gradually recognizes that he is such an artist, camouflaging the "hollow reality" of his paintings "under craftsmanship and good taste." He is a concrete example of the "static artist" described by Fowles in *The Aristos*.

The story culminates in a "point of fulcrum" for David Williams, but, failing to act at the critical moment, he loses the "chance of a new existence." Rejecting this chance, failing to seize it, David sadly realizes that he has arrested his further development as an artist. "Crippled by common sense," he has failed to embrace mystery, exploit hazard, and discover a way to self-renewal. The possibilities confronting Nicholas Urfe and Charles Smithson at the end of their ordeals appear closed to David. The conclusion of "The Ebony Tower" is final, not open-ended. As he goes to meet his wife at the airport, David awakens from the "dream" of a freer, more vital mode of existence. He has "a numbed sense of something beginning to slip inexorably away. A shadow of a face, hair streaked with gold, a closing door." With an inward, "drowning cry," David awakens to "jackbooted day" and "surrenders to what is left: to abstraction."

Like "The Ebony Tower," Fowles's next story, "Poor Koko," ends with an extended epiphany, or revelation, on the part of the main character. Like David Williams, the protagonist of "Poor Koko" makes a discovery whose meaning extends beyond his personal life. David realizes that abstract painting is one symptom of the malaise in contemporary culture—a retreat from human concerns and reality into the "ebony tower." Similarly, the highly literate narrator of "Poor Koko" recognizes in what happens not only his own failure but the failure of his generation and the breakdown of society. He makes this discovery when he travels to a country cottage in North Dorset, which has been lent to him by friends so that he may finish, without interruption, his critical biography of Thomas Love Peacock (a nineteenth-century novelist admired by Fowles). Just after the narrator arrives at the cottage, a thief breaks in, thinking the cottage empty. The young robber ties up the narrator, but does not harm him. In fact, as the thief goes about his business, selecting things of value, he engages the narrator in a long conversation, even offering to make him a cup of coffee before he leaves. Before he goes, the young man suddenly, and without warning, destroys all the books, documents, notes, and drafts the narrator has accumulated—over a period of four years—for his book on Peacock.

This violent attack on his manuscript rather than on his person presents the narrator with an enigma he is still trying to solve nearly a year after the event. He keeps asking himself what could possibly have been the thief's motive. He arrives, finally, at a "tentative conclusion" that he relates to the reader. Being a man of letters, he focuses his attention on the verbal evidence. He recalls what the young man said to him and,

what is more, what he might have been trying to say to him in the crude jargon adopted by contemporary, alienated youth. "Man, your trouble is you don't listen hard enough," the thief had told him. In that rebuff the narrator now recognizes "a tacit cry for help." He admits to himself that he was "guilty of a deafness." His manuscript thrown into the fire, he now perceives that "what was really burned was my generation's 'refusal' to hand down a kind of magic," the power of language. He blames himself, as a member of that generation, for such a catastrophic breakdown of social and cultural values. The younger generation, he perceives, has been deprived of the most vital source of personal energy and power a culture can bestow. They have been left to "doubt profoundly their ability to say" what they think and believe. The strongest evidence for the narrator's argument resides in the narrative medium of the story itself. The narrator's measured, precise delineation of feeling and perception, and the compassionate insight at which he ultimately arrives, could not be shared, or realized, had not the author's language worked its special magic here.

While the narrator of "Poor Koko" solves, at least to his own satisfaction, the enigma of what has happened to him, the mystery of the next story—aptly titled "The Enigma"—is not solved, but abandoned. In the process of investigating the inexplicable disappearance of John Marcus Fielding, a prominent London member of Parliament, a young police sergeant named Jennings discovers for himself and the reader what Fowles had previously suggested in *The Magus*: the quest for answers to a mystery, rather than the answers themselves, pours energy into the seeker. While Michael Jennings searches for clues to a possible "sexual-romantic solution" to the M.P.'s disappearance, he unwittingly embarks on an amorous adventure of his own. *Cherchez la femme*, advises another M.P. whom Jennings questions about Fielding's disappearance; but the woman Jennings finally discovers is not the abstract one for whom he thought he was looking. His investigation leads instead to a remarkable young woman, Isobel Dodgson, who is the former girlfriend of the vanished man's son. Jennings is immediately taken with her; and the mystery of love proves the abiding enigma of this story.

Not only is Isobel Dodgson exceptionally pretty and quick-witted; she also possesses the electric vitality and independence that characterize a self-motivated individual in Fowles's world. A fledgling writer, Isobel is aware of the parallels between the "game" of detection in which Jennings is engaged and the conventions of the detective-story genre. "Let's pretend," she suggests to him, that "everything to do with the Fieldings, even you and me . . . is in a novel. A detective story. . . . Somewhere there's someone writing us, we're not real. He or she decides who we are, what we do, all about us." Playfully taking up the writer's part in this predictable genre of fiction, Isobel teasingly suggests to Jennings a potential lead in the case—that is, her possible complicity in Fielding's disappearance. As the reader already realizes, however, Fowles's story transcends the narrow conventions of the detective story. Jennings rejects Isobel's playful solution as an obviously false lead, remarking that "it's not how I read her character." That Jennings has begun to "read" Isobel's character suggestively implicates the act of literary interpretation in the processes of life. In both life and literature readers seek meaning and a satisfactory mode of representing discoveries to themselves as well as to others.

The lack of a central lead or a neat key to Fielding's disappearance prompts Isobel to observe: "If our story disobeys the unreal literary rules, that might mean that it's actually truer to life." For at the heart of life, as Fowles suggests throughout his fiction, lurks insoluble mystery. The uncertainty of real existence distinguishes actual human beings from conventional literary characters. The latter, because their fates are thoroughly "written" by a creator intensely interested in them, lack the freedom of real individuals inhabiting an apparently indifferent universe. It is also possible, in Fowles's view, to allow oneself to be "written" by a social system or a fixed code of conventions in real life. By unthinkingly conforming to a system of rules governing both thought and action, human beings can forfeit their freedom and unknowingly transform themselves into social puppets. In "The Ebony Tower," David realizes that, having allowed himself to be so written, he is an "artificial man" rather than a free one. By implicitly equating authorial control—being written—with social determinism, Fowles again raises the important question: how does an author who explicitly provokes his reader's awareness of the literary artifice hope to grant to his literary puppets a measure of personal freedom? One way is to insist that those of his characters who reflect human freedom—Maurice Conchis, Lily de Seitas, Sarah Woodruff, Henry Breasley, and perhaps the vanished man Fielding—retain

an aura of mystery about them. They are, by virtue of their unpredictable humanity, not wholly solvable or determinable, either by the reader or by the author. The real mystery or enigma at the heart of Fowles's fiction provokes the reader to seek his own answers and thus partake of the energy that mystery generates. In the words of Conchis, mystery "pours energy into whoever seeks the answer to it."

Abandoning the search for the solution to an abstract problem, Jennings recognizes the priority of the enticing mystery before him: "The act [Fielding's disappearance] was done; taking it to bits, discovering how it had been done in detail, was not the point. The point was a living face with brown eyes, half challenging and half teasing; not committing a crime against that." Part of Isobel's attraction for Jennings is her inscrutable air of independence. Her effect on him in some ways resembles Sarah's on Charles Smithson: "Something about [Isobel] possessed something that he lacked: a potential that lay like unsown ground, waiting for just this unlikely corn-goddess; a direction he could follow. . . . An honesty." The power Jennings perceives in Isobel is associated with the source of growth, fertility, or fruition in nature. A "corn-goddess" whose vital power promises to nurture new life in him, Isobel recalls Lily de Seitas, who appears before Nicholas, the seeker in *The Magus*, "like Demeter, Ceres, a goddess" on her "corn-gold" throne.

The final story of the collection, "The Cloud," is the most evanescent structurally and thematically. The opening paragraph, with its concrete evocation of a summer's day in rural France, proves nothing short of deceptive. In a matter of hours the azure sky of this "noble day, young summer soaring, vivid with promise," will be transformed by the precipitous appearance of a mysterious cloud, "feral and ominous"—the "unmistakable bearer of heavy storm." The style of the opening paragraph is deceptive as well. Its realistic tone and point of view will abruptly give way to a series of shifting narrative perspectives. To begin with, the reader is given a glimpse of the central characters at close range. On a terrace two young women lie outstretched on beach chairs in the sun; three other people, a woman and two men, are ranged about an outdoor table, while three children play below on the lawn. No sooner is this picture sketched than the point of view shifts to a position "across the river," from which the narrator gazes with a painter's detachment at the distant composition of these "eight personages" in a "leafy" and "liquid" landscape. The harmony of this composition suggests to the narrator a Gustave Courbet painting; the tranquillity, however, is more apparent than real. "So many things clashed, or were not what one might have expected," he says, slyly adding, "If one had been there, of course." As soon as the narrator reminds the reader that he is indeed not "there" in the scene, he mysteriously finds himself—without any helpful transition—back in the midst of these "eight personages." The authorial sleight of hand reminds Fowles's readers that they are in a fictive universe, where imagining is the only form of being anywhere.

No matter from which perspective the characters are viewed—and in this story the perspective keeps changing—the sense of their interrelationships and ulterior motives is fleeting and elusive. The indistinct contours of the cloud after which the story is named come to suggest the impalpable human emotions lying beneath the visible surface of reality. A vaporous floating island adrift in the azure sky, the cloud also connotes the essential isolation of each of the characters, even as they embark on a group picnic by the river. Most isolated of all is the story's major character, a bitter young woman named Catherine, first glimpsed sunbathing on a beach chair. She is the recently widowed sister of Annabel Rogers, who lives with her husband Paul and their two children in a charming old mill by a river in central France. Visiting them are Paul's friend Peter; Peter's girlfriend, Sally; and his son by a former marriage. Still mourning the loss of her husband and consumed with bitterness over his suicide, Catherine resents the presence of the other guests; she feels both superior and hostile to their casual talk. Since the suicide of her husband, she has lost all sense of continuity in her life. For her, everything has become "little islands, without communication, without farther islands to which this that one was on was a stepping-stone, a point with point, a necessary stage. Little islands set in their own limitless sea. . . . And the fear was both of being left behind and of going on." The terror and isolation Catherine feels but cannot express to anyone are revealed in the fairy tale about a lost princess that she tells to her little niece. The princess, having gone on a picnic with her royal family, falls asleep in the forest: "And when she woke up it was dark. All she could see were the stars. She called and called. But no one answered. She was very frightened."

At the end of "The Cloud," Catherine, like the lost princess, has been left alone by the other picnickers, who assume she has already started home. By this time, having noticed the ominous cloud that has suddenly appeared in the sky, they are eager to get back before it starts "thunder-and-lightning all night." As the picnickers, without Catherine, start walking back, the narrative viewpoint once again shifts "across the river." The reader watches the characters disappear from the scene, leaving the meadow empty. The landscape is silent, the composition of figures now removed from the setting. All that is left is "the river, the meadow, the cliff and cloud." No one, not even the reader, can see where Catherine is lying. The ambiguous final sentence of the story echoes a line from the fairy tale Catherine told to her niece: "The princess calls, but there is no one, now, to hear her." Catherine, it seems, is lost forever; perhaps she will commit suicide, a possibility that has haunted her throughout the day. Perhaps she is doomed not to death, but to that prison of despair from which she cannot call out—or, like the princess, calls out when it is already too late. The events of this story lead to no visible climax. Only the charged atmosphere of unspoken fear, hate, and desire conveys the menace lurking in the otherwise bucolic landscape. The symbolic embodiment of these elusive psychic realities is the cloud. A sign of the bad weather to come, the cloud also serves as a harbinger of impending human disaster.

As he announces the sudden appearance of the ominous cloud on the horizon, the narrator remarks: "And the still peaceful and windless afternoon sunshine . . . seems suddenly eerie, false, sardonic, the claws of a brilliantly disguised trap." In this story, the false "trap" of appearances has been staged by the author, but with obvious reference to the deceptions of both nature and art—most particularly, the deceptive surface "realism" of landscape painting. In "The Cloud," Fowles evokes the wilderness of the solitary human heart lurking beneath the innocent landscape, a wilderness, insubstantial but real, that every true writer seeks to embody in the concrete physical environment. In "The Cloud" imagery, style, and structure create a vivid impression of this protean reality without fixing it in final form.

In the *New York Times Book Review*, Theodore Solotaroff qualified his warm praise of these stories by comparing them to Fowles's previous novels: "None of the four long stories . . . has the originality of those two novels [*The Magus* and *The French Lieutenant's Woman*] or even the tour de force quality of Fowles's *The Collector* . . . and they do tend to have a kind of relaxed, mopping-up feeling about them." Solotaroff's critical reservations may say less about the intrinsic value of *The Ebony Tower* than they do about the disadvantage any writer faces when he breaks with his past practices and tries out a new form or style. Although Fowles returned in his next work, *Daniel Martin* (1977), to the novel form, he was still committed to breaking new literary ground. His description of the novel as "a long journey of a book" is apt, for its writing occupied him for years. (During those years he also conceived and wrote *The Ebony Tower* and completed his revision of *The Magus*—both of which were published before *Daniel Martin*.) Like much of Fowles's other fiction, this novel is patterned on the quest motif, the main character's search for an authentic self. *Daniel Martin* also reflects the author's journey toward greater authenticity as a writer. By his own admission, this novel is Fowles's most personal work. Aware of the obvious parallels between himself and his character, Fowles says: "I was brought up in a Devon village, the one in the book. Quite a lot of my ideas are spoken by [Daniel Martin]. I gave him two or three of my interests." The "authenticity" as well as the psychological intensity of this novel originate not in its autobiographical elements, however, but in Fowles's immediate and searching presentation of the main character's inner life.

A few years after the publication of *The French Lieutenant's Woman*, Fowles told an interviewer that he now wanted "to write more realistically. *The Collector* was a kind of fable, *The Magus* was a kind of fable, and *The French Lieutenant's Woman* was really an exercise in technique." He added, "of course style is *an* essential preoccupation for any artist. But not to my mind *the* essential thing. I don't like artists who are high on craft and low on humanity. That's one reason I'm getting tired of fables." Interestingly, he was preparing the final version of *The Magus*, attempting to atone for his literary "crimes" against language and craft in that "adolescent" book, at the same time that, in *Daniel Martin*, he was trying to move away from too much preoccupation with style and craft. Aware that his special gift as a writer was "for narrative"—a gift for telling stories that made people listen—Fowles had begun to wonder whether he had abused this gift by writing novels full of "literary gymnastics." While his earlier "betrayal of the word" had compelled him

to rewrite *The Magus* one more time, his quest for a more authentic style in *Daniel Martin* apparently grew out of an awareness—now that he had mastered the techniques of literary invention—that craft alone is not enough. In an interview in 1977, shortly after *Daniel Martin* was published, Fowles referred to the novel as his "penance." The word suggests that for him this "journey of a book" was a kind of pilgrimage, an act of literary contrition for the artistic "sin" of having exploited or hidden behind his talent for narrative invention. *Daniel Martin* is not simply nor unartfully constructed; its design is extremely complex. But, unlike Fowles's previous novels, this one does not proceed with rapid forward momentum, catching the reader up in its ingenious twists and turns. Critics have, in fact, faulted the novel for its long paragraphs of unwieldly introspection and lack of dramatic tension. Fowles's intention, however, is clear. There is nothing superficially compelling about the action or plot of this long, ruminative novel.

The protagonist of *Daniel Martin* is an English playwright turned screenwriter. The idea for a novel about a screenwriter apparently took shape during Fowles's visit to Hollywood in 1969. He had gone there to discuss plans for filming a motion picture of *The French Lieutenant's Woman*. (Many abortive attempts to bring the novel to the screen were made prior to the version released in 1981.) With a half hour to kill before his appointment with the head of production at Warner Brothers, Fowles wandered around the studio lot. Since nothing was being filmed, all the sets were empty. He had an intense impression of vacuity, and that sense of emptiness about the moviemaking industry inspired him to begin *Daniel Martin*.

A man in his late forties, Daniel Martin has arrived at a "point of fulcrum" in his personal and professional life. Although materially successful, with an established career in films, he is overcome by a sense of defeat and moral failure. It is, he says, "as if I was totally in exile from what I ought to have been." In an attempt to recover that neglected and abandoned self, Dan begins to contemplate, with considerable trepidation, the possibility of writing a novel about his life. The novel that Fowles's reader holds in his hand appears, at first, to be the one Dan ultimately succeeds in writing. By the end of the novel, however, Dan has not yet begun to work on it. Instead, in the last paragraph of Fowles's novel, Dan suddenly thinks of an apt concluding sen-

The EBONY TOWER

John Fowles

Dust jacket for Fowles's 1974 collection of "variations both on certain themes in previous books . . . and in methods of narrative presentation"

tence for his projected work. Then, in the last sentence of *Daniel Martin*, the real author steps in to comment on his character's discovery of a last sentence: "In the knowledge that Dan's novel can never be read, [that it] lies eternally in the future, his ill-concealed ghost has made that impossible last [sentence of Dan's] his own impossible first." Daniel Martin's "ill-concealed ghost" is Fowles himself, who refers the reader to the "impossible first" sentence of his novel. This isolated fragment—"Whole sight; or all the rest is desolation"—makes little sense to the reader when he first encounters it. The full meaning only emerges after he has read Fowles's closing paragraph and returns to the opening of *Daniel Martin* to read the sentence a second time. Fowles's "journey of a book" thus describes a circle, tracing the archetypal pattern of the quest itself. In *The Magus*, Fowles describes this circular pattern, quoting from the last poem in T. S. Eliot's *Four Quartets* (1943), "Little Gidding": "And the end

of all our exploring / Will be to arrive where we started / And know the place for the first time."

At the end of *Daniel Martin*, the protagonist finds himself—like Fowles's other "seekers," Nicholas Urfe and Charles Smithson—poised on the brink of a possible new life, the "chance of a new existence." In contrast to Fowles's other novels, *Daniel Martin* concludes with a definitive happy ending—in the form of the main characters' reconciliation. In another sense Fowles still refuses to offer fixed solutions for his characters or readers. By self-consciously introducing himself, Dan's "ill-concealed ghost," into the novel's concluding sentence, Fowles reminds us that his character's projected novel is not the one, *Daniel Martin*, just read. Daniel Martin's book must lie "eternally in the future." Dan's past has been joyfully redeemed, but the future still holds its mysteries.

Most important, however, is the vision of wholeness achieved by Dan at the end of the novel. The discovery of "whole sight" is a culmination of his journey toward self-integration. To be whole Dan must recover that lost, or potential, self from which he has felt "exiled." The stages of this journey toward recovery and integration are embodied in both the events and the narrative structure of the novel. *Daniel Martin* astutely traces a mind's digressive movement back and forth over the critical events of a lifetime. These events loom like islands in the sea of Dan's consciousness, and he journeys back to them in memory while time carries him forward into the future.

In *Islands* (a long essay featuring a series of photographs of the Scilly Islands, published in 1978), Fowles remarks that the structures of his novels all seem to recall the voyage of consciousness to different islands in time and memory: "I have always thought of my own novels as islands, or as islanded. I remember being forcibly struck . . . by the structural and emotional correspondences between visiting . . . different islands and any fictional text: the alternation of duller passages . . . the separate island quality of other key events and confrontations—an insight, the notion of islands in the sea of story." Although all of Fowles's novels loom as a series of islands in their author's mind, none has a structure more closely resembling this description than *Daniel Martin*. This "journey of a book" does not trace the linear movement one associates with a train or car, but the apparently wayward, drifting motion of a sailboat—tacking its way through a populous archipelago and halting at various points of interest. "Forward Backward" is the title of an early chapter in *Daniel Martin*, describing Dan's return to Oxford, England, where an old friend of his is dying of cancer. The friend, Anthony Mallory, is someone from whom Dan has been estranged for many years; in his last hours Anthony wishes to redress old wounds and make amends. The journey to Oxford from London, a literal progression forward in time, is for Dan a journey backward into the past. Here he must confront not only Anthony and his wife, Jane—with whom Dan was in love years ago, when they were students at Oxford, and whom he knows he should have married—but also buried regrets, fears, and guilt. Up until this moment he has been living in flight from his past, fearing to face up to himself or to atone for past betrayals. Giving up writing plays for a career in films has also offered escape: "Film excludes all but now; permits no glances away to past and future; is therefore the safest dream. That was why I had given so much of my time and ingenuity to it."

The telephone call that brings Dan to Oxford from Hollywood, where he has been working on a script, is the catalyst for his delayed confrontation with the past and his lost self. When he hears, over the transatlantic telephone wires, the voices of Jane and her sister, Nell (Dan's ex-wife), he already knows that the sea, and the voyage, have claimed him: "The decision is on him, almost before he knows it is there, and he feels—the image is from seeing, not experience—like a surfer, suddenly caught on the crest, and hurled forward." The surfer, riding the crest of the wave *back* to shore, is literally engaged in the "forward backward" movement that symbolizes Dan's inner voyage toward recovery of the past and "what he ought to have been."

The forward-backward movement of the novel's narrative also reflects the special Englishness of Dan's, and his race's, elusive nature. These special qualities comprise, according to Fowles, the basic subject of *Daniel Martin*. As Fowles has Dan realize in the novel, the reserve of the English is a manifestation of their "peculiarly structured imagination, so dependent on undisclosed memories, undisclosed real feelings." The real life of the English, Dan observes, takes place beneath the surface of the visible and present: "We are above all the race that live in flashback, in the past and the future; and by a long blindness I had got myself into the one artistic profession [filmmaking] where the essence of En-glishness, this psychological and emotional equivalent of the flashback (or flash-forward, flash-aside) lay completely across the natural grain of the medium—which was a constant flowing through nowness, was chained to the present image." The Englishman's characteristic withdrawal into the privacy of the inner self is also expressed in Dan's love of the "sacred combe"—the hidden valley or forest retreat that provides sanctuary from the strictures of the everyday world. To this green world, a mythical Sherwood Forest, the English psyche retreats to encounter and be nourished by the essential mysteries of life. In *The Tree* (1979), an essay Fowles wrote to accompany a series of evocative photographs of trees, he describes the green refuge of forest and wood as "the best analogue of prose fiction." He adds, "Some such process of retreat from the normal world—however much the theme and surface is to be of the normal world—is inherent in any act of artistic creation, let alone that specific kind of writing that deals in imaginary situations and characters. And a part of that retreat must always be into . . . a complexity beyond daily reality, never fully comprehensible or explicable, always more potential than realized."

Dan's decision to write a novel is thus an expression of his "longing for a medium that would tally better with this real structure of my racial being and mind . . . something dense, interweaving, treating time as horizontal, like a skyline; not cramped, linear and progressive." Such a medium is embodied in the novel *Daniel Martin*. "Dense" and "interweaving" like a forest interior, the novel not only intertwines events from different time periods but also alternates between different narrative points of view. The narrative shifts from third to first person, from "he" to "I" and back as Dan intermittently engages in the "attempt to see oneself as others see one—to escape the first person, to become one's own third." His desire to escape the first person also manifests his fear of subjectivity, of "emotion and unreason." He knows that "the objectivity of the camera corresponded to some deep psychological need in him." This need for distance is akin to the emotional detachment Nicholas Urfe assiduously cultivates in *The Magus*. In some ways Daniel Martin represents a middle-aged version of Urfe, burdened by a sense of personal defeat and failure made heavier by his greater years and experience. The emotional rebirth, or recovery, of self that both characters undergo is, therefore, associated with their renewed apprehension of mystery—the fertile source, the green world, of "emotion and unreason."

The novel's frequent shifts in narrative point of view also serve to remind the reader of that authorial presence, Dan's "ill-concealed ghost," standing in the wings, waiting to declare himself at the end of the novel. As soon as Dan decides that "anything would be better than to present" his hypothetical novel "in the first person," the chapter breaks—and the next paragraph begins with the sentence, "I was also very tired that morning." It is not Dan but his author, Fowles, who is in ultimate control. This particular shift to first person occurs, moreover, just after Dan recalls the name Simon Wolfe, the name he is thinking of using for the main character in his projected novel. Later this "mythical Simon Wolfe" reappears in his thoughts as "S. Wolfe"; as several critics have noted, S. Wolfe is an anagram for Fowles. Fowles's self-conscious references to the acts of reading and writing again draw attention to the analogies that exist between life and art. Consciousness makes all human beings readers and writers of reality—writing so that they may be read and interpreted by others. In *Daniel Martin* this literary and existential process is reflected at all levels of the text. Behind the characters and events of the novel is glimpsed the shadowy presence of the author, John Fowles (S. Wolfe)—whose self, vision, and imagination have written the world of *Daniel Martin* into being.

In one sense, the novelist's characters are all versions, or representations, of his inmost self. They are the masks he invents for the purpose of defining what that self is, knows, experiences. In *Daniel Martin*, then, the author's role is recapitulated by Fowles's central character. As the narrating persona of the novel, Daniel Martin is engaged in the act of "writing himself." But writing himself in the present implies reviewing and interpreting his past. As he sets about doing this, Dan realizes that he has always been writing, producing, and acting versions of himself. He sees the Oxford student Dan Martin as a tour de force creation—with the author playing the role and serving as the audience, too. "I was writing myself, making myself the chief character in a play, so that I was not only the written personage, the character and its actor, but also the person who sits in the back of the stalls admiring what he has written." The description evokes both the world of the theater and the myth of Narcissus, who gazed with solipsistic admiration at his reflection in the pool. It also describes Dan's deep psycholog-

ical need for what he calls "the objectivity of the camera." By detaching his public self, the one who performs and acts in the world from his innate sense of being, Daniel Martin has sought to live at safe remove from the wellsprings of his deepest emotions. Of course, all versions of the self are to some degree masks constructed to act in the world, or to protect the individual from its harsh pressures. But some masks are more valuable, or more harmful, than others. Some, like Dan's glib persona at Oxford, may inhibit personal or artistic development by masking a human being's deepest impulses even from himself. Dan thus distinguishes between the "mask of excuse, a sacrificial pawn," behind which the wearer takes refuge from himself, and the mask that serves as "an emblem of some deep truth, or true presentiment."

The drama and destiny of the self are not the only issues confronted in *Daniel Martin*, however. Fowles appears more concerned than ever before with the relationship of the individual to his society, and with the necessary balance between personal freedom and social restraint—what he calls the "printed text of life." Recalling a "gratuitous sexual act" committed years earlier as a student at Oxford, Dan makes the following observation: "Our surrender to existentialism and each other was also, of course, fraught with evil. It defiled the printed text of life; broke codes with a vengeance; and it gave Dan a fatal taste for adultery, for seducing." The "printed text of life" is a communal code, created and validated by individuals united in a common concern, the health and welfare of their society. Coming of age during the years immediately following World War II, most of Dan's generation rebelled against the text and "broke codes with a vengeance." By doing so they helped to usher in the "age of self." "All that my generation and the one it sired have ever cared a damn about," Dan observes, "is personal destiny; all the other destinies have become blinds."

Like Gustave Flaubert's *A Sentimental Education* (1869), which Fowles has acknowledged as an influence on his novel, *Daniel Martin* is both the record of a character's personal history and the cultural history of a generation and its failures. Dan's recognition of the narcissism infecting him and his generation appears to convey his author's concern for the ultimate well-being of an entire culture. Significantly, in *Daniel Martin* the sexual-romantic relationships of the protagonist are, unlike those in Fowles's previous novels, linked to family relationships—relationships that bind the individual to society and the generations to each other. When Dan returns to England from America, he breaks off an affair with a younger woman and begins to pick up the pieces of his aborted, mangled friendship with Jane. In the tortuous process of their eventual reconciliation and the gradual awakening of an affinity that lay in ruin for decades, Dan must examine and rebuild other relationships, too: the one with his daughter, Caro; with Jane's children; even with his ex-wife, Nell.

This "journey of a book" involves, then, not only Daniel Martin's quest for an integrated self, but also his gradual reintegration with others. The bonds existing between Dan's isolated self and others, in both his family and society at large, must be recovered in the quest for wholeness. Dan's renewed sense of loyalty and attachment suggests, within the context of this novel, the necessary commitment required of each individual if a sane and healthy social order is to be achieved. Fowles appears to say that a compromise between the needs of the self and the requirements of society is necessary. Dan comes to recognize, therefore, that compromise is not a denial of personal freedom but its realization in the actual world: "The only true and real field in which one could test personal freedom was present possibility. Of course we could all lead better, nobler . . . lives; but not by positing them only in some future perfect state. One could so clearly only move and act from today, *this* present and flawed world."

Daniel Martin's journey is a quest to discover "what had gone wrong, not only with Daniel Martin, but his generation, age, century; the unique selfishness of it, the futility, the ubiquitous addiction to wrong ends." What Dan accomplishes by reentering his past and attempting to put right what had gone wrong has a larger significance, suggesting the possibilities for moral and social regeneration. Anthony Mallory, Dan's dying friend, articulates the connection between personal and social history that Fowles develops throughout the novel. "I do have the strangest kind of optimism about the human condition," Anthony says. "I can't explain it. It's . . . just that we shall come through. In spite of all our faults. If only we learn that it must begin in ourselves. In the true history of our own lives." Dan's decision to write a novel about his true history appears to confirm Anthony's view that human progress begins "in ourselves."

When Dan, in Hollywood, receives the unexpected call summoning him to Anthony's bedside, he senses that a "door in the wall" of his existence has suddenly opened, "as in a fiction." He recognizes that this phone call breaks all laws of probability and plausibility, laws that he, as a writer, "might have flinched at breaking if he had been inventing the situation." Yet, in this chance "unsettling of fixed statistical probability," Dan ultimately perceives "a release from mire, a liberation, a yes from the heart of reality to the supposed artifice of art." This "yes from the heart of reality" is tinged by irony, of course, since the phone call occurs not in reality but within the artifice of Fowles's novel. As a metaphor for existence, however, this artifice contains its own reality, conveys its own truth. By introducing this chance opportunity, this suddenly opened door into Daniel Martin's existence, Fowles knows he is breaking more than the code "of fixed statistical probability." He is self-consciously breaking with that overriding sense of doom and defeat that permeates so much contemporary fiction.

Apocalypse and absurdity seem indelibly written into the texts of life currently produced by the most noted writers of this age. It is, as Dan observes, "like some new version of the Midas touch, with despair taking the place of gold. This despair might sometimes spring from a genuine metaphysical pessimism, or guilt, or empathy with the less fortunate. But far more often it came from a kind of statistical sensitivity . . . since in a period of intense and universal increase in self-awareness, few could be happy with their lot." Perhaps the "cultural fashion" of despair, Fowles suggests, is really a symptom of the "age of self," resulting from the extraordinary attention now focused on personal happiness, comfort, and reward. Rejecting the excesses of this age, then, Daniel Martin—and behind him his author, Fowles—refuses to create his novel in "deference to a received idea of the age: that only a tragic, absurdist, black-comic view . . . of human destiny could be counted as truly representative and serious." The thread of optimism that runs through this novel, affirming the possibilities for moral and social regeneration, suggests that Fowles wants to introduce more than formal innovations into contemporary fiction. In *Daniel Martin* he attempts to free the novel not only from traditional conventions for depicting reality but also from a popular, doom-laden vision of reality itself. The "yes from the heart" of Fowles's novel may well embody the affirmation life can yield when established ways of seeing, as well as writing, give way and the resources of the individual are contemplated anew.

Readers of *Daniel Martin*, as Robert Huffaker points out, "have responded to the book generally less enthusiastically than they greeted his more flamboyant works." The more subdued character of this novel is a direct result of Fowles's decision to guard his integrity as an artist rather than to exploit his talents as a storyteller. Although *Daniel Martin* did not repeat the outstanding popular success of *The French Lieutenant's Woman*, several distinguished critics have regarded it as Fowles's most artistically ambitious work to date. Since the publication of *Daniel Martin* in 1977, the author has focused on nonfiction works. Several of these present extensive, often wide-ranging commentary to accompany a series of photographic studies on a particular subject. Both *Islands* and *The Tree* (1979) attest to the truth of Fowles's assertion that he "came to writing through nature." In *The Enigma of Stonehenge* (1980), Fowles turns his attention from natural to man-made wonders. One of the most intriguing artifacts of Stone Age civilization, Stonehenge is the "technological masterpiece" of Neolithic man. Standing on the Salisbury Plain in Wiltshire, England, are large circular formations consisting of huge upright stone slabs and lintels. The function of these massive stones, weighing as much as forty-five tons apiece, has long been the subject of scholarly speculation, and Fowles adds his own voice to the discussion of this ancient enigma. He provides both a detailed account of the archaeological evidence dating the phases of Stonehenge's construction and a survey of the various religious and scientific accounts that have arisen, from medieval times to our own, to explain the original function of this stone ruin.

In the book's final pages, however, Fowles characteristically shifts the focus of his discussion from what is known about Stonehenge to what is still unknown: "There are not yet enough facts about it to bury it in certainty, in a scientific, final solution to all its questions. Its great *present* virtue is precisely that something so concrete . . . so individualized, should still evoke so much imprecision of feeling and thought." In an "increasingly 'known,' structured, ordained, predictable world," the enigma of Stonehenge—like the mysteries embodied in nature or great works of art—offers the human imagination "a freedom, a last refuge of the self." Here, as in his earliest fiction,

Fowles identifies the quest for self and freedom with the presence of mystery and the energy it pours into the seeker. His own quest, it is clear, has centered on the imaginative adventures—and the very real risks—of writing fiction.

As a literary explorer, Fowles has investigated a wide range of styles, techniques, and approaches to writing; the history of this exploration is recorded and embodied in the rich variety of his published work. He has affirmed the resources of language and at the same time delineated the strictures inherent in representing reality within literature and art. By acknowledging these limitations, yet continuing to struggle against them, Fowles has indeed proved himself a dynamic rather than a static artist. Generations of readers will doubtless continue to be enlightened as well as entertained by his fiction.

Interviews:

Roy Newquist, "John Fowles," *Counterpoint* (New York: Simon & Schuster, 1964), pp. 217-225;

Richard Boston, "John Fowles, Alone But Not Lonely," *New York Times Book Review*, 9 November 1969, pp. 2, 52, 53;

Daniel Halpern, "A Sort of Exile in Lyme Regis," *London Magazine*, 10 (March 1971): 34-46;

James Campbell, "An Interview with John Fowles," *Contemporary Literature*, 17 (Autumn 1976): 455-469;

Mel Gussow, "Talk With John Fowles," *New York Times Book Review*, 13 November 1977, pp. 3, 84, 85.

Bibliography:

John Fowles: A Reference Companion (New York: Greenwood, 1991).

References:

Robert Alter, "*Daniel Martin* and the Mimetic Task," *Genre* (Spring 1981): 65-78;

Ronald Binns, "John Fowles: Radical Romancer," *Critical Quarterly*, 15 (Winter 1973): 317-334;

Malcolm Bradbury, "John Fowles's *The Magus*," in *Sense and Sensibility in Twentieth-Century Writing*, edited by Brom Weber (Carbondale: Southern Illinois University Press, 1970), pp. 26-38; republished as "The Novelist as Impresario: John Fowles and His Magus," in *Possibilities: Essays on the State of the Novel* (Oxford: Oxford University Press, 1973), pp. 256-271;

Patrick Brantlinger, Ian Adams, and Sheldon Rothblatt, "The French Lieutenant's Woman: A Discussion," *Victorian Studies*, 15 (March 1972): 339-356;

Dwight Eddins, "John Fowles: Existence as Authorship," *Contemporary Literature*, 17 (Spring 1976): 204-222;

Constance B. Hiett, "*Eliduc* Revisited: John Fowles and Marie de France," *English Studies in Canada*, 3 (Fall 1977): 351-358;

Robert Huffaker, *John Fowles* (Boston: G. K. Hall, 1980);

Barry N. Olshen, *John Fowles* (New York: Frederick Ungar, 1978);

William J. Palmer, *The Fiction of John Fowles* (Columbia: University of Missouri Press, 1974);

Elizabeth D. Rankin, "Cryptic Coloration in *The French Lieutenant's Woman*," *The Journal of Narrative Technique*, 3 (September 1973): 193-207;

Roberta Rubinstein, "Myth, Mystery, and Irony: John Fowles's *The Magus*," *Contemporary Literature*, 16 (Summer 1975): 328-339;

Robert Scholes, "The Orgastic Fiction of John Fowles," *Hollins Critic*, 6 (December 1969): 1-12;

Theodore Solotaroff, "John Fowles' Linear Art," review of *The Ebony Tower*, *New York Times Book Review*, 10 November 1974, pp. 2-3, 20;

Richard Stolley, "The French Lieutenant's Woman's Man: Novelist John Fowles," *Life*, 68 (29 May 1970): 55-58, 60;

Katherine Tarbox, *The Art of John Fowles* (Athens: University of Georgia Press, 1988);

David H. Walker, "Subversion of Narrative in the Work of Andre Gide and John Fowles," in *Comparative Criticism: A Yearbook*, volume 2, edited by E. S. Shaffer (Cambridge: Cambridge University Press, 1980), pp. 187-212;

Ian Watt, "A Traditional Victorian Novel? Yes, and Yet . . . ," review of *The French Lieutenant's Woman*, *New York Times Book Review*, 9 November 1969, pp. 1, 74, 75;

Peter Wolfe, *John Fowles, Magus and Moralist* (Lewisburg, Pa.: Bucknell University Press, 1976).

Dick Francis

(31 October 1920 -   )

This entry was updated by Gina Macdonald (Loyola University in New Orleans) from her entry in
DLB 87: British Mystery and Thriller Writers Since 1940: First Series.

BOOKS: *The Sport of Queens: The Autobiography of Dick Francis* (London: Joseph, 1957; revised, 1968; New York: Harper, 1969; revised again, London: Joseph, 1974);

Dead Cert (London: Joseph 1962; New York: Holt, Rinehart, 1962);

Nerve (London: Joseph, 1964; New York: Harper, 1964);

For Kicks (London: Joseph, 1965; New York: Harper, 1965);

Odds Against (London: Joseph, 1965; New York: Harper, 1966);

Flying Finish (London: Joseph, 1966; New York: Harper, 1967);

Blood Sport (London: Joseph, 1967; New York: Harper, 1968);

Forfeit (London: Joseph, 1969; New York: Harper, 1969);

Enquiry (London: Joseph, 1969; New York: Harper, 1969);

Rat Race (London: Joseph, 1970; New York: Harper, 1971);

Bonecrack (London: Joseph, 1971; New York: Harper, 1972);

Smokescreen (London: Joseph, 1972; New York: Harper, 1973);

Slay-ride (London: Joseph, 1973); republished as *Slayride* (New York: Harper, 1974);

Knock Down (London: Joseph, 1974); republished as *Knockdown* (New York: Harper, 1975);

High Stakes (London: Joseph, 1975; New York: Harper, 1976);

In the Frame (London: Joseph, 1976; New York: Harper, 1977);

Risk (London: Joseph, 1977; New York: Harper, 1978);

Trial Run (London: Joseph, 1978; New York: Harper, 1979);

Whip Hand (London: Joseph, 1979; New York: Harper, 1980);

Reflex (London: Joseph, 1980; New York: Putnam's, 1981);

Twice Shy (London: Joseph, 1981; New York: Putnam's, 1982);

Dick Francis (photograph by Mary Francis)

Banker (London: Joseph, 1982; New York: Putnam's, 1983);

The Danger (London: Joseph, 1983; New York: Putnam's, 1984);

Proof (London: Joseph, 1984; New York: Putnam's, 1985);

Break In (London: Joseph, 1985; New York: Putnam's, 1986);

A Jockey's Life: The Biography of Lester Piggott (London: Joseph, 1985; New York: Putnam's, 1986);

Bolt (London: Joseph, 1986; New York: Putnam's, 1987);

Hot Money (London: Joseph, 1987; New York: Putnam's, 1988);

The Edge (London: Joseph, 1988; New York: Putnam's, 1989);

Straight (London: Joseph, 1989; New York: Putnam's, 1989);

Longshot (London: Joseph, 1990; New York: Putnam's, 1990);

Comeback (London: Joseph, 1991; New York: Putnam's, 1991).

OTHER: "Dead Cert," in *Best Racing and Chasing Stories*, edited by Francis and John Welcome (London: Faber & Faber, 1966), pp. 86-101;

"The Midwinter Gold Cup," in *Best Racing and Chasing Stories 2*, edited by Francis and Welcome (London: Faber & Faber, 1969), pp. 143-151;

The Racing Man's Bedside Book, edited by Francis and Welcome (London: Faber & Faber, 1969);

"The Gift," in *Winter's Crimes 5*, edited by Virginia Whitaker (London: Macmillan, 1973), pp. 104-130;

"Nightmares," in *Ellery Queen's Searches and Seizures*, edited by Ellery Queen (New York: Davis, 1977), pp. 141-149;

"The Day of the Losers," in *John Creasey's Crime Collection 1980*, edited by Herbert Harris (London: Gollancz, 1980);

The Dick Francis Treasury of Great Horseracing Stories, edited by Francis and Welcome (New York: Norton, 1990).

SELECTED PERIODICAL PUBLICATION—
UNCOLLECTED: "Can't Anybody Here Write these Games? The Trouble with Sports Fiction," *New York Times Book Review*, 1 June 1986, p. 56.

Author of twenty-nine novels, which have been translated into nearly two dozen languages and which have sold more than twenty million copies, Dick Francis is unequaled at making horse racing come alive. In fact, Philip Larkin (*Times Literary Supplement*, 10 October 1980) calls his novels "brilliant vignettes," and admirers such as John Welcome (*London Magazine*, March 1980) point out that in his work "one can hear the smash of birch, the creak of leather and the rattle of whips." He asserts that no one can touch Francis at capturing the "tragedies and occasional triumphs," "the seductive beauties" of the track, and infusing them with a significance beyond their domain: "a microcosm of the contemporary world." Julian Symons has argued (*New York Times Book Review*, 29 March 1981) that what Francis does best is to capture the "thrills, spills and chills of horse racing." His prose is lucid, his plots ingenious, intricate, and carefully conceived. His dialogue captures the nuances of class and region as he throws together the echelons of equine sports: owners, trainers, jockeys, stable lads, bookmakers, and touts.

His basic formula is predictable: competent stoics, out of love or loyalty or a sense of fair play and decency, are forced to come to terms with a hidden evil, one at first only suspected but then clearly defined by injury or death. His heroes must face physical pain or psychological trauma and must summon up their inner strength, their resilience, and their sheer grit to unravel the mystery, save their friends, prove themselves, or simply defeat evil. His villains are always motivated by greed or insanity, or, as in *Break In* (1985), both. Despite his standard approach, Francis's works are never the same. His plots remain fresh, unexpected, solid. They move forward briskly, with an admirable sense of timing, and are lent variety by his interweaving of racing and other concerns: mining, photography, banking, computer science, aviation, accounting, art, antiques, yachting, private investigation, acting, writing, and the wine business. Francis's books are not simply novels of suspense, but, as Edward Zuckerman has so aptly called them (*New York Times Magazine*, 25 March 1984), "novels of character and manners."

Richard Stanley Francis was born on 31 October 1920 at Coedcanlas, his maternal grandfather's farm near Tenby, Wales. His father, George Vincent Francis, who had been a professional steeplechase jockey before World War I, was later manager of W. J. Smith's stables at Holyport, near Maidenhead.

Francis learned to ride at age five and showed horses at age twelve. An unenthusiastic student, he quit school at age fifteen, vowing to become a professional jockey, and, in preparation, helped race, train, transport, and show horses for his father, first at Holyport, then at the family stables near Wokingham. During much of World War II he was an airplane mechanic. In the later years of the war he flew fighter planes, troop-carrying gliders, and Wellington bombers for the Royal Air Force. After the war he returned to racing, first as an amateur (tacitly taking under-the-table "gifts" from grateful owners), then as a professional. The conflict between amateurs and professionals, which he personally ex-

Dust jacket for the first American edition of Francis's novel set in Moscow

perienced, provides tension in many of his novels. Standing five feet, eight inches tall and weighing 150 pounds, Francis was too large to ride in flat races and so made the steeplechase his specialty. After riding seventy-six horses to victory during the 1953-1954 racing season, he won the title of champion jockey. The same year he began riding for Elizabeth, the Queen Mother.

Francis had long been a devotee of detective fiction, in his youth reading Sir Arthur Conan Doyle, Nat Gould (a pre-World War I English racing writer), and Edgar Wallace. In maturity he began to read writers such as Alistair MacLean, Desmond Bagley, Gavin Lyall, and Michael Underwood, each of whom competently captures a world of expertise. But Francis never considered writing until forced to retire from steeplechasing at age thirty-six. He had just before suffered an unusual incident at the Grand National, when Devon Loch, the Queen Mother's horse, per-

haps frightened by the roar of the crowd, fell on its stomach ten strides from the winning post—and that after clearing the last fence of the grueling four-and-a-half-mile course. Losing the race remains a sore spot, with Francis's nightmare that of being remembered as the man who lost the Grand National in so spectacular a way. Shortly after, Francis had a horse fall on top of him, kick him in the stomach, and break his wrist. His doctor recommended retirement. Until that time he had had an illustrious career as a jockey, having ridden 350 winners and having served as the Queen Mother's first jockey. However, as Francis himself points out in a 1983 *Writer* interview, after age thirty-five "the human body doesn't allow you to bounce back" from falls "thirty or forty times a year at forty miles an hour," the average for most steeplechase jockeys.

After the agent son of a friend of his mother had encouraged him to write his autobiography, and then the sports editor of the *London Sunday Express* had persuaded him to try his hand at covering the track, Francis finally decided to try to make a living as racing correspondent and did so, working for the *Sunday Express* for sixteen years. The position allowed him to move in familiar circles, but the difficulties of walking "a fine edge" in dealing with one's friends and acquaintances as "raw material" that the racing correspondent-hero of *Forfeit* (1969) complains about clearly reflect Francis's feelings. Consequently, while still a correspondent, Francis decided to attempt mystery writing to help pay for the education of his two sons and improve the family finances. He has turned out a novel a year ever since. Francis feels that journalism taught him a crisp, disciplined style that, together with his own obsession with precision and timing, has made his novels terse, fast paced, and solid. Nonetheless, racing remains his first love. When Sid Halley, in *Whip Hand* (1979), quotes a former champion who took thirty years to get over his yearning for racing, it is probably Francis speaking of his own sense of loss. At the track he takes pleasure in watching the tactics of jockeys; at home he works out those tactics on paper. As he pointed out in the interview with Zuckerman, "Having a book on the best-seller list is very nice, but there's nothing nicer than jumping over large fences on a good horse and looking through his pricked ears for the next ones." In a 1990 *Writer* interview Francis compares writing novels to "riding a race." He points out, "You keep your high moments until the last furlong and then you produce your horse to win. When you're jumping the big fences, you're placing your horse to meet that fence. When you're writing your story, you're placing your words so that the reader will be excited at the right moment and, then, easing off after you've jumped the fence."

Francis claims his method is to think of a plot by midsummer, do his research in the fall, and start writing around 1 January when the family goes to Fort Lauderdale, Florida; he does his first draft in longhand, then reads it aloud on tape, types it up, and submits his manuscript by late April. He discusses his plots a good deal with his wife, Mary Margaret Brenchley, whom he married in 1947. She researches new fields of expertise, makes suggestions about details and credibility, and helps him with the final editing. Sometimes he does not know how he will end his story until he actually sits down with his exercise book and starts writing, and most of his minor characters and subplots develop during that process. Since the early 1970s he and his wife have traveled around the world for his research, once going to Australia for a promotional campaign that produced *In the Frame* (1976) and later to Johannesburg, South Africa, to judge the National Horse Show, see a gold mine, and visit a game reserve (the basis for *Smokescreen*, 1972). A trip to see the fjords of Norway produced *Slay-ride* (1973; published in the United States as *Slayride*, 1974); a visit to Moscow, a city he observed with distaste, led to *Trial Run* (1978). Travel in America spawned *High Stakes* (1975), which takes place in part in Florida, and *Blood Sport* (1967), a tale of kidnapping, which is set in London, New York, Kentucky, Las Vegas, and California (Francis took a Greyhound bus cross-country to see the lay of the land). The Francises' own private air-charter business provided background for *Rat Race* (1970), Mary took up painting for *In the Frame*, and both spent time in pharmacological laboratories preparing for *Banker* (1982). A meticulous writer, he prides himself on his accuracy and claims, in fact, to have made only one error since beginning his publishing career, miscalling the London School of Music the London College of Music. His works incorporate experiences from his own life, though he claims never to have had any sinister dealings at the track, only a halfhearted attempt at a bribe made by a bookmaker who wanted him and his brother to stop a horse. He agreed with Brigette Weeks that his heroes "are all very similar" because, although their characters are built up "out of a number of peo-

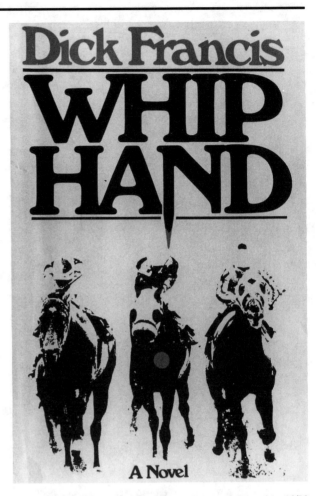

Dust jacket for the first American edition of Francis's 1979 novel featuring the one-handed ex-jockey Sid Halley, who was introduced in Odds Against (1965)

ple," they are like someone he would like to meet or be like himself; they are male because he feels unable to place himself "in a woman's mind," though feminists find his treatment of women egalitarian and balanced and praise his depiction of such important human issues as birth control, aging, and sexual needs as sensitive and unconventional.

Francis's novels combine the best of the classical and the hard-boiled detective fiction traditions: 1) country truths with city vice; 2) ratiocination with personal involvement; 3) an unquestionably upright, genteel hero of sound principles who is tough, hard-boiled, cynical, and down-to-earth, capable of violence, and mistrusted by the police; 4) an objective search for a pattern of clues amidst red herrings and a carefully reasoned elimination of suspects with a personal motivation for seeking justice, a crusade in which the search involves questions of loyalty and personal betrayal and ends with personal solutions; 5) offstage deaths with active violence and a physical confrontation between investigator and criminal. The combination of the two traditions is part of what gives the Francis adventure novel its power and appeal.

Though the particulars change from novel to novel, the Francis hero is basically the same: a seemingly common man who proves himself uncommon. He may be upper class or working class, but he always reflects a mixture of the values of both classes, yet is not totally a part of either world. He values decency, hard work, competence, practicality, and amiability, and is contemptuous of snobbery, hypocrisy, and bullying. Francis describes him as "compassionate and likeable, with a sense of humor and a lively eye." He is often an amateur rather than a professional, riding more for the joy of the sport than for the income, and his choice of vocation or avocation involves physical labor and hobnobbing amicably across class barriers. He does not particularly care about power or prestige; he judges men by who they are and what they can do, not by money or class. He is self-disciplined and resourceful, introspective, and usually in his thirties. He is also a loner (for example, the hero in *Enquiry* [1969] is said to have eyes that are "dark and sort of smiley and sad and a bit withdrawn"), but in spirit he is allied with other men of principle. He instinctively protects the weak and the innocent, and is willing to risk reputation, career, and life to do so. What one of the characters says about the protagonist in *Slay-ride* applies to all Francis heroes: "Give him one fact and he guesses the rest."

Francis's hero's interest in crime grows out of his personal sense of moral outrage. In *Flying Finish* (1966) he is appalled by the cold-hearted villainy of throwing men out of planes in mid flight, just because they *might* know too much, and disturbed that his friend, a decent man, believes the best of everybody, "even with villainy staring him in the face," all because of his "illogical faith in human goodness." In *Dead Cert* (1962) he approves of a retired sergeant major who, when faced by murderous thugs demanding protection money, not only effectively protects himself and his family but organizes the community, helping them train guard dogs and hiring a judo expert to protect the children on their way to school. In *Slay-ride* he is angered by the callous beating of a scared and pregnant young woman and sympathizes with a guilt-ridden youngster who kills to save himself and

who is deeply wounded by his father's ruthlessness. He also mourns a treacherous friend who betrayed him and nearly destroyed him. In *In the Frame* he wants "to smash in the heads of all greedy, callous, vicious people who cynically devastated the lives of total strangers. Compassion was all right for saints. What I felt was plain hatred, fierce and basic." This anger leads him to spend money and effort, travel halfway around the world, and face near death to help a friend; he criticizes the modern attitude that "anyone who tries to right a wrong" is "a fool" who would be much better off not meddling, not getting involved, not accepting moral responsibility, and asks, when "I see the hell he's in" and know "there's a chance of getting him out," "how can I just turn my back?"

Francis's villain is a social climber, a ruthless person who wants money, rank, and title, but lives in too flashy a fashion so all seems overdone. He is impeccably turned out. His car is expensive and garish. He bears a pretentious name such as Trevor Deansgate, Ivor den Relgan, Hedley Humber, or Quintus. He values possessions more than people. He is rather a snob and either seems too good to be true (like the "golden boy" of *Smokescreen*) or has shady associates who reflect his true nature. Sometimes his greed drives him mad, and the animal behind the facade takes over. Like the villains of the Conan Doyle stories, he exists by way of contrast with the detective-hero and is sometimes a cruel, sadistic bully (like Grimsby Royden in "The Adventure of the Speckled Band"), driven by greed, jealousy, and an inherent evil. The description of Kraye in *Odds Against* (1965) is typical: "Even though I was as far as he knew an insignificant fly to swat, a clear quality of menace flowed out of him like a radio signal. The calm social mask had disappeared along with the wordy, phony surface personality." What lies beneath is the dangerous, sadistic, amoral villain—"the boa constrictor" behind the guise of "grass snake."

The Francis hero, on the other hand, is loyal, honorable, self-aware, and at times self-sacrificing, a man who values friendship and who desires to stand on his own merits; but he is also a man who knows what he wants, even if it does not meet the conventional social expectations. He will do all he can to win the love of the girl he finds attractive, but he has a strong sense of fair play and will not gain an unfair advantage over a rival by telling the girl's parents he is wealthy or a lord. His powers of close observation and deduc-

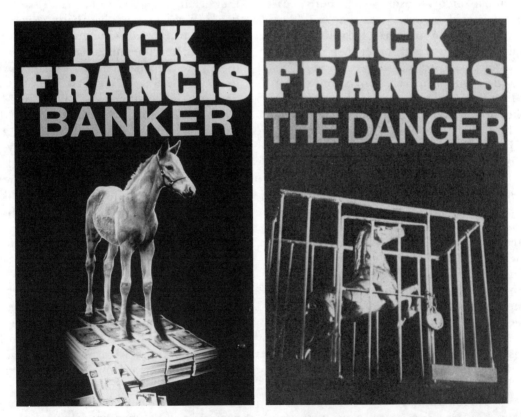

Dust jackets for the first editions of three of Francis's many books set in the world of horse racing

tion are highly developed, but his reasoning often involves instinctive leaps of the imagination; for example, the hero of *Dead Cert* is said to have "an unerring instinct for smelling out crooks." He may be tortured by self-doubt and insecurities and openly deny his heroic instincts, but beneath his quiet, nondescript exterior is an inner core that is tough, resilient, and undefeatable. In *Flying Finish* the hero is described as "ice on a volcano," and his friends agree. Often the hero's brush with villainy results from his kind heart. He is capable of enduring extreme physical punishment and not only surviving but being able to laugh at it. In *Rat Race* (1970) he braves it out: "I've been bruised before and I've broken my collar-bone before. It doesn't last long!" But he adds ruefully to himself that it was indeed highly "unpleasant" while it lasted, though he can feel better about personal damage if he inflicts a little himself: "They took with them some damaged knee cartilage, aching larynxes, and one badly scratched eye."

Francis's setting is usually peaceful, rural, idyllic, his central character in tune with nature and animals. He eulogizes the glories of taking racehorses for their morning exercise, the simple pleasures of unity of man and beast, the wind in one's hair, and the sun on one's back. His descriptions of the racetrack reflect a classical view of nature as controlled and tamed, with white picket fences, manicured turfs, and well-groomed horses. The stables usually are near a city but far enough out for the air to be fresh and invigorating. Within the setting, city men, greedy and corruptible, may betray these rural values with blackmail, bribes, threats of violence, and foul play, fixing bets and fixing races. In doing so they force authority to control everyone's freedom. *Whip Hand* looks behind the beauty and ritual of the track to capture the bleaker side: "People ready to bribe, people with the ready palm. Anguished little hopefuls and arrogant big guns. The failures making brave excuses, and the successful hiding the anxieties behind their eyes. All as it had been, and was, and would be, as long as racing lasted."

Francis builds on both English and American detective traditions in his focus on justice. In *Dead Cert* Alan York allows Uncle George to commit suicide rather than be placed in an insane asylum or be dragged through a homicide trial that would be injurious to and painful for his family. He also punishes the dishonest jockey, Sandy, for guilt by complicity when the law cannot touch

him, tossing him off his horse in mid race, to be bruised, battered, and broken. In *Rat Race* Matt Shore, who has once before broken air-flight regulations to deliver needed supplies to impoverished Latin American refugees, now breaks them again to rescue Nancy, noting that he always told himself to stay out of trouble but never listened: "I had just broken two laws and would undoubtedly be prosecuted again by the Board of Trade. I wondered if I would ever learn to keep myself out of trouble." In *Forfeit* James Tyrone, intoxicated by whiskey forced down his throat, fuzzily thinks, "Got to stop him smashing up our lives, smashing up other people's lives." Someone, somewhere, had to stop him, and Tyrone does so, causing a car wreck that kills the key villains. He feels guilty when sober but realizes that his deed has ended crimes that the law would have had trouble confirming. In *Longshot* (1990), in turn, John Kendall, despite a suspicious police inspector, chooses silence after a murderer's faked accident because "Nothing could be gained.... Much would be smashed. They all would suffer. The families always suffered most. No child would become a secure and balanced adult with a known murderer for father."

Another Francis hallmark is his emphasis on the intrinsic and extrinsic rewards of competence and skill that go beyond barriers of class, race, and sex. For Francis, the best person is one who is well rounded and versatile; he can move with ease among all classes, knowing that competence, not class, makes the man, and that a person should ultimately be judged on what he is as an individual, not on what his origins are. In *Trial Run* someone describes the hero as looking like "one of those useless la-di-das in the telly ads," but he performs with the reflexes and coolheadedness of a professional. In the majority of Francis's books his characters demonstrate competence in racing. They are able to recognize their horse's potential despite appearances. Because they know the horse, the course, and the psychology of racing, they can get the best performance from an animal, no matter what its quirks. They also know how to fall and how to deal with injuries both to horse and man. But usually they are also competent in other areas as well. If they are pilots, they fly with mechanical precision, understanding the versatility and the limitations of the aircraft. They know flight patterns and navigational devices beyond a simple mechanical ability with instruments so that even under primitive conditions they can maintain a high level of preci-

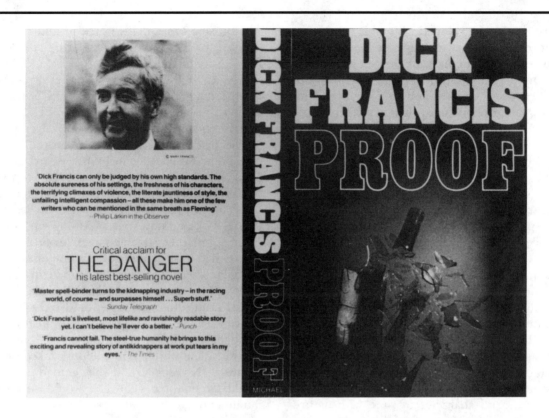

Dust jacket for the first edition of Francis's 1984 novel

sion. Such familiarity with their machinery is so much a part of them that they can recognize intuitively when anything is amiss. In *Rat Race*, for instance, Matt senses a bomb on board the plane because the slight weight has been enough to alter the way the plane feels in flight. Francis's boatmen are easy masters of their boats and their situations. The painter in *In the Frame* knows that "if you mix flake white, which is lead, with cadmium yellow, which contains sulfur, . . . you get a nice pale color to start with, but the two minerals react against each other and in time darken and alter the picture." The inquisitive and capable author of survival manuals in *Longshot* knows how to forage and survive in jungle and desert, island and mountaintop, and even his crazed opponent can transform wood into exquisite shapes and forms. Clearly, for Francis, competence involves understanding one's limits as well as one's potential, so one can recognize when someone else is a better jockey, a better aviator, or a more astute businessman. Such competence also involves a process of character building. As men learn to handle unexpected situations and are forced to develop physical and mental strength and agility to deal with every possibility, they are also forced to make moral decisions, to develop a code of loy-

alty, and to learn to listen to their inner voice.

However, as one might expect, Francis's focus on competence also means a focus on the realities of a profession rather than the idealized public view of it. Hence, while Francis does show readers the winner and all his glory, he also emphasizes that there are more losers than winners, that winning is not always a comfortable experience, that being a jockey is a hard, demanding job. He portrays trainers having to endure criticism from owners and jockeys, owners being duped by unscrupulous trainers or jockeys, and jockeys being used by owners and trainers. He also demonstrates the high potential for physical injury in horseracing, a potential that, as a steeplechase jockey, he learned about firsthand. He has broken his back, arm, and wrist once each, his nose five times, his collarbones about six times each side, and his ribs uncountable times. He also has cracked his skull and crushed some vertebrae and has had horses throw him, kick him, and fall on top of him. According to Zuckerman, he once won two races and rode in ten others with an untreated broken arm; he just couldn't be bothered with doctors.

A Francis novel depends on contrasts between the competent and the incompetent. Some of his upper-class figures are naive, simplistic, bumbling dabblers, who judge on superficial appearances. His university professors (like Chaner in *Rat Race*) are out-of-date, unreliable men trying to sound like a combination of Marx and a Liverpool street punk. In fact, whenever a character resorts to polysyllabic diction and spouts unintelligibly about the nature of the universe, he should be immediately suspected of ignorance, pretension, and perhaps villainy. Francis's villains often become criminals because of their inability to thrive honestly. The experienced, competent pilot is contrasted with the capable beginner and the flashy but unskilled incompetent (easily recognized by his bad landing and poor attitude). The successful female horse trainer, who wins male admiration, is played off against the woman who is incompetent at love and incompetent at dealing with a man's world. Competent crooks who almost get away with fraud and murder are set against incompetent ones who cannot hang on to money, who try too many scams at once, and who make too many mistakes, though often all are denigrated as limited. "The worst vandals are always childish," says the hero of *Enquiry*. The naive and trusting endanger themselves and those around them and are foils to those whose sense of instinct comes from knowledge and experience.

Cynicism is absent when Francis treats romance. His heroines may differ in physical appearance or social background, but they immediately win the hero's attention and heart. They always have an inner fire that sets them apart from other women and a compassion that involves them in others' problems. They are always competent at what they do but often are vulnerable in some way, whether it be due to disease or injury, difficult relatives, a recent bereavement, or merely an inability to speak English. Their vulnerability brings out hidden strengths in the heroes. In *For Kicks* (1965), for example, the trusting and innocent young daughter of an English lord unwittingly destroys the hero-spy's cover, but he knowingly sacrifices his own safety to protect her. Often there are other weak, vulnerable, but sympathetic characters in the background, such as a sister with leukemia, a brother who is an alcoholic, a youngster ignored by parents, an older woman helpless in the face of economic or physical threats, a husband who mourns his dead spouse, a simpleminded stable lad.

The language of a Francis novel is straightforward, with a good balance between action, description, and dialogue. Francis enjoys parallel series, mainly in sets of threes, such as "gentle, generous, and worried," or "bribed, bludgeoned, or blackmailed." He employs the terminology of specialized fields, but with explanations, so that the reader shares in the expertise of the characters. Occasionally there are biblical allusions, such as the hero sowing the wind and reaping the whirlwind (*Dead Cert*). He also uses Shakespearean references. In *Blood Sport*, for example, the hero, who contemplates suicide but always puts it off because of obligations, not fear, remarks, "I haven't a horse. Nor a Kingdom to give for one." Francis enjoys word games and crossword puzzles and frequently employs puns. The title *For Kicks*, for example, plays on the protagonist's motive in acting and the physical beating he must endure, kicked for kicks, while the title *Break In* refers to both the training of a young horse and a burglary. The title *Proof* (1984) means both evidence and percentage of alcohol, and the title *Longshot* refers to an unexpected win at the track, a long shot with a bow and arrow, and a far-out guess about motive and act.

The narrative voice in a Francis novel is always first person, the point of view of his central character. It is this first-person perspective that hurtles the action forward, that infuses it with a sense of moral concern, that adds wit and compassion. It is also difficult to control, for the problem is always how to reveal the heroic character of the protagonist without making him seem egotistical, how to suppress conclusions in order to hold suspense without leaving the reader feeling cheated. Francis has learned to do this well. His opening lines are always clever attention getters.

Francis's techniques and themes have undergone continual development. His first novel, *Dead Cert*, which got an advance of three hundred pounds sterling (about seven hundred dollars at the 1960s exchange rate), made Francis's reputation as a mystery writer and set the pattern which has made him famous. Many still consider it his best work, though there is clearly competition for the title. Its hero, self-effacing but tenacious and unrelentingly compelled to face danger for the sake of right, is based on a real person whom Francis knew. In fact, Francis reports that he had to be very careful to keep his character fictitious because his tendency was to copy him too closely from his real-life model. A surreal quality dominates much that is memorable: "the mingled smells of hot horse and cold river mist," an isolated string of riders, severed from re-

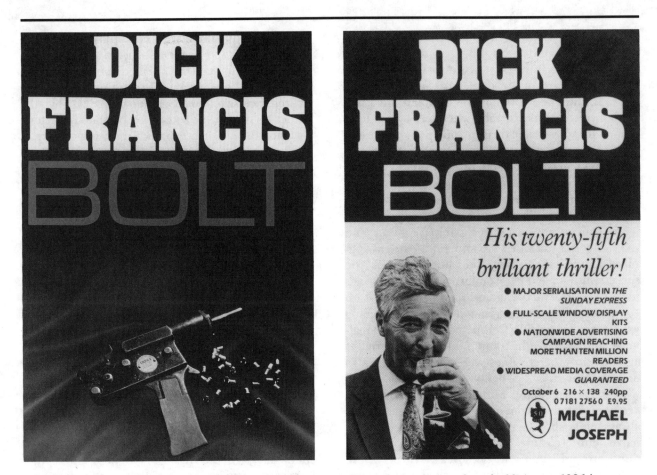

Dust jacket for the first edition of Francis's 1986 novel and publisher's advertisement from the 23 August 1986 issue of Bookseller

ality by a "silent, surrounding whiteness" and suddenly the thrashing legs of a fallen champion. The satiric treatment of class snobbery, the contrasting portraits of casual friendships, and the underlying concept of illusion hiding reality raise *Dead Cert* above the level of pulp fiction and give it seriousness and depth without losing the excitement and pleasure of the mystery genre.

Nerve (1964), which was selected to be a *Reader's Digest* condensed book, is a study of character under pressure. It begins with the suicide of an aging jockey. The rest of the book unravels the motivation and despair behind that act. Rob Finn, the protagonist, the tone-deaf son of a musical family, is a beginning jockey, enough of a neophyte to be elated when asked to be a second-string rider: "Give me a horse and a race to ride it in, and I don't care if I wear silks or . . . pajamas. . . . I don't care if I don't earn much money, or if I break my bones, or if I have to starve to keep my weight down. All I care about is racing . . . , racing . . . and winning, if I can." But after six of his mounts in a row have made a showing

far below their usual capabilities, a fact that has outraged owners, considerably diminished his reputation, and led to accusations of lost nerve, he begins to understand the perspective of the suicide victim and decides to take action. He uncovers a calculated destruction of jockeys, then doctored sugar cubes, and finally a jealousy and a hatred that explain who and why. But before he makes the final discovery, he is hung on harness hooks, doused with icy water, and left to freeze in a cooler. Only sheer determination helps him overcome seemingly impossible odds. Here the motive of the villain is not profit but revenge and madness, and interest for the reader comes more from the psychological study of the hero than from the villain's exposure.

In *For Kicks* a restless young Australian, Daniel Roke, forced by his parents' death into giving up his career dreams and devoting himself to providing and caring for his young siblings, is by chance offered an opportunity to play stable-hand in England in order to investigate a new, undetectable stimulant for racehorses. Feeling like a "dull, laborious prig" caught in a prosperous trap (managing a stable), and sick of being sensible, Roke agrees. He cultivates a cockney accent, changes clothes and hairstyle, grows sideburns, and begins to behave in a shifty, insolent way to insinuate himself among the rougher sort. Francis brings the phrase "clothes make the man" to life as he shows the hero's precipitous decline from gentleman to down-and-outer on the make. Here the "aggressive egalitarianism" Francis so admires in Australians meets the English class structure at its most rigid; Roke must restrain his rebellious instincts and submit for awhile in order to overthrow the most abusive of class offenders: the clever, well-born psychopath whose bullying aggression is dismissed as high spirits and the climbing money men who make up for their own insecurities by their snobbery and their wanton spending. His ruse works. While experiencing a Dickensian life of torture, humiliation, and servitude in the worst of stables, Roke methodically studies the facts, follows them to their logical conclusions, and tests a chain of assumptions step by step. In a violent and terrifying sequence of events he solves the case, uncovering Pavlovian conditioning carried out in a most sadistic way, only to find himself jailed for murder. Again, despite the Holmesian pattern of ratiocination and the suspenseful climax, character and class conflict provide the main interest, as Roke discovers the strengths and weaknesses that make him what he is by instinct: a democratic man and a born hunter.

Odds Against and *Whip Hand* share a protagonist (the first time Francis had written two books about the same character), Sid Halley. Francis wrote the screenplay of the television version, "The Racing Game," and was delighted with Mike Gwilym's performance as Halley. However, in his interview with Weeks he rejected any plan to write another Sid Halley book because he prefers to build characters as he plans plot, so that "If I started with a ready-made character like Sid, I should be lost." (Jockey Kit Fielding's appearances in *Break In* and *Bolt* [1986] signal that Francis has had a change of opinion.) A champion jockey turned detective after losing his hand in a racing accident, Halley is nearly killed in the first few pages of *Odds Against;* his father-in-law tries to revive his interest in life and help him regain his self-confidence by involving him in a plan to save the racetrack at Seabury from a particularly underhanded and fraudulent management takeover, one strengthened by seeming accidents:

tanker collisions, collapsed drains, stable fires, and exploding boilers. Halley's strategy is for his father-in-law to denigrate him so the villains will grossly underrate him—to their dismay. As Halley plays sleuth, he learns to trust his instincts and accept his inner wounds—in part by helping a young woman with a scarred face do the same. By not accepting personal defeat, he turns the villains' secret connivings against them and saves a track whose executives had too easily accepted defeat. Both *Odds Against* and *Whip Hand* treat the humiliation of the handicapped and the shattering viciousness of class snobbery with sensitivity and grace.

In *Whip Hand* several top racehorses, brilliant two-year-olds, prove undistinguished as three-year-olds and die young from heart problems. Halley, pursuing a new career as private investigator and building his growing reputation for tenacity and cleverness, is indirectly called in on the case by his estranged, embittered former wife. Aided by his cheerful, irreverent sidekick, Chico Barnes, Halley links the horses' poor performance to a deadly, artificially induced swine disease. In the process he is caught up in an exciting balloon race presided over by a true eccentric and spends a good deal of time adjusting to the wonders and limitations of his new mechanical hand. The book effectively captures the two key tensions of the Francis novel: the excitement of a horse race as the rider feels the ripple of muscles, "the striving bodies, uniting in one . . . the balance . . . the stretching brown neck, the mane blowing in my mouth, my hands on the reins," and the fear of physical injury as the villain tries to humiliate and break his victim. Francis waxes eloquent about the "feeling of oneness with horses" and the passion for winning; but he also captures the human cost: divorce, injury, the wrench of loss when dreams must be discarded. In this book Halley is paralyzed by fear for his remaining hand: "All the fear I'd ever felt in all my life was as nothing compared with the liquefying, mind-shattering disintegration of that appalling minute. It broke me in pieces. . . . And instinctively, hopelessly, I tried not to let it show."

Flying Finish on the simplest level is about a scam to take advantage of a tax loophole by transporting the same racehorses and brood mares back and forth by air—under false papers, a scheme adopted wholeheartedly by other, more sinister thugs, who transport defectors for a fee. But the novel's real interest is in Henry Grey, soon to be Lord Grey. He sickens of friends and

Dust jacket for the first American edition of Francis's 1987 novel about racing and family strife

opportunities that exist only because of his rank and of women who pursue him for title and wealth, and he seeks to prove himself as a man. He throws over an easy office position for a laborer's job (managing horse air transport) and races horses for a cut of the winnings. He finds his beloved in Italy, a working woman who has never heard of his family or title. The real test of Grey's manhood comes when he discovers he was hired because it was assumed he would be lazy and unobservant; his competence and hard work make him too aware of inconsistencies in flights and horses transported, too curious about the disappearance of acquaintances who covered the same territory. He is a threat to a lucrative and illegal business. Attempts to distract his attention by playing on his sense of fair play, his class guilt, and his fear of pain fail, and when the villains move in to eliminate him, he draws on all his knowledge and resources to withstand pain, puzzle out a method of coping, and rescue himself and his friend. The emphasis is on his options,

step-by-step, and the psychology that motivates him to react as he does. He has no qualms about brutally destroying the sadistic thug who tortured him, nor about taking off in a plane in which he had never trained. He may feel the weakness seeping into his limbs and shiver from exhaustion and fear; he may reject his choice as childish and vainglorious; but he somehow finds the strength and determination to face impossible odds and take the right action—for his country, for his friend, and for himself.

The protagonist of *Blood Sport* is a world-weary bachelor, an active intelligence officer, skilled in European languages, perceptive about human motives and human weaknesses, and artful at placing bugs, breaking and entering, and arranging "accidents." He hurtles himself fearlessly into investigation and action, half in love with death. He dives into dangerous waters to save a drowning man and survives being sucked through a weir; he guides a nervous horse along a narrow ledge in the dark, heedless of its terrifying height; he faces would-be murderers without giving ground: "You will not, whatever you do, recover the horse," he says into the barrel of a rifle. His skill at deductive reasoning and intuitive leaps of the imagination is Holmesian in nature, as too is his skill at collecting and interpreting statistics and facts. He always acts with care and caution, setting up a timed schedule, arranging minute details, even counting and collecting each of the shells expelled from his Luger, though his friend lies dead beside him. Those around him often accuse him of reading their minds because of his uncanny sensitivity to their secrets and emotions. He is a hunter, most at home with other hunters. His challenge in *Blood Sport* is to recover first one, and then two more, thoroughbred studs stolen over a ten-year period. Against all odds he does so, tracing clues overlooked by others, first in England, then in Kentucky and Nevada, until they lead first to a dude ranch, then to a reputable stud farm. Along the way he uncovers blackmail, fraud, and murder. But it is the protagonist himself, not the mystery, exciting though its unraveling may be, that makes *Blood Sport* one of Francis's finest efforts. The hero is detached enough to admire the artistry of his opponent, realistic enough to realize when prosecution is impossible, and cold-blooded enough to know how to reap vengeance without consulting the police or breaking the law. A naive young girl on the verge of womanhood helps both the protagonist and the wife of his em-

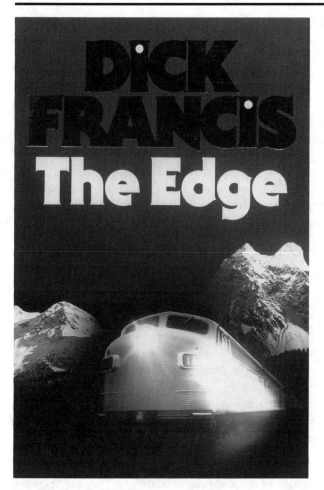

Dust jacket for the first edition of Francis's 1988 novel, in which a security operative for the British Jockey Club disguises himself as a railway waiter

ployer come to terms with that "gray-black octopus," depression, whose "tentacles" reach out and suck "into every corner of the spirit until" life becomes "unbearable" and death seems "the only possible relief."

Forfeit builds on family trauma. Francis's wife, who contracted polio in 1949 while pregnant with their first child, was in an iron lung for five weeks. Out of that experience, Francis produced the character of Elizabeth, a lovely young woman, much in love, her life ahead of her, suddenly stricken by polio, ninety percent paralyzed, permanently confined to an iron lung. Her husband's attempts to cope with his physical needs, with his guilt, and with his love form a key part of this work. He is James Tyrone, a writer for the *Sunday Blaze*, turned sleuth when a fellow writer dies "accidentally" from a fall. The dead writer's past record and his notebooks tell of blackmailing bookmakers, encouraged by a South African mobster, playing with people's lives and finances.

Investigation uncovers daughters threatened with rape and sons threatened with kidnapping to pressure owners into withdrawing horses from running and to force newspaper reporters into giving controlled tips. After his veiled hints in an aggressive exposé and his steps to hide a famous racehorse for its protection, Tyrone is savagely beaten, then blackmailed for adultery, but he does not take aggressive action until the villains trick his mistress and endanger his helpless wife. In the novel's resolution Tyrone not only routs the villains but comes to terms with his own weaknesses.

Enquiry, as its title suggests, centers on an official inquiry into race fixing, but the panel is rigged and the evidence manufactured. The accused are at first too shocked to defend themselves; facing financial ruin and social ostracism, one contemplates suicide, while the other determines to fight back. The odds may seem hopeless, but protagonist Kelly Hughes is ready to redeem his reputation "or die in the attempt." And he almost does so, from carbon-monoxide poisoning and multiple dislocations—hip, knee, and ankle. He methodically traces the faked evidence and intentional errors to their multiple sources, checks out old enemies (vindictive bookmakers and jealous jockeys), and faces hostility and abuse with aplomb. This is a novel about courage and the human will. The situation tests friendships and men's willingness to stand up to authority and power. It is also a novel about class. Lord Ferth, an aristocratic racing patron, is stunned to find a jockey who attended university and who can talk eruditely of the history of politics and about the nature of aggression. Ferth learns to face the fact that justice should not depend on good manners and that "men in power positions" are not "infallibly truthful." The snobbish daughter of a moneyed trainer learns to concentrate on character, not accent, and to see that judging people "by their voices" and origins is wrong; she must, for the first time, deal with another class, throwing off "the fetters" in her mind and the "iron bars" in her soul. In the process she learns to love a man for who he is and what he is. When Hughes asks her, "Would you consider coming down to my level?," she responds, "Are you speaking literally, metaphorically, intellectually, financially, or socially?," but later she discovers that mean-spirited, "kinky" blue bloods are really inferior to "gutsy," considerate, strong-hearted men of working-class origins.

Rat Race was not very popular with the critics, who found it a bit disappointing because of the negative attitudes of its protagonist, Matt Shore, but it is a convincing study of a man who has almost given up on life. Condemned by the Board of Trade for humane but illegal acts, divorced, disillusioned, he has lost his sense of joy in his work and has tried to practice stoic detachment by cutting himself off from human emotions. He chauffeurs the wealthy racetrack crowd but feels contempt for most of them. The novel is interspersed with brief, satiric portraits of aristocrats. Shore sees his battle for dominance over a rival company as nature's "pecking order" at work and himself as a rat "trapped on a treadwheel" going in circles. And yet his virtues shine through. His humane act was smuggling food and medical supplies to starving refugees. He is competent and careful—a man who knows his business well. Despite his self-admonitions not to get involved, his automatic tendency toward deduction, coupled with intuition and instinct, help him get passengers off a flight before a bomb explodes, deal kindly with a leukemia victim (twin sister of the heroine), talk Nancy (the heroine) down when her airplane's electric system is sabotaged, and ferret out motives and villains so that, at the close of the book, he has rediscovered himself and his values and has learned to love again.

Bonecrack (1971), set at a prestigious racing stable in Newmarket, is a briskly paced story of syphilitic-induced megalomania that gains tension from a conflict of generations. The hero, a sober-minded businessman, Neil Griffon, a former antique dealer turned accountant-troubleshooter for small companies in financial difficulty, returns to the home he had left fourteen years before to manage his father's stables while the old man recovers from a car accident. His relationship with his father is antagonistic and competitive, with the old man never forgiving his son for attaining his freedom and making a success of his life on his own. He resents his son's assistance in his time of need and does his best to undermine his son's efforts and thereby prove to the world his own superiority. His son, in turn, finds that managing a stable and training horses is a pleasurable, instinctive skill he thought he had lost. This father and son relationship is contrasted to that of an Italian-Swiss mobster, Rivera, who gives his spoiled only child everything in order to curtail the son's freedom and to maintain his own ascendancy. When the son decides he wants to become a champion jockey, the fa-

ther kidnaps Neil Griffon to force an arrangement, breaks the legs of Griffon's horse to prove his threats are real, and ultimately tries to murder the stable's leading jockey to make way for his son. But he does not count on Griffon's competence and courage, for, while seeming to partly acquiesce, Griffon quietly collects evidence that could damn Rivera and ruin his son's career chances. He teaches the mobster's son that success as a jockey cannot be bought but must be won by hard work, determination, self-control, clear thinking, and talented horsemanship; forces him to recognize in others skills he has not yet honed; chides him when he fails for want of trying; praises him when he demonstrates real care, and thereby uses him as a pawn in his struggle to save his own father's stables and diminish Rivera's power. Griffon's girlfriend remarks that "anything which smells of challenge is your meat and drink," and Griffon rises to the occasion.

Illusion becomes reality in *Smokescreen* as an initial movie take—the hero handcuffed to the steering wheel of a tiny sports car in the blazing desert heat—is played out for real in the scorching sun of Kruger National Park, South Africa: six days without food or water, only a growing rage and a will to survive. The protagonist, Edward Lincoln, "Linc" for short, is a successful actor whom Francis describes as "patient, powerful, punctual, professional and puritanical." An experienced stuntman and a close observer of human nature, he works hard at turning out a professional performance. A family man, he also works hard at being a good husband and parent. His explosive temper is usually indulged only "on behalf of someone else." Linc can handle snobs and fans with equal finesse. At the request of a terminally ill family friend he agrees to investigate the unexpected losing streak of a group of thoroughbred flat racers in South Africa. After two murder attempts disguised as accidents (one involving his being knocked out in a gold-mine shaft shortly before a scheduled blast), he realizes he has been lured to the killing ground by a deceptively charming man, "cold and ruthless as ice," one more savage than the beasts around him. The descriptions of South Africa, the discussions of the controversies of apartheid, the carefully contrasted characters, and the portrait of a good man who must protect the weak by exposing the dangerous beast beneath the civilized facade mark this book as an interesting and effective variation on Francis's traditional concerns.

The protagonist of *Slay-ride*, British investigator David Cleveland, in Norway to find and vindicate a missing jockey accused of grand theft, finds his small boat intentionally overturned and himself left to drown; later he is knifed, and his car is bombed as he uncovers murder and then an oil-stock swindle. Readers get a British view of Norway: shock at the cold, at horse races that are literally in the dark, at liquor-licensing laws "madder . . . than Britain's." The book is well worth reading for the final image of a man, bound to a sleigh, flying though space, down to his death in a cold, Nordic sea.

The refrain of *Knock Down* (1974; published in the United States as *Knockdown*, 1975) is "Bash me, I bash back," the words of Jonah Dereham, a former steeplechaser turned bloodstock agent, whose toughness and honesty in a basically dishonest business make him the object of a concerted campaign to turn him crooked or break him. Here Francis captures the inner workings of a business that functions on the basis of reputation and trust and hence is open to wholesale manipulation and dishonesty. The sales-ring scenes are convincing, as are the "ruthlessness, rudeness, and rows" behind the scenes. The book is a straightforward exposé of the nasty reality behind the shining facade of bloodstock sales. Dereham is advised that there is no place left for the individualist, that one must join the firm or forge an agreement, and that bucking the system is passé, that business is a Darwinian world in which "invaders" single out the strong to overcome so that the weak will then submit quietly. Critics complained of the multiple plot threads, but Francis does carefully interweave them as they move inexorably toward a final confrontation. Bound together with webbing to keep his shoulder from dislocating, a plight Francis still shares, Dereham finds himself the object of an unrelenting series of attacks. First he is mugged, then forced to sign away a sales slip for a new purchase. Later a horse worth seventy thousand pounds is loosed from his stable at night and is nearly killed. An attempt to steal Dereham's next purchase only fails by chance. His brother, an alcoholic, is fed liquor, the family stables are burned down, and lies and rumors are spread to reduce his clientele. But the villains have chosen the wrong man to try to break; Dereham is outraged, not only by the personal attacks, but by the viciousness of men who demand kickbacks and then enforce their demands with rumors that drive down prices, turning a business that is built on

dreams into a swindle. His counterattack conclusively exposes past swindles and makes use of the villains' own key tool: rumor.

The fact that the hero in *High Stakes* is a toy manufacturer new to racing (having only recently acquired a string of racehorses) provides an excuse for Francis to teach newcomers about the racing scene, but most particularly about the multiple fiddles a crooked trainer has at his command, especially collusion between trainer and bookmaker to their mutual profit. It begins with the neophyte, Steven Scott, giving his trainer the sack and, as a result, immediately having his prizewinner stolen and his name besmirched in the press. With no legal remedy possible he enlists carefully chosen friends to help him go after the criminals. Using a Florida look-alike, they exchange nag for champion and thereby set a trap that elicits a confession, undoes the villains, and vindicates Scott. The risks are great and the final costs even greater: Scott's toy factory demolished, his friend injured and nearly killed, his own life jeopardized. But the experience jars Scott's complacency and brings him love, maturity, and a new, exciting career.

In the Frame begins with a violent and seemingly senseless murder, the after-product of a burglary: "a harmless girl, come to harm." The police clearly suspect the husband, who is so in shock that life has lost all meaning for him. The cousin, Charles Todd, determines to prove them wrong and does so, tracking down a series of coincidences that lead to Australia, art fraud, and international burglary. He discovers "a mobile force of thieves shuttling containerfuls of antiques from continent to continent, selling briskly to a ravenous market." The "supermarket" villains chat amiably with middling wealthy tourists about their art collections back home, sell them a genuine painting, substitute a fake, then recover the lot in a carefully planned burglary. To unravel the web of this monolithic spider, Todd joins forces with an old school friend, a mad artist, being with whom was "like a toboggan run, downhill, dangerous, and exhilarating." Together they flush out the villains, gather their evidence (breaking and entering and absconding with it), and, before finally letting the police in on the action, nearly get themselves maimed or killed. The setting allows Francis to explore cultural differences, as he captures the unique and elastic diction of Australians, explains the origins of Australian male chauvinism (two-thirds of the best seats in the members' stands reserved for males only,

Dick Francis, late 1980s (photograph by Mary Francis)

a division that has since been removed), praises Australian wines, and provides precise images of Australian cities.

Risk (1977) is dedicated to the memory of Lionel Vick, a professional steeplechase jockey and certified accountant, who obviously inspired Francis's portrait of the main character Roland Britten. Britten is an amateur steeplechase jockey, enamored of racing but well aware of his limitations, a rider who, in a run of luck, gives a good horse its head and wins time and again—to the consternation of dishonest trainers and bookmakers. Because he is an honest man, he is beset by enemies who are angered by his unwillingness to take bribes, both as jockey and as accountant, and by his instinctive ability to recognize a swindle or a fiddle, no matter how artfully disguised. When he is kidnapped and imprisoned in dark, isolated quarters, first below deck on a sailboat, later in a covered van, he begins to consider who among the felons and frauds he has exposed might want not simply revenge but freedom of ac-

tion to perpetuate another fraud. Britten's knowledge of bank accounts, stables, and training yards means a wide field of possibilities, but the list of suspects narrows when his partner joins the action. This book has powerfully rendered portraits of men and women making the most of life's challenges: a quiet, unobtrusive man coping with the terrors of total darkness, isolation, seasickness, and despair finds he is made of "sterner stuff" than he believed; a dowdy, middle-aged headmistress finds the courage to save a life, investigate a crime, and explore her potential as a woman; a young girl learns to see behind the facade, admit her father's weakness, and make her own life without him.

In *Trial Run* Randall Drew, a Warwickshire gentleman farmer, banned from racing because he wears eyeglasses, is recruited by British Intelligence to go to Moscow to determine whether or not it is safe for a member of the royal family, an equestrian aiming for the Olympics, to attend. Drew is disturbed by the cold, the food, the queues, the regimentation, the inherent suspicion, the carefully controlled faces, and the daily fear and harshness of life in Moscow; yet as a reputable horseman, he gains acceptance and respect that make him a fearful antagonist, and, in battling a terrorist plot to embarrass both the British royal family and the Russian regime, he gains common cause with Russian patriots. This book laments the social, political, and economic conflicts that warp one's youth and transform disturbed youngsters into weak, irresponsible adults bent on striking out at authority—no matter what the cost to others.

Reflex (1980), a Book-of-the-Month-Club selection, whose initial hardback edition sold eighty-five thousand copies, marked a breakthrough in Francis's popularity, and deservedly so, for it is one of his finest efforts. Paperback rights sold for $440,000. Since *Reflex* (the title of which refers to camera type as well as to an involuntary response), Francis's novels have automatically been best-sellers in America. In the novel Philip Nore, a disillusioned, aging jockey and amateur photographer, stumbles on a blackmailing scheme built on corruption and murder and unwittingly sets himself up as the next target. Nore's mother, disowned by her own mother for stealing her young lover, had passed her son from friend to friend until she eventually died of a heroin overdose. Nore's much despised grandmother wants him to find a sister, Amanda, whom he never knew existed, so the sister can inherit the fortune the grandmother wishes to keep out of the hands of her homosexual son and her illegitimate grandson. Nore, instead, gets caught up in investigating curious negatives left by a skilled but seemingly amoral photographer, negatives that suggest blackmail and murder. The description of Nore's process of discovery through his photographic skill is excellent. Ultimately his investigation interlocks with the search for his sister and for his parentage so that, in dealing effectively with the foibles and vices of others, he stops a heroin dealer (among other wrongdoers), regains his self-respect, and acquires a sense of family and roots. This book is an especially powerful study of the influence of one man on another, as Nore learns "his [own] mind, his intentions, his beliefs," solves "his puzzles," and fires "his guns."

In contrast to *Reflex*, Francis's next novel, *Twice Shy* (1981), is one of his weakest efforts, possibly because the evil characters are not deeply evil. They are a father and son team, both minor thugs, and as such unworthy of the hero's effort.

The novel is also weakened by being split into two parts, separated not only by fourteen years, but by different protagonists, so character development is much more limited than is usually possible in a full-length novel. In the first half a young physicist, Jonathan Derry, discovers that a cassette of Broadway music handed him by a friend is really a computer program for a handicapping system that works. When his friend is killed in a boat explosion and his wife has a nervous breakdown, Derry, instead of using the cassette to make a fortune for himself, seeks to trace the tape's rightful owners to return their property. As a result his wife is kidnapped, and a rescue scene ensues. At this point the book leaps forward to after Derry's departure to California, when his racing-enthusiast brother, William, assumes the burden of the tape and finally ends the train of violence. The final image of the villainous son, permanently brain-damaged, is pathetic and dissatisfying. In Francis's other novels the villain has been warped but intelligent, weak and incompetent in some areas, but highly skilled in others. In this novel there is a sense of not merely ineptitude but limited mental capabilities. It is as if Francis has brought together all his usual ingredients for mystery and adventure but has somehow lost the moral thread that gives them strength and substance.

In *Banker* (1982) the first-person narrator-hero is Tim Ekaterin, thirty-two years old, an alert, sharp-minded banker on his way up in his family's famous London firm. He is skilled at managing enormous sums of money and at making correct decisions about risky loans. The novel covers a span of three years in which the world of thoroughbred racing and merchant banking are interwoven. *Banker* begins with Tim's immediate superior stepping into the courtyard fountain and hallucinating paranoid fantasies—the result of an overdose of medication for Parkinson's disease. Tim considers the proposition of a reputable stud-farm owner, Oliver Knowles, who wants a five-million-pound loan to buy a star-quality racing stallion, Sandcastle. As the plot advances and Sandcastle's foals are born deformed, readers learn a great deal about investments, horse disease, stud-farm management, pharmacology, and herbal lore. This plot has been called one of Francis's most intricate, for it involves two murders, the solution to which rests on a bottle of shampoo, several tightly spun subplots concerning office politics, a sixteen-year-old would-be murderer, a miracle worker who restores dying horses to health, and Tim's quiet passion for his ailing boss's wife. Unlike the typical Francis hero, Tim Ekaterin has never experienced physical pain and is "unconvinced" of his own mortality until he finds himself locked in a stall with a crazed horse, its forelegs crashing down so close they brush his hair. Francis's method in formulating this book is typical of his most recent pattern. Approached by a fan, Jeremy H. Thompson, a UCLA professor of pharmacology, Francis was intrigued by the professor's knowledge of drugs that were safe for people but fatal for horses (a reversal of his method in *Trial Run* where drugs safe for horses kill humans); during the same general period, an important banker in a nearby box at the Cheltenham race meeting suggested a merchant banking focus. After extensive research, aided by London banking officials, he produced *Banker*.

In *The Danger* (1983) Andrew Douglas, star operative for a British antikidnapping agency, travels the world recovering kidnap victims in some way connected with the racing world. He recovers three victims in the novel: the jockey daughter of a rich industrialist, the three-year-old son of a racehorse owner, and the senior steward of the Jockey Club of England. As self-effacing "consultant," Douglas liaises with overanxious police, who are willing to sacrifice the victim to capture the criminal; with relatives torn by grief and then later resentful of the disruption of their lives and the crippling ransom that decimates their finances; and with the victims, who endure physical and psychological injury. Francis is particularly skillful in showing the psychological state of the kidnap victims. In the first case police interference almost costs the life of the victim; in the second Douglas and a friend trace clues to a boathouse and effect a rescue; but by the third, Douglas has so narrowed the field, postulating a kidnapping crime lord with racing connections, that he himself is kidnapped and learns the hard way the truths of his training manual. The final descriptions of hunter and hunted share the detail of Geoffrey Household's classic treatment of the same subject in *Rogue Male* (1939).

Proof, the story of a wine merchant enlisted by police to detect fraudulently labeled wines, was derived in part from Francis's thirty years of discussing wine with his brother-in-law Dick Yorke and local merchant Margaret Giles, visits to the Australian wine regions in the Barossa Valley, and an awareness of the notorious European wine-fraud scandals of the 1970s. Tony Beach (a

grieving widower, son and grandson of war-hero jockeys, and owner of a liquor store), while catering wine at a training farm, witnesses a horse van plunge down a hill into a tent filled with wealthy imbibers. The plot leads directly to an explanation of this bizarre incident. *Proof* is well researched and gives readers a sense of the day-to-day business of a British liquor store and describes French vintages and Scotches, but it has limited dialogue, no love interest, and less memorable action and fewer merits than most Francis novels. Beach, in aiding the police, must deal with hijacking, murder, and a near drowning. Nevertheless, his self-doubts seem strained and the final discovery of his idealized father's humanity too predictable.

Francis's *Break In* and *Bolt* return to the track. Steeplechase jockey Kit Fielding, a dour loner but a trusted friend of a princess whose horses he races, is the central character of both books. In *Break In* he enlists royal assistance to discover the motive for a scandal sheet attack on his twin (Holly) and her beleaguered husband, Bob Allardeck, a horse trainer near bankruptcy, but in the end he unravels the threads of a complex plot himself. In *Bolt* he returns the royal goodwill, however, by providing the strength to help Princess Casilia and her family stand up to the blackmail, threats, and violence that are part of a would-be business takeover by a power-mad arms merchant. In traditional Francis style both books include vivid descriptions of English steeplechase racing, romance beset by class differences, telling comments on lineage and class, and conspiracies based on unbounded ambition. The misuse of the press and the inhumanity of loan sharks dominate *Break In*, while the villainy of arms merchandising and the irrationality of revenge dominate *Bolt*. The intricate plot of *Break In* involves the seething hatred of feuding clans (Fielding vs. Allardeck), the telepathic bonds of twins, character assassination, illegal wiretaps, break-ins, bribery, and sabotage. The book opens with a tough race in which Fielding struggles body and soul against a truculent brute of a horse with winning style; it concludes with an even tougher competition in which Fielding employs the skills of mass-media video splicing to bridle an embittered brute of a man whose winning style depends on the destruction of others. The feud continues in *Bolt* but with a nastier edge that forces Fielding to go beyond the law to safeguard those he loves. To force the princess and her husband to sign over their company, the arms merchant, who believes "every conscience has its price," tries acid, a near-fatal push off a second story, and a bomb to frighten and compel, while his vengeful counterpart arranges for their champion horses to be put down with a "bolt," a so-called "humane killer." Fielding proves his "capacity for endurance" and his nerve, as he sets himself up as bait and turns the villains' own weapons against them.

Hot Money (1987), extending a pattern begun in *Break In* and *Bolt*, emphasizes family relationships, a topic always of concern to a Francis hero but one often left undeveloped as the alienated protagonist moves away from his family group to form new connections, whether romantic or convivial. Here the hero, Ian Pembroke, does the opposite, rebuilding his relationship with his estranged father, Malcolm, and acting as the only common bond between his father's three living divorced wives and his seven children and their assorted spouses: an embittered clan, few of whom have much in common beyond a pressing need for their sire's money. Horse racing is only a background concern, with Ian a jockey and with Malcolm learning to enjoy the sport, as father and son deal with murder plots, their own somewhat prickly relationship, and the pain of knowing that some blood relative wishes one or both of them dead. Francis's achievement here lies in showing that unhappy families are not all alike; this one is riven by the disagreements and contrary ambitions of a varied set of people, all recognizably Pembrokes, yet with genetic predispositions twisted and rearranged by personal history and circumstance. As a result, *Hot Money* is one of Francis's finest novels.

Tor Kelsey of *The Edge* (1988) is another of Francis's quietly competent, resilient heroes whose performance continually dumbfounds his associates. Despite an inherited fortune, Kelsey chooses the challenge of the security operative game, working undercover for the British Jockey Club to anticipate trouble and moving with ease between classes. He enjoys the comfort money can buy but relies on the day-to-day strains of a working man's toil to give his life meaning. His forte is his ability to blend chameleonlike with his environment, and in the course of the novel he masquerades as a wealthy horse owner, a congenial actor assisting with a staged murder, and a self-effacing waiter on The Great Canadian Transcontinental Mystery Race Train. Doing so allows him to thwart a disgruntled railway saboteur, salvage the honor and the horse (but not the insane

son) of a troubled racing family, and trap a deceptively charming blackmailer (Julius Apollo Filmer) who brutishly thrives on wielding power through threats, intimidation, and violence. A broken shoulder blade does not stop Kelsey from making the case against the "slippery" Mr. Filmer cast-iron by allowing himself in his role as innocent waiter to be knocked out in front of significant and vocal witnesses.

Straight (1989) and *Longshot* (1990), vintage Francis, demonstrate his growing strength as a writer certain of his authority, his method, and his values. In *Straight* jump rider Derek Franklin, grounded by a smashed ankle and overcome by the unexpected death of his brother (killed by falling scaffolding), inherits a reputable jewel firm, some winning racehorses, innumerable mechanical and electronic gadgets, persistent enemies (including a drug lord), and a troubled magistrate mistress; as a result he is caught up in a series of events that puzzle, anger, and challenge him. As his brother's second-in-command, Annette Adams, and her associate, June, introduce him to the mysteries of the gem trade, Derek finds himself trying to second-guess a dead brother, "a man of secrets" with "a mind like a labyrinth." The answers involve betrayed trust, bent employees, crooked horse trainers and horse owners, and several criminal schemes. But Derek, who is "straight through and through," looks at things "straight" and thereby finds a fortune in missing diamonds and explains the muggings, break-ins, attacks, and shootings that plague him. In doing so he gains a new expertise and lays his brother to rest.

The hero of *Longshot*, John Kendall, is also breaking new ground. A successful writer of survival manuals for an adventure-travel agency, he first yearns for the greater challenge of writing novels and later, as the action progresses, that of being a professional jockey. Short on funds, he agrees to live in the Berkshire home of famed horse trainer Tremayne Vickers, study his methods under his direct tutelage, and write his biography. This agreement involves him in a jealous rivalry and a police investigation, each of which almost costs him his life. Feeling as if he has been given "a walk-on part" in a play that is already "in progress," he quickly adjusts to the Vickerses' eccentric household, conducting research, cooking, working horses, and teaching two teenagers the harsh realities of survival and the necessity of preparation, equipment, knowledge, and a proper mindset. A careful, methodical man, Kendall finds his quiet competence and commonsensical advice put to the test, not in the wilds of distant lands but in rural England, where, beneath "the day-to-day surface of ordinary life" lie hidden horrors—silent, deadly two-legged "sharks" who transform his guidebooks for survival into recipes for murder.

Francis's outlook in both these books is grimmer than usual, with villainy presented as normal in a savage, amoral world. In *Straight*, Derek Franklin learns that honesty and courage can provoke evil and thereby prove deadly, for, as his brother noted before his murder, "The bad scorn the good and the crooked despise the straight." A crooked horse trainer thinks "Everyone can be bought," a respected artist steals the wallet of a dying friend, and a sympathetic policeman notes that "there isn't always an understandable reason" for violence and hatred. In *Longshot* young Gareth Vickers observes that every man is really two people, one a secret, darker self. The older Kendall confirms that appearances are deceptive, motives mixed, strength sometimes a handicap, weakness sometimes the key to survival, and the "bedrock and everlasting design of nature" a brutal Darwinian encounter in which every tomorrow is "a struggle."

Francis had in progress for more than ten years a biography of English jockey Lester Piggott but had agreed not to publish it until that eleven-time British flat-racing champion had given up the sport. When Piggott retired in 1985, *A Jockey's Life: The Biography of Lester Piggott* was published. Piggott is in certain respects the model of the Francis hero, a man who has striven against difficulties, who has devoted his life to racing, who for Francis sums up the ideals of the sport of kings.

Through time the Francis novel has lost its early focus on sadistic physical violence, and, although there is still violence, the later books concentrate more specifically on psychological stress—emotional conflict and self-doubt. The hero is less a man who can endure torture than one who has the strength to face self-doubt, fear, and human inadequacy and still survive and thrive. His later books strive more for a psychological study of a just and decent man than for a dramatic presentation of heroic action. They also try to teach readers about different places and different fields, about bearing one's crosses and showing moral fortitude and courage. There is a world-weary, stoic quality to his heroes that is part of Francis's statement about dealing with life. His

journalist understands that the story he fights to piece together for Sunday will light fires and wrap fish and chips on Monday. His actor realizes that there is really little significant difference between the first take and the fifty-first take and that the "realism" of the movie theater fails to even approximate reality. His books' compelling action keeps Francis at the top of the best-seller list, but as Barry Bauska (*Armchair Detective*, July 1978) points out, while his work remains "splendidly readable," he has evolved into "less a writer of thrillers and more a creator of literature."

Francis's popularity and success in England and America is not hard to account for. Besides the obvious fact that he is a first-rate novelist, one who has mastered all the technical tools of his craft, his underlying theme is a successful blend of old-world tradition and elegance and new-world innovation and energy. Francis marries the British ratiocinative detective tradition with Chandleresque loners who suffer massive physical punishment or deep inner stress in the pursuit of truth. The corruptions of the city and of excessive, self-indulgent wealth (themes in many American hard-boiled works) contrast with the calm decencies of English country life.

Francis's heroes make the ultimate accommodation to the new democratic realities. The world of horse racing provides a fine metaphor for a class-divided society whose different levels must nevertheless cooperate if common goals are to be attained. In *Slay-ride,* when Arne asks Cleveland, "Do you know so many rich people?," after Cleveland has just rejected a wealthy man's rudeness as atypical, Cleveland replies: "Meet them every day of the week . . .; they own racehorses." In *Break In* Fielding rises above money and class to mix easily with touts and princesses, chatting companionably with stable boys and fellow jockeys as well as with the blue bloods on whom his business depends. As Francis continually emphasizes, racing needs the efforts of stable lads as well as millionaires, of photographers and drivers as well as jockeys. Yet the material rewards—such as they are for the majority of participants—are distributed with gross inequality, as a few profit hugely, while large numbers sacrifice their efforts for minimal rewards. Francis's emphasis on the nonmaterial benefits of the racing life, the almost sensual descriptions of everyday activity, help justify and rationalize the material inequities. There is a sense of belonging in his books, a sense of loyalty to racing that is akin to patriotism. Francis's heroes offer the hope so necessary to stability of the racing world or society in general, the hope generated by the intrinsic rewards of competence.

Since Francis's heroes are defined by their ability to perform under pressure with a high degree of efficiency, if not grace, the blending of the hard-boiled and the ratiocinative traditions of mystery writing in his work can be said to have a political end. The future belongs to the competent. The new technocrats will transcend impoverished backgrounds, limited education, and formerly forbidden careers. The class system will be smashed, not by Marxist posturing or by class struggle, but by applied knowledge. Democracy will consist of a middle ground—rather like a race meeting—where elevated and humble will mix amicably in the pursuit of profit and fun, and where the star players will reap the rewards for their competence in proportion to their suffering and devotion. Francis is not the first writer to see life as a horse race, but his vision is certainly the most complete and thoroughly rendered.

Interviews:

"Dick Francis," *New Yorker*, 45 (5 March 1969): 29-30;

Deryck Harvey, "A Word with Dick Francis," *Armchair Detective*, 6 (May 1973): 151;

Brigette Weeks, "Writing Mystery Novels," *Writer*, 96 (August 1983): 11-12;

Edward Zuckerman, "The Winning Form of Dick Francis," *New York Times Magazine*, 25 March 1984, pp. 40, 50, 54, 60-62;

"Dick Francis: An Interview," *Writer*, 103 (July 1990): 9-10.

References:

Pete Axthelm, "Writer with a Whip Hand," *Newsweek*, 97 (6 April 1981): 98;

Melvyn Barnes, *Dick Francis* (New York: Ungar, 1986);

Barry Bauska, "Endure and Prevail: The Novels of Dick Francis," *Armchair Detective*, 11 (July 1978): 238-244;

Ronald Blythe, "Literary Lairs: Ronald Blythe on the Realm of the British Writer," *Architectural Digest*, 42 (June 1985): 98-103;

Robert Cantwell, "Mystery Makes a Writer," *Sports Illustrated*, 28 (25 March 1968): 76-78;

J. Madison Davis, *Dick Francis* (Boston: Twayne, 1989);

Fred Hauptfuhrer, "The Sport of Kings? It's Knaves that Ex-Jockey Dick Francis Writes Thrillers About," *People* (7 June 1976): 66-68;

Judy Klemesrud, "Behind the Best Sellers," *New York Times Book Review*, 85, 1 June 1980, p. 42;

Marty S. Knepper, "Dick Francis," in *Twelve Englishmen of Mystery*, edited by Earl F. Bargainnier (Bowling Green, Ohio: Bowling Green University Popular Press, 1984), pp. 222-248;

Jack Newcombe, "Close-up: Jockey with an Eye for Intrigue," *Life*, 66 (6 June 1969): 81-82;

"Riding High," *Forbes*, 117 (15 April 1976): 100;

Alvin P. Sanoff, "Finding Intrigue Wherever He Goes," *U.S. News & World Report*, 124 (28 March 1988): 56;

Michael N. Stanton, "Dick Francis: The Worth of Human Love," *Armchair Detective*, 15 (Spring 1982): 137-143.

Thom Gunn
(29 August 1929 -   )

This entry was written by Blake Morrison for
DLB 27: Poets of Great Britain and Ireland, 1945-1960.

SELECTED BOOKS: *Fighting Terms* (Oxford: Fantasy Press, 1954; revised edition, New York: Hawk's Well Press, 1958; London: Faber & Faber, 1962);

The Sense of Movement (London: Faber & Faber, 1957; Chicago: University of Chicago Press, 1959);

My Sad Captains (London: Faber & Faber, 1961; Chicago: University of Chicago Press, 1961); republished with *Moly* (New York: Farrar, Straus, 1973);

Selected Poems, by Gunn and Ted Hughes (London: Faber & Faber, 1962);

Positives (London: Faber & Faber, 1966; Chicago: University of Chicago Press, 1967);

Touch (London: Faber & Faber, 1967; Chicago: University of Chicago Press, 1968);

Poems 1950-1966: A Selection (London: Faber & Faber, 1969);

Moly (London: Faber & Faber, 1971); republished with *My Sad Captains* (New York: Farrar, Straus, 1973);

Jack Straw's Castle (London: Faber & Faber, 1976; New York: Farrar, Straus, 1976);

Selected Poems 1950-75 (London: Faber & Faber, 1979; New York: Farrar, Straus & Giroux, 1979);

The Passages of Joy (London: Faber & Faber, 1982; New York: Farrar, Straus & Giroux, 1982);

The Occasions of Poetry: Essays in Criticism and Autobiography (London: Faber & Faber, 1982);

The Man with Night Sweats (London: Faber & Faber / New York: Farrar, Straus & Giroux, 1992).

OTHER: *Poetry from Cambridge 1951-52*, edited by Gunn (London: Fortune Press, 1952);

Five American Poets, edited by Gunn and Ted Hughes (London: Faber & Faber, 1963);

Selected Poems of Fulke Greville, edited by Gunn (London: Faber & Faber, 1968; Chicago: University of Chicago Press, 1968);

Ben Jonson: Poems, edited by Gunn (Harmondsworth: Penguin, 1974).

The paradox of Thom Gunn's achievement is best characterized by the ambiguities inherent in the word *fashion*. He is a "fashioning" poet, in the old-fashioned sense—a writer preoccupied by the problems of "shaping," "determining," and "controlling" both in life and in art. But somewhat to his surprise and quite without opportunism he has also turned out to be a chronicler of fashion—a poet in whose work one can discern various trends of postwar culture: Sartrean existentialism; youth subculture; the communal aspirations of the 1960s; the consumption of hard and soft drugs. He is not a polemical poet, nor one who has been active in political movements; yet future social historians and cultural anthropologists wanting to learn about the texture of our times will probably find it more useful to turn to his work than to that of the other British poets who also emerged in the 1950s—Philip Larkin, Ted Hughes, Geoffrey Hill, Peter Redgrove, Charles Tomlinson. What one finds in Gunn's work is not just an unusual receptivity to the aspirations and transformations of our age but also a traditional set of humanist concerns. He is at bottom a philosophical poet, addressing himself to perennial questions of love, identity, freedom, and choice, but finding his answers in the immediate (and often deviant) present.

Gunn was born in 1929 in Gravesend, Kent, and christened Thomson William (Thom for short). His father, Herbert Smith Gunn, was a journalist with the Beaverbrook press, a gregarious and successful man who moved up from provincial papers such as the *Kent Messenger* to become editor of the *Evening Standard* in 1944 and later, in the 1950s, editor of the *Daily Sketch*. Gunn's mother, Ann Charlotte Thomson Gunn, had also worked as a journalist until the births of Thom and his younger brother Alexander (Ander, as he is known). An independent woman, something of a socialist and feminist, she was a voracious reader and passed on to Thom the idea "of books as not just a commentary on life but a part of its continuing activity." Gunn has

better read at eleven than most people are at thirty-five. As a boy he read Louisa May Alcott, Charles Kingsley, and John Masefield; in his early teens Christopher Marlowe, John Keats, John Milton, Alfred, Lord Tennyson, and George Meredith. Most crucial of all perhaps was his discovery of a broad range of poetry in W. H. Auden's anthology *The Poet's Tongue* (1941), given to him by an enlightened English teacher at Bedales school in Hampshire, to which he was evacuated for four terms during the World War II Blitz bombings of London (the larger part of his education was spent at University College School in London). He had also written from an early age (he recalls character sketches done at eight and a short, "curiously sophisticated novel" he wrote at twelve), and from sixteen onward he took his writing seriously, though "the results were immature and dispiriting."

After he left school, Gunn spent two years' National Service in the British army from 1948 through 1950 (National Service was at this time compulsory for young British men). It is tempting to date his fascination with soldiers from this period, but he himself dates it earlier, to just after the Blitz, when he enjoyed "eyeing the well-fed and good-looking GIs who were on every street, with an appreciation I didn't completely understand." (In the poem "The Corporal" he goes even further: "Half of my youth I watched the soldiers.") After completing National Service he went to Paris for six months, worked for the Metro in a low-paid office job, read Marcel Proust, and attempted a Proustian novel of his own. Despite this apparent precocity, Gunn judges that when he went up to read English at Trinity College, Cambridge, in 1950, at the age of twenty-one, he was "strangely immature, a good deal more so than any of my friends."

Once there, however, he grew up quickly, becoming part of a lively and challenging circle of undergraduates who edited and wrote for the university magazine *Granta* and who were later to make their names as writers and literary journalists: Karl Miller, Nicholas Tomalin, Mark Boxer, John Coleman, John Mander, and Tony White. The abrasive Miller was especially influential— "When I wrote a new poem I would give it to him for criticism, and he would pin it to the wall above his desk for several days before he told me what he thought of it. . . . He matured my mind amazingly"—and Tony White, later a translator, odd-job man, and dropout, was to become a life-long friend. "Looking back on that time, I can

said that his was a happy childhood and that he had a special fondness for Hampstead, a well-to-do part of London to which the family moved when he was eight: a couple of his poems celebrate the spacious heath for which Hampstead is renowned and which he frequented as a child and teenager. There were, however, two darker events in his childhood about which he has been more reticent: the divorce of his parents shortly after they had moved to Hampstead and the death of his mother when he was fourteen. It is hard not to see a link between these events and the lonely (compensatorily macho) personae of his early poems. An uncollected undergraduate poem, "Mother Love," describes a boy who finds nothing but loneliness "as soon / As the old line of his mother's was permanently closed down."

Throughout his childhood and adolescence, Gunn read widely: according to his father he was

see it all as a bit incestuous," Gunn has said: "we promoted each other consistently." But he has also said that he received "more education from my contemporaries than from my teachers." The one teacher he remembers with respect is F. R. Leavis, whose lectures he attended and whose "discriminations and enthusiasms helped teach me to write, better than any creative-writing class could have. His insistence on the realized, being the life of poetry, was exactly what I needed."

Gunn's first book, *Fighting Terms* (1954), is the product of these Cambridge years: he wrote all the poems in it between 1951 and 1953, when he received his B.A. Like most undergraduate collections it has not worn particularly well: Gunn himself has rightly said that it was received more kindly than it deserved because he had somehow been cast in the role of the new "Cambridge poet," of whom great things were expected. In retrospect the collection looks affected, cerebral, and overclever, a combination epitomized in the refrain from "Carnal Knowledge": "You know I know you know I know you know." Several poems are no more than elaborations of single metaphors or setting up of riddles: the reader is invited to decode or unscramble, to discern that the strange landscape described in "Without a Counterpart," for example, is that of the human body. The most common conceit in the book is love treated as war. As in "To His Cynical Mistress," sex becomes the battle of two human wills, lovers' ruses are military stratagems, seduction is a matter of conspiracy and maneuver:

> And love is then no more than a compromise?
> An impermanent treaty waiting to be signed
>   By the two enemies?
> While the calculating Cupid feigning impartial-
>   blind
> Drafts it, promising peace, both leaders wise
> To his antics sign but secretly double their
>   spies.

If that poem points to the influence of John Donne (and its title to Andrew Marvell), others betray the presence of William Shakespeare, Ben Jonson, Fulke Greville, Auden, William Empson, William Butler Yeats, and Robert Graves. Such indebtedness gives the poems an air of bookish sophistication, even world-weariness—"For a Birthday" begins as if the poet were seventy, not twenty-four, "I have reached a time when words no longer help"—but such seeming sophistication cannot disguise an opposite strain of callowness and crudity, evident, for example, in the slickly

rhyming "La Prisonniere," which is based on the same pop-song image that Cliff Richard was later to make famous in "Livin' Doll": "Now I will shut you in a box / With massive sides and a lid that locks. / Only by that I can be sure / That you are still mine and mine secure."

Yet the book is far from being a complete embarrassment. The obsession with soldiers, the themes of will and choice, and the strange accounts of metamorphosis anticipate the concerns of the mature Gunn. There are, moreover, poems that stand up well by any standards. "Wind in the Street" nicely animates the cliché of the browsing shopper—"I only came . . . to look round"—and enlarges it with a suggestion of "uncommitted" existential questing. "The Secret Sharer" recounts an actual experience of disembodiment, or double selfhood, which Gunn had in Cambridge. "Lerici" strikingly contrasts the lives of Percy Bysshe Shelley and George Gordon, Lord Byron, celebrating the Romantic energy of Byron over the "submissive" qualities of Shelley (a characteristically Leavisian preference). "Incident of a Journey" is an unlikely but suggestive amalgam of Wilfred Owen's "Strange Meeting" and Edith Piaf's "Je ne regrette rien." Above all there is the book's opening poem, one of the author's best, which features the sort of existential hero to whom Gunn at this period was drawn—the professional soldier willing to fight on any side and "subject to no man's breath"—and who is powerfully mysterious about the nature of the wound (emotional? physical? intellectual?) that is now incapacitating him. Few first books can boast opening lines as authoritative as these from "The Wound":

> The huge wound in my head began to heal
> About the beginning of the seventh week.
> Its valleys darkened, its villages became still:
> For joy I did not move and dared not speak;
> Not doctors would cure it, but time, its patient skill.

Fighting Terms created a stir in 1954 not just because it marked the emergence of a bold new individual talent, but because it was identified with a new spirit of realism and irreverence in English poetry. Gunn shared with other recent arrivals—Philip Larkin, Kingsley Amis, Donald Davie, John Wain—a preference for tight verse forms, a respect for the tough and reasonable, and a distrust of the neoromanticism that Dylan Thomas and others had made fashionable in the 1940s (though Thomas himself Gunn did admire). Various articles of the time, most crucially a 1954 piece by Anthony Hartley in the *Spectator*, gave these writers a corporate identity and public image, which Robert Conquest's anthology *New Lines* (1956) consolidated: they became known as The Movement. Gunn himself was well aware of the publicity surrounding The Movement but regarded the group as largely a journalistic invention (or convention) and was somewhat surprised to find himself being called one of its main members: whereas Amis, Larkin, and Wain did know each other fairly well, Gunn had met hardly anyone who was supposed to be part of the group. Nonetheless, it is easy to see why Gunn should have been incorporated. A poem such as "Lines for a Book," which mocks at sensitives such as Stephen Spender and adopts brutally hardheaded attitudes, is typical of brusque Movement ideology. It is also the early poem of his that Gunn now most regrets:

> It's better
> To go and see your friend than write a letter;
> To be a soldier than to be a cripple;
> To take an early weaning from the nipple
> Than think your mother is the only girl.

Whatever the extent of Gunn's affiliations with The Movement, links of one sort were effectively broken when, in the same year as his first book was published, 1954, he departed for the United States. His chief reason for going seems to have been his involvement with Mike Kitay, an American he had met at Cambridge and who was to become a steady companion. (Gunn was already a homosexual in Cambridge, though he found it hard to admit this fact to his friends and adopted a heavily heterosexual persona in the early poems.) A creative-writing fellowship at Stanford made the transatlantic move possible, and for a year Gunn lived in Palo Alto, thirty miles south of the city in which he was eventually to settle, San Francisco. It was a productive year, one in which he wrote most of his second book and fell under the spell not only of California but of Yvor Winters: "It was wonderful luck for me that I should have worked with him at this particular stage of my life, rather than earlier when I would have been more impressionable or later when I would have been less ready to learn." Gunn was soon to become conscious of his mentor's rigidity about poetry—"The rigidity seemed to be the result of what I can only call an increasing distaste for the particulars of existence"—but for the moment the partnership flourished, as

his well-known poetic tribute, "To Yvor Winters, 1955," testifies:

> You keep both Rule and Energy in view,
> Much power in each, most in the balanced two:
> Ferocity existing in the fence
> Built by an exercised intelligence.

This poem appeared in Gunn's second collection, *The Sense of Movement* (1957), a book that he has described as "a second work of apprenticeship," "more sophisticated" but "less independent" than the first. This comment is, up to a point, fair: the existentialism of Jean-Paul Sartre and Albert Camus, with its vocabulary of *will, choice, freedom, action, self-determination,* and *individualism,* is more intrusive in this volume than in *Fighting Terms.* On the other hand, Gunn's first book is largely lacking in a temporal context, whereas his second is vividly contemporary, adopting as subject matter motorcycle gangs, Elvis Presley, jukeboxes, cafés, cityscapes, street markets, and leather fashions. In what was a fairly conservative period of British poetry, such "lowlife" contemporaneity involved Gunn in a considerable risk: he had been hailed as a strenuous traditionalist but was now seemingly to be placed with American Redskins rather than English Palefaces, with Allen Ginsberg and Jack Kerouac rather than Larkin and Davie. Formally, however, Gunn remained buttoned up, and this tension was indeed the key to the volume: myths of wild men explored in rigidly restrained meter, American motorcyclists celebrated in structures that took Marvell's mower poems as a model. So, too, Gunn's frantic commitment to the new was held in check by a series of historical allegories about Merlin, Saint Martin, Jesus, and Julian the Apostate, and by a superb Chekhovian period piece, "Autumn Chapter in a Novel":

> Through woods, Mme Une Telle, a trifle ill
> With idleness, but no less beautiful,
> Walks with the young tutor, round their feet
> Mob syllables slurred to a fine complaint,
> Which in their time held off the natural heat.

This is one of the few poems in the book to show a sneaking regard for inaction. Elsewhere Gunn is in constant danger of elevating action and movement excessively high above thought, especially at the end of the book's celebrated opening poem, "On the Move," the philosophical implications of which do not bear close examination. Gunn is aware of the poem's moral problem—

may not the restless activity of the motorcycle gang be to no purpose? may it not indeed be positively harmful to others?—but this awareness does not prevent him from identifying strongly with the gang's motto of movement for movement's sake:

> At worst, one is in motion; and at best,
> Reaching no absolute, in which to rest,
> One is always nearer by not keeping still.

This last line is fine rhetoric, but Gunn cannot have failed to realize that it is also untrue: movement can take one further away as well as toward. He may not have defined it quite in this way, but his problem for the next few years lay in shaking off the hoodlum philosophy to which his early allegiance to existentialism, in combination with a natural leaning to the violent and militaristic, had driven him. By 1957 some readers were already beginning to find his attraction to strong leaders and romantic overreachers to be fascistic, and he was himself aware of unpalatable elements in his work. The problem was in part a formal one: meter and rhyme tended to enforce his emphasis on control and will. As he himself later put it: "in metrical verse it is the nature of the control being exercised that becomes part of the life being spoken about. It is poetry making great use of the conscious intelligence, but its danger is bombast—the controlling music drowning out everything else."

In the late 1950s, his first two books behind him, Gunn began to experiment with syllabic and free verse so as to develop what he called a "more humane" impulse in his work. It was not, in terms of poetry, a very productive period: he found it a struggle to master free forms. He was also, one suspects, finding it hard to adjust to life in the United States, much though he was excited by it, so that in personal terms, too, this was a restless and at times unhappy period of his life: a fairly tedious year's teaching in San Antonio, Texas (1955-1956); graduate work at Stanford, by the end of which (in 1958) Gunn had still failed to complete his Ph.D. and had become disenchanted with Yvor Winters; two years living in Oakland while teaching at Berkeley (1958-1960); a trip to Italy on a Somerset Maugham award (1959); then finally some months away in Berlin (1960), after which Gunn returned to make his home in San Francisco. Gunn was reviewing regularly for *Poetry* and *Yale Review* during these years, but by about 1964 he had become "dissatis-

fied with the business of making comparatively fast judgments on contemporary poets," and since then he has reviewed very little; he especially regrets a hastily dismissive verdict on William Carlos Williams, a poet who was soon to become important to him. He could not have been very happy, either, about what was being said about his own poetry back in England, where his name was being linked with that of Ted Hughes, who had been at Cambridge just after him and whose first book, *Hawk in the Rain,* was published to great acclaim in 1957. The two were spoken of by A. Alvarez, Edward Lucie-Smith, and others as the originators of a new school of violence in poetry—not toughly reasonable like The Movement, but unreasonably tough: aggressive, amoral, drawn to fascism and Nazi regalia. There was some justice in the Hughes-Gunn pairing, for there are verbal and thematic parallels in their early work. (The 1962 joint selection of their poetry brought out by Faber and Faber was a huge success and has gone on to sell more than one hundred thousand copies.) But for Gunn, who was in the late 1950s and early 1960s trying to remake and humanize himself, it must have indeed been tough to be the subject of this sort of attention: the last thing he wanted was a "New Brutalist" label.

My Sad Captains (1961) was at least some sort of answer. The book is deliberately divided into two parts: the "old phase" of metrical verse and Sartrean will in part 1; the new phase of syllabics and "tenderness" in part 2, suitably introduced by a poem called "Waking in a Newly Built House." The implied clean break was, of course, a simplification: Gunn's previous book had already contained two poems in syllabics ("Market at Turk" and "Vox Humana"), just as later books were to revert to meter. But the book does undoubtedly mark a turning point, and not only its second half: the fine opening poem, for example, "In Maria Del Popolo," reverts to a familiar Gunn theme—man in his struggle against nothingness—but now concedes that contemplation, not action, may be the best means of resistance. The braggarts and tough guys who stalk the book's pages seem seedier and less confident than their predecessors, to be pitied rather than admired: fallen rakes in middle age, young black jackets whose tattoo-motto reads "Born to Lose." Human relationships generally are revalued, the selfishness and subterfuge Gunn formerly saw dominating them giving way to the possibility of gentleness, as in "The Feel of Hands":

The hands explore tentatively,
two small live entities whose shapes
I have to guess at. They touch me
all, with the light of fingertips

testing each surface of each thing
found, timid as kittens with it.
I connect them with amusing
hands I have shaken by daylight.

Above all Gunn is for the first time attentive to the natural world; its minutiae—snails, forest ferns, grass blades—are painstakingly described. The concluding title poem is thus a fitting farewell to Gunn's existential heroes (such as Alexander, Brutus, Coriolanus, Byron) and to the idolatry of action: as they "withdraw to an orbit / and turn with disinterested / hard energy," so too Gunn seems to attain a new detachment and disinterest. He will no longer propagandize on behalf of the brave and strong. Clarity becomes his new touchstone, a clarity that he finds present in the California light itself:

on fogless days by the Pacific,
there is a cold hard light without break

that reveals merely what it is—no more
and no less. That limiting candour,

that accuracy of the beaches,
is part of the ultimate richness.

"Limiting candour" does not sound like an exciting poetic program, and *My Sad Captains* is far from being Gunn's best book. But it is the most important transitional collection, the one that made his subsequent development possible.

With three collections under his belt and steady employment teaching at Berkeley, Gunn had now reached some sort of plateau and had begun to think of San Francisco as his home: he was no longer the English traveler abroad, but an émigré, or settler. Ironically, however, his next two books were both made possible by the one year in the 1960s that he spent away from San Francisco—a year from mid 1964 to mid 1965, when he lived in London. Though then in his mid thirties, Gunn was living in London for the first time as an adult—"A London returned to after twelve years"—and its importance to him is admitted in his autobiographical essay, "My Life up to Now" (in *The Occasions of Poetry*, 1982), and in his "Talbot Road" sequence of poems (from *The Passages of Joy*, 1982) about the West London street and large Victorian house where he stayed.

For those, like him, interested in youth culture generally and rock music in particular, this was an exhilarating time to be in Britain, the years of "Swinging London," "Carnaby Street," and the Beatles: "barriers seemed to be coming down all over, it was as if World War II had finally drawn to its close, there was an openness and high-spiritedness and relaxation of mood I did not remember from the London of earlier years."

As well as seeing a good deal of his Cambridge friend Tony White, who lived nearby, Gunn also visited his brother Ander and family in Teddington. He was much taken with Ander's photographs, and the two decided to collaborate on a book of poems and photographs commemorating contemporary English urban life. *Positives* (1966) cannot be considered one of Gunn's serious collections, and indeed nothing from it was included in his *Selected Poems* of 1979. As he has said, "I was never very sure whether what I was writing opposite the photographs were poems or captions," and some of the text does not seem to work as either. But the poems on subjects in which Gunn had already a proven interest—teddy boys, motorcyclists, pop singers, the subculture of male youth generally—have moments of genuine power: an arrogant young man gesturing at the camera, "inviting experience to try him"; a group of teenage boys shown huddled by a warehouse, their bodies "increasing in secret society"; and two concluding poems about an old tramp-woman, the first a memory of hop picking in Kent that echoes her present destitution ("she worked all day along the green / alleys, among the bins"), the second a haunting premonition of death:

Something approaches, about
which she has heard a good deal.
Her deaf ears have caught it, like
a silence in the wainscot
by her head. Her flesh has felt
a chill in her feet, a draught
in her groin. She has watched it
like moonlight on the frayed wood
stealing toward her
floorboard by floorboard. Will it hurt?

Let it come, it is
the terror of full repose,
and so no terror.

At the back of *Positives* lies Gunn's growing admiration in the early 1960s for William Carlos Williams: he has said that he wanted to "anglicize" Williams, to write free verse poems of "fragmentary inclusiveness" about Britain in the mid 1960s. *Positives* does this with modest success and much visual support.

The year in London also enabled Gunn to complete "Misanthropos," the centerpiece of his next full-fledged collection, *Touch* (1967). This sequence of seventeen linked poems presents a life stripped to primitive essentials. A skeletal narrative recounts how the seemingly solitary survivor of a global war exists by himself until, to his surprise and even dismay, he encounters a group of about forty other survivors. The circumstances of the global war, and the man's escape from it, are not fleshed out: the poem is instead a meditation on first and last things, on what it would be like to be the last representative of the human race—and thus in effect the first one, Adam. It is an ambitious poem for which William Golding's novel *The Inheritors* (1955) is the acknowledged model (one notices the influence especially in sections 12 through 15) and which Ted Hughes's poem "Wodwo" also resembles. But both these texts point up the weaknesses of Gunn's: his poem has not their richly sensuous response to the natural world; its philosophizing takes place in a void or dust bowl. Most of the other poems in *Touch* are also disappointing, lacking in personality and bite, as if Gunn's turning away from the brutal and willed had left him without a subject and without a tone of voice. The collection is dominated by an ethic of the random and all-inclusive propounded in "Confessions of the Life Artist"— "Whatever is here, it is / material for my art," "You control what you can, and / use what you cannot." Fine in principle, this theory in practice results in a collection where few poems stand up as *poems, as artifacts.* The one distinguished work in the collection, arguably the best in Gunn's whole oeuvre and good enough to make one happy to pass over the rest of *Touch,* is the title poem, a superb example of free verse and in its last lines a pointer to the communal idealism that also dominates his next book:

What I, now loosened,
sink into is an old
big place, it is
there already, for
you are already
there, and the cat
got there before you, yet
it is hard to locate.
What is more, the place is
not found but seeps

from our touch in
continuous creation, dark
enclosing cocoon round
ourselves alone, dark
wide realm where we
walk with everyone.

Gunn returned to San Francisco in mid 1965 to find that he had been given tenure at Berkeley. A year later, however, he decided to give up his job, evidently feeling that a full-time teaching position was no longer compatible either with his poetry writing or with the kind of life he wanted to lead. Possibly the atmosphere in San Francisco, as heady as and even more optimistic than the London he had left, had something to do with it. There was also his involvement with the drug LSD, which he seems to have taken then for the first time and which helped to make those years, as his excited description suggests, "the fullest years" of his life: "Raying out from the private there was a public excitement at the new territories that were being opened up in the mind. . . . We tripped . . . at home, on rooftops, at beaches and ranches, some went to the opera loaded on acid, others tried it as passengers on gliders, every experience was illuminated by the drug. . . . These were the fullest years of my life, crowded with discovery both inner and outer, as we moved between ecstasy and understanding. It is no longer fashionable to praise LSD, but I have no doubt at all that it has been of the utmost importance to me, both as a man and as a poet." For a brief golden moment in San Francisco, drug taking, utopian politics, and "flower power" happily coexisted and created optimism in Gunn and others about communal living and the perfectibility of man.

As a poet, his dilemma was to find a way of speaking of these newfound experiences, images, and ideas. Drug experiences, being "essentially non-verbal," were difficult to transcribe: "Metre seemed to be the proper form for the LSD-related poems, though at first I didn't understand why. Later I rationalized about it thus. The acid trip is unstructured, it opens you up to countless possibilities. . . . The only way I could give myself any control . . . was by trying to render the infinite through the finite, the unstructured through the structured." Yet there was the problem of clarifying and articulating the nexus of ideas in which, partly because of drugs, he had become interested: "trust, openness, acceptance, innocence." The difficulty resulted in a temporary writing block, release from which—as he recounts in the essay "Writing a Poem" (in *The Occasions of Poetry*)—came about through the experience of seeing a naked family (father, mother, and small son) on a deserted Pacific beach. The encounter is memorialized in his poem "Three," and the parents in it, who have "had to learn their nakedness," become a sort of symbol for and inspiration to his work of the period. They not only confirm the possibility of innocence repossessed but are an emblem of what Gunn now thinks poetry should be—clean, naked, open, trusting, fused with the natural world.

The position Gunn had reached by the end of the 1960s was thus very different from that he had held in his first two books. *Fighting Terms* and *The Sense of Movement* had depicted the natural world as a threatening void; his heroes were those, whether motorcyclists or emperors, whose machines or mechanistic wills could overpower it; human achievements in life and art were a matter of subduing and ordering and subduing— "much that is natural to the will must yield." *Moly,* published in 1971, embodies Gunn's more hopeful vision of a fruitful union between man and nature, and between writing and living. The poem "From the Wave," for example, celebrates surfing (and by implication poetry) as a process not of defeating the natural but of riding it, harnessing it, working in consort with it. Watching surfers, he writes:

Their pale feet curl, they poise their weight
  With a learn'd skill.
It is the wave they imitate
  Keeps them so still.

The marbling bodies have become
  Half wave, half men,
Grafted, it seems, by feet of foam.

Moly is dominated by such images of merging and metamorphosis, of centaurs, pantheists, men and women (and men and animals) in sexual union. Once aloof, moated, "condemned to be an individual," Gunn now embarks on a thrilling mission to dissolve, melt, commune, share, belong. This is, in part, the meaning of the title: when Hermes gave Odysseus the drug moly, it broke Circe's spell of confinement and subordination. The collection is about being set free into a new, more expansive universe.

The title has a second, connected meaning: it implies an analogy between the releasing powers of moly and those of LSD. There are at least a half-dozen poems in *Moly* that specifically de-

scribe LSD experiences, and several more are indirectly indebted to the drug. In none of these could Gunn be accused of self-indulgence, of the transcription of merely private dreamworlds. He always edges the poems into the public domain to which he believes LSD belongs. ("By 1968 taking the drug was no longer an unusual experience, probably hundreds of thousands had had at least one experience with it, and many more knew about it without having taken it, so to write about its effects was not any more to be obscure or to make pretentious claims to experience closed to most readers.") The opening of "The Fair in the Woods" is a good example of his public mode, its perfect iambics echoing the opening of Thomas Gray's "Elegy Written in a Country Churchyard" (1751): "The curfew tolls the knell of parting day" (Gray); "The woodsmen blow their horns, and close the day" (Gunn). But the poems are public also because they are set in public places (a fair, a rock festival) and because they affirm a brave new social order of openness and trust:

Open on all sides, it is held in common,
The first field of a glistening continent
Each found by trusting Eden in the human:
The guiding hand, the bright grey eyes intent.

Gunn in his earlier work had praised "uncommitted" men with the courage of their lack of convictions. It was an easier stance than the one he takes here, which means holding convictions that are Edenic, vulnerable, and, in retrospect, even gullible. But the courage makes this his most affirmative book, and his tight poetic structures help contain his utopianism to make it also, arguably, his best work. There are several strong poems at its center ("The Sand Man," "Three," "Words," "From the Wave"), and it ends superbly with "The Discovery of the Pacific," about a young couple resting at the end of their pioneering journey to the West Coast, and with "Sunlight," an ode that in its final lines provides Gunn with his most eloquent and beneficent moment:

Great seedbed, yellow centre of the flower
Flower on its own, without a root or stem,
Giving all colour and all shape their power,
Still recreating in defining them,

Enable us, altering like you, to enter
Your passionless love, impartial but intense,
And kindle in acceptance round your centre,
Petals of light lost in your innocence.

Thom Gunn, 24 June 1970 (photograph by Alden)

Moly is a buoyant book, "high" on the Edenic impulse of the late 1960s. By the time it appeared in 1971, however, that buoyancy had subsided. Already in 1970, while he was living for a spell in a loft apartment on Prince Street in New York (he commuted to Princeton, where he taught), Gunn had felt the beginnings of a change: "It was the time of numerous bombings—I saw a rather famous townhouse go up in smoke—and of the invasion of Cambodia. The feeling of the country was changing, and one didn't know into what. I went back to England for a few months of the summer, and when I returned to San Francisco I felt something strange there too: there was a certain strain in attempt-ing to preserve the euphoria of the sixties, one's anxieties seemed obstructive. I had a couple of rather bad trips on LSD that taught me no end of unpalatable facts about myself, to my great edi-fication." This was the tenser, more contradictory atmosphere that Gunn and many others experi-enced, both privately and publicly, in the early 1970s. On the one side was a feeling of unease and violence, a desire (during the Nixon era) to draw back into the self. On the other was "edifica-tion," clear-sightedness and a chastened but persis-tent belief that "everything that we glimpsed— the trust, the brotherhood, the repossession of innocence, the nakedness of spirit—is still a possi-bility and will continue to be so." In personal terms Gunn moved between the pain of losing his friend Tony White (who died at forty-five from injuries sustained in an accident while playing soccer) and the joy of discovering new friends, between the upheavals and nightmares that accompanied a move from one side of San Francisco to the other and his occasional association with a new sort of hedonistic community at a rundown resort in Sonoma County.

Tragedy versus joy, 1960s meliorism against 1970s disenchantment—these are the fluctuating feelings that lie behind Gunn's next book, *Jack Straw's Castle*, published in 1976 and dedicated to the memory of Tony White. The book opens strongly with two poems that show the persistence of that fascination with cityscapes underlying the earlier "In Praise of Cities" and *Positives*. "Diagrams" describes Indian construction workers "with wrenches in their pockets and hard hats"; "Iron Landscapes" explores oppositions of iron and water, stability and fluidity, the virtues of constancy and the dangers of stubborn resistance. Even in these poems Gunn's persona seems darker and more resolute in mood than in *Moly*, and the shift is confirmed in the first of the book's two long sequences, "The Geysers." Initially the change is scarcely visible: the poem's opening two sections have rapturous, *Moly*-like celebrations of men merged in pantheistic union and are infected with the same pleasure that Gunn brings to his description of the background to the poem: "In the early seventies I went a few times with friends to the area in Sonoma County, north of San Francisco, known as the geysers. . . . We camped anywhere, on the flanks of the hills, which were warm even at night, or in the woodland, or beside the cool and warm streams. Everyone walked around naked, swimming in the cool stream by day and at night staying in the hot baths until early in the morning. Heterosexual and homosexual orgies sometimes overlapped: there was an attitude of benevolence and understanding on all sides that could be extended, I thought, into the rest of the world." But in section 3 the poem becomes more disquieting: the speaker's encounter with the rock and heat that underlie the geyser's watery pleasures brings him to a recognition of forces beyond his control: "Up here a man might shrivel in his source." Section 4 ushers in the disorder augured here, the verse changing abruptly from meter and rhyme into free-verse fragments, and the speaker losing his individuality and his sense

of the past in an "uneasy" (part ecstatic, part terrifying) orgy of communal bathing:

I am part of all
                    hands take
                                        hands tear and twine

I yielded
            oh, the yield
                                what have I slept?
my blood is yours the hands that take accept.

The lesson to be drawn is not that the chilly self should not be surrendered, but that the surrender may be painful and traumatic—more so than the similarly communal vision of *Moly* had implied.

The element of nightmare in "The Geysers" recurs more strongly in the second section of the collection and its second long sequence, "Jack Straw's Castle," which has obsessive images of the poet being assaulted, imprisoned, burned up, annihilated. Here the speaker has not expanded his mind but found it imprisoning him; he has not moved into an airy region of self-transcendence but has been returned to the dark "core" or "source" or "dungeon" of selfhood; he has not fellow hedonists and bathers for companions but Charles Manson, Medusa, and the Furies; and he finds not a joyous release through the senses but an oppressive regime of sweat, fungus, sour breath. In this prison he faces a horrific series of receding mirror images:

I am the man on the rack.
I am the man who puts the man on the rack.
I am the man who watches the man who puts
                            the man on the rack.

In the third section of the book there is a return to daylight and poise and to a hope that seems stronger for its having been put through the ordeal of the previous section. "The Idea of Trust," for example, is an archetypal 1970s riposte-poem: that someone might steal "the money and dope / of the people he'd lived with" could not have been acknowledged in the headier days of the 1960s. Facing up to the fact now, Gunn is not, however, merely disillusioned—he takes seriously, as a sort of plausible philosophical position, the culprit Jim's definition of trust as "an intimate conspiracy," and he implies that those who choose to share possessions must be prepared to lose them. Gunn seems to believe that the abolition of privacy is an ideal worth pursuing, but one must be clear that it involves risk and pain. In this final section he also finds room for at least one poetic persona who moves unambiguously from gloom and boredom to "joy," "love," and sensual fulfillment: the persona is that of a dog, Yoko, seen welcoming home his human master. The poem brilliantly overcomes the problems of anthropomorphism that usually attend such exercises to become, as its author intended, a "completely doggy" poem: in it Gunn escapes most convincingly the self that imprisons him elsewhere in the collection. Overall, however, *Jack Straw's Castle* is Gunn's most disturbing book, veering alarmingly between extremes of self-absorption and self-erasure. It is a book of middle age, both literally (written while he was in his mid forties) and because of a new note of brooding and revaluation.

Throughout his career Gunn has shown an impressive ability to move off in unexpected directions. Sometimes they seem to surprise even him; it was probably no exaggeration when he wrote, a year after the publication of *Jack Straw's Castle*, that he had "no idea" what his next book would be like, nor that as late as 1980 he was claiming, "I don't see a pattern for my next book yet." So, too, even those intimate with his work, and those who had been reading his new poems as they appeared in periodicals in the late 1970s, must have been taken aback by the shape and content of *The Passages of Joy* when it appeared in 1982. Gunn's life-style had changed little during the period of its composition: he continued to live in San Francisco and to make occasional trips to London and other places; he added to a stream of earlier prizes and awards (a Rockefeller grant in 1966, for example, and a Guggenheim Fellowship in 1971, the prestigious W. H. Smith Award given to his *Selected Poems* of 1979), yet on average he continued to earn an income, as he puts it, "about half of that of a local bus driver or street sweeper." He came to believe more strongly than ever that writing was for him not a pose (as it had perhaps begun) but an integral part of his life, a way of understanding himself and others. But for all this steadiness and continuity, the new book was a distinct departure, being plainer and more direct than any of its predecessors and, in particular, franker about its author's homosexuality.

Yet *The Passages of Joy* is not a confessional book in the sense that confessionalism in poetry has come to be understood. Gunn has expressed his admiration for T. S. Eliot's theory of poetic im-

personality and has expressed his skepticism about the demand that a poet have a "distinctive voice" ("Distinctiveness can look after itself, what I want is a voice that can speak about anything at all"). One of the poems in *The Passages of Joy*, "Expression," attacks young poets who have modeled themselves on confessional precursors:

> They write with black irony
> of breakdown, mental institution,
> and suicide attempt, of which the experience
> does not always seem first-hand.

But *The Passages of Joy* is the book in which Gunn "comes out" as a homosexual and is confessional in the sense that he speaks candidly for the first time about his sexual experiences with, and attraction to, other men, as in "Sweet Things":

> How handsome he is in
> his lust and energy, in his
> fine display of impulse.
> "How about now?" I say
> knowing the answer. My boy
> I could eat you whole. In the long pause
> I gaze at him up and down and
> from his blue sneakers back to the redawning
> one-sided smile. We know our charm.
> We know delay makes pleasure great.

One must not exaggerate the homosexual element in the book, as some reviewers did. Only a few of the poems are explicitly about homosexual encounters or venues; heterosexual relationships are also described in poems such as "Adultery" and "His Rooms in College" (though interestingly such relationships are unhappy); and the lines of Samuel Johnson from which Gunn takes his title—"Time hovers o'er, impatient to destroy, / And shuts up all the Passages of Joy"—are on one level to be taken simply as a memento mori, as a reference to mortality and the decay of the flesh. But of course the secondary meaning of these lines is indeed sexual: the passages, as Gunn has said, refer to "the nine channels with their nine holes through which we get most of our physical joys," and it is the joys of the eighth and ninth passages (the penis and the anus) that are highlighted. Moreover it is very difficult to imagine the book's occasionally demotic frankness before the decensorship of the 1960s and the widespread "gay liberation" campaign in the United States and Europe in the late 1970s. As Gunn says in his essay "Homosexuality in Robert Duncan's Poetry": "Most homosexual

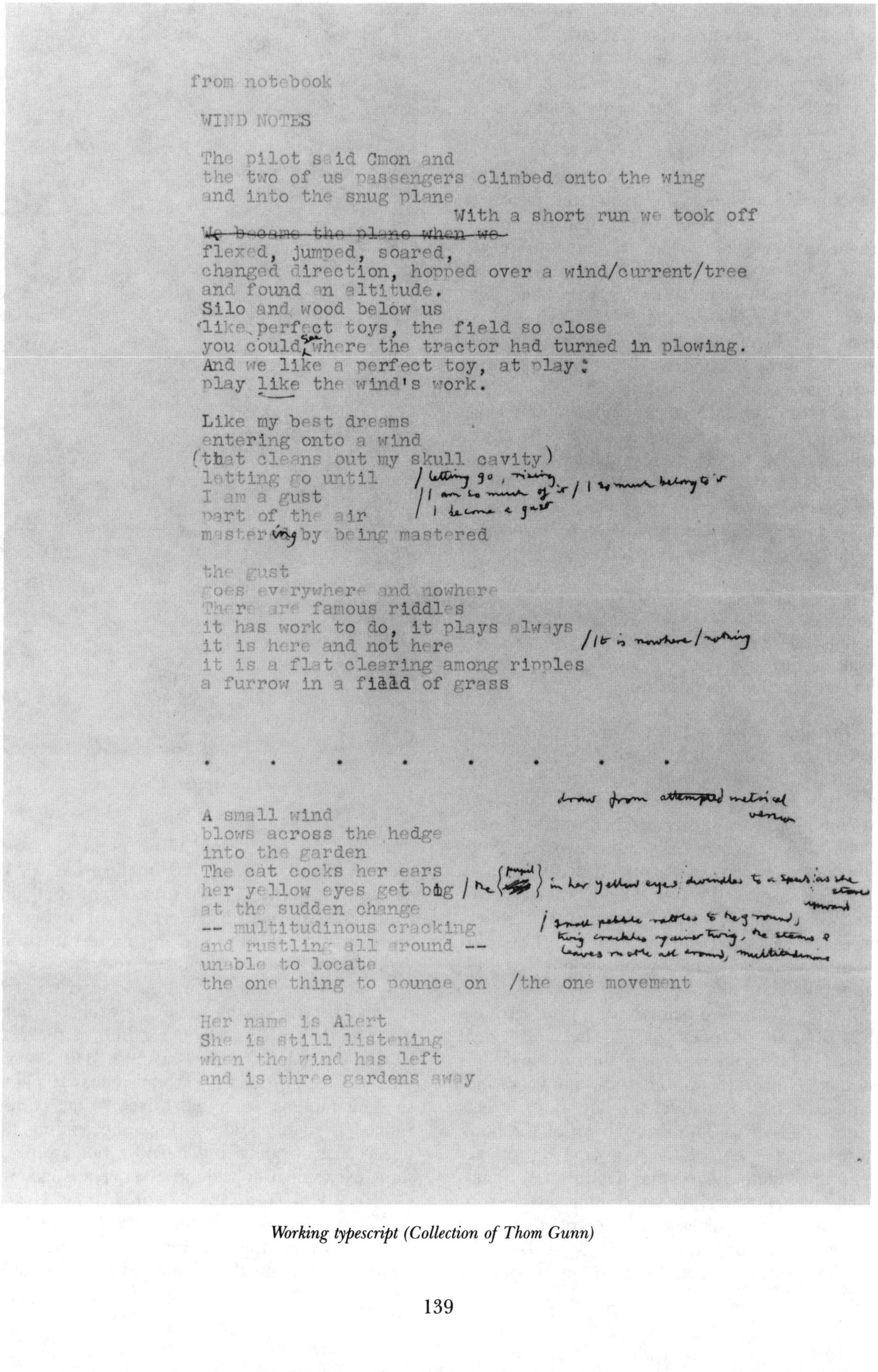

from notebook

WIND NOTES

The pilot said Cmon and
the two of us passengers climbed onto the wing
and into the snug plane
               With a short run we took off
~~We became the plane when we~~
flexed, jumped, soared,
changed direction, hopped over a wind/current/tree
and found an altitude.
Silo and wood below us
like perfect toys, the field so close
you could, where the tractor had turned in plowing.
And we like a perfect toy, at play:
play like the wind's work.

Like my best dreams
entering onto a wind
(that cleans out my skull cavity)
letting go until   / letting go, rising
I am a gust   / I am so much of it / so much belong to it
part of the air   / I become a gust
mastering by being mastered

the gust
goes everywhere and nowhere
There are famous riddles
it has work to do, it plays always
it is here and not here   / It is nowhere / nothing
it is a flat clearing among ripples
a furrow in a field of grass

.   .   .   .

                         draw from attempted metrical version

A small wind
blows across the hedge
into the garden
The cat cocks her ears
her yellow eyes get big / The {pupil} in her yellow eyes dwindles to a speck as she
at the sudden change
-- multitudinous cracking   / small pebble rattles & they round,
and rustling all around --   twig crackles against twig, the stems &
unable to locate   leaves rustle all round, multitudinous
the one thing to pounce on   /the one movement

Her name is Alert
She is still listening
when the wind has left
and is three gardens away

Working typescript (Collection of Thom Gunn)

writers until at least the 1960s dealt with autobiographical and personal material only indirectly. One method was for a poet to address his work to an unspecified you, giving an occasional ambiguous hint about what was really going on to those in the know only. (This is what Auden did, and what I was to do later.)"

In *The Passages of Joy* Gunn adopts no such subterfuges: throughout he hymns the pleasures of male companionship, with himself undisguisedly at the center. The "coming out" is reflected in a style of "coming clean"—a poetic mode that eschews metaphor, symbol, and allegory and relies instead on anecdote, casual observation, and plain speech, "the real language of men." In "Song of a Camera" Gunn implies that his art may be that of a camera—the chance shot, the cut from life, the art that shows simply what it sees, leaving the audience to supply the adjectives and adverbs of moral judgment. But like the camera's, this is an art more artful than it seems—there is the subtlety of the line breaks in the opening "Elegy" to dead friends, for example, that carries the poem's grief:

> They keep leaving me
> and they don't
> tell me they don't
> warn me that this is
> the last time I'll be seeing them.

The Passages of Joy did not have a particularly good reception in England, where some reviewers felt that too many of the resources of Gunn's art had been stripped away and others that there was coming to be a rather tired antiestablishment air about his preference for dramatis personae located on the fringes of society—a drug dealer, a taxi driver, a pinball player, a bodybuilder, a volunteer in a mental institution. But it is a collection that seems less plain the more one lives with it: it appears to hide nothing, but it does have hidden depths.

Ten years passed before Gunn produced another volume of poetry. *The Man with Night Sweats* (1992) again deals with homosexual subject matter and themes, but this volume, as one might expect, also analyzes the horrifying effects of the AIDS virus. The first section of the book continues in the vein of *The Passages of Joy*, with reflections on the pleasures and hedonism of homosexual love. However, the concluding section consists of a sequence of elegies to the poet's friends who have died of AIDS. A review of *The Man with Night Sweats* in the *Economist* summarized it

Thom Gunn, 1991

thus: "In the past, Mr. Gunn's poetry has often seemed to lack warmth; his intellect has been in control. Now the close witnessing of that 'difficult, tedious, painful enterprise of dying' has given his poetry more life and more raw human vigour than it has ever had before."

Gunn's overall reputation as a writer, from the perspective of the 1990s, is probably not as great as the initial acclaim for him in the 1950s would have led one to suspect. His work is taught widely in British schools; he has persuasive champions such as Clive Wilmer; he is ranked by many critics among the leading half-dozen British poets: but he does not arouse the same excitement or wide interest as, for example, Geoffrey Hill, Ted Hughes, or Seamus Heaney. There are in part extraliterary explanations. Like Auden, Gunn chose to make his home in the United States, and though he did not time his departure as badly as Auden, a prejudice against his "defection" persists. One can see it, for instance, in the English critic Colin Falck's part-chiding, part-pleading assessment of *Jack Straw's Castle*: "If Gunn could put away the vacant counter-cultural slovenliness of his Californian ethic . . . he might be able to recover the faith which once tied him in with English poetry's finest traditions. . . ." But for Gunn the choice "English or American?" is not a meaningful one: he belongs to both cultures (and countercultures); his Californian ethic is not a superficial grafting but part of the texture of his life. He continues to be better known in England than in the United States, of course, and it is more common (and commonsensical) to measure his achievement against that of British contemporaries than against the Allen Ginsbergs and Gary Snyders. In the end, however, he deserves to be seen as one in a long and distinguished line of modern poets for whom the term "Anglo-American" is a perfectly proper description—Eliot, Ezra Pound, Auden, Sylvia Plath, Charles Tomlinson, and Donald Davie are others.

Interviews:

Ian Hamilton, "Four Conversations," *London Magazine*, 4 (November 1964): 64-70;

Hilary Morrish, "Violence and Energy," *Poetry Review*, 57 (Spring 1966): 32-35;

W. I. Scobie, "Gunn in America," *London Magazine*, 17 (December 1977): 5-15;

John Haffenden, *Viewpoints: Poets in Conversation* (London: Faber & Faber, 1981).

Bibliography:

Jack W. C. Hagstrom and George Bixby, *Thom Gunn: A Bibliography 1940-78* (London: Rota, 1979).

References:

Alan Bold, *Thom Gunn and Ted Hughes* (Edinburgh: Oliver & Boyd, 1976);

Alan Brownjohn, "The Poetry of Thom Gunn," *London Magazine*, 3 (March 1963): 45-52;

Martin Dodsworth, ed., *The Survival of Poetry* (London: Faber & Faber, 1970), pp. 193-215;

Colin Falck, "Uncertain Violence," *New Review*, 3 (November 1976): 37-41;

G. S. Fraser, "The Poetry of Thom Gunn," *Critical Quarterly*, 3 (Winter 1961): 359-367;

P. R. King, *Nine Contemporary Poets* (London: Methuen, 1979), pp. 77-106;

John Mander, *The Writer and Commitment* (London: Secker & Warburg, 1961), pp. 153-178;

John Miller, "The Stipulative Imagination of Thom Gunn," *Iowa Review*, 4 (Winter 1973): 54-72;

Blake Morrison, *The Movement: English Poetry and Fiction of the 1950s* (Oxford: Oxford University Press, 1980);

Neil Powell, "The Abstract Joy: Thom Gunn's Early Poetry," *Critical Quarterly*, 13 (Autumn 1971): 219-227;

John Press, *Rule and Energy* (Oxford: Oxford University Press, 1963), pp. 191-201;

M. L. Rosenthal, *The New Poets* (Oxford: Oxford University Press, 1967), pp. 251-257;

"Testimony at the End of the Day," review of *The Man with Night Sweats*, *Economist*, 22 February 1992, p. 88;

Clive Wilmer, "Definition and Flow," *PN Review*, 5 (Spring 1978): 51-57.

Papers:

There is a collection of Gunn's manuscripts at the University of Maryland.

Seamus Heaney
(13 April 1939 -   )

This entry was updated by Robert Buttel (Temple University) from his entry in
DLB 40: Poets of Great Britain and Ireland Since 1960: Part One.

BOOKS: *Eleven Poems* (Belfast: Festival Publications, Queen's University, 1965);

Death of a Naturalist (London: Faber & Faber, 1966; New York: Oxford University Press, 1966);

A Lough Neagh Sequence, edited by Harry Chambers and Eric J. Morten (Didsbury, Manchester: Phoenix Pamphlets Poets Press, 1969);

Door into the Dark (London: Faber & Faber, 1969; New York: Oxford University Press, 1969);

Boy Driving His Father to Confession (Farnham, Surrey: Sceptre Press, 1970);

Night Drive (Crediton, Devon: Richard Gilbertson, 1970);

Servant Boy (Detroit: Red Hanrahan Press, 1971);

Wintering Out (London: Faber & Faber, 1972; New York: Oxford University Press, 1973);

The Fire i' the Flint: Reflections on the Poetry of Gerard Manley Hopkins (London: Oxford University Press, 1975);

Stations (Belfast: Ulsterman Publications, 1975);

North (London: Faber & Faber, 1975; New York: Oxford University Press, 1976);

Bog Poems (London: Rainbow Press, 1975);

In Their Element, by Heaney and Derek Mahon (Belfast: Arts Council of Northern Ireland, 1977);

After Summer (Old Deerfield, Mass.: Deerfield Press, 1978);

Robert Lowell: A Memorial Address and Elegy (Boston & London: Faber & Faber, 1978);

Field Work (Boston & London: Faber & Faber, 1979);

Hedge School: Sonnets from Glanmore (Salem, Ore.: C. Seluzichi, 1979);

Selected Poems 1965-1975 (Boston & London: Faber & Faber, 1980); republished as *Poems: 1965-1975* (New York: Farrar, Straus & Giroux, 1980);

Preoccupations: Selected Prose 1968-1978 (Boston & London: Faber & Faber, 1980);

Sweeney Praises the Trees . . . (New York, 1981);

The Rattle Bag: An Anthology of Poetry, selected

© 1981 Layle Silbert

with Ted Hughes (London: Faber & Faber, 1982);

Sweeney Astray (London: Faber & Faber, 1984; New York: Farrar, Straus & Giroux, 1984);

Station Island (London: Faber & Faber, 1984);

The Haw Lantern (London: Faber & Faber, 1987; New York: Farrar, Straus & Giroux, 1987);

The Government of the Tongue: Selected Prose 1978-1987 (New York: Farrar, Straus & Giroux, 1988);

The Place of Writing (Atlanta: Scholars Press, 1989);

The Cure at Troy (London: Faber & Faber, 1990);

New and Selected Poems: 1966-1987 (New York: Farrar, Straus & Giroux, 1990);

Seeing Things (London: Faber & Faber, 1991).

RECORDING: *The Northern Muse,* by Heaney and John Montague, Claddagh Records, 1969.

OTHER: *Soundings: An Annual Anthology of New Irish Poetry,* edited by Heaney (Belfast: Blackstaff, 1972);

Soundings II, edited by Heaney (Belfast: Blackstaff, 1974).

SELECTED PERIODICAL PUBLICATIONS—
UNCOLLECTED: "Out of London: Ulster's Troubles," *New Statesman,* 1 July 1966, pp. 23-24;

"Old Derry's Walls," *Listener,* 24 October 1968, pp. 521-523;

"A Poet's Childhood," *Listener,* 11 November 1971, pp. 660-661;

"The Trade of an Irish Poet," *Guardian,* 25 May 1972;

"Deep as England" [on Ted Hughes], *Hibernia,* 1 December 1972, p. 13;

"Seamus Heaney Recalls When Li'l Abner Breezed in from Castledawson," *Education Times,* 20 December 1973;

"John Bull's Other Island," *Listener,* 29 September 1977;

"Treely and Rurally," *Quarto,* 9 (August 1980): 14;

"English and Irish," *Times Literary Supplement,* 24 October 1980, p. 1199;

"Osip and Nadezhda Mandelstam," *London Review of Books,* 20 August - 2 September 1981, pp. 3-6;

"Above the Brim: On Robert Frost," *Salmagundi,* 25th Anniversary Issue (Fall 1990 - Winter 1991): 275-294.

From the beginning critical as well as popular acclaim has greeted each volume of Seamus Heaney's poetry. Who would have predicted in 1966, when his first full-length book appeared,

the impact such poetry would have? It is, after all, a poetry manifestly regional and largely rural in subject matter and traditional in structure—a poetry that appears to be a deliberate step back into a premodernist world of William Wordsworth and John Clare and to represent a rejection of most contemporary poetic fashions.

Indeed, one generally favorable review of *Door into the Dark* (1969), Heaney's second volume, points with dry irony to the notion of retrogression: "Turbines and pylons for the 1930s: bulls for the 1960s. It's an odd progression." Perhaps, though, it is this very sense of return to a natural world and traditional forms that explains the popular response to Heaney's work (sales for each of the volumes have ranged from fifteen thousand to thirty thousand). Here is a poetry as superficially accessible as Frost's poetry is superficially accessible: one can almost hear the sighs of relief emanating from those readers discouraged by the complexities of modernist and postmodernist poetry. But it is not quite so understandable that most critics—scattered murmurings of dissent aside—would lean in the direction of Robert Lowell's assessment that Heaney is "the most important Irish poet since Yeats," an accolade that the poet himself, who seems to eschew self-advertising, must bear somewhat uneasily. Part of the explanation may be that reviewers and critics themselves have been captivated by the appeal of the subject matter, the Irish because it confirms the native experience and the Americans and British because it is exotic, a part of the charm of Irish culture to the outsider.

The appeal of the poems to critics is perhaps not so surprising if the favorable reception of Ted Hughes's early work, itself based on a brute natural world exotic to the London or New York reviewer or academic critic, is recalled. Heaney himself certainly found elements in Hughes's work that he could adapt to his own uses and that pushed him toward the possession of his own voice. A more likely explanation is that critics have been disarmed by Heaney's consummate skill in exploiting the resources of language and poetic technique, thereby transcending the limitations of the local and traditional. Suffice it to say at this point that the effect of his impressive output (nine full-length volumes of poetry to date—not counting two volumes of selected poems—plus extensive critical commentary, autobiographical pieces, translations, and edited works) has been remarkable. For a comparable leap into poetry's spotlight the meteoric rise of Dylan Thomas (a poet who presented another version of the Celtic world) comes to mind, but Heaney, with a sure trust in his origins and a steady hold on his identity, has resisted so far the blandishments of fame.

The imprint of the poet's origins is indelibly fixed in his work. As he said, his "quest for precision and definition, while it may lead backward, is conducted in the living speech of a landscape I was born with," and he has quoted the poet in *Timon of Athens* more than once: "Our poesy is as a gum which oozes / From whence tis nourished." The landscape he was born with, as the oldest of nine children of Margaret and Patrick Heaney, had at its center Mossbawn, the place of the family farm in county Derry, Northern Ireland, about thirty miles northwest of Belfast. This landscape offered a definite sense of place and tradition, of habits that arose in a remote past and became part of the local rhythm. Heaney has reflected that "Wordsworth was lucky and . . . I was lucky in having this kind of rich, archetypal subject matter . . . as part of growing up."

The landscape also offered reminders of ancient conflicts and losses, some reaching back in history to the threshold of myth. Old tensions also extended right into the present. Although his family was part of the Catholic majority in the local area, living in relative harmony with the Protestants (a Protestant neighbor on presenting the Heaneys a gift of rosary beads from Rome said, "I stole them from the Pope's dresser"), Heaney was at an early age conscious of living in what he has called the "split culture of Ulster." Between the villages of Castledown and Toome, he was "symbolically placed between the marks of English influence and the lure of the native experience, between 'the demesne' [representing English and Unionist power] and the [native] 'bog'. . . . The demesne was walled, wooded, beyond our ken."

The cultural split Heaney was heir to was defined not only by political, religious, and social divisions but also by a linguistic one: the townlands of Broagh and Anahorish were to the poet "forgotten Gaelic music in the throat, *bruach* and *anach fhior uisce*, the riverbank and the place of clear water," while Grove Hill and Back Park, English names insinuated into the area, evoked "a version of pastoral." Part of Heaney's linguistic richness derives from this sense of doubleness; perhaps rather fancifully he has said, "I think of the personal and Irish pieties as vowels, and the literary

Front cover for Heaney's first full-length book, which C. B. Cox of the Spectator *called "the best first book of poems I've read for some time"*

awareness nourished on English as consonants," verbal elements he wished to combine in an expression of his "whole experience." Despite the taciturnity which he has attributed to the people he grew up among, he emerged from Mossbawn with a rich verbal hoard.

He left home in 1951 to become, under the auspices of the 1947 Education Act, a boarder at St. Columb's College in Londonderry on a scholarship, thus beginning an ongoing process of deracination which has fed a nostalgia for his native locale. He carried with him, however, a wealth of anecdotes, local lore, stories heard at cattle fairs, limericks, sentimental and patriotic verses and songs which he recited on occasion at family gatherings. At school he had received training in Gaelic, and he became an avid reader, even though this practice caused him to be the butt of some good-natured amusement at home. He consumed a variety of reading material, from comic books to Robert Louis Stevenson's *Kidnapped* (1866), the first book he owned. At St. Columb's he not only studied Latin but, under a very good English teacher, read William Shakespeare, Geoffrey Chaucer, Wordsworth, and John Keats as well as T. S. Eliot's "The Hollow Men."

Leaving St. Columb's in 1957 to enter Queen's University, Belfast, he carried with him both the impressions of his childhood world that would become such an important part of the substance of *Death of a Naturalist* and the latent talent for transforming remembered experience into poems. But his development at Queen's, where he studied until 1961, when he received a first-class honors degree in English language and literature, and in the year following (1961-1962), when he took a postgraduate course of study leading to a teacher's certificate at St. Joseph's College of Education in Belfast, was an essential prelude to the writing of those poems.

For one thing, he read more extensively in the English literary tradition, but at the same time he discovered the Irish tradition, especially its poetry—William Butler Yeats, of course, but in a very different mode Patrick Kavanagh, whose "The Great Hunger" strongly impressed him as one way to make effective poetry out of the sort of native Irish subject matter familiar to him; he was struck similarly by the work of Austin Clarke, Richard Kell, Thomas Kinsella, John Montague, Richard Murphy, and Richard Weber in *Six Irish Poets* (1962), edited by Robin Skelton.

Meanwhile he began at Queen's to try his hand at writing poems himself, some of which he published in the university magazines under the unassertive pen name Incertus. The uncertainty behind these apprentice pieces, recalling Keats and the Georgians or imitative of Dylan Thomas or Gerard Manley Hopkins ("Minute movement millionfold whispers twilight / Under heaven-hue plum-blue and gorse pricked with gold"), is understandable. In "Lines to Myself" he would insist on a more sinewy style ("Avoid the lilting platitude. / Give us poems, humped and strong, / Laced tight with thongs of song").

He was responding to a variety of poets, including R. S. Thomas, but two poets in particular seem to have inspired him to find his own voice, to have certified for him the kind of poetry he was instinctively ready to write, based as it was on nature and the local, based too on Kavanagh's dic-

tum that "parochialism [as opposed to provincialism] is universal; it deals with fundamentals." Frost was one of these pivotal poets: according to Benedict Kiely, Heaney told him "that the first poet who ever spoke to him was Robert Frost." Ted Hughes, whose poetry Heaney encountered around 1962, was the other. When Heaney, in a 1972 article, says that "Hughes brought back into English poetry an unsentimental intimacy with the hidden country," that in Hughes's poetry "racial memory, animal instinct and poetic imagination all flow into one another" with an "exact sensuousness," and that Hughes interjected into the "typically standard English intonations of contemporary verse . . . an energetic, heavily stressed, consciously extravagant and inventive northern voice," he is in effect pointing to attributes of his own work.

One further catalyst during his early development was the English writer Philip Hobsbaum, who had recently come to teach at Queen's, where he formed a group of young writers under his aegis and acted as a literary midwife, encouraging the neophyte writers into poetic maturity. Heaney, during his year at St. Joseph's and while some of his first poems were beginning to be published outside the university, joined the group, which included, among others, Derek Mahon and Michael Longley, with whom he became friends. The group, which was part of a general efflorescence of the arts in Ulster at the time, "generated a literary life," says Heaney, much needed in Belfast. Here definitely was reinforcement for his poetic urgings, which were to culminate shortly in *Death of a Naturalist*.

While he was teaching at St. Thomas's Secondary School, in Ballymurphy, Belfast (1962-1963), some of the first poems that he would collect in *Death of a Naturalist* were published ("Turkeys Observed" in the *Belfast Telegraph*, "Mid-Term Break," about the death of one of Heaney's younger brothers, in *Kilkenny Magazine*, and "Advancement of Learning" in the *Irish Times*). From 1963 through 1966 he was lecturer in English at St. Joseph's College. It was during these years that he was associated with the Hobsbaum group and began to become firmly established in the literary world. Three of his poems published in the *New Statesman* in December 1964 came to the attention of Faber and Faber, which would become his chief publisher, and he began to write reviews and other pieces for the *New Statesman*, the *Listener*, and other periodicals. These years brought a series of fulfillments: in 1965 his *Eleven Poems,* a pamphlet, was published by Festival Publications, Belfast, and in August of the same year he was married to Marie Devlin; in May of 1966 *Death of a Naturalist,* for which later in the year Heaney would receive the E. C. Gregory Award, appeared, and in July his son Michael was born.

Of the poems that accumulated during these few years and were collected in *Death of a Naturalist,* the most impressive are those which concentrate on the youthful shocks of recognition and initiation, falls from innocence to an awareness of mortality, decay, and corruption recalled in the perspective of the older, more knowing speakers; then, as a kind of progression, a few of the poems trace the onset of love and ensuing marriage. Some of the poems are chiefly vivid descriptions of the sheer force in natural phenomena such as a waterfall or a trout; others present a disturbing or threatening confrontation with animality. Violence, human as well as natural, is a significant issue in many of the poems. It appears in the form of British behavior during the mid-nineteenth-century famine (in "At a Potato Digging" and "For the Commander of the 'Eliza' ") and in the barely repressed rage of an emotionally warped present-day Protestant dockworker ("Docker"). Childhood encounters with the killing of animals occur in "The Early Purges" and "Dawn Shoot." But another important emphasis in the collection is on control, on ordering, with a focus on special kinds of rural knowledge and skill, often with aesthetic implications, as in "Diviner," where the diviner's hazel switch stirs in response to hidden, mysterious currents.

Many poems focus on the aesthetic act. Thus the first poem in the volume is a declaration of poetic intent, a deliberate choice of the craft of writing over the customary family dedication to farming; in fact it uses the analogy of the farm chore of digging for the act of writing ("Between my finger and my thumb / The squat pen rests. / I'll dig with it"): the speaker desires the same skill in his craft as his father and grandfather, whom he remembers "Nicking and slicing neatly . . . / . . . going down and down / For the good turf," had in theirs. The suggestion is that of technique as the means of probing down into poetic as well as natural substance. The technique should be so true to the object that the separating between it and art is eliminated, as in "In Small Townlands," which has to do with landscape painting: "Loaded brushes hone an edge / On mountain blue and heather grey" or "The

Seamus Heaney, late 1960s (photograph by Jerry Bauer)

splintered lights slice like a spade."

Heaney is at his most successful in this first volume when word, metaphor, and prosody create with uncommon precision the physicality of the object or activity observed. Early on he found his talent for producing a seemingly palpable rendering of the sensuous world. Here in "Churning Day," for example, is the texture of cream and then the heat of the animal source of the cream accentuated by reference to the cool earthenware receptacles for it: "A thick crust, coarse-grained as limestone rough-cast, / hardened gradually on top of the four crocks / . . . / After the hot brewery of gland, cud and udder / cool porous earthenware fermented the buttermilk." Words and sounds in an image in "Death of a Naturalist" seem almost as densely tangible as "the warm thick slobber / of frogspawn that grew like clotted water" that they describe. "Thick slobber" tellingly conveys the soft, repellent gelatinousness of the spawn; "clotted water" requires of the reader an act of mental metamorphosis which "transforms" the water into more substantial form. By such means Heaney captures the essence of things in language. In this title poem he also captures a visceral sense of the dread felt by the young boy in the poem when he falls from the innocence of schoolroom lessons on the tadpoles the class had collected and comes upon the disgusting reality (heightened by the sexual connotations) of the grown "gross-bellied frogs ... cocked / On sods; their loose necks pulsed like sails. Some hopped: / The slap and plop were obscene threats." All of Heaney's early talents and energies are concentrated in this poem; it is the volume's chief triumph, and he was shrewd in calling attention to it in the title.

Other poems, however, strive for effect and leave an effect of striving. One notes, for example, an overdetermined use of images based on projectiles and explosives: a trout is likened to "a fat gun barrel"; blows of a hand on a cow "plump like a depth-charge / far in her gut"; when in "In Small Townlands" the painter "unlocks the safety catch / On morning dew, on cloud, on rain," "The spectrum bursts, a bright grenade." In instances such as these the poet seems overzealous for the imagistic impact that would shatter the restriction of the traditional forms within which he was working.

Aware now of his vulnerability to charges of such excessively dramatic imagery, Heaney has recently said of "Digging," the poem wherein he says he first found his voice and got his feelings ("my *feel*") into words, that "there are a couple of lines in it that have more of the theatricality of the gunslinger than the self-absorption of the digger" (that is, the pen is held between finger and thumb "snug as a gun"). Of course he was assuming various stances in the process of locating his voice. Some of the attempts fail to rise above well-crafted conventional verse; others leave an impression of forced virtuosity that was part of the risk-taking leading to his natural virtuosity.

If the volume is uneven, it gives play nevertheless to what was essentially a new and authentic voice that managed to make the potentially archaic experience of the backcountry immediate and vital to contemporary urban and modernist literary sensibilities. The reception was not unqualified—one reviewer would rather snidely refer to "mud-caked fingers in Russell Square," the intellectual center of London and the home of his publisher, Faber and Faber—but generally it was favorably received as a promising book, original in its poetic grasp of the youthful response to the physical world. The favorable reception was subsequently confirmed by additional awards: the Cholmondeley Award in 1967, the Geoffrey Faber Memorial Prize in 1968, and the Somerset Maugham Award also in 1968.

Another important event for Heaney in 1966 was his appointment as lecturer in English (modern literature) at Queen's University, Belfast. It was in this year too that he began contributing to educational broadcasts on BBC radio and television. This was a connection he maintained for some years. He would compile in 1974, for example, an issue of *Explorations* (published by BBC Radio for Schools), on "Words Working," with his commentary on language interwoven with examples from Irish and English writers as well as a story by Maxim Gorky and "Home Burial" by Robert Frost. The compilation reflects Heaney's ardent belief in the power of language. Moreover, the thoughtful, unpatronizing commentary and arrangement of the material suggest his sincere commitment to teaching. Indeed, he has a reputation for taking his teaching duties seriously, whether at the secondary or university level. Anyone who has attended one of Heaney's poetry readings would expect his articulateness and the warm, easy rapport he establishes with his audience to make him a gifted teacher. His educational responsibilities, however, did not prevent him from writing the poems that he gathered for *Door into the Dark* in 1969; nor did his increased parental responsibilities: his second son, Christopher, was born in February 1968.

Door into the Dark represents both continuity with *Death of a Naturalist* and the opening of new and more complex territory in the poet's work. One notices many images of graphic physical detail similar to those in the first volume. The clay in "Bann Clay" when mined becomes "Slabs like the squared-off clots / Of a blue cream." But the poem is more than descriptive: the alluvial clay becomes an emblem of deposits laid down in a timeless process that would later embed "Mesolithic / Flints"; the speaker, recalling the cleaning of a drain ditch, "Till the water gradually ran / Clear on its old floor," still "labours" in his mind toward the primeval substratum. "Bogland," the final poem in *Door into the Dark* and an anticipation of Heaney's archaeological and anthropological impulse which was to emerge more fully in *Wintering Out* (1972) and *North* (1975), moves down through history and geological time in the peat which preserves "the Great Irish Elk" and butter still "salty and white" toward origins, the ultimate mysterious source—the "Wet centre" which is "bottomless." That is, if the poems in the first volume depend primarily upon the impact of the accurately observed phenomenal world, in this second volume Heaney plunges into the unconscious, into myth, and into the dark submerged currents of being and supernatural awareness.

The volume opens with three poems ("Night-Piece," "Gone," and "Dream") which are marked by obsessive and disturbingly vivid imagery evoking dread, loss, and primal guilt. "Dream," for instance, surrealistically portrays the speaker's hacking with a billhook at a huge, apparently phallic stalk and then at a man's head until the steel stopped "In the bone of the brow," a Cain-like act. Here the dread in some of the poems in *Death of a Naturalist* is intensified and carried further in a Freudian direction. These first three poems open the door into part of what the poet means by the word *dark* in this second book. He means a variety of things. "The Forge," from which the title for the volume comes (the poem begins, "All I know is a door into the dark"), concerns the inner sanctum of the blacksmith's trade, which bears associations with myth, ritual, and art: his anvil is "somewhere in the centre," "Horned as a unicorn," an "altar / Where he expends himself in shape and music." He is an alien to the outside world "where traffic is flashing in rows," and has a knowledge similar to that held much earlier by the monks "In Gallarus Oratory" (an ancient unmortared stone chapel on the Dingle Peninsula in the southwest of Ireland). The oratory holds a "core of old dark"; "When you're in it alone / You might have been dropped, a reduced creature / To the heart of the globe." The monks came out of that dark center spiritually renewed to find nature mystically purified and freshened, "The sea a censer, and the grass a flame." The phrase "heart of the globe" brings to mind the first words in Heaney's essay "Mossbawn" (*Preoccupations*, 1980) wherein he recalls his first environment: "I would begin with the Greek word, *omphalos,* meaning the navel, and hence the stone that marked the centre of the world, and repeat, *omphalos, omphalos, omphalos,* until its blunt and falling music becomes the music of somebody pumping water at the pump outside our back door." The poems in *Door into the Dark* emanate from a religious sensibility that has come to value myth. In an interview published in 1981 Heaney says, "I'm not what you'd call a pious Catholic, I don't go to Mass much, and the doctrines of the Faith aren't my constant reading" but then adds, "I've never felt any need to rebel or do a casting off of God . . . , because I think in this day anthropologists have

Dust jacket for Heaney's 1969 book, in which the poet moves away from the accurate observation of the phenomenal world that characterized his first collection into the unconscious, the mythical, and the supernatural

taught us a lot, to live with our myths."

A notion of myth informs many of the poems in *Door into the Dark.* The historical events in the sonnet "Requiem for the Croppies," for instance, assume a mythic or archetypal dimension. The croppies (so called for their short-cropped hair), who had carried on a heroic guerrilla campaign until in the abortive uprising of 1798 they were slaughtered by the occupying forces on Vinegar Hill, compare with sacrificial fertility gods, for the barley they had carried in their pockets for their meager rations "grew up out of the grave." (Heaney gives the historical, political meaning: "The oblique implication was that the seeds of violent resistance sowed in the Year of Liberty had flowered in what Yeats called 'the right rose tree' of 1916.") This is not to say that Heaney is programmatic about myth; the mythic is simply one result of his search for significant patterns, his recognition of underlying energies, and his perception of the wondrous in the ordinary. "Undine" is spoken by the water sprite of the title, who acquires a soul by marrying a mortal and bearing his child: the farmer who opened up the ditches and drains for the water to flow "dug a spade deep in my flank / And took me to him"; "I alone / Could give him subtle increase and reflection"; "Each limb / Lost its cold freedom. Human, warmed to him." And the girls in "Girls Bathing, Galway 1965" as they gaily wade ashore, apparently free for the moment from "fear of flesh and sin," are associated with the ancient goddess of love: "So Venus comes, matter-of-fact."

Certainly one of the main concerns in the volume is with the various manifestations of the life force, especially having to do with sexuality and the procreative, as the two previous examples suggest. Consequently the role of women receives poignant attention, as in "Mother," in which a pregnant farm wife expresses her feelings of fatigue and frustration, trapped as she is in the stifling round of chores and impatient to be free of carrying the restive new life within her. The pathos of her situation is caught in her response to the "jingling bedhead" now used as a gate in the fence: "it does not jingle for joy any more." Similarly, the wife in "The Wife's Tale" sensitively expresses her feelings of being divided from her husband's businesslike pride in his achievements. Heaney also brings a tender awareness to two love poems, "Night Drive" and "At Ardboe Point." The unlicensed bull in "The Outlaw" has no human ambivalence about his role in the procreative process; he mechanically exerts his brute sexual power as he "slammed life home" before he "resumed the dark, the straw,"—the dark, that mysterious source which seems part of the cycle of mortality and rebirth, spiritual and imaginative as well as physical.

Heaney focuses on this cycle in *A Lough Neagh Sequence*, the most ambitious work by the poet up to this point and the most impressive. This sequence, published separately in pamphlet form in 1969, encompasses the main themes in *Door into the Dark* and is a long poem or a suite of seven interrelated poems in various stanza forms and lengths. Some of the sections rhyme, some do not. The sequence celebrates the men who fish for eels in the huge "marvelous" lake. They are, despite their matter-of-fact attitude, caught up in a timeless, instinctual ritual; a mystical aura surrounds their labors. They are moved by the same forces that move the eels: the wakes of the boats "are enwound as the catch / On the morning water"—"And when did this begin? / This morning, last year, when the lough first spawned? / The crews will answer, 'Once the season's in.' " In the unfolding of the sequence the eels, which find their way through the dark to the dark bottom of the lake, both completing the cycle of their existence and initiating another one (the female is "lost / once she lays / ten thousand feet down in / her origins"), come to be fearsome emblems of mortality, sexuality, and the disturbingly nonhuman. But at the same time they also suggest the wonder of existence.

In technique and conception the sequence gathers the poet's resources into the major achievement of his early development. Not the least of this achievement is his continued ability to convey the physical, which for Heaney is not divorced from the metaphysical: the eels, thrown into a barrel, become "a knot of back and pewter belly / That stays continuously one / For each catch they fling in / Is sucked home like lubrication." Not all the poems in this volume reach the depth and subtlety of this sequence. Some of them do little more than confirm what the poet had mastered in *Death of a Naturalist*. "Thatcher," whose artisan performs his magical business of stitching the thatch into "a sloped honeycomb" with "his Midas touch," is no real advance over the artisan poem "The Diviner" in the earlier volume.

Heaney does not entirely escape the risk of overfamiliarizing his readers with the ground of his preoccupations, the danger of turning his own repertoire into a cliché of itself—thus some of the guardedness mingled in the general critical praise that welcomed *Door into the Dark*. The most negative response was that by A. Alvarez, piqued at Faber and Faber for inflating the reputations of young poets by publishing them—the same complaint another critic had upon the appearance of the first volume—but this response did not keep *Door into the Dark* from becoming the Poetry Book Society Choice for 1969.

Almost immediately Heaney's poetic stance was to come under the heavy pressure of events in Northern Ireland. Referring to "Requiem for the Croppies," he has said that he "did not realize at the time that the original . . . murderous encounter between Protestant yeoman and Catholic rebel was to be initiated again in the summer of 1969, in Belfast, two months after the book [*Door into the Dark*] was published." The Heaney family had a temporary reprieve from the sulphurous

Seamus Heaney (drawing by Jacqueline Morreau; collection of Bernard Stone, The Turret Book Shop)

strife that has been the dominant fact of existence in Northern Ireland since 1969, and the chance to encounter a new geographical and cultural terrain, by going in the academic year of 1970-1971 to California, where Heaney was guest lecturer at the University of California at Berkeley. There he encountered a politically charged atmosphere that, for all its differences, echoed the one in Belfast: "I could see," he says, "a close connection between the political and cultural assertions being made at the time by the minority in the north of Ireland and the protests [against the Vietnam War and social injustice] . . . going on in the Bay Area." He saw also that the poets took part in the protests and that poetry could be a force, "a mode of resistance."

At the same time the examples of Gary Snyder, Robert Duncan, and Robert Bly pointed to the mythological in ways that reinforced his own orientation toward myth. Finally, he feels that the exposure to American poetry, especially that of William Carlos Williams, helped to loosen his own verse in *Wintering Out* and to give it a more relaxed movement so that it ceased being "as tightly strung across its metrical shape." The

source of his writing was still in Ireland, however: while in Berkeley he began writing a series of twenty-one prose paragraphs that draw on his childhood; these would be published in pamphlet form in Belfast (1975) with the title *Stations*. Not long after their return from California, Ann Saddlemeyer, a Canadian friend, offered the Heaneys an opportunity to rent a cottage she owned in Glanmore, county Wicklow, in the Irish Republic. This offer opened the prospect for Heaney of a total commitment to the career of writing, and the result was that in 1972, shortly before the publication of *Wintering Out*, Heaney resigned his secure position at Queen's University, and the family moved south.

Before the move, however, Heaney had been writing the poems of *Wintering Out*, wrestling with the question of poetry's adequacy in the face of violence (in a 1972 *Guardian* essay he quotes Shakespeare's "How with this rage shall beauty hold a plea?"); he became conscious of an attempt to move from the "personal, rural childhood poetry" to "wider . . . , public connections." In the dedicatory poem of the volume (which would become the fourth part of "Whatever You Say Say Nothing" in *North* [1975]) the poet approaches head-on the violence in Belfast, using some of the stock imagery and irony that twentieth-century poets, following W. H. Auden chiefly, have developed to convey the horror and futility of war: a scene of machine-gun posts in the mist defining "a real stockade" calls up "déjà-vu, some film made / of Stalag 17." The sardonic ironies of the third and final stanza register the numbed despair of the city: "Is there a life before death? That's chalked up / on a wall downtown. Competence with pain, / coherent miseries, a bit and sup, / we hug our little destinies again." This is competent enough, and the futility behind the poem is readily granted, but the idiom of the poem is not natural to Heaney. The strain is more pronounced in "A Northern Hoard," a five-poem sequence which with nightmare imagery conflates details of contemporary violence with those of primeval savagery and includes motifs concerning the violation of nature and spiritual emptiness. The effect is strident and melodramatic, the rhetoric is clotted, and the style a pastiche, with reminders of Auden and Wilfred Owen ("the din / Of gunshot, siren and clucking gas / Out there beyond each curtained terrace / Where the fault is opening") and Yeats ("What could strike a blaze / From our dead igneous days?").

Heaney's solution for coping poetically with the new round of sectarian and political violence was to be more indirect in his "search," as he has said, "for images and symbols adequate to our predicament." These he found by stepping back historically, so that he would avoid "plying the pros and cons of the Ulster situation in an editorializing kind of way" and instead probe the "roots of the political myths" and lay a claim for the native by drawing inspiration from the linguistic source, the "etymology, vocabulary, even intonations" of place. Given his predilection for digging into origins and the lure of language itself for him, this was a more rewarding strategy. This way he could "politicize the terrain and the imagery of the first two books." Looking back, Heaney found sure identities and loyalties, and, as in "Bog Oak," geniuses of the place who maintained their authenticity and traditional ways despite the cruelties that Edmund Spenser and other usurpers imposed upon them. "How / you draw me into your trail," says the speaker addressing the subject of "Servant Boy," who is "wintering out" (the phrase which became the book's title).

At the same time, in several of the poems Heaney employs images of pious closeness to the land and to nature. "Land" is one of these poems in which one notes a spiritual affinity with place, with the "phantom ground." Moreover, the very sounds of the land, its natural music and place names, create a numinous aural identity: the swollen Moyola River in "Gifts of Rain" is "an old chanter," "bedding the locale / in the utterance," musically "breathing its mists / through vowels and history."

The poet in some of the poems revels almost giddily in the mysterious power of words; he seems inspired by a faith in language as a process of transubstantiation—nature, experience, feelings incarnate in words, in the texture of the poem. Using techniques derived from this faith, he repossesses the terrain by bedding the locale in the utterance. The tone tends toward reverent elegy and is fused with a mood of trance, of dreamlike recall. The poems are allusive, sometimes enigmatic, but the spirit of place and its beings emerge as haunting, vital presences. The effects are enhanced by the freer movement of the two- or three-stress lines (part it seems of what Heaney learned from William Carlos Williams).

Two poems extend the probe into origins by exploiting anthropological material Heaney came upon in P. V. Glob's *The Bog People* (1969), a study, with compelling photographs, of pre-

served bodies of Iron Age men and women punitively or sacrificially slain and unearthed from Danish and other peat bogs in northern Europe. Here were archetypal "emblems of adversity," to use Heaney's term, correlative with the victims in Ulster, and the poet could feel an intimate contact with an underlying northern mythos which lent a universality to his concerns. The subject of "The Tollund Man," with "his peat-brown head, / The mild pods of his eye-lids, / his pointed skin cap," who was a "Bridegroom to the goddess" sacrificed in a fertility ritual, becomes a symbol of the pain and pathos of the human condition, a saint to whom the speaker would pray to bring to life ("germinate") those "ambushed" victims slaughtered in Ulster. "Nerthus" celebrates a carved wooden icon, exposed to the weather and isolated, of the sort the Bog People used in their worship of the goddess of the title. Its four lyrically affecting lines, including the northern dialect words "kesh" and "loaning," suggest an austere beauty and lonely stoicism. These two poems were the forerunners of a whole series of bog poems in the ensuing volume *North*.

In the variousness of *Wintering Out*, Heaney displays other sympathies, especially in a group of five poems that conveys a deep compassion for the trapped, the rejected, the lost, or alienated, all women. "Limbo" and "Bye-Child" portray the desperate results of the shame felt by women who have borne illegitimate children. In them images of a cosmic emptiness occur: the drowned infant in "Limbo" joins "a cold glitter of souls / through some far briny zone"; the boy in "Bye-Child," confined to a henhouse and incapable of speech, offers "gaping wordless / Of lunar distances / Traveled beyond love." "Maighdean Mara," the legendary mermaid who must leave the sea to marry the man who steals her magic garment, suffers "man-love nightly / In earshot of the waves" and "milk and birth" before retrieving her garment and returning to the sea. And "A Winter's Tale" presents a young girl who is from one point of view pathetically deranged but from another is a spirit of the place, close to nature, a harbinger of spring. "Shore Woman," like "The Wife's Tale" in *Door into the Dark*, concerns the difficulty of marriage from a wife's point of view. This difficulty is the issue in "Summer Home," where with a very personal, almost confessional tone the speaker expresses dismay and guilt over some disturbing rift with his wife for which he has tried to atone. The poem is very modern in its freer form and its vivid but unexplained references and images.

The rest of the poems in *Wintering Out* are for the most part capably executed but not as engaging as the poems already noted; several of them would fit unobtrusively into the first two volumes. The titles "Wedding Day," "Mother of the Groom," "Navvy," "First Calf," "The Wool Trade," "Linen Town," and "Veteran's Dream" suggest something of the nature and range of subjects in these poems. The critical response to *Wintering Out* was rather ambivalent: mingled with the praise were some reservations. The complaint, which has threaded its way through the criticism of Heaney's work, that despite his undeniable gifts he has restricted his range too severely, appears in the commentary on this volume. Alan Brownjohn, for example, saw a retrenchment; although admiring the book, he hoped it represented "a mode from which Heaney's remarkable talent will move on." And Patricia Beer was unhappy over his continued exploitation of the regional and rural: "In 'Westering,' . . . written in California, he takes one look at an 'official map of the Moon' and he darts straight back to 'the last night / In Donegal.' " Such criticism, however, was not to deter Heaney from following his own urgings in the three volumes which have followed.

Between the publication of *Wintering Out* and *North* Heaney and his family, with their third child, Catherine Ann, born in 1973, continued to live at Glanmore, aided by the Writer in Residence Award from the American Irish Foundation in 1973 (the year in which he also received the Denis Devlin Award) and the E. M. Forster Award in 1975. During these years, as he attempted to earn his living as a writer, he gave numerous poetry readings in the United States and England, wrote essays, and edited two poetry anthologies: *Soundings: An Annual Anthology of New Irish Poetry* (1972) and *Soundings II* (1974). Also he had begun, as part of his interest in Irish roots, a translation of the Middle Irish romance *Buile Suibhne*, which concerns the mythic northern Irish king Sweeney, who is driven into a mad despair out of which he utters a poetry of precisely rendered pain, in an idiom congenial to Heaney's own proclivities.

In *North*, Heaney brought together two groups of poems, one in which, "Kinned by hieroglyphic / peat," he steps "through origins" ("Kinship") to summon mythic, prehistorical, and historical identities, and the other and shorter one in which the subject matter is biographical and contemporary, dealing with the relation between the divisive, anguishing realities of Northern Ireland and the role of the poet. *North* opens, however, with a pair of preliminary poems, "Mossbawn: Two Poems in Dedication," to the poet's mother, Mary Heaney. The mother in "Sunlight" baking scones and the men preparing seed potatoes in "The Seed Cutters" (in sonnet form emphasizing the aesthetic pattern in which the speaker would capture them) are engaged in mundane rituals that are part of a timeless rhythm; they are like the eel fishers in *A Lough Neagh Sequence*.

Marked by love and sympathetic response, these poems offer a redemptive note against which the pattern of struggle, loss, and mortality in the ensuing poems must be read. Antaeus in the poem named after him, which begins part 1, and in "Hercules and Antaeus," the poem which closes part 1, is an archetype of the resister whose strength against the imperialist Hercules (seeker of "the golden apples and Atlas") depends on his closeness to the earth that "wombed" him. In "Hercules and Antaeus," though, Hercules wrenches him from his element, "the cradling dark, / the river-veins, the secret gullies / of his strength," to make him in defeat, "a sleeping giant, pap for the dispossessed." Perhaps he will awaken and lend his original strength to the dispossessed, but meanwhile he is a subject for elegies whose defeat anticipates the deaths of Balor, Byrthnoth, and Sitting Bull, sufferers, like the Irish, one can infer, at the hands of superior aggrandizing powers. In one group of the sixteen poems between these two, Heaney with an anthropological obsession unearths more of the Nordic trove he had cut into in "The Tollund Man" and "Nerthus" in *Wintering Out*.

These bog poems (eight of them, published in a limited edition entitled *Bog Poems* in 1975) explore with almost morbid fascination victims of pagan rites and punishments. They are described with all the graphic exactitude characteristic of Heaney's style: "I can feel the tug / of the halter at the nape / of her neck, the wind / on her naked front. / It blows her nipples / to amber beads" ("Punishment"). The speaker's sympathy for the "Little adulteress" pulls him erotically: "I almost love you"; "I am the artful voyeur / of your brain's exposed / and darkened combs, / your muscles' webbing." But as he compares her with "your betraying sisters" in the present who have presumably been punished, "cauled in tar,"

Covers for Heaney's 1975 book. After he completed this volume, Heaney told an interviewer, "I don't know if I could have written another bog poem."

for consorting with British soldiers, he feels himself caught between the "civilized outrage" at which he "would connive" and his understanding of "the exact / and tribal, intimate revenge" to which the Iron Age adulteress had been subjected. Similarly, the preserved figure in "The Grauballe Man" is not only associated with the Dying Gaul but also with "the actual weight / of each hooded victim, / slashed and dumped" in the current revenge killings in Northern Ireland. In "Bog Queen," perhaps the most reverently elegiac and vividly detailed of these poems—it epitomizes the group—the eponymous speaker says, "My diadem grew carious, / gemstones dropped / in the peat floe / like the bearings of history." She is part of a universal pattern moving through time.

In other poems Heaney takes up more recent history. For example, "Ocean's Love to Ireland" (an ironic play on Sir Walter Ralegh's "The Ocean's Love to Cynthia" in honor of Queen Elizabeth) uses the metaphor of sexual assault for the invasion and subjection of Ireland by England. Heaney has drawn on John Aubrey's account of Ralegh's attack on a maid of honor; in the poem he backs a maid to a tree "As Ireland is backed to England / And drives inland / Till all her strands are breathless: / 'Sweesir, Swatter! Sweesir, Swatter!' " (Sweetsir, Sir Walter!), she exclaims in her poignant, panicky desperation. It is a defeat for poetry and language too: "The ruined maid complains in Irish" and "Iambic drums / Of English beat the woods where her poets / Sink like Onan." Heaney's consciousness of this defeat no doubt fed his consuming interest in the buried linguistic and poetic resources. The "tongue" of a Viking longship tells the speaker in "North" to "Lie down / in the word-hoard" and to "Keep your eye clear / as the bleb of the icicle." In "Bone Dreams" the speaker pushes back "through dictions, Elizabethan canopies," "Norman devices," and so on "to the scop's / twang, the iron / flash of consonants / cleaving the line."

Certainly in the poems in part 1 of *North* the poet achieves an urgent, taut control of the acutely visualized and sensually rendered material. The result is a terse, affecting lyricism. The intensity of the poems derives from what Heaney has referred to as his entrancement with the material, but at the same time the interest led to a near surfeit of archeological imagery and Nordic vocabulary. Having completed *North,* he came to feel a "self-consciousness about the bogs and so forth." He also felt a need to open up the narrow poetic lines of two and three stresses and escape from a "sense of constriction."

The fulfilling of this need would produce a shift of style in *Field Work* (1979), the next volume. Meanwhile, in the much shorter part 2 of *North* Heaney had already used a style in a lineage with that of "Docker" in *Death of a Naturalist* and "The Other Side" in *Wintering Out.* In *North,* "Whatever You Say Say Nothing" is characterized by a contemporary, colloquial, ironic idiom: "I'm writing just after an encounter / With an English journalist in search of 'views / On the Irish thing.'" The four-part poem sardonically and despairingly comments on the warped, muted, and false speech produced by the divided culture and hatred in Ulster. The six-poem sequence "Singing School," which comprises the major part of part 2, presents key moments in the writer's development, stabs of consciousness beginning with the homesickness at St. Columb's upon first being away from home. A central theme is the conflict between art and actuality as exacerbated by life in Northern Ireland. No easy solution exists for the writer. In the final poem the setting is Wicklow, with the speaker aware of having missed "The once-in-a-lifetime portent," some transcendent illumination, "The comet's pulsing rose." "Neither internee nor informer," he has become an inner "émigré," "a wood-kerne [a renegade resister of the colonizers of Ulster] / Escaped from the massacre" who feels "Every wind that blows." Evoked is a note of self-criticism and lost opportunity; the poet is suspended in a difficult position, "weighing and weighing / My responsible *tristia.*"

Heaney's ambiguous status as an "émigré" may well have contributed to the rather cool,

even sour, reception of *North* by critics in Belfast. The reception elsewhere, however, was mostly positive as in Anthony Thwaite's praise in the *Times Literary Supplement* of the "pure and scrupulous tact" of the poems. "They are solid, beautifully wrought." Popular response is measurable by the six thousand copies sold in the first month; also the book won the W. H. Smith Award and the Duff Cooper Prize, which was presented, in accordance with Heaney's wishes, by Robert Lowell. It was also the Poetry Book Society choice.

In 1975, Heaney returned to teaching, assuming a position at Caryfort College, a teacher-training institution in Dublin, where he became head of the English department. In the following year, after four years in Glanmore, he and his family moved to Dublin, acquiring a house along the bay, about halfway between the center of the city and Dun Laoghaire. Meanwhile, Heaney kept up his transatlantic ties, frequently giving readings of his poems in America. The connection with America became stronger after 1981, when he resigned his position at Caryfort College and began in February 1982 a five-year arrangement to teach each spring semester at Harvard, where he had already taught in the spring semester of 1979. The arrangement is now permanent, with Heaney acquiring the title Boylston Professor of Rhetoric and Oratory. Yet another tie with America was Robert Lowell, with whom the Heaneys became close during the last few years of Lowell's life.

Lowell's poetry, indeed, seems to have had a considerable influence on the style of Heaney's *Field Work.* In this volume Heaney wished to change the note of his verse: "I was hoping I could get a technique to fortify the quotidian into a work." He desired to include elements of his "usual nature," his more social, convivial self. "Hence," he says, "the more domestic love poems." For these, Heaney had the example of Lowell's Lizzie and Harriet poems along with the American poet's work generally. Lowell's manner does not obtrude but, rather, colors Heaney's own procedures with a subliminal presence. One catches it perhaps in the acutely realized quotidian detail of "The refrigerator whinnied into silence" in "The Skunk" or in "The Otter" in the deft touch of the colloquial word "smashing" in "I loved your wet head and smashing crawl, / Your fine swimmer's back and shoulders" and in the natural fluency of the varied line lengths of the unrhymed four-line stanzas of this poem. The ease and control of the versification are paral-

Successive drafts for "North" (Collection of Seamus Heaney): Draft 1

Northerners

NORTH ~~ATLANTIC~~ NTIC

I returned to that long strand,
curved like a ~~shod,~~ hammered under light, *the beaten shod of the bay*
and found only the secular
powers of the Atlantic thundering. *~~towards~~*

I faced the unmagical
invitations of Iceland,
the pathetic colonies ~~nf~~
of Greenland

And suddenly those ~~beautiful~~ *fabulous*
adventurers, those lying
in Orkney and Dublin
measured against their long

swords' rusting, those in the solid
belly of ~~iron~~ stone ships,
those hacked and glinting
in the gravel of thawed streams

were ocean-deafened voices
warning me off, cursing
the mysterium of water.
The longship's swimming tongue

instructed me
~~against epiphanies —~~ *it said Their looms running*
geography and trade,
thick-witted couplings and revenges, *~~believe both~~*

the hatreds and the ~~terror~~ *terror*
of the althing, lies and women,
exhaustions nominated peace,
~~poets~~ incubating the spilled blood.

Heaney

Draft 3

NORTH ATLANTIC

I returned to that long strand,
curved like a shod, hammered under light,
and found only the secular
powers of the Atlantic thundering.

I faced the unmagical
invitations of Iceland,
the pathetic colonies ~~nf~~
of Greenland

And suddenly those beautiful
adventurers, those lying
in Orkney and Dublin
measured against their long

swords' rusting, those in the solid
belly of ~~iron~~ stone ships,
those hacked and glinting
in the gravel of thawed streams

were ocean-deafened voices
warning me off, cursing
the mysterium of water.
The longship's swimming tongue

instructed me
against epiphanies —
geography and trade,
thick-witted couplings and revenges,

the hatreds and the terror
of the althing, lies and women,
exhaustions nominated peace,
poets incubating the spilled blood.

Draft 2

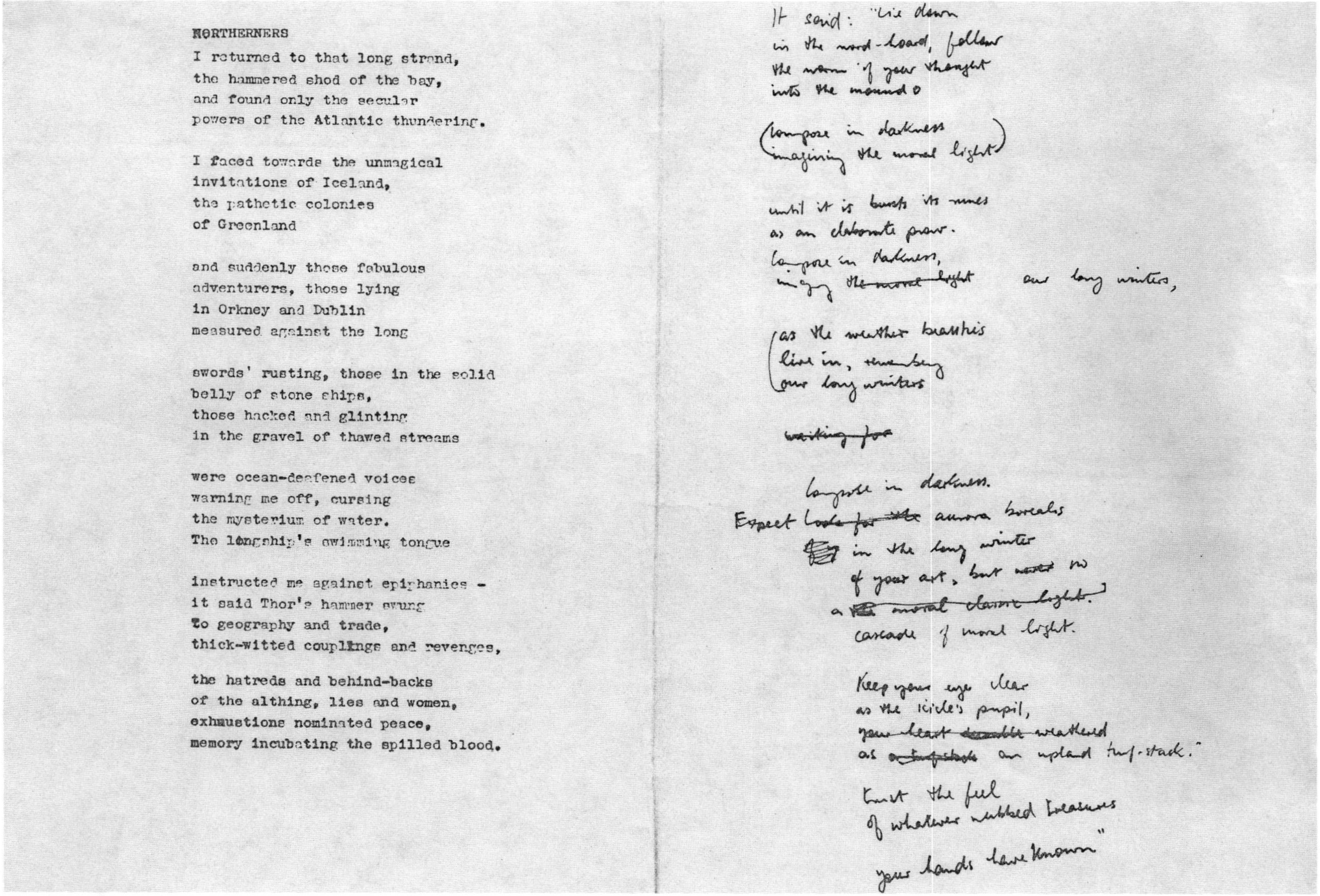

NORTHERNERS

I returned to that long strand,
the hammered shod of the bay,
and found only the secular
powers of the Atlantic thundering.

I faced towards the unmagical
invitations of Iceland,
the pathetic colonies
of Greenland

and suddenly those fabulous
adventurers, those lying
in Orkney and Dublin
measured against the long

swords' rusting, those in the solid
belly of stone ships,
those hacked and glinting
in the gravel of thawed streams

were ocean-deafened voices
warning me off, cursing
the mysterium of water.
The longship's swimming tongue

instructed me against epiphanies -
it said Thor's hammer swung
to geography and trade,
thick-witted couplings and revenges,

the hatreds and behind-backs
of the althing, lies and women,
exhaustion nominated peace,
memory incubating the spilled blood.

Draft 4

NORTH

I returned to a long strand,
the hammered shod of a bay,
and found only the secular
powers of the Atlantic thundering.

I faced towards the unmagical
invitations of Iceland,
the pathetic colonies
of Greenland
and suddenly/those fabulous
viking adventurers,/those lying
in Orkney and Dublin/
measured against/their long swords

rusting,/those in the solid
belly of stone ships,
those hacked and glinting
in the gravel of thawed streams
were ocean-deafened voices
warning me, *that* cursing *the mystery*
mythique of violence.
the mysterium of water.
The longship's swimming tongue
declared
instructed me against epiphanies -
it said Thor's hammer swung
to geography and trade,
thick-witted couplings and revenges,

the hatreds and behind-backs
of the althing, lies and women,
exhaustions nominated peace,
memory incubating the spilled blood.

It said:"Lie down
in the word-hoard, follow
the worm of your thought
into the mound.

Compose in darkness.
Expect aurora borealis
in the long *winter* of your art
but no cascade of metal light.

Keep your eye clear
as the icicle's *purl, like to the icicle,*
trust the feel of whatever nubbed
treasure your hands have known."

NORTH

I returned to a long strand,
the hammered shod of a bay,
and found only the secular
powers/of the Atlantic *A* thundering.

I faced the unmagical
invitations of Iceland,
the pathetic colonies
of Greenland, and suddenly

those fabulous raiders,
those lying in Orkney and Dublin
measured against
their long swords rusting,

Those in the solid
belly of stone ships,
those hacked and glinting
in the gravel of thawed streams

were ocean-deafened voices
warning me, *cursing the necessary* *lifted again*
mystique of violence, *in silence and sopping*
The long-ship's swimming tongue

declared against epiphanies - *was* *lift-out gathered* *tongues with knowledge -*
it said Thor's hammer swung
to geography and trade,
thick-witted couplings and revenges,

the hatreds and behind-backs
of the althing, lies and women,
exhaustions nominated peace,
memory incubating the spilled blood.

It said,"Lie down
in the word-hoard, follow *tongue into*
the worm of your thought *of the shuttles and gleam*
into the mound. *of your brain's cold furrows*

Compose in darkness.
Expect aurora borealis
in the long foray of your art
but no cascade of light.

Keep your eye clear
as the blep of the icicle,
trust *whatever* *of whatever nubbed treasure*
treasure/your hands have known."

leled by the tact in the handling of tone which so gracefully combines love, admiration, tenderness, and sensuality while avoiding mawkishness in the intimate expression. The husband, holding his wife in his embrace, thinks of her as "my palpable, lithe / Otter of memory / In the pool of the moment." The indelible vividness of the physicality retained in the memory ("And suddenly you're out, / Back again, intent as ever, / Heavy and frisky in your freshened pelt, / Printing the stones") adds to the intensity of the present moment. This otter is sublimely erotic. Similarly, in "The Skunk" the memory of one of those black-and-white creatures seen when the speaker was alone in California "came back to me last night, stirred / By the sootfall of your things at bedtime, / Your head-down, tail-up hunt in a bottom drawer / For the black plunge-line nightdress."

Not all these marriage poems (as Heaney has referred to them) strike this sensual, erotic note: "Polder" concerns an embrace of reconciliation following a "sudden outburst and . . . squalls"; "A Dream of Jealousy" relates a dream of sexual transgression and unatonable guilt; the four-part title poem "Field Work" leads through a subtle skein of images (circles and rings, vaccination mark, moon, sunflower) toward a private ritual of initiation that marks the back of the wife's hand with the "sticky juice" of a flowering currant leaf and earth mold, "like a birthmark," so that "stained, stained / to perfection," she is identified in her complex association with nature. These love poems frequently hint at or explicitly draw a linguistic or poetic relation, providing a distancing effect that lowers the threat of sentimentality. "Polder," for instance, plays metaphorically on the Dutch title word for a piece of reclaimed land and on two other words of Dutch origin, *bosom* and *fathom*. In "The Harvest Bow," the plaited object of the title could have, the speaker says, the motto "the end of art is peace"; from it he gleans *the unsaid off the palpable.* And the palpable physicality of the "otter" in its poem is caught not only in the memory but in the language of the poem, "Printing the stones" (a reminder in this respect of Ted Hughes's "The Thought-Fox," in which the "hot stink of fox" attains its verbal immediacy as "The page is printed").

This concern with memory and the present, as well as with the relation between nature and language, helps to shape the centerpiece of *Field Work*, the Glanmore sonnet sequence, ten intricately interwoven poems which both ruminate on

and quietly celebrate nature and the art of poetry. The sequence takes advantage of the withdrawal to Glanmore to be deliberately rural and pastoral. The mode follows an ancient tradition: when Heaney claims in the first sonnet that art is a "paradigm of earth new from the lathe / Of ploughs," he speaks in the lineage of Theocritus and Virgil. He also speaks in the lineage of his own early poems—for the image is akin to that of digging with his pen in the *Death of a Naturalist* poem "Digging." What he wants from the "hedge-school of Glanmore" is "to raise / A voice caught back off slug-horn and slow chanter / That might continue, hold, dispel, appease." He desires in this second sonnet a tactile immediacy of language in keeping with the mystery in things: "Sensings, mountings from the hiding places, / Words entering almost the sense of touch." In the fifth sonnet the speaker is an "etymologist of roots and graftings." Childhood sensings resonate in the memory and stir a Wordsworthian nostalgia for the fresh intensity of early experience: "I fall back to my tree-house and would crouch / Where small buds shoot and flourish in the hush." Woven into the sonnets is a sacramental view of the earth that characterizes much of Heaney's poetry. In sonnet 3, however, indulgence in the Wordsworthian is humorously deflated when the husband begins to refer to Dorothy and William and the wife interrupts: "You're not going to compare us two . . . ?"

The husband has his wife much in mind in these poems, particularly in the final three. In sonnet 8 a thunderstorm brings thoughts of death and old violences. He ponders the mysterious force that moves through things: "What welters through this dark hush on the crops?" Then his mind leaps to a memory of an old woman in France rocking "A mongol [child] in her lap" as she sang, and suddenly this image of human care set against thoughts of death and obscure forces in nature stirs him to desire and arousal: "Come to me quick, I am upstairs shaking. / My all of you birchwood in lightning." In sonnet 9 domestic and pastoral tranquillity is upset by a black rat swaying "on the briar" outside the kitchen window "like infected fruit" and disturbing the poet's wife. The "burnished bay tree at the gate, / Classical," with all its literary associations, is "hung with the reek of silage." Considering the thought of "Rats speared in the sweat and dust of threshing," the speaker suddenly and urgently asks, "What is my apology for poetry?" The justification would seem to be poetry's human pur-

Dust jacket for the American edition of Heaney's 1980 book, which gathers poems published in Death of a Naturalist, Door into the Dark, Wintering Out, *and* North

pose: to come to terms in the art of the poem with the very disruptive elements in experience that violate classical decorum. Poetry clarifies, renews, redeems. When at the end of the sonnet the husband sees his wife in a strange new perspective—her face through the briar and window "Haunts like a new moon glimpsed through tangled glass"—the domestic is transfigured as the husband has a sudden vision of his wife's beauty and mystery.

In the final sonnet of the sequence the relationship of the couple acquires further definition through their kinship with literary and mythic pairs: "Lorenzo and Jessica in a cold climate. / Diarmid and Grainne waiting to be found." Images of threat, isolation, exposure, and mortality mark the speaker's dream of the pair's sleeping on Donegal turf banks in a drizzle until the dreaming shifts to the first night they spent together "in that hotel / When you came with your deliberate kiss" (Heaney has Thomas Wyatt's "They Flee from Me" in mind here). Love and the erotic assume their intensity against the transient and un-

certain. The poem arrives at complex recognitions of the pain as well as loveliness involved in sex, of the separateness of as well as the bond between the two beings, and of the similarity of sexual release to a deathlike repose: the last line, "The respite in our dewy dreaming faces," recalls the earlier line describing the lovers sleeping in Donegal "Like breathing effigies on a raised ground." The whole sequence weaves together its complex of themes concerning nature, language, memory, poetry, and love. In these sonnets, so masterfully and fluently fulfilled, poetry does seem to redeem the painful, disrupting contingencies of existence. Glanmore becomes the focus for a series of meditations on timeless, universal issues, while the poems themselves become an unself-conscious extension of a traditional mode.

The troubles in Ulster are offstage in this sequence, but "an army helicopter patrolling" intrudes in "Triptych" recalling "The helicopter shadowing our march at Newry," while "The Toome Road" recalls a convoy of armored cars that invaded the early morning rural quiet. The impact of the conflict in the North, however, seems most deeply felt when it has struck down individuals close to the poet, as in three elegies, one for a cousin and each of the others for a friend. The elegiac mode is congenial to Heaney's sensitivity to human loss and his compassion for victims, whether Bog People, abused children, women, or those slain in the long history of struggle in Ireland. Although these three poems convey an understated anger and bitterness, their main function is to mourn and to celebrate the vital individuality of the three senselessly killed men—the shy, independent eel fisherman in "Casualty," the sensitive farmer cousin in "The Strand at Lough Beg," who in life was "scared to find spent cartridges" of hunters on his way "to fetch the cows," and the clownish "Prince of no-man's land" in "A Postcard from North Antrim," who had dropped out, then joined the hippy scene in Sausalito before returning to be a social worker in Belfast and stop with his "candid forehead" a "pointblank teatime bullet." Heaney seems much more comfortable with this function of poetry than with the notion that poetry can change things socially and politically.

In three other elegies Heaney pays tribute to two poets and a musician. These artists are models of creative commitment and chance taking, especially Robert Lowell, memorialized in "Elegy," himself "the master elegist" whose music set a course "wilfully across / the ungovernable and dangerous," and one hears in this poem as part of its praise deliberate imitations of Lowell's music, as in "You drank America / like the heart's / iron vodka." Another model is the gifted composer and chief impetus in the recent revival of Irish music honored in "In Memoriam Sean O'Riada," who is referred to as "trusting the gift, / risking gift's undertow." The tribute to the minor poet who died in the trenches of World War I, "In Memoriam Francis Ledwidge," reaches back for an understanding of a figure before Heaney's time who is "our dead enigma," a Catholic who left his natural locale to die in a "Tommy's uniform," in whom "all the strains / Criss-cross in useless equilibrium." The poem laments the waste and the loss of a lyrical voice; poetry, not military action, is the proper sphere for the poet.

Yet *Field Work* ends not on the elegiac note of this poem but with "Ugalino," a translation from cantos 32 and 33 of Dante's *Inferno*. Earlier, in the more humorous vein of "An Afterwards," the poet's wife "would plunge all poets in the ninth circle," to backbite one another "Like

Ugalino on Archbishop Roger." "Ugalino," however, unsparingly renders the horror of Dante's deepest level of depravity. As depiction of evil it points to the rage with which poetry must contend, and as poetry it points to imperatives other than the lyric. Dante's whole *Commedia* aims at a transcendent peace and places in perspective Heaney's much more modest attempt to achieve peace as the end of art.

Generally, reviewers of *Field Work* treated Heaney as a major figure. Harold Bloom in his *Times Literary Supplement* review, after weighing Heaney's achievement by favorably comparing it with the admittedly superior achievements of William Butler Yeats, Wallace Stevens, Walt Whitman, and other major poets in their fortieth years, goes on to wonder "how remarkable a poet [he] may yet become, if he can continue the steady growth of an art as deliberate, as restrained, and yet as authoritative and universal as the poems of *Field Work*." Denis Donoghue in his front-page review in the *New York Times Book Review* is of like mind: Heaney "has learned his trade so well that it is now a second nature wonderfully responsive to his first. And the proof is in *Field Work*, a superb book, the most eloquent and far-reaching book he has written." Helen Vendler, too, in her long essay in the *New Yorker* treats Heaney as a poet of important stature. Representing the mostly favorable British response is Alan Brownjohn in *Encounter*: *Field Work* is "Heaney's most varied and startling collection, balancing courage and affirmation with a lurking uneasiness and foreboding; and showing increasingly impressive technical range and control."

At the other and less populated end of the critical spectrum one finds Calvin Bedient in *Parnassus* and Marjorie Perloff in the *Washington Post Book World* complaining that Heaney lacks a firm point of view and depth. He is for Bedient only "potato deep" and, with few exceptions, "a poet merely of the desire for profundity"; he offers "deliberate myth-making, not the stab of astonishment." Perloff says that, like Dylan Thomas, he "makes a little substance go a long way" and that "there is not much variation or breadth" in his poems; she also claims that he is too self-consciously "aware that [he] is making a poem." Such negative responses as these—with Bedient's the more persuasive of the two—provide an astringent dose of skepticism against a too-ready trend toward adulation. Heaney, after all, has at times reveled indulgently in the descriptive powers of what John Montague has called his "extraor-

Dust jacket for Heaney's 1984 book that Blake Morrison called "intense, superstitious, pantheistic, even mystical, and at times very difficult to decipher"

dinary auditory and tactile imagination"—but given such powers who would always be able to avoid temptation? Also, he has moved precariously along the edges of nostalgia and sentiment. Still, Bedient, who wishes for greater passion and daring, a leap beyond what Heaney does so modestly and readily, qualifies his basically negative stance by saying that the poet's strength lies in "making most of real but limited advantages."

Other critics see a much wider range of advantages, of course, but at a minimum those advantages would have to include an authentic and trustworthy voice and a superlative technique in using the words and music of poetry for capturing "the music of what happens" ("Song"). One should not expect to find in Heaney a philosophical poet; he is not like Wallace Stevens an "inquisitor of structures." As he has said, "I don't think my intelligence is naturally analytic or political." He probes feelings, states of consciousness,

being. Against the burden of memory and guilt, of longings, responsibilities, and loyalties, of the complexities of love and the human relationship to nature, he searches for moments of perfected being, of accord. Finally, his work represents an assertion, or reassertion, of the traditional (as currently in painting one notices a reassertion of the representational).

Significantly, both Bloom and Bedient single out for praise "The Harvest Bow," a poem very much in the pastoral tradition: Bedient discovers "unusual scope and power in the ending"; Bloom calls it a "perfect lyric," Heaney's "masterpiece so far." "Song," a briefer lyric, also belongs to this tradition. Here is the second of its two stanzas:

> There are the mud-flowers of dialect
> And the immortelles of perfect pitch
> And that moment when the bird sings very close
> To the music of what happens.

We hear Heaney's voice surely, but the poem also seems timeless in style, a contemporary variation within a venerable lineage.

Following *Field Work* Heaney published *Selected Poems 1965-1975* and *Preoccupations: Selected Prose*, both in 1980, and then in 1982 he received the twelve-thousand-dollar biennial Bennett Award sponsored by the *Hudson Review*. Also in 1982 Queen's University, Belfast, his alma mater, conferred upon him an Honorary Doctor of Letters degree. *Preoccupations* offers candid and engaging accounts of his poetic origins and development; the critical essays on other poets are also revealing of his own interests. One comes from the book with a heightened sense of Heaney's whole poetic enterprise.

Another of his preoccupations has been the medieval Irish work *Buile Suibhne*, which concerns the mad king Sweeney who, cursed by the cleric Ronan for having flung a psalter into a lake, is transformed into a bird-man and undergoes exile, lonely wandering, and physical hardships. Heaney's vividly rendered English version of the work, *Sweeney Astray* (1984), reveals a heartfelt affinity with the dispossessed king who responds with such acute sensitivity, poetic accuracy, and imaginative force to his landscape. His plight has made Sweeney a connoisseur of pain and the few sensuous pleasures he derives from nature, its lovely watercresses, for example.

In 1984 Heaney published *Station Island*, his first collection of new poems since *Field Work* in

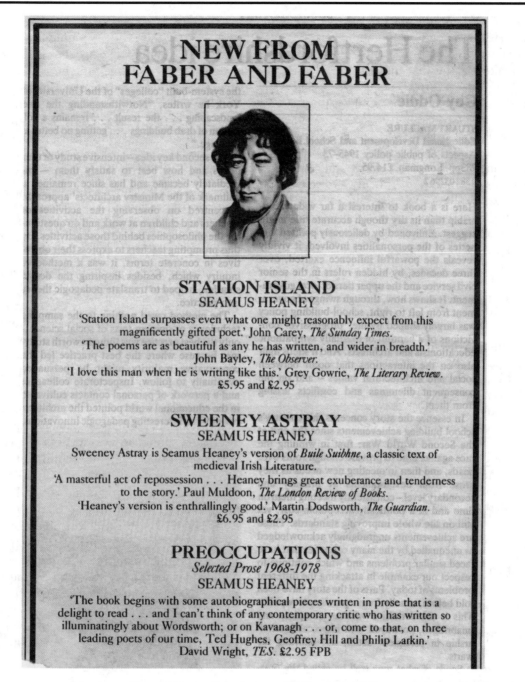

Times Literary Supplement, *30 November 1984*

1979. These poems exhibit, for one thing, the gift for presenting objects with the imagistic precision that one finds in his work from the beginning. Indeed, a lobster in "Away From It All"—"articulate twigs, a rainy stone / the colour of sunk munitions"—would not be out of place in *Death of a Naturalist,* the first volume. *Station Island* is characterized too by the recurring sympathies and pieties, the hauntings, inklings, and plangent memories, the yearnings and epiphanies encountered in the earlier volumes. Heaney in these poems courts, as he has so often before, the mythic and the mystical. Threading its way through this volume also is a personal drama of guilt, lost innocence, and lost moral and religious certainty played against the redemptions of love, faith in the integrity of craft and of dedicated individuals, and ties with the universal forces operating in nature and history.

The volume is composed of three parts: a

gathering of various poems very much in keeping with Heaney's oeuvre; "Station Island," a twelve-part sequence set on a three-day pilgrimage of penitential fasting and prayer at Lough Derg, where the pilgrim encounters would-be alter egos, as Heaney referred to them at a reading, ghosts as diverse as a shopkeeper victim of sectarian violence, a priest, and James Joyce—all reminiscent of Dante's meetings with souls of the dead in the *Divine Comedy*; and "Sweeney Redivius," a series of poems "voiced for Sweeney," as Heaney says in a note, a rich byproduct of Heaney's translation of the *Buile Suibhne*. That the poet took the title of the central sequence for the whole volume points to its importance. Here he assumes a confessional stance ("as usual, I had somehow broken / covenants, and failed an obligation") and expresses feelings of guilt, wry self-criticism, inadequacy, and remorse.

In general, the tone is devout and properly purgatorial, which is no doubt partly what prompted Blake Morrison to say in his *Times Literary Supplement* review that *Station Island* "is a religious book and no getting around it—intense, superstitious, pantheistic, even mystical, and at times very difficult to decipher. . . . it gives us a rather different poet from the one we thought we knew." Actually, the poet is not very different: we still hear the essential Heaney voice (even in some of the words he puts in Joyce's mouth) and find not unusual variations on his central themes. Also, the religious intensity is undercut in the final section of the "Station Island" sequence when Joyce deflates the persona's penitential solemnity: "And don't be so earnest, / let others wear the sackcloth and ashes." Much of the elusiveness dissolves, too, so that the sequence becomes a complex though accessible narrative concerned not only with spiritual inadequacy, which includes a failure of personal response to the pattern of violence in the North, but also with atonement. The sequence is also a pilgrimage of the persona as poet coming to terms with himself, attempting to perfect his artistic sensibility. It is fitting in this regard that his penance is to translate a poem by Saint John of the Cross, which is just what he does in section 9—the spiritual and poetic acts thus conjoined. He is then ready for the bracing advice he receives from Joyce, the aesthetic father figure.

It is clear from this advice that Heaney sees the need for a new beginning, a transcendence beyond the stage of his present accomplishment.

Joyce advises greater daring: "Take off from here"; "Let go, let fly"; "it's time to swim / out on your own." While the reviews of *Station Island* have generally acclaimed the book, hints of reservation arise, as when Nicholas Christopher in the *New York Times Book Review*, after saying that "it is clear that we are in the hands of a master," adds, "He makes it all seem too easy." Blake Morrison in his *Times Literary Supplement* review is more pointedly qualified in his acclaim when he says of part 1 of the volume that "we get roughly what we were expecting, though a bit less than we might have hoped" and that some of the poems "are familiar because they echo, perhaps too closely, earlier treatments of the same theme."

Nevertheless, Heaney, whatever the criticism, continues to produce a new volume of poems every few years. *The Haw Lantern* (1987) maintains the incisively sensual and lyrical voice that is so unmistakably his. It has drawn mixed reviews: some, as usual, glowing, and some registering disappointment, complaining that the poet is too entrenched in his customary strategies. In 1991 another volume, *Seeing Things*, appeared. Meanwhile, his popularity remains high as he accumulates honors and distinctions. In 1990 he received one of six Lannam Foundation awards of thirty-five thousand dollars. In 1989 he was elected professor of poetry at Oxford University—an Irishman honored at one of the pinnacles of the British establishment. This mark of status has rankled some of his Irish peers, inspiring in one case a scathing pamphlet damning Heaney for being a darling of the English reading public (as well as of American academics), but then he is in a long tradition of Irish writers who have flourished in the British literary scene, showing the Britons new possibilities for poetry in their mother tongue.

Interviews:

Seamus Deane, "Unhappy and at Home," *Crane Bag*, 1, no. 1 (1977): 61-67;

James Randall, "An Interview with Seamus Heaney," *Ploughshares*, 5, no. 3 (1979): 7-22;

John Haffenden, *Viewpoints: Poets in Conversation with John Haffenden* (London & Boston: Faber & Faber, 1981), pp. 57-75;

Frank Kinahan, "An Interview with Seamus Heaney," *Critical Inquiry*, 8 (Spring 1982): 405-414;

June Beisch, "An Interview with Seamus Heaney," *Literary Review*, 29 (Winter 1986): 31-42.

References:

A. Alvarez, "A Fine Way with the Language," *New York Review of Books*, (6 March 1980): 16-17;

Alvarez, "Homo Faber," *Observer*, 22 June 1969;

Anthony Bailey, "A Gift for Being in Touch," *Quest* (January-February 1978): 38-46, 92-93;

Calvin Bedient, "The Music of What Happens," *Parnassus*, 8 (Fall/Winter 1979): 109-122;

Harold Bloom, "The Voices of Kinship," *Times Literary Supplement*, 8 February 1980, pp. 137-138;

Edward Broadbridge, ed., *Seamus Heaney* (Copenhagen: Danmarks Radio, 1977);

Terence Brown, "Four New Voices: Poets of the Present," in *Northern Voices: Poets from Ulster* (Totowa, N.J.: Rowman & Littlefield, 1975; Dublin: Gill & Macmillan, 1975), pp. 171-213;

Robert Buttel, *Seamus Heaney* (Lewisburg, Pa.: Bucknell University Press, 1975);

Ciaran Carson, "Escaped from the Massacre?," *Honest Ulsterman*, 50 (Winter 1975): 183-186;

William Cookson and Peter Dale, eds., *Agenda*, Seamus Heaney Fiftieth Birthday Issue, 27 (Spring 1989);

Neil Corcoran, *Seamus Heaney* (London & Boston: Faber & Faber, 1986);

Tony Curtis, ed., *The Art of Seamus Heaney* (Bridgend, Mid Glamorgen: Poetry Wales Press, 1982);

Denis Donoghue, "Poets Who Have Learned Their Trade," *New York Times Book Review*, 2 December 1979, pp. 1, 45-46;

Douglas Dunn, "Mañana Is Now," *Encounter*, 45 (November 1975): 76-81;

Irwin Ehrenpreis, "Digging In," *New York Review of Books*, 8 (October 1981): 45-46;

John Wilson Foster, "The Poetry of Seamus Heaney," *Critical Quarterly*, 16 (Spring 1974): 35-48;

Mark Patrick Hederman, "Seamus Heaney: The Reluctant Poet," *Crane Bag*, 3, no. 2 (1979): 61-69;

Robert H. Henigan, "The Tollund Man on Bogside: Seamus Heaney's Political Objective Correlative," *Publications of the Arkansas Philological Association,* 7 (Fall 1981): 48-60;

Benedict Kiely, "A Raid into Dark Corners: The Poems of Seamus Heaney," *Hollins Critic,* 7 (October 1970): 1-12;

Edna Longley, "Fire and Air," *Honest Ulsterman,* 50 (Winter 1975): 179-183;

Longley, "Heaney: Poet as Critic," *Fortnight* (December 1980): 15-16;

Longley, "Stars and Horses, Pigs and Trees," *Crane Bag,* 3, no. 2 (1979):

Michael Longley, "Poetry," in *Causeway: The Arts in Ulster,* edited by Longley (Belfast: Arts Council of Northern Ireland, 1971), pp. 95-109;

Derek Mahon, "Poetry in Northern Ireland," *Twentieth Century Studies* (November 1970): 89-93;

Arthur E. Mcguinness, "The Craft of Diction: Revision in Seamus Heaney's Poems," in *Image and Illusion: Anglo-Irish Literature and its Contexts,* edited by Maurice Harmon (Portmarnock, County Dublin: Wolfhound Press, 1979), pp. 62-91;

Blake Morrison, *Seamus Heaney* (New York & London: Methuen, 1982);

Darcy O'Brien, "Seamus Heaney and Wordsworth: A Correspondent Breeze," in *The Nature of Identity: Essays Presented to Donald E. Haydon by the Graduate Faculty of Modern Letters,* edited by William Weathers (Tulsa: University of Tulsa Press, 1981), pp. 37-46;

Jay Parini, "Seamus Heaney: The Ground Possessed," *Southern Review,* 16 (Winter 1979): 100-123;

Marjorie Perloff, "Seamus Heaney: Peat, Politics and Poetry," *Washington Post Book World,* 25 January 1981, pp. 5, 11;

Salmagundi (Special Feature: Seamus Heaney), 80 (Fall 1988): 3-101;

Anthony Thwaite, "Neighborly Murders," *Times Literary Supplement,* 1 August 1975, p. 866;

Helen Vendler, "The Music of What Happens," *New Yorker,* 57 (28 September 1981): 146-157;

Andrew Waterman, "Ulsterectomy," in *Best of the Poetry Year 6,* edited by Dannie Abse (London: Robson, 1979), pp. 42-57.

Geoffrey Hill

(18 June 1932 -   )

This entry was written by Vincent B. Sherry, Jr. (Villanova University) for
DLB 40: Poets of Great Britain and Ireland Since 1960: Part One.

BOOKS: [Poems], Fantasy Poets, no. 11 (Oxford: Fantasy Press, 1952);

For the Unfallen: Poems 1952-1958 (London: Deutsch, 1959; Chester Springs, Pa.: Dufour, 1960);

Preghiere (Leeds: Northern House, 1964);

Penguin Modern Poets 8, by Hill, Edwin Brock, and Stevie Smith (Harmondsworth: Penguin, 1966);

King Log (London: Deutsch, 1968; Chester Springs, Pa.: Dufour, 1968);

Mercian Hymns (London: Deutsch, 1971);

Somewhere Is Such a Kingdom: Poems 1952-1971 (Boston: Houghton Mifflin, 1975);

Brand: A Version for the Stage, adapted from Henrik Ibsen's play (London: Heinemann, 1978; revised edition, Minneapolis: University of Minnesota Press, 1981);

Tenebrae (London: Deutsch, 1978; Boston: Houghton Mifflin, 1979);

The Mystery of the Charity of Charles Péguy (London: Agenda/Deustsch, 1983; New York: Oxford University Press, 1984);

The Lords of Limit: Essays on Literature and Ideas (London: Deutsch, 1984; New York: Oxford University Press, 1984);

Collected Poems (Harmondsworth: Penguin, 1985; New York: Oxford University Press, 1986);

The Enemy's Country (Oxford: Clarendon Press, 1991).

PLAY PRODUCTION: *Brand*, adapted from Henrik Ibsen's play, London, National Theatre, April 1978.

RECORDING: *The Poetry and Voice of Geoffrey Hill*, Caedmon, 1979.

OTHER: "Isaac Rosenberg" and "Allen Tate," in *Concise Encyclopedia of English and American Poets and Poetry*, edited by Stephen Spender and Donald Hall (London: Hutchinson, 1963), pp. 278, 326-327.

© *Jerry Bauer*

SELECTED PERIODICAL PUBLICATIONS—UNCOLLECTED:

POETRY

"Homo Homini Lupus: after Anne Hébert's 'Les Offensés,' " *Agenda*, 15 (Winter 1977-1978): 64.

NONFICTION

"Letter from Oxford," *London Magazine*, 1 (May 1954): 71-75;

"Robert Lowell: Contrasts and Repetitions," *Essays in Criticism*, 13 (1963): 188-197;

"The Dream of Reason" [on William Empson], *Essays in Criticism*, 14 (1964): 91-101;

" 'I in Another Place': Homage to Keith Douglas," *Stand*, 6, no. 4 (1964): 6-13;

" 'The Conscious Mind's Intelligible Structure': A Debate," *Agenda*, 9-10 (Autumn-Winter 1971-1972): 14-23;

"Gurney's Hobby," *Essays in Criticism*, 34 (April 1984): 97-128;

"C. H. Sisson," *PN Review 39*, 11, no. 1 (1984): 11-15.

Geoffrey Hill is a poet with a capacity for paradox. He combines the two opposing tendencies of British verse in the postwar period, displaying an excellent formal control, like the Movement poets of the 1950s, and an awareness of the violence of language in relation to history, like Ted Hughes and others writing since the 1960s. But Hill has lived largely apart from the public world of literary trends, lecturing and writing as an academic on subjects ranging from Renaissance literature to the religious dimensions of art. A solitary perfectionist, he has fashioned poems with the solidity, gravity, and finality of Roman inscriptions. His impulse toward technical experimentation, his concern with history and religion, his touches of cosmopolitan irony: these are the traits of a neomodernist poetry that is complex, richly allusive, formally innovative.

Geoffrey William Hill was born to William George and Hilda Beatrice Hands Hill in Bromsgrove, a small market town in Worcestershire; he was raised in the adjacent village of Fairfield, where his father served as a police constable. He attended the local Church of England school and began singing in the choir when he was seven, an experience often echoed in his poetic use of liturgical song. An only child, he developed early on the habit of going for long walks alone. Deliberating and composing poems while walking was a later practice he anticipated as an adolescent, carrying Oscar Williams's *A Little Treasury of Modern Poetry* (1946) "in my jacket pocket all over Worcestershire for several years until it disintegrated: I think there was probably a time when I knew every poem in that anthology by heart."

Hill had developed a strong feeling of locality in Worcestershire, and when he went up to Oxford in 1950 to read English, he felt "socially very much isolated and ill-at-ease." The literary friendships that would shape the Movement from Oxford, the formative triangle of Philip Larkin, John Wain, and Kingsley Amis, had already made room for the newer, looser confederation of A. Alvaraz, Adrian Mitchell, George Mac-Beth, Alan Brownjohn, and Anthony Thwaite.

Although Hill published poems in the Oxford magazine *Isis*, he only skirted the periphery of the literary society. He immersed himself instead in the traditional English language and literature syllabus of the time. Studious, disciplined, he let his poems grow as a slow, interiorized process. But as poems appeared in *Isis*, and another was broadcast on the BBC Home Service, he drew the attention of Donald Hall, then president of the Oxford University Poetry Society, who would become his friend, sympathetic critic, and influential advocate for his work.

Hill's poetry combines the conventional and experimental impulses in postwar verse. He can, for example, use fixed forms to accommodate rhythms and syntax that are fractured, psychologically elliptical, often elusive. The poems work symbolically but mysteriously, avoiding final statements and single positions, displaying a strong taste for paradox. An active paradox in his work is the contrast between its disciplined formal qualities and its violent historical content, the various wars and tyrannies of English, European, and American history. With the American poet Allen Tate, Hill utters the "formal pledge" of art against "aimless power," maintaining that poetic form may stand as a model of order against the larger, darker forces of a chaotic history or a void metaphysics. Morality is not preached in his poetry, then, but practiced in the art of writing it: "Poetry is responsible. It's a form of responsible behaviour, not a directive. It is an exemplary exercise."

In 1952, as Hill was entering his third year at the university, Hall suggested that he submit poems to the Fantasy Press, founded earlier that year at Oxford to bring out work by beginning poets (including Elizabeth Jennings, Thom Gunn, and Donald Davie). A pamphlet of five poems was published that autumn. This early work is highly self-conscious, concerned with the role of the poet and the nature of poetry, studied in prosody and regulated in form. But the affinities with the tight formalism of the Movement end where the mythic resonance and allusive range begin, reminding one more of Isaac Rosenberg and William Blake, poets he acknowledges in two of the poems. His apprenticeship in the Oxford syllabus of traditional literature gave him volume and depth as a poet as well as a sense of his place in literary tradition. "I think of you, as of my heritage," the young poet announces in "To William Dunbar," the first poem in the pamphlet, and four of the five pieces contain titles or epigraphs recognizing older poets.

"Genesis: A Ballad of Christopher Smart" is the centerpiece of the pamphlet. This five-part sequence, which took shape "over a period of weeks in a series of long one-day walks in Worcestershire," conflates the landscape of the poet's childhood with that of Genesis in the Bible. Like God's, the young poet's words create a world. Ironically, Hill fits this ideal conception to the myth of a lost paradise, but, along the same lines, suggests that poetry may assume a Christlike redemptive function, although he will not claim such an office for himself. These shifts in attitude and perspective already show the suitability of the sequence for paradox and dialectic, a potential Hill would realize fully in his later books. He likewise anticipates his later statement, that poetry's moral function lies not in content but in technique, in "God's Little Mountain." Here the poet, swept up into the region of the angels, lacks the grace to tell what he has seen. No visionary prophet, the poet is a craftsman whose art is the revelation, a principle to which the high degree of workmanship in the poems bears witness.

Hall reprinted "Genesis" in an early issue of *Paris Review* and helped to extend Hill's reputation beyond Oxford. But the publication of the pamphlet did not alter Hill's social circumstances at the university. He made several good friends, among them Jonathan Price and Alistair Elliot, but he remained ill at ease socially. He received his B.A. with first-class honors in English in 1953, and remained at Oxford for the following year. In the spring of 1954 he published a "Letter from Oxford" in *London Magazine*, a prose piece that is strangely picturesque and poignant, reflecting both his love of Oxford scenes and his estrangement from Oxford society. "And here, amid so many thousands of young people bent on the pursuit of love and happiness, here is the place of all places on earth to be very lonely and very unhappy." This estrangement, the letter also hints, derived in some part from his class background.

In 1954 Hill was appointed lecturer in English at Leeds University. The academic climate at Leeds was superior; the English department, chaired by Bonamy Dobrée, included eminent scholars such as G. Wilson Knight and Douglas Jefferson. Hill now showed himself as conscientious and scrupulous a lecturer as he was a poet. His courses in Shakespeare and the study of poetry were taught with equal erudition and presence.

To his students he seemed remote, lofty; to many, inspiring. By the late 1950s his weekly lectures became events not to be missed, often attended by students outside the English department. The story goes that young ladies used to sit in the front rows to take down the lectures verbatim, with suitable pauses for Hill's coughs, lingering glances through the windows, snorts of derision, and exclamations. The lectures were difficult, allusive, never linear; they were not constructing a single theory; they were the texture of an individual sensibility that was complex, learned, rich. At the end he would sweep up his notes and return, it seemed, to an aerie of god-like learning from which he descended once a week.

Hill was able to continue writing poetry during the academic term at Leeds, for, composing slowly, he could carry poems in mental drafts while going about his academic work. He married Nancy Whittaker in 1956, and during the 1960s their family grew to four children. Through the 1950s he published poems in *Hudson Review, Poetry, New Statesman*, and the annual P.E.N. anthologies of new poems in 1956, 1957, and 1958. In 1957 the influential anthology *New Poets of England and America*, edited by Hall, Louis Simpson, and Robert Pack, included seven poems by Hill, the youngest British poet in the collection. In 1958 he finished *For the Unfallen: Poems 1952-1958*, which contained three poems from his early pamphlet, and André Deutsch published it in the autumn of 1959.

The new work displays a new, deepened sense of history as well as a continued interest in religion and myth. Thus the title refers to the unfallen in World War II as well as to those unfallen from grace. But the consolations of religion do not diminish the anxieties of history. The violent past, imaged in "The Distant Fury of Battle," still reaches the present and determines it. To this historical determinism there are two attitudes, typically paradoxical, set out in "Solomon's Mines." The past is both a rich resource and an enervating drain on the present. The positive attitude provides mood, title, and persona for "Merlin," where the poet, like the ancient magician-priest, exchanges gifts with the Muse of History, opening with a full-dress ritual invocation: "I will consider the outnumbering dead." But his disenchanted view of history is stronger. In the six-poem sequence "Of Commerce and Society," the mines of history become "The Lowlands of Holland," where the old English folk song provides an image for a continent sunken into its past, its ancient decay manifest in the two world wars, its old order inseparable from its decadence.

Hopes for a new order evoke the figure of the artist-savior in the third poem of the sequence, "The Death of Shelley." But the next extinguishes Shelley's millennial fervor, as the poet, speaking ironically in his own person, apologizes lamely for the Jewish Holocaust; he attributes it to "Jehovah's touchy methods" and pleads "At times it seems not common to explain." Thus the concluding piece, "The Martyrdom of Saint Sebastian," represents the poet as an exhausted aesthete, a victim who "Catches his death in a little flutter / Of plain arrows," where the cliché matches the impotence of the poet's tongue. But explaining history may be only an ideological exercise, and as such more devious than ignoring it. Thus "Requiem for the Plantagenet Kings" suggests that explanations are only eloquent decorations of sordid facts: "Men, in their eloquent fashion, understood" the rationalizations of the Norman takeover. This is the first poem (1955) to display what would become Hill's characteristic syntax—discontinuous, abrasive, jagged: an instrument cutting through eloquence to disclose the hard truths of the skeptic. This severe style prevails in other poems preoccupied with Christianity, myth, history, art, love, and death.

Predictably, several reviewers found this austerity uncongenial, the difficulties insurmountable. Roy Fuller complained of poems "impenetrable and uncommunicative" and disliked the surfaces "from which so much that is human and revealing has been carefully erased." But G. S. Fraser praised the impersonal perfectionism: "Every word, in these poems, compels the mouth to shape it with love and care. I hardly know what the man is like behind the words; but I salute a master rhetorician." In 1960 Dufour Editions brought out the volume in America, where Carolyn Kizer expressed wary approval, conceding the accomplishment but claiming that Hill "had too much acclaim already." But his advocates already included the young Alvarez, who hailed *For the Unfallen* as "one of the three or four important first books of poetry to appear in the fifties," a judgment echoed in retrospect by reviewers of his later books. The first edition sold quickly in England, where it was republished in September 1960, again in June 1971, and in September 1979. It won the E. C. Gregory Award for Poetry in 1961.

Dust jacket for Hill's 1968 book, which includes poems that range remarkably from the austerities of "Funeral Music" to the comic eroticism of "The Songbook of Sebastian Arrurruz"

Hill received author's copies of his first book at the University of Michigan, where he had arrived several weeks earlier as a visiting lecturer for 1959-1960. Hall, then teaching at Michigan, facilitated the exchange, having created considerable interest in Hill's poems by reading some of them (instead of his own) on a public occasion. At Michigan, Hill became friends with Allan Seager, novelist and biographer of the American poet Theodore Roethke, and in his next major collection Hill dedicated a poem to Seager on the American Civil War, which developed as a natural complement to Hill's interest in the English Wars of the Roses. His admiration for the American poet Allen Tate resulted in his entry on Tate (as well as Isaac Rosenberg) in an encyclopedia of English and American poetry edited by Hall and Stephen Spender.

After his return to England, Hill became acquainted with Jon Silkin, who had arrived at

Leeds on the nonacademic Gregory Fellowship in Poetry in 1958, and would continue there as a "mature student" until 1965. Helped by the resources of the Gregory fund, Silkin was creating a lively writing environment at Leeds. He drew younger student poets to the university, including Ken Smith and Jeffrey Wainwright, publishing some of their work in *Stand*, which he edited, and involving them in some of the editorial deliberations. Hill, though not directly connected with *Stand*, was a radiating influence in this milieu. To the younger writers at the time he could seem difficult, argumentative, high principled, a bit "prickly"; in retrospect, he seems to have been a moral, a cultural, a literary touchstone. A younger poet, once he understood he could disagree with Hill, usually felt his own viewpoint improved, clarified, by having come to grips with Hill's.

In 1964 Silkin asked Hill to publish a small collection in the Northern House Poets, the series of pamphlets he had initiated earlier that year at Leeds with Ken Smith and Andrew Gurr, a lecturer at Leeds. Hill consented and arranged the eight poems for *Preghiere*, which, like others in the series, was beautifully hand set on a flatbed press at the Department of English.

"Preghiere," meaning "prayers" in Italian, suggests that poetry may be a form of prayer, the poet a type of priest, his practice a channel of grace and a means of spiritual transcendence. Thus the power of poets to transcend political oppression through a spiritual art is the concern of the first three poems, which, grouped later with another as "Four Poems Regarding the Endurance of Poets," form a natural sequence. The first, "Men Are a Mockery of Angels," commemorates Tommaso Campanella (1568-1639), the imprisoned Italian priest and poet whose tough, ascetic craft served to liberate him spiritually; Hill's trim octets and regimented six-syllable lines embody that ascetic impulse. With the irony characteristic of his best sequences, however, the next poem undercuts this ideal and indicates that it is pure hypothesis. "Domaine Public" views the last days of the French poet Robert Desnos at the Nazi camp at Terezin; his starvation mocks the concept of redemptive discipline. "A Prayer to the Sun," written in memory of Miguel Hernandez, a poet Francisco Franco imprisoned in the 1930s, reasserts the redemptive possibilities of poetry in three short emblem pieces shaped typographically in the form of crosses.

"Three Baroque Meditations" evidence the same conflicts. Here the poet appears in his "Flesh of abnegation" as an ascetic radical, whose "poem / Moves grudgingly to its extreme form," typified by rigid syllabic. But in the next piece, the monologue of "The Dead Bride," the wife of a famous poet punctuates his high ascetic ideals, defaming

His sacramental mouth

That justified my flesh
And moved well among women
In nuances and imperatives.

A dramatic speaker like the bride also becomes a device for balancing the idiomatic and formal ranges of language. Thus the poet-speaker of "Ovid in the Third Reich" mixes clichés with literary diction, colloquial uncertainty with stylized finality:

I love my work and my children. God
Is distant, difficult. Things happen.
Too near the ancient troughs of blood
Innocence is no earthly weapon.

The new, open dramatic element running through the pamphlet was not enough to waylay criticism for Hill's difficulty and obscurity. The *Times Literary Supplement* labeled him a "disappointingly ingrown talent," the poems "mandarin and rarefied." At the same time, however, Hill's creative use of idiom and cliché was appreciated by Christopher Ricks in the first substantial critical essay on the poetry, "Cliché as 'Responsible Speech'; Geoffrey Hill." Later, in an omnibus review for *New Statesman*, Ricks acknowledged the difficulty of Hill's language but recalled T. S. Eliot's dictum that genuine poetry can communicate before it is understood. Roger Hecht's praise in *Poetry* was unqualified: "*Preghiere* is further confirmation, were it needed, that Geoffrey Hill is beyond question one of the very finest poets now at work." His deliberate obliquity struck Hecht as an effective strength. "Mr. Hill's poems are . . . made brilliant by a fury a great part of which is suppressed," a perception repeated by C. H. Sisson in an elegant conceit: "It is as if the shock of experience were received into a great volume of water, so that the surface trembling is no more than indicative."

Through the mid 1960s at Leeds, Hill conformed to a fairly regular rhythm of teaching and writing; "my professional work has had a ben-

Front cover for Hill's 1971 book, which confirmed, for reviewer Michael Schmidt, Hill's status "as one of the most original poets to have emerged in recent years"

eficial effect on my creative work," he maintains, "in the sense of putting in my way happy discoveries which I might not have made if I'd not been a teacher of English literature." As an example he cites his sonnet sequence on the Wars of the Roses, "Funeral Music," which he was composing during these years: "in order to give a lecture course on Shakespeare I found myself re-reading the *Henry VI* plays at exactly the right time; discovering the power of a certain kind of rhetoric which I'd been educated to think of as inferior to Shakespeare's later work. This came at a time when my thoughts were beginning to stir toward the writing of the sequence 'Funeral Music.'" He varied his routine by visiting the University of Ibadan in Nigeria during the early months of 1967, a period of crisis preceding the outbreak of the Nigerian civil war. He met the poet Christopher Okigbo, author of *Labyrinths*, a few months before he was killed fighting for the Biafran army.

Despite the turmoil Hill returned to England with the manuscript for *King Log*, including all the poems in *Preghiere*, nearly complete. Deutsch again accepted and published it in August 1968.

Aesop's fable of King Log and King Stork contrasts two kings of opposite qualities: the contemplative, gentle, do-nothing King Log and the active, rapacious, care-nothing King Stork. The frogs of a pond, dissatisfied with King Log, ask for a change and, ironically, receive something much worse. Most of the poems in the volume chronicle the reign of King Stork, focusing on forms of power unenlightened by human virtue. Historically, the subjects range from the medieval to the modern worlds, and the political and spiritual ruthlessness of the earlier age sets the mood. In style and form, the poems repeat this experience of power. They can be authoritative to the point of arrogance, demanding complete submission on the part of the reader. At the same time, however, several poems, such as those on Campanella and Hernandez in "Four Poems Regarding the Endurance of Poets," associate poetry with formal goodness. Thus the experience of reading enacts a dialectic between ascetic virtue and worldly power, and some poems take up this tension as their chief concern.

The speaker of "Ovid in the Third Reich" acts out this tension between artistic virtue and worldly power; he claims the innocence of his art, in the excerpt quoted earlier, but also discloses, with dramatic irony, the guilt of his compliance under Adolf Hitler. "Annunciations," whose title suggests a messianic role for the poet, follows "Ovid in the Third Reich"; ironically, however, the "Word," like the poet of the Third Reich, goes with the times, goes on vacation: "The Word has been abroad, is back, with a tanned look." But the Marxist ideal, that poetry should reflect history and explain it, is fulfilled with consummate irony in "History as Poetry." For his poetry, with its love of violent sensation, abrupt paradox, and bullying difficulty, partakes fully of the ruthless world of history. There are the "tongue's atrocities" to match history's.

Hill's sequence of eight blank-verse sonnets on the English Wars of the Roses, "Funeral Music," stands at the center of the volume. Variously narrative, dramatic, and meditative, the perspectives shift freely from soldiers' accounts of the Battle of Towton in 1461 to ceremonial views of executions. The first sonnet opens graphically with the decapitation of John Tiptoft, Earl of Worcester, echoing his request for three blows of the ax to symbolize the Trinity. This juxtaposition of ritual and violence recalls the central tension in *King Log* between asceticism and power, a tension that generates the design and style of the sequence. There is the decorous, formal procession of the sonnets on one hand, on the other the searing "Postscript: King Stork," an expository essay that, with its abrasive details and fierce rhythms, revels in the gore of violent historical facts. Stylistically, Hill frequently pierces the ornate Elizabethan diction of his verse with colloquial exclamations, as in the first lines of sonnet 3, "They bespoke doomsday and they meant it by / God . . . ," a style Hill aptly characterizes in his postscript as "a florid grim music broken by grunts and shrieks."

King Log ranges remarkably from the austerities of "Funeral Music" to the comic eroticism of "The Songbook of Sebastian Arrurruz," where an apocryphal Spanish poet relates the loss of his wife to the practice of his craft. It is a seriocomic tale graced by a shy, introverted sensuality:

> Why do I have to relive, even now,
> Your mouth, and your hand running over me
> Deft as a lizard, like a sinew of water?

Arrurruz reputedly died in 1922, without the benefit, Hill has noted elsewhere, of reading T. S. Eliot's *The Waste Land* or James Joyce's *Ulysses*. Thus he stands as an unknown, eccentric figure on the periphery of literary modernism. This persona provides a human immediacy for ironies couched more obliquely in other poems.

But most of the poems do not display such human directness; several critics could see nothing but its absence. Martin Seymour-Smith found "frigid, carefully executed, super-literary poems" where a "barrier of confident recondite language screens the reader from all human energy." At the same time, the *Times Literary Supplement* admired "the struggle to write more simply and directly of people." Likewise, for Martin Dodsworth the passionate "simplicity" of several poems, notably "The Songbook of Sebastian Arrurruz," accounted for "the excellence of *King Log*." Robin Skelton's mixed response was typical. He admired the technical rigor but resented the obscurity, was alienated but awed by the austere intensity, and for the most part accepted the difficulty as the signature of a strange genius.

After returning from Africa in 1967, Hill resumed teaching at Leeds and began work immediately on his next book, *Mercian Hymns* (1971).

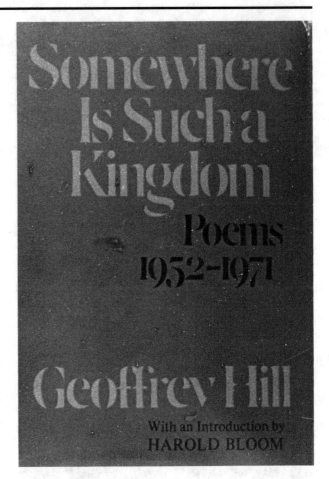

Dust jacket for the American edition of the poems in Hill's first three full-length books. In his introduction to the volume Harold Bloom asserted that Hill should "survive all but a handful (or fewer) of American poets now active" and "should be read and studied for many generations."

This sequence of thirty short prose poems "took me almost three years to the day to complete"; it was the "one book which came relatively quickly." The quickening "excitement of *Mercian Hymns*," he has observed, "was to find that I was meditating on my roots in a double sense." For the sequence blends history and autobiography, combining legends of the eighth-century Mercian king Offa with imagined episodes from Hill's childhood in his own narrative Mercia.

Linking the figures of the medieval king and the modern child is the perception that the child's fantasies of power, his gratuitous cruelty and egoistic whims, underlie the adult king's structures of command. The epigraph from C. H. Sisson, which soberly compares the behavior of private persons with the conduct of government, is thus developed ironically by Hill: the boy's possessiveness and violent retributions anticipate the kingly machinations of power, just as his toy prefigures his kingdom:

> After school he lured Ceolred, who was sniggering
> with fright, down to the old quarries, and
> flayed him. Then, leaving Ceolred, he
> journeyed for hours, calm and alone, in his
> private derelict sandlorry named *Albion*.

Likewise, children act out a savage parody of justice in "Offa's Laws." By a similar analogy, brutal folk customs precede the rituals of kingship in the phantasm of "Offa's Bestiary." Or, looking forward, Offa's fears of political intrigue anticipate a modern man's petty, fantastical insecurities. Offa thus becomes a timeless figure of the struggle to hold psychological as well as political power. Presenting the king as all aspects of man, from the perennial child to the infirm adult, Hill confirms his common human nature, eliciting from the reader not a moral judgment but a psychological understanding.

Correspondingly, history in *Mercian Hymns* is not a medium for moral lessons but a realm of exploration and discovery. "Digging" into archaeological strata occurs throughout the sequence as a metaphor for this exploration, beginning with the poet's childhood: "invested in mother-earth," he would tunnel like the mole into "the Roman flues, the long-unlooked-for mansions of our tribe." The unearthed coins of Offa's realm are his solids of discovery, his "ransacked epiphanies." With unknown images and ancient inscriptions, these coins emerge from the "rune-stone's province," and to Hill the past speaks this magic language of runes. Helping to re-create this sense of mystery are various forms of the Anglo-Saxon riddle. In "The Naming of Offa," for instance, Hill adapts the practice of the medieval acrostic, or letter-riddle. "A laugh; a cough. A syndicate. A specious gift. . . . The starting-cry of a race" all echo the unwritten letters *o, f, f, a*: sounds of laughing or coughing, the initials of an organization, an offer, "They're off!" In a larger sense, too, Hill builds a riddle into the design of the book. The thirty poems are numbered in sequence but untitled; a list of scene-setting, informative but prosaic titles is wedged, as though hidden, between the text and the notes; the reader must probe each piece for its subject, examine it like a crusted coin, experience the mystery of the past, and achieve the kind of discovery a historian seeks in treating the same materials. In fact, Hill researched his material only while writing, letting the poem in process shape the line of in-

quiry, opening the past with a sense of intuitive discovery. Thus the reader's discovery reenacts the poet's process of composition.

In the same year as *Mercian Hymns*, Hill published a long discursive essay on rhythm, "Redeeming the Time," a natural complement to his experiments with poetic cadence in the prose poems. He shapes his "Mercian Hymns" as "versets," intends them to be heard as a "pitched and tuned chant," and names them after the Mercian Hymns in *Sweet's Anglo-Saxon Reader* (1959, fourteenth edition), a collection of biblical passages, psalms and canticles primarily, whose cadenced Anglo-Saxon translations retain the rhythmical, poetic qualities of the original. Like the Anglo-Saxon, Hill's prose tends to run in brief rhythmic units of juxtaposed phrases, not in long continuous rhythms. These cadences can verge on the ceremonial tones of Scripture, but Hill creates this decorum in order to fracture it, just as he contrasts the ritual king with the private person, the legendary figure with the petulant child. In the opening section, for example, the poet engages in the literary ritual of the Anglo-Saxon bard, singing the praises of the patron king in a cadenced heroic catalogue, when the king's vanity interrupts the liturgy: " 'I liked that,' said Offa, 'sing it again.' " The alternation between these liturgical and personal voices helps to create pace in the sequence, shaping the "cross-rhythms" and "counterpointings" Hill values in his rhythm essay. Like the best of his rhythms, it is poised in paradoxical and ironic perceptions.

This technical excellence drew high praise in the *Times Literary Supplement*: "brilliantly exact verbal organizations." But Hill's virtuosity proved bothersome to Ian Wedde, who protested that pyrotechnics obscured Hill's subject, that the Sisson epigraph promised a "large treatment of a large theme" and the sequence provided only "brilliant notes towards this intention." To Wedde the riddles were coy, the subtleties barren. But Christopher Ricks claimed that the difficulty was intrinsic to the material, purposive; the poems "speak of crypts and they are cryptic; they are about patience and they ask it." Michael Schmidt voiced the majority opinion: the ingenuities of *Mercian Hymns* confirmed Hill "as one of the most original poets to have emerged in recent years."

Matching this recognition was a growing list of literary awards: the 1969 Hawthornden Prize and the 1970 Geoffrey Faber Memorial Award for *King Log*; the 1971 Whitbread, Heinemann, and Alice Hunt Bartlett awards for *Mercian*

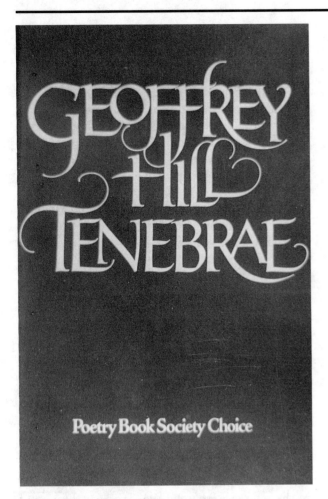

*Dust jacket for Hill's 1978 book. While some reviewers ob-
jected to the religious ambiguities of the poems, Donald Hall
saw them as a strong point of the book: "If in the end he has contradicted everything that he has written, including his own contradictions, he has made an articulated structure, or representation, of the modern mind unable to find rest or resolution,
defeated and beautiful in stillness."*

Hymns. Leeds University elected him to the Chair
of English Literature in 1976. Several years earlier, Jonathan Galassi, then at Houghton Mifflin,
arranged for an American edition of his collected
poems, and his American readership increased in
1975 with the publication of *Somewhere Is Such a
Kingdom: Poems 1952-1971.* This volume includes
all the poems in his three full-length books, in
the original order; however, without explanation
it omits the epigraphs to the volumes. The title is
taken from the American poet John Crowe Ransom and alludes, though ironically in Hill's case,
to a world of tranquillity and concord above the
turmoil of history. The American critic Harold
Bloom added "An Introduction: The Survival of
Strong Poetry," viewing the place of history and literary tradition in Hill's poetry, promulgating his

own (Freudian) notion of poets struggling with
their literary fathers. Looking forward, Bloom
predicted that Hill should "survive all but a handful (or fewer) of American poets now active,"
and "should be read and studied for many generations." American reviewers, Richard Howard for
one, generally hailed this "powerful new voice."
At the same time, some, such as Howard, complained of poems "compressed to the point . . .
of being clogged." "One gets the impression,"
repeated Irvin Ehrenpreis, "of muffled out-
cries rather than furious eloquence." But John
Matthias's review in *Poetry* stressed Hill's sense of
his reader, like Samuel Taylor Coleridge's, as a
"fellow-labourer" in the difficult art of poetry,
and concluded that "Hill is, as anyone who has
made the effort to read him understands, a magnificent poet." "The best poet now writing in England," echoed Christopher Ricks in the *New York
Times Book Review.*

Hill's poetry had found an important admirer in Sir Peter Hall, director of the National
Theatre in London. In late 1975 Hall and John
Russell Brown, a script director, approached Hill
to do a verse translation of Henrik Ibsen's poetic
drama *Brand* (1866). Hill had never read the play
and knew no Norwegian. He was to collaborate
with Inga-Stina Ewbank, the Norwegian scholar
at London University. Their routine marked a
new departure for Hill, working to schedules
and deadlines that had never mattered in his poetry. Beginning in the summer of 1976, Ewbank
supplied him regularly with blocks of literal translation, which he refashioned as he followed her
notes on points of connotation, imagery, and
rhythm. Remarkably, he produced nearly six thousand lines of verse in little more than a year; the
pace led to a kind of exhausted "euphoria." His
original interest in the project fired into a passionate enthusiasm for the technical challenge he perceived in the translation. He felt Ibsen searching
for a meter supple enough to modulate between
ecstasy and farce, just as his mythic hero Brand is
alternately a messiah and a fool. But Ibsen's regular tetrameter, rendered directly into English
verse, seemed too mechanical for these purposes.
Thus Hill remade it into a short, predominantly
three-beat unit, a plastic, flexible instrument adequate to the range of emotions in the play. The National Theatre in London staged the first production in April 1978, though its emphasis on visual
spectacle tended to diminish the verbal art. A
later production on the tiny stage of the University Theatre at Leeds reduced the action to sym-

bolic gestures and enhanced the role of the language. The Heinemann edition of the play was edited in line with the first London production, but a second edition, published by the University of Minnesota Press, restored nearly the full text of Hill's version.

From 1971 through 1978, Hill was at work on several poetic sequences, though the *Brand* project largely preempted his poetry in the last two years of this period. In the spring of 1976, before he began translating, he traveled through India, where he jotted down notes for several poems on the British colonial presence, to be incorporated into a sequence nearly five years in the making, "An Apology for the Revival of Christian Architecture in England." As *Brand* was nearing production, he collected his various sequences and some shorter poems, and in October 1978 Deutsch published *Tenebrae*.

"Tenebrae," meaning "darkness" in Latin, refers to the somber ritual on Good Friday evening, when candles are ceremonially extinguished to symbolize the death of Christ. A mood of brooding meditation thus prevails in the volume. There is a kind of liturgical propriety in *Tenebrae*, matched by a literary decorum unseen since *King Log*: a return to closed forms, especially the sonnet, and extensive echoing and paraphrasing of earlier literature.

The opening series, "The Pentecost Castle," consists of fifteen short lyrics, some modeled loosely, others very closely, on religious poems of sixteenth-century Counter-Reformation Spain. These poets were rewriting popular profane verse as spiritual lyrics; to this purpose they employed the medieval allegory of love, viewing physical desire as a symbol, an anticipation, of divine love. A poem based on Juan del Encina's lyric, for example, pictures a woman as a heron who, pierced by the "blade" of physical love, ascends in a symbolically spiritual flight; she

> goes seeking the high rocks
> where no man can climb
> where the wild balsam stirs
> by the little stream
>
> the rocks the high rocks
> are brimming with flowers
> there love grows and there love
> rests and is saved.

As though to modernize the medieval concept, Hill attaches a two-part epigraph from William Butler Yeats and Simone Weil—Yeats asserting

the primacy of physical desire, Weil the importance of spiritual love. But the poems do not attempt to sound a modern voice. Rather, Hill sets out to refine and perfect the poetic diction of the Spanish Golden Age: elegant but spare, rich but precise.

"Lachrimae, or Seven tears figured in seven passionate Pavans" borrows its title from John Dowland's composition (circa 1600) for viols and lute. These seven sonnets move with the somber elegance of his pavanes; the cadence is even, displaying a steady rather than a shifting caesura, allowing the verse line to coincide with units of syntax and sense. But the sonnets are also, in Dowland's word, "passionate." The verse has a sensuous quality, like the music, and the religious meditation often achieves a passionate intensity.

For Hill's concern in "Lachrimae" is acutely personal, unlike the somewhat dated conception behind "The Pentecost Castle." When asked to characterize his own religious experience in relation to his poetry, he refers (in a way characteristic of his impersonality) to the vision of a modern Italian poet: "a heretic's dream of salvation expressed in the images of the orthodoxy from which he is excommunicate." In the sequence he enlarges this feeling of exclusion, and increases its significance, as he dwells on the disjunction between man and God. He envisions a *deus absconditus*, a God aloof from the human condition, typified in the figure of Christ withdrawn cavalierly from the human pains of the Crucifixion:

> You are the crucified who crucifies,
> self-withdrawn even from your own device,
> your trim-plugged body, wreath of rakish thorn.

But as God withdraws from history, man must enter it and claim responsibility for his own destiny. Some of the best poems in *Tenebrae* return to the concrete historical world in light of this perception. It was the perception of the German theologian Dietrich Bonhoeffer (1906-1945), whom Hill commemorates in the short poem "Christmas Trees," recalling his death in a Nazi prison camp after his alleged part in a plot to kill Hitler. The piece originally formed part of a cantata text set to music and performed in Emmanuel Church, Leeds, in 1975, a public occasion that amplified the warning in the last lines:

> Against wild reasons of the state
> his words are quiet but not too quiet.
> We hear too late or not too late.

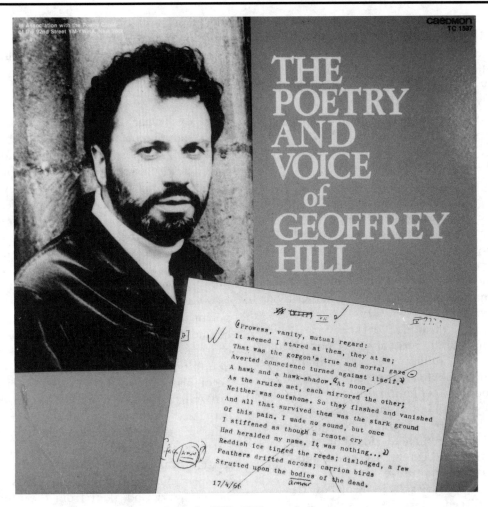

Cover for Hill's 1979 record album

This historical orientation continues in the sequence of thirteen titled sonnets, under the general title "An Apology for the Revival of Christian Architecture in England." Here Hill views the "sad serenity and elegance of the eighteenth-century country house" in terms of the social system required to support it. The sequence mixes nostalgia for a faded ideal and assessment of its human price. "Damon's Lament for his Clorinda (Yorkshire 1654)" places these pastoral characters as peasants in a Yorkshire landscape; but Hill's figures lead far less than Arcadian lives, a disparity matching the contrast between the pastoral ideal of the country house and the rural laborers who upheld it. The broad historical scope of the sequence includes three sonnets, "A Short History of British India (I, II, III)," where oppressed Indian peasants stand as counterparts to a battered English tenantry. Beginning in the notes Hill scribbled during his trip to India, these poems are

crowded with religious icons and cultural rituals, reshaped slowly as he brooded over his observations. One source of creative energy for these poems may have been the profound emotional experience he underwent in the East India Company graveyard in Calcutta, where the tombstones, likes icons, seemed to call up the complex history of the British colonial presence.

A sequence of eight pieces in mixed forms, "Tenebrae," comes at the end of the volume, just as the ritual of Tenebrae concludes the day. These poems are touched by a mood of somber introspection. The three pieces set to music and sung (with "Christmas Trees") at the church service in Leeds in 1975 may be the best. These have a recognizable musical, liturgical structure: the chiming antiphonies of the fourth poem, "O light of light, supreme delight; / grace on our lips to our disgrace," or the cadenced litany of the sixth, shaping the isolation felt during the Tenebrae service:

Dust jacket for Hill's 1984 collection of critical writings, which provides a framework for exploring his poetry

this is a raging solitude of desire,
this is the chorus of obscene consent,
this is a single voice of purest praise.

But for these paradoxes, typical of Hill's best poetry, the liturgical style may seem a mannered,
unsupple instrument.

    Several reviewers of *Tenebrae* shared the dis-
appointment of Paul Breslin, who saw Hill regress-
ing from the open style of *Mercian Hymns* into
the "convolutions of his earlier, more formal
poems." Craig Raine objected to the "traditional
diction" and considered it false to filter intense
personal sentiments through the "frigid" formu-
las of sixteenth-century religious poetry. This
learned, allusive style caused Vernon Young to typ-
ify Hill as a "poet's poet, readily appreciated in
the Academy by those overwhelmed by his erudition." The difficulty of the poems led, inevitably,
to misreadings. Hayden Carruth, for example,
mistook the intensity of religious feeling for impassioned belief, and hailed *Tenebrae* as "the best
book of devotional poetry in the modern high
style since Eliot's *Ash-Wednesday*." Others per-

ceived the ambiguity in Hill's religious views but
objected to it: "A unifying statement is presumably not the poet's aim," Frederick Grubb complained laconically. But several important reviewers, notably Michael Schmidt, Peter Davison at
Atlantic Monthly, and Donald Hall in *Poetry*, valued the ambivalence as a strength and acclaimed
the book highly. Hall wrote: "If in the end he
has contradicted everything that he has written, including his own contradictions, he has made an articulated structure, or representation, of the modern mind unable to find rest or resolution,
defeated and beautiful in stillness." *Tenebrae* also
won the 1979 Duff Cooper Memorial Prize.

    In 1980 Hill was elected fellow of
Emmanuel College, Cambridge, and university
lecturer in English, and moved to the college. He
has since completed a poem in one hundred quatrains, *The Mystery of the Charity of Charles Péguy*,
first published in the *Times Literary Supplement* (4
February 1983) and later as a special edition by
Agenda magazine in cooperation with Deutsch. Followed by a short prose appreciation of Péguy's
life, the poem is a homage to Péguy as a man

and a poet, as a visionary who preserved the integrity of his inspiration outside the literary coteries of his day. A socialist but a committed nationalist, a Catholic but not of orthodox subscription, Péguy conveyed a distinctive vision of France, an ideal of *L'ancienne France* based on a mystical sense of the French soil and a heroic conception of the peasants, like his parents, who labored on it. Following his own patriotic ideals, he died at the age of forty-one, "an aging infantry lieutenant of the Reserve, on the first day of the first Battle of the Marne in September 1914." Although Hill is not engaged in hagiography here, there is a fundamental sympathy between the two men, beginning in their formative experiences. The poem bears a dedication to Sarah Ann Hands (1869-1967), Hill's much-loved maternal grandmother, who, raised in the cottage industry of nail making, typifies the common people Péguy celebrated.

Since Péguy's ideal belongs to the preindustrial past, the poem might easily have become an elegy of cultural decline, the voice one of embattled conservatism. But Hill's fundamental sympathy with the French poet allows him to present the vision as a living sensibility, to recreate its felt particulars, to avoid both the weakness of nostalgic sentiment and the temptation to polemical defense. He conveys the severe beauty and epic bleakness of this view with something of its original intensity, for example, as he represents its conception of time, a *durée* of living and dead souls of the nation:

> Drawn on the past
> these presences endure; they have not ceased
> to act, suffer, crouching into the hail
> like labourers of their own memorial.

> or those who worship at its marble rote,
> their many names one name, the common "dur"
> built into duration, the endurance of war;
> blind Vigil herself, helpless and obdurate.

The poem, though not discursive or argumentative, demonstrates a recurring concern with the political responsibilities of poetry, sometimes, ironically, with the political liabilities and misreading of poetic speech. By 1914 Péguy, previously a supporter of the socialist deputy Jean Jaurès, was "calling for his blood," though only, Hill wryly observes in the essay, "figuratively, it must be said"; but "a young madman, who may or may not have been over-susceptible to metaphor, almost immediately shot Jaurès through the head." Thus the first section opens with the scene of this assassination, asking the essential question of the poet's responsibility for his words:

> Did Péguy kill Jaurès? Did he incite
> the assassin? Must men stand by what they write
> as by their camp-beds or their weaponry
> or shell-shocked comrades while they sag and cry?

Likewise Péguy, as a poet, "spoke to the blood" of his conationals; consequently, "the metaphors of blood begin to flow" with the advent of the 1914 war, calling others to a death like his in the beetroots of the Marne:

> So you spoke to the blood. So, you have risen
> above all that and fallen flat on your face
>
> 5
>
> among the beetroots, where we are constrained
> to leave you sleeping. . . .

This awareness of the violence of language in relation to history recalls the concerns and practices of Hill's earlier poetry, notably the sonnets in "Funeral Music." Once again, these poems utter the "formal pledge" of art against the chaos of history; the quatrains, flexible but firm, consort and contrast with the violence they represent.

Hill has received an increasing number of requests to read his poetry, and for this purpose has visited the United States, the former Soviet Union, Canada, and Poland. A collection of his essays and reviews, planned for his fiftieth birthday in 1982, was delayed for two years. The volume, *The Lords of Limit: Essays on Literature and Ideas*, was published by André Deutsch in 1984. His critical prose forms a coherent whole with his poetry, stressing his belief in poetic form, his disbelief in single message or directive, the importance of a questioning irony, and his sense of his reader as a "fellow-labourer." Collected, the prose provides a first framework for scholars exploring the poetry.

Already his work has begun to receive the type of patient, scholarly explication it deserves. The degree of difficulty in his poetry, it is now commonly agreed, measures the individuality of his attitudes, the uniqueness of his voice. These qualities should sustain a growing body of critical commentary. Hill remains, however, a rather isolated, unassignable genius; his high standards have prescribed but limited his fame: only a select clerisy of devoted "fellow-labourers" has attempted to penetrate his sometimes imposing surfaces. But to confront the work is to be impressed, moved, and awed even before understanding it. The consensus is that Hill's reputation will accrue like his own poems, at his own pace: he does not write quickly, and throw away; he shapes slowly, and saves.

Interviews:

Blake Morrison, "Under Judgment," *New Statesman*, 8 February 1980, pp. 212-214;

John Haffenden, *Viewpoints: Poets in Conversation with John Haffenden* (London & Boston: Faber & Faber, 1981), pp. 76-99.

References:

John Bayley, "A Retreat or Seclusion," *Agenda*, Geoffrey Hill Special Issue, 17 (Spring 1979): 38-42;

Calvin Bedient, "On Geoffrey Hill," *Critical Quarterly*, 23 (Summer 1981): 17-26;

Merle Brown, *Double Lyric: Divisiveness and Communal Creativity in Recent English Poetry* (New York: Columbia University Press, 1980), pp. 20-72;

Martin Dodsworth, "Geoffrey Hill's New Poetry," *Stand*, 13 (Winter 1971): 61-63;

Thomas H. Getz, "Geoffrey Hill: History as Poetry; Poetry as Salutation," *Contemporary Poetry*, 4 (1982): 4-23;

Donald Hall, "Naming the Devils," *Poetry*, 136 (May 1980): 102-110;

Henry Hart, "Geoffrey Hill's *The Mystery of the Charity of Charles Péguy*: A Commentary," *Essays in Criticism*, 33 (October 1983): 312-338;

Seamus Heaney, "Now and in England," *Critical Inquiry*, 3 (1977): 471-488;

Cathrael Kazin, " 'Across a Wilderness of Retrospection': A Reading of Geoffrey Hill's 'Lachrimae,' " *Agenda*, Geoffrey Hill Special Issue, 17 (Spring 1979): 43-57;

Grevel Lindop, "Myth and Blood: The Poetry of Geoffrey Hill," *Critical Quarterly*, 26 (Spring & Summer 1984): 147-154;

Wallace D. Martin, "Beyond Modernism: Christopher Middleton and Geoffrey Hill," *Contemporary Literature*, 12 (Autumn 1971): 420-436;

John Matthias, "Such a Kingdom," *Poetry*, 128 (July 1976): 232-240;

William S. Milne, " 'Creative Tact': Geoffrey Hill's *King Log*," *Critical Quarterly*, 20 (Winter 1978): 39-45;

Milne, " 'Decreation' in Geoffrey Hill's 'Lachrimae,' " *Agenda*, Geoffrey Hill Special Issue, 17 (Spring 1979): 61-71;

Milne, "Geoffrey Hill's *Mercian Hymns*," *Ariel*, 10 (January 1979): 43-63;

Milne, " 'The Pitch of Attention': Geoffrey Hill's *Tenebrae*," *Agenda*, Geoffrey Hill Special Issue, 17 (Spring 1979): 38-42;

Robert Morgan, "The Reign of King Stork," *Parnassus*, 4 (Spring-Summer 1976): 31-48;

John Peck, "Geoffrey Hill's *Tenebrae*," *Agenda*, Geoffrey Hill Special Issue, 17 (Spring 1979): 13-24;

Christopher Ricks, "Cliché as 'Responsible Speech': Geoffrey Hill," *London Magazine*, 4 (November 1964): 96-101;

Ricks, *Geoffrey Hill and "The Tongue's Atrocities"* (Swansea, Wales: University College, 1978);

Peter Robinson, ed., *Geoffrey Hill: Essays on His Work* (Milton-Keynes, U.K.: Open University Press, 1985);

Sibyl Severance, "The Structure of Understanding: Geoffrey Hill's *Funeral Music*," *Contemporary Poetry*, 4 (1981): 46-65;

Jon Silkin, "The Poetry of Geoffrey Hill," *Iowa Review*, 3 (Summer 1972): 108-128;

C. H. Sisson, "Geoffrey Hill," *Agenda*, 13 (Autumn 1975): 23-28;

Stephen Utz, "The Realism of Geoffrey Hill," *Southern Review*, 12 (Spring 1976): 426-433;

Jeffrey Wainwright, "An Essay on Geoffrey Hill's *Tenebrae*," *Agenda*, Geoffrey Hill Special Issue, 17 (Spring 1979): 4-12;

Wainwright, "Geoffrey Hill's 'Lachrimae,' " *Agenda*, 13 (Autumn 1975): 31-38;

Andrew Waterman, "The Poetry of Geoffrey Hill," *British Poetry Since 1970: A Critical Survey*, edited by Peter Jones and Michael Schmidt (New York: Persea Books, 1980), pp. 85-102;

A. K. Weatherhead, "Geoffrey Hill," *Iowa Review*, 8 (Fall 1977): 104-116;

Clive Wilmer, "An Art of Recovery: Some Literary Sources for Geoffrey Hill's *Tenebrae*," *Southern Review*, 17 (January 1981): 121-141.

P. D. James
(Phyllis Dorothy James White)

(3 August 1920 -   )

This entry was updated by Bernard Benstock (University of Miami) from his entry in
DLB 87: British Mystery and Thriller Writers Since 1940: First Series.

BOOKS: *Cover Her Face* (London: Faber & Faber, 1962; New York: Scribners, 1966);

A Mind to Murder (London: Faber & Faber, 1963; New York: Scribners, 1967);

Unnatural Causes (London: Faber & Faber, 1967; New York: Scribners, 1967);

The Maul and the Pear Tree: The Ratcliffe Highway Murders, 1811, by James and T. A. Critchley (London: Constable, 1971; New York: Mysterious, 1986);

Shroud for a Nightingale (London: Faber & Faber, 1971; New York: Scribners, 1971);

An Unsuitable Job for a Woman (London: Faber & Faber, 1972; New York: Scribners, 1973);

The Black Tower (London: Faber & Faber, 1975; New York: Scribners, 1975);

Death of an Expert Witness (London: Faber & Faber, 1977; New York: Scribners, 1977);

Innocent Blood (London: Faber & Faber, 1980; New York: Scribners, 1980);

The Skull beneath the Skin (London: Faber & Faber, 1982; New York: Scribners, 1982);

A Taste for Death (London: Faber & Faber, 1986; New York: Knopf, 1986);

Devices and Desires (London: Faber & Faber, 1989; New York: Knopf, 1990).

OTHER: "Ought Adam to Marry Cordelia?," in *Murder Ink: The Mystery Reader's Companion,* edited by Dilys Winn (New York: Workman, 1977), pp. 68-69;

"A Fictional Prognosis," in *Murder Ink: The Mystery Reader's Companion,* edited by Winn (New York: Workman, 1977), pp. 339-342;

"Dorothy L. Sayers: From Puzzle to Novel," in *Crime Writers* (London: British Broadcasting Corporation, 1978), pp. 64-75.

SELECTED PERIODICAL PUBLICATION—
UNCOLLECTED: "A Series of Scenes," in "How I Write My Books," compiled by H. R. F.

P. D. James (photograph by Nigel Parry)

Keating, *Writer's Digest,* 63 (October 1983): 26-27.

The coming-of-age of a mature crime fiction in England, to which P. D. James has contributed prominently, can be attributed to a variety of disparate causes: the rapid changes in a society that had appeared for so long as monolithic; the end of the death penalty; the reaction of writers of fiction against experimentation; the shift of emphasis in psychology from science to a study of the human enigma; the persistence of inexplicable evil; the demise of the pure puzzle mystery; and the necessity that British detective fiction confront the presence of violent action that had become so much a characteristic of the American thriller. In her writings P. D. James expresses aspects of all of these factors, and since the first appearance of her fiction in 1962 she has established a major reputation in Britain and only to a slightly lesser extent in America, rivaled only by that of Ruth Rendell. According to dust-jacket blurbs, James and Rendell are the queens of contemporary detective fiction, just as were Dorothy L. Sayers and Agatha Christie of the previous generation. Furthermore, journal reviews praise James as a masterful writer and storyteller, even though her work is considered popular rather than serious. James has been instrumental, along with other writers of the last three decades, in narrowing the gap between crime fiction and serious fiction, between what Sayers had separated as "literature of escape" and "literature of expression."

The James canon of eleven novels is by no means homogenous: a progression of changes in style, mood, and scope can be discerned along the way, as well as variations in the investigative focus of her novels. Adam Dalgliesh (spelled *Dalgleish* in the first book, but not thereafter), whom she created as her New Scotland Yard inspector, remained her primary detective for the first four books, but her fifth introduced a young woman as private investigator. The more romantic book reviewers quickly predicted a love affair in the future for the twenty-two-year-old Cordelia Gray and Dalgliesh (twice her age), reading between the lines of their closing confrontation in *An Unsuitable Job for a Woman* (1972). The next two novels return exclusively to Adam Dalgliesh; Cordelia Gray is barely mentioned. A new departure is taken in the eighth novel, in which neither of the two plays any part: *Innocent Blood* (1980) is a psychological crime thriller without a detective even peripheral to the action, much less as the central focus. But Cordelia Gray returns as the operative in the ninth novel, Adam Dalgliesh in the tenth and eleventh—and the sentimental reviewers and readers have remained frustrated in their anticipation of romance. James's outspoken admiration for Sayers might have had a hand in the assumption of a love affair imitating that of Lord Peter Wimsey and Harriet Vane, but she has persisted in her es-

tablished separation of Adam and Cordelia. Her two characters do share a love for church architecture and for natural flowers, but in a short piece in *Murder Ink: The Mystery Reader's Companion* (1977) entitled "Ought Adam to Marry Cordelia?" James remains noncommittal, commenting: "I can only say that I have no plans at present to marry Dalgleish [*sic*] to anyone. Yet even the best regulated characters are apt occasionally to escape from the sensible and controlling hand of their author and embark, however inadvisably, on a love life of their own."

P. D. James is the pen name of Phyllis Dorothy James White, who was born in Oxford, England, on 3 August 1920, the daughter of Sidney and Dorothy May Hone James. (In *Innocent Blood* the main character is a young potential writer who combined for her own pen name, "Phillippa Ducton," the first name given to her by her adoptive parents and the surname that she has eventually learned is actually hers—a hybrid that suggests an aspect of P. D. James's choice for herself.) Her father was an official of the Inland Revenue, and the family moved to Cambridge where she attended the Cambridge High School for Girls. At the age of sixteen James went to work in a tax office, but a few years later she became an assistant stage manager at the Festival Theatre in Cambridge. (*The Skull beneath the Skin* [1982] is her only work to date with some aspect of a theatrical setting.)

In 1941 Phyllis James married Ernest Conner Bantry White, a physician who served in the Royal Army Medical Corps during World War II. White returned to England in 1945 a mental invalid and remained so until his death in 1964. In 1949, when her daughters were five and seven years old, Mrs. White became the main financial support of the family, working for the newly established National Health Service and eventually being promoted to the position of hospital administrator. Medical administration became her career and would prove valuable for clinical settings in many of her detective novels: *Shroud for a Nightingale* (1971) is situated in a teaching hospital for nurses; *A Mind to Murder* (1963) in a London psychiatric clinic; *The Black Tower* (1975) in a home for the critically disabled. *Death of an Expert Witness* (1977) is located in a forensic laboratory, reflecting the author's subsequent career. In 1968 she entered the Home Office after being selected from an open competition for senior-level applicants: she served as a principal first in the Police Department and later in the

Dust jackets for the first American editions of two of James's novels from the 1970s

Criminal Policy Department, experiences that constantly made their way into the verisimilitude of her fiction. She has also served as a magistrate in inner London. She retired in 1979 and has been devoting herself full-time to her writing, a factor that does not reflect itself in any greater frequency of publication but in the larger format of her books since that time.

The extended format also allies James with Sayers, whose *Gaudy Night* (1936) purposely offended the traditions of the genre with its length and sustained intensity. Unlike Sayers, James does not avoid making her mystery contain a murder: the 454-page *A Taste for Death* (1986) begins with the discovery of two throat-slashed corpses and ends with violence and death as well. The fully mature James novel opens into the lives of its characters with depth and analytical insight, including the police officials along with the victims and the suspects. American reviewers in particular have balked at this superseding of the purity of the genre. The reviewer of *A Taste for Death* in

the *New York Times* (23 October 1986), who credits the author with "demonstrating an increasing grasp of emotions and themes that normally lie beyond the genre of the detective thriller," finds "a falling off" in *The Skull beneath the Skin* and is perplexed by the "plot complication, thematic digression, character articulation and details, details, details" of *A Taste for Death*. That James creates a vast and intricate cross section of English life in the 1980s and probes the hidden corners of various characters may well be the achievement of this novel rather than its limitation.

In becoming a critically acclaimed and publicly acknowledged master of the detective novel James has achieved a popularity that exceeds that of her detectives (unlike the creators of Sherlock Holmes, Lord Peter Wimsey, and Inspector Maigret). Not that Dalgliesh and Gray are inconsequential personalities, but they do not have the eccentric touches that had once been considered essential for the detective hero of fiction, until at least the 1930s. Instead of providing Adam Dalgliesh, for example, with an initial set of outré characteristics to be repeated as the givens of his personality throughout the novels, James presents him and sustains him as something of an enigma, rationally understandable perhaps but nonetheless enigmatic in his private self. The Dalgliesh story as such evolves through the eight books in which he appears (with just a disturbing afterthought in *An Unsuitable Job for a Woman*). At the Dalglieshian center may reside the fact that his wife and son died in childbirth in the early years of his career, disclosed to the reader in *Cover Her Face* (1962) as Dalgliesh's private recollection. In that initial novel Detective Chief Inspector Dalgliesh is a proven veteran of the Metropolitan CID, whose "first big case" had been seven years ago. He pursues his investigation with cold precision: "I'll see the body first. The living will keep" are his first words. He is intent on uncovering all hidden secrets remorselessly, insisting that a murder investigation takes precedence over all private affairs (of course keeping the privilege of his own privacy intact). But he can also be extremely gentle with the suffering and even sympathetic with the murderer, in this case a particularly fine person.

Not all the "facts" about Dalgliesh are permanent: the "30-foot sailing boat" that serves as relaxation after the case in *Cover Her Face* has been solved never surfaces again; perhaps it was sold along with an Essex cottage mentioned in *A Mind to Murder*. In the recent novels he lives in a flat "high above the Thames in the City," which is never described in detail. James's *A Mind to Murder*, her second novel, opens at a sherry party given by Dalgliesh's publisher, and only because a murder has been committed across the square is Dalgliesh involved. In having to leave the party he has to drop his plan to ask a young woman to dinner, a woman whose mother he had arrested three years before (in *Cover Her Face*). Only when the new case is solved, not particularly to Dalgliesh's credit, does he pick up where he had left off and make the phone call. In *Unnatural Causes* (1967) he is torn by his commitments to the woman, who has been his mistress for a while, and he goes off to contemplate whether to ask her to marry him. What had been intended as a meditative holiday evolves into a nasty murder case that almost costs him his life. At its conclusion he writes a poem to the woman, but it never gets sent since her letter arrives telling him that she is leaving for America. Sharing his life proves difficult for Adam Dalgliesh, and his unstinting

commitment to his profession bars any rival commitment. In the succeeding books he remains unmarried but has a vague series of sexual affairs along the way. The pull of the past is particularly pointed in *A Mind to Murder:* on "the anniversary of his wife's death, Dalgliesh called in at a small Catholic church behind the Strand to light a candle. His wife had been a Catholic."

Devices and Desires intensifies and extends the Adam Dalgliesh case history, especially as he is continually reminded of his childhood. More introspective than ever, he cannot avoid seeing facets of himself everywhere he turns, but mostly in an old rectory: "So he had lived in childhood and adolescence in the same country rectory," also noting that it "was a world he relinquished with small regret." He also remembers himself as a nine-year-old in preparatory school, but mostly as a "lonely only child" at home, the "much-wanted only child of elderly parents, burdened by their almost obsessive parental concern and overconscientiousness." The death of his wife and child are brought home to him when the detective chief inspector on whose "patch" he is uncomfortably intruding is awaiting the birth of his first child, an event that takes place at the end of the case, much to his exulting and to Dalgliesh's realization of envy. The memory of his dead wife, "which for years, a traitor to grief and to their love, he had resolutely tried to suppress because the pain had seemed unbearable," returns, although he cannot visualize her face, but his "newborn son's face he could still recall vividly and sometimes did in his dreams." As for a new love in his life, it is only obliquely hinted at throughout *Devices and Desires*.

The professional Dalgliesh is succinctly delineated in *A Mind to Murder*, from the opening statement that "he had never yet known the taste of defeat" to the concluding humility after tracking the wrong murderer (whom he nonetheless apprehends in the act of attempted murder): "If this case doesn't cure me of conceit, nothing will." *A Mind to Murder* is a rare instance in which he does not adhere to his stated methodology, the time-honored caution not to theorize in advance of the facts. Dalgliesh particularly prides himself on the speed with which he solves his cases, and when this one seems somewhat bogged down, he feels impatient: James narrates, "There followed a hiatus in the investigation, one of those inevitable delays which Dalgliesh had never found it easy to accept. He had always worked at speed. His reputation rested on the pace as well as the success of the cases. He did not ponder too deeply the implications of this compulsive need to get on with the job. It was enough to know that delay irritated him more than it did most men." An inherent contradiction begins to show itself in Adam Dalgliesh: the stolid policeman respectful of the facts and doggedly determined to "get on with the job" undercut by the impatient perfectionist with a strong belief in his instinctive powers—the man of conceit.

In James's third novel, *Unnatural Causes*, Dalgliesh not only returns to full form but does so despite the apparent evidence that the victim has died a natural death. He then describes himself as "stupidly persistent, blindly following his hunch in the teeth of the evidence." It leads him into physical danger as he confronts the murderer ("It was at that moment that he sensed a warning, the unmistakable instinct for danger. It was as much part of his detective's equipment as his knowledge of firearms, his nose for an unnatural death. It has saved him time and time again and he acted on it instinctively").

The biographical information on Dalgliesh accumulates from volume to volume: whereas in the first Chief Inspector Dalgliesh's ten-year-old sorrow is the basic piece of biography, in the second Superintendent Dalgliesh's career as a publishing poet becomes germane, while in the third he has published his second volume of verse, and readers learn that he is a parson's son. It is as the son of a cleric that he finds himself involved in a series of murders in *The Black Tower*, murders well disguised as suicides or natural deaths. On convalescent leave he responds to a call to visit a sickly old priest who had been his father's curate, only to find him dead. The grim series of deaths obsesses him, and as he attends one of the funerals he remembers the funeral of a fourteen-year-old contemporary, a friend who had murdered his family and killed himself. Only Dalgliesh and the curate had been at the grave; Dalgliesh's own parents were away on holiday, and the townspeople were hostile toward the young parricide. This shared experience at age fourteen had established a bond with his father's curate that Dalgliesh hopes to continue in his frustrated inquiries into the events surrounding his death. No stranger to churches, and indeed an enthusiastic surveyor of church architecture, he nonetheless confesses to being an unbeliever: "All these problems are easier for people who believe in God," he comments. "Those of us who don't or can't have to do the best we can. That's what the law

is, the best we can do. Human justice is imperfect, but it's the only justice we have."

In *Shroud for a Nightingale* Dalgliesh is chief superintendent; in *The Black Tower* he has become a commander, and his rise in prestige has made him something of a legend at New Scotland Yard, while the people whom he encounters in his cases know him as a poet. ("The Yard's wonder boy," comments a character in *Death of an Expert Witness*, "descends from the clouds. Well, let's hope that he works quickly.") Yet in *A Taste for Death* readers learn that he has not written poetry for some time, and he is even twitted for the failure of his muse. His self-dissection is even more mordant: he calls himself "the poet who no longer writes poetry. The lover who substitutes technique for commitment. The policeman disillusioned with policing." That disillusionment reaches its nadir in *The Black Tower*. Dalgliesh has recovered from an illness that mistakenly had been diagnosed as terminal and had made his decision to resign from the force. His obsession with the old curate's death, however, makes his an active investigation despite himself. Although both his physical strength and his will prove to be weak, his success against the odds is achieved. "The truth is, he thought, that I don't know what, if anything, I'm investigating, and I only spasmodically care. I haven't the stomach to do the job properly or the will and courage to leave it alone." Self-analysis can become very much a part of his personality, and he despairs of getting the case officially opened since he has no facts to present to the police: "He couldn't say: I, Adam Dalgliesh, have had one of my famous hunches—I disagree with the coroner, with the pathologist, with the local police, with all the facts." Only the murderer respects Dalgliesh's hunches and attempts to kill him, but not until he learns that Dalgliesh has decided to remain on the police force. Dalgliesh cunningly plans ways to make sure that if he is killed his death will be laid at his murderer's door, and he succeeds in sending the murderer to his death instead. Now hospitalized for a flesh wound, Dalgliesh hallucinates the hospital stay with which the novel opens. Physical danger has become a hallmark from the third book on and is no respecter of gender: Cordelia Gray comes close to death in both her cases. James has opted out of the genteel puzzle mystery in favor of American preferences for violence and danger at the resolution.

Very much his own person and insisting on a privacy that is close to total aloofness, Dalgliesh

Dust jackets for the first editions of four of James's novels featuring Adam Dalgliesh

is seen in different ways by the women with whom he comes in contact. In *A Mind to Murder* a woman psychiatrist blushes after noting that "He's about forty, I should think. Tall and dark. I liked his voice and he has nice hands." A senior nurse in *Shroud for a Nightingale* muses: "Probably he would be thought handsome by most women, with that lean bony face, at once arrogant and sensitive. It was probably one of his professional assets, and being a man he would make the most of it." But a beautiful and rather coldhearted woman in *Death of an Expert Witness* sums him up in a discussion with her brother, who asks:

"Was Dalgliesh offensive?"
"No more offensive than I to him. Honours even, I should have said. I don't think he liked me."
"I don't think he likes anyone much. But he's considered highly intelligent. Did you find him attractive?"
She answered the unspoken question.
"It would be like making love to a public hangman."

Dalgliesh indeed solicits such occasional negative responses, especially from some of the more unlikable people whom he meets. But it is the reaction of those who have to work with him that proves to be the most diagnostic—and caustic.

In James's first two novels, which are rather benign considering the sinister qualities of their successors, Dalgliesh's working relationships disclose very little. His sergeant in both is a man named Martin who is "ten years older than his chief and it was unlikely now that he would gain further promotion." All that readers learn is that "Dalgliesh and Martin worked together for too many years to find much talking necessary and they moved about the flat almost in silence," searching for clues. When the nondescript Sergeant Martin is replaced by Sergeant Masterson in *Shroud for a Nightingale*, particular judgments are made: "Masterson respected him. . . . He thought him very able. . . . he disliked him heartily. He suspected that the antipathy was mutual." Dalgliesh occasionally displays a fondness for good food and in this context wins some points with Masterson, who "thought that they never got closer to liking each other than when they were eating and drinking together." But there is hardly enough there for friendship, and Masterson eventually feels the brunt of Dalgliesh's wrath. Masterson's case against him is later summed up: "Dalgliesh who was so uncaring

about his subordinates' private life as to seem unaware that they had any; whose caustic wit could be as devastating as another man's bludgeon."

Death of an Expert Witness introduces Detective-Inspector the Honourable John Massingham as Commander Dalgliesh's assistant, the rank reflecting the new system at the Metropolitan Police. He is the son of a peer who has made the odd choice of the police force instead of the army. Massingham does not like his superior any better than did his predecessors, and he is surprised when other people seem to like Dalgliesh ("God knows why. At times he's cold enough to be barely human"). Dalgliesh's own verdict at the end of the case is that he "wished never to see Massingham again. But he would see him again and, in time, without even caring and remembering." Oddly enough, he chooses Massingham for his special squad in *A Taste for Death*, along with a female assistant, Kate Miskin, who has heard a great deal about her boss and sums up the conclusion at New Scotland Yard: "He's a bastard, but a just bastard." Dalgliesh's brief appearance in *An Unsuitable Job for a Woman* brings him into contact with his superior, the assistant commissioner, and the verdict there is presented with ironic humor: "The two men disliked each other but only one of them knew this and he was the one to whom it didn't matter."

Locating the essentials of Adam Dalgliesh, the inner man concealed so deftly by the professional personality, has not been easy for James's readers, although there have been some clues along the way. As early as *Unnatural Causes*, in which he is battling his own doubts between his job and a possible marriage and at best interfering with the local inspector on a case that is not his own, he has a moment of self-doubt: "Suddenly he felt again some of the uncertainties and the inadequacies which had tormented the young Detective Constable Dalgliesh nearly twenty years ago." In *Shroud for a Nightingale*, in a moment of frank conversation with a sympathetic listener, he is prodded into admitting that "I can't interest myself in anything which I not only don't understand but know that I have no prospect of ever understanding." The degree to which self-doubt determines his temporary decision to resign, as he half-unconsciously pursues an uninvited inquiry in *The Black Tower*, careful not to tread on the toes of the local police, can only be gauged by his ultimate success and decision not to leave his job, but to "get on with it." Now, with his extended appearance in *A Taste for Death*, where read-

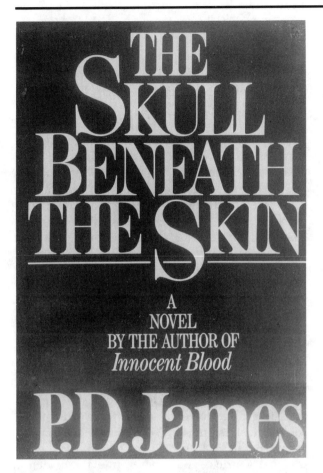

Dust jacket for the first American edition of one of two James novels featuring Cordelia Gray. The other is An Unsuitable Job for a Woman.

ers learn that his mother died when he was fifteen, there are additional clues, particularly as he associates himself with the victim, someone he had known and about whom he becomes almost as obsessional as he had over the dead priest. "We're alike even in this," Dalgliesh muses: "If he had a splinter of ice in the heart, then so have I." At a fairly leisurely moment he contemplates the escapism of a self-indulgent couple and realizes that he, too, has "his own contrivances for keeping reality at bay." The conflict between his job and his self, the basic contradiction, perhaps, between the poet (now lapsed) and the policeman (dominant, but never quite certain—Massingham ranks his interests as "his poetry, his job and his privacy. And probably in that order"), never resolves itself. At a low moment he thinks: "And if I tell myself that enough is enough, twenty years of using people's weakness against them, twenty years of careful non-involvement, if I resign,

what then?" Between arrogant self-confidence fostered by his success, and moments of despondency when he realizes the futility of life, Adam Dalgliesh makes his balanced observations, not without a touch of irony: "It was odd, he sometimes thought, that a man morbidly sensitive about his own privacy should have chosen a job that required him to invade almost daily the privacy of others."

More than even in the most extreme instances in which human beings are shown to be hermetically isolated from each other (as in *The Black Tower* and *Death of an Expert Witness*), *Devices and Desires* is peopled with aloof, constrained, unresponsive characters (one minor figure is described by her fiancé as "that blond, remote, self-contained beauty"), but none more so than Dalgliesh, who admits that he "couldn't tolerate twenty-four hours in which the greater part wasn't spent entirely alone." As he participates in a murder case in which he has no official jurisdiction, he is the close observer more than the investigating detective, analyzing people rather than clues or evidence, wondering "whether it was ever possible to know another human being except on the most superficial level." At a moment of desperate danger another minor character has the same observation, realizing that "she had never known Caroline, could never know her, never begin to understand what in her past, perhaps in her childhood, had led to this dangerous conspiracy." As in *Unnatural Causes* and *The Black Tower*, the scene is a wild and remote coastal area where Dalgliesh is on holiday, but not from himself. A perceptively astute tramp (one of James's most perfect incidental characters) challenges Dalgliesh by wondering, "from what are you escaping on this isolated headland? If from the violence of your job, you have been singularly unlucky." What Dalgliesh and the others are incapable of eluding is summed up near the end by the culminating question: "Can we never break free of the devices and desires of our own hearts?"

The Cordelia Gray narratives weave their way through the later Dalgliesh narratives as well: as a private investigator she is significantly distanced from the New Scotland Yard man yet inadvertently influenced by him at every turn. At the opening of *An Unsuitable Job for a Woman* she finds that she has inherited the detective agency where she had started as a typist and quickly been made a partner by her boss, Bernie Pryde, who prides himself at having learned his trade from Dalgliesh at the CID—from which he had been sacked (by Dalgliesh). Pryde idolizes his former boss and passes on words of wisdom constantly, to Cordelia Gray's silent anger:

> Sometimes she had wondered whether this paragon had actually existed or whether he had sprung impeccable and omnipotent from Bernie's brain, a necessary hero and mentor. It was with a shock of surprise that she had later seen a newspaper picture of Chief Superintendent Dalgliesh, a dark, sardonic face which, on her closer scrutiny, disintegrated into an ambiguity of patterned micro dots, giving nothing away. Not all the wisdom Bernie so glibly recalled was the received gospel. Much, she suspected, was his own philosophy. She in turn had devised a private litany of disdain: supercilious, superior, sarcastic Super; what wisdom, she wondered, would he have to comfort Bernie now.

Pryde commits suicide, and Dalgliesh never acknowledges his death. Cordelia claims her legacy as a responsibility and the only job she had, not quite realizing that she also inherits Dalgliesh's "wisdom" through a dead intermediary.

Cordelia's life is as open a book as Dalgliesh's is a closed one. Her past is established in the opening sections of An Unsuitable Job for a Woman: her mother died just after her birth; her father, a militant radical engaged in clandestine politics, has her fostered out to various families; a mistake of identity has her educated in a Catholic convent; the opportunity to attend Cambridge is vetoed by her father, who claims her; she has two sexual affairs with young comrades; her father's death frees her to return to London, where she goes to work for the Pryde Agency. Only in The Skull beneath the Skin, published ten years later than the first book in which she is featured but allowing only for a gap of less than a year in Cordelia's life, are readers informed that her father was a famous Marxist lecturing from university platforms. The sale of his Paris apartment provides enough money for Cordelia's new flat on the Thames, inadvertently making her Dalgliesh's neighbor (she is aware that "they shared the same river").

In both novels Cordelia Gray finds herself investigating murders when her initial assignments were decidedly less demanding than that, and despite her inexperience, not to mention her gender, her investigations are successful. In both cases, however, the solutions are not neat, textbook resolutions: in the first she finds herself concealing the killing of the murderer she had unmasked, and in the second she faces an uphill court battle if the murderer is ever to be convicted. (In the interim her agency deals with hunting down lost pets.) In both cases the slight twenty-two-year-old Cordelia is nearly murdered—in a well and in a cave—and each time she employs strategy, determination, and physical courage to survive. In the well she realized that she "was alive and capable of thought. She had always been a survivor. She would survive," and in the cave "she fought like a desperate and cornered beast. The sea was death, and she struggled against it with all she could muster of life and youth and hope." These qualities immediately and permanently identify Cordelia Gray.

As a young woman engaged in a profession reserved for mature and physically powerful men, Cordelia comes under everyone's scrutiny. In The Skull beneath the Skin the police even treat her as a suspect until Dalgliesh disabuses them of that opinion: thereafter she is only suspected of being an impressionable female with an unchecked imagination. Various people inform her that hers is "an unsuitable job for a woman," a comment she ignores. Nonetheless, the cynical murderer in An Unsuitable Job for a Woman, positive that Cordelia could never find the evidence to have him arrested, scoffs even after she has proven her courage and her deductive powers, and even a woman she aids in the process misunderstands her motives: "I thought you might have acted in the service of justice or some such abstraction." Cordelia Gray responds, "I wasn't thinking of any abstraction. I was thinking about a person," a young unfortunate who, like Cordelia, had been orphaned.

A sympathetic male character in The Skull beneath the Skin provides the most objective evaluation of Cordelia. In observing her he realizes that "despite those candid, almost judgemental eyes, the disconcerting honesty, the impression of controlled competence, she was at heart a sensitive child," noting also "how sweet she was, with that gentle, self-contained dignity." The local police sergeant, on the other hand, is far more wary: "She's attractive. Like a cat. . . . Self-contained and dignified." In An Unsuitable Job for a Woman Dalgliesh interviews her, knowing full well what she has done in her cover-up (she had used his methods, following a hunch as she knew he would have, and consequently he is able to follow her lines of thought as if they were his own). When the murderer for whom Cordelia perjured

Book 4 section 7

responds as if I were the one doing the favour. What is it about this job that makes people grateful that I can act like a human being?'

The two men waited in silence, but the tea came very quickly. So that, he thought, accounted for the delay in opening the door. She had hurried at his knock to put on the kettle. They sat ~~round~~ *at* the table in stiff formality waiting while Albert Nolan ~~had~~ *raised himself stiffly from his chair and* edged his way painfully into his seat. The effort set up a new spasm of shaking/ *Without speaking his wife poured his tea and set the cup before him.* He didn't grasp ~~his cup~~ *it*, but bent his head and slurped his tea noisily from the side. His wife didn't even look at him. There was a half-cut cake which she said was walnut and marmalade, and she smiled again when Dalgliesh accepted a slice. It was dry and rather tasteless, rolling into a soft dough in his mouth. Small pellets of walnut lodged in his teeth and the occasional sliver of orange-peel was sour to the tongue. He washed it down with a mouthful of strong, over-milked tea. Somewhere in the room a fly was making a loud intermittent buzz.

He said:

'I'm sorry that I have to trouble you, and I'm afraid it may be painful for you. As I explained on the telephone, I'm investigating the death of Sir Paul Berowne. A short time before he died he had an anonymous letter. It suggested that he might have had something to do with your granddaughter's death. That's why I'm here.'

Mrs Nolan's cup rattled in her saucer. She put both hands under the table like a well-behaved child at a party. Then she glanced at her husband. She said:

'Theresa took her own life. *I thought you'd know that, sir.*'

415

Page from the revised typescript for A Taste for Death *(Collection of P. D. James)*

herself is killed in a road accident, Dalgliesh's concern in his job of uncovering is moot. She had withstood his interrogation well: "She had resisted the momentary temptation to change her story. Bernie had been right. She recalled his advice; the Superintendent's advice; this time she could almost hear it spoken in his deep, slightly husky voice: 'If you're tempted to crime, stick to your original statement.' " To his superior Dalgliesh reports that his investigation is closed, indicating, "I don't think that young woman deludes herself about anything. I took to her, but I'm glad that I shan't be encountering her again." He is, of course, theorizing in advance of the facts: when he is hospitalized Cordelia sends him flowers that she had picked, fresh flowers rather than the cut flowers he detests, and in his delirium at the end of *The Black Tower* he worries over not having thanked her for them.

There is no evidence for a long time that their paths have ever crossed again, but he is obviously in her thoughts: she tries unconvincingly to dismiss her attraction by labeling him a father-surrogate. When she knows that the police are investigating her and her agency she tries to imagine that it is Dalgliesh climbing her stairs but knows that he is too important these days for so menial a job: "From the rarefied and mysterious heights of hierarchy which he now inhabited, any such chore was unthinkable. She wondered whether he would read about the crime, whether he would learn that she was involved." The local inspector is quite caustic in identifying Commander Dalgliesh: "The Commissioner's blue-eyed boy, darling of the establishment," but he nonetheless acknowledges Dalgliesh's impressive accomplishments ("He could have had his own force by now . . . if he hadn't wanted to stick to detection"). His transmittal of Dalgliesh's assessment of the suspect is highly revealing of the personal evaluation concealed in his professional one:

> He knows the girl, Cordelia Gray. They tangled together in a previous case. Cambridge, apparently. No details offered and none asked for. But he's given her and that agency a clean bill. Like him or not, he's a good copper, one of the best. If he says that Gray isn't a murderess, I'm prepared to take that as evidence of a sort. But he didn't say that she's incapable of lying, and I wouldn't have believed him if he had.

(In *A Taste for Death*, when gossip reaches Dalgliesh about "Adam Dalgliesh, poet-detective, with Cordelia Gray at Mon Plaisir," the commander merely comments: "Your readers must lead very dull lives if they can find vicarious excitement in a young woman and myself virtuously eating duck à l'orange.")

As forceful and delightful as her two detectives are, they do not overshadow the fictions in which they are central, and with the publication in 1980 of *Innocent Blood* James wrote her only nondetective novel to date, proving that she could sustain a long narrative without a detective as its focal point. Nor is *Innocent Blood* a traditional crime novel: a murder *had* taken place, but that was ten years in the past; a vengeance killing is being planned, making the novel in part a type of inverse crime novel, but it misfires when the knife is plunged into the neck of the victim who had already committed suicide. As James has explained, one of the inspirations for the novel came from the passing of the "Legislation for Children Act of 1975," which "gave eighteen-year-old adoptive children in England and Wales the right to set out on the journey of exploring who their real parents were by having access to their birth certificates." James's eighteen-year-old is a young woman not unlike Cordelia Gray, rebelling against her unloving adoptive parents and persistent in finding out her own identity. That her father died in prison, convicted of having raped a twelve-year-old girl, and her mother was soon to be released from prison, having killed the rape victim, seems to bother her less than the news that her mother had violently mistreated her as a child, necessitating her adoption *before* the rape and murder. The father of the dead girl meanwhile stalks the released murderer, who now lives with her daughter. All the elements of the crime novel are there, and all the motifs, techniques, and individual touches of a James mystery are there as well. "I think it shows the influence of the detective story," James has commented, "in that it is a book which does in fact have clues—clues to personality, clues to events that have happened."

There are numerous characteristics that make a James mystery recognizable, the most prominent being the setting, what James has called a sense of place. Few of her books are located in London. Until such late works as *Innocent Blood* and *A Taste for Death*, only *A Mind to Murder* was set in London, with no real incorporation of the city ambience; these two recent books, however, powerfully evoke the areas around Paddington, Notting Hill, and West Kensington, particularly the Holland Park section where James now lives. The scene of her first novel is rather conventional, an Elizabethan manor house in an Essex village, but that was before James began to realize her potential for Gothicism. Only with the third book does the Gothic become a vital, though never controlling, element in her fiction. *Unnatural Causes* is situated in the East Anglian region that James particularly loves, from childhood summers and her own Southwold cottage, and she has even written an article for one of the posh Sunday newspapers in which she traces the routes and scenes of that novel. For *Devices and Desires* the scene shifts from Suffolk to Norfolk, to a converted windmill that Dalgliesh inherited from his Aunt Jane. The neighboring buildings include a ruined Benedictine abbey, a cottage on the site of the residence of a burned Protestant martyr, a delapidated caravan, and the newly built nuclear reactor. The Dorset coast provides the mood setting for her starkest novel, *The Black Tower*, where an asylum for the dying crippled, staffed by attendants in monks' habits, is claustrophobically sequestered from the nearby sea. Also in the same area is the setting for *The Skull beneath the Skin* but in this case in a restored castle on a forbidding island off the coast. The location of the hospital in *Shroud for a Nightingale* is of less importance than the doomed building itself, while the wild fen country plays its atmospheric role in *Death of an Expert Witness*. By contrast, *An Unsuitable Job for a Woman* is very much a nostalgic evocation of the beauties of Cambridge, but not without its stark outposts and byroads.

Once she realized her talent and taste for the Gothic, James has never relented in using it, although she employs it judiciously. She evokes the sounds of smugglers' horses along coastal roads and the bells of long-drowned churches causing the "stirring of an atavistic fear of darkness and the unknown" in *Unnatural Causes*, a work that begins with a drifting dinghy containing the body of a neatly dressed corpse whose hands have been hacked off at the wrists. (The grisly opening also proves potent in later James novels—Cordelia finding Bernie Pryde's dead body in the office when she arrives for work; an elderly spinster and a ten-year-old boy finding two corpses with throats slashed in the church vestry—a contrast to some of the openings of her more genteel mysteries.) In *Unnatural Causes* a storm that rages along the East Anglian coast terrifies a crippled woman in her vulnerable cliff-side cottage as she arms herself against what she believes is a

murderous intruder, although she herself is the murderer.

James has a keen eye for architectural structures and reads them as emblematic of the lives of their inhabitants; a concern in her fiction is the impact of the past on the present and the violation of the past by the present. The Gothic effect is immediate for the convalescent Dalgliesh as he approaches the area of the black tower: "He sensed something strange and sinister in its emptiness and loneliness which even the mellow afternoon sunlight couldn't dispel." Two recent deaths and three that follow them are reinforced by the legend of the death of the builder of the tower who while alive immured himself within it awaiting the Second Coming but tore his fingers to the bone attempting to undo his interment. The ghostly sounds emanating from the tower frighten even Dalgliesh, but he uses the sound of the rasping torn branches to good advantage when he is in a death struggle with the murderer. A grisly death in the island castle cave also sets a precedent in *The Skull beneath the Skin*, for it claims a new victim at the resolution of the novel—and almost claims Cordelia as well. Like *The Black Tower*, *Shroud for a Nightingale* also begins with an approach to a "Castle Perilous," although the building is merely a hospital that had been created out of a country house. A dark and rainy early January morning finds the visitor driving toward Nightingale House: "She felt strangely isolated in the dim quietness and suddenly she was touched with an irrational unease, a bizarre sensation of journeying out of time into some new dimension, borne onwards towards an uncomprehended and inescapable horror." (Within the hour she will witness the violent death by poisoning of a nurse during a demonstration of intragastric tube feeding.) The house itself is the basic Gothic structure. After the three murders, as well as the bludgeon attack on Dalgliesh, the walls of this House of Usher are doomed to fall. The architectural structure had been desecrated in its transition into a hospital, for which it was quite unsuited, and when the visitor returns after the case has been resolved, she finds that the "house looked as if it had been clumsily cut into two by a giant's claw, a living thing wantonly mutilated." The building is being pulled down, for the nurse's training school has been relocated. The murderer's cottage in *Unnatural Causes* is perceived by Dalgliesh as "an ugly building, as uncompromisingly square as a doll's house," and it is destined to be tumbled into the sea by violent nature—a nature as violent but without the same purposeful maliciousness as its occupant. Even incidental abodes in *Devices and Desires* contribute to the collection of unsuitable dwellings, such as the one that "faced inland, a square, uncompromising building with a cobbled yard instead of a front garden, and picture windows which destroyed any period charm it might once have had," as well as a "forbidding, almost sinister little box of crude red brick."

Both Adam Dalgliesh and Cordelia Gray have an eye for architecture and decor, as does Phillippa in *Innocent Blood*, as they evaluate their surroundings. They are able to appreciate a house that is "simple but strongly formalized in design," a room that is beautifully proportioned, a row of cottages that displays "unity of age, architecture and height," but each cottage "charmingly individual." A solicitor's office building may display "solid affluence, tradition and professional rectitude," but his own office mirrors the man himself: the room is "poky, stuffy and untidy." In James such contrasts often are diagnostic of a violation, a falling-off, a failure to keep faith. The death cottage in *An Unsuitable Job for a Woman*, in which Cordelia camps out during her investigation, has been superstitiously neglected but was in the process of being rescued and restored when its occupant was killed ("It was, she thought, a curious place, heavy with atmosphere and showing two distinct faces to the world like facets of a human personality"). Dalgliesh encounters the same dichotomy when he arrives at the forensic laboratory that a nineteenth-century benefactor has made from his own manor house. As he admires the "excellent example of late seventeenth-century domestic architecture," his escort comments, "Agreeable, isn't it? But wait till you see what the old man did to some of the interior." What he sees is a despoliation of the contours for pragmatic purposes, making makeshift work space out of elegance, proportion, and spaciousness, a compromise noted in many professional buildings that he enters, even those of the government in Whitehall. Whereas the old buildings with "Gothic splendour" he assumes were "infuriating and uncomfortable to work in," the new ones reveal an intention "to express confident authority tempered by humanity," but "he wasn't sure that the architect had succeeded. It looked more suitable for a multinational corporation than a great Department of State."

For the cheerful and sanguine Cordelia Gray the viewings of the three dwellings are diagnostic, including the two-faceted cottage in which she takes refuge. The main house to which the cottage belongs is a "large Victorian edifice of red brick," and she wonders why "anyone should have wanted to build such an intimidatingly ugly house, or, having decided to do so, would have set down a suburban monstrosity in the middle of the countryside. . . . Even the rock plants burgeoned like morbid excrescences." Major ambiguity is found in a house in which the victim had been reared and where his father, his murderer, still lives and runs a major laboratory:

> The house was obviously Georgian, not perhaps the best Georgian but solidly built, agreeably proportioned and with the look of all good domestic architecture of having grown naturally out of its site. The mellow brick, festooned with wisteria, gleamed richly in the evening sun so that the green of the creeper glowed and the whole house looked suddenly as artificial and unsubstantial as a film set. It was essentially a family house, a welcoming house. But now a heavy silence lay over it and the rows of elegantly proportioned windows were empty eyes.

A constant undercutting of the potentially positive delineates an important aspect of the James novels. There are frequent negative descriptions of ugly edifices, the smug bourgeois, and the insipid poor, but the subtle undermining of a manor house is particularly characteristic of James.

While regarding the Victorian dwelling Cordelia wonders if "perhaps it had replaced an earlier more agreeable house," and indeed many of the buildings that serve as the central stage of the Jamesian dramas have been converted from something else, and each is either in the process or in potential danger of being reconverted, abandoned, or demolished. Numerous indications of an old order having changed, and now in the flux of changing once again, with a loss of continuity and a greater degree of depersonalization, permeate the mood of her novels generally, but nowhere as subtly as in *Death of an Expert Witness*. The new employee, a bright woman of eighteen, is impressed that the forensic laboratory has a long and unbroken history, but the new director has replaced the portrait of the founder with a modern painting intended to discomfort his staff. (Paintings hung in residential dwellings and offices are carefully scrutinized by each of the James protagonists and are significant indicators throughout—when Phillippa of *Innocent Blood*

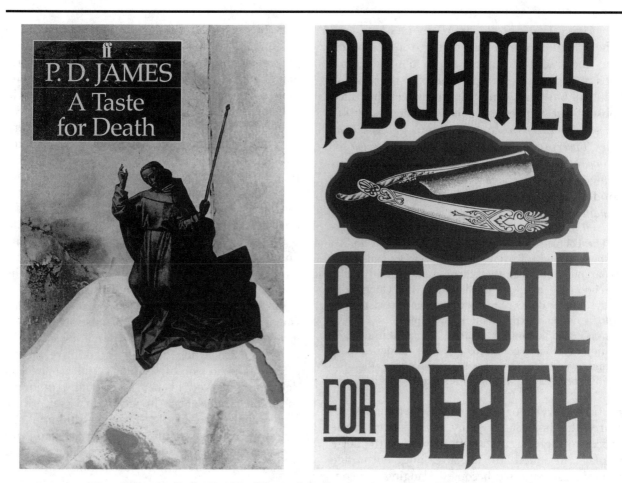

Dust jackets for the first British edition and the first American edition of James's 1986 novel

leaves her adoptive home for the flat she rented for her real mother, she takes with her only a valued and valuable painting.) The disruption within the administration of the forensic lab is making its effects known, and a new structure is in the process of being built on the grounds. At present it is a dangerous area, with warning signs to the staff not to use it as a shortcut. Yet when she finds herself in danger, Brenda Pridmore, a young employee, cuts through it in the dark and manages to terrify herself to the extent that she rushes into the chapel for succor—only to discover a hanging corpse. She survives her experience but does not return to her job.

Two architectural creations loom large in *A Taste for Death*, both by famous nineteenth-century designers but fictionalized by James for her particular settings: a Romanesque church in Paddington credited to Arthur Blomfield and a four-story residence on Campden Hill Square attributed to Sir John Soane. The church has as its vicar an unkempt priest who has lost his faith to the same extent as the church has lost its parishion-

ers, and yet it is here that one of the victims has had a religious conversion and is brutally murdered, along with a tramp who used it as a haven. The house, greatly admired by Dalgliesh, is nonetheless assessed by him as a dwelling in which none of the residents, except for the eighty-two-year-old grande dame, has endowed it with any element of individual personality. These buildings declare their elegance as architectural achievements but not as reflections of their constituent humanity. In her work James strongly implies that only those places in which someone has devoted time and effort, a measure of love and attention (transferred intact from builder to resident), an indication of an individual personality or the shared love of the occupants, have a human resonance and an element of beauty. The destructive defeat caused by poverty, the aesthetic indifference derived from bourgeois complacency, or the callous results of narrow ambition can turn any residence into a demeaning hovel or an architectural horror, relentlessly reflecting the lives within.

Her variants on Edgar Allan Poe's House of Usher theme seem representative for her of either fine traditions fading out or obsolete traditions still dug in, of ugly buildings retained or beautiful buildings cannibalized. Stables that once housed fine horses have either been sold off (*Cover Her Face*) or converted into garages (*The Black Tower*) or laboratories (*An Unsuitable Job for a Woman*). Renovations, when they do suggest an element of progress, are inefficacious, as in the London address of one of the shadier suspects in *Unnatural Causes:*

> The cobbled entrance was uninviting, ill-lit and smelt strongly of urine. . . . The premises had apparently once been the headquarters of a driving school and a few tattered notices still clung to the garage doors. But they were dedicated now to a nobler purpose, the improvement of London's chronic housing shortage. More accurately, they were being converted into dark, under-sized and over-priced cottages soon, no doubt, to be advertized as "bijou town residences."

Even the Liverpool Street railway terminus is not spared this Jamesian scrutiny, when it was "in the process of being rebuilt—'improved,' as the large displays designed to reassure and encourage proclaimed—and had become a clanging and confusing maze of temporary walkways and direction signs in which it was difficult to actually find the trains."

The basic milieu of the James mysteries is unmistakably that of the upper middle class, particularly among those of professional status, physicians and scientists, writers and technicians, and even a member of Parliament, but the sociological perspective is often much broader. When Phillippa in *Innocent Blood*, reared in upper-middle-class comfort, begins her trek in search of her parents, a train takes her eastward from London, and she views "rows of drab houses with blackened bricks and patched roofs from which sprang a tangle of television aerials, frail crooked fetishes against the evil eye; layered high-rise flats smudged in a distant drizzle of rain; a yard piled high with the glitter of smashed cars in symbolic proximity to the regimented crosses of a suburban graveyard; a paint factory; a cluster of gasometers; pyramids of grit and coal piled beside the track; wastelands rank with weeds; a sloping green bank rising to suburban gardens with their washing lines and toolsheds and children's swings among the roses and hollyhocks."

In describing and analyzing the social scene in England, using her skills as a former employee of the Criminal Policy Department and her expertise in the juvenile courts, James nonetheless has no fixed political perspective as such, and one can believe her statement to Julian Symons (in a review of *A Taste for Death*) that at various times she has voted Conservative, Labour, and Liberal: a strong humanitarian thrust is tempered by a sense of tradition and a mood of caution. More recently, James's more traditional attitudes may have hardened, as Dalgliesh faces the nuclear reactor and muses on the present: "This is the music of 1988; these are our heroes; that building on the headland is our architecture," and later "he found himself wondering, as he had before in his life, at man's insistent need for ritual, for the formal acknowledgement of each rite of passage." Nor does the professional sociologist necessarily fare particularly well, especially in *Innocent Blood*, where Phillippa's adoptive father, a famous professor of sociology and a television debater, is viewed by her as cold and unloving (he depicts himself as "invincibly arrogant in the high renaissance of the heart")—although she not only returns to him but goes to bed with him. Scrutiny of the social scene is balanced, and even undercut, by James's fascination with aberrant psychology, particularly in her later works. The *New York Times* reviewer of *A Taste for Death* may have balked at the book's resolution, which not only shifts from the detective format to an inverse crime story but also has as its revealed murderer a "psychopath" (also dismissed as an "erratic madman"), yet the murderer becomes so psychologically authenticated as he discloses his motivations that the charge of authorial arbitrariness seems unfounded. James rarely opts for the *surface* motives for murder, although enough suspects have them, but more and more often finds motivation within the realm of hate and love, within the personal rather than the social realm. Human fallibility, instead of greed, ambition, or desire, is frequently at the core of the crime. In *Shroud for a Nightingale* the matron exonerates a nurse who considers herself guilty of theft ("Every one of us has some incident in our lives that we're ashamed and sorry about"); soon after, Dalgliesh exonerates the matron on the basis of a valid alibi, and she responds: "I know it's foolish to feel such relief at not being under suspicion when one knows anyway that one is innocent. Perhaps it's because none of us is innocent in any real sense." What she is concealing is that she had stood trial for war crimes at Nuremberg, and she knows that her close associate has killed a nurse who knew this fact. The associate has murdered and will murder again, as well as attack Dalgliesh, out of love, a love that she has used as blackmail in her demanding friendship with the matron. She is discovered to have killed herself, but Dalgliesh knows—although he is unable to prove—that she has been murdered by the matron, who eventually does commit suicide. In its profound and perverse manifestations, love often proves to be potentially dangerous in James's novels.

It is interesting to note that the first four James books have a woman as the murderer (there are two murderers in *Shroud for a Nightingale*), although there is also a male accomplice in one instance and a male attempting murder in another. That women are not exempt from criminality in her work is particularly underscored by the fact that she presents women as having strong capacities for emotional commitment and emotional frustration. James's nicest murderess is the mother in *Cover Her Face* (she is also the nicest of all the suspects); she throttles an infuriatingly disruptive element in her household, a maid who threatens the sanctity of the family. When Dalgliesh has eliminated all of the other suspects she quietly confesses, having waited until her terminally ill husband has died so that she could be free to be imprisoned. Although no one had apparently suspected her as such, there was a reluctance among the family and friends to encourage the police in their investigation, as if the necessity to bring the murderer to justice was in itself an aberration of human justice. "Then why not leave it to the police?" one of the most perceptive suspects comments; "Their greatest difficulty will be to get enough evidence to justify a charge." An equally sympathetic murderess, although a far more complex character, emerges at the end of *Devices and Desires*, where Dalgliesh only "suspects" her, while the investigating detective prefers two other women as the murderers, all three now dead.

In James's fiction, that a murder is sometimes not so much an antisocial act as a corrective undercuts the concept that society must avenge every homicide and protect itself from anyone with homicidal tendencies. Dalgliesh muses on the idea that "Every death benefited someone, enfranchised someone, lifted a burden from someone's shoulders, whether of responsibility, the pain of vicarious suffering or the tyranny of love. Every death was a suspicious death if one looked only at motive, just as every death, at the last, was a natural death." Yet in *The Black Tower* five murders have been committed—and the murder of Dalgliesh is attempted—by a murderer protecting his acquired affluence, attained through illicit drug trafficking. The "tyranny of love" is hardly operative in *The Black Tower* as it is in *Shroud for a Nightingale*, *A Mind to Murder*, *A Taste for Death*, and *Devices and Desires*: the need to assure the comfort of a terminally ill mother by preventing a change in a will and the obsessive dependence on a sister's love produce two very different kinds of killers. In controlling her narratives James opts for the modernist tendency of allowing her suspects to reveal their thoughts to the reader without precipitously revealing their guilt, so that the mother in *Cover Her Face* can reveal her "honest mind" as she "explored . . . this revelation that a loyalty which the family had all taken for granted had been more complicated, less acquiescent than any of them had suspected and had at last been strained too far." In effect, this is a confession but only apprehended by a reader exploring psychological motivations instead of the more traditional ones.

Twice in the James canon a four-element package of motives is presented as all-inclusive: in *Unnatural Causes* Dalgliesh remembers his "old chief" insisting on the "four L's—love, lust, loathing and lucre" and concludes that "superficially that was true enough." The key element in this case is loathing, the least traditional of the four and the one that eventually explains the ghastly murder and mutilation. Hate hides itself more successfully than love, but few writers of detective fiction would ever feel secure enough in using it as a motive for murder unless they could provide the psychological portraits that have become James's particular strength. To educate her readers on the potency of hatred she has the most innocent of the suspects turn on one of the more obvious ones and declare, "I don't think you hated him that much." The murderer herself is even more precise in her taped confession, when she gloatingly states that "it was convenient that there should be at least two people at Monksmere, both spiteful, both aggrieved, both with an obvious motive." When Dalgliesh in *A Taste for Death* reiterates the verdict of "an old detective sergeant," there is a new emphasis (perhaps intended to both lead and mislead the reader): "Love, Lust, Loathing, Lucre, the four Ls of murderer, laddie. And the greatest of these is lucre." The complexity of *A Taste for Death* is such that both the murderer and the woman who provides him with an alibi harbor hatred and love—the latter invariably misdirected—but that securing wealth for his beloved sister also means securing it for himself as well. In effect, all four L's are operative, given the various lies and concealments practiced by the suspects. One of them Dalgliesh dismisses as displaying "arrogance, aggression, sexual jealousy. . . . But not hate." Dalgliesh has developed a sixth sense about hate, noting that "this murderer didn't kill from expediency. There had been hatred in that room. Hate isn't an easy emotion to hide." Conversely, in *Death of an Expert Witness* Dalgliesh again quotes his mentor ("the first detective sergeant I worked under") as saying: "They'll tell you that the most destructive force in the world is hate. Don't you believe it, lad. It's love. And if you want to make a detective you'd better learn to recognise it when you meet it."

The conventional notion, which is propagated through most of the history of detective fiction either explicitly or implicitly, has been the assumed redressing of balance with the apprehension of the murderer, especially in the years of capital punishment (an eye for an eye, a death for a death, returns the world to normality). Yet the problem has been complicated by the two persistent extremes: the victim more heinous than the murderer and the murderer, usually the multiple murderer, who is particularly vile. James deals with both extremes, the first in *Cover Her Face, Death of an Expert Witness*, and *Devices and Desires*, and the second in *The Black Tower* and *A Taste for Death*, as she investigates an intricately unpleasant society, uncovering the "sad sludge of a dead world." Dalgliesh is aware of the dangers of such uncoverings: in *Death of an Expert Witness* he is told by the retiring controller of the Forensic Science Service, "You chaps usually bring as much trouble with you as you solve. You can't help it. Murder is like that, a contaminating crime. Oh, you'll solve it, I know. You always do. But I'm wondering at what cost." The same observation is made with bitterness by the murdered man's mistress in *A Taste for Death*, again to Dalgliesh: "but what about your victims? I expect you'll catch Paul's murderer. You usually do, don't you? Does it ever occur to you to count the cost?"

Despite the precision with which James practices her craft, no rational or scientific touchstone is applied to the society she dissects, and, as with many other writers of the genre, she reveals a fasci-

nation with death, a vision of "the skull beneath the skin," a phrase from Renaissance revenge tragedian John Webster which has been transmitted in the present century with a quasi-religious note by T. S. Eliot. (Even before using it as the title of her ninth novel, James employs the phrase in *The Black Tower*, and she uses it again, in *A Taste for Death*.) Religion plays an important role in all of James's novels, from the love of English church architecture shared by her two protagonists, though neither professes to being religious, to the sham religion of *The Black Tower* and the persistence of the religious in *A Taste for Death*. In *Death of an Expert Witness* a lovely Wren chapel is used for fornication and later for a murder, and in *A Taste for Death* the throat slasher strikes again and shoots the vicar. The book ends with the devout parishioner, who found the dead bodies in the church, trying to pray, despite her realization that she had probably lost her faith. James told Symons that she was an Anglican, and "quite a religious person," but the most pervasive aspect of the religious in her novels is the underlying persistence of evil, stronger throughout than even the most dire of sociological causes and the most pronounced of psychological causes. Few of the books are without some speculation that evil or wickedness is an entity in itself and basically at the bottom of the homicidal horror. Even before the murder in *Cover Her Face* has been discovered, the perpetrator of the crime has a feeling that "the imminence of evil took hold of her and she had to pause for a second before she could trust her voice." Yet it is the need to care for her dying husband that keeps her from immediately confessing to the crime of manslaughter.

Whatever role unmitigated evil has been allowed to play in the detective subgenre, where hardheaded and logical deduction has been expected to hold sway despite an almost supernatural atmospheric aura at times, it has been given prominence as the result of criminal tendencies rather than the cause. On occasion in a James novel it is that aura that pervades, perhaps suggesting something more, as when Dalgliesh senses that "no corner of Nightingale House was free of the oppressive atmosphere of evil; the very plants seemed to be sucking their manna from the tainted air" and has his sensation corroborated at the end when the visitor watches it being demolished: "It was a horrible house; an evil house. It should have been pulled down fifty years ago." In the tradition of the Gothic tale a house is imbued with evil, and the act of demolition is also the act of exorcism. Dalgliesh feels the same emanations in the dead priest's cottage where he takes his temporary residence (as Cordelia did in the dead youth's cottage): "He could almost believe that he smelt the presence of evil." As a detective he mistrusts the nonrational ("It was an alien factor which he half resented and almost wholly distrusted"), yet it leads him to the conclusion that the priest had been murdered. Cordelia comes to the same conclusion about the presumed suicide victim whose cottage she inhabits: "Evil existed—she hadn't needed a convent education to convince her of that reality—and it had been present in this room. Something here had been stronger than wickedness, ruthlessness, cruelty or expedience. Evil." (Her convent education parallels Dalgliesh's parsonage childhood.) Cordelia discovers that the murder was done with ruthlessness and cruelty and for expediency, and the murderer taunts her with her own human complicity: "If you are capable of imagining it, then I'm capable of doing it. Haven't you yet discovered that about human beings, Miss Gray? It's the key to what you would call the wickedness of man."

Gray is naturally more receptive than Dalgliesh to the concept of evil as it is embodied in an evil human being. In *The Skull beneath the Skin* she examines poison-pen letters and considers their effect on the receiver, both the maliciousness of the intender and the vulnerability of the intended: "in all societies there was an atavistic fear of the malevolent power of a secret adversary working for evil, willing one to failure, perhaps to death. There was a rather horrible and frightening intelligence at work here"—the closest she comes to accepting a demonic presence. Later she discusses evil with the dying man who befriended her, specifically in religious terms, acknowledging to herself that "it was when she had finally stared into the face of his murderer [that of the youth in *An Unsuitable Job*] that she had known about evil." Ironically, the writer of the poison-pen letters does not intend death as his result but covers up someone else's inadvertent murder and now finds himself in the process of attempting to murder the slayer (and Cordelia) to keep him quiet. Aware of multiple ironies, he explains that he was being blackmailed and staked everything in keeping the money that he inherited despite his violation of the tax laws that would deprive him of all his gains. It was a charitable act that had brought him back from tax exile, and that act of charity was now resulting in his

criminal acts. It was "a simple act of filial kindness," and yet it was the germinating cause of malevolence and murder: "Evil coming out of good, if those two words mean something to you." In *Innocent Blood* Phillippa hears her mother describe her father's rape of the twelve-year-old girl and thinks, "He had made use of what was good and kind in her to destroy her. If evil existed, if those four letters placed in that order had any reality, then surely here was evil."

With eleven novels James is at the zenith of her career. She is probably the most complex writer of detective fiction in England today, and her achievements have been appropriately acknowledged. Four of her books have been made into television films; she was awarded an OBE in the Queen's Birthday Honours in 1983; and in 1985 she was elected a fellow of the Royal Society of Arts and an associate fellow of Downing College, Cambridge. She has written her first play, *A Private Treason* ("there is a crime within it," she has acknowledged, "although it is not a mystery story as such"), produced in Watford in April 1985. Her most interesting departure, however, is *The Maul and the Pear Tree: The Ratcliffe Highway Murders, 1811* (1971), coauthored with her then supervisor at the Home Office, T. A. Critchley. In it they examine an old case that excited incredible interest in England at the time, including questions in Parliament. Bloody crimes were committed for which a suspect was arrested, but he died by his own hand instead of that of the executioner. To James and Critchley it remains an unsolved crime, and they investigate the documents in the case with careful scrutiny, unsatisfied with the reported result but still unable to determine the total facts of the case. It is both a history and a condemnation of archaic police methods and of inhumane behavior toward others. Published in England in 1971, it has only recently been published in America, attesting to James's newly acquired stature on this side of the Atlantic.

There are some new departures in the most recent work, almost as if P. D. James were feeling restricted within the conventions of even the more expanded detective novel: several of the characters are allowed to bare their thoughts to the reader, revealing important aspects of their past lives to the extent that even Dalgliesh never learns the underlying motivation for the murder; two murder investigations track each other for the first half of the book; minor personages take on fascinating characteristics; and the "alternate" detective's life figures importantly, as does his rivalry with Dalgliesh. That a surprising lesbian relationship surfaces late in the plot—only to be discovered as a false trail leading away from a terrorist plot that brings Dalgliesh into an uncomfortable alliance with MI5—may indicate that James is straining against the conventions of the genre where on other occasions she was able to supersede them with finesse. But most important is the expanded portrait of Adam Dalgliesh, who has inherited a fortune that could mean his separation from Scotland Yard (but no indication that this is his intention) and has lost "his last surviving relative, an aunt whom he liked and respected, but he had never thought that he had really known her, and now he never would. He was a little surprised how much he minded." Perhaps even more significant is his new stature as a respected poet: "After four years of silence his new book of poetry, *A Case to Answer and Other Poems*, had been published to considerable critical acclaim." And there are intriguing clues to Dalgliesh in love: "Certainly he wanted some people to read him, one person in particular, and having read the poems he wanted her to approve."

James's commitment to the detection format, which had been put in question by the writing of *Innocent Blood* and the speculation that she might join her rival and admirer Ruth Rendell in some sort of alternation of detective and nondetective fiction, seems to remain firm after the publication of the latest Cordelia Gray and Adam Dalgliesh books. When she was pointedly asked about that commitment, she told Symons, "I write detective stories. I hope they're novels, too, and I don't see any contradiction in that. But if I felt there *was* a contradiction, if the detective element got in the way of the novel and I had to sacrifice one or the other, then the detective element would have to go. I hope and believe I shan't have to make such a choice." Her sense of what she is doing as a detective novelist can best be viewed in what she wrote in *The Skull beneath the Skin*, where the case under investigation can be read to pertain to the novel under construction:

> Murder, the unique and ultimate crime, was seldom the most interesting forensically or the most difficult to solve. But when you did get a good one there was no excitement like it: the heady combination of a manhunt with a puzzle; the smell of fear in the air, strong as the metallic smell of blood; the sense of randy well-being; the fascinating way in which confidence, personality, morale, subtly changed and deteriorated under its contaminating impact. A good murder was what police

work was about. And this promised to be a good one.

Despite her professed preference for what she terms "literary realism" and the exacting verisimilitude of her settings and details, James is instinctively aware of the gap between real life and good fiction, and the murders she plots are invariably replete with excitement and the qualities she lists. A good murder is what her novels are about.

Interviews:

Barbara Bannon, "PW Interviews: P. D. James," *Publishers Weekly*, 209 (5 January 1976): 8-9;

Patricia Craig, "An Interview with P. D. James," *Times Literary Supplement*, 5 June 1981, p. 4079;

Dale Salwak, "An Interview with P. D. James," *Clues*, 6 (Spring-Summer 1985): 31-50;

Rosemary Herbert, "A Mind to Write," *Armchair Detective*, 19 (1986): 340-348;

"Detective Stories Affirm the Sanctity of Life," *U.S. News & World Report*, 24 November 1986;

M. Stassio, "No Gore, Please—They're British," *New York Times Book Review*, 9 October 1988.

References:

Jane S. Bakerman, "Cordelia Gray: Apprentice and Archetype," *Clues*, 5 (Spring-Summer 1984): 101-114;

Bakerman, "From the time I could read, I always wanted to be a writer," *Armchair Detective*, 10 (1977): 55-57, 92;

Bernard Benstock, "The Clinical World of P. D. James," in *Twentieth-Century Women Novelists*, edited by Thomas F. Staley (London: Macmillan, 1982), pp. 104-129;

SueEllen Campbell, "The Detective Heroine and the Death of her Hero: Dorothy Sayers to P. D. James," *Modern Fiction Studies*, 29 (Autumn 1983): 497-510;

M. Cannon, "Mistress of Malice Domestic," *New York Times Book Review*, 27 April 1980, p. 50;

S. L. Clark, "*Gaudy Night*'s Legacy: P. D. James's *An Unsuitable Job for a Woman*," *Sayers Review*, 4 (1980): 1-11;

Lillian De La Torre, "Cordelia Gray: The Thinking Man's Heroine," in *Murderess Ink*, edited by Dilys Winn (New York: Workman, 1977), pp. 111-113;

K. Flett, "Murder, She Writes," *Harper's Bazaar* (September 1989);

Richard B. Gidez, *P. D. James* (Boston: G. K. Hall, 1986);

Donald Goddard, "The Unmysterious P. D. James," *New York Times Book Review*, 27 April 1980, p. 28;

Bruce Harkness, "P. D. James," in *Essays in Detective Fiction*, edited by Benstock (London: Macmillan, 1983), pp. 119-141;

Erlene Hubly, "Adam Dalgliesh: Byronic Hero," *Clues*, 3 (Fall-Winter 1982): 40-46;

Hubly, "The Formula Challenged: The Novels of P. D. James," *Modern Fiction Studies*, 29 (Autumn 1983): 511-521;

Nancy Carol Joyner, "P. D. James," in *Ten Women of Mystery*, edited by Earl F. Bargainnier (Bowling Green, Ohio: Bowling Green University Popular Press, 1981);

Thomas Lask, "Another Aspect of a Mystery Writer," *New York Times*, 8 February 1980, p. 27;

Dennis Porter, "Detection and Ethics: The Case of P. D. James," in *The Sleuth and the Scholar: Evolution of Current Trends in Detective Fiction*, edited by Barbara A. Rader and Howard G. Zetler (Westport, Conn.: Greenwood Press, 1988), pp. 11-18;

Norma Siebenheller, *P. D. James* (New York: Ungar, 1981);

Christine W. Sizemore, "The City as Mosaic: P. D. James," in *A Female Vision of the City: London in the Novels of Five British Women* (Knoxville: University of Tennessee Press, 1989), pp. 152-187;

Julian Symons, "The Queen of Crime," *New York Times Magazine*, 5 October 1986;

Patricia A. Ward, "Moral Ambiguities and the Crime Novels of P. D. James," *Christian Century*, 101 (16 May 1984): 519-522;

Robin W. Winks, "P. D. James: Murder and Dying," *New Republic* (31 July 1976): 31-32.

Philip Larkin

(9 August 1922 - 9 December 1985)

This entry was updated by Bruce K. Martin (Drake University) from his entry in
DLB 27: Poets of Great Britain and Ireland, 1945-1960.

SELECTED BOOKS: *The North Ship* (London: Fortune Press, 1945; enlarged edition, London: Faber & Faber, 1966);

Jill (London: Fortune Press, 1946; revised edition, London: Faber & Faber, 1964; New York: St. Martin's Press, 1964);

A Girl in Winter (London: Faber & Faber, 1947; New York: St. Martin's Press, 1963);

XX Poems (Belfast: Privately printed, 1951);

[Poems] Fantasy Poets, no. 21 (Oxford: Fantasy Press, 1954);

The Less Deceived (Hessle, Yorkshire: Marvell Press, 1955; New York: St. Martin's Press, 1960);

The Whitsun Weddings (London: Faber & Faber, 1964; New York: Random House, 1964);

All What Jazz. A Record Diary 1961-68 (London: Faber & Faber, 1970; New York: St. Martin's Press, 1970);

High Windows (London: Faber & Faber, 1974; New York: Farrar, Straus & Giroux, 1974);

Required Writing: Miscellaneous Pieces 1955-1982 (London: Faber & Faber, 1983);

Collected Poems, edited, with an introduction, by Anthony Thwaite (London: Marvell Press/Faber & Faber, 1988; New York: Farrar, Straus & Giroux, 1989).

RECORDINGS: *Listen presents Philip Larkin reading The Less Deceived*, Listen LPV 1 (Hessle, Yorkshire: Marvell Press, 1959);

Philip Larkin reads and comments on The Whitsun Weddings, Listen LPV 6; the Poets Voice series, edited by George Hartley (Hessle, Yorkshire: Marvell Press, circa 1966);

British poets of our time, Philip Larkin; High windows; poems read by the author, Argo PLP 1202 (London: Arts Council of Great Britain and the British Council, circa 1975).

OTHER: *The Oxford Book of Twentieth-Century English Verse*, edited by Larkin (London: Oxford University Press, 1973).

photograph by Alan Marshall

SELECTED PERIODICAL PUBLICATIONS—UNCOLLECTED: "Wanted: Good Hardy Critic," *Critical Quarterly*, 8 (Summer 1966): 174-179; "It could only happen in England," *Cornhill*, 1969 (Autumn 1971): 21-36.

In a time when popular reception of poetry is perhaps more tenuous than in any period since the Wordsworthian revolution, Philip Larkin has managed to capture a loyal, wide, and growing audience of readers. He has been acclaimed England's "unofficial poet laureate" and "laureate of the common man," as a representative spokesman for the British sensibility since World War II. He emerged as the center, if not the starting point, of most critical debate over postwar British verse. He is the best known and most acclaimed—critically and popularly—of the figures who made up the so-called Movement in the early 1950s and as an avowed enemy of the literary modernism scorned by The Movement. His scant four collections of poems, written over thirty years, as well as the two novels he brought out shortly after the war continue to go into new printings, hardcover and paperback, on both sides of the Atlantic. While he denied being a "Great Poet," only Ted Hughes among his English contemporaries rivals him in terms of international recognition. For all of his self-proclaimed insularity, Larkin is known and has been responded to as no other British poet since Dylan Thomas.

Two incidents from Philip Larkin's career illustrate the tone of his life, at least as he chose to project it in his writing. The first occurred shortly after he had had his small collection *XX Poems* (1951) published at his own expense. At first wondering why the writers and critics to whom he had sent copies failed to acknowledge them, he soon discovered that, because of a postal rate hike of which he had been unaware, the copies had been received with postage due. Self-deprecating irony, as well as a strong sense of ill-timing and chances missed, connect this incident with the personality seen in so many of his poems.

Also revealing are the circumstances attending his 1982 *Paris Review* interview. With his well-known reluctance to grant interviews, he insisted that, rather than meet his interviewers face-to-face, he be sent a series of questions, the first set of which he took five months in answering. The paradox of his consenting to the interview but on such a condition—his sense of a place on the literary map yet his refusal to be a public figure—accords with the combination of wariness and fascination toward all relationships, even the most private, seen throughout his poetry.

Philip Arthur Larkin was born in Coventry, England, on 9 August 1922, to Sydney and Eva Emily Day Larkin. Whether his childhood was "unspent," as he claimed in one of his wittier poems ("I Remember, I Remember"), there is no way of telling. His father's job as the city treasurer afforded the family a measure of solidity and financial security. His activities included the typical routines of young friends, games of football and cricket, seaside holidays. Family trips to Germany when he was a teenager established a distaste for foreign travel that persisted. To the extent that Larkin remembered his childhood at all, he remembered it as more boring than unhappy. However, he recalled vividly the misery brought on by nearsightedness, which went undetected for a long time, and by stuttering, which continued well into adulthood.

Perhaps these difficulties help account for his rather patchy academic performance at King Henry VIII School in Coventry, which he attended throughout the 1930s. Most certainly they relate to the shyness he attributed to himself as a child and as an adult, as well as to the preoccupation with the solitude-society issue evident in so many of his poems. Despite—or perhaps because of—such defects, Larkin soon began cultivating habits of wide reading and a lively imagination, both of which fed a youthful interest in writing. His father's well-stocked library put him in touch with authors considerably advanced for a schoolboy of the time—including George Bernard Shaw, D. H. Lawrence, Somerset Maugham, and George Moore—and these young Larkin supplemented with frequent trips to the public library.

For Larkin serious writing began sometime not too late in his period at King Henry VIII School, with a class assignment to write a poem, and quickly developed into a nightly routine. Though he dismissed his school writings as typically adolescent, from 1933 until leaving school in 1940 he contributed regularly to the *Coventrian*, the school magazine. In late 1940 he made his first appearance in print outside school publications with a poem in the *Listener*.

The autumn of 1940 also saw Larkin's arrival at Oxford and the beginning of a vital stage in his personal and literary development. The power of his experience there is suggested by one of his most moving poems, "Dockery and Son," written twenty years after he left Oxford, which turns on his frightening realization of how much time has elapsed and how much has changed since his university years and on how he can never return. In his introduction to the 1964 edition of his novel *Jill* (first published in 1946), Larkin spoke eloquently of how wartime Oxford served to mature the young undergraduate. For the first time in his life he was introduced to circles of friends who were especially interested in things which especially interested him. While he recalled feeling surrounded by thousands of people cleverer than he, apparently he was able to hold his own—judging from the reports of close friends he made there, such as Kingsley Amis and John Wain—and eventually to distinguish himself academically, with a first-class honors degree in English (1943). The opportunity to specialize in English proved a chance to exercise an interest which had been held partly in check by the broader school curriculum he had encountered prior to Oxford.

Oxford stimulated Larkin's bent toward writing, too. He contributed to student literary magazines and to anthologies of student poetry. Despite his wariness of the Oxford "Aesthetes"—and his preference for the "hearties" among his fellow students—he attended poetry readings and lectures. Yet the most dramatic result of his time at Oxford came after he took his degree. The poems composing *The North Ship* (1945), as well as his two novels, *Jill* (1946) and *A Girl in Winter* (1947), were all completed within two years of his leaving Oxford. So intense an outburst of activity, which he attributed to "creative relief" at being freed from academic pressure, surely must be credited in part to that same Oxford atmosphere and experience.

Larkin recalled how a few months after he left Oxford, the Ministry of Labour politely inquired what he was doing with himself. Having failed the physical exam for the military, he nevertheless felt obligated to answer in some definitive fashion and happened to notice a newspaper advertisement for a small-town librarian's job in Shropshire. As a result, he became the town librarian for Wellington, a job that partly inspired the rather grim setting in *A Girl in Winter,* in which the main character likewise joins the library staff in a city, where she feels alone and unappreciated.

Thus began his career as librarian. Three years later, in 1946, Larkin went to Leicester, as assistant librarian at University College, and, according to Kingsley Amis, he served as the model for Jim Dixon in *Lucky Jim* (1954). Larkin expressed some skepticism about Amis's claim, though the years at Leicester were his most frustrating as a writer. He was able to take an Oxford M.A. in 1947. The best years—or at least the best conditions for writing—came, he felt, when he went to Belfast in 1950, as sublibrarian at Queen's University.

The youthful style and outlook informing the poems in *The North Ship* resulted directly

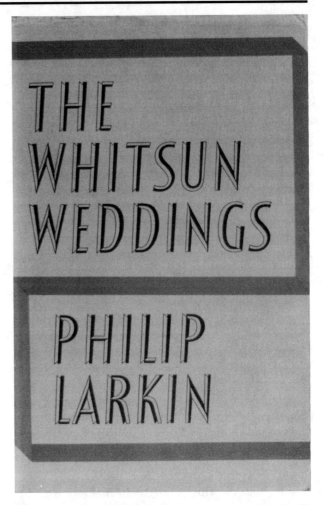

Dust jacket for Larkin's 1964 book, the central volume in his poetic canon

from an Oxford encounter, and subsequent consultations, with Vernon Watkins, friend of Dylan Thomas and disciple of Yeats, who impressed upon the younger poet the importance of Yeats as a poetic model. Larkin's first collection was invited by the owner of the small Fortune Press. He later remarked that, despite his excitement at the time, the circumstances of his book's publication were "next door to a vanity press." And, reflecting on the poetry itself, he said, "It seems amazing that anyone should have offered to publish it without a cheque in advance and a certain amount of bullying."

Most readers have found the poems of *The North Ship* greatly inferior to what Larkin was to write later. Generally they reflect an infatuation with Yeatsian models, a desire to emulate the Irishman's music without having undergone the experience upon which it had been based. Indeed, Larkin confessed to "limbering up" with his edition of Yeats—significantly the 1933 edition, which lacks the final poems—each evening before he began working on poems for *The North Ship*. Most of those poems are vaguely plaintive. They speak of love affairs terminated or threatened by unspecified causes, of an unfriendly natural environment, and of a pervasive atmosphere of doom—perhaps a natural result of their being written in wartime. Such complaints, ungrounded by particulars of setting or motivation, however, ultimately appear self-indulgent whimpering, the products of a sensibility bent upon being unhappy and unable to face up to the possibility of relief or self-help. Such a poetry, its arguments and situations appearing so senseless, is forced to depend on image and prosody. Yet, even in these it generally fails, as there is a monotony of predictable rhymes and stanzas, of uninterestingly bleak images, and of wearisome tone throughout the collection. The emphasis in a few poems upon dream and vision introduces only another dimension of dullness to the collection's landscape, a landscape without social reality or humor. Potentially concrete settings—such as the train carrying the Polish air girl (number twelve), the snowy field through which the girl is dragged (number twenty), or the railway platform on which the man stands (number twenty-two)—invariably give way to vague expressions of misgiving or despair. Because the speaker in these poems exists only as a voice mouthing complaints—and not as a character with either compelling dilemmas or qualities of personality beyond self-pity—he inspires at best uninterest, and at worst extreme annoyance.

Larkin later saw in *The North Ship* several abandoned selves, including the would-be Yeatsian. The process by which such abandonment occurred, and by which the central Larkin mode emerged, was long and tortuous. He collected some of *The North Ship* poems, along with several newer ones, in a manuscript titled "In the Grip of Light," which he unsuccessfully attempted to publish in 1947. "I didn't choose poetry: poetry chose me," he told an interviewer. This remark has special relevance to the period 1946-1950, when he experienced extreme frustration in trying to determine what he ought to be writing. Part of his problem stemmed from having written and published two novels in a relatively short time, *Jill* having come out in 1946 and *A Girl in Winter* the next year. Where *Jill* was little noticed at the time, except by Oxford insiders, the second novel, Larkin's first book under

the Faber and Faber imprint, was reviewed widely and quickly commanded a coterie of admirers.

Such success would understandably inspire an author barely into his mid twenties to attempt a third novel, which is precisely what Larkin did for the next five years. His failure to get very far with that project led to his gradual abandonment of another one of his selves. Because he retained his admiration for the novelist's craft—he continued to insist that novel writing is much more demanding than the writing of poetry and that a novel is a much more impressive achievement than any number of poems—this dismissal of the novelist-self must have been especially difficult.

Nevertheless, he did dismiss it, and in the process perhaps unwittingly came upon something he preferred over novel writing. His notebooks for this period record the slow beginning, developing, and revising of poems that would not appear in print for several years. For Larkin the chief difficulty was to find a kind of poetry which could satisfy the various, and deeper, selves which remained. Yeats had clearly proven a dead end. Indeed, by this time he seems to have relegated *The North Ship* to that category already containing his juvenilia. He needed a newer concept of poetry, as well as a definitive model, to fill the vacuum created by the dismissal of Yeats.

The solution appears to have come through his discovering, or rediscovering, the poetry of Thomas Hardy. Though Larkin had admired Hardy's fiction, he had brushed aside the poetry as gloomy and inelegant. His rethinking of this position, according to Larkin himself, began with his reading Hardy's "Thoughts of Phena At News of Her Death," which quickly led to a rereading and reappraisal of other Hardy poems he had forgotten. While he had had his ear for prosody sharpened by other models—notably Yeats and Auden—he had his feel for content sharpened by encountering Hardy. Hardy taught him not to be afraid of the obvious and commonplace in his writing—indeed, to nurture them—and, above all, to engage only actually felt emotion in his poems. Armed with this basis for what ultimately would become his mature poetic, and stimulated by moving to Belfast in 1950, he rather quickly completed and gathered together those pieces that would become *XX Poems*. "I felt for the first time I was speaking for myself," he explained.

Despite the mailing mishap, and despite the fact that *XX Poems* received almost no critical attention when it appeared, this small pamphlet proved extremely important to Larkin's development as a poet. For one thing, he retained half of its contents for *The Less Deceived* (1955); thus the basis for that collection's phenomenal success was already set several years before its publication. Poems such as "At Grass," "If, My Darling," and "Deceptions," all of which first appeared in *XX Poems,* have remained popular and critical favorites among Larkin's writings and have continued to find their way into anthologies. They mark his advance away from vague plaintiveness toward specified setting, character, and moral issues, as well as toward a kind of diction, primarily telling metaphor, which reinforces such specificity.

Larkin referred to his novels as "oversized poems" in their preciseness of detail and language. Equally valid is the notion of his mature poems as miniature novels, in terms of the concrete fictional quality they exude. Although based on a retired racehorse—or, to be more precise, on a newsreel of a famous racehorse in retirement—"At Grass" moves through a long series of realistic particulars defining the British obsession with "Cups and Stakes and Handicaps" to an implicit comparison of horses with people and the question of how our adjustment to life's later passages measures up to theirs. "If, My Darling" more amusingly shows its speaker caught in mock worry over what might happen were his girlfriend to "jump, like Alice" into the cesspool he knows the stream of his consciousness to be. The metaphors with which he renders his mind and its workings operate as credible expressions of guilt plaguing a witty young man caught between old-fashioned love and emancipated sexuality. The poem's effect depends on an ironic perspective central to *Jill*—Larkin's novel about a naive undergraduate newly arrived at Oxford—but wholly absent from *The North Ship* poems. Relatedly, the exclusion from *The Less Deceived* of those pieces in *XX Poems* that hearken back most to the poems of *The North Ship* reflects Larkin's growing confidence in realism, irony, and humor as components of the poetry he wished to write.

Of the earlier poems retained in *The Less Deceived,* none is more powerful than "Deceptions," originally titled "The Less Deceived." Here again is the lesson of Hardy through concrete fictionality, the poem's essence of person and place. Here, too, is Larkin's fusion of his fiction into his verse in the issues of moral responsibility and disillusionment which the poem shares with *A Girl in Winter.* The germ of the poem—a passage from

Henry Mayhew's *London Labour and the London Poor* (1851-1864), where a young prostitute movingly recalls being kidnapped, drugged, and raped to initiate her into her trade—spurred Larkin to consider, through almost-emblematic metaphors, the profound grief she must have felt, but then to observe how, compared with the exactness of her suffering, her attacker's desire must have involved "erratic" readings of whatever satisfaction the attack would bring him. He concludes therefore that, whatever her pain, she was less deceived than her attacker, "stumbling up the breathless stair / To burst into fulfillment's desolate attic." Larkin's rendering of the distinction between suffering and desire, and its various ramifications, takes on significance far beyond the girl, the rapist, or even the nineteenth century in which he found them.

The 1955 publication of this and about two dozen other poems as *The Less Deceived* proved a mild sensation in poetry circles. The owner of the small Marvell Press, George Hartley, had written Larkin for a collection, and once published it gained instant notice and favorable comment in many reviews, very quickly sold out the first printing, and went into several additional printings. Its author became recognized as a significant poet. Additionally, after the appearance of *The Less Deceived* Larkin began to have poems, reviews, and occasional essays published in periodicals much more frequently. Clearly his long-sought poetic was succeeding.

The newer poems in *The Less Deceived* further solidified the issues and techniques toward which he had been moving and which afterward came to be identified with him. Perhaps foremost among such techniques, especially in comparison with *The North Ship,* is the engaging "I" of Larkin's mature poetry. Whether humorous or serious, the speaker in most of these poems presents a compelling contrast to the bland personality in Larkin's earlier verse. The result is that subjects only vaguely developed before take on a vividness, a viewpoint, and a feeling to which the reader can respond readily.

Various poems dealing with relationships illustrate these later tendencies and techniques. In the wittily titled "Lines on a Young Lady's Photograph Album" a young man's excitement over his girlfriend's finally allowing him to examine old snapshots of herself turns to the realization that he is on his way out of her life. Only in a sadly ironic sense will a photo permit him to hold her. "Unvariably lovely there, / Smaller and clearer as

1/35

But much less quickly noticed was the noise
            The weddings made
Each station that we stopped at: sun destroys
Your interest for what's happening in ~~the~~ shade,
And down the long cool platform whoops and skirls
Might have been porters larking with the ~~mails~~,
~~Or pan-hung climbers;~~ ~~when we started, though,~~
~~They slowly~~ ~~passed~~ ~~fathers, mothers~~ ~~girl~~
~~Their clothes grotesquely new, in altitudes~~
~~Emotions, tense, or tried,~~ ~~watching us go.~~

                    Once
                  ~~~~

Or pan-hung climbers; ~~then~~   we started, though,
~~We~~ ~~They~~ passed ~~~~ them   ~~~~ fathers grinning, mothers and ~~g~~

In parodies of fashion, heels and veils, —
~~All~~ ~~irresolutely, to do to~~   watching   us go.

But much less quickly noticed was the noise
            The weddings made
Each station that we stopped at: sun destroys
           The   or
~~Your~~ interest ~~for~~ what's happening in shade,
And down the long cool platform whoops and skirls
          I took for
~~Might have been~~ porters larking with the mails,
        went on reading
And ~~I~~ ~~pan-hung climbers~~. Once we started, though,
We passed them, grinning and pomaded, girls
In parodies of fashion, heels and veils —
        posed
All ~~took~~ irresolutely, watching us go,

                                            4 v

~~when they watching?~~

Page from a draft for "The Whitsun Weddings" (Collection of Philip Larkin)

the years go by." In "Maiden Name" one sees perhaps the same character at a later stage in his life and in his relationship with his former lover, as he meditates, with philosophical bitterness and cynicism, on the strange implications of the name change wrought by marriage and on how only her old name "shelters" his fidelity to her as she was, in her youthful beauty. In each of these instances the speaker examines a personal dilemma in terms of conceptual complexities surrounding it. In "Reasons for Attendance" and "Places, Loved Ones" Larkin again developed the viewpoint of the outsider looking in, or back, on possible relationships he has lost, but with the character more aware of his power to rationalize and thus less satisfied with the answers such power yields.

Much of the mature art of Philip Larkin turns on telling metaphors, particularly as the credible "I" uses them to define a feeling or problem. In one poem he calls his work a toad and wonders why he does not "drive the brute off " with his wits, as others seem to do. Elsewhere he labels his skin an "Obedient daily dress" and thinks of the old age as a sort of "white swaddling." Then, in "Whatever Happened?" he combines two metaphorical patterns—the passage of a ship through a dangerous latitude and the developing of a photograph—to suggest a traumatic experience and the later attempt to make sense of it.

All such poems deal at least in part with the riddle of time, which by the mid 1950s had become one of Larkin's preoccupations. Because those lyrics concerned with relationships tend to question the irrevocability of previous choices, they necessarily ask in what sort of medium choices develop and harden. While in "I Remember, I Remember" Larkin deprecated his youth by wittily inverting the clichés of romantic poetry and fiction, he also suggested there that time and the human proneness to illusion and self-deception conspire to make memory highly unreliable. The same process by which the perspective afforded by time turns out to misrepresent events as experienced is, of course, at the center of "Whatever Happened?" Yet another poem, "Triple Time," gave Larkin the opportunity to develop the puzzle of time even further, as he observed how the present ("a time unrecommended by event") is, ironically, both the future once wildly anticipated and the past soon to be recalled with nostalgia or regret.

Several attributes of the entire collection coalesce in "Church Going"—the single piece of writ-

ing most responsible for establishing, and sustaining, Larkin's reputation. Naturally it exhibits the realistic detail of setting and motivation of most of the other poems in *The Less Deceived*. As Larkin's longest poem to that time, it incorporates into its very structure the honesty and self-scrutiny increasingly evident in his writing. Its agnostic speaker admits himself to be "bored and uninformed" and discovers in his puzzling over the attraction old churches have for him—which amounts almost to an irresistible magnetism—an empiricist basis for his own set of religious values. Here, too, is Larkin's careful orchestrating of stanzas, the play between stanza and syntax which by this time had become for him a central technical resource, and the careful placing of metaphors—which, in fact, do not occur until very late in the poem, when the speaker is well toward solving his puzzle.

Republished in the *Spectator* soon after its initial appearance, "Church Going" quickly became celebrated as the definitive Movement poem, in the traditional aspects of its form (notably stanza, rhyme, and subdued imagery) and the modest dimensions of its subject and resolution. The Larkin character in "Church Going" became a prototype of the thoughtful postwar Englishman: skeptical of the merely material comfort afforded by the welfare state yet equally dubious of the promise held out by political, religious, or artistic extremists. To a generation of sensitive readers in England and America "Church Going" defined the spirit of secular humanism.

The years between the initial appearance of *The Less Deceived* in 1955 and the publication of *The Whitsun Weddings* in 1964 were probably the most eventful of Larkin's career. Just as the earlier book was coming out, he left Belfast to accept the position of librarian at the Brynmor Jones Library at the University of Hull, a situation that apparently suited him for over a quarter-century. His affection for that area of England he expressed in "Here," the opening poem of *The Whitsun Weddings*. The poem's panoramic tribute to Hull's common people ("A cut-price crowd, urban yet simple") and their way of life extends to the surrounding countryside, where one is said to have a sense of "unfenced existence: / Facing the sun, untalkative, out of reach." Later Larkin explained that literary celebrity had made him even more appreciative of Hull, as strangers eager to see or meet him (especially Americans) tended to be discouraged by the difficulty of getting there by rail. As for his library position—

which he has referred to as "that nice little Shetland pony of a job you so confidently bestride in the beginning [which] suddenly grows to a frightful Grand National Winner"—he liked its combining of academia and administration and definitely preferred it to the alternatives of teaching or giving readings by which other poets are forced to earn their livings. In his years at Hull, Larkin saw buildings erected and collections and staff expanded, for which he felt considerable pride of accomplishment.

In addition to his professional work and the writing of poetry—which continued at a steady if modest pace—Larkin's first decade at Hull included his debut as a jazz writer. Though beginning with occasional reviews of books on jazz, in 1961 he became a regular reviewer of jazz recordings for the *Daily Telegraph,* an assignment which lasted well into the 1970s. The first eight years of the *Daily Telegraph* reviews were later assembled into a collection titled *All What Jazz* (1970). His enthusiasm for jazz had begun back in the mid 1930s, when, according to Larkin, the emotional impact of the great jazz artists on sensitive youth was comparable to that of the great romantic poems a century earlier. So obsessed with jazz was he as an adult that, adapting Baudelaire, he claimed he could live a week without poetry but not a day without jazz.

Besides providing apparently boundless listening pleasure, jazz represented for Larkin what he termed a "telescoped art," since, though not even a century old, it had passed through stages which took centuries to unfold in painting or poetry. Specifically, he saw in the shift from traditional to progressive jazz an analogue to the move from realism to modernism in the other arts, a move he came to dislike intensely. Thus Charlie Parker joined the modernists of other art forms as a special target of Larkin's invective. In his introduction to *All What Jazz* he criticized the products of modernism ("whether perpetrated by Parker, Pound or Picasso") as "irresponsible exploitations of technique in contradiction of human life as we know it," adding that modernism "helps us neither to enjoy nor endure. It will divert us as long as we are prepared to be mystified or outraged, but maintains its hold only by being more mystifying and more outrageous: it has no lasting power."

He held in similar scorn the industry of explication that had grown up from the mystique of modernism: "The terms and the arguments vary with circumstances, but basically the message is:

Don't trust your eyes, or ears, or understanding. They'll tell you this is ridiculous, or ugly, or meaningless. Don't believe them. You've got to work at this: after all, you don't expect to understand anything as important as art straight off, do you? I mean, this is pretty complex stuff: if you want to know how complex, I'm giving a course of 96 lectures at the local college, starting next week. . . ." For Larkin, continuity and clarity—rather than violent discontinuity or obscurity—were the proper aims of human art, in keeping with the aims of human life. Modernism in most of its manifestations he rejected as elitist, pretentious, and antihumanist.

Given this poetic of continuity, *The Whitsun Weddings* represents an extension of, rather than a departure from, *The Less Deceived.* In fact, none of Larkin's three mature collections differs markedly from the other two in any respect. More than the books of most other contemporary poets, they partake of the same character, which is rooted in traditional technique, gentle irony, and sympathy with the commonplace. With *The Whitsun Weddings,* the feel of continuity with the earlier poems is especially genuine, as newer pieces began appearing in periodicals almost immediately after the publication of *The Less Deceived* and continued at the steady rate of two to four each year until the later collection was pulled together. After *The North Ship,* the notion of distinctive phases in Larkin's career as poet becomes virtually impossible to sustain.

Commercially, as well as artistically, *The Whitsun Weddings* proved an even greater success than its predecessor. It quickly won favorable opinions in influential quarters, went into several printings, and gained awards for its author, including the Arts Council Triennial Award and the Queen's Gold Medal for Poetry. Such notice, of course, depended in part on the reputation gained Larkin earlier by *The Less Deceived.* Nevertheless, most reviewers saw in the newer book a sharpening of the talent which had first delighted them ten years before. Yet, because the debate over The Movement was at its height, Larkin had begun to have detractors, in both England and the United States, who regarded him as representative of a narrowness of vision infecting postwar Britain.

Without question *The Whitsun Weddings* represents the full fruition of Philip Larkin's search for a comfortable poetic and style. In every way it is his central book. More consistently there than even in *The Less Deceived* did he define the

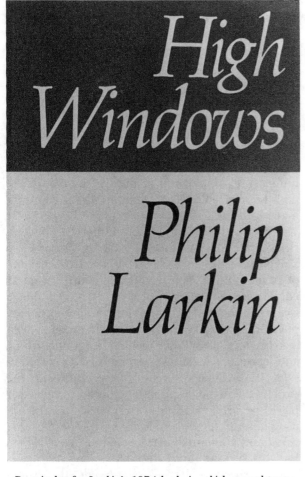

Dust jacket for Larkin's 1974 book, in which several poems signal a return to his early Yeatsian mode

ably, "MCMXIV," while picturing the details of the Edwardian England which disappeared with the beginning of World War I, invests that picture with a degree of reverence only possible to one growing up with the worship of "The Great War" and viewing prewar times from the perspective of several decades.

In *The Whitsun Weddings* Larkin managed a much wider range of tones and effects than before. This greater variety is due in part to the greater proportion of either third-person poems or first-person poems featuring characters not to be equated with Larkin himself. "A Study of Reading Habits"—the speaker of which has moved from naive romanticism through sensationalism and now finds himself bored by the all-too-familiar routine of realism—illustrates Larkin's playful irony. Besides "Toads Revisited," a sort of sequel to his earlier critique of the work ethic, he added the more topical and biting satire of "Naturally the Foundation Will Pay Your Expenses," an attack on academic gamesmanship. Another new piece, "Mr. Bleaney," illustrates an extreme of the chillingly effective Larkin poem, as its speaker, upon renting a seedy room, reflects at length with scorn at the former tenant's simplemindedness and then realizes, with muted horror, that he has chosen the same "hired box" but without even the saving naiveté of the simpleton.

All of these poems are essentially negative in resolution. As if to counter such a tendency and to suggest a set of positives even behind such irony and gloom, three poems—"Love Songs in Age," "An Arundel Tomb," and "The Whitsun Weddings"—turn on the possibility of strength and triumph. The first describes a widow's rediscovering the romantic sheet music of her youth as she empties out the piano bench. After being momentarily tempted by the songs into their attendant ideal of love—"still promising to solve, and satisfy, / And set unchangeably in order"—she recognizes in herself a realism which can no longer tolerate such youthful illusions, so that "to cry, / Was hard, without lamely admitting how / It had not done so then, and could not now." An equally sensible valuation of love comes in "An Arundel Tomb," where Larkin finds in the sculptor's detail of clasped hands on the tomb of an earl and countess that emblem of love in all its forms, profane as well as sacred, which transcends the ephemera of life that they, and we, consistently overvalue. "What will sur-

world of his poetry as postwar Britain. By the time he was writing his best poems, England had been recovering from the war; postwar prosperity accelerated the movement into mass culture which had begun for Britain between the wars, to produce a society immersed in consumer goods and a sense of the contemporary, but not at all certain how to bear the burden of its considerable past.

Much of this emergence of mass culture was captured by Larkin in *The Whitsun Weddings*, as he devoted entire poems to such mundanely contemporary subjects as stylish billboards ("Essential Beauty") or an American evangelist's crusade through England ("Faith Healing"), graffiti on a sexy resort poster ("Sunny Prestatyn"), big-city ambulances ("Ambulances"), and even a workingman's department store featuring "Bri-Nylon Baby-Dolls and Shorties" ("The Large Cool Store"). Even poems devoted to historically more remote topics suggest a very recent viewpoint. Not-

vive of us is love," he concludes in this moving meditation.

Perhaps more than any of his other poems except "Church Going," the title piece of *The Whitsun Weddings* suggests the richness and emotional power of his writing. Interestingly, the central figure seems to be Larkin himself, recounting his own discovery. The occasion was a train journey from the north of England—presumably Hull—into London on a Whitsun Saturday afternoon. With loving detail worthy of a chronicler of contemporary England, where for most people trains are the principal mode of travel, Larkin traces his pilgrimage through the Lincolnshire countryside, through towns and suburbs, and gradually into the urban sprawl of London. Paralleling this movement is an adventure of mind and emotion, by which the narrator-protagonist slowly becomes aware of the newlyweds being picked up at each station and of the "frail travelling coincidence" linking his life with the profound changes beginning in all of theirs. Initially unaware and then cautiously curious, he ultimately comes to feel at least temporarily involved in these marriages. The warmth of his recollecting what clearly has been a meaningful realization for him is tempered, though, by the somewhat saddening irony that only a bachelor like himself can have the solitude and perspective to appreciate so tenuous a connection. Certainly the newlyweds have not noticed him. The unmarried observer, a staple in Larkin's poetic world, thus enjoys only a curious and highly limited kind of communion with those he observes.

The years following *The Whitsun Weddings* saw Larkin repeatedly honored as probably Britain's principal living poet. Thus the BBC feted him with a special "Larkin at 50" broadcast in 1972. Not the least of such recognitions was his being asked to edit *The Oxford Book of Twentieth-Century English Verse*, published the next year. Indeed, by the time *High Windows* (1974) appeared, the pattern of his career had become so clear to critics that the regular appearance of a Larkin collection roughly ten years after the last was fully anticipated.

The object of this waiting interested all of his readers and pleased most. The majority of the *High Windows* poems reflect a continuing observation of contemporary English life. Thus the subject of "The Building" emerges only gradually as a modern hospital, for the reader first is taken through the urban scene: "Traffic; a locked church; short terraced streets / Where kids chalk

games, and girls with hair-dos fetch / Their separates from the cleaners." Such contemporaneousness extends throughout the collection. Here one finds, also, the same Larkin emphasis on continuity with the past, in particular poems—notably "To the Sea" and "Show Saturday," which celebrate the British rituals of seabathing and country shows, respectively—and in the traditional forms in which virtually all the poems are cast. That poem which is arguably the most radical in terms of subject and tone, "The Card-Players," employs the same sonnet form as one of the collection's quietest pieces, "Friday Night in the Royal Station Hotel."

The characters of the poems also link with Larkin's earlier writings. "Forget What Did," where he expresses relief at having stopped keeping his diary, exhibits the same self-deprecating tone as several prior poems. "This Be the Verse" connects with all of Larkin's earlier speculations on the source of human error, as well as with the wariness of family humorously expressed by several speakers in the other collections. And *High Windows* reveals the same literary personality as before, a Larkin definitely in middle age but still brooding on his solitude, on choices made long ago and on the strange, troubling fruits of time—all in the same wryly humorous, bitingly sympathetic tone as before.

Yet almost all critics sensed a difference here, at least of degree. In a sense, if there was continuity and sameness, it spelled out a vital difference. Many of the newer poems revealed a significant shift in age of the persona from that in the earlier poetry. Here the Larkin emphasis is not merely on time passing or on his being caught somewhere in middle age—anywhere from thirty to fifty—but on his moving into old age. If earlier he had seemed prematurely, though humanely and perhaps wisely, concerned with aging and death, such concern seemed timely in *High Windows*. Thus the stocktaking of the more recent poetry, as in "Sympathy in White Major" and "Money," took on a starker and maybe more desperate coloring. Though "High Windows," one of the most moving and beautiful of these last lyrics, looked back to the sense of human community affirmed in "Church Going" and "The Whitsun Weddings," it rested on more final considerations as well as it ultimately focused on "the deep blue air, that shows / Nothing, and is nowhere, and is endless." Nor is it an accident that this poem recounts a habitual discovery, implying perennial forgetting and a desperate need to remember; the "When" of the opening line ("When I see a couple of kids") clearly means "Whenever." As before, the Larkin speaker is unmarried and alone, but here the prospect of death is more of a reality for him: "Sad Steps" ends not with simply the puncturing of romantic illusion, but with the recognition that this illusion "is for others undiminished somewhere." Contrary to his rejection of love and the crowd in so many previous poems—albeit an uneasy rejection—in "Vers de Societe," he joins the party once scorned, as he explains:

> Only the young can be alone freely.
> The time is shorter now for company,
> And sitting by a lamp more often brings
> Not peace, but other things.

An awareness of "other things" is further suggested by the greater topicality of his last collection. Where Larkin's previous poetry contained virtually no reference to contemporary historical events, several of the *High Windows* selections depend almost entirely on such reference for their effects. Two argue didactically against developments in contemporary Britain: "Going, Going" against the encroachment of litter and tourists threatening to turn England into the "first slum of Europe," and "Homage to a Government" against the British government's decision to close its last military bases east of the Suez. A third poem, "Annus Mirabilis," while not directed to a specific event, refers to such historical particulars as the ban on *Lady Chatterley's Lover,* the Beatles' first album, and possibly the Profumo Scandal, as its speaker complains in typical Larkin fashion of having just missed out on the sexual revolution. In "Posterity" Larkin for the first time made use of another development from contemporary history, his own rise to literary prominence, in satirically describing an opportunistic young American scholar ("Jake Balakowsky, my biographer") bent on "doing" Larkin ("one of those old-type *natural* fouled-up guys") to gain academic tenure.

Though striking, such topicality is scarcely so startling as the emblematic-symbolic quality of several other *High Windows* poems. Many critics have seen in this development Larkin's return to his Yeatsian mode, and indeed he said of one of these poems, "Solar," that it was "more like *The North Ship*" than anything he had written for many years. Certainly "Solar" and several others— including "Dublinesque," "How Distant," and "The Explosion"—depend on lyric suggestiveness

more than concrete realism and on image more than metaphor. Though poems from *The Whitsun Weddings* and *The Less Deceived* resemble them in these regards, they seem to go beyond the others in avoiding a rooted and defined speaker and in evoking vaguely Platonic impressions. However, despite this Yeatsian flavor, each of these later poems manages sadness without the annoyingly personal plaintiveness of *The North Ship* and without the imagistic monotony plaguing that collection. Each moves from concrete particulars to its own symbolic suggestion. In each Larkin maintained prosodic and syntactical control. Each is recognizably, if not typically, a Larkin poem.

Larkin repeatedly expressed the wish to write the kind of poetry ordinarily not associated with him. The topical and imagistic poems in *High Windows*—not to mention the surrealistic "Card-Players"—suggest that he perhaps succeeded. But between the publication of *High Windows* and his death from throat cancer in December 1985, he wrote practically no new poems and often complained of the Muse's having abandoned him. Indeed, his last book published in his lifetime, *Required Writing* (1983), which won the 1984 W. H. Smith Literary Award, is a collection of prose pieces written between 1955 and 1982. His final literary triumph came posthumously with the publication of his *Collected Poems* (1988), which won a degree of broad critical acclaim and commercial success in England and the United States rarely enjoyed by a book of poetry.

Larkin's integrity as a poet would prevent him from writing, or at least publishing, a poem in which he could not believe; he was most vocal in renouncing earlier work, such as *The North Ship,* despite critical acclaim. And while there is some confusion over the matter of Larkin's being offered the poet laureateship in 1984, it appears that he turned it down, partly because he felt it an inappropriate honor for someone who would likely write no further poetry.

It is this same honesty that made him admired. Besides the charge of narrowness and insularity, the most frequent complaint against Larkin's poetry is that it is cold and unfeeling. But anyone reading carefully much of his mature work must agree with Larkin himself that, if anything, it sometimes borders on the sentimental. At his best, though, he projects a humane concern with the basic problems troubling his readers: love, loneliness, aging, personal and cultural discontinuity, and the need for metaphysical comfort in a culture bereft of metaphysics. Larkin's decision to write no more poetry is perhaps regrettable. That he gave us so many moving and quietly elegant poems clearly is not.

Interviews:

Ian Hamilton, Interview with Larkin, *London Magazine,* new series 4 (November 1964): 71-77;

Dan Jacobson, "Philip Larkin—a profile," *New Review,* 1 (June 1974): 25-29;

Miriam Gross, "A Voice of Our Time," *Observer Review,* 16 December 1979, p. 35;

John Haffenden, "The True and the Beautiful: A conversation with Philip Larkin," *London Magazine,* 20 (April/May 1980): 81-96;

Robert Phillips, "The Art of Poetry XXX: Philip Larkin," *Paris Review,* no. 84 (Summer 1982): 42-72.

Bibliography:

B. C. Bloomfield, *Philip Larkin: A Bibliography* (London & Boston: Faber & Faber, 1979).

References:

Calvin Bedient, *Eight Contemporary Poets* (London, New York & Toronto: Oxford University Press, 1974), pp. 69-94;

Donald Davie, "Landscapes of Larkin," in his *Thomas Hardy and British Poetry* (London, New York & Toronto: Oxford University Press, 1972), pp. 63-82;

Seamus Heaney, "Now and in England," *Critical Inquiry,* 3 (1976-1977): 471-488;

Lolette Kuby, *An Uncommon Poet for the Common Man. A Study of Philip Larkin's Poetry* (The Hague: Mouton, 1974);

Guido Latre, *Locking Earth to the Sky. A Structuralist Approach to Philip Larkin's Poetry* (Frankfurt am Main, Bern & New York: Peter Lang, 1985);

Bruce K. Martin, *Philip Larkin* (Boston: Twayne, 1978);

Andrew Motion, *Philip Larkin* (London & New York: Methuen, 1982);

James Naremore, "Philip Larkin's 'Lost World,' " *Contemporary Literature,* 15 (Summer 1974): 331-343;

Dale Salwak, ed., *Philip Larkin. The Man and His Work* (London: Macmillan / Iowa City: University of Iowa Press, 1989);

Anthony Thwaite, ed., *Larkin at Sixty* (London: Faber & Faber, 1982);

David Timms, *Philip Larkin* (New York: Barnes & Noble, 1973);

Chad Walsh, "The Postwar Revolt in England Against Modern Poets," *Bucknell Review,* 13 (December 1965): 97-105;

A. Kingsley Weatherhead, "Philip Larkin of England," *ELH,* 38 (December 1971): 616-630;

Terry Whalen, *Philip Larkin and English Poetry* (Vancouver: University of British Columbia Press, 1986).

Papers:

A manuscript notebook for 5 October 1944 - 10 March 1950 is held in the British Library Department of Manuscripts. An archive of letters and other manuscript materials is housed in the Brynmor Jones Library at the University of Hull.

John le Carré
(David John Moore Cornwell)
(19 October 1931 -   )

*This entry was written by Joan DelFattore (University of Delaware) for
DLB 87: British Mystery and Thriller Writers Since 1940: First Series.*

BOOKS: *Call for the Dead* (London: Gollancz,
1961; New York: Walker, 1962); republished as *The Deadly Affair* (Harmondsworth:
Penguin, 1964);

A Murder of Quality (London: Gollancz, 1962;
New York: Walker, 1963);

The Spy Who Came In from the Cold (London:
Gollancz, 1963; New York: Coward-McCann, 1964);

The Looking-Glass War (London: Heinemann,
1965; New York: Coward-McCann, 1965);

A Small Town in Germany (London: Heinemann,
1968; New York: Coward-McCann, 1968);

The Naive and Sentimental Lover (London: Hodder
& Stoughton, 1971; New York: Knopf,
1971);

Tinker, Tailor, Soldier, Spy (New York: Knopf,
1974; London: Hodder & Stoughton, 1974);

The Honourable Schoolboy (London: Hodder &
Stoughton, 1977; New York: Knopf, 1977);

Smiley's People (London: Hodder & Stoughton,
1980; New York: Knopf, 1980);

The Little Drummer Girl (New York: Knopf, 1983;
London: Hodder & Stoughton, 1983);

A Perfect Spy (London: Hodder & Stoughton,
1986; New York: Knopf, 1986);

Vanishing England, by le Carré and Gareth H. Davies (Topsfield, Mass.: Salem House, 1987);

The Russia House (London: Hodder & Stoughton,
1989; New York: Knopf, 1989);

The Secret Pilgrim (London: Hodder & Stoughton,
1991; New York: Knopf, 1991).

OTHER: Bruce Page, David Leitch, and Phillip
Knightley, *The Philby Conspiracy*, introduction by le Carré (Garden City, N.Y.: Doubleday, 1968), pp. 1-16.

SELECTED PERIODICAL PUBLICATIONS—
UNCOLLECTED: "Dare I Weep, Dare I
Mourn," *Saturday Evening Post*, 240 (28 January 1967): 54-56, 60;

John le Carré (photograph by Stephen Cornwell)

"What Ritual Is Being Observed Tonight?," *Saturday Evening Post*, 241 (2 November 1968):
60-62, 64-65.

John le Carré (pseudonym of David John
Moore Cornwell) is the author of realistic spy stories resembling those of Eric Ambler and Graham Greene. His best-known novels are *The Spy
Who Came In from the Cold* (1963) and the George
Smiley trilogy: *Tinker, Tailor, Soldier, Spy* (1974),
The Honourable Schoolboy (1977), and *Smiley's Peo-*

ple (1980). Le Carré was born in Poole, Dorset, on 19 October 1931. His father, Ronald Thomas Archibald Cornwell, had left school at the age of fourteen and embarked upon a series of financial speculations which were often unsuccessful and occasionally illegal. As le Carré later remarked (*Time*, 3 October 1977), "He was like Gatsby. He lived in a contradictory world. There was always credit, but we never had any cash, not a penny. My father would occupy a house and default, then move to another one. He had an amazing, Micawber-like talent for messing up his business adventures." When le Carré was still a child, his father was convicted of fraud and sentenced to his first prison term. Shortly afterward le Carré's mother, the former Olive Glassy, left her husband and moved in with one of his business associates. Cornwell later divorced her and remarried twice, and le Carré did not see his mother again until he was twenty years of age. He and his brother, Tony, spent some time with relatives who refused to discuss either parent, and le Carré later claimed that his earliest experience of espionage was his attempt to piece together, from the little that he and his brother managed to overhear, some explanation for his mother's desertion and his father's frequent absences. He concluded at one point that his father must be a spy, called away to perform dangerous missions for the good of his country.

As a result of his family's frequent moves le Carré never settled into one school or felt at home with one group of friends. At first he had the companionship of his brother, two years his senior, upon whom he was very dependent; but later their father, deciding that his sons should be more self-sufficient, sent them to boarding schools thirty miles apart. Although the two boys usually spent Sundays together, bicycling to a point halfway between the two schools, le Carré felt abandoned. This sense of isolation, which he experienced through most of his childhood and youth, is reflected in the loneliness and alienation of his fictional protagonists.

Le Carré's last preparatory school was Sherborne, in Dorset (scene of the musical film *Goodbye, Mr. Chips*, 1969). There he was a reasonably successful student, and at the age of sixteen he won his first award for literature, the school prize for English verse. However, at this point he decided that he had had enough of school life, and he informed the headmaster that he would not return to Sherborne for his final year. Thoroughly annoyed, his father sent him to Switzer-

Dust jacket for the first edition of le Carré's 1963 best-seller featuring George Smiley

land, where they had relatives, in order to spend a year studying German language and literature at the University of Bern.

On his return to England in 1949 le Carré joined the army and was assigned to the intelligence corps. Because of his proficiency in German he was sent to Vienna, where he encountered Eastern European refugees who had been imprisoned by both the Axis and the Allies. He also encountered Royal Air Force officers who, having bombed Berlin four years earlier, had returned to assist with the airlift and relief programs. The ironic inconsistencies of political institutions, and the ruthless disregard of those in power for the rights and well-being not only of their enemies and victims but also of their own agents, made a lasting impression on le Carré and became the major themes of his best work. "It was," he observed in *Time*, "like reading the right book at the right time. I saw the right *things* at the right time."

When he left the army le Carré was persuaded by his father to resume his university studies. Despite, or perhaps because of, his own legal difficulties, Cornwell wanted both of his sons to be lawyers. Le Carré's brother had read law at Cambridge and had been called to the bar, but he had left immediately afterward for North America. (He eventually became one of the directors of a Manhattan advertising agency.) Le Carré himself, who had no interest in the law, read modern languages at Lincoln College, Oxford. In 1954, while he was still at Oxford, le Carré married Alison Ann Veronica Sharp, daughter of a field marshal in the Royal Air Force. Shortly after his marriage he accepted a teaching position at Millfield Junior School in Glastonbury, Somerset, but after a year he returned to Oxford, where he took a degree in modern languages in 1956.

After taking his degree le Carré spent two years at Eton as a tutor in French and German. As he told *Current Biography* (1974), his reactions to Eton were mixed: "In some ways, those who knock the upper classes have no idea how awful they are. Eton, at its worst, is unbelievably frightful. It is intolerant, chauvinistic, bigoted, ignorant. At its best, it is enlightened, adaptable, fluent, and curiously democratic." He left Eton in 1958 and attempted to make a living as a painter and illustrator, but without success. He had no desire to return to teaching, so when he saw an advertisement for late entrants into the Foreign Office, he answered it. Largely because of his proficiency in French and German he was accepted.

While commuting by train between the Foreign Office in London and his home in Great Missenden, Buckinghamshire, le Carré wrote his first novel, *Call for the Dead* (1961; republished as *The Deadly Affair*, 1964). It introduces George Smiley, the brilliant, prosaic spy who was to become le Carré's series protagonist. Le Carré's conception of the character is clear and virtually complete in the introductory chapter of *Call for the Dead*: he is a nearsighted, unobtrusive middle-aged man, deceptively mild and painstaking to the point of genius. Smiley is the antithesis of the glamorous spy-hero epitomized by Ian Fleming's James Bond. A timid and inexpert driver, he wears expensive but ill-fitting clothing and is often cuckolded by his wife, who addresses him as "my darling teddy-bear" or "toad." His hobby, like le Carré's, is doing scholarly research on obscure seventeenth-century German poets.

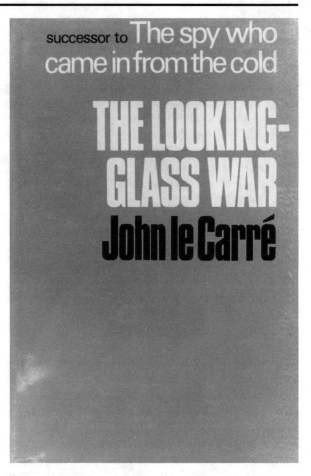

Dust jacket for the first edition of le Carré's 1965 novel

Although Smiley is a member of the British Secret Service, *Call for the Dead* is essentially a detective story rather than a spy story. Smiley, having cleared a member of the Foreign Office, Samuel Arthur Fennan, of the charge of being a Communist sympathizer, learns that Fennan is believed to have committed suicide and soon suspects that he has been murdered. The chief clue is suggested by the title of the novel: the dead man had requested a wake-up telephone call for the morning following his supposed suicide. With the help of Peter Guillam and Inspector Mendel, who also appear in later stories, he identifies both Fennan's murderer and the head of an East German spy ring. However, in his single-minded determination to solve the case, Smiley commits an act of ruthlessness which appears to him, upon reflection, to have been a betrayal of his principles and of his humanity. In order to avoid further conflicts between his duty and his honor, he resigns from the Secret Service. *Call for the Dead* thus includes a comparatively simple and straightforward version of themes which were to appear in le Carré's later novels in increasingly elaborate and sophisticated forms: the tension between man and his institutions, the sacrifice of truth to expediency, and the loss of humanity in the drive for efficiency. Further, Smiley's personal dilemma and the corresponding conflicts of supporting characters in the novel illustrate le Carré's tendency to incorporate into the traditional suspense-story format an unusual depth of characterization, not by endowing his characters with a wide range of personal quirks or external mannerisms, but by identifying in them a consistent and complex philosophical or ethical viewpoint.

In 1967 *Call for the Dead* was filmed under the title *The Deadly Affair*, with James Mason in the role of Smiley, who is for no apparent reason renamed Charles Dobbs. Simone Signoret, Maximilian Schell, and Lynn Redgrave also appear. Sidney Lumet directed the film, which is a reasonably faithful adaptation of the novel, although it is an uneven production, wavering between suspense and fast-paced action on one hand, and pointless, didactic conversation on the other.

When *Call for the Dead* was accepted for publication, its author had to choose a pseudonym because members of the Foreign Office were not encouraged to publish fiction under their own names. He used one of his middle names and a name he claims to have appropriated from a sign in a London shop window. Since "le carré" means "the square," the name may have suggested a slangy pun on his realistically unglamorous portrayal of life in the Secret Service, as opposed to the gimmicks-girls-and-guns approach of Fleming, whose James Bond books were approaching the height of their popularity when le Carré wrote *Call for the Dead*.

In 1961 le Carré was posted to the British embassy in Bonn, where he served as second secretary; and, while commuting between his home and his office, he wrote his second novel. Like many second novels, it is not quite as good as the first. *A Murder of Quality* (1962) is a detective story in which Smiley, having resigned from the Secret Service, investigates at the request of a friend the murder of a schoolmaster's wife. The murder victim, like Daphne du Maurier's Rebecca, is first portrayed as having been an exemplary woman and then, gradually, is exposed as having been a scheming virago; and her murderer is, in a sense, her victim. As he does in *Call for the Dead*, Smiley persists in seeking answers to seemingly unimportant questions upon which, in the end, the solution rests. However, because he

possesses, in the words of one of his former superiors, "the cunning of Satan and the conscience of a virgin," Smiley is unprepared for the human consequences of his professional success. Having applied himself single-mindedly to solving the murder puzzle, he realizes as he confronts the murderer that he does not want to hand this man over to be hanged, but the realization comes too late.

Le Carré, who had been a schoolmaster himself, was praised for his trenchant portrayal of the British public school community which serves as the background for this novel. However, although—or perhaps because—many of the characters in it are based on single individuals rather than on composites or types, they are more shallow than the supporting characters in le Carré's earlier novel. Further, because Smiley faces no convincing personal dilemma until the end of the story, it lacks the sustained internal conflict of le Carré's best work.

Both *Call for the Dead* and *A Murder of Quality* enjoyed a reasonable degree of critical and commercial success, but le Carré, who by the mid 1960s had three sons, found it impossible to give up his position in the Foreign Office to become a full-time writer. Therefore, his third novel, like its predecessors, was written when he could spare the time from his official duties. When *The Spy Who Came In from the Cold* was published, le Carré, who was then a British consul in Hamburg, is said to have laughingly instructed his accountant to inform him if his bank balance ever reached twenty thousand pounds, the sum he felt that he had to have in reserve before he could afford to resign. Much to his surprise the book was a best-seller. His balance rose far above the required figure, and in February 1964 he became a full-time writer.

The Spy Who Came In from the Cold received the most enthusiastic reviews accorded to any novel of espionage since Eric Ambler's *The Mask of Dimitrios* (1939). Graham Greene, with whom le Carré is often compared, called it "the best spy novel I have ever read"; J. B. Priestley wrote that it is "superbly constructed with an atmosphere of chilly hell"; and Anthony Boucher declared that it places le Carré "beside Ambler and Greene in the small rank of writers who can create a novel of significance, while losing none of the excitement of a tale of sheer adventure." Le Carré also received the Crime Writers' Association's Gold Dagger Award for 1963 and the W. Somerset Maugham Award for 1964. The commercial suc-

*Dust jacket for the first American edition of le Carré's
1968 novel*

not only as a professional target but also as a personal antagonist. He finds, however, that the plan does not proceed as Control had said it would; and then he realizes, gradually and reluctantly, that Control had never intended that it should. Leamas is caught in a magnificently conceived multiple-cross: not only does he find himself in a situation in which nothing outside himself is as it seems to be; not only does he, in carrying out orders which he believes will lead to one result, unwittingly and unwillingly contribute to bringing about its opposite; but, in the very act of disobeying Control's orders and taking steps to abort his plan, Leamas completes the plan, because by defying Control at that particular point he does exactly what Control had expected and hoped he would do. However, although Control succeeds in double-crossing his opponents by triple-crossing his own agent, Control appears only briefly in the novel and is seldom even mentioned. As a result, the novel centers almost exclusively on characters who have no means of determining or even of anticipating the effects of their own actions. The novel thus projects the vision of a Hardyesque, absurd universe in which free will is negated by ignorance, self-determination is an illusion, and trust is an act of insanity.

Le Carré solved the enormous technical problems involved in presenting a story of this complexity by focusing very closely on the character of Leamas, so that the reader views events through Leamas's eyes and usually penetrates a particular layer of plot only when he does. As a result, although *The Spy Who Came In from the Cold* is occasionally bewildering, the confusion does not concern what is happening, but why it is happening; and that confusion is in itself an integral part of the story's meaning. Further, the close identification of Leamas's perceptions with the plot itself and with the reader's experience of the story contributes to the psychological depth which le Carré, like Ambler and Greene, succeeded in incorporating into an essentially cerebral form of literature.

The film rights to *The Spy Who Came In from the Cold* were purchased by Paramount shortly after the novel was published, and in 1965 the film was released. It stars Richard Burton as Alec Leamas, with Claire Bloom, Oskar Werner, Sam Wanamaker, Cyril Cusack, and Bernard Lee in supporting roles. This film, which is extremely faithful to the book, was made in grainy black and white to emphasize the harsh realism of the

cess of the book was as great as its critical success, and within ten years the worldwide sales of *The Spy Who Came In from the Cold* had reached twenty million copies.

Unlike le Carré's earlier work, *The Spy Who Came In from the Cold* is not a detective story but a novel of espionage. It introduces the recurrent character of Control, the unscrupulous and unfeeling head of the Secret Service, which Smiley is eventually prevailed upon to rejoin. Smiley is not, however, the protagonist of this novel, although he appears briefly. Its protagonist is Alec Leamas, former head of the British spy network in East Germany. Leamas is requested by Control to take the leading role in an attempt to discredit Hans-Dieter Mundt, head of operations for the East German Abteilung, who was responsible for the elimination of all the agents who had made up Leamas's network. Leamas willingly undertakes the destruction of Mundt, whom he regards

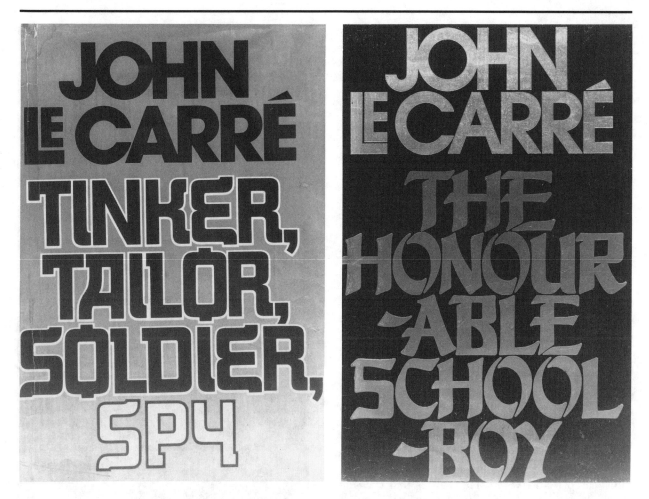

Dust jackets for the first American editions of le Carré's 1974 novel, in which Smiley comes out of retirement to locate a mole in the Circus, and its 1977 sequel

story. The absence of color and the comparative slowness of the action also serve to underline the contrast between this film and the romantic spy films epitomized by the James Bond series. Although it was not a box office success when it was first released, *The Spy Who Came In from the Cold* is considered by most critics to be a landmark in the development of the realistic spy film. The screenwriters, Paul Dehn and Guy Trosper, were nominated for the Writers Guild Award.

The success of *The Spy Who Came In from the Cold* catapulted le Carré into the celebrity circuit, where he was distracted by people who wanted to lionize, interview, photograph, gush over, or shake hands with him. He promptly withdrew to Crete, and then to Vienna, to work on his next book.

Le Carré's fourth novel repeats the central themes of *The Spy Who Came In from the Cold*, but it lacks the complexity and the brilliance of its predecessor. *The Looking-Glass War* (1965) con-

cerns a minor and almost extinct branch of the British Secret Service, whose chief, Leclerc, tries to revitalize his department and to bolster his own ego by sending an agent into East Germany to investigate a rumor of Russian troop activity. The mission is quite unnecessary from an operational point of view, but Leclerc is anxious to assert his right to run agents, thus challenging the monopoly of the Circus, the branch of the Secret Service run by Control. In an apparently uncharacteristic burst of generosity, Control provides Leclerc with a radio set and crystals to be used by the agent, Leiser. However, the set is twenty years out of date, and Leiser, poorly trained and poorly equipped, has almost no chance of survival. As he crosses into East Germany he finds it necessary to kill a young border guard, which focuses the attention of the police on the area and unnerves Leiser himself. Upset by the police activity and by his own guilt for having killed the guard, Leiser not only broadcasts very slowly, but also forgets to change crystals and frequencies when communicating with his superiors, who have remained on the West German side of the border. When Control learns, through connections in the Foreign Office, that the East German police have picked up Leiser's signal and are ready to arrest him during his next broadcast, he delightedly sends Smiley to West Germany to inform Leclerc and his associates that they must abandon Leiser. Control's continued monopoly over the running of agents is thus assured.

In *The Looking-Glass War* le Carré abandoned the single narrative viewpoint of *The Spy Who Came In from the Cold* to portray a variety of responses to the central themes of treachery, duplicity, and abandonment. Leclerc, like Control, is concerned with the success of the mission only as it affects his own prestige and that of his department; he abandons Leiser with a shrug of the shoulders and sets about salvaging what he can of his department's importance. An alternative point of view is provided by Leclerc's naive young associate, Avery, who, horrified by Leclerc's casual abandonment of Leiser, weeps for Leiser and for his own lost ideals. Smiley, too, abhors the callous indifference with which the men in power view individual agents, but his understanding of the duplicity involved is much more sophisticated than Avery's. He realizes that the service's breach of faith with Leiser goes much deeper than simple abandonment because he knows that Control, in addition to providing an antiquated radio set, had deliberately warned the East German police to listen for Leiser's signal. He also realizes that it is futile to respond to such duplicity, as Avery does, by trying to obstruct it or by weeping over it. Leiser never quite understands what has happened to him but retains his humanity and performs his futile mission with genuine, if misguided, courage.

Although *The Looking-Glass War* provides the complexity of a variety of viewpoints, it is in some respects a short story padded into a novel. Individual episodes, such as Leiser's period of training, are stretched far beyond the requirements of plot, theme, or effect; and conversations whose only purpose is the exploration of moral or ethical concepts slow the action of the novel and give it an undertone of didacticism. However, despite its faults *The Looking-Glass War* is an entertaining novel which explores, from a complicated and technically demanding perspective, the mechanism of betrayal. The book received mixed reviews, but, aided perhaps by the

Dust jacket for the first edition of le Carré's 1980 Smiley novel

momentum from *The Spy Who Came In from the Cold*, it became a best-seller, and le Carré received the Mystery Writers of America Edgar Allan Poe Award for 1965.

In 1970 *The Looking-Glass War* was made into a film by Columbia Pictures, starring Christopher Jones, Pia Degermark, Ralph Richardson, and Anthony Hopkins. Unlike the film of *The Spy Who Came In from the Cold*, the film of *The Looking-Glass War* is quite different from the novel on which it is based. Leiser, who is a nondescript middle-aged man in the novel and whose age and appearance are an important part of his characterization, appears in the film as a conspicuously handsome young man who is frequently seen shirtless. The screenplay was written by the director of the film, Frank R. Pierson, who inserted action scenes that serve no apparent purpose except to provide opportunities for stunt work. The film is confusing and episodic, exaggerating the faults of the novel and bypassing its virtues.

In a few of the scenes in *The Looking-Glass War*, such as those relating to the domestic situations of the characters involved in the plot, le Carré introduced elements of the "straight" novel as opposed to the thriller. He moved further in this direction in his next book, *A Small Town in Germany* (1968), in which the defection of Leo Harting, a minor official in the British embassy in Bonn, is considered from several viewpoints. Like *Call for the Dead* and *A Murder of Quality*, *A Small Town in Germany* involves a great deal of detective work, but here the detective and espionage genres are more integrated, as an investigator from the Security Department in London attempts to discover what has become of Harting and of the top-secret file that disappeared with him. These composite thriller elements are wedded to the "straight" novel by means of the emphasis that le Carré places upon the personal and, in some cases, romantic motivations underlying activities which appear, on the surface, to be purely political. For example, Harting has a personal grudge against Karfeld, leader of a German antiparliamentary movement, whom he hopes to destroy by means of the circumstances of his own defection. Meadowes, an embassy official, is at odds with investigator Alan Turner because of an extremely unpleasant incident involving Meadowes's daughter; and the reaction of the head of chancery, Bradfield, to Harting's defection is influenced by Bradfield's knowledge that Harting has been his wife's lover. The personal motivations thus revealed add depth to the characters and poignancy to otherwise uninteresting episodes and contribute to the plausibility of the story by creating the illusion of a behind-the-scenes look at a real-life political news item. Further, the emphasis that le Carré places on personal motivations makes it clear that the action of the novel is not based on the characters' responses to events impinging on them, as is often the case in pure thrillers, but on conflicts created by the interplay of the characters themselves. However, the continuity and the total effect of *A Small Town in Germany* suffer from le Carré's failure to blend rather than alternate the literary genres he was combining. Much of the novel is presented as a series of dramatic action scenes followed by explanations of their personal or romantic background, which has the effect of superimposing on the genuine complexity of the story an element of unnecessary and unproductive structural confusion.

A Small Town in Germany became a bestseller, although neither this novel nor *The Looking-Glass War* enjoyed the success of *The Spy Who Came In from the Cold*. Critical response to *A Small Town in Germany* was mixed. Some reviewers felt that le Carré's own experience as a consul in Bonn, where his responsibilities had included reporting on political movements within Germany, contributed greatly to the plausibility and sophistication of the political background of the story; and that, in addition to sustaining interest as a spy story, *A Small Town in Germany* provided interesting and valid sociological commentary on British institutions and customs. Others, however, felt that the novel lacks excitement, and that in combining several fictional genres it fails to do justice to any. Malcolm Muggeridge, one of the severest of these critics, condemned the entire book as "remarkably silly."

After moving steadily in the direction of the "straight" novel in his first five books, le Carré finally abandoned the thriller genre altogether in his sixth book to write a psychological/romantic story, *The Naive and Sentimental Lover* (1971), based in part on a short story, "What Ritual Is Being Observed Tonight?," which he had published in the *Saturday Evening Post* in 1968. Some critics believe that *The Naive and Sentimental Lover* is a roman à clef, responding to *Some Gorgeous Accident*, a novel written by a friend of le Carré's, James Kellavar.

Le Carré told *Current Biography* that both the title and the central conflict of *The Naive and Sentimental Lover* are based on Friedrich von Schiller's observation that "a poet either *is* nature, and naive, or *seeks* nature, and is sentimental." The sentimental lover in the novel is Aldo Cassidy, a successful manufacturer of baby carriage accessories; the naive lover is Shamus, an unconventional and highly colorful artist. Both men are in love with a woman aptly named Helen. Although it is not a thriller, *The Naive and Sentimental Lover* expresses many of the same themes as le Carré's earlier work, particularly with reference to the conflict between individuals and the institutions that trap and betray them. Nevertheless, the novel was critically and commercially unsuccessful. The reviewer for the *Times Literary Supplement* (24 September 1971) called the book " a disastrous failure," and the reviewer for the *Spectator* (6 July 1974) called it "appalling." Shortly after the publication of *The Naive and Sentimental Lover* le Carré and his first wife were divorced, and both promptly remarried. Le Carré's second wife, Valerie Jane Eustace, had been an editor employed by the publishing firm of Hodder and Stoughton in London. Their son, Nicholas, was born in 1972.

After the negative reception of *The Naive and Sentimental Lover* le Carré decided to return to a combination of the "straight" novel and the thriller, and to his original protagonist, George Smiley. In *Tinker, Tailor, Soldier, Spy* Smiley, having been forced to retire from the Circus because of a change of administration following the death of Control, is drawn back into the world of British espionage when Oliver Lacon, a civil servant acting as liaison between the Secret Service and the appropriate ministries in Whitehall, asks him to investigate a rumor that the security of the Circus has been breached by an Englishman acting as a Russian agent-in-place: in espionage jargon, a "mole." The plot was suggested by the scandal which had erupted in 1963 when Kim Philby, a senior and highly placed member of British intelligence, escaped to Moscow after years of unsuspected treachery.

The presence of the mole, whose code name is "Gerald," is suggested to Control by fragmentary but highly suspicious bits of evidence. Further, the nature of the mole's activities and the quality of the material to which he evidently has access make it clear to Control that the mole must be one of five people: Percy Alleline, a Circus official who would become chief after Control's death, code-named Tinker; Bill Haydon, head of London Station, code-named Tailor; Roy Bland, code-named Soldier; Toby Esterhase, head of the Acton Lamp-lighters organization (couriers, overseas supplies, communications), code-named Poorman; or Smiley himself, code-named Beggarman. Smiley is eliminated from the list of suspects because of the circumstances surrounding his enforced retirement from the Circus after Control's death; and, with the help of Peter Guillam, still in the Circus but in disfavor with the new administration, Smiley sets out to track down the mole.

Because Smiley's search for the mole, Gerald, takes the form of painstaking, often tedious burrowing through Circus records and through the sometimes rambling recollections of former Circus employees, and because it involves a limited number of clearly identified suspects, *Tinker, Tailor, Soldier, Spy* is an excellent example of the blending of detective-fiction conventions into a

novel of espionage. Further, in this novel le Carré finally succeeds in effectively incorporating elements of "straight" fiction into a thriller plot. *Tinker, Tailor, Soldier, Spy* is, in many respects, a novel of manners centering around the inhabitants of Britain's secret world, detailing their habits of dress, speech, and social intercourse. Because these observations are actually clues to the identity of Gerald, however, they not only provide human interest but also further the plot. Similarly, Smiley's relationship with his unfaithful wife, Ann, closely parallels his experience with the Circus, which simultaneously attracts and betrays him. It also parallels Gerald's relationship with the country of his birth and with his Russian masters, and it serves as an integral part of the plot against England. This plot was conceived by Karla, head of the branch of Soviet Intelligence which corresponds to the Circus, and carried out by Gerald. Unlike *The Looking-Glass War* and, to a lesser degree, *A Small Town in Germany*, which merely add elements of "straight" fiction to a thriller plot, *Tinker, Tailor, Soldier, Spy* is a thriller which is, equally and inseparably, a "straight" novel.

The structure of *Tinker, Tailor, Soldier, Spy* resembles that of a set of Russian dolls, each opening up to reveal a smaller doll inside. Each layer of the plot thus presented reveals not only new factual material, but also new insight into the philosophical or ethical basis of the novel. Unlike le Carré's earlier work, notably *The Spy Who Came In from the Cold* and *The Looking-Glass War*, *Tinker, Tailor, Soldier, Spy* comes to grips with some of the fundamental ideological distinctions between the Communist world and the free world. It also explores the fact that these distinctions do not cease to exist even when the men who control the free-world institutions are themselves ruthlessly ambitious. As Smiley confronts the trapped mole at the end of the novel and listens to his poorly presented and entirely unconvincing assertions about the moral superiority of the Eastern monolith over the crass commercialism of the West, Smiley's own vaguely humanitarian liberalism begins to harden into the conviction that, although many of Gerald's criticisms of the West are accurate, his final evaluation is not. Gerald, having exploited, on Karla's orders, Ann's infidelity to Smiley, describes Smiley's continued love for Ann as his one point of vulnerability, "the last illusion of the illusionless man." By introducing into the conflict between Smiley and Karla the opposition between love, vulnerability, and

Cambridge Circus, London, site of the Circus

human decency on one hand, and ruthlessly rational and perhaps irresistible efficiency on the other, le Carré sets up the terms for the continuing rivalry between Smiley and Karla which forms the basis of his next two novels.

Most of the reviews of *Tinker, Tailor, Soldier, Spy* were wildly enthusiastic, applauding its suspenseful complexity and its depth of characterization and comparing it favorably with *The Spy Who Came In from the Cold*. Predictably most of the negative or mixed reviews focused on the novel's ideological and social commentary, accusing the novel of superficiality and of mongrelizing the genre; but these represented the reactions of a small minority of readers. Although le Carré's work had al-

ways been realistic—or at least plausible—*Tinker, Tailor, Soldier, Spy* was particularly noted for this quality. An official of the Central Intelligence Agency is quoted in *Time:* "We know that our work plays havoc with our personal lives. We know that an awful lot of what we have to do is slogging through file cards and computer printouts. Poor George Smiley. That's us."

Although *Tinker, Tailor, Soldier, Spy* is much too intricate to be adapted into a two-hour film, it was produced as a miniseries by London Weekend Television. The producer of the series, Richard Bates, was adamant in his insistence on retaining the grimly realistic spirit of the novel and avoiding all temptations to glamorize the story for television. The series, starring Alec Guinness in a superbly underplayed performance as Smiley, won both critical and popular acclaim.

The story begun in *Tinker, Tailor, Soldier, Spy* is resumed in *The Honourable Schoolboy*, in which Smiley, now caretaker chief of a demoralized and largely ineffectual Circus, seeks to restore its prestige by undertaking a long and intensive search whose object is to determine what materials have been falsified or destroyed by Gerald, thus revealing the areas of Circus intelligence regarded by Karla as sensitive enough to require suppression, even at the risk of Gerald's exposure. The paper-chase and interview methods of *Tinker, Tailor, Soldier, Spy* are repeated here, yielding at last the knowledge of a "gold seam"— a series of secret Soviet payoffs. Smiley sends Jerry Westerby, a reporter who occasionally works for the Circus and who appeared briefly in *Tinker, Tailor, Soldier, Spy* as one of Gerald's victims, to investigate rumors of a connection between the Russian payoffs and a Hong Kong millionaire, Drake Ko.

Beneath Smiley's determination to restore the prestige of the Circus is a growing personal rivalry between him and Karla, his opposite number in the Russian secret service. Smiley rejects completely what he regards as Karla's absolutist and antihumanitarian methods, but he finds himself faced with the alternatives of displaying a certain degree of ruthlessness himself or of losing to Karla. He compromises gradually, becoming withdrawn and secretive, balancing professional priorities against the rights and well-being of individuals, reassuring himself that it is necessary to be "inhuman in defence of our humanity . . . harsh in defence of compassion . . . single-minded in defence of our disparity." Smiley does in fact retain a surprising amount of gentleness and compassion, even as chief of the Circus. The narrative voice, whose interruptions constitute one of the novel's chief stylistic flaws, repeatedly assures the reader that Smiley is doing as well as anyone could do under the circumstances, and that his critics in the service and in Whitehall fail to understand the pressures with which he must deal. Nevertheless, Smiley himself is dissatisfied with his own performance, and in a letter to his estranged wife, he writes, "I honestly do wonder, without wishing to be morbid, how I reached this present pass. . . . Today, all I know is that I have tried to interpret the whole of life in terms of conspiracy. That is the sword I have lived by, and as I look round me now I see that it is the sword I shall die by as well. These people terrify me, but

Dust jacket for the first American edition of le Carré's 1983 novel

I am one of them. If they stab me in the back, then at least that is the judgment of my peers." His peers do indeed stab Smiley in the back; and, despite the success of the Hong Kong operation, he is ousted from the Circus once again by an ungrateful ministry.

The Honourable Schoolboy sustains the level of characterization set in *Tinker, Tailor, Soldier, Spy*, particularly in its depiction of Westerby, the title character. He is, in some respects, a foil for Smiley: unintellectual but instinctively shrewd and emotionally vital, he respects the judgment of those he calls "the owls"—Smiley and the other upper-level policymakers in the Circus— acknowledging their superior grasp of the total operational picture. He is, however, too empathetically imaginative to carry out their orders when faced with the actual human beings whose weaknesses and failings he has been sent to exploit. If Karla resembles one side of Smiley in his brilliance, dedication, and persistence, Westerby resembles Smiley's benignly humanitarian side. Although he does not condemn Smiley himself, because he recognizes Smiley's essential decency and realizes that he himself does not understand the reasons for Smiley's orders, Westerby rejects Smiley's position, as Smiley once rejected Control's. Inevitably Westerby's simplistic and sympathetic approach to the complex and ruthless world in which he moves costs him his life; and, in view of Smiley's action in le Carré's next novel, it is possible to see in Westerby's death the impending compromise of Smiley's own humanitarian ideals.

Since much of the action in *The Honourable Schoolboy* takes place in Southeast Asia, le Carré made five visits to that area to collect background material for his book. On one occasion, exposed to automatic weapons fire in Cambodia, he rolled under a truck and lay there making notes of his sensations on index cards. Although much of this firsthand material provides the novel with color and immediacy, le Carré included so much background description that parts of the book read like a travelogue. He also wrote a lengthy and largely unnecessary opening sequence, apparently for the sole purpose of creating the character of Old Craw, a reporter, modeled on a real-life journalist, Dick Hughes. These scenes, together with the often didactic interruptions of the narrative voice, are no more than padding for an already overly long novel.

Largely because of its verbosity and its consequent loss of focus, *The Honourable Schoolboy* did not enjoy the enthusiastic reception which had been accorded to *Tinker, Tailor, Soldier, Spy*. Further, several reviewers pointed out specific examples of overwriting and mixed metaphors. Clive James, for example (*New York Review of Books*, 27 October 1977), mentions le Carré's description of a conversation between Smiley and a former Circus employee, Sam Collins: " 'Now at first Smiley tested the water with Sam—and Sam, who liked a poker hand himself, tested the water with Smiley.' Are they playing cards in the bath?" Nevertheless, most reviewers noted the fine interplay of characters and the sustained suspense which are the novel's strongest points. *The Honourable Schoolboy* became the Book-of-the-Month Club selection for October 1977, and it superseded *Tinker, Tailor, Soldier, Spy* as the highest-grossing espionage novel ever written. Le Carré received two major awards for *The Honourable Schoolboy:* The Black Memorial Award and the Crime Writers' Association's Gold Dagger Award.

In the final volume of the trilogy, *Smiley's People*, Smiley discovers that his opponent, Karla, has an emotionally disturbed daughter whom he has secretly sent out of Russia to avoid the political embarrassments which her condition would cause him if she remained there. In the course of establishing and maintaining her false identity in Switzerland, Karla orders the deaths of several people, including Smiley's friend and former agent, Vladimir. Called out of retirement to investigate Vladimir's murder, Smiley grasps this opportunity to accomplish the utter defeat of Karla: his enforced defection to England. However, in bringing about this result Smiley is forced to exploit Karla's love for his daughter even more ruthlessly than Karla once exploited Smiley's love for his wife. Although Smiley repeatedly bolsters his resolution by recalling the horrors which Karla, in his single-minded ambition, has ordered, he cannot escape the realization that if what Smiley condemns in Karla were all of Karla, Smiley would not have been able to defeat him. It is not Karla's cruelty, but the one vestige of affection which redeems him from utter inhumanity that leads to his destruction.

By the time he wrote *Smiley's People* le Carré had become so adept at combining the detective, espionage, and "straight" fictional genres that most readers had ceased even to take note of it. Many of the events in *Smiley's People*, like those in *Tinker, Tailor, Soldier, Spy* and *The Honourable Schoolboy*, are based on the conventions of detective fiction: a paper chase, interviews, the discovery and investigation of clues, and the pursuit and eventual capture of the prey. On the other hand, Smiley's uncertainty about the purity of his motives and the right-mindedness of his actions adds to the externally oriented suspense of the conventional thriller a dimension of internal tension usually associated with the "straight" novel. Moreover, the action of *Smiley's People*, like that of its predecessors, is generated by the interplay of rounded characters rather than by a series of more or less implausible or unexpected external events.

Le Carré's next novel, *The Little Drummer Girl* (1983), was a significant departure from his earlier work. Asked why he had abandoned Smiley, he said that Guinness's portrayal of the character in the television adaptations of *Tinker, Tailor, Soldier, Spy* and *Smiley's People* had been so convincing that he could no longer envision Smiley apart from Guinness. As some reviewers observed, however, a more obvious explanation is

Dust jacket for the first edition of le Carré's first novel to be serialized in the Soviet Union

that the Smiley story had run its course, at least for the moment. Le Carré's first female protagonist, Charlie, is an intelligent, sensitive, but somewhat scatterbrained young actress who is active in a variety of political movements that she barely understands. As befits her profession, she not only engages in an elaborate charade but also falls in love with a succession of masks. Recruited by Israeli intelligence to infiltrate a Palestinian terrorist organization, she finds that neither cause nor individual has only one face.

Like earlier le Carré novels, *The Little Drummer Girl* blurs the distinction between "them" and "us," between action and motivation, and between honor and betrayal. The substitution of a comparatively naive and idealistic protagonist for the cynical Smiley recalls Leamas and Westerby,

but Charlie has less chivalry and a correspondingly better chance of survival. Like Leamas and Westerby, she is occasionally victimized by her employers; and, like them, she is aware that she is playing a role but unaware of its real dimensions and goals. Nevertheless, her responses to her gradual disillusionment include not only anger, but also some recognition of the inevitable ambivalence that underlies political interactions. Despite her initial political shallowness, Charlie becomes, in some ways, one of the most instinctively perspicacious of le Carré's characters. She never sees the clear outlines within which other characters in the novel move, but the novel opens the possibility that her multilayered, affective, frequently muddled visions of reality may not be altogether removed from the truth.

Le Carré's next novel, *A Perfect Spy* (1986), is written in an ironically autobiographical mode that features flashbacks detailing the relationship between the protagonist, Magnus Pym, and his father. Like le Carré's father, Ronald Thomas Archibald Cornwell, Richard Thomas Pym is a charmingly manipulative swindler who never quite understands why good intentions are not a fully acceptable substitute for reliable behavior. Taught from childhood that betrayal is not inconsistent with love, Magnus Pym becomes a natural betrayer—first a spy and then, in an inevitable progression, a double agent. All of le Carré's novels include layers of betrayal, but *A Perfect Spy* is truly an anatomy of betrayal, dwelling in detail on its origins, progression, distinguishing characteristics, and consequences. Le Carré's plotting has never been simple, but *A Perfect Spy* is one of his most complex novels. The narrative alternates between a long apologia that Magnus Pym is writing to his son, Tom, and an account of the search for Pym that the British and the Czechs are conducting. In the epistolary segments Pym seeks an understanding of himself; in the rest of the novel others seek an understanding of him. Eventually, these internal and external searches, which initially seek to explain how he has arrived at his present point in life, focus on the reasons he must now die. Since *A Perfect Spy* is the most intimate of le Carré's novels, this gradual perception of the inevitability of Pym's death should elicit a much more vivid affective response than is characteristic of most spy fiction. The absence of such a response is, perhaps, the most serious consequence of the novel's major flaw: like all of le Carré's novels, this one is word-heavy.

Even in the love scenes, apparently intended to be evocative and touching, words pile up dauntingly. For example, this paragraph occurs early in the description of Pym's relationship with his wife, Mary: "He is watching her and when she catches sight of him he bursts out laughing and shuts her mouth with passionate kisses doing his Fred Astaire number, then it's upstairs for a full and frank exchange of views, as he calls it. They make love, he hauls her to the bath, washes her, hauls her out and dries her, and twenty minutes later Mary and Magnus are bounding across the little park on the top of Dobling like the happy couple they nearly are, past the sandpits and the climbing-frame that Tom is too big for, past the elephant cage where Tom kicks the football, down the hill towards the Restaurant Teheran which is their improbable pub because Magnus so adores the black-and-white videos of Arab romances they play for you with the sound down while you eat your couscous and drink your Kalterer. At the table he holds her arm fiercely and she can feel his excitement racing through her like a charge, as if having her has made him want her more." The line between poetry and verbosity may be hard to define in the abstract, but there can be little doubt about the side of that line on which passages like this one fall. As Bruce Allen observed in his *Christian Science Monitor* review, "This may be a major novel that nobody will be able to finish."

A Perfect Spy was made into a television miniseries that portrays Magnus Pym as a basically good-natured but befuddled betrayer. Like the production of *Tinker, Tailor, Soldier, Spy*, the adaptation of *A Perfect Spy* is faithful to the novel in its setting and tone as well as in its characterizations and plot. It is particularly effective in capturing the experience of physical wandering and psychological wandering that is so essential to the sense of Pym's story.

Although some readers believed that *The Little Drummer Girl* and *A Perfect Spy* had signaled the end of le Carré's Soviet plots, those readers were proven wrong when, in 1989, le Carré's *The Russia House* was published. The protagonist of this novel, Barley Blair, is a marginally successful publisher who often travels to the Soviet Union because his company's book list includes some works by Soviet authors. Blair resembles Eric Ambler's best-known protagonists in that he is a nonprofessional who suddenly finds himself caught up in espionage and counterespionage. Le Carré had been slowly progressing in this direction, be-

ginning with the journalist-courier Westerby in *The Honourable Schoolboy* and continuing with the actress-recruit Charlie in *The Little Drummer Girl*. Blair is an entirely innocent bystander until the secret world is literally thrust upon him in the form of a package sent to him by a dissident Russian scientist and author nicknamed "Goethe," with whom he had once shared a drunken Sunday outside Moscow. Embedded in the rambling literary manuscript is information on how the Soviet Union's weapons systems work—or, more precisely, on how they fail to work. In sending this information to the West, Goethe envisions slowing down the arms race by disillusioning the British and American political establishments about the strength of the Russian military threat. In a sense this is the obverse of le Carré's earlier theme that the West is as morally impoverished as the East. Now the message is that the East is as technologically impoverished as the West.

Once the information is in British and American hands, there is a mad scramble to confirm it, deny it, get more of it, and/or bury it, all at once. Of particular concern are certain American politicians described as "Bible-belt knuckle-draggers who take it into their heads to pillory Goethe's material because it endangers Fortress America." Mimicking such politicians, who are described as having hair between their toes, one of Blair's interrogators drawls, "This li'l ole planet just ain't big enough for two super-powers, Mr. Brown. Which one do *you* favor, Mr. Brown, when poo-ush comes to sheu-uve?" ("Mr. Brown" is Blair's code name.) This novel thus adds to le Carré's recurrent themes of personal ambition, international rivalry, and interservice bickering a new element of deliberately preserved ignorance based on xenophobia and mindless militarism. The point that the novel is making on this issue is suggested by its first epigraph, a quotation from Dwight David Eisenhower: "Indeed, I think that people want peace so much that one of these days governments had better get out of their way and let them have it."

Amid all these waves of conflict, Blair struggles to maintain his balance, his humanity, and his concern for Katya, Goethe's politically naive courier. As the plot of *The Russia House* develops, echoes of le Carré's earlier novels, especially *The Spy Who Came In from the Cold* and *The Looking-Glass War*, become evident. For example, the narrator of *The Russia House*, Palfrey, plays much the same role in the plot of this novel that Smiley plays in *The Looking-Glass War* and, to a lesser ex-

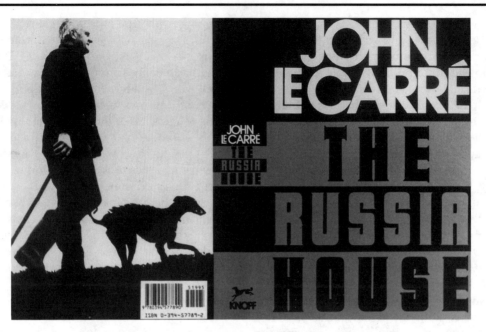

Dust jacket for the first American edition of le Carré's 1989 best-seller

tent, in *The Spy Who Came In from the Cold*. Like Smiley, Palfrey is a scholarly middle-aged man with an unsuccessful love life and a correspondingly low level of self-esteem and interpersonal trust. Despite the cynicism that results from that description, Palfrey, like Smiley, represents the voice of sanity, reason, and humanity in a world that contains very little of these qualities. Smiley does not narrate any of the novels in which he appears, as Palfrey narrates *The Russia House*, but it seems as if le Carré has need of a character of this type to provide the light by which the actions of others can be evaluated. Further, just as Smiley is often on the fringes of the espionage world—retired, resigned, about to resign—Palfrey serves in the rather tangential role of legal adviser to the secret service. This allows le Carré to comment on the action of the novel by means of a character who, while remaining involved enough to know what is going on, is independent of direct lines of authority and does not quite represent the establishment.

The ending of *The Russia House* can be read as an upbeat revision of *The Spy Who Came In from the Cold*, at least from the point of view of the main character, since he avoids the traps set for him by the secret service of his own country and saves the woman he loves. If he betrays his country to accomplish this, which is left unclear, perhaps in the world of this novel that country deserved to be betrayed. In any case, this novel, unlike *A Perfect Spy*, deals with some elements of

human triumph rather than with unredeemed betrayal.

The Russia House was, in accord with Mikhail Gorbachev's policy of openness, serialized in the Soviet Union in the magazine *Ogonyok*, and a 1990 movie version of the novel, starring Sean Connery and Michelle Pfeiffer, was filmed on location in Moscow. A *New York Times* feature article (22 May 1989) focused on the relationship between the improvement of East-West relations and le Carré's novel, which clearly transcends the cold-war themes of his earlier work. In a rare interview, le Carré observed, "We had no contingency plan for the end of the cold war. . . . The notion that peace should break out was one that was never seriously contemplated. We really have to make the choice of whether we're going to help them out of the ice or stamp them on their fingers every time they try to crawl out." The same ideas appear at greater length in a cover article in *Newsweek* (5 June 1989). There, le Carré is quoted as opposing Margaret Thatcher's "chauvinistic revival," stating, "I'm deeply pessimistic about what Mrs. Thatcher has done to our national soul." As these examples indicate, one of the few things about *The Russia House* that is entirely unambiguous is its political relevance.

The *Newsweek* article, by Tom Mathews, describes *The Russia House* as being "faster and leaner than anything le Carré has done in years," while a *New York Times* (18 May 1989) book review by Christopher Lehmann-Haupt objects that "there's a little too much emphasis on language." *The Russia House* is certainly less bulky, physically and syntactically, than its immediate predecessors, and it contains some effective and blessedly brief descriptions. Of Blair, for example, Palfrey says, "He has people inside himself who really drive him mad" and "his mind leaves the room and you wait on tenterhooks to see whether it will come back." The novel even includes a few examples of le Carré's infrequent use of humor; for example, Goethe describes himself to Blair by saying, "I'm a moral outcast. . . . I trade in defiled theories." "Always nice to meet a writer," Blair replies. Nevertheless, as the *New York Times* review indicates, this novel exhibits le Carré's almost indefinable tendency toward a quality that most reviewers see as verbosity.

In the course of le Carré's publishing career, which has spanned more than thirty years, he has moved from writing comparatively plot-oriented detective spy stories to producing complex political and psychological novels that qualify him for consideration as a "serious" author. This development is discernible not only in his writing in general, but also in the evolution of his best-known character, George Smiley. In *Call for the Dead* Smiley is a rather fuzzily portrayed detective/spy; in *Smiley's People* he approaches the level of a tragically flawed character who has sold his soul but does not quite know when or how it happened. The post-Smiley novels continue le Carré's trend toward writing "serious" novels in which characters happen to be spies, as the characters created by other authors happen to be psychiatrists or airline pilots. The greatest drawback to his writing is, as critics and reviewers have repeatedly pointed out, the insistent heavy-handedness of his style. Although this quality is modified significantly in *The Russia House*, his persistence in writing lengthy novels that include verbose and apparently pointless descriptive passages, innumerable tangents, and a plethora of poorly defined minor characters is intriguing if not perverse. It is as if he is convinced that this style will work if he can only get it right—and, considering the unquestionable success of his books, that may be true. In any case, this combination of brilliance and diffusiveness makes a final assessment of le Carré's work difficult. What is certain, however, is that he occupies a place among the most commercially—and, on the whole, the most critically—successful writers of espionage fiction, and deservedly so.

References:
Tony Barley, *Taking Sides: The Fiction of John le Carré* (Philadelphia: Open University Press, 1986);
Eric Homberger, *John le Carré* (London & New York: Methuen, 1986);
Peter Lewis, *John le Carré* (New York: Ungar, 1985);
David Monaghan, *The Novels of John le Carré: The Art of Survival* (New York: Blackwell, 1985);
Monaghan, *Smiley's Circus: A Guide to the Secret World of John le Carré* (London: Orbis, 1986);
Peter Wolfe, *Corridors of Deceit: The World of John le Carré* (Bowling Green, Ohio: Bowling Green University Popular Press, 1987).

Doris Lessing

(22 October 1919 -   )

This entry was updated by Paul Schlueter from his entry in
DLB 15: British Novelists, 1930-1959: Part One.

BOOKS: *The Grass Is Singing* (London: Joseph, 1950; New York: Crowell, 1950);

This Was the Old Chief's Country (London: Joseph, 1951; New York: Crowell, 1952);

Martha Quest (London: Joseph, 1952);

Five: Short Novels (London: Joseph, 1953);

A Proper Marriage (London: Joseph, 1954);

Retreat to Innocence (London: Joseph, 1956; New York: Prometheus Books, 1959);

The Habit of Loving (London: MacGibbon & Kee, 1957; New York: Crowell, 1958);

Going Home (London: Joseph, 1957; New York: Ballantine, 1968);

A Ripple from the Storm (London: Joseph, 1958);

Fourteen Poems (Northwood, Middlesex: Scorpion, 1959);

In Pursuit of the English: A Documentary (London: MacGibbon & Kee, 1960; New York: Simon & Schuster, 1961);

Play with a Tiger (London: Joseph, 1962);

The Golden Notebook (London: Joseph, 1962; New York: Simon & Schuster, 1962);

A Man and Two Women (London: MacGibbon & Kee, 1963; New York: Simon & Schuster, 1963);

Martha Quest and A Proper Marriage (New York: Simon & Schuster, 1964);

African Stories (London: Joseph, 1964; New York: Simon & Schuster, 1965);

Landlocked (London: MacGibbon & Kee, 1965);

A Ripple from the Storm and Landlocked (New York: Simon & Schuster, 1966);

Particularly Cats (London: Joseph, 1967; New York: Simon & Schuster, 1967);

The Four-Gated City (London: MacGibbon & Kee, 1969; New York: Knopf, 1969);

Briefing for a Descent into Hell (London: Cape, 1971; New York: Knopf, 1971);

The Story of a Non-Marrying Man and Other Stories (London: Cape, 1972); republished as *The Temptation of Jack Orkney and Other Stories* (New York: Knopf, 1972);

The Summer Before the Dark (London: Cape, 1973; New York: Knopf, 1973);

Memoirs of a Survivor (London: Octagon, 1974; New York: Knopf, 1975);

A Small Personal Voice: Essays, Reviews, and Interviews, edited by Paul Schlueter (New York: Knopf, 1974);

Collected Stories, 2 volumes (London: Cape, 1978); republished as *Stories*, 1 volume (New York: Knopf, 1978);

Shikasta (London: Cape, 1979; New York: Knopf, 1979);

The Marriages Between Zones Three, Four and Five (London: Cape, 1980; New York: Knopf, 1980);

The Sirian Experiments (London: Cape, 1981; New York: Knopf, 1981);

The Making of the Representative for Planet 8 (London: Cape, 1982; New York: Knopf, 1982);

Documents Relating to the Sentimental Agents in the Volyen Empire (London: Cape, 1983; New York: Knopf, 1983);

The Diary of a Good Neighbour, as Jane Somers (New York: Knopf, 1983; London: Joseph, 1983); republished as part of *The Diaries of Jane Somers* (London: Joseph, 1984; New York: Knopf, 1984);

If the Old Could . . . , as Jane Somers (London: Joseph, 1984; New York: Knopf, 1984); republished as part of *The Diaries of Jane Somers*;

The Good Terrorist (London: Cape, 1985; New York: Knopf, 1985);

Prisons We Choose to Live Inside (Montreal: CBC Enterprises, 1987; London: Cape, 1987; New York: Harper & Row, 1987);

The Wind Blows Away Our Words (London: Pan, 1987; New York: Vintage, 1987);

The Making of the Representative for Planet 8: An Opera in Three Acts, with Philip Glass (New York: Dunvagen Music Publishers, 1988);

The Fifth Child (London: Cape, 1988; New York: Knopf, 1988).

Collection: *The Doris Lessing Reader* (New York: Knopf, 1988; republished with different contents, London: Cape, 1989).

OTHER: "The Small Personal Voice," in *Declaration*, edited by Tom Maschler (London: MacGibbon & Kee, 1957), pp. 11-27;

Each His Own Wilderness, in *New English Dramatists: Three Plays*, edited by E. Martin Browne (Harmondsworth, U.K.: Penguin, 1959);

Olive Schreiner, *The Story of an African Farm*, afterword by Lessing (Greenwich, Conn.: Fawcett, 1968), pp. 273-290;

Lawrence Vambe, *An Ill-Fated People: Zimbabwe Before and After Rhodes*, foreword by Lessing (London: Heinemann, 1972; Pittsburgh: University of Pittsburgh Press, 1972), pp. xiii-xxi;

The Singing Door, in *Second Playbill Two*, edited by Alan Durband (London: Hutchinson, 1973).

SELECTED PERIODICAL PUBLICATIONS—UNCOLLECTED: "Myself as Sportsman," *New Yorker*, 31 (21 January 1956): 78-82;

"Being Prohibited," *New Statesman and Nation*, 51 (21 April 1956): 410-412;

"The Kariba Project," *New Statesman and Nation*, 51 (9 June 1956): 647-648;

"Flavours of Exile," *London Magazine*, 4 (February 1957): 41-48;

"London Diary," *New Statesman*, 55 (15 March 1958): 326-327; (22 March 1958): 367-368;

"Desert Child," *New Statesman*, 56 (15 November 1958): 700;

"Crisis in Central Africa: The Fruits of Humbug," *Twentieth Century*, 165 (April 1959): 368-376;

"Ordinary People," *New Statesman*, 59 (25 June 1960): 932;

"African Interiors," *New Statesman*, 62 (27 October 1961): 613-614;

"Smart-Set Socialists," *New Statesman*, 62 (1 December 1961): 822, 824;

"Homage for Isaac Babel," *New Statesman*, 62 (15 December 1961): 920, 922;

"What Really Matters," by Lessing and David Storey, *Twentieth Century*, 172 (Autumn 1963): 96-98;

"My Father," *Sunday Telegraph*, 1 September 1963; abridged as "All Seething Underneath," *Vogue* (15 February 1964): 80-81, 132-133;

"An Elephant in the Dark," *Spectator*, 213 (18 September 1964): 373;

"Zambia's Joyful Week," *New Statesman*, 68 (6 November 1964): 692, 694;

"Allah Be Praised," *New Statesman*, 71 (27 May 1966): 775, 778;

"On Our Side," *New Statesman*, 74 (6 October 1967): 437-438;

"A Few Doors Down," *New Statesman*, 78 (26 December 1969): 918-919;

"A Deep Darkness," *New Statesman*, 81 (15 January 1971): 87-88;

"Ant's Eye View," *New Statesman*, 81 (29 January 1971): 149-150;

"What It Cost," *New Statesman*, 81 (28 May 1971): 739-740;

"An Ancient Way to New Freedom," *Vogue*, 158 (July 1971): 98, 125, 130-131;

"The Education of Doris Lessing," *Observer*, supplement, 26 September 1971, pp. 53-55;

"If You Knew Sufi . . . ," *Guardian* (Manchester), 8 January 1972, p. 12;

"What Looks Like an Egg and Is an Egg?," *New York Times Book Review*, 7 May 1972, pp. 6, 41-43;

"In the World, Not of It," *Encounter*, 39 (August 1972): 61-64;

"Vonnegut's Responsibility," *New York Times Book Review*, 4 February 1973, p. 35;

"Life, To Be Lived Not Feared," *New York Times Book Review*, 23 September 1973, pp. 16, 18;

"On *The Golden Notebook*," *Partisan Review*, 40, no. 1 (1973): 14-30;

"The Way of Mecca," *Books and Bookmen*, 19 (April 1974): 22-24;

"Sufi Philosophy and Poetry," *Books and Bookmen*, 20 (October 1974): 38-39;

"The East's New Dawn," *Books and Bookmen*, 20 (June 1975): 26-27;

"The Ones Who Know," *Times Literary Supplement*, 30 April 1976, pp. 514-515;

"Looking Backward from the Future," *Mother Jones*, 4 (November 1979): 51-58;

"Our Minds Have Become Set in the Apocalyptic Mode," *Guardian*, 14 June 1982, p. 9;

"These Shores of Sweet Unreason," *Guardian*, 25 September 1982, p. 11;

"Writing Under Another Name," *Granta*, 13 (Autumn 1984): 175-180;

"Impertinent Daughters," *Granta*, 14 (Winter 1984): 51-68;

"Learning to Love Books," *New Society*, 9 May 1985, pp. 190-192;

"Autobiography (Part Two): My Mother's Life," *Granta*, 17 (Autumn 1985): 225-238;

"A Reporter at Large: The Catastrophe," *New Yorker*, 63 (16 March 1987): 74-90, 93;

"Events in the Skies," *Granta*, 22 (Autumn 1987): 14-17;

"Womb Ward," *New Yorker*, 63 (7 December 1987): 41-43;

"Three Women of Herat," *Times Educational Supplement*, 5 February 1988, p. 26;

"Afghanistan: Agony of a Nation," *Times Educational Supplement*, 5 February 1988, p. 26;

"Events in the Skies," *Harper's*, 276 (March 1988): 30-32;

"How Women Can Help Save the Planet," *New Scientist*, 118 (21 April 1988): 59;

"The Real Thing," *Partisan Review*, 55 (Fall 1988): 555-580;

"The Lost Call of the Veld," *Independent* (London), 14 January 1989, p. 27;

"Zimbabwe Mobilises the Agents of Change," *Independent* (London), 18 January 1989, p. 12;

"Zimbabwe Struggles to Make Old Customs Match New Laws," *Independent* (London), 19 January 1989, p. 12;

"Among the Roses," *Ladies' Home Journal*, 106 (April 1989): 96, 99-100, 103, 105;

"On Salman Rushdie: A Communication," *Partisan Review*, 56 (Summer 1989): 406-408.

Doris Lessing burst upon the British literary scene in 1950 with her first novel, *The Grass Is Singing*, and she has remained at the top ever since. In the past four decades, her work has had a profound and lasting influence on both women and men, and the critical acclaim enjoyed by her books has grown to the point where she has been frequently nominated for the Nobel Prize for Literature. In her work she has spoken out courageously for the humanist vision she associates with the major nineteenth-century writers and, more recently, for inner psychic phenomena and for mysticism. Her writing has been uniformly alert to the necessity for the split, fragmented individual to achieve wholeness, and her more recent novels have identified her as a kind of prophet for the sensitive, intelligent, "emancipated" reader. Increasingly a private person, she has been reluctant to divulge biographical information, preferring to have her work speak for itself.

Doris May (Tayler) Lessing was born 22 October 1919 in Kermanshah, Persia (now Bakhtaran, Iran), one of two children born to Alfred Cook Tayler, who had been a bank clerk in England before World War I, and Maude McVeagh Tayler, who nursed her husband following the amputation of a leg as a result of wounds suffered in the battle of Passchendaele. Tayler had worked for the Imperial Bank in Persia, but with a better education for the children in mind, the family moved to Rhodesia (now Zimbabwe), where Lessing's younger brother, Harry, still lives. The Taylers settled in an isolated area one hundred miles west of the Mozambique border, where Tayler was unsuccessful as a farmer; for some twenty years the family lived in poverty. As a child Doris was sent to the Dominican convent school in Salisbury (now Harare) and later to a government school for girls, also in Salisbury. At the age of twelve or thirteen she moved back home because of eye trouble and subsequently was self-educated. At age sixteen she began working for the telephone company, having taught herself to type. In the late 1930s she began working for a

Doris Lessing

firm of attorneys in Salisbury, where she taught herself shorthand; she subsequently worked for the Rhodesian parliament as a secretary and in 1947 as a typist on a Cape Town (South Africa) newspaper, the *Guardian*. Even after moving to London in 1949, she worked as a part-time typist (and took in boarders) to make her way financially.

In 1939 Lessing married Frank Wisdom, who eventually rose to become master of the High Court in Salisbury, a civil service position in the Ministry of Justice. This marriage, which lasted for four years, resulted in two children, Jean and John, who still live in Rhodesia. In 1945 she married Gottfried Lessing, a half-Jewish German Communist who immigrated to Rhodesia during World War II. Their son, Peter, was born in 1947. In 1949 the family left for England and Gottfried moved on to East Germany, where he rose to become the commissar of trade. He later became ambassador to Uganda and was accidentally killed in May 1979 during the revolt

against Idi Amin. Lessing has never remarried; since 1949 she has lived with Peter in various residences in London.

The Grass Is Singing (1950) is a relatively uncomplicated novel about white settlers in Rhodesia, with the title derived from section 5 of T. S. Eliot's *The Waste Land* (1922). Lessing's novel focuses on Mary Turner, who has been killed by her houseboy; most of the novel is an elaborate flashback to her childhood, her acceptance of her unmarried state, her intentional, even desperate grasping for emotional stability by marrying Dick Turner, a farmer, when she is thirty, and her subsequent life on an isolated, impoverished farm. There she seems incapable of adjustment, and her cruelty to the native workers and the mental and economic deterioration of the couple and their farm put them at a level only slightly different, in the eyes of the other white farmers, from the natives themselves. The farm is finally sold to a neighbor, and Mary is killed by Moses, who confesses to the killing and is arrested.

For many English and American readers, *The Grass Is Singing* was the first candid dramatic presentation of apartheid, with the horror emphasized through the matter-of-fact acceptance of the racial system, even by well-intentioned whites who have emigrated from England to Rhodesia. Before her marriage Mary Turner had never had any direct contact with blacks but, like other whites, had developed a "code" of behavior toward them; in general this code suggested that blacks are not trustworthy, that whites should not get too close to them, and that the system could never be altered without wreaking chaos upon the nation. Mary, incapable of any self-respect or authority, fears Moses, and the relationship gradually changes to the point where he is dominant, with his power taking on the same malevolent nature her own behavior previously had reflected. Though Moses wants "revenge" for the treatment he has suffered, he knows as well that he cannot escape punishment; Mary, in fearing anything "personal" between herself and Moses, ironically has taunted Moses sexually, the one particularly forbidden personal area and the one that has tormented Mary since childhood. Her obsessions become hatred combined with a temptation of the forbidden, and her gradual disintegration becomes a stoical, masochistic kind of acceptance of punishment and death.

Critical reception of *The Grass Is Singing* was overwhelmingly favorable, with critics pointing out not only the expected parallels with Eliot—atmospheric conditions, especially the thunder, are integrally tied in with Mary's deterioration and death—but also with *Lady Chatterley's Lover* (1928) by D. H. Lawrence, an author with whom Lessing has often been compared and discussed. Mary Turner is unlike any of Lessing's later female protagonists in her passive willingness to endure unquestioningly the wasteland of her life and surroundings; unlike the later heroines, Mary Turner demonstrates no desire for or understanding of the nature of freedom—real or imagined—in a person's life. Characterization in the novel is sometimes limited to stereotypes, but in the psychological portrayal of a haunted, driven woman, Lessing is excellent, and, in the more limited understanding of the forces at work upon Moses, she does as good a job as a non-native, even one growing up in such a milieu, could have reasonably been expected to do. While the whites in the novel have the economic and political power, the blacks have the moral edge. In most respects, this is a relatively successful first novel.

But it was in the expansive (five volumes running about eighteen hundred pages) "Children of Violence" series about Martha Quest, in many respects a close fictional double for Lessing herself, that Lessing's talents had their most significant showplace. Lessing has observed that the series is a "study of the individual conscience in its relations with the collective," a point she noted that was overlooked by initial critics of the first volume in the series, many of whom preferred to find autobiographical parallels. Such parallels do exist, for Martha Quest, like Lessing, was born in 1919, grew up in rural Rhodesia, married twice (with obviously intentional parallels in the names of Lessing's and Martha Quest's husbands), became a Communist and later left the party, and immigrated to England in 1949. Citing such parallels is one matter; trying to equate author with protagonist is quite another, and what Lessing has done in the series is to take elements of her own early and later life and transform them into a sequence fully equal to recent saga or series novels by C. P. Snow, Anthony Powell, and others. Lessing's five-part sequence was published over a period of some seventeen years, with the first three parts published in fairly rapid succession (1952, 1954, 1958), a seven-year gap until the next volume (1965), and four more until the culminating volume (1969). While most critics feel that Lessing's 1962 *The Golden Notebook* is her greatest single work, her achievement in the "Children of Violence" series is undeniably also a major one, with the final volume, *The Four-Gated City*, often singled out for particular acclaim because of its apocalyptic and psychic elements; it and its immediate predecessor in the series followed publication of *The Golden Notebook* and therefore necessarily reflected some of Lessing's profoundly analytical evaluation of a mature woman's life and psyche.

The first novel in the sequence, *Martha Quest* (1952), resembles a conventional Bildungsroman or initiation novel, and while some of the details about Martha do fit this category, Martha's mature years transcend by far the youthful Martha's learning experiences. We first meet Martha at age fifteen as she attempts to break away from what appears to her to be a too-confining, too-genteel home, especially to leave her domineering, self-righteous, hypocritical, and possessive mother; until Martha is able to leave the home, following her years in school, she

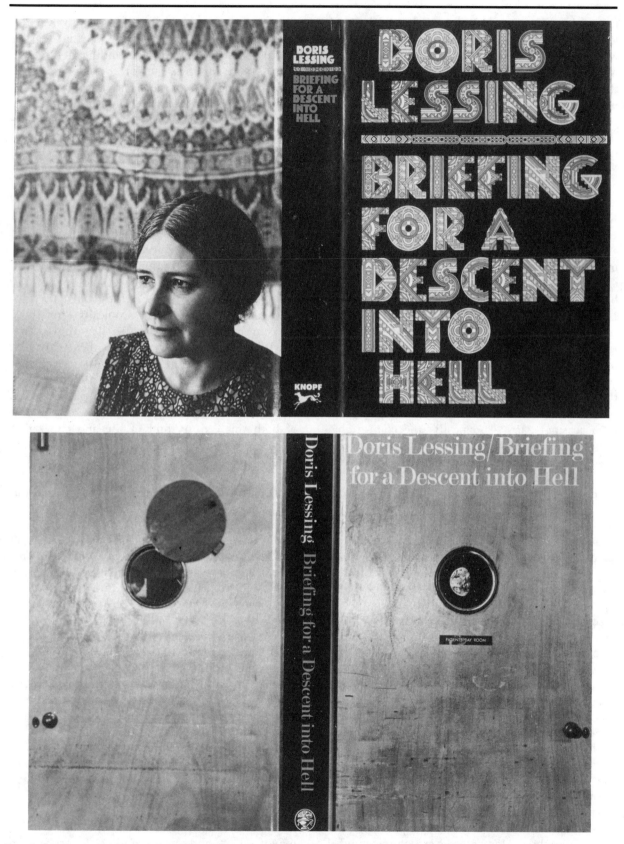

Dust jackets for the British and American editions of Lessing's 1971 novel. Her only novel to that date with a male protagonist, it was influenced by the theories of psychiatrist R. D. Laing.

must simply endure the tensions. Instead of going to the university, however, Martha begins working in Zambesia (as Salisbury is called in the novel), leaving forever the small-mindedness of the rural area and, she hopes, the deeply felt prejudices and provincialism as well. Like Lessing, Martha has been an omnivorous reader, and much of her reading has focused on a naive understanding of emancipation and justice. She in time joins a leftist clique where she meets a Jewish youth with whom she has her first sexual experiences; she then meets and marries Douglas Knowell (a close similarity in name to that of Lessing's first husband, Frank Wisdom).

A Proper Marriage (1954), the second volume in the sequence, presents the young couple as socially active, Martha as pregnant, and her husband as a fighter in the first years of World War II. The many Royal Air Force men stationed near Zambesia lead Martha and her left-wing friends to consider ways of abolishing the "colour bar," for the British fliers, she finds, are less concerned with rigid racial categorization than are the white settlers, even those who had emigrated from England. After Martha's baby is born, she is increasingly active politically; the comfortable life that she and Douglas, now returned from duties in Europe, share is more and more frustrating and stifling, and, despite interference by her parents, especially by her mother, Martha decides to leave her husband.

The third volume, *A Ripple from the Storm* (1958), shows Martha increasingly active with European refugees. One of the refugees, a Jew who had left Germany before Hitler's pogroms, is Anton Hesse (whose name parallels that of Lessing's second husband, Gottfried Lessing), who becomes Martha's second husband as a means of escaping the deportation with which he is threatened. Hesse, a Communist, rules the left-wing group of which Martha is a part; this loveless marriage, too, is doomed to failure, and the left-wing group splits into militants (such as Martha and Anton), moderates (roughly equivalent to Social Democrats), and the Labour party (affiliated with the white labor unions).

Landlocked (1965) begins near the end of the war, and, though Martha and Anton are still married, they have separate identities and lives. A variety of other refugees are brought into the novel, especially Thomas Stern, a Jew from Poland, with whom Martha has her one meaningful romantic and sexual relationship. Stern leaves for Israel, returns to Africa, and dies of a fever

when he goes out into the wilderness to live with the natives. Many others from Martha's earlier life also die in this novel, including her father. Martha and Anton are divorced, she finds herself increasingly out of touch with the younger radicals, and she plans to immigrate to England.

In *The Four-Gated City* (1969), Martha is living in London and working as the secretary-mistress of Mark Coldridge, a noted writer. Postwar London is described as relentlessly bleak, chaotic, and economically deprived. The title for this novel comes from a vision Martha has in the first novel in the sequence in which she sees a "golden city, tree-lined, four-gated, dignified . . . where black and white and brown lived as equals, and there was no hatred or violence." Such a utopian vision becomes inverted at the end of *The Four-Gated City*, because Coldridge plans a utopian sanctuary—in Africa, ironically—for those who survive the ultimate battle. We are told that the British Isles are destroyed in the 1970s and, in the powerful closing pages of the novel, that the earth itself is destroyed in the 1990s through either atomic weaponry or nerve gas or both. Lessing's searing apocalyptic portrait of the end of both this century and of life and civilization themselves are her way of portraying—not for the last time in her fiction—the end of the entire mad mentality of the world.

With the five-part series ranging from its initial realistic portrayal of a romantically inclined teenage girl down through the awesome final pages, it is quite obviously difficult to speak of all five parts as a unified piece of work in formal terms. Yet there are elements that tie together all five, aside from Lessing's clear intention all along of showing how Martha's youthful vision also becomes a part of her middle-aged years. For despite whatever experiences and major changes there may be in Martha's life, she at all times remains an independent seeker after individual identity and values, particularly those shared by some of Lessing's other heroines in the name of "freedom," imagined or real. Much of Martha's childhood was spent trying to rationalize and understand her mother's twisted mentality, and this is also her concern as she moves beyond friends, husbands, groups, and countries to her final years in England.

In *The Four-Gated City*, Martha realizes the limits of normal rational attempts to bring order out of chaos, and the alienation she feels from the world around her soon extends to much of what is called the "real" world. Indeed, her own frequent inability to focus on her identity, which goes back to her earliest years, suggests that for Martha there is not only a "split" in herself—more fully developed thematically in *The Golden Notebook*—but that schizophrenia is endemic around her. Martha, for example, learns of hidden psychic dimensions that she had not explored previously, such as ESP and telepathy (also used by Lessing in some of her later work). Martha has tried to emancipate herself from some of the entanglements of conformist institutions throughout her life, but no relationship, even the closest in human terms, such as husband-wife or mother-child, really enables her to feel "free." Just as she says that she set her own daughter "free" by leaving her in Rhodesia, so a pilot's attempt to gain "freedom" causes him to crash accidentally in England and therefore to obliterate the entire country. However poorly defined and deemed incapable of actually being experienced, such freedom is at the heart of much of Lessing's fiction. True, she is equivocal about mankind's chances of ever actually achieving either freedom or the ideal state of brotherhood identified with a utopian form of escape such as a four-gated city, for holocaust and death are far more rampant in the final volume of the sequence than are positive emotional and psychic experiences.

On more formal grounds, there are elements that both unify and diffuse all five novels. There are, for instance, references in the last volume to events and characters in earlier volumes in the sequence, though these are not as extensive as one might have wished since so much of what occurs in *The Four-Gated City* is intentionally far removed from the relatively simple world of Martha's youth and young adulthood in Rhodesia. As with people in the real world, Martha simply outgrows the physical and emotional need to reflect upon her earlier relationships and commitments. Fictionally, however, this does not work as well as it might, and the chief criticism offered regarding the final volume has been its diffuseness, the radically different emphases in the different volumes that led some critics to impute contradictions on Lessing's part. Thematically the five volumes cohere, and Lessing evidently laid the foundations for all five before the first was ever published, with her statement about "the individual conscience in its relation to the collective" as meaningful in terms of total annihilation and destruction as in smaller social groups.

Still, seventeen years can alter an author's perspective, and Lessing's work has undeniably changed directions at various points in her career. The problem in "Children of Violence" is simply that we conventionally anticipate some degree of use of a unified series of reflections on Martha's earlier life. But Martha—perhaps like Lessing too, though one can only speculate—prefers not to look back at previous stages in her life, whether they were filled with mistakes or, less often, with moments of joy and satisfaction. Martha's notoriously poor memory, mentioned from *Martha Quest* onward, is no doubt tied in with this rejection of the past and with persistent, tenacious looking toward the future, for some of the early events in her life were so unpleasant that she says she could not endure trying to remember them. Such repression or blocking is not unusual in real life, nor even in fictional presentations of character; but Lessing is so adamantly concerned with focusing on what will happen next that the unity of the sequence suffers somewhat. Not even the deaths of those for whom Martha felt some genuine affection recur in her thoughts, and in the fifth part of the sequence, Martha's changed environment, which one would think would necessarily lead her to reflect, seems instead to have obliterated all vestiges of her earlier life; indeed, the chief carryover from the earlier volumes is Martha's detestable mother, who comes briefly into the narrative. Since Martha's concern is with surviving (again in common with other Lessing protagonists), nostalgic reflection is of less concern than the infinite possibilities of uncharted directions that her mind might yet take her. For since *The Four-Gated City* has only the relatively passive Martha as a primary carryover from the earlier volumes—after all, the setting, the other characters, the time period covered in the novel are all different—this last novel seems almost as if it is about another heroine; it may possibly have been Lessing's need to complete the series that led to the creation of such a self-contained, even obtrusive part-of-a-series novel as *The Four-Gated City*, but it definitely affects the reader's expectation that either a Bildungsroman or a series novel has been concluded satisfactorily.

Ironically, it is not until *The Four-Gated City* that Martha really has some kind of rewarding, sustaining work to do; prior to this volume she has moved from one unsatisfying involvement to another, utilizing her reading, in common with many of Lessing's other heroines, as her chief means of finding a meaningful existence in something other than a limited, conventional role as-

"Her intelligence is formidable, her integrity monumental and her operating methods wholly uncompromising. She has not spared herself and she will not spare the reader."
                    —John Leonard writing in *The New York Times* about *The Four-Gated City*

"She is a writer of considerable native power, a 'natural' writer in the Dreiserian mold, someone who can close her eyes and 'give' a situation by the sheer force of her emotional energy."
                    —Joan Didion reviewing *Briefing for a Descent into Hell* in *The New York Times Book Review*

"Of all the postwar English novelists Doris Lessing is the foremost creative descendant of that 'great tradition' which includes George Eliot, Conrad, and D. H. Lawrence: a literary tradition that scrutinizes marriage and sexual life, individual psychology and the role of ideology in contemporary society."
                    —Richard Locke writing in *The New York Times* about *The Temptation of Jack Orkney*

"She is prophetic, but not in a vague, exhortatory, passionate mode. Her judgments are practical, based on sound observation, and her grasp of what is actually happening in the world is ministerial. She is one of the very few novelists who have refused to believe that the world is too complicated to understand."
                    —Margaret Drabble in *Ramparts*

Alfred A. Knopf

Dust jacket for the American edition of Lessing's popular 1973 novel, criticized for its didacticism

signed her by society. Openness to change is one of Lessing's chief emphases in her presentation of character, and Martha's radical alterations between the first and the last books in the sequence can be better appreciated if the reader keeps that in mind rather than anticipates a mere continuation of the same events occurring to the same person. For while Martha explores the possibilities of marriage and politics, among other concepts, Lessing manipulates her so that such activities merely become more encumbrances in the path to psychic wholeness and self-understanding. And the fact that this "path" takes as long as it does through such circuitous detours, tedious and claustrophobic though they may be at times, merely enhances Lessing's desire to show how Martha's gradually broadened perspectives and experiences parallel not only the typical adult's widened world but, even more, the sharp contrast between the narrow confines of a colonial, essentially rural world and the complicated, expansive urban world hurtling toward its own destruction.

In 1956 Lessing published an intriguing minor work, one she has subsequently and repeatedly disowned and refused to allow to remain in

print. *Retreat to Innocence* concerns Julia Barr, ingenuous daughter of Sir Andrew Barr, who becomes involved (sexually and politically) with Jan Brod, a Jewish Czech Communist. Jan eventually returns to Czechoslovakia, and Julia marries a young Briton solely for the sake of creature comforts. As in Lessing's other works, there is a conflict of generations, but in this novel there is also a different sort of conflict, an inversion: Julia rejects the bourgeois, romantic life one would identify with her roots, while Jan considers "personal relations" more important than any other value. Julia, we are told, is a split person, and at the novel's end she realizes that she cannot do anything with an "undivided mind." Julia tries to be unconventional and "emancipated," yet she eventually "retreats" to a safer, more innocent world of conventionality. To some extent Lessing explores the nature of freedom in this novel, with Jan especially aware of the freedom he will lose by returning to Europe. Yet Jan is the wholly dedicated Communist, more so than any other character in Lessing's fiction (for example, he has written a quarter-million-word allegory combining the story of Jesus and Communist theory); hence he reflects a commitment that Julia, in all her privilege and comfort, can never understand or feel. No doubt part of Lessing's reasons for rejecting this novel is the fact that she herself left the Communist party of England the year after the book was published. Before the book appeared, she left on a seven-week return trip to Rhodesia, which resulted in *Going Home* (1957). No doubt *Retreat to Innocence* seemed to her, as to many readers since, more a tract or apologia for communism than a convincing work of fiction.

The Golden Notebook (1962) has generally been acclaimed Lessing's masterpiece, though it is considerably less accessible than any of her earlier novels or most of her subsequent ones. It is a complex maze of differing perspectives on the same woman's life and circumstances and structurally is an exceedingly carefully controlled series of overlapping "notebooks." Lessing has said that "the point [in this book] was the relation of its parts to each other" and that its "meaning is in the shape." Her original intent was to write a short formal novel that would enclose the rest of her material in the book, but since the formal novel is "ridiculous" when it "can't say a damned thing," she split up the material not included in the short formal novel into four "notebooks," each concerned with a different though similar aspect of one woman's life, and then in turn divided each notebook into four parts. The result is a technique in which first a part of the short novel—called "Free Women"—is given, then one part each of the black, red, blue, and yellow notebooks, a pattern that is repeated four times. Then there is a short section of the entire novel, also called "The Golden Notebook," followed by the concluding "Free Women" section, which ends the novel. Hence the reader can either read from page 1 to the end of the book, or, if the reader wishes, read all the parts of each notebook and "Free Women" together; either way, the conclusion is that *The Golden Notebook* is a complex, infinitely rewarding work.

Anna Freeman Wulf—Lessing's names are often symbolic, as was the case with Martha Quest—is one of the most consciously self-analytical and questioning characters in modern fiction. She senses the lack of order in her life, the sheer lack of coherence and pattern, so she opens up her "split" psyche into four notebooks, written records of successive stages of her life reflecting not only differing time spans but also varying moods: the black notebook basically covers her experience in colonial Africa; the red her time spent as a Communist; the yellow a fiction-

alized account of an alter ego named Ella; and the blue primarily a factual diary account of "real" life. "Free Women" is ostensibly "written" by Anna as a work of fiction, though it too deals with a character named Anna Wulf. And while there are admittedly major parallels between Anna and Lessing herself, in no sense is the novel "the confessions of Doris Lessing." Rather, it is a tightly controlled account of the mad, aggressive forces at work on the mind and soul of a sensitive, committed woman with an artistic bent—and with writer's block. All four of the notebooks are written in the first person and cover roughly the period from 1950 to 1957; the fifth notebook (the "golden" one) deals only with events in 1957, as do the "Free Women" passages.

Since the novel offers such a variety of perspectives on Anna Wulf's circumstances, with successive layers of narrative paralleling the "actual" events in Wulf's life (something like a nest of Chinese boxes), it is difficult at times to determine exactly what "happens." The ending of the novel, for example, offers at least two interpretations as to what Anna does after she attains psychic wholeness, and the Ella and "Free Women" passages are clearly efforts to present an alter ego even further removed from the reader than Anna Wulf herself. Inconsistencies also abound, though nothing that would alter Lessing's intent. The point is that Lessing probes deeply into the psyche of Anna Wulf as a means of getting to those levels of experience that are split as the first step toward restoring wholeness. Through constant self-analysis and probing, Anna reevaluates life in Africa, with all its injustice, hatred, and native heroes and villains, as one particular "commitment" made by Anna. Her allegiance to communism—like Lessing's—presumably began as idealism; both Wulf and Lessing subsequently left the party before the general exodus in 1956 (the date of the Twentieth Congress, at which Nikita Khrushchev denounced Joseph Stalin). The pressures felt by Anna in the party tend only to fragmentize her further. Love and sex and marriage are also examined, for Anna and her alter egos are alike in sensing disappointment at having to pay a price for their monogamous emotional and sexual identities; in particular the lack of "freedom" in such relationships drives Anna to even further doubt and inner examination. It is only when Anna meets Saul Green, an American Jew, that she finds a substantial relationship; when Anna and Saul separate, each gives the other the first sentence of a prospective

Doris Lessing, circa 1975

novel, with Saul's serving as the first sentence of Anna's "Free Women." Lessing offers a far more candid appraisal of male-female relationships in the sections of this book dealing with romantic and sexual matters than was conventional three decades ago, and so the passages in which women discuss orgasms and lovemaking offer a remarkably frank rejection of anything other than "committed sex" for a woman.

As a means of regaining psychic equilibrium, Anna Wulf consults a Jungian lay psychoanalyst, Mrs. Marks, also called "Mother Sugar." Her name, too, is suggestive of Anna's commitment to Marxism, but she does assist Anna in eliminating her frightful nightmares—Lessing's protagonists often have vivid dream lives that serve contrapuntally to parallel their mundane existences—through encouraging her to use the medium with which Wulf as a writer is most familiar: words. Wulf thereafter descends into her private

hell in which she frantically attempts to use writing as a further form of therapy, not only her own experiments to try to get all of her experience onto paper but also a maniacal cutting-out of newspaper articles and an obsessive, feverish accumulation of such clippings. Only when Anna turns from such compulsive, private uses of language to a more public form—as in the writing of a novel—does she begin to regain her sanity.

Lessing's landmark essay "The Small Personal Voice," written in 1957 and often reprinted since, is instructive in this context, for it applies implicitly to this novel in particular. While Lessing may not agree today with everything she offered in this early personal credo, her contention that commitment to writing is necessary because of today's confusion of values leads her to cite some of the great nineteenth-century novels—such as those by Leo Tolstoy, Stendhal, Honoré de Balzac, Fyodor Dostoyevski, and others—as the source of her humanistic conviction that such books reflect a compassion, warmth, humanity, and love of people that are just as necessary today. Further, if the novel is to regain its greatness, Lessing feels, the writer has a responsibility to choose for evil or to strengthen good, especially because the writer must recognize each human being as an individual, not merely as a part of any collective. Such a critical stance does not require that the writer become a propagandist for a cause, political or otherwise, nor does he or she regress by making such a commitment. The writer, she feels, must become an "instrument of change for good or bad" and an "architect of the soul." And what Anna Wulf experiences in the transition to a new sense of psychic balance closely fits this credo, especially in her personal struggle and victory over the fragmented portions of her psyche that have almost destroyed her; indeed, so powerfully is this presented by Lessing that *The Golden Notebook* seems worthy to stand in the same line of fictional descent from the novels of a century ago that she singled out for emphasis in the essay.

Throughout her career as a writer, Lessing has espoused various philosophic allegiances, and, not surprisingly, her fiction reflects these commitments. *Retreat to Innocence*, as mentioned, is an explicitly pro-Marxist work, but since her defection from the Communist party, she has disowned that novel. *The Golden Notebook* reflects a Jungian interest, partly in the nature of the psychoanalyst whom Lessing's protagonist in that novel consulted. At various times critics have singled out other influences as well; the Jungian remains the most pervasive, but an Eriksonian theory has been discussed by Ellen Cronan Rose at some length as it influenced the "Children of Violence" series. *Briefing for a Descent into Hell* (1971), the novel published after *The Golden Notebook* and the last two parts of "Children of Violence," shows a distinct correlation to and dependence on the work of the late psychiatrist R. D. Laing.

When *Briefing for a Descent into Hell* was published, critics noticed the contrasts between it and Lessing's previous work; even though the same dominant themes of mental imbalance and psychic phenomena that were used in *The Golden Notebook* and in *The Four-Gated City* are to be found here as well, there are some major differences. For one thing, *Briefing for a Descent into Hell* has as its protagonist one of the few men who have served this purpose in any of Lessing's longer fiction: Charles Watkins is a classics professor at Cam-

bridge University, and his mental and emotional "journey" and eventual restoration to psychic health constitute the book's plot. Lessing called this book "inner-space fiction," a label intended to suggest that it is Watkins's mental health rather than any actual physical journey that is at the heart of the book. Lessing thus attempts to probe beneath the accumulated layers of social pretense and conventional reaction to the kind of experience that frequently disguises any analysis of deeper reality in a person's psyche, any movement from "insanity" to "sanity."

The narrative presents Watkins endlessly circling the Atlantic on a raft, after a "Crystal," an extraterrestrial spaceship, abducts his companions but leaves him. He eventually arrives at an obscure island, an uncharted paradise, where he finds the ruins of a prehistoric city. Strange creatures combining characteristics of rats and dogs invade the city, followed by apes; war between these two species results in great bloodshed, but Watkins is flown to safety by a huge white bird, which then takes him back to a clearing where he again sees the Crystal, this time claiming him too and bringing him back to "reality." At this point, about one-third of the way into the book, Watkins is transported to a gathering of Greek deities who are debating methods of sending celestial representatives down to earth to become infants, directly parallel to William Wordsworth's "Ode: Intimations of Immortality from Recollections of Early Childhood" (1807), in which developing human life necessarily results in the loss of innate innocence and divinity as the children age; the title of the novel refers to the "briefing" such creatures share prior to their being sent "down" to a "poisonous Hell," that is, to earth. Mercury reflects on the others' willingness to subjugate themselves by such a mission and especially about the impossibility of their being affected by earthly existence. Truth, Mercury says, will be a part of humanity's "new soon-to-be-developed equipment," not because of man's own influence but because of the "celestial light" that is equated both with God and with a lucid understanding of the meaning of life on earth.

Watkins is then found wandering aimlessly in the streets of London and is admitted to a mental hospital, where the greater part of the book occurs. Suffering from amnesia, he cannot remember his previous life as a professor, though he can recall presumed other "existences" that in reality never occurred: serving as a guerrilla fighter in Yugoslavia during World War II, for instance.

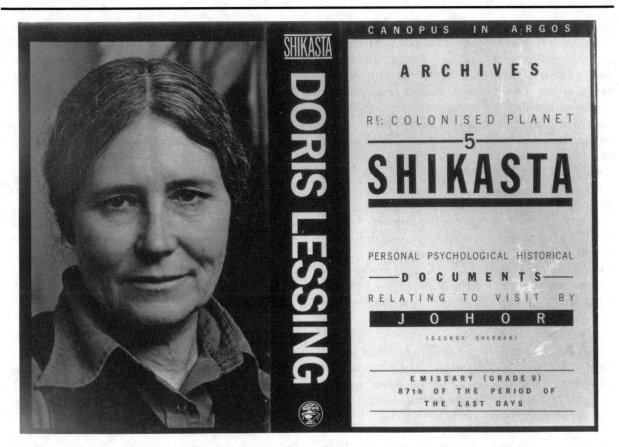

Dust jacket for Lessing's 1979 novel, the first in the series called "Canopus in Argos: Archives"

Extensive medical treatment, including the use of drugs, results in his recalling nothing at all of his academic life, his family, his friends; shock treatment, though, does work, and all too abruptly the book ends. The assumption here is that Watkins's "dream" life is more authentic and real than his actual one, certainly more dramatically memorable than his relatively quiet life as a professor; two intrusions upon his consciousness by his physicians are ignored as not really "there," though one of the physicians does manage to break through. The shock treatment suggests that Watkins has gone through a mental breakdown, caused by unspecified pressures, but his fantasy world remains for him a far more desirable and authentic world than the routine one he normally inhabits.

Some of Lessing's images in this novel are shockingly effective and illustrate quite well the extent to which Watkins has descended into "madness." While in the deserted city, for instance, he sees one of the rat-dog creatures simultaneously giving birth, trying to defend herself and her brood (killing some of them in the process), and being sexually attacked by her antagonist, a fright-

ening combination of birth, copulation, and death in a single act. And during the Yugoslavian part of the book, Watkins's lover is killed by a doe protecting her own offspring, again combining the two opposite experiences. For the "descent" to which the celestial creatures must humble themselves is itself a matter of entering into life through the act of birth and eventual acceptance of the inevitability of death—in other words, the normal human experience.

Watkins once observes that the sea had been the "well of sanity" before he was washed ashore, and "sanity" thereafter becomes whatever cosmos Watkins finds most real at the particular moment, which is why his university seems unreal to him. Hence Watkins is perched between two kinds or spheres of consciousness, once even seeing his two identities merged into one. Psychic wholeness, therefore, is Lessing's emphasis here as in *The Golden Notebook*, for man, despite the extremes to which he is driven, is ultimately still no more free or whole than he has ever been. At one point Watkins envisions a "broth of microbes" becoming volitional and intelligent, suggesting not only a dystopian future for earth but, even more, a perpetual, unsolvable cleavage in man, between his sense of human harmony and his desire for individual experience. The celestial gathering suggests that harmony is the only way in which mankind can endure, but human aggression, greed, and irrationality instead become the pattern called Life.

The fact that *Briefing for a Descent into Hell* deals with schizophrenia necessarily ties it in with the work of R. D. Laing; many parallels can be found in Lessing's fictional version of psychoanalytic theory, but the particular parallels between the last chapter of Laing's *The Politics of Experience* (1967), "A Ten-Day Voyage," and this novel are especially close. Laing, too, discusses "inner space," he provides a list of "directions" that a schizoid person could use in the path to complete recovery, and, even more important, he does this through the medium of a character named Watkins. The schizophrenic for Laing takes a "trip" in which he experiences hallucinations about weird animals and "gods," but then decides to return to "normality." As Laing says (with his emphasis), "Can we not see that *this voyage is not what we need to be cured of, but that it is itself a natural way of healing our own appalling state of alienation called normality?*"

The sense of the apocalyptic that was so prominent in *The Four-Gated City*, in which the end of life on earth is posited, is just as real in *Briefing for a Descent into Hell*, though now in personal emotional and intellectual terms rather than in world conflagration. Watkins's descent into madness (the hell of his own mind) has been a mental deterioration with no corresponding breakthrough into light, not, that is, until he experiences electroshock therapy. Lessing observes in an afterword to the novel that she knew such a person, one with an unusual degree of sensitivity to experience, but that such a person must necessarily be a handicap in a society like ours, which favors the "conforming, the average, the obedient." She observes that various therapists disagree among themselves as to the most efficacious form of treatment and that education attempts to categorize and label all of existence instead of allowing for individual awarenesses and experiences. Again, as in *The Four-Gated City*, Lessing suggests that such nonconformist perceptiveness may ultimately be more real than that which is more commonly recognized and accepted as conventional, predictable, and safe as desired and rewarded by a conformist society. For the visionary—the one who, through a schizoid

state, breaks through the limits placed upon him or her by society's conformist pressures—both regresses to a presocietal state and is squelched by the institutions we call civilized. The goal from society's perspective is normality, and any means can be used—even shock therapy—to restore the prodigal one to what society calls "adjustment." It is not surprising that Watkins is only vaguely aware of the psychic possibilities that lie within him, for it has always been in society's best interests to try to enforce such conformity, even among those who, like Watkins, belong to whatever aristocracy the world enjoys today. And if a professor of classics can be made to fit in once again to the restraints of social conformity, one can only wonder about the circumstances of less prominent people who must adapt with even less understanding of their true condition. In all cases, the psychic journey of such a "traveler" is freer, less loaded down with the trivial encumbrances of civilization, and infinitely more concerned with the "personal" as Lessing had used the term before, with a corresponding diminishing of the sociopolitical, so that *Briefing for a Descent into Hell* becomes an even more crucial transitional work than *The Four-Gated City* was—tied as the former novel necessarily was to earlier events in Martha Quest's life and circumstances—and a clear foretaste of her more recent "space fiction" novels.

Even more crucial, both in terms of *Briefing for a Descent into Hell* and Lessing's subsequent work, is her interest in the Sufis, particularly in the work of Idries Shah. She has published essays and reviews about Sufi thought, with one overriding emphasis: the absolute need for human beings to eliminate the patterns of preconditioned thinking that have so long imprisoned them and to open themselves to the higher thinking that can come about through the unique mystical perceptions that transcend rational discourse and thought. Being open to such impulses seems to be Lessing's focus, with such openness necessarily resulting in an extreme kind of individualism in which the person must trust his or her own sensations, experiences, and opinions above anything else. She includes a Sufi epigraph in *Briefing for a Descent into Hell*, and most of Lessing's protagonists from Martha onward challenge the accepted ideas and convictions of the established world around them; most of them, moreover, attempt to record their inner, nonrational sensations, such as Watkins's tape recordings or the voluminous notes maintained by both Martha and Anna

Wulf. When these characters attempt to "alter" the reality in which they must exist day by day, they are quickly made to feel that they must capitulate and adjust to society if they are to survive. Some of her characters, such as Mark Coldridge in *The Four-Gated City*, are trapped by their conventional thinking and so cannot make the necessary leap of faith to a freer, less limited means of perception. Hence the real, permanent part of human beings, their inner perceptions, are made to bend to the accumulated weight and influence of social reality. And in *Briefing for a Descent into Hell*, which moves from the most mundane aspects of earthly life to the most grandiose manifestations of "outer" space, out into the cosmos itself, we have a pattern that was to occupy Lessing in much of her subsequent fiction, especially in *Memoirs of a Survivor* (1974).

Restoration of psychic health is also the focus of *The Summer Before the Dark* (1973), which has the ironic distinction of being both one of Lessing's most popular—and profitable—novels (since superficially at least it is among her most readable and accessible) and one of the most severely criticized. Critics observed that Lessing seemed less sure of her handling of the dream metaphor in the novel, for one thing, or that she seemed to be saying much the same thing, but less persuasively, as in her preceding novels, almost as if she were overtly imitating herself, never quite sure whether she was writing another realistic novel like her earliest ones or a symbolic one like the more recent books. The protagonist, Kate Brown, seems considerably less interesting than Martha or Anna, she is certainly less open to inner experience, and she seems much duller. The book is an account of Kate's gradual awakening at age forty-five into a self-conscious "liberation" that leads her to emulate Henrik Ibsen's Nora: she ventures out of her home for a series of radically different (for her) experiences, only to return, at the novel's end, wiser if not chastened. Kate has been the sustainer of the family, self-sacrificing, passive, solitary, and ultimately tough-minded; when she feels she is no longer needed, her depression leads her, in a moment of crisis, to leave her home for a summer. The members of her family have gone their respective directions, with her husband, a noted neurologist, off to California for a lengthy conference. She takes a job with an international organization to serve as a translator of Portuguese, the language she grew up with. On one of her travels, to Turkey and then to Spain, she enters into an af-

fair with a sickly young man, after which she eventually returns to London more fully accepting of her own aging and eventual death.

Once her family has dispersed, Kate no longer feels needed or essential to the home; the emotional exhilaration formerly felt in the marriage has diminished, at least in part because of her husband's affairs with younger women. The position she takes as translator is itself a sort of mothering, and as she links up with the young man, Lessing's account of their conversation and affection becomes monotonously banal. Determined to resolve whatever has caused her malaise, Kate returns anonymously and completely disheveled to London, taking a cheap room in Bloomsbury, where she meets Maureen, a beautiful young woman trying to decide whether to get married or follow a career, the same choice Kate has had to make. Kate, in short, has descended as far from her previously secure status as she could, and in trying to help Maureen she is the "blind leading the blind" since all she can do is to mother the younger woman in interminable talk sessions. Kate then returns home, and in this regard she seems to be Lessing's version of a typical middle-aged woman who discovers late in life that she has never done anything but serve as wife and mother and who realizes, intentions notwithstanding, that all she can do is to effect a kind of compromise in returning home. She is as confused as the young people in the hotel, even at the novel's end, and so one wonders whether she has learned anything through her summer sojourn. One has no hint at all that Kate is qualitatively changed in any way through her summer away from her family, and, if one is to take the title as meaningful, she merely returns to the "dark"—to her conventional life and eventual death.

The very clichéd nature of the plot suggests that Lessing was writing more a didactic tract for a particular understanding of liberation than a convincing novel, for Kate at no point becomes anything but an ordinary, dull (though intelligent), trapped (in her own eyes at least), and predictable character. She is conventionally disgusted at pollution and other dehumanizing elements of the modern world; she suffers a mysterious, unnamed ailment (her own "dark night of the soul"); she feels hatred toward men and the institution of marriage as a result of her own family experiences; and the book offers no innovative answers to the dilemma such women find themselves in when they are alone. We never quite feel with Kate Brown as she tries to figure out the reasons for her malaise, nor does her self-conscious summer-long emancipation become persuasive; merely longing for freedom and peace does not allow a character in a novel to make these joint desires a vital part of her being.

Yet the book, despite these disclaimers, does have some of the quality of Lessing's earlier work. Kate is resourceful, and her dreams reflect the substance of other dreams in Lessing's work; in this case, Kate dreams of laboriously trying to save a seal that beached itself, but only through great effort—and many repetitions of the dream in one guise or another—does she save the seal by helping it return to the sea. But if the seal returns to health, Kate seems to decline, for in the course of a short summer she has not only endured a minor bout with the disease her young lover had (possibly hepatitis, judging from the symptoms) but has grown ugly, and her hair has turned particularly straggly and unappealing. Kate's obvious talents and flair make the work she takes on wholly satisfying to her and convincing to the reader—but just as suddenly as the work is taken on it is dropped, with no hint that she will continue it after she returns home. Does this reflect any real change for the better to Kate, or does it offer any hint that her life will be anything but a waste thereafter? By far the most persuasive parts of the novel are in the early chapters in which Kate is trying to find some answer for her feeling of being unneeded, and this is as sharply drawn and reminiscent of Lessing's earlier work as the latter portions seem tacked on for sheer didactic effect. Kate does not go through an epiphany akin to Martha Quest's eventual acceptance of her moral dimension to her life in which she becomes an "instrument of change"; Kate simply seems to give up, with only darkness to await her.

Those who praised this novel—critical opinion was more sharply divided than for any other Lessing novel, before or since—pointed out the authenticity of Kate's experience, and, indeed, this authenticity is superior to Lessing's formal achievement in the novel; the thematic, psychological truths in the book, qualified as they are, seem distinctly superior to Lessing's artistry. True, the book has been praised as a satiric, ironic, and parodistic work, but the fact that the heroine is too insubstantial and limited to carry the weight of introspection and self-analysis that Lessing attributes to her, not to mention the unconvincing profound change she allegedly experiences, ulti-

mately makes it much less of a significant work than it could have been.

Memoirs of a Survivor (1974), by sharp contrast, was much more successful on any terms; it remains one of Lessing's most discussed, praised, and ultimately important works. Her protagonist is once again a strong, solitary, middle-aged woman, this time unnamed, who is trying to maintain as normal a life as possible in a British city, presumably London, following a catastrophic war. Her first-person narrative is filled with the mundane details of survival, but she is suddenly and inexplicably given a twelve-year-old girl to care for. Much of the book covers the subsequent two years in their life together, years in which the girl, Emily, undergoes dramatic physical and emotional changes; the spindly girl-child is transformed into a sexually active, no longer innocent girl-woman. Emily is truly a "child of violence," but the implication is that she, like the narrator, is an innocent victim of that violence, and as a result of war and deprivation both her values and behavior are forever altered. The narrator's "memoirs" tell how the technologically advanced world has disintegrated and how the remaining alternatives are complete annihilation or radical alteration in values and behavior.

About half the novel is taken up with the gradual breakdown of civilized life in the city, the kind of circumstance dreadful to contemplate and the usual stock in trade of novelists writing about postcatastrophe survival. These portions of the book are relentlessly realistic and detailed; they closely resemble many similar accounts and offer little that suggests a radical departure from a stock science-fiction plot. Capitalism comes in for its share of the responsibility for the breakdown of society, for the greed motive is rampant. The feeling that the end of an era is upon the world is pervasive in these parts of the book, and Lessing implies that this is inevitable given the inequitable chasm between the fortunate and the unfortunate. The children are most flexible in adapting to an entirely new social system, squatters' rights are more important than legal ownership, and both possessions and talents are barterable. Older humans, part of the precatastrophe thinking, find that their values are either radically outmoded or necessarily altered, and the narrator is among the latter group. For if survival itself is the highest good, then any means toward that survival—even children feasting on corpses—can be justified. The adults in the book find it impossible to accept such realities, though they do recognize the necessity of restoring some semblance of order if life that is recognizably human is to endure. The new circumstances in society as it is presented in the novel require a correspondingly new set of values, though this need not imply anarchy. Emily and her lover Gerald, in fact, become the pioneers in helping the survivors to make the adjustment between older ways of thinking and the requirements of future survival; only the young can make the necessary adjustment easily because they have the fewest vestiges of tradition to cast off. And in these portions of the novel Lessing excels at showing both the horror of such a society and the innovative techniques for survival; in these respects, the novel becomes a kind of *Whole Earth Catalog* for the end of civilization.

But the second half of the book offers a different dimension to the narrator's view of reality, and in this respect Lessing's increasing concern with nonphysical phenomena is evident. The narrator concentrates on a section of her living-room wall where there had once been paint and wallpaper and envisions an alternate form of reality. These visions, not unlike the dreams Lessing's previous protagonists have often had, allow the narrator to "see" through the wall into the vacant apartment next door. What she sees there is a series of tableaux from her own presumed earlier life, when she too was named Emily. She sees a hexagonal room with a worn carpet on the floor; if she can find a piece of carpet from a pile of such pieces on the floor, the rug can be restored to "life," and, therefore, by implication, the colorful qualities of life that have been exterminated by the exigencies of survival can be re-created. Far from being mere wishful thinking or nostalgia for what had been, this sharp contrast between the mundane dullness of real life and the vivid possibilities for what could yet be becomes once again a form of therapy similar to what writing had been for Anna Wulf in *The Golden Notebook*: a means of reconciling her fantasy life with physical reality. For the nameless narrator, as "Emily," experiences a sequence of events, as visualized through the wall, that closely parallel the normal stages of development in a child's life; indeed, these are the same stages that are endlessly experienced throughout human history on a larger scale and, presumably, throughout what remains of that history in the novel.

Lessing, always somewhat pedantic in offering a didactic solution to the horrors life inflicts upon her characters, here too suggests a form of remediation. For in the narrator's travels into the room beyond the wall, she symbolically rids herself of patterns of behavior (and therefore of thinking) that governed her life prior to the postcatastrophe reality in which she finds herself. That is, by attempting to discard and therefore transcend the pictures of conventional childhood and its concomitant psychological pressures, she eventually confronts an idealized, apotheosized vision of a godlike creature, an ethereal woman who floats through the rooms of the visionary apartment. This transcendent vision dominates and takes over the narrator's consciousness, and, as the narrator completely subordinates herself to this apparition, a sort of paradise is regained and the wraith protects the narrator and the other characters who join her behind the wall, a total, mystical merger of pure mind and blemished world. As in those parts of Lessing's earlier work in which dreams are emphasized, the visionary world becomes far more real than the mundane realities surrounding the characters.

For the real world of war and pestilence and cannibalism is completely absorbed and transcended by the euphoric inner world. Such an allegorical transformation of outer into inner is not wholly satisfactory by any means, for surviving in one sense can seem to mean sheer escapism into schizophrenia, as in *Briefing for a Descent into Hell*. Lessing evidently intends more than such a simplistic reductionism, and once again her intent seems to have been based on Sufi thought to which she has increasingly been attracted and devoted. Detailed examinations of this commitment have been made (as suggested by the essays by Nancy S. Hardin and Dee Seligman); a brief summary of Lessing's position requires a radical adjustment from the normal, linear thinking so common in the West to a greater sense of the total integration of the intuitive to the rational so that the way we think is altered. The room beyond the wall is not another world; it is a different dimension of the same reality found on this side of the wall. Such a Platonic vision of a mystical union of the divine with the mundane is presumably an evolutionary step beyond the rational order, to which Lessing attributes the chaos in this novel, into a properly cultivated degree of sublimity of experience. While there is much more that could be offered in such a summary of a Sufi position, it is clear that Lessing has deliberately taken and used such a perspective as a means of suggesting how survival can and must occur. Not all of her fiction in the 1970s and 1980s reflects the same Sufi concept, but there is no doubt whatsoever that Lessing has assimilated Sufi teaching; she has frequently written about it, and her more recent fiction uniformly can be analyzed with profit from such a perspective. It is ironic, in a way, that Lessing, who was born in Persia, who was subsequently denied permission to return to Rhodesia because the accident of birth made her an "Asiatic," now espouses a form of Islam that originated in Persia.

In 1979 Lessing began a series of "space fiction" books that broke completely new ground for her. For even though elements of science fiction were found in some of her earlier novels, notably *The Four-Gated City* and *Memoirs of a Survivor*, her readers had little idea of the direction this new series would take her. Five books in the series—*Shikasta* (1979), *The Marriages Between Zones Three, Four and Five* (1980), *The Sirian Experiments* (1981), *The Making of the Representative for Planet 8* (1982), and *Documents Relating to the Sentimental Agents in the Volyen Empire* (1983)—have appeared, but it is not certain that the series has been completed. Lessing has offered surprises before, but nothing thus far of the sort these five volumes have given to her readers. For these books combine some of the elements that have concerned her in the past, notably the untapped inner psychic resources presumably available to all beings and a pessimistic view of human history, along with some novel conceptions, such as the idea that competing evil and benign influences from far out in space directly determine events on earth—and on other planets—through active intervention by ageless beings. The intervention is not consistent, however, and the rise and fall of human epochs and civilizations reflect variously the influence of one interstellar race or another. Those from Canopus call Earth "Shikasta" (the "broken or damaged place"), while those from Sirius call it "Rohanda" ("the beautiful").

The series is called "Canopus in Argos: Archives," with some of the volumes bearing cumbersome subtitles. The first, *Shikasta* (short for *Re: Colonised Planet 5, Shikasta: Personal, Psychological, Historical Documents Relating to Visit by JOHOR (George Sherban), Emissary (Grade 9), 87th of the Period of the Last Days*), is far and away Lessing's most didactic, tedious, and prolix novel; no matter how concerned with "message" she was in her earlier works, she always presented humans interacting and conversing. But *Shikasta* is a long sequence of documents, diaries, reports, and records with little dialogue and relatively little

attempt to delineate human character in believable situations. Earthly history is seen from a cosmic perspective, with various recognizable epochs in that history presented from an "objective" point of view; by far the most intriguing parts of the book are those glimpses into twentieth-century events as seen from this perspective. Lessing is clearly one of those writers whose galactic empires are directly responsible for events on earth, and her positing good and evil worlds in opposition to each other and as equally eager to influence earth is a kind of Manichaeanism that one rarely encounters in modern science fiction. Indeed, these books have been relatively ignored by critics of science fiction because they seem more like allegory than science fiction, because of their sheer old-fashioned didacticism, or because of their lack of character development and involvement. True, Lessing does give human guise to her narrator, Johor, but more than the name "George Sherban" is needed before he comes completely alive for the reader; for a narrator, even one incorporating in his own account the history of earth from its beginnings to its catastrophic third world war, is bound to appear somewhat more omniscient than most humans, and therefore some degree of verisimilitude is lost. Lessing's attempt to make this omniscience believable through the framework of documents that we can and do recognize, such as "sacred books" rationalizing the existence of evil, including portions of the Bible, is only partially successful; nor does her term for the quality that has been lost on Earth, the "substance-of-we-feeling" (often merely labeled SOWF), serve any purpose other than that provided by such traditional words as *love* or *grace*. The planet Shammat is directly responsible for this decline on Earth, especially since a degenerative disease called individualism has also taken hold.

Johor materializes as George Sherban to take a direct part in earthly events, especially to guide Earthlings away from Shammat's influence; he does this through becoming a part of an English family involved in charitable work, and some of the documents are unrewarding journal entries by Sherban's fourteen-year-old sister, Rachel. Sherban is concerned with trying to divert this "century of destruction" from its inevitable course, and some of Lessing's most imaginative writing in *Shikasta* concerns a ceremony, a trial, between the darker and lighter races of humanity and between the young and the old, as if such easy dichotomies are in some way symbolic of the struggle between good and evil on earth. Lessing remarks in a brief introduction to the novel that it got its impetus through the Old Testament, and in this case she seems to have had the Edenic myth in mind; but in the documents we find that, both when earth was called Rohanda (and was inhabited by benign giants who lived for thousands of years) and later when it got the name Shikasta, a "fall" occurred; now, with the diminution of SOWF and mankind's tendency toward self-destruction, we are given a detailed accounting of the end of human history—or at least of the "last days" in which a mere remnant of mankind will survive to try again.

What Lessing has assembled in *Shikasta*, then, is less a convincing novel and more a thin allegory in which the gods determine, in some unnamed Calvinistic sense, humanity's destiny; all that humanity can do is to flounder irresponsibly from one catastrophe to the next when divine guidance is rejected. The reader is startled to find Lynda Coldridge (from *The Four-Gated City*) brought in, but little is done with this intrusion from the earlier work. And Lessing presents all of this with such a cosmic solemnity that the result, for many readers and critics, is simply dull. Lessing has always been a moralist, a deadly serious writer with little sense of humor; but in *Shikasta* this tendency was brought to fruition and her deep, prophetic seriousness resulted in a work that—by itself—was simply not very convincing as fiction. In retrospect, some of the frustrating loose ends in *Shikasta* make more sense since they are tied together in the later volumes, but by itself it was a most unpromising beginning for a series.

Fortunately, the second novel in the sequence is as light and moving as the first was heavy and tedious. *The Marriages Between Zones Three, Four and Five* is also heavily allegorical, but is deeply human in the sense that the reader is given convincing, moving portrayals of characters caught up in passions and influences that they cannot completely understand. Among other things, this novel is a touching love story and contains some of Lessing's most rhapsodic, finely wrought prose. One of the frustrations experienced in reading *Shikasta* was the sense that mankind, in some unexplained fashion, would continue to survive, no matter how completely successive wars and other forms of devastation ravaged the earth. In *The Marriages Between Zones Three, Four and Five* both the suspense and our feeling of objectivity are heightened because events presumably do not take place on earth and because we are not sure what will result as the novel continues. The finely shaped sense of psychological analysis found in Lessing's earlier works is also found in *The Marriages Between Zones Three, Four and Five*, as is a limited, noncosmic focus on a small number of characters rather than all life in the universe.

In *Shikasta* various numbered zones were mentioned, with the highest—Zone Six—akin to Hades or some other residing place for the dead; the lower the number of the zone, presumably the more ethereal and spiritual. This conceit is carried out successfully in *The Marriages Between Zones Three, Four and Five*. An order comes from the indistinct rulers of the cosmos, the Providers, that Al-Ith, the queen of Zone Three, must marry Ben Ata, the king of Zone Four, and raise an heir. As Zone Three is sweet, pure, lovely, harmonious, lush, peaceful, telepathic, and spontaneous, so Zone Four is militaristic, crude, spartan, obsessed with duty and obedience, and insensate. Hence the marriage combines not just individuals with conflicting values but, even more, whole societies with clashing ways of life. As the newlyweds learn to tolerate and adjust to each other—psychically, sexually, experientially—the reader is given details of their respective lands and outlooks on relations with the absolute. Love, sex, nationalism, eschatology, and psychic phenomena are among the qualities that differ in the two zones, but the marriage and the birth of a child effectively bring the two lands closer together in a compromise based on mutual self-interest. Human emotional involvements such as sensual love are especially effectively drawn, for while the book is an epithalamium, a celebration of marriage, it is also a book offering interpretations from many perspectives: theological, psychological, philosophical, mythical. It succeeds simply as fantasy, but much of Lessing's success is also due to the reader's profound identification with Al-Ith; for, after the birth of the child, Ben Ata is again ordered to marry, this time with the barbaric queen of Zone Five, presumably the closest to sheer animalistic or demonic life; even Ben Ata is appalled at the prospect. Al-Ith must return without her child to her own zone, but she no longer fits in, so great has been the mutual adjustment she and her husband have made. She is sent to a distant corner of Zone Three, where she longingly spends her days, looking up to the even more ethereal, rarefied land of disembodied souls, Zone Two, to which she travels at the novel's end.

Little explicitly ties *The Marriages Between Zones Three, Four and Five* in with *Shikasta* other than the reference to the zones and to the fact that the Providers seem akin to the Sirians. These characters are in a quasi-earthly planet in their profound, clearly human emotional relationship with each other and in the reader's inevitable sense that Al-Ith's innate joy and vitality are unjustly delimited for reasons that parallel earth's own gradual descent into barbarism. True, the merger of Al-Ith's nature, the very high, must necessarily be combined with Ben Ata's, the very low, and therefore synthesized into a kind of vitality offering eventually greater rewards for both lands. Presumably an even further synthesis is suggested by Ben Ata's subsequent marriage, though the cavalier disposal of Al-Ith remains a perplexing, unclear turn in the plot. The novel is a far stronger work of fiction than *Shikasta*, and it can easily be read independently of the rest of the series as fable, folktale, or allegory. Lessing does not moralize, nor does she offer any kind of cosmic message or explanation for the events in the novel, for as myth it is sufficient unto itself. No matter how successful the series as a whole might be considered, there is no doubt that *The Marriages Between Zones Three, Four and Five* is one of her most affecting, moving works and that it demonstrates a mellower perspective than any of her earlier work.

The Sirian Experiments stands somewhere between the first two in quality. On the one hand, it contains far too much of the endless and sometimes dull reports about earth's early history and the great rivalry between empires for influence over earth and its peoples; these reports are offered by Ambien II, a female member of the Sirian colonial administration, and they focus primarily on earth's early history, whereas most of the reports in *Shikasta* concern the twentieth century. Ambien II is also far more prone to errors in judgment or action than Johor, and only slowly do we see that she, too, is learning the true significance of the cosmic actions of which she is both a participant and an observer. She is often seen in connection with Klorathy, a Canopean administrator, but he is infinitely more patient, introspective, and omnisciently benevolent than she is; only as Ambien II discovers the significance of the rise and fall of civilizations and cultures are we able to share her wonderment at such strange worlds: a version of Atlan-

tis, ruled by women; Central American cults (evidently Mayan/Aztec) in which human sacrifice is practiced; hordes of barbarians devastating peaceful empires; and even a happy, peaceful utopian society on one side of a mountain range with a dystopian one on the other. Ambien II, as part of the "group mind" that rules the Sirian empire, finds that the Canopeans are superior in intellectual and moral qualities but that she and her fellow Sirians impute the unworthiest of motives to their benevolent actions. Hence Ambien II is sometimes forced to recant or to acknowledge error, and she is even ousted from "the Five" because of her disobedience to their will.

Lessing acknowledges in a preface to this novel that the changes in Ambien II parallel the changes in the universe (especially earth, by whatever name it is called) as the dominance of the Canopean empire is reluctantly accepted. "I could like Ambien II better than I do," Lessing comments; "some of her preoccupations are of course mine. The chief one is the nature of the group mind, the collective minds we are all part of. . . ." In this sense Lessing seems to revert to her announced intent for the "Children of Violence" series, as already discussed; and in this preface she refers to the "odd" notion that each person is unique and self-determined. And while a Jungian concept of race memory is evident in *The Sirian Experiments*, for the most part Lessing is concerned with phenomena such as telepathy as a means of higher beings communicating between themselves, the inability of such beings to envision death for themselves (since they are for all practical matters immortal), and the kind of willfulness that is equated with evil. The great contrast between opposing cultures is especially well seen in the differing views held about earth: the Sirians consider Rohanda a world to visit, exploit, and use as a place for experimentation; the Canopeans, taking the longer view of life, look to the ultimate "Golden Age" which will inevitably await Shikasta under the proper cosmic supervision.

If the sequence of reports in *The Sirian Experiments* is as tedious at times as in *Shikasta*, the several major sections of the book in which human discourse and activity occur are among the more fascinating. This is especially so in Ambien II's contacts with Nasar, a Canopean administrator so affected by the evil of Shammat that his usefulness and virtue are radically diminished. And her conversations and physical contacts with Klorathy, infrequent as they are in the book, combine high drama (in the contrast between celestial perspectives) and affectionate, underplayed lovemaking. Indeed, it is the very human qualities reflected by these demigods that give this book its greatest charm and appeal, for these qualities contrast sharply with the more objective accounts given in the reports. All too often, though, Lessing prefers to tell rather than to dramatize, and the result is page after page of what we *should* conclude about these creatures, their worlds, and their worldviews, not what we are persuaded to believe through careful, consistent character interaction and discourse.

True, Ambien II is strong, vigorous, and ultimately independent (in her willingness to deviate from official Sirian policy), and in this respect Lessing has created another in her series of such women. While infinitely less concerned with freedom than her predecessors (in a cosmic sense, the term simply has no meaning), she is as dedicated and competent as could be expected short of perfection. And in her dry, efficient manner, she offers a perspective about earthly history that we come to feel is both reliable and accurate. For instance, the latter parts of the novel present some of the cataclysmic events of this century, such as the two world wars and racial hatred in southern Africa. No doubt one of Lessing's intents in the book is to present the irrationality of much human activity and history as seen from the more balanced perspective of those who will ultimately bring both harmony and destruction to the world, for from this perspective earth is of exceedingly minor importance and could be annihilated as easily as other entire worlds are in the book.

The fourth volume in the series, *The Making of the Representative for Planet 8*, is an extremely short work (124 pages with a 20-page afterword by Lessing), again about a world of creatures who while clearly not human do manifest the emotional uncertainties and confusion identified with Earthlings. In its barest sense, this novel is about the death—through freezing—of a planet. Doeg, the narrator, is one of forty Representatives of various skill classes on Planet 8 who have been informed by Johor (narrator for *Shikasta*) that the planet's inhabitants must prepare for a radical alteration in their existences and that they will be taken to Rohanda, a compatible planet. Soon their planet begins to cool toward its certain death, and Lessing is superb in her descriptions of changes in her characters' physical and emotional lives, in alterations in the chain of life and

the food supply, and in an understanding of what their celestial masters expect of them. Lessing's afterword clearly indicates that much of her impetus for these descriptions comes from Robert Scott's ill-fated Antarctic expedition in 1910-1913, and most of the novel matches what we know of that continent.

Yet Lessing again suggests that even the overlords themselves, such as Johor, are merely pawns in a larger scheme of things and that even their power to influence whole universes is limited. As Rohanda becomes Shikasta (that is, as earth deteriorates ethically and physically), it becomes clear that the mass evacuations promised Planet 8 are not to occur, and the only outcome is total annihilation of all life on the planet. In the process of dying, though, the Representatives find a much greater degree of understanding of their plight and of the common substance of shared experience that was described earlier in *Shikasta*. As the planet dies and becomes a lump of cosmic ice, Doeg realizes that even his world takes on a myriad of guises and possibilities, that a "perpetual shifting and changing" is merely a stage in the ultimate development of possibilities in life, not a fixed, static, final stage of development. As Lessing observes in her afterword, earthly concepts of nationalism, of national pride and historical process, are often summed up in one person; just as Scott's associate Edward Wilson is such a person for her, so Doeg becomes the means of his planet's assimilation into universal process as a necessary, inevitable, and wholly nonethical evolutionary stage. Just as the animals on Planet 8, as well as the humanoid creatures themselves, adapt to survive before all hope is lost, so, presumably, did those creatures on Antarctica that were studied by the first expedition to that frozen land.

Lessing offers compelling, even shocking, visions of the future in these two novels, and her handling of Johor and the doomed planet in the latter work suggests both that there are connections between the novels and that her high seriousness in describing earth's own decline and ultimate demise is as profoundly apocalyptic as ever. And even if there is no hope (as commonly understood) for the inhabitants of Planet 8, Lessing seems as fiercely concerned with the larger cosmic picture as before.

The fifth (and possibly final) volume in the "Canopus in Argos: Archives" series, *Documents Relating to the Sentimental Agents in the Volyen Empire*, combines the bureaucratic reports so abundant in

Shikasta with heavy-handed satire about the debasing and abuse of language. Lessing clumsily strikes out at such obvious targets as political jargon, wartime sloganeering, and high-sounding platitudes intended to placate the populace. Victims of such linguistic excess—the "sentimental agents" of the book's title—dry out in a Hospital for Rhetorical Diseases, but little attempt is made to distinguish, for example, between such patriotic appeals as Winston Churchill's "We shall fight on the beaches" and inflammatory speech used to arouse mobs, and her characters utter such dated profundities as "Wow!," "Cool!," "Neat!," "Right on!," and "What a drag!" Language identified with Christianity is said to be useless, as is a "dirge" beginning "We shall overcome," but Lessing's satire falls flat.

The documents in the novel do carry the story more than those in *Shikasta*, to be sure, though Lessing's point—that empires rise and fall—has been made abundantly clear in the series by this stage. Lessing's spokesman, Klorathy, represents the beneficent world of Canopus and thus takes a longer view of empires' ups and downs than do the planets' inhabitants; he represents reason and balance in language, and it is he who advises the Volyens to survive conquest by adjusting to their invaders. Since the Volyens are said to be defeated through rhetorical excess, there is much opportunity for him to offer such advice. But the easy satiric targets offer little challenge and no opportunity for humor, thus suggesting that Lessing may simply have let this series dwindle to a close with this volume.

Whether or not one cares to take Lessing's jeremiads seriously, they do make for endlessly provocative reading, for this series is a retelling of cosmic and earthly history far more ambitious than most recent fiction—or science fiction, for that matter. Far from being mere escapist fiction or some other form of conventional space narrative, the series offers a further glimpse into her prophetic view of human history and activity; even when dull, flawed, overwritten, and in need of acute editing, the series offers a qualified hope for earth from the point of view of those who have some power of determination in such matters. One can say with some certainty, however, that she will continue to offer didactic, complex, ultimately moral, highly evocative glimpses of her own evolving sensitivity as a woman and as a writer, and that, while these future works will have no more of a mass following than most of her previous books, their collective influence

on modern fiction and individual experience will persist.

Lessing wrote the two "Jane Somers" novels, *The Diary of a Good Neighbour* (1983) and *If the Old Could . . .* (1984), as a deliberate attempt, she has said, to see whether an "unknown" author can get published today; indeed, more critical attention was given to the hoax than to the novels themselves. The novels are slight efforts, though the first is somewhat more interesting than the second; Lessing's effort to fool the publishing world and thus the reviewers can only be considered a hoax that failed, for the prank proves merely that established authors receive more attention than do alleged novices. *The Diary of a Good Neighbour* focuses on a sophisticated woman journalist who befriends and interviews a poor elderly woman, in time coming to accept personal responsibility for her welfare. And *If the Old Could . . .* describes the journalist's meeting a strange, fascinating man at an underground station. She wordlessly falls in love with him and has a hopeless affair. Despite the books' high seriousness, they are little more than soap-opera depictions of urban life.

The title character of *The Good Terrorist* (1985) is a gullible, thirty-six-year-old, middle-class drudge of a revolutionary who is primarily concerned with making her group's "squat" comfortable and tidy. Protagonist Alice Mellings seems much younger than her age and is only marginally more appealing than the others in her group, who are mostly two-dimensional caricatures. Her actions merely range from crying at society's ills to cursing her parents for their too-comfortable existences to spray-painting slogans on walls to expressing her need to be a part of the movement by getting involved in the setting of a car-bomb. Though the book represents a welcome return to Lessing's earlier realism, it is at most a reversal of the idealism found in the Martha Quest novels in its contemptuous rejection of her characters' misguided urge for social betterment. Alice is simply self-deceived rather than filled with conviction, as is ironically illustrated by her efforts to reject her parents' middle-class life-style by imposing the same life-style on the other revolutionaries, and though much of her story is potentially rich and relevant, it trivializes both the genuineness of some nonconformists' convictions and the dangers of terrorism.

Again demonstrating her interest in different literary genres, Lessing wrote the short novel *The Fifth Child* (1988) as her foray into horror fiction. David and Harriet Lovatt, an ordinary British couple, have four normal children before the birth of Ben, a vicious "goblin" of a monster-child, a genetic throwback whom Lessing has called a "Neanderthal." Critics called the work a terrifying "moral fable," though characters such as Ben are familiar in horror fiction. The Lovatts' comfortable middle-class life, and eventually their moral certainties, are radically altered by Ben's amorality and cruelty. Ben is kept drugged in an institution, but Mrs. Lovatt guiltily removes him and takes him home, where he is certain to continue killing and injuring others.

Lessing has noted that this choice between abandoning a child and the great emotional and physical pain the child brings to the family when he is a part of it constitutes "one big moral question" in the novel. Though variously interpreted in social and political terms by critics, the novel does suggest society's moral deterioration insofar as Ben seems to fit in with other maladjusted, violence-prone youths in what Lessing calls the "barbarous eighties," a time of moral and societal breakdown that will inexorably lead to an even worse future. Though the novel has little of the psychological or mythic richness of some of her earlier books, it is an absorbing fable and raises some valid, provocative questions.

Lessing's work has changed radically in format and genre over the years, then, and she has been more and more willing to take chances fictionally by tackling unusual or taboo subjects. Yet throughout her career she has maintained her high seriousness (and relative humorlessness) and her prophetic urgency. For more than three decades she has focused on the solitary, compulsive person, usually a woman, who has been driven by various personal pressures to the breaking point, to schizophrenia or some other radical shock. Only through an equally radical revaluation of personal identity has that character been able to be restored to psychic health. But Lessing's books are ultimately fictions, not clinical diagnoses or case studies, and her ability to create believable characters in crisis, particularly as various inadequate commitments and causes are considered and then rejected, is superb. And while it is commonplace to note that Lessing is not a stylist, that she is repetitive, that her fiction too easily reflects her own enthusiasms at particular moments, and that she is too verbose, prolific, and in need of editing and pruning, the fact remains that she is among the most powerful and compelling novelists of our century. Her pace

has not slackened significantly now that she is in her seventies, and if anything she is embarked on more adventurous forays at a time when she could permit her previous career and some three dozen books to sustain her reputation as a major figure in contemporary English literature.

So far as that reputation is concerned, in fact, one should note that the slow trickle of critical analysis a mere ten or twenty years ago has now reached the flood stage: dissertations and books appear with regularity, and scholars from around the world have formed the Doris Lessing Society and participate in the publication of the *Doris Lessing Newsletter* (neither of which Lessing encourages or approves of in any way; she firmly believes that it is her task to write and to have that writing speak for itself). She is opposed to biographical inquiry, she rarely permits interviews, and she adamantly refuses to allow some of her earlier work to remain in print. Yet as more and more of her books, especially *The Golden Notebook*, are translated into other languages, she finds entirely new audiences and critical acclaim. On a personal level, after many years of determined, conscientious dedication to her craft, she is now relatively comfortable. Her stature as a major writer, therefore, is secure; any additional readership, study, or recognition she receives will only establish that reputation more securely and open up new opportunities for probing the mind and craft of an exciting, endlessly rewarding writer.

Interviews:

Thomas Wiseman, "Mrs Lessing's Kind of Life," *Time & Tide*, 42 (12 April 1962): 26-29;

Robert Rubens, "Footnote to *The Golden Notebook*," *Queen*, 21 August 1962, p. 31;

Roy Newquist, Interview, *Counterpoint* (Chicago: Rand, McNally, 1964), pp. 413-424;

Florence Howe, "A Talk with Doris Lessing," *Nation*, 6 March 1967, pp. 311-313;

Joseph Haas, "Doris Lessing: Chronicler of the Cataclysm," *Panorama Magazine, Chicago Daily News*, 14 June 1969, pp. 4-5;

Jonah Raskin, "Doris Lessing at Stony Brook: An Interview," *New American Review 8* (New York: New American Library, 1970), pp. 166-179;

Marilyn Webb, "Feminism and Doris Lessing: Becoming the Men We Wanted to Marry," *Village Voice*, 4 January 1973, pp. 1, 14-17, 19;

Joyce Carol Oates, "A Visit with Doris Lessing," *Southern Review*, 9 (October 1973): 873-882;

Howe, "A Conversation with Doris Lessing," *Contemporary Literature*, 14 (Autumn 1973): 418-436;

C. J. Driver, "Profile 8: Doris Lessing," *New Review*, 1 (November 1974): 17-23;

Francis Wyndham, "The Doors of Perception," *Sunday Times* (London), 18 November 1979, p. 41;

Minda Bikman, "A Talk with Doris Lessing," *New York Times Book Review*, 30 March 1980, pp. 1, 24-27;

Nissa Torrents, "Testimony to Mysticism," translated by Paul Schlueter, *Doris Lessing Newsletter*, 4, no. 2 (1980): 1, 12-13;

C. W. E. Bigsby, *The Radical Imagination and the Liberal Tradition* (London: Junction Books, 1981), pp. 190-208;

Lesley Hazelton, "Doris Lessing on Feminism, Communism, and 'Space Fiction,' " *New York Times Magazine*, 25 July 1982, pp. 20-21, 26-29;

Bernd Dietz and Fernando Galván de Reula, "A Conversation with Doris Lessing," *Revista Canaria de Estudios Ingleses*, 6 (April 1983): 89-94;

Eve Bertelsen, Interview, *Journal of Commonwealth Literature*, 21, no. 1 (1986): 134-161;

Paul Barker, "A Golden Notebook of 70 Years of Dreams," *Independent* (London), 16 October 1989, p. 19.

Bibliographies:

Catherina Ipp, *Doris Lessing: A Bibliography* (Johannesburg: University of Witwatersrand, 1967);

Selma Burkom, "A Doris Lessing Checklist," *Critique*, 11 (1969): 69-81;

Agate N. Krouse, "A Doris Lessing Checklist," *Contemporary Literature*, 14 (Autumn 1973): 590-597;

Burkom and Margaret Williams, *Doris Lessing: A Checklist of Primary and Secondary Sources* (Troy, N.Y.: Whitston, 1973);

Carol Fairbanks Myers, *Women in Literature: Criticism of the Seventies* (Metuchen, N.J.: Scarecrow Press, 1976), pp. 117-121;

R. S. Roberts, "A Select Bibliography on Doris Lessing," *Zambesia: The Journal of the University of Rhodesia*, 4 (December 1976): 99-101;

J. Pichanik, A. J. Chennells, and L. B. Rix, eds., *Rhodesian Literature in English: A Bibliography 1890-1974/5* (Gwelo, Zimbabwe: Mambo, 1977);

Holly Beth King, "Criticism of Doris Lessing: A Selected Checklist," *Modern Fiction Studies*, 26 (Spring 1980): 167-175;

Dee Seligman, *Doris Lessing: An Annotated Bibliography of Criticism* (Westport, Conn.: Greenwood, 1981).

References:

Marie Ahearn, "Science Fiction in the Mainstream Novel: Doris Lessing," in *Proceedings of the Fifth National Convention of the Popular Culture Association, St. Louis, Mo., March 20-22, 1975*, edited by Michael Marsden (Bowling Green, Ohio: Bowling Green University Popular Press, 1976), pp. 1227-1296;

Dagmar Barnouw, "Disorderly Company: From *The Golden Notebook* to *The Four-Gated City*," *Contemporary Literature*, 14 (Autumn 1973): 491-514;

Nancy Topping Bazin, "The Moment of Revelation in Martha Quest and Comparable Moments by Two Modernists," *Modern Fiction Studies*, 26 (Spring 1980): 87-98;

Ralph Berets, "A Jungian Interpretation of the Dream Sequence in Doris Lessing's *The Summer Before the Dark*," *Modern Fiction Studies*, 26 (Spring 1980): 131-145;

Eve Bertelsen, ed., *Doris Lessing* (Johannesburg: McGraw-Hill, 1985);

Douglas Bolling, "Structure and Theme in *Briefing for a Descent into Hell*," *Contemporary Literature*, 14 (Autumn 1973): 550-564;

Dorothy Brewster, *Doris Lessing* (New York: Twayne, 1965);

Ellen W. Brooks, "The Image of Woman in Lessing's *The Golden Notebook*," *Critique*, 15, no. 1 (1973): 101-109;

Selma Burkom, " 'Only Connect': Form and Content in the Works of Doris Lessing," *Critique*, 11, no. 1 (1969): 51-68;

John L. Carey, "Art and Reality in *The Golden Notebook*," *Contemporary Literature*, 14 (Autumn 1973): 437-456;

Valerie Carnes, " 'Chaos, That's the Point': Art as Metaphor in Doris Lessing's *The Golden Notebook*," *World Literature Written in English*, 15 (April 1976): 17-28;

Lorelei Cederstrom, "Doris Lessing's Use of Satire in *The Summer Before the Dark*," *Modern Fiction Studies*, 26 (Spring 1980): 117-129;

Cederstrom, " 'Inner Space' Landscape: Doris Lessing's *Memoirs of a Survivor*," *Mosaic*, 13 (Spring/Summer 1980): 115-132;

Carol P. Christ, *Diving Deep and Surfacing: Women Writers on Spiritual Quest* (Boston: Beacon, 1980), pp. 55-73;

Margaret Drabble, "Doris Lessing: Cassandra in a World Under Siege," *Ramparts*, 10 (February 1972): 50-54;

Betsy Draine, "Changing Frames: Doris Lessing's *Memoirs of a Survivor*," *Studies in the Novel*, 11 (Spring 1979): 51-62;

Draine, "Nostalgia and Irony: The Postmodern Order of *The Golden Notebook*," *Modern Fiction Studies*, 26 (Spring 1980): 31-48;

Draine, *Substance Under Pressure: Artistic Coherence and Evolving Form in the Novels of Doris Lessing* (Madison: University of Wisconsin Press, 1983);

Bernard Duyfhuisen, "On the Writing of Future-History: Beginning the Ending in Doris Lessing's *The Memoirs of a Survivor*," *Modern Fiction Studies*, 26 (Spring 1980): 147-156;

Doris L. Eder, "Doris Lessing's *Briefing for a Descent into Hell*," *Contemporary Literature*, 14 (Autumn 1973): 550-564;

Katherine Fishburn, "The Nightmare Repetition: The Mother-Daughter Conflict in Doris Lessing's *Children of Violence*," in *The Lost Tradition: Mothers and Daughters in Literature*, edited by Cathy N. Dandson and E. M. Brown (New York: Ungar, 1980), pp. 207-216;

Fishburn, *The Unexpected Universe of Doris Lessing: A Study in Narrative Technique* (Westport, Conn.: Greenwood, 1985);

Judith Kegan Gardiner, *Rhys, Stead, Lessing and the Politics of Empathy* (Bloomington: Indiana University Press, 1989), pp. 83-120, 143-155;

James Gindin, *Postwar British Fiction* (Berkeley: University of California Press, 1962), pp. 65-86;

Nancy S. Hardin, "Doris Lessing and the Sufi Way," *Contemporary Literature*, 14 (Autumn 1973): 565-581;

Hardin, "The Sufi Teaching Story and Doris Lessing," *Twentieth Century Literature*, 23 (October 1977): 314-326;

Evelyn Hinz and John J. Teunissen, "The Pieta as Icon in *The Golden Notebook*," *Contemporary Literature*, 14 (Autumn 1973): 457-470;

Molly Hite, *The Other Side of the Story: Structures and Strategies of Contemporary Feminist Narratives* (Ithaca, N.Y.: Cornell University Press, 1989), pp. 55-102;

Ingrid Holmquist, *From Society to Nature: A Study of Doris Lessing's "Children of Violence"* (Gothenburg, Sweden: Gothenburg Studies in English, 1980);

Florence Howe, "Doris Lessing's Free Women," *Nation*, 200 (11 January 1965): 34-37;

Joseph Hynes, "The Construction of *The Golden Notebook*," *Iowa Review*, 4 (Summer 1973): 100-113;

Nancy Joyner, "The Underside of the Butterfly: Lessing's Debt to Woolf," *Journal of Narrative Technique*, 4 (September 1974): 204-211;

Carey Kaplan and Ellen Cronan Rose, eds., *Approaches to Teaching Lessing's "The Golden Notebook"* (New York: Modern Language Association, 1989);

Kaplan and Rose, eds., *Doris Lessing: The Alchemy of Survival* (Athens: Ohio University Press, 1988);

Sydney J. Kaplan, *Feminine Consciousness in the Modern Novel* (Urbana: University of Illinois Press, 1975), pp. 136-172;

Frederick J. Karl, "Doris Lessing in the Sixties: The New Anatomy of Melancholy," *Contemporary Literature*, 13 (Winter 1972): 15-33;

Karl, "The Four-Gaited Beast of the Apocalypse: Doris Lessing's *The Four-Gated City*," in *Old Lines, New Forces: Essays on the Contemporary British Novel, 1960-1970*, edited by Robert K. Morris (Rutherford, N.J.: Fairleigh Dickinson University Press, 1976), pp. 181-199;

Jeannette King, *Doris Lessing* (London & New York: Arnold, 1989);

Mona Knapp, *Doris Lessing* (New York: Ungar, 1984);

Barbara F. Lefcowitz, "Dream and Action in Lessing's *The Summer Before the Dark*," *Critique*, 17 (December 1975): 107-120;

Marian V. Libby, "Sex and the New Woman in *The Golden Notebook*," *Iowa Review*, 5 (Fall 1974): 106-120;

Marjorie J. Lightfoot, "Breakthrough in *The Golden Notebook*," *Studies in the Novel*, 7 (Summer 1975): 277-284;

Lightfoot, " 'Fiction' vs. 'Reality': Clues and Conclusions in *The Golden Notebook*," *Modern British Literature*, 2 (Fall 1977): 182-188;

Michael Magie, "Doris Lessing and Romanticism," *College English*, 38 (February 1977): 531-552;

Lois Marchino, "The Search for Self in the Novels of Doris Lessing," *Studies in the Novel*, 4 (Summer 1972): 252-261;

Herbert Marder, "The Paradox of Form in *The Golden Notebook*," *Modern Fiction Studies*, 26 (Spring 1980): 49-54;

M. Mark, "Reports from the Front," *Village Voice*, 2 October 1978, pp. 127-128, 131-132;

Alice B. Markow, "The Pathology of Feminine Failure in the Fiction of Doris Lessing," *Critique*, 16, no. 1 (1974): 88-100;

Frederick P. W. McDowell, "The Fiction of Doris Lessing: An Interim View," *Arizona Quarterly*, 21 (Winter 1965): 315-345;

Ellen Morgan, "Alienation of the Woman Writer in *The Golden Notebook*," *Contemporary Literature*, 14 (Autumn 1973): 471-480;

Robert K. Morris, *Continuance and Change: The Contemporary British Novel Sequence* (Carbondale: Southern Illinois University Press, 1972), pp. 1-27;

Anne M. Mulkeen, "Twentieth Century Realism: The 'Grid' Structure of *The Golden Notebook*," *Studies in the Novel*, 4 (Summer 1972): 262-274;

Patrick Parrinder, "Descents into Hell: The Later Novels of Doris Lessing," *Critical Quarterly*, 22 (Winter 1980): 5-25;

Jean Pickering, "Marxism and Madness: The Two Faces of Doris Lessing's Myth," *Modern Fiction Studies*, 26 (Spring 1980): 17-30;

Pickering, *Understanding Doris Lessing* (Columbia: University of South Carolina Press, 1990);

Dennis Porter, "Realism and Failure in *The Golden Notebook*," *Modern Language Quarterly*, 35 (March 1974): 56-65;

Nancy Porter, "Silenced History: *Children of Violence* and *The Golden Notebook*," *World Literature Written in English*, 12 (November 1973): 161-179;

Annis Pratt, "The Contrary Structure of Doris Lessing's *The Golden Notebook*," *World Literature Written in English*, 12 (November 1973): 150-161;

Pratt and L. S. Dembo, eds., *Doris Lessing: Critical Studies* (Madison: University of Wisconsin Press, 1974);

Elayne A. Rapping, "Unfree Women: Feminism in Doris Lessing's Novels," *Women's Studies*, 3 (1975): 29-44;

Barbara H. Rigney, *Madness and Sexual Politics in the Feminist Novel: Studies in Brontë, Woolf, Lessing, and Atwood* (Madison: University of Wisconsin Press, 1978), pp. 65-89;

Ellen Cronan Rose, "Doris Lessing's *Citta Felice*," *Massachusetts Review*, 24 (Summer 1983): 369-386;

Rose, "The End of the Game: New Directions in Doris Lessing's Fiction," *Journal of Narrative Technique*, 6 (Winter 1976): 66-75;

Rose, *The Tree Outside the Window: Doris Lessing's Children of Violence* (Hanover, N.H.: University Press of New England, 1976);

Roberta Rubenstein, "Briefing on Inner Space: Doris Lessing and R. D. Laing," *Psychoanalytic Review*, 63 (Spring 1976): 83-93;

Rubenstein, "Doris Lessing's *The Golden Notebook*: The Meaning of Its Shape," *American Imago*, 32 (Spring 1975): 40-58;

Rubenstein, *The Novelistic Vision of Doris Lessing* (Urbana: University of Illinois Press, 1979);

Robert F. Ryf, "Beyond Ideology: Doris Lessing's Mature Vision," *Modern Fiction Studies*, 21 (Summer 1975): 193-201;

Lorna Sage, *Doris Lessing* (London & New York: Methuen, 1983);

Margaret Scanlan, "Memory and Continuity in the Series Novel: The Example of *Children of Violence*," *Modern Fiction Studies*, 26 (Spring 1980): 75-85;

Paul Schlueter, "Doris Lessing: The Free Woman's Commitment," in *Contemporary British Novelists*, edited by Charles Shapiro (Carbondale: Southern Illinois University Press, 1964), pp. 48-61;

Schlueter, *The Novels of Doris Lessing* (Carbondale: Southern Illinois University Press, 1973);

Dee Seligman, "The Four-Faced Novelist," *Modern Fiction Studies*, 26 (Spring 1980): 3-16;

Seligman, "The Sufi Quest," *World Literature Written in English*, 12 (November 1973): 190-206;

Seligman, "A Visit to Rhodesia," *Doris Lessing Newsletter*, 1 (Winter 1976): 1,7;

Elaine Showalter, *A Literature of Their Own: British Women Novelists from Brontë to Lessing* (Princeton: Princeton University Press, 1977), pp. 298-319;

Rotraut Spiegel, *Doris Lessing: The Problem of Alienation and the Form of the Novel* (Frankfurt, Bern, Cirencester [U.K.] & New York: Peter Lang, 1980);

Mark Spilka, "Lessing and Lawrence: The Battle of the Sexes," *Contemporary Literature*, 16 (Spring 1975): 218-240;

Claire Sprague, *Rereading Doris Lessing: Narrative Patterns of Doubling and Repetition* (Chapel Hill: University of North Carolina Press, 1987);

Sprague, " 'Without Contraries Is No Progression': Lessing's *The Four-Gated City*," *Modern Fiction Studies*, 26 (Spring 1980): 99-116;

Sprague, ed., *In Pursuit of Doris Lessing: Nine Nations Reading* (New York: St. Martin's Press, 1990; London: Macmillan, 1990);

Sprague and Virginia Tiger, eds., *Critical Essays on Doris Lessing* (Boston: G. K. Hall, 1986);

M. C. Steele, *Children of Violence and Rhodesia: A Study of Doris Lessing as Historical Observer* (Salisbury: Central Africa Historical Association, 1974);

Judith Stitzel, "Humor and Survival in the Novels of Doris Lessing," *Regionalism and the Female Imagination*, 4 (Fall 1978): 61-68;

Stitzel, "Reading Doris Lessing," *College English*, 40 (January 1979): 498-504;

Lynn Sukenick, "Feeling and Reason in Doris Lessing's Fiction," *Contemporary Literature*, 14 (Autumn 1973): 515-535;

Alvin Sullivan, "*The Memoirs of a Survivor*: Lessing's Notes Toward a Supreme Fiction," *Modern Fiction Studies*, 26 (Spring 1980): 157-162;

Alan Swingewood, "Structure and Ideology in the Novels of Doris Lessing," in *The Sociology of Literature: Applied Studies*, edited by Diana Laurenson (Keele, U.K.: University of Keele, 1978), pp. 38-54;

Jenny Taylor, ed., *Notebooks/Memoirs/Archives: Reading and Rereading Doris Lessing* (London & Boston: Routledge, 1982);

Michael Thorpe, *Doris Lessing*, Writers and their Work, no. 230 (London: Longmans for the British Council, 1973);

Thorpe, *Doris Lessing's Africa* (London: Evans, 1978);

Thorpe, "Martha's Utopian Quest," in *Conference of Commonwealth Literature*, edited by Anna Rutherford (Aarhus, Denmark: University of Aarhus, 1971), pp. 101-113;

Virginia Tiger, "Advertisements for Herself," *Columbia Forum*, 3 (Spring 1974): 15-19;

Martin Tucker, *Africa in Modern Literature: A Survey of Contemporary Writing in English* (New York: Ungar, 1967), pp. 175-183;

Marion Vlastos, "Doris Lessing and R. D. Laing: Psychopolitics and Prophecy," *PMLA*, 91 (March 1976): 245-258;

Barbara B. Watson, "Leaving the Safety of Myth: Doris Lessing's *The Golden Notebook* (1962)," in *Old Lines, New Forces: Essays on the Contemporary British Novel, 1960-1970*, edited by Morris (Rutherford, N.J.: Fairleigh Dickinson University Press, 1976), pp. 12-37;

Ruth Whittaker, *Doris Lessing* (London: Macmillan, 1988; New York: St. Martin's Press, 1988);

Michele W. Zak, "*The Grass Is Singing*: A Little Novel About the Emotions," *Contemporary Literature*, 14 (Autumn 1973): 481-490.

Papers:

The University of Tulsa Library has typescripts for *Memoirs of a Survivor* and the story "The Temptation of Jack Orkney," as well as some letters.

John Mortimer

(21 April 1923 -   )

This entry was updated by Gerald H. Strauss (Bloomsburg University) from his entry in
DLB 13: British Dramatists Since World War II: Part Two.

BOOKS: *Charade* (London: Bodley Head, 1947; New York: Viking, 1987);

Rumming Park (London: Bodley Head, 1948);

Answer Yes or No (London: Bodley Head, 1950); republished as *The Silver Hook* (New York: Morrow, 1950);

Like Men Betrayed (London: Collins, 1953; Philadelphia: Lippincott, 1954; New York: Viking, 1987);

The Narrowing Stream (London: Collins, 1954; New York: Viking, 1989);

Three Winters (London: Collins, 1956);

With Love and Lizards, with Penelope Mortimer (London: Joseph, 1957);

Three Plays (London: Elek, 1958; New York: Grove, 1962)—includes *The Dock Brief, What Shall We Tell Caroline?*, and *I Spy*;

The Wrong Side of the Park (London: Heinemann, 1960);

Lunch Hour and Other Plays (London: Methuen, 1960)—includes *Lunch Hour, Collect Your Hand Baggage, Call Me a Liar*, and *David and Broccoli*;

Two Stars for Comfort (London: Methuen, 1962);

The Judge (London: Methuen, 1967);

A Flea in Her Ear, translated from Georges Feydeau's play (London & New York: French, 1968);

Cat Among the Pigeons, translated from Feydeau's play (London: French, 1970);

A Voyage Round My Father (London: Methuen, 1971);

Come As You Are (London: Methuen, 1971)—includes *Mill Hill, Bermondsey, Gloucester Road*, and *Marble Arch*;

The Captain of Köpenick, translated from Carl Zuckmayer's play (London: Methuen, 1971);

Knightsbridge (London: French, 1973);

Collaborators (London: Eyre Methuen, 1973);

Will Shakespeare (London: Hodder & Stoughton, 1977);

The Lady from Maxim's, translated from Feydeau's play (London: Heinemann, 1977);

The Bells of Hell (London: French, 1978);

Rumpole of the Bailey (Harmondsworth, U.K.: Penguin, 1978);

The Trials of Rumpole (London: Penguin, 1980; New York: Penguin, 1982);

Rumpole's Return (London: Penguin, 1980; New York: Penguin, 1982);

Clinging to the Wreckage: A Part of Life (London: Weidenfeld & Nicolson, 1982; New Haven: Ticknor & Fields, 1982);

Rumpole for the Defense (London: Penguin, 1982; New York: Penguin, 1984);

In Character (London: Allen Lane, 1983);

Rumpole and the Golden Thread (London & New York: Penguin, 1983);

The First Rumpole Omnibus (London: Penguin, 1983)—includes *Rumpole of the Bailey, The Trials of Rumpole*, and *Rumpole's Return*;

Edwin and Other Plays (London: Penguin, 1984)—includes *Bermondsey, Marble Arch, The Fear of Heaven*, and *The Prince of Darkness*;

Paradise Postponed (London & New York: Viking, 1985);

Three Boulevard Farces (London: Penguin, 1985)—includes *A Little Hotel on the Side, A Flea in Her Ear*, and *The Lady from Maxim's*;

Character Parts (London: Viking, 1986);

Rumpole's Last Case (London: Penguin, 1987);

The Second Rumpole Omnibus (London: Viking, 1987)—includes *Rumpole for the Defense, Rumpole and the Golden Thread*, and *Rumpole's Last Case*;

Summer's Lease (London & New York: Viking, 1988);

Rumpole and the Age of Miracles (New York: Penguin, 1989);

Rumpole à la Carte (London: Viking, 1990);

The Rapstone Chronicles: Paradise Postponed and Titmuss Regained (London: Viking, 1991).

PLAY PRODUCTIONS: *The Dock Brief* and *What Shall We Tell Caroline?*, Hammersmith, Lyric Opera House, 9 April 1958 (transferred to London, Garrick Theatre, 20 May 1958), 99 [performances];

John Mortimer and son, 1962 (photograph by Mark Gerson)

I Spy, Salisbury, Salisbury Playhouse, 16 March 1959;

The Wrong Side of the Park, London, Cambridge Theatre, 3 February 1960, (transferred to London, St. Martin's Theatre, 16 May 1960), 173;

Lunch Hour, Salisbury, Salisbury Playhouse, 20 June 1960; London, Criterion Theatre, 13 February 1961, 64;

Two Stars for Comfort, London, Garrick Theatre, 4 April 1962, 189;

Collect Your Hand Baggage, London, London Academy of Music and Dramatic Art, December 1962;

A Flea in Her Ear, translated from Georges Feydeau's play, London, Old Vic (National Theatre), 8 February 1966;

The Judge, Hamburg, Deutsches Schauspielhaus, 29 January 1967; London, Cambridge Theatre, 1 March 1967, 77;

Cat Among the Pigeons, translated from Feydeau's play, London, Prince of Wales's Theatre, 15 April 1969, 103;

Come As You Are (*Mill Hill*, *Bermondsey*, *Gloucester Road*, and *Marble Arch*), London, New Theatre, 27 January 1970, 278;

A Voyage Round My Father, London, Greenwich Theatre, 25 November 1970; London, Haymarket Theatre, 4 August 1971, 501;

The Captain of Kopenick, translated from Carl Zuckmayer's play, London, Old Vic (National Theatre), 9 March 1971;

I, Claudius, adapted from Robert Graves's *I, Claudius* and *Claudius the God*, London, Queen's Theatre, 11 July 1972, 61;

Collaborators, London, Duchess Theatre, 17 April 1973, 167;

Heaven and Hell (*The Fear of Heaven* and *The Prince of Darkness*), London, Greenwich Theatre, 27 May 1976;

The Bells of Hell, London, Garrick Theatre, 27 July 1977, 69;

The Lady from Maxim's, translated from Feydeau's play, London, Lyttleton Theatre (National Theatre), 18 October 1977;

John Mortimer's Casebook (*Dock Brief*, *The Prince of Darkness*, and *Interlude*), London, Young Vic, 6 January 1982;

When That I Was, Ottawa, Ontario, Arts Centre, 16 February 1982;

A Little Hotel on the Side, translated from Feydeau's play, London, Olivier, 9 August 1984;

Die Fledermaus, translated from Carl Haffner and Richard Genée's libretto, London, Royal Opera House, 9 January 1989.

MOTION PICTURES: *Ferry to Hong Kong*, screenplay by Lewis Gilbert and Vernon Harris with additional dialogue by John Mortimer, Rank, 1959;

The Innocents, screenplay by Truman Capote and William Archibald from Mortimer's adaptation of Henry James's *The Turn of the Screw*, Twentieth Century-Fox, 1961;

Guns of Darkness, adapted from Francis Clifford's *Act of Mercy*, Warner Brothers, 1962;

I Thank a Fool, adapted by Mortimer and others from Audrey Erskine-Lindop's novel, M-G-M, 1962;

Lunch Hour, London Films, 1962;

The Running Man, adapted from Shelley Smith's *The Ballad of the Running Man*, Columbia, 1963;

Bunny Lake Is Missing, adapted by John Mortimer and Penelope Mortimer from Evelyn Piper's novel, Columbia, 1965;

A Flea in Her Ear, translated and adapted from Georges Feydeau's play, Twentieth Century-Fox, 1968;

John and Mary, adapted from Mervyn Jones's novel, Twentieth Century-Fox, 1969.

TELEVISION: *David and Broccoli*, BBC, 1960;

The Encyclopedist, BBC, 1961;

A Choice of Kings, Associated Rediffusion, 1966;

The Exploding Azalea, Thames Television, 1966;

The Head Waiter, BBC, 1966;

The Other Side, BBC, 1967;

Desmond, BBC, 1968;

Infidelity Took Place, BBC, 1968;

Swiss Cottage, BBC, 1972;

Knightsbridge, BBC, 1972;

Rumpole of the Bailey, BBC, 1975;

A Little Place off Edgware Road, *The Blue Film*, *The Destructors*, *The Case for the Defense*, *Chagrin in Three Parts*, *The Invisible Japanese Gentlemen*, *Special Duties*, and *Mortmain*, adapted from Graham Greene's stories, Thames Television, 1976;

Will Shakespeare series, Associated Television, 1978;

Brideshead Revisited, adapted from Evelyn Waugh's novel, Granada Television, 1981;

The Ebony Tower, Granada Television, 1984;

Paradise Postponed, Thames Television, 1986;

Summer's Lease, Thames Television, 1989.

RADIO: *Like Men Betrayed*, BBC, 1955;

No Hero, BBC, 1955;

The Dock Brief, BBC, 1957;

Three Winters, BBC, 1958;

Call Me a Liar, BBC, 1958;

Personality Split, BBC, 1964;

Education of an Englishman, BBC, 1964;

A Rare Device, BBC, 1965;

Mr. Luby's Fear of Heaven, BBC, 1976.

OTHER: *A Choice of Kings*, in *Playbill Three*, edited by Alan Durband (London: Hutchinson, 1969).

SELECTED PERIODICAL PUBLICATIONS—UNCOLLECTED: "End or Change Stage Censorship," *Plays and Players*, 9 (September 1962): 22;

"After the Chamberlain," *Author*, 81 (Summer 1970): 70-71;

"I, Claudius," *Plays and Players*, 19 (September 1972): i-xvi.

John Mortimer has said that comedy "is the only thing worth writing about in this despairing world," which "is far too serious to be described in terms that give us no opportunity to laugh." Indeed, since his first play in 1958, he has written a succession of comedies of manners, sex farces, and Chekhovian one-acts that, as he intended, "chart the tottering course of British middle-class attitudes in decline." But within the "narrow seam" that he has chosen as his stage province, Mortimer has created some memorable moments in the theater. Whereas such farces as *Marble Arch* (1970) and *Mill Hill* (1970) are mere whimsies, at least four other plays are notable achievements: *The Dock Brief* (1958), *The Judge* (1967), *A Voyage Round My Father* (1970), and *Collaborators* (1973). He has gained his largest audience and

Program title page, cast list, and synopsis of scenes for the first London production of Mortimer's first full-length play

earned his most widespread critical acclaim for television adaptations, including those he did of Evelyn Waugh's *Brideshead Revisited* (1981) and of his own novels *Paradise Postponed* (1986) and *Summer's Lease* (1989). Most popular, however, has been the continuing series of teleplays, starting in 1979, that Mortimer has adapted from his stories of Horace Rumpole, the irreverent Old Bailey barrister who usually defends the friendless and succeeds despite expectations of failure.

John Clifford Mortimer was born in Hampstead, London, the son of Kathleen May Smith Mortimer and Clifford Mortimer, a barrister who pursued his profession even after he became blind when John was a boy. Educated at Harrow School in Middlesex from 1937 to 1940 and Brasenose College, Oxford, from 1940 to 1942, Mortimer was called to the bar in 1948 and began practicing law in London, becoming Queen's Counsel in 1966 and Master of the Bench, Inner Temple, London, 1975. He retired from the law in 1986 to write full-time. As a barrister, he frequently argued for the defense in freedom of speech and press cases, and partly

through his efforts the stage censorship powers of the Lord Chamberlain were abolished with the passage of the Theatres Act of 1968, which, he believes, raised the status of playwrights "to the most carefully protected of all public performers." Despite his beliefs and activities regarding stage censorship, in his own plays he has not been inclined to test the accepted boundaries of propriety.

While with the crown film unit during World War II, he worked as an assistant director and scriptwriter. After the war he wrote six novels, three of which were republished in the 1980s. *Charade* (1947; republished 1987) is set during World War II and features a young man with a film unit that is making an army training documentary. The witty narrative develops into a mystery when a crew member dies in what may or may not be an accident. Another early novel, *Like Men Betrayed* (1953; republished 1989), also was done as a radio play (BBC, 1955), Mortimer's first of many such dramas. *The Dock Brief*, produced by the BBC Third Programme in 1957, won the Italia Prize in 1958 and was brought to the stage in 1958 as part of a double bill with

What Shall We Tell Caroline?, Mortimer's first play written specifically for theater.

The Dock Brief is about an old barrister whom success has eluded for fifty years, and who may be, Mortimer has speculated, "a distant cousin of a far more extrovert creation, 'Rumpole of the Bailey,' whom I wouldn't begin to think about for another fifteen years." He is randomly chosen to defend a man accused of murdering his wife. In a jail cell the two men assume the roles of judge, witnesses, and jurors as they rehearse their trial strategy. Later, however, when he is in the courtroom, the barrister becomes tongue-tied and loses the case; but his client is freed because the attorney's incompetence has rendered the whole business "ever so null and void." Rationalizing that the counsel's "dumb tactics" had won the day, the pair of misfits leave the cell whistling and dancing. This is a funny yet sad play, an example of Mortimer's contention that comedy be "truly on the side of the lonely, the neglected, the unsuccessful" and that it be "against established rules and against the imposing of an arbitrary code of behaviour upon individual and unpredictable human beings." In a real sense his attitude toward comedy reflects his legal philosophy. According to Mortimer, "I wanted to say something about the lawyer's almost pathetic dependence on the criminal classes, without whom he would be unemployed, and I wanted to find a criminal who would be sorrier for his luckless advocate than he was for himself." *The Dock Brief* was revived in 1982 as part of *John Mortimer's Casebook*, which also includes *The Prince of Darkness* (1976) and a new play, *Interlude*. The triple bill is an indictment of three pillars of society: the law, the church, and medicine.

In *What Shall We Tell Caroline?*, a sensitive character study, a curmudgeonly headmaster always at odds with his wife reveals a well-hidden tenderness when he convinces an assistant to continue a pretended affair with her: "If we stopped quarreling over her now . . . think how empty her poor life would be." During much of the domestic sparring, their eighteen-year-old daughter, toward whom they have been overprotective, silently observes the goings-on, but at the play's close she announces her departure for London, where she will live and work. Caroline's escape from the stifling environment ("There's an awful, deceptive silence about people in this house, a goading tormenting, blank silence," says her father) anticipates Mrs. Morgan's desertion of her husband in *I Spy* (1959) and Paddy's flight to

Paris in *Collect Your Hand Baggage* (1962), two other short plays which followed in a few years. Further, variants of the ménage à trois motif are common in Mortimer's works, such as *Bermondsey* and *Gloucester Road* (two 1970 sex farces), *Collaborators*, and *The Wrong Side of the Park* (1960). In all, the characters are like those in *The Dock Brief*: possessed of a comic vitality touched with pathos, these sympathetically drawn people have trouble communicating with others and coping with life, and the accommodations they make only superficially resolve their domestic difficulties. Except for *The Dock Brief* these plays are about unhappy marriages, matches from which all romance has long since departed. (Mortimer's 1949 marriage to Penelope Fletcher—a novelist, first as Penelope Dimont and then as Penelope Mortimer—ended in divorce in 1971; he remarried the same year, to Penelope Gollop.)

In *The Wrong Side of the Park*, his first full-length treatment of the ménage à trois theme, the central character, according to Mortimer, is the London house where he lived. It also features "an anglicized Blanche Dubois" who is married to a "dull dog" and lives in squalor with her inlaws. Attracted to a lusty boarder who resembles her first husband, she fantasizes about her previous marriage. But in a happy ending that is somewhat contrived she becomes reconciled to life with her present mate, who is made to seem better than he really is. Reviewers saw it as an interesting attempt to provide an aura of originality to hackneyed material; but the play is too long, for Mortimer had not yet learned to sustain characters, plot, and action through a full-length work. ("In a one act play," he has said, "the enthusiasm has no time to die.")

Two Stars for Comfort (1962), his next full-length play, is not tediously long, though one critic has dismissed it as "a whimsical sermon," while another has called it "an effectively astringent attack on sentimental make-believe." A solicitor-turned-publican seduces young girls, but his freewheeling life leads to conflict with others (including his wife), who effectively destroy his joie de vivre and force him to come to terms with the unpleasant realities of life. A reworking of an early unpublished novel, this is the first of his plays in which Mortimer portrays the law as a repressive force.

The Judge also examines the notion of the law as repressor and develops more fully the contrast between opposing ways of life. Mortimer's nameless high court judge (who has a reputation

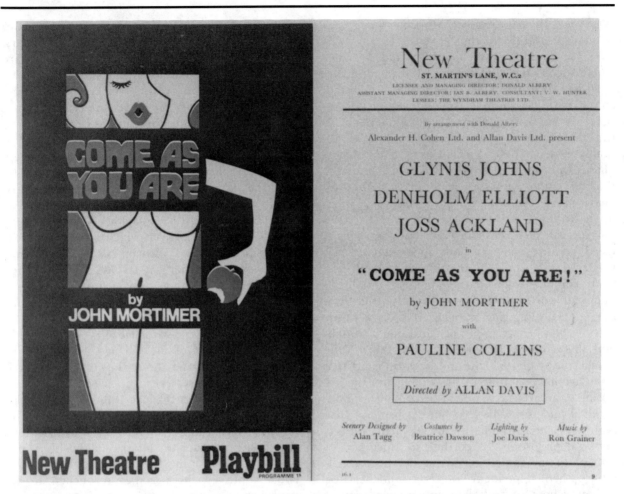

Program cover and title page for the first production of Mortimer's 1970 set of sex farces

for severity) returns to his birthplace for his last assize before he retires; obsessed with guilt for having abandoned in his youth a local girl he thought was pregnant, he has come home to be judged instead of to judge. Unlike him, the girl, Serena, enjoys life, running an antique shop that also provides a variety of questionable services. Mortimer skillfully develops character-revealing and tension-building episodes that provide a context for the judge's attempts to force a confrontation with Serena, which he achieves in the penultimate scene: refusing to accept Serena's forgiveness, he demands in vain that she "proceed to judgement." When he tells her, "I'm not fit to be a judge," she retorts, "That's all you are fit for," and he collapses into a doctor's arms. Less well made than Mortimer's earlier plays (there are too many scenes and changes of locale), *The Judge* has been criticized for diffuseness; as one critic put it, "Conditioned by his naturalistic habits, his plotting is ill served by his non-naturalistic structure." While it is correct to criticize Morti-

mer for such a curious mix of realism and nonrealism, this play is a memorable study of obsession and a disturbing look at how people in the legal profession sometimes function.

The law also is central in the autobiographical *A Voyage Round My Father*, which spans more than twenty years and dramatizes the symbiotic relationship between the playwright and his blind father. Other shaping forces also are in the play: the teachers, the military experiences, the girls, the friends; and all closely parallel real people and events. Despite the complexity of the drama of two lives, this play is not diffuse. Mortimer avoids the fragmentation of many separate scenes; rather, his episodes flow into each other, united by the son as a reflective narrator who bridges past and present and provides a clearly defined point of view.

The succession of episodes in this play, which was a critical and popular success when originally staged and which Mortimer adapted for television in 1982, begins with the young son being

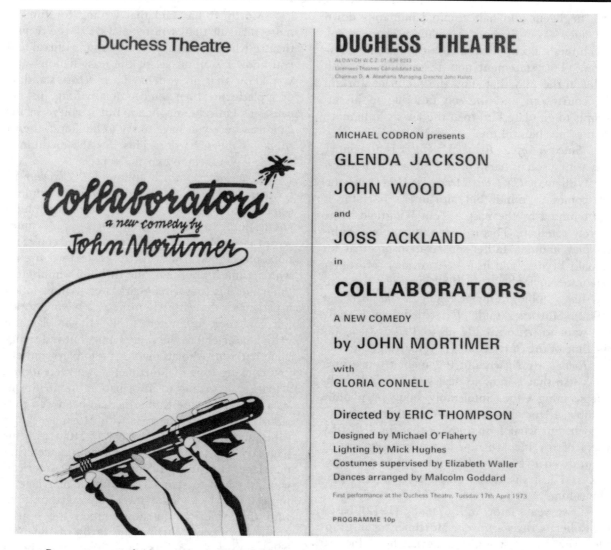

Duchess Theatre

Collaborators
a new comedy by
John Mortimer

DUCHESS THEATRE

ALDWYCH W.C.2. 01-836 8243
Licensees Theatres Consolidated Ltd.
Chairman D. A. Abrahams Managing Director John Hallett

MICHAEL CODRON presents

GLENDA JACKSON

JOHN WOOD

and

JOSS ACKLAND

in

COLLABORATORS

A NEW COMEDY

by JOHN MORTIMER

with
GLORIA CONNELL

Directed by ERIC THOMPSON

Designed by Michael O'Flaherty
Lighting by Mick Hughes
Costumes supervised by Elizabeth Waller
Dances arranged by Malcolm Goddard

First performance at the Duchess Theatre, Tuesday 17th April 1973

PROGRAMME 10p

Program cover and title page for the first production of Mortimer's comedy about a married screenwriting team who begin to live their script

taught to whistle by a girl named Iris (who reappears in an adolescent initiation scene) and then proceeds to his school experiences with a simpleminded headmaster and masters who still suffer the aftereffects of World War I shell shock and battle fatigue. Years later, through the intercession of two lesbians who run a bookshop, the son gets a wartime position as an assistant director with a propaganda film unit. He meets Elizabeth, a film writer whom he marries when she is divorced. Soon after meeting Elizabeth, he decides to study law. Intermingled with these events is a series of episodes involving the blind father, an iconoclast whose world is bound by his garden and the courtroom, in each of which he strives to dominate: the earwigs that prey upon his plants and the barristers for the opposition. Though he pretends

not to take much of life very seriously, the father has a sense of dignity that proscribes mention of his blindness, and he engages in selfless acts of kindness toward children and animals. Not a demonstratively affectionate husband or parent, he does sometimes express his feelings, about marriage for instance: "You know, the law of husband and wife might seem idiotic at first sight. But when you get to know it, you'll find it can exercise a vague medieval charm." And in the same speech he says to his son: "Learn a little law, won't you? Just to please me. . . ." The son's reaction (as narrator, to the audience) reveals the first of several conjunctions of the views of father and son: "It was my father's way to offer the law to me—the great stone column of authority which has been dragged by an adulterous, careless, negligent and half criminal humanity down the ages—as if it were a small mechanical toy which might occupy half an hour on a rainy afternoon." This statement notwithstanding, the episodes in the play that show the father at work in the courtroom and the son faltering in his attempts to emulate him treat the law as little more than a "mechanical toy."

Since *A Voyage Round My Father* is a memory play with a son as narrator and *raisonneur*, Tennessee Williams's *The Glass Menagerie* (1944) inevitably comes to mind, but Mortimer's narrator is not haunted by the past as Tom Wingfield is; he merely retells it. This is a frankly autobiographical play about a father-son relationship that (as Ronald Bryden said in a 1970 review) "Mortimer celebrates lovingly." In a 1982 interview concerning his autobiography, *Clinging to the Wreckage* (1982), Mortimer said: "I decided that I really did want to write my life up to 1970, which was the time of the *Oz* trial and a new marriage and *Voyage Round My Father*, but the main trouble in a book like that is how to deal with yourself without seeming either intolerably smug or phonily humble. It remains to be seen whether I've managed it, but what I do know is that the first fifty years of my life are now lost to me. By writing them down I've made them into public property, just as I lost my father when I wrote that play about him."

Two years later, in *I, Claudius* (1972), based on Robert Graves's novels, Mortimer again grapples with a large mass of material; here, too, he avoids separate scenes. According to him, the play explores "what the theatre can do in terms of time without having scenes . . . and time is elastic." The stage play emerged from his screenwriting activities, for in the early 1960s he had prepared a screenplay based on the Graves books, with Peter Sellers slated to play the lead. When nothing came of the film project, and Tony Richardson gained the film rights to the books, Mortimer and Richardson wrote another script. But they failed to get financial backing for the film and decided to do a play. Mortimer's stage treatment is not based on the film script and includes portions of the books which were not covered in the screenplay. His personal epic, *A Voyage Round My Father*, is a more successful play than his nevertheless popular Roman epic, which, according to one critic, "galloped, no other word for it, at a pace undignified for either humans or history."

Mortimer has said that writing for films is more difficult than writing plays: "If you're in a theatre where you know everything is unreal and you know it's all an act of the imagination—and you know that all you have are actors standing on a platform—then you can do anything, just because it's entirely imaginary. But if you're in the cinema where you have to try to be literal, then I think it's much harder. This way the medium is so free—you have to explain so little."

Collaborators, which followed *I, Claudius* by a year, similarly has links with Mortimer's screenwriting as well as other autobiographical connections. In *Clinging to the Wreckage*, Mortimer writes about Henry Winter, a pacifist and conscientious objector who was his closest Oxford friend, who became a physician, and through whom Mortimer met his first wife. Years later, Winter killed a patient's wife, with whom he was having an affair, and then committed suicide. In the play, the main character has the same name, but is a struggling barrister who also writes radio plays and enjoys cooking (one of Mortimer's own recreational activities, according to information about him in *Who's Who*); his wife Katherine had been wed previously (which was the case with Mortimer's first wife); and he is moving toward an affair with his secretary as a means of escape from his teetering marriage. He runs into Sam Brown, an American who asks him to script a film about marriage, a project that becomes a three-way collaboration, with the American intruding upon the household, alternately courting the favor of the husband and wife. Before long, the script being performed for Mortimer's audience becomes indistinguishable from the one the characters are writing, just as the reality of their lives becomes intertwined with the fiction of the film script. By the final curtain the foreign intruder is gone, the husband's nubile secretary has been scared off, and the married couple is alone—scarred by their domestic sparring and wearied by children grown tall enough "to eat the pornography" (which is moved to a higher shelf). Having collaborated on their screenplay, they are ready now to collaborate anew on another project, their marriage. Comparisons with Edward Albee's *Who's Afraid of Virginia Woolf?* (1962) are inevitable, for there is a similarity of situation and pacing; but Mortimer's play is wittier than Albee's.

As he neared the start of his third decade as a writer for the stage, Mortimer became slightly less realistic, and he continued to be interested in the shorter comic play. *Heaven and Hell*

Program cover and title page for the first production of Mortimer's full-length version of The Prince of Darkness

(1976) is a double bill comprised of *The Fear of Heaven* and *The Prince of Darkness*. The first is about two Englishmen who think they are in heaven because the ceiling of their Italian hospital room has a celestial fresco. The second, set in a London rectory, is in the tradition of the 1970 *Come As You Are* sex farces, but with a religious twist and a mod view of the devil and sin. A reviewer who thought the forty-minute curtain raiser, *The Fear of Heaven*, was a belabored one-joke play regretted that Mortimer "could not enlarge his second play to full length." He did so, and *The Prince of Darkness* became *The Bells of Hell* (1977), of which another commentator said: "Now stretched to full length, it is so thin as to be transparent." Others agreed with this judgment. This same reviewer also characterized the dialogue as "flabby and unwieldy," a rare criticism of Mortimer's work, for he has been most

often praised for the richness, fluency, precision, and appropriateness of his style (whereas the slightness and artificiality of his plots have been noticed with some frequency). According to Mortimer, "there is no substitute for the long and lonely work of the writer, writing words which must be delivered with total accuracy if the whole mood and color of the play is not to vanish in a well-meaning blur." This credo is most apparent in *When That I Was* (1982), a one-man play, whose character is Jack Rice, an old actor at Shakespeare's Globe.

Translating works by Georges Feydeau also has made Mortimer more keenly aware of the nuances of speech. He has said: "you have to write totally Engish dialogue and yet persuade the audience somehow to believe that what they're hearing is like French which they can understand perfectly. There are certain jarring notes you can

3

JACK RICE (cont)

Alex Cooke. I hope you be not here, Alex. You pale palled streak of
Puritan, forever telling us that "All flesh is as the grass" and "wine
is a betrayer". You played our heroines and I longed, when I was a child,
to have such parts off you. And I succeeded /Oh, to be sure I am not

I have stood here in skirts and painted lips and felt from the ground
and the boxes a /united/ throb of lust for my petticoated person and the
great gales of merriment that greeted our finest sallies and shook the
very galleries with laughter!

*[Ghostly sound of ~~applause~~ laughter and applause.
JR looks out fearfully, into the darkness]*

*Not now! Not now plays and players be outlawd
by order of the Puritan Parliament ... A four hour
sermon on the evils of fornication is the nearest we come to comedy
I have not been an actor / Actors are only fit to
be whipped as sturdy vagabonds. I have been
[assume Preachers voice) .... Sexton Rice,
Key Holder and Tombs Tender of the Church of St
Barnabas hith out. No Graven Saints, no
coloured glass, and a rod for any child caught
laughing ...
[Sound of animals]
Greetings ... master Ass. My Lords sheep ...
I beg to inform your worships, and my Lady sow
and all her ~~litter~~ honourable litter*

Page from a draft for When That I Was, *Mortimer's one-character play*

strike in a Feydeau translation which would suddenly make the audience think that they weren't in Feydeau-land. But at the same time the language must be sufficiently contemporary and colloquial for them to enjoy it for its own sake." His work with Feydeau prepared him for a later translating task: an English version of the Johann Strauss operetta *Die Fledermaus* (1874) for Covent Garden (1989).

According to Ronald Hayman, Mortimer "has oscillated between writing safe plays, catering for the West End audience, and dangerously serious plays, which might have alienated the public [he] had won." Indicative more of his versatility than of his limitations, this ambivalence is shared by Mortimer with many of his contemporaries. He can be praised for clever conception and deft management of situations, characters that are believable even when they are largely stereotypes, and dialogue that abounds with witticisms; and all of his plays, not just his ambitious ones, but the whimsies too, are the work of a perceptive social conscience.

In 1969 Mortimer described a play as "a demonstration, in which an audience can recognize something about themselves." The same can be said for the interviews of prominent people he has done for London newspapers—collected in *In Character* (1983) and *Character Parts* (1986)—and the novels he began writing in the 1980s. As in his early fiction, mystery and detection motifs are also dominant in *Paradise Post-poned* (1985), *Summer's Lease* (1988), and *Titmuss Regained* (1991), but these books are also social commentaries in the manner of Charles Dickens, Graham Greene, Vladimir Nabokov, Anthony Trollope, and Evelyn Waugh, all of whom Mortimer has acknowledged as influences. Indeed, almost all of his work—drama and fiction—reflects a Dickensian humanism, the sense that one should feel sorry for the less fortunate. This philosophy is even present in the *Rumpole of the Bailey* stories and teleplays, which are "founded on the Sherlock Holmes stories," Mortimer has said, and have a "Sherlockian" structure. Though detective fiction, Rumpole's adventures reflect Mortimer's strong social conscience. In these as elsewhere, he offers his audiences many insights into themselves and others at the same time that he makes them laugh.

References:

Gordon Gow, "Talking About *I, Claudius*," *Plays and Players*, 19 (April 1972);

Ronald Hayman, *British Theatre Since 1955: A Reassessment* (Oxford: Oxford University Press, 1979);

Rosemary Herbert, "The Art of Fiction CVI: John Mortimer," *Paris Review*, 109 (Winter 1988);

Herbert, "Murder by Decree," *The Armchair Detective*, 20 (Fall 1987);

Sheridan Morley, "Brisk Business at the Bar," *Times* (London), 4 January 1982.

Iris Murdoch

(15 July 1919 -)

This entry was updated by John Fletcher (University of East Anglia) from his entry in
DLB 14: British Novelists Since 1960: Part Two.

SELECTED BOOKS: *Sartre, Romantic Rationalist* (Cambridge: Bowes & Bowes, 1953; New Haven: Yale University Press, 1953);

Under the Net (London: Chatto & Windus, 1954; New York: Viking, 1954);

The Flight from the Enchanter (London: Chatto & Windus, 1956; New York: Viking, 1956);

The Sandcastle (London: Chatto & Windus, 1957; New York: Viking, 1957);

The Bell (London: Chatto & Windus, 1958; New York: Viking, 1958);

A Severed Head (London: Chatto & Windus, 1961; New York: Viking, 1961);

An Unofficial Rose (London: Chatto & Windus, 1962; New York: Viking, 1962);

The Unicorn (London: Chatto & Windus, 1963; New York: Viking, 1963);

The Italian Girl (London: Chatto & Windus, 1964; New York: Viking, 1964);

A Severed Head [play], by Murdoch and J. B. Priestley (London: Chatto & Windus, 1964);

The Red and the Green (London: Chatto & Windus, 1965; New York: Viking, 1965);

The Time of the Angels (London: Chatto & Windus, 1966; New York: Viking, 1966);

The Italian Girl [play], by Murdoch and James Saunders (London & New York: French, 1968);

The Nice and the Good (London: Chatto & Windus, 1968; New York: Viking, 1968);

Bruno's Dream (London: Chatto & Windus, 1969; New York: Viking, 1969);

A Fairly Honourable Defeat (London: Chatto & Windus, 1970; New York: Viking, 1970);

The Sovereignty of Good (London: Routledge & Kegan Paul, 1970; New York: Schocken, 1971);

An Accidental Man (London: Chatto & Windus, 1971; New York: Viking, 1971);

The Black Prince (London: Chatto & Windus, 1973; New York: Viking, 1973);

The Three Arrows and The Servants and the Snow: Plays (London: Chatto & Windus, 1973; New York: Viking, 1974);

The Sacred and Profane Love Machine (London: Chatto & Windus, 1974; New York: Viking, 1974);

A Word Child (London: Chatto & Windus, 1975; New York: Viking, 1975);

Henry and Cato (London: Chatto & Windus, 1976; New York: Viking, 1977);

The Fire and the Sun: Why Plato Banished the Artists (Oxford: Clarendon, 1977);

The Sea, The Sea (London: Chatto & Windus, 1978; New York: Viking, 1978);

A Year of Birds: Poems (Tisbury, Wiltshire: Compton, 1978);

Nuns and Soldiers (London: Chatto & Windus, 1980; New York: Viking, 1981);

The Philosopher's Pupil (London: Chatto & Windus, 1983; New York: Viking, 1983);

The Good Apprentice (London: Chatto & Windus, 1985; New York: Viking, 1986);

Acastos: Two Platonic Dialogues (London: Chatto & Windus, 1986);

The Book and the Brotherhood (London: Chatto & Windus, 1987; New York: Viking, 1988);

The Message to the Planet (London: Chatto & Windus, 1989; New York: Viking, 1990).

PLAY PRODUCTIONS: *A Severed Head,* by Murdoch and J. B. Priestley, Bristol, Theatre Royal, 7 May 1963;

The Italian Girl, by Murdoch and James Saunders, Bristol, Bristol Old Vic, 29 November 1967;

The Servants and the Snow, London, Greenwich Theatre, 29 September 1970; adapted by Murdoch as an opera libretto, music by William Mathias, Cardiff, Cardiff New Theatre, 15 September 1980;

The Three Arrows, Cambridge, Arts Theatre, 17 October 1972;

Art and Eros, London, Olivier Theatre, 2 April 1980;

The Black Prince, London, Aldwych Theatre, 25 April 1989.

Iris Murdoch (photograph by Jerry Bauer)

OTHER: "Something Special," in *Winter's Tales 3* (London: Macmillan, 1957; New York: St. Martin's Press, 1957), pp. 175-204.

SELECTED PERIODICAL PUBLICATIONS—
UNCOLLECTED: "Nostalgia for the Particular," *Proceedings of the Aristotelian Society*, 52 (1952): 243-260;

"Vision and Choice in Morality," *Proceedings of the Aristotelian Society*, supplement, 30 (1956): 32-58;

"The Sublime and the Good," *Chicago Review*, 13 (Autumn 1959): 42-55;

"A House of Theory," *Partisan Review*, 26 (Winter 1959): 17-31;

"The Sublime and the Beautiful Revisited," *Yale Review*, 49 (December 1959): 247-271;

"Against Dryness: A Polemical Sketch," *Encounter*, 16 (January 1961): 16-20;

"Art is the Imitation of Nature," *Cahiers du Centre de Recherches sur les Pays du Nord et du Nord-Ouest*, 1 (1978): 59-65.

One of the dominant figures of postwar British literature, Iris Murdoch continues to divide the critics; for example, one of the professors of English at Cambridge University, Frank Kermode, thinks highly of her work, while another, Christopher Ricks, has reviewed it extremely unfavorably. But she has forestalled some of the critics, at least on the crucial issue of the quantity against the quality of her output. Reviewing Sartre's *Being and Nothingness* in 1957, she concluded with these rather prophetic words: "writers of brief and meticulous articles will always look askance at writers of large, unrigorous, emotional volumes; but the latter, for better or worse, have the last word." She had herself by then published two novels (*Under the Net*, 1954, and *The Flight from the Enchanter*, 1956), a monograph, and a handful of philosophical articles. Some thirty-five years and almost as many books later, she herself has become, in the eyes of several critics, a writer of large, unrigorous, emotional volumes. Fecundity such as hers has not often been seen since the days of Charles Dickens, William Makepeace Thackeray, or Wilkie Collins.

Some critics wonder if she is not a modern Collins, an entertaining and accomplished novelist but a fearfully uneven one. How is it possible, her detractors ask, to publish a long novel almost every year and not succumb to facile effects and slick repetition? It is certainly not difficult to criticize some of her books and show how they fall below her usual standards. Reviewers on the whole—with a few distinguished exceptions—greet each new novel as enthralling and funny but excessively complicated and ultimately unconvincing. And academic critics have tended to stop short of any serious confrontation with her work.

Perhaps what makes academics uneasy is a feeling that, despite all the notorious symbolism and the heady moral theorizing, Iris Murdoch is basically a lightweight, even frivolous, novelist, a sort of intellectuals' Georgette Heyer. After all, they say, how can anyone be serious who takes such obvious delight in playing elaborate tricks on her readers? Some critics feel that these antics do not square with an obvious fascination with character and plot (in that order) and an abiding preoccupation with love, reconciliation, and redemption. Yet those critics forget that Henry James too had his mystery plots; that Jane Austen enjoyed teasing her readers; or that Dickens often employed improbable characters and plots while being deeply concerned, himself, with Murdoch's same recurring themes. Are the games Thackeray plays with the reader over Becky Sharp all that different from those Murdoch plays with her enchanters, ingenues, or old lechers? In other words, she draws eclectically on the English tradition and at the same time extends it in important ways.

She is at her best, perhaps, where a perfect "machine"—of a plot—coincides with a satisfying moral concern, in the manner of the greatest English novelists from George Eliot to E. M. Forster; and she is accordingly at her weakest in books such as *The Time of the Angels* (1966), in which the "machine" is so intricately built that it gets out of hand, or *The Sandcastle* (1957), in which the moral thrust becomes too obtrusive. Nevertheless, she is an exceptionally clever

writer—perhaps the most intelligent novelist the English have produced since Eliot—and she is liable, if he is not constantly on the alert, to catch the reader coming and going. In *The Sacred and Profane Love Machine* (1974)—the very title should put one on his guard—the tragic plot resolves (or perhaps dissolves) into farce. The author's way of getting rid of Harriet at Hanover Airport can be seen as sleight of hand, the deus ex machina of an incompetent novelist unable otherwise to extricate her characters from an impossible position—that is, if one takes the plot as serious exploration of middle-class adultery rather than as what it is: a machine, reality metamorphosed into fiction, whose laws are very different from those of life.

A more sophisticated objection to Murdoch's work is that it is not experimental enough: she is most often mentioned in the same breath as Angus Wilson or Kingsley Amis, novelists who make no bones about using traditional methods. But she has in fact much more in common with Vladimir Nabokov, with whom no one thinks of comparing her. Her books, like his, are craft-built fictional engines; only superficially are they social satire or realistic documentation. Her choice of the writers who have influenced her most bears out this assessment. For whereas Wilson makes it clear that his main influences are Dickens and Emile Zola, Murdoch cites as early models Samuel Beckett and Raymond Queneau—hardly writers one would place in the realist tradition. She also owes great debts to William Shakespeare, Leo Tolstoy, Fyodor Dostoyevski, and Henry James. She may write novels that at first read like cruel and witty studies of contemporary upper-middle-class London or Oxford society, but on closer inspection they usually turn out to be something different: not allegories exactly, but decidedly symbolic and universal.

Iris Murdoch was born in Dublin, Ireland, on 15 July 1919 but left Ireland while she was still a child. However, she is of Anglo-Irish parentage on both sides; her father, Wills John Hughes Murdoch, was an Irish cavalry officer in World War I and later a British civil servant. Her mother was Irene Alice Richardson Murdoch. Further back, her ancestors were mainly Anglo-Irish landowners, farmers, and soldiers. Because she was an only child, she had what she has called imaginary siblings, who, no doubt, inspired her to tell herself stories. She spent her holidays in Ireland as a child but says she finds it hard to write about her country of birth, whose current trou-

IRIS MURDOCH

the
SACRED & PROFANE
LOVE MACHINE

*Dust jacket for the American edition of Murdoch's 1974
novel, in which reality is metamorphosed into fiction*

bles she finds "too terrible," and indeed her only
attempt at treating the subject, not an entirely successful one, is her historical novel of the 1916
Dublin Easter Rebellion, *The Red and the Green*
(1965). She grew up in the London suburbs of
Hammersmith and Chiswick; she attended the
Froebel Educational Institute in London and
went from there, at age thirteen, to Badminton
School, a girls' public school of liberal tradition
in Bristol. She started writing for the school magazine almost immediately, and her earliest known
published piece appeared in that journal in 1933.
Murdoch was one of only two scholars—that is,
students holding bursaries, or scholarships—in
the school. A former teacher at Badminton
School, Leila Eveleigh, recalls: "She was very
homesick [at first] or else just bewildered and
Miss Baker's [the school principal's] therapy for
that was, in her case, work in the garden under
the care of the lady head gardener. I used to
meet her pricking out seedlings in the green-
house quietly and painstakingly." Murdoch was,

according to Miss Eveleigh, good scholastically,
particularly so in classics and English, a fine
hockey player, interested and gifted in painting
(she contributed some woodcuts to the magazine), and, though not particularly musical, prepared to "have a go." She appears to have been
particularly close to Miss Baker, with whom she
kept in touch for many years afterward, inscrib-
ing copies of her books to the woman she always
addressed affectionately as "BMB" and presenting her with a "colourful strong poster-like" painting of Lynmouth harbor, where the school was
transferred during the war.

Murdoch went up to Somerville College, Oxford, in October 1938 on an exhibition (that is, a
junior bursary), the Harriet Needham Exhibition.
The school of which she had been Head Girl still
heard from her, and indeed her writing continued to appear in its magazine for some time.
The following entry, although written in the
third person, was contributed by Murdoch herself: "Iris Murdoch is at Somerville. She is taking
Classics and loves her work passionately, and generally takes a zestful interest in the life of the University. She too suffers from a shortage of time
and finds a day of twenty-four hours quite insufficient for her needs. She takes an active part in
the life of the College and represents the First
Year on the Junior Common Room Committee.
She is a member of the Somerville Debating Society and also of the Dramatic Society, in whose production of 'The Winter's Tale' next term she is to
take the part of Polixenes. She is too busy to play
any regular games, but this term is learning
to ply a very pretty punt pole on the Isis. The
Classical Association, the Arts Club, and the
B.U.L.N.S. claim other parts of the day, but her
main activities are political and literary. She is a
very active member of the Labour Club and
helps to run the Somerville branch. For four
terms she was advertising manager to 'Oxford Forward,' the progressive University weekly, and
now continues her connection as a contributor.
She has recently joined the staff of the
'Cherwell,' and hopes next term to subedit that
paper. Any time which remains is devoted to the
Discussion of Life." The last sentence may have
been recalled later with affectionate irony in *The
Flight from the Enchanter* when the heroine,
Annette, abruptly determines to leave her finishing school and tells the principal, "I have learnt
all that I can here. . . . I shall go out into the
School of Life." The principal, perhaps like an
older and wiser Murdoch, replies drily, "As for

the institution which you call the School of Life, I doubt . . . whether you are yet qualified to benefit from its curriculum."

Whether or not she benefited from the curriculum of the "School of Life," Murdoch did very well at Oxford, where she read classical moderations and "Greats" (ancient history, classics, philosophy) and took a first-class honors degree in 1942. She was also very left-wing, and, in fact, joined the Communist party of Great Britain for a time, an action which in the later 1940s led officials to deny her a visa to the United States when she was awarded a scholarship there. This political activity has continued to the present day. She was fiercely hostile toward American involvement in Vietnam and is an active writer of letters to the London *Times*. Her attitudes are not, however, dogmatic or even clear-cut; she opposed the Labour government's policy over comprehensive (all-ability) schools, arguing that socialism and selection are quite compatible and deploring the destruction of the old grammar schools, which, she said, enabled bright students from poor homes to make the most of their potential (or, as the proponents of "comprehensivisation" would claim, join the establishment).

On leaving Oxford she worked as a temporary wartime civil servant (assistant principal) in the Treasury for a couple of years; from this period, no doubt, she derived her extensive knowledge of the British civil service: several of her characters work for that elitist and secretive organization. In 1944 she joined the United Nations Relief and Rehabilitation Administration—at school she had been an enthusiastic supporter of the former League of Nations—and shortly after the end of the war in Europe was sent first to Belgium and then to Austria, where she worked in a camp for displaced persons. (This experience is also recalled in *The Flight from the Enchanter*, where Nina, the refugee dressmaker, has been born to the east of a line arbitrarily drawn by the Allies and so risks deportation and return to a land abandoned to the Red Army.) During her stay in Belgium, Murdoch met Jean-Paul Sartre, the subject of her first book, *Sartre, Romantic Rationalist* (1953), and in Austria she met Raymond Queneau, who became a close friend.

Having failed to gain entry to the United States (one can only speculate how different her literary career might have been if, at this very formative stage of her life, she had been exposed to American culture), she spent a year, more or less as a dropout, in London, during which she read

much Immanuel Kant and no doubt developed even further her extensive acquaintance with almost every corner of that capital city, a knowledge which has stood her in good stead for the settings of several of her novels; one critic has even spoken of her "London novels" as almost a distinct subgenre. She returned to academic life in 1947, when she held the Sarah Smithson Studentship in philosophy at Newnham College, Cambridge; although until then she had considered archaeology or art history as a career, she was now committed to philosophy. On the termination of the scholarship in 1948, she was appointed tutor in philosophy and fellow of St. Anne's College, Oxford, a post she held until she gave up full-time teaching in 1963. She continued, however, as a part-time philosophy teacher at the Royal College of Art in London until 1967. She was elected a member of the Aristotelian Society, a rather exclusive club of academic philosophers, in 1947, but she allowed her association with it to lapse in the early 1960s. By then her career had changed to that of full-time writer, but she continues to practice philosophy on the fringes of academe: she published her latest academic work, *The Fire and the Sun: Why Plato Banished the Artists*, in 1977, and in 1982 she gave the Gifford Lectures at the University of Edinburgh. *The Fire and the Sun* is about Plato, who has come to exercise a deep influence on her; before that she was much preoccupied with Sartre and existentialism, without ever fully espousing what she sees as existentialism's ethics of irresponsibility. At Cambridge she met Ludwig Wittgenstein, who was a major influence on her development as a philosopher, even though she did not adopt his logical positivism.

In the ten years following her graduation from Oxford, she wrote four novels; she discarded three, and one was rejected by a publisher. In 1954, however, *Under the Net* appeared and was an immediate success. Since then Murdoch has written more than twenty other novels, nearly all of them successful with the reading public.

Fiction is not, however, all the creative writing she has done. There are good if largely uncollected poems; many philosophical-literary essays (the best are collected in *The Sovereignty of Good*, 1970); and three original plays, *The Servants and the Snow* (first produced in September 1970), *The Three Arrows* (October 1972), and *Art and Eros* (April 1980). She has also adapted three of her novels for the stage: *A Severed Head*, written in collaboration with J. B. Priestley (1963); *The Italian Girl*, done with James Saunders (1967); and *The Black Prince* (1989). *A Severed Head* also became a motion picture (Columbia, 1971), and *The Servants and the Snow* she adapted as an opera libretto for the composer William Mathias (first performed at the Cardiff New Theatre on 15 September 1980). Of Murdoch's writing for the stage, it is fair to say that she is good at creating atmosphere but—rather like Sartre in his plays—tends to set up debates in dialogue form so that, curiously, her drama is less dramatic than her fiction. She is also not very good at dramatic plots; the resolutions are somewhat contrived and sudden, lacking the forceful internal logic of the novels. Revelations tend to come so fast at the end that they are merely melodramatic, lacking the ironies with which they are associated in the fiction.

Probably the greatest influence on her writing has been her husband, John Oliver Bayley, currently Thomas Warton Professor of English Literature at Oxford, whom she married in 1956. (Her first fiancé was apparently killed in the war.) Murdoch and John Bayley enjoy an intimate, even symbiotic, intellectual relationship; they are particularly close in their fascination with Shakespeare and with what Bayley has called "the characters of love." The concept of literary personality—and a proper respect for it—is central to Bayley's humanism, as it is also to Murdoch's. The authors he most fervently admires, Shakespeare and Tolstoy, endow their characters with the greatest freedom to be themselves. This idea is strongly reminiscent of Murdoch's admonition in a well-known essay, "The Sublime and the Beautiful Revisited," published shortly before her husband's book, *The Characters of Love*, that "a novel must be a house for free characters to live in." It is evident that Murdoch and Bayley share one of the most fruitful literary and critical partnerships of our time.

Murdoch's own ideas about literature have unfortunately not been collected, but her most famous essay, "Against Dryness," first published in *Encounter* for January 1961, has been widely reprinted; it argues polemically for a return to rounded characters and stable values in the novel. As in so much of her writing, she reveals an analytical mind in combination with an Irish heart, steely intellect with emotional warmth. An immensely intelligent and learned person, she would obviously have become a professor or the mistress of an Oxbridge college if she had chosen to remain in academic life. But her passion-

ate interest in people and concern for moral issues have impelled her instead to leave the university environment in order to concentrate on the witty, intelligent, and compassionate novels for which she is best known. And since she has not had any children herself, her books, in a sense, as in the last century for George Eliot, are her children.

She is a keen gardener, devoting her afternoons (she writes mostly in the morning) to her garden in the village north of Oxford where she lives; her particular passion is roses, about which she reveals herself knowledgeable in *An Unofficial Rose* (1962). She is reputed to be a jujitsu expert and lists her hobby in *Who's Who* as learning languages, like her hero Hilary Burde in *A Word Child* (1975). She describes herself as an ex-Christian (Badminton School had a strong religious life) with inclinations toward Buddhism, a faith which is featured in both *The Nice and the Good* (1968) and *An Accidental Man* (1971). She has traveled widely around the world, and it is perhaps Japan which has left the deepest mark on her writing, a mark that appears with especial prominence in *A Severed Head* (1961) and *The Three Arrows*. She has served as a member of the Formentor Literature Prize Committee and has delivered lectures in several countries.

One of her most recent lectures has been expanded to monograph length in the book on Plato, *The Fire and the Sun*, about which Peter Conradi comments, "Murdoch permits herself only a pyrrhic victory in her single combat with Plato over the question of the relations between art and truth . . . the depiction of artists in her books is always a suspicious one." Conradi's assertion is borne out by the closing sentences of the lecture: "Plato feared the consolations of art . . . [and] we live now amid the collapse of many . . . structures, and as religion and metaphysics in the West withdraw from the embraces of art, we are it might seem being forced to become mystics through the lack of any imagery which could satisfy the mind. Sophistry and magic break down at intervals, but they never go away and there is no end to their collusion with art and to the consolations which, perhaps fortunately for the human race, they can provide; and art, like writing and like Eros, goes on existing for better and for worse."

Her first published novel, *Under the Net*, fully supports that statement and remains for many readers her finest and most characteristic work. It is easy to see why. The tone, not only of

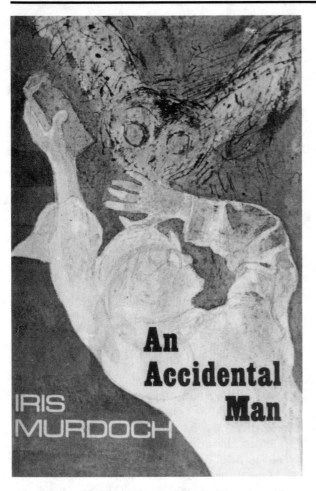

Dust jacket for Murdoch's 1971 novel, about a man who survives through destroying others

guage? I discovered Beckett long ago, at the beginning of the war. I remember being in an Oxford pub and hearing someone recite the passage from *Murphy* which begins: 'Miss Counihan sat on Wylie's knees. . . .' I was immediately enslaved. I got the book and read it. . . . The influence of that book, together with Queneau's *Pierrot*, upon *Under the Net* should be obvious. I imitated these two great models with all my heart." It is worth looking into the matter more closely in order to discover something about the nature of Murdoch's particular kind of comic fiction.

All three novels are comic in a wry way. Pierrot at the end of his complicated tale bursts into laughter; Murphy wills that his mortal remains be flushed down the particularly noisy lavatory of the Abbey Theatre, Dublin, during the performance of a piece, but otherwise "without ceremony or show of grief"; and Jake, unable at the end to explain a law of genetics to Mrs. Tinckham, laughingly calls it "just one of the wonders of the world." As befits comic novels, all three have intricate plots. And, as for their heroes, Murphy, though passive, is relatively central, for all things lead to him, whereas Pierrot is just a spectator in his own story. Jake is something between the two: a baffled onlooker whose actions marginally affect the plot.

The tone of all three novels is similar: a kind of Chaplinesque sadness is pervasive under the drollery. It is not easy to read unmoved the accounts of Murphy's actual dissolution (his ashes are scattered about a barroom floor) or Pierrot's unrequited passion for Yvonne or Jake's final break with Madge. What Jake says of himself applies to all three heroes: "my happiness has a sad face."

Finally, in all three books language is a comic protagonist in its own right. Murdoch's verbal self-consciousness is particularly endearing. She plays cleverly with clichés, for example, as in the words italicized here: "I had acquainted Hugo with something which he needed to know, and we had exchanged *not unfriendly* words. We had even had an adventure together in the course of which I had *acquitted myself at least without shame*. In a sense it could be said that the *ice was broken* between us. But it is possible to break the ice without *burying the hatchet*." The hero can see "no living being" in Farringdon Street; "not a cat, not a copper," glosses Murdoch, who is fond, too, of syllepsis: "He held his head well and the bottle by the neck."

this novel but of much else in her large output, is established in the following passage in *Under the Net*: "The movement away from theory and generality is the movement toward truth. All theorizing is flight. We must be ruled by the situation itself and this is unutterably particular. Indeed it is something to which we can never get close enough, however hard we may try as it were to crawl under the net. . . ." *Under the Net*—the image in the title comes from Wittgenstein's *Tractatus* (1922)—is an attempted demonstration of that remark in fictional terms; and those terms owe much to Samuel Beckett's *Murphy* (1938) and Raymond Queneau's *Pierrot mon ami* (1943), two novels which hold pride of place on her hero Jake Donaghue's bookshelf. The debt is made even clearer by the dedication of *Under the Net* to Raymond Queneau, and by the following avowal in response to interviewer Harold Hobson's question, "You admire Beckett?": "Enormously. But why did he stop writing in the best lan-

All three writers, as one might expect, are given to an appealing form of donnish humor. Beckett expects his reader to grasp this musical metaphor before sweeping on: "The decaying Haydn, invited to give his opinion of cohabitation, replied: 'Parallel thirds.' But the partition of Miss Counihan and Wylie had more concrete grounds." Likewise, Queneau gives just enough clues to enable the cognoscenti to pick up his many classical allusions.

Similarly, Murdoch expects the reader to know his Rimbaud and what is meant by the Cerberi; she even requires her readers to be as fluent in French as she is: "The *flaneurs* were flaning." The language, in all three novels, is often of such wit that it is hard to refrain from bursting into laughter: for example, at Murphy spluttering over his tea in the cafe like "a flushing-box taxed beyond its powers."

It is clear that Murdoch has studied her masters fruitfully: the filiation, as she told Harold Hobson, is indeed obvious. Her "torments of a morbid self-scrutiny" is a very Beckettian phrase, and "some of my friends think that Finn is cracked, but this is not so" is reminiscent of her older compatriot's comic pedantry. Jake's "dreamy unlucrative reflexion" which he enjoys "more than anything in the world" is like Pierrot's; Murphy would accept delightedly the epithet "unlucrative," although he would repudiate any suggestion of dreaminess. He would, however, concur with Jake's thought that "the quenching of thirst is so exquisite a pleasure that it is a scandal that no amount of ingenuity can prolong it."

But there is a more serious side to comedy that is never far from the minds of the creators of these characters: "If fantasy and realism are visible and separate aspects in a novel, then the novel is likely to be a failure. In real life the fantastic and the ordinary, the plain and the symbolic, are often indissolubly joined together, and I think the best novels explore and exhibit life without disjoining them." So declared Murdoch to Harold Hobson later in the interview quoted above. *Under the Net* is an illustration of the indissolubility of the fantastic and the ordinary, the plain and the symbolic. Jake seeks to impose his own pattern on life, and life resists Jake's pattern: "I would be at pains to put my universe in order and set it ticking, when suddenly it would burst again into a mess of the same poor pieces, and Finn and I would be on the run." He fantastically misconstrues events and characters, mistaking the substance for the shadow, and thereby loses his best friend and two girls who have a distinct fondness for him. If only he had known, he thinks, he might have behaved differently: "I had had a wrench that dislocated past, present and future." Fiction is perverse, "like life": X loves Y, who is keen on Z, and Z loves W, who is keen on X. In these circumstances—a grotesque parody of Racine's tragedy *Andromaque* (1667)—"love requited," as *Murphy* has it, "is a short circuit." The moral is hard to bear: " 'Some situations can't be unravelled,' said Hugo, 'they just have to be dropped. The trouble with you, Jake, is that you want to understand everything sympathetically. It can't be done. One must just blunder on. Truth lies in blundering on.' " The end mocks all "contrived finalities" because Jake has made the mistake of "having conceived things as I pleased and not as they were." Fortunately in comic fiction the world is never quite so serious, and the damage can usually be repaired: "The ground was strewn with legless torsos and halves of men and others cut off at the shoulders, all of whom, however, were lustily engaged in restoring themselves to wholeness by dragging the hidden parts of their anatomy out from under the flat wedges of scenery, which lay now like a big pack of cards." For, after all, we are in a world of make-believe, and not life itself. Queneau adopts a light-hearted attitude to the quirks of fate, which he exaggerates. The ends are then studiously tied up, in spite of the humorous disclaimer that they are not; "he saw," Queneau writes, "the guileless novel he'd taken part in," a novel that "could have had a dramatic plot but didn't." He is mistaken; nevertheless, it is true that when the play is done, "when the bodies have been carried from the stage and the trumpets are silent . . . an empty day dawns which will dawn again and again." So, too, Celia is graciously accorded a thirteenth and final chapter in which to pick up once more the threads of her life after Murphy's demise and take what pleasure she can in "that unction of soft sunless light on her eyes that was all she remembered of Ireland."

"The end is in the beginning and yet you go on," Hamm declares in Samuel Beckett's *Endgame* (1957), meditating ironically on Heraclitus. The essence of the postmodern comic aesthetic (which Murdoch obviously shares) is that it emphasizes this continuity in things. Comedy begins, and ends, in medias res, untidily, like life. And yet not quite like it; for a work of art, whatever its aesthetic, is self-conscious in a way that

Dust jacket for Murdoch's 1973 novel, which concludes, "Art tells the only truth that ultimately matters"

life is not. "The above passage," intrudes Beckett's narrator after the paragraph which Murdoch heard being read in an Oxford pub, "is carefully calculated to deprave the cultivated reader." Likewise, Queneau's narrator knowingly winks at the seasoned novel-fancier: "the classic train launched its familiar wail." And Jake feels that nothing is more paralyzing than a sense of historical perspective, especially in literary matters; he had contrived, he says, to stop himself just short of the point at which it would have become clear to him that the present age was not one in which it was possible to write a comic novel.

The theme of each novel centers on a clearly defined symbol. In *Murphy* this is Murphy's mind, which is pictured "as a large hollow sphere, hermetically closed to the universe without," a figure of Murphy's profound, if happy, alienation. The central presence in *Pierrot mon ami* is the mysterious chapel overshadowed by the garish vulgarity of Uni-Park. *Under the Net* is domi-

nated by Jake's friendship with Hugo, obligingly underlined for us by the author as "the central theme of this book." His conversations with Hugo lead to Jake's writing *The Silencer*, the "genuine" work to which he will return after so many years of hack-writing; and it is their friendship which lies, disastrously, at the heart of the novel's complex of human relationships.

The maturity, elegance, and stylishness of this first published Murdoch novel are impressive—as are its easy familiarity with other contemporary comic masterpieces and the authority and seriousness of its moral concern. All these qualities recur in the later novels in varying degrees. Indeed, one may divide these works into two broad categories: the more populous category is that of the ironic tragedy; the other is that of the bittersweet comedy, of which *Under the Net* is the first and perhaps the best. Although Murdoch does not write to formula, her novels do have certain abiding themes and techniques. Her techniques are heavily reliant on surprise, suspense, and other dramatic devices. She always writes a highly readable novel, with a strong, gripping narrative and (for the most part) vivid and convincing characters. But at the heart of her stories there is always a moral problem, which, being among the least directive of writers, she sets before the reader for his or her judgment. Her fundamental concerns are with the definition of goodness, the nature and language of art, the relation between contingency and design, and the workings of love and sacrifice in human relationships. She is fascinating and possibly unique, too, in being willing to write in an open and to some extent repetitious way, risking elements of reduplication.

It has often been noticed by critics that there are several "nuns" and many "soldiers" in Murdoch's fiction, either literally or metaphorically. Other figures also recur, like the young and rather foolish virgin, the insecure but morally intransigent boy, the weary and disillusioned middle-aged man, the rapacious and no-longer-quite-so-young female, the old man laden with regrets and unrepented sins, and so on; but it would be misleading to suggest a whole typology, even a worked-out scheme. The point is that Murdoch is concerned above all with moral issues and dilemmas, and since these tend to recur in different guises from one novel to the next, it is not unnatural that the characters who wrestle with them tend to bear a family resemblance to each other.

The Flight from the Enchanter is an early—though distinctly major—novel, with a particularly pregnant title. Each character has some person, idea, illusion, or object by which he is possessed, and each tries to break the spell, to flee the enchanter; for both "flight" and "enchantment" are recurrent themes in Murdoch's fiction. In this novel, a pert young girl finds out the hard way that life is a serious business, and a well-meaning older woman burns her fingers through meddling in the lives of others. The girl frivolously attempts suicide, and a tragic misunderstanding leads to the successful suicide of another and worthier character. As in *Cosi fan tutte* (1790) by Mozart, we find here a disturbing combination: under the effervescent comedy we detect a serious argument about ends and means, expediency and morality.

Expediency and morality are at the heart of *The Sandcastle* as well. Mor, a middle-aged married schoolmaster, falls in love with a young woman painter, but his formidable wife and precocious children lay their plots with such skill that he fails, when the crunch comes, to run off with her. He and his lover are made very unhappy by this failure, but Murdoch is not writing a sentimental love story, so it is strongly implied by the narrator that Mor does—if not the right thing—then at least the only thing that makes sense in the light of all the circumstances. But within the narrative a harsh verdict is also expressed, by the old man whose portrait the painter has been painting: " 'Coward and fool!' said Demoyte. 'Nothing was inevitable here. You have made your own future. . . . Do not deceive yourself. You may meet her once more by accident in ten years' time at a party when you are fat and bald and she is married.' " As part of the trick that his wife has played on him, the schoolmaster will stand for Parliament as a Labour candidate. "If you drop this plan," Demoyte warns him, "if you let her [your wife] cheat you out of that too, I'll never receive you in this house again." But he need not worry: it is clear that Mor will stand by the decision which has been forced upon him. And that, in Murdoch's world, is perhaps more important than the pursuit of personal happiness.

Murdoch's ironic tragedies, as the term implies, contain much that is funny and even farcical. In *The Bell* (1958), for instance, the arrival of the Bishop to christen the new bell is in the finest tradition of English comedy, a scene worthy of P. G. Wodehouse. And yet *The Bell* is a serious, even tragic novel, with one attempted and one successful suicide and at least one life ruined during the course of the work. But as is so often the case in Murdoch, if some of the characters go under, others—and often the less obviously or immediately admirable—survive. This is particularly true of the easygoing, even sluttish heroine of *The Bell*, Dora Greenfield, who would be rather unlikable if her husband, Paul, were not apparently even more unpleasant; it is she, however, with whom the narrator begins and ends the story, and it is she who is selected to survive. And almost by virtue of that fact, she becomes progressively more admirable in the reader's eyes. Murdoch clearly takes much pleasure in questioning our moral attitudes in this way. The leader of the lay community at Imber Court, Michael Meade, seems at first to be a worthy man, but gradually his weakness and self-indulgence are exposed by the cool and even merciless progression of the narrative, so that in the end nothing is quite as clear-cut as it appears at first to be. Paul Greenfield is perhaps not such a cruel cad, after all; the aspirant nun Catherine is revealed to be harboring violent erotic feeings for Michael Meade; and the wastrel Nick, her brother, is in a real sense ennobled by his suicide.

The questioning of moral attitudes and, as in *The Sandcastle*, standing by decisions rather than blindly pursuing personal happiness are important considerations in *A Severed Head*. Here Honor Klein, the heroine, says to her lover at the end when, after many hazards and misunderstandings, they come together, "This has nothing to do with happiness, nothing whatever." In the novel, a group of characters each rearrange their relationships at least once and in some cases twice during the course of the action. Specifically, the hero, Martin Lynch-Gibbon, realizes that he loves neither his wife, Antonia, nor his mistress, Georgie, but instead loves Honor Klein, who happens to be the half-sister of the lover of Martin's own wife. Palmer Anderson, the brother in question, starts the novel as the lover of both Honor, his half-sister, and Antonia Lynch-Gibbon, and he ends it leaving for New York in the company of Martin's ex-mistress, Georgie Hands. Having run away from Palmer, whose attitude toward her changes dramatically once Martin has discovered him and Honor in bed together, Antonia herself goes back briefly to Martin before declaring that her true passion is Alexander, Martin's brother, who has been her occasional lover for many years. But before he leaves for Rome with her, Alexander has had time to become engaged to Georgie Hands and provoke her to attempt suicide. The only character not linked sexually to any other (although it is implied she has her own affairs elsewhere) is Rosemary, the divorcée sister of Martin and Alexander. And the only two characters who have nothing sexually to do with each other are Alexander and Honor Klein. Otherwise, Antonia loves Martin, Palmer, and Alexander; Georgie loves Martin, Alexander, and Palmer; and Honor is loved by Palmer and Martin: all in that order. Honor's attachments are referred to in the passive voice because she is the rather mysterious dynamo who generates the tensions which cause the others to act; she herself takes no initiatives, except perhaps at the very end when, having seen the others off the stage, she calls on Martin with the evident intention of offering herself to him.

This complex plot, inevitably rather crude sounding in summary, is by no means as frivolous as might appear at first sight. In the final pairings each hitherto morally blind partner (Martin, Antonia, and Georgie) is linked up with a lucid one (respectively Honor, Alexander, and Palmer), undoubtedly for his or her good. It is undeniably better for Martin to grow up into full moral adulthood: he has tended in the past to take refuge in filial relationships with women. The shock of Antonia's adulteries, of Georgie's misadventures culminating in her departure in Palmer's company, and above all of his own demonic passion for the "severed head," Honor, hurls him brutally but salutarily from his cosy Eden. (In mythology, the Medusa's head, cut off by Perseus, turned people who looked at it into stone.) As for Antonia, she has to stop enjoying the possession of three men, who flatter different facets of her personality, and settle for one of them. And Georgie, abandoned by one brother after the other, learns the hard way that a woman makes herself a doormat at her peril. Under the surface comedy of this game of musical beds, therefore, lies a closely argued moral statement: that to play with people is to hurt them, that to abase oneself in love is to invite humiliation, and that only upon mutual respect can a mature and adult love be based. Under the dazzling appearance of comic contingency, too, lies the tougher substance of an almost tragic determinism: one can never really escape from the enchanter but only remain under his or her spell.

The enchanter in *An Unofficial Rose* (1962) is a young charmer called Lindsay (who, like many of Murdoch's heroines, has an androgy-

nous name). Randall, a rose-grower, leaves his wife for Lindsay, and his father sells a family heirloom in order to supply Randall with the money he needs to finance his affair in style. The father's motive for this extraordinary action lies in the fact that, many years before, he had failed to leave his own wife for an enchanter who has since become a well-known novelist and (not wholly incidentally) the protector and employer of young Lindsay. So Randall gets his heart's desire because his father once suffered a fatal lack of courage in not grasping his. As for poor worthy Ann, Randall's long-suffering wife, she is courted by a soldier who cannot quite bring himself to seduce her, and who leaves her, tortured by the awareness that "he was paying the penalty . . . for being an officer and a gentleman." The rather surprising moral of this novel seems therefore to be that the deserving will not get their just deserts and that the unworthy will have heaped upon them what they have not merited.

The Unicorn (1963) is undoubtedly one of the best of Murdoch's early novels, certainly one of the most closely studied. Written during the first decade of her career as a novelist, it can usefully stand for them all in terms of symbolism, magic and mystery, and the theme of first love. It is a thriller in the Wilkie Collins lineage crossed with a "romantic" novel of the *Jane Eyre* (1847) variety (with a youngish woman arriving at an ancient castle inhabited by an older man). There are even touches of *Wuthering Heights* (1847) and no end of allusions to "La Dame a la licorne" (the famous tapestry in Paris), to castles perilous, and to courtly love. But all such allusions are handled ironically, and no single theme offers a key. Once again we are shown that fiction is not life, but a construct of life's elements; and once again we find the author winking at us through the fine weave of her own tapestry, as we see in this passing remark: "It had undeniably the qualities of a wonderful story."

The Italian Girl (1964) is not a wonderful story, as most critics agree. It is one of Murdoch's shortest novels and undoubtedly her weakest. Uncle Edmund returns to the family home after a long absence to attend his mother's funeral, and soon he becomes involved in bizarre goings-on which include the impregnation of both his mature sister-in-law and his young niece by the same male charmer, and the frenzied affair between his brother and the charmer's eccentric sister. After events which are more than usually melodramatic, Edmund discovers that, far from being sexually frigid himself, he is in love with the "Italian girl," the housekeeper who is the latest incarnation of a long line of Italian governesses whom his mother hired. There is no attempt on Murdoch's part to underplay the overt Freudianism of the relationship between an immature adult "son" and his surrogate mother.

The Time of the Angels (1966) shares the weaknesses of *The Italian Girl*, notably an excessively melodramatic plot. The new rector of a riverside parish in London insists on receiving no one, not even his own brother, and we soon discover why: having abandoned his mistress (the black housekeeper, Pattie), he is having an affair with his own daughter. The only sympathetic and even believable inhabitant of this chamber of horrors is the janitor, a Russian refugee called Eugene who lives immured in his memories of prerevolutionary Russia, and he is left to clear out the rectory when its other inhabitants have moved away on the death by suicide of the incestuous rector who has lost his faith in God.

Opinions are divided about Murdoch's only historical novel, *The Red and the Green* (1965). Although like the other novels of the mid 1960s it betrays an uncertainty of direction, it is more impressive than either *The Italian Girl* or *The Time of the Angels*. This is perhaps because Murdoch is self-confessedly ambivalent about Ireland: on the one hand she is Irish, at least by descent, and on the other she feels a sort of appalled recoil at the "miserable stupid mixed-up country betrayed by history and never able to recover from the consequences," such as the reemergence of terrorism, a situation which so offends her rational mind. That a great deal of herself went into this sober yet moving account of the 1916 rebellion cannot be doubted: she clearly needed to write this otherwise rather uncharacteristic book in order to exorcise the exasperatingly muddled romanticism which she inherits from her ancestors and which, her critics would say, mars some of her novels. This necessity is revealed not only by the tone of the novel but also by a detail such as the use of Murdoch's own mother's maiden name, Richardson, as the maiden name of the mother of one of the leading characters. Nevertheless, perhaps because the subject of the Easter Rising is an emotional one as far as she is concerned, she does not resist the temptation to have some fairly startling sexual goings-on. The *Times Literary Supplement* reviewer was, however, unfair in calling the book an "implausible bedroom farce"; nearer the mark is critic Donna Gerstenberger's comment

Iris Murdoch (photograph by Sophie Fallows)

that Murdoch was performing at less that her best in this novel by "accept[ing] romanticized absolutes about historical events" and "see[ing] value in such judgments." This tendency may account for the novel's sentimentality; on the other hand, the historical basis of the material gives the novel a sharp tragic structure and allows it to deal with issues largely unclouded by the symbolism which dogs the other novels of this period of her career.

Murdoch returned to full form with *The Nice and the Good* (1968). This story opens literally on a pistol shot (echoes of Stendhal, except that the civil service rather than politics is involved, and this is hardly a concert). Octavian is burping over his Friday lunch, savoring the afterglow of belched burgundy, and looking forward to his regular weekend at his Dorset country house when he hears a sound that he recognizes from his army days—the report of a discharged revolver. Joseph Radeechy, one of Octavian's subordinates, has shot himself in a nearby office, as his colleague Richard Biranne at once comes to inform Octavian.

An opening as dramatic as this surpasses even Wilkie Collins for surprise. What follows is less like Collins and more like Honoré de Balzac—the filling-in about who Octavian is, what sort of household he heads, who Paula (Richard Biranne's divorced wife) is, and so on. But still within the Collins mode is the art with which very little transpires about Radeechy himself for many pages to come. That is the mystery which, like the secret in Collins's masterpiece, *The Woman in White* (1860), is held back and forms the heart of the novel.

Still, like all Iris Murdoch's works, this is more than just a perverse pleasure to read. It is a morality: a quasi-Shakespearean comedy (particularly reminiscent of *A Midsummer Night's Dream*) with a happy ending, but much concerned with a crucial nuance in human affairs between the "nice" and the "good." The meaning of this fundamental Murdochian distinction is given obliquely in a number of places: it is the apparent good as opposed to the genuine good, or, in love, the self-gratifying contrasted with the impersonal. Few of Murdoch's characters aspire to the "good" and even fewer attain it: most settle for the "nice," often blissfully unaware of the possibility of another mode of being. Nevertheless, people do need to learn to seek the right path to love, indeed the only path to love: the way of unselfishness. In this novel, Ducane stumbles belatedly upon that path as a result of his brush with death when he plunges into the sea-cave to save Pierce from drowning.

In one of Murdoch's bittersweet comedies, *Bruno's Dream* (1969), a rather feckless character gets the nice girl while the upright (and rather uptight) Miles does not, but there is a certain rough justice about it: "We've all paired off really, in the end," one of the characters realizes; "Miles has got his muse, Lisa has got Danby. And I've got Bruno. Who would have thought it would work out like that?" (The answer to that rhetorical question is, of course, easy: the novelist.) The blurb on the dust jacket of *Nuns and Soldiers* (1980), almost certainly inspired by the author herself, fits not only that novel but all the bittersweet comedies in one way or another: "All the characters are forced into some degree of heroism, and at last muddle and lies are cleared away, and sins are forgiven, though not everybody gains his heart's desire." To that, one need only add that those who do gain their heart's desire are not evidently the most worthy.

The very title of the next novel, *A Fairly Honourable Defeat* (1970), contains a harsh irony (and one missed, incidentally, by Penguin's blurb writer): Rupert's defeat is not honourable at all; it is cruel and messy, like life, and in any case is overshadowed by the greater defeat of good (Tallis) by evil (Julius). Unlike *The Nice and the Good*, this novel has an unhappy ending; and like so many of the others, it is dominated by an enchanter. This particular manipulator, Julius King, exploits the vanity, mendacity, and cowardice of his fellow creatures in a situation where imperfect beings are related to each other by deep if obscure bonds. Julius does not get his comeuppance as the reader expects (and perhaps hopes), no doubt because he is, in the novel's symbolism, God, or at least fate.

At the heart of *An Accidental Man* lies a theme inaugurated by Henry James: that of transatlantic misunderstanding. Ludwig Leferrier, expatriate American and potential Vietnam draft dodger, resigns his Oxford fellowship and returns to face the music, ignoring the baffled incomprehension of his English fiancée and her upper-middle-class parents. This is also, except for *The Red and the Green*, Murdoch's most political novel to date. Technically, it is one of her most stunning: the extensive use of letters and of unattributed dialogue to advance the narrative is strikingly new; it bears out her consistent claim that she is by no means satisfied to reproduce the forms of the novel as she has inherited them but has a definite interest in experimenting with different styles and devices, each novel making its own technical innovation (more than perhaps might appear).

Similarly, *The Black Prince* (1973) is, like so many great modern works, a portrait of the artist, although in this case a rather parodic one, since the artist-hero in this book is a retired tax inspector in love with a college student. Still, like Marcel Proust's *A la recherche du temps perdu* (1913-1927), it tells the story of its own composition; and like James Joyce's *Ulysses* (1922), it reflects and meditates upon a masterpiece of classic literature, in this case *Hamlet* (whence the "black prince" of the title—nothing to do, as the reader at first mistakenly thinks, with Edward III's son, the character of English history and everything to do with the god Apollo, who appears in the story as a "Mr Loxias"). But the closest affinities it has are perhaps with Nabokov's *Lolita* (1958). Like Humbert Humbert, the narrator of *The Black Prince* is a conceited and literate deviant who transports his immature loved one away from home and family before being cruelly punished for his pains. *The Black Prince* is a self-styled "celebration of love"; but it is also an unremitting exposure of that other face of love: hatred. And following Nabokov, Murdoch tells the story of this unhappy, even doomed, love affair in the context of an elaborate reflection about art. She may well be unaware of—certainly unconcerned about—parallels between her book and *Lolita*; in any case establishing influence is of secondary importance. What putting these two major contemporary works side by side chiefly shows is that Murdoch is no less a "modern writer" than Nabokov; she is as much concerned as he is with the nature and status of art. At the end of *Lolita*, Humbert invokes what he calls "the refuge of art" and claims it as the only immortality which he and his Lolita may hope to share. The reader may compare with that statement the last words of *The Black Prince*: "Art tells the only truth that ultimately matters. It is the light by which human things can be mended. And after art there is, let me assure you all, nothing." Even allowing for a hint of self-deprecating irony here, the tone is very similar, and the respect for art as the only available salvation just as great; indeed, Murdoch's confidence is perhaps even greater than Nabokov's: it is after all Humbert Humbert who speaks, in *Lolita*, of "the melancholy and very local palliative of articulate art."

Humbert Humbert's melancholy tone is more at home in *A Word Child* (1975), a sad, ironic tale of a brilliant boy from a deprived background who, by winning various scholarships, makes it to a fellowship at Oxford University, only to lose it all through an affair (with a colleague's wife) that has disastrous consequences. We meet Hilary Burde later in life, when he has "buried" himself in an obscure government office in Whitehall, doing a job well below his ability. His dull but peaceful existence is shattered when his old rival in love is appointed to head the section in which he works. Perhaps rather incredibly, history then proceeds to repeat itself, and Hilary is once again the instrument in provoking an accident which makes his chief a widower for a second time. Hilary is thrust even further into social obscurity, but there is a hint that he will, at the last, be redeemed by the selfless and unreciprocated love of his mistress, Thomasina, who seems to be breaking down his bitter cynicism by persuading him to marry her. This curious, melodramatic story once again reveals that all is not so simple as it appears in Iris Murdoch's world. As we have seen, she herself strongly approves of an educational system based on selection by bursaries and other such means; but her novel is a surprisingly telling indictment of what can happen to a person of great gifts (in this case, as the title implies, a talent for languages) who is raised above his or her normal social environment before attaining sufficient moral and emotional maturity to enable him or her to cope with the enormous pressures involved. Thus the novel has a particularly British obsession with class and social background, and as such it may hold less interest than other Murdoch titles for readers outside England.

In *Henry and Cato* (1976), one of Murdoch's ironic tragedies, Cato the austere priest is cut down to size, and his self-indulgent, easygoing, and even feckless friend Henry inherits wealth and landed property and marries the beautiful fresh young girl he really has no moral right to. Or hasn't he? Cato's highmindedness cannot prevent the violent death of Joe, the "beautiful" boy from a deprived background whom Cato wishes to "save" less out of Christian charity, it soon becomes clear, than out of a homosexual infatuation which the boy cynically encourages. So perhaps Henry, who is ethically much more modest, is not as undeserving of life's bounties as might at first sight appear. This is perhaps the most Dickensian of Iris Murdoch's novels: the broad humor of the characterization is often similar (Lucius is rather like the sponger Skimpole in *Bleak House* 1851), the low-life urban setting reminds one of *Little Dorrit* (1857), and the way the characters are introduced and the surprises engineered is characteristic of Dickens's manner. And just as Pip ends up, in *Great Expectations* (1861), older, sadder, and much wiser, so Henry and Cato, two very different prodigal sons, return home at last, chastened, punished, and rewarded in varying degrees. But Murdoch, if she is rewriting Dickens in terms of the 1970s, is doing so very much tongue in cheek.

Perhaps Murdoch's most mature exploration of the theme of personal redemption is *The Sea, The Sea* (1978), which won the coveted Booker literary prize. A massive novel—over five hundred pages long—it is a major achievement, even by this novelist's high standards. Her steady output has been maturing as well as deepening in quality over the years, but this book is one of her best. Certainly its only close rival is *The Black Prince*; and, like *The Black Prince*, it is the story of an obsessive love, an infatuation of tragic proportions.

But whereas fifty-eight-year-old Bradley Pearson, the narrator-hero of the earlier novel, was enslaved by a girl barely out of her teens who could almost have been his granddaughter, Charles Arrowby, the more recent teller of his own sad tale, is a retired theatre director who meets again the girl he loved when he was a boy: Hartley, his own Annabel Lee (as Humbert Humbert would put it). Unfortunately for Charles—but then this is the bittersweet world of Iris Murdoch, where every situation is suffused with irony, and not the cloying universe of Georgette Heyer—Hartley has not been pining for *him* all those years; in fact, she is happily married to a former staff sergeant who evidently (evident, that is, to all but Charles) gives her a very satisfying sex life.

The story of how this monumental and indeed dangerous misunderstanding—the classic quid pro quo of all good comedy—is resolved constitutes the basic plot of the novel. But there are other elements, other themes. For example, we are made very conscious that Charles, not surprisingly for a former actor, is a kind of magician, a comic, even rather parodic, Prospero-figure: allusions to *The Tempest* abound, as did echoes of *Hamlet* in *The Black Prince*. Charles is a very destructive magician, though, and he has to recognize, at the end, that he has intervened frivolously, even wantonly, in the destinies of Hartley, of her adopted child, Titus, of his friends Peregrine and Rosina, Gilbert and Lizzie: the list of the people whom his monstrous egoism has damaged or destroyed is seemingly endless.

The theme of the dangerous enchanter is, of course, familiar from other Murdoch novels. So is the presence of the sea—not only the cruel sea lamented by one great poet, Gerard Manley Hopkins, but "*la mer, la mer, toujours recommencée*" celebrated by another: Paul Valéry's famous line from *The Graveyard by the Sea* haunts readers of this novel, and it is significant that the sea, such an important feature elsewhere in Murdoch's world, figures prominently here too. The title actually refers to the cry (*Thalassa, thalassa!* [The sea, the sea]), recorded by Xenophon, of the retreating Greek army when at last they saw the sea over which they could escape. The sea, a means of solace and refuge, is also cruel. It destroys people (young Titus is tragically, senselessly drowned), but it also cleanses, and that indeed is its principal function. Charles returns from his so-journ by the sea a sadder, lonelier, but wiser and better man; in a psychological as well as physical sense, his long summer vacation has done him good. The leading themes are fourfold and related: that of self-deception versus self-understanding; of art versus reality; of reconciliation and love versus enmity and hatred; and of the mysterious, even the magical, versus the familiar and the mundane.

The first theme is obvious enough, in that Charles is patently deceiving himself in believing that Hartley wishes to leave her husband after so many years of marriage. One of the finer ironies of this book is the way Charles sees Hartley as a woman locked up in her nightmares, whereas it soon becomes apparent to the reader how deeply enmeshed Charles is in his own. "It's something childish, it isn't part of the real world," Hartley tells him when he reminds her so insistently of their feelings for each other long ago; and of course she is right. The real world is husband Ben, the little house with roses round the door and a stuffy overheated atmosphere inside, the collie dog, and the cucumber sandwiches for tea: a world Charles, who never married, cannot begin to understand. A significant detail that shows this up in sharp relief is the visit he pays the house at six p.m. one day. "Six o'clock for me meant drinks," he says. "I had imagined it would be a sensible and humane time to call. In fact I had interrupted their evening meal." His reaction speaks volumes not only for the different worlds in which he and Hartley have grown up and lived out their lives, but also for his obtuseness, lack of tact, and deficiencies of understanding. His awakening, when it finally comes, is hurtful to his self-esteem: "I had deluded myself throughout by the idea of reviving a secret love which did not exist at all. . . . How much, I see as I look back, I read into it all, reading my own dream text and not looking at the reality." Reality, indeed, is what the reader, not the narrator, has been aware of almost from the beginning. But by a fine paradox, Charles's movement from self-deception to enlightenment is also a movement, for the former actor, from reality to art: Charles's story, begun as a kind of memoir or journal, becomes a novel (that is, a work of art) of which he is simultaneously the leading character and the creator. "So I am writing my life, after all, as a novel!" he realizes about one-third of the way through; like so many narrator-heroes in modern literature since Proust's Marcel and including Nabokov's Humbert Humbert, he is working like an alchemist to transmute his life into art under our very eyes.

But the development is not only an aesthetic one: it has, as always with Murdoch, a moral dimension also. What is here referred to as "the relentless causality of sin" is broken, albeit at great human cost. Charles becomes resigned to Hartley's second and final departure from his life (as he himself says, though without at the time sensing the full force of the parallel, he is a "crazed Orpheus" and she a "dazed Eurydice"). Additionally, he makes his peace at the last with those he has misjudged (like his cousin James, who saves his life when he falls into the sea) and with those he has harmed (such as Peregrine and Rosina, whose marriage he had callously broken up several years before). The child he had lost before he even knew of its existence (Rosina's, which she aborted to spite him) and the "son" he loses so soon after finding him (Titus, whom he had planned to raise on his own) may finally be replaced with the help of Angie, the impetuous virgin who presses him to let her give him an heir.

There is thus, in spite of everything, something magical about all these events. The pilgrimage of human life, Charles perceives at the end, is "demon-ridden," but the demons are not necessarily always hostile. James appears to live in easy familiarity with them, and it is perhaps with their assistance that he saves Charles from drowning; certainly something very odd happens when Charles gives himself up for dead and is, quite miraculously, saved. There is indeed more to heaven and earth than is dreamt of in his philosophy; and in common with her usual practice (as in *The Bell* or *The Unicorn*), Murdoch leaves that particular mystery unexplained.

As is so often the case in Murdoch's world, Charles begins the painful process of self-understanding only after he has been snatched from the jaws of death. Thus ends what Charles himself calls "another story of death and moral smash-up," although it is only fair to point out that he is thinking more of Henry James's *The Wings of the Dove* (1902) than of his own book-in-the-making. But the description, whatever it makes of James's masterpiece, does not quite fit *The Sea, The Sea*: a death does occur, but there is a hint of the promise of new life being created with and through Angie; and if there is "moral smash-up," it is the essential prelude to moral regeneration. The same is true of *Nuns and Soldiers*, like *The Sea, The Sea* "very much a love story," in which Gertrude and Tim, against all odds—and

particularly the rooted conviction of their friends and relations that Tim is not morally or socially worthy of Gertrude—not only fall in love but marry and stay almost wickedly happy together. Such an outcome may seem "awfully bad form" to the other characters in the story, but it is one in which Murdoch evidently takes some delight; she likes to show the morally self-righteous getting their comeuppance. In this, as in other ways, she has much in common with her revered master, James: what could be more unsettling than the discomfiture of Isabel Archer in *The Portrait of a Lady* (1881), of the clever girl who is so morally sure of herself and others? But what could be more exhilarating than Isabel's ennobling realization that she has been grossly manipulated and crudely if effectively misled? In Murdoch, as in James, people are on the whole made better by their sufferings, even someone as initially unprepossessing as Tim in *Nuns and Soldiers*.

It is quite clear that Murdoch writes novels not to advance a cause, expound a philosophy, or portray a society; still less to ensure a future for the English novel, although her intricate plots, particular brand of humor, and sophisticated stance toward her reader may well indicate a way forward that younger novelists can exploit. She writes in order to solve fictional problems. "There is a grace of certainty about being in love," she says in *Bruno's Dream*; "there is a grace of certainty in art but it is very rare." If her subject matter is usually love, especially its more bizarre manifestations—and in the more recent novels, notably *The Book and the Brotherhood* (1987) and *The Message to the Planet* (1989), religion has also become a major preoccupation—her true concern is with art and with what she calls "the grace of certainty" that is so rare in art. She is right: it *is* very rare. But, fortunately for us, it is occasionally to be encountered in the works of Iris Murdoch, the only Henry James our age deserves or is likely to produce.

Interviews:
Bookman, November 1958, p. 26;
Sunday Times (London), 17 May 1959;
John O'London's, 4 May 1961, p. 498;
Contemporary Literature, 18 (1977): 129-140;
Studies in the Literature Imagination, 11 (1978): 115-125;
Listener, 27 April 1978, pp. 533-535.

Bibliography:
John Fletcher and Cheryl Bove, *Iris Murdoch: A De-*

scriptive Primary and Annotated Secondary Bibliography (New York: Garland, forthcoming 1992).

References:

Frank Baldanza, *Iris Murdoch* (New York: Twayne, 1974);

Malcolm Bradbury, "A House Fit for Free Characters: Iris Murdoch and *Under the Net*," in his *Possibilities: Essays on the State of the Novel* (London & New York: Oxford University Press, 1973), pp. 231-246;

A. S. Byatt, *Degrees of Freedom: The Novels of Iris Murdoch* (London: Chatto & Windus, 1965; New York: Barnes & Noble, 1965);

Colette Charpentier, *Le Thème de la claustration dans The Unicorn d'Iris Murdoch: Etude lexicale et sémantique* (Paris: Didier, 1976);

Peter J. Conradi, *Iris Murdoch: The Saint and the Artist* (Basingstoke, U.K.: Macmillan, 1986);

Donna Gerstenberger, *Iris Murdoch* (Lewisburg: Bucknell University Presses, 1975; London: Associated University Presses, 1975);

Steven G. Kellman, *The Self-Begetting Novel* (London: Macmillan, 1980), pp. 87-93;

Frank Kermode, *Modern Essays* (London: Fontana, 1971), pp. 261-266;

Modern Fiction Studies, special Murdoch issue, 15 (Autumn 1959);

William Van O'Connor, *The New University Wits and the End of Modernism* (Carbondale: Southern Illinois University Press, 1963), pp. 54-74;

Rubin Rabinovitz, "Iris Murdoch," in *Six Contemporary British Novelists*, edited by George Stade (New York: Columbia University Press, 1976), pp. 271-332;

Lorna Sage, "Female Fictions: The Women Novelists," in *The Contemporary English Novel*, edited by Malcolm Bradbury and David Palmer (London: Edward Arnold, 1979), pp. 68-74;

Richard Todd, *Iris Murdoch: The Shakespearean Interest* (New York: Barnes & Noble, 1979; London: Vision Press, 1979);

Peter Wolfe, *The Disciplined Heart: Iris Murdoch and Her Novels* (Columbia: University of Missouri Press, 1966).

Papers:

The manuscript and typescript drafts of most of the novels, together with other papers both published and unpublished, are held at the University of Iowa, Iowa City. The Bodleian Library, Oxford, possesses the manuscript of the Romanes lecture, which was revised and published as *The Fire and the Sun: Why Plato Banished the Artists*.

V. S. Naipaul

(17 August 1932 -   )

This entry was updated by Joseph Caldwell from his entry in DLB Yearbook: 1985.

BOOKS: *The Mystic Masseur* (London: Deutsch, 1957; New York: Vanguard, 1959);

The Suffrage of Elvira (London: Deutsch, 1958);

Miguel Street (London: Deutsch, 1959; New York: Vanguard, 1960);

A House for Mr Biswas (London: Deutsch, 1961; New York: McGraw-Hill, 1961); republished with author's foreword (New York: Knopf, 1983);

The Middle Passage: Impressions of Five Societies— British, French and Dutch—in the West Indies and South America (London: Deutsch, 1962; New York: Macmillan, 1962);

Mr Stone and the Knights Companion (London: Deutsch, 1963; New York: Macmillan, 1964);

An Area of Darkness (London: Deutsch, 1964; New York: Macmillan, 1965);

The Mimic Men (London: Deutsch, 1967; New York: Macmillan, 1967);

A Flag on the Island (London: Deutsch, 1967; New York: Macmillan, 1967);

The Loss of El Dorado: A History (London: Deutsch, 1969; New York: Knopf, 1970);

In a Free State (London: Deutsch, 1971; New York: Knopf, 1971);

"The Overcrowded Barracoon" and Other Articles (London: Deutsch, 1972; New York: Knopf, 1973);

Guerrillas (London: Deutsch, 1975; New York: Knopf, 1975);

India: A Wounded Civilization (New York: Knopf, 1977; London: Deutsch, 1977);

A Bend in the River (London: Deutsch, 1979; New York: Knopf, 1979);

"The Return of Eva Perón" with "The Killings in Trinidad" (New York: Knopf, 1980; London: Deutsch, 1980);

Among the Believers: An Islamic Journey (New York: Knopf, 1981; London: Deutsch, 1981);

Three Novels (New York: Knopf, 1983)—includes *The Mystic Masseur, The Suffrage of Elvira,* and *Miguel Street*;

Finding the Centre (London: Deutsch, 1984); republished as *Finding the Center* (New York: Knopf, 1984);

V. S. Naipaul, circa 1983 (photograph by Thomas Victor)

The Enigma of Arrival (New York: Knopf, 1987; London: Viking, 1987);

A Turn in the South (New York: Knopf, 1989; London: Viking, 1989);

India: A Million Mutinies Now (London: Heinemann, 1990; New York: Viking, 1991).

SELECTED PERIODICAL PUBLICATIONS— UNCOLLECTED: "Violence in Art: The Documentary Heresy," *Twentieth Century*, 173 (Winter 1964-1965): 107-108;

"A Note on a Borrowing by Conrad," *New York Review of Books*, 29 (16 December 1982): 37-38;

"An Island Betrayed," *Harper's*, 268 (March 1984): 61-72;

"Among the Republicans," *New York Review of Books*, 31 (25 October 1984): 5, 8, 10, 12, 14-17;

"My Brother's Tragic Sense," *Spectator*, 258 (24 January 1987): 22-23;

"Our Universal Civilization," *New York Review of Books*, 38 (31 January 1991): 22-25;

"Argentina: Living with Cruelty," *New York Review of Books*, 39 (30 January 1992): 13-18;

"The End of Peronism?" *New York Review of Books*, 39 (13 February 1992): 47-53.

"Half the writer's work . . . is the discovery of his subject." With this statement V. S. Naipaul declares his purpose as a writer and the object of his craft—the imaginative shaping of experience into an affecting and intelligent narrative that reveals a truth to its writer. Naipaul has pursued his goal vigorously from the earliest days of his career as a writer, when, while free-lancing on the BBC radio program "Caribbean Voices," he sat at a borrowed typewriter and typed out the first sentence of the first book he completed, the collection of stories he titled *Miguel Street* (1959).

In his "Prologue to an Autobiography," the first of two personal narratives that make up *Finding the Centre* (1984), Naipaul recalls his beginner's lack of confidence that prevented him from numbering his pages and made him single-space the lines he typed to give the illusion of print. That day in the BBC free-lance room, Naipaul says, he was lucky; the first sentence of the story "Bogart," simple and full of promise, led to the second, to the third, and on until the story was told. With the encouragement of his colleagues, he wrote enough stories to complete a book and tried to have it published. Though he could not interest a publisher in this work and though he continued to lack confidence in his ability as a writer, Naipaul wrote three novels. Since Naipaul first began writing in 1954, it has been his only profession. He has continued to write, to discover, to learn.

Vidiadhar Surajprasad Naipaul was born 17 August 1932 at Lion House, the home of his mother's family, in the central Trinidad town of Chaguanas. Vidiadhar was the first son and second child of Seepersad and Bropatie Capildeo Naipaul, who had married in 1929. The marriage was an unhappy match. At the time of his son's birth, Seepersad was estranged from his wife and was living in the neighboring town of Montrose.

Seepersad became local correspondent for the *Trinidad Guardian* in 1929. In 1934, under the strains of a public humiliation related to one of his articles written in 1933, disagreement with

his wife's family on matters of religion and politics, and his resignation from the *Guardian*, Naipaul suffered a nervous breakdown from which he never fully recovered. For the next four years he held various jobs around Chaguanas. Naipaul rejoined the *Guardian* staff in 1938 and moved his family to Port of Spain. He died there of a heart attack in 1953.

The move to Port of Spain benefited V. S. Naipaul. There he was enrolled at Tranquility Boys School, where he began the education that eventually got him off the island of Trinidad. Naipaul was an excellent student and sat for one of the classes offering a scholarship. Scoring third highest in the 1942 island-wide competition, he won a free place at Trinidad's Queen's Royal College, where he began attendance in January 1943. Upon his graduation in April 1949, the Trinidad Education Board awarded him a special scholarship to attend college in Great Britain. In 1950 he left Trinidad to take his place at University College, Oxford, where he earned a degree in English in 1954. The death of his father the previous year and the uncertainties of his job with the BBC contributed to the sense of desperation that led him to write, from varied memories of his life on Trinidad, the story that inaugurated his career as a writer.

Miguel Street comprises a series of vignettes narrated by an educated adult who looks back with bitterness upon his boyhood residence in a poor Port of Spain neighborhood. The narrator reports the behavior of several characters who live on the street—such as Morgan, a pyrotechnician of genius who prefers to be thought of as a funnyman; Laura, mother of eight children by seven fathers; and Man-man, the street madman, who, after a religious conversion, undergoes a mock crucifixion. He records his boyhood impressions in an ironic, humorous style that gives the impression that, even as a boy, he was more mature than the adults whose behavior he observed and admired. *Miguel Street* has no continuity of plot and relies for unity on the consciousness of the narrator as he records his growth from awestruck child to restless young man. It describes his awakening need to escape from the constraints of a provincial place to the larger world. This accounts for the bitter irony with which the stories are told. The narrator, from a distant place and with the enlightened detachment of education, regrets the unstimulating background that kept him innocent for too long and made his greatest ambition to be nothing

Poster advertising Naipaul's controversial account of Islam in Iran, Pakistan, and Indonesia

more than a man like Hat, the ignorant but charming leading citizen of Miguel Street.

Despite his bitterness the narrator does have sympathy for those who cannot escape their backgrounds. Just before he leaves the island to study abroad on scholarship, he answers his mother's charge that he is becoming too wild by saying, "Is just Trinidad. What else anybody could do here except drink?" From his vantage he understands the truth of his statement: a place devoid of possibility does not excite ambition. This knowledge helps him to realize that he is not better, but better off, than those he left behind.

Miguel Street, written in 1954 but published in 1959, was given the 1961 Somerset Maugham Award. Typical of its reception was George McMichael's statement in the *San Francisco Chronicle* that "Miguel Street is the Bowery, the Tenderloin, the Catfish Row of Trinidad's Port of Spain—its citizens a loony multitude whose knavery often rises from real kinship with pathos and tragedy. . . ." Most reviewers noted the narrator's sympathy for the poor folk with whom he grew up, but few commented on his ironic tone.

Ganesh, a character mentioned briefly in *Miguel Street*, became the main character of *The Mystic Masseur* (1957), one of two novels written after but published before *Miguel Street*. It chronicles Ganesh's rise from humble beginnings as a "massager" to fame as a powerful but disillusioned politician. The narrator, a student living in London, recalls his first youthful visit to Ganesh for treatment of a foot injury. Ganesh at this time was a struggling amateur, inept but friendly. As a premium Ganesh had given the boy a book he had written, *101 Questions And Answers On The Hindu Religion*, which later sparked the narrator's interest in Ganesh's career. His book, really a pamphlet, lent legitimacy to Ganesh's claim that he was a writer. More important, it signaled that Ganesh had the ambition and drive to achieve fame.

From writer Ganesh progressed to mystic masseur, from healer of spiritual ills to politician. Ganesh began to eradicate the record of his past once he had won a place on the legislative council; he suppressed his autobiography, *The Years of Guilt*, which accounted for his years as a struggling healer. As his influence and importance grew, his idealism concerning fame and the application of power shriveled. When the narrator meets Ganesh again on a railroad platform in England, he has become G. Ramsay Muir, M.B.E., a man wearied by his total corruption. His fame and power are not what he imagined they would be, and they give him no pleasure. Though saddened that Ganesh has drifted so far from his simple dream of fame, the narrator retains sympathy and admiration for him.

The Mystic Masseur was awarded the John Llewelyn Rhys Memorial Prize in 1958. The *Times Literary Supplement* reviewer remarked, "Naipaul possesses a remarkably acute ear for dialogue and dialect, a pleasantly poker-faced sense of humor, and considerable feeling for, as well as insight into, his characters. At the moment his strength seems to lie in the presentation of individual episodes and scenes, and not to be entirely equal to the strain of a full-length novel. . . ." Naipaul later agreed with this assessment of his early work. Anthony Quinton's appraisal of the book for *New Statesman and Nation*—"Yet another piece of intuitive or slap-happy West Indian fiction as pleasant, muddled and inconsequent as the Trinidadian Hindus it describes"—represented the opinion of reviewers who felt that Naipaul's setting and characters were too exotic for the common reader, and that he was not truly testing his talent by practicing what they considered genre fiction.

The Suffrage of Elvira (1958), the story of an election in an obscure but representative district of Trinidad, offers scathing commentary on the corruption of island politics. Democracy, granted to the island in 1946, "had taken nearly everybody by surprise and it wasn't until 1950, a few months before the second general election under universal adult franchise, that people began to see the possibilities." Surujpat "Pat" Harbans seeks the support of Chittaranjan to gain the Hindu vote and of Baksh for the Muslim vote. Baksh and Chittaranjan assure Harbans that he will have their support—for a price. Harbans's worries over the mercenary tendencies of his campaign staff are complicated by the influence of two Jehovah's Witnesses who convince the Spanish constituency not to participate in the election, the threat of *obeah* (island witchcraft) embodied by the miserable pariah dog Tiger, and the cost of bribes to cabdrivers, who threaten to strike on the day of the election if Harbans does not raise their fee. The campaign proves expensive, but, as was expected, Harbans wins.

One episode exemplifies the corruption, absurdity, and cynicism that Naipaul claims characterized local politics in Trinidad at this time. To celebrate his victory, Harbans buys a Jaguar and drives it to the ceremonial presentation of a case of White Horse Scotch whiskey to his campaign staff. At the ceremony a crowd of disaffected (because unbribed) voters who have noted the change in Harbans's attitude toward them—accessible and friendly during his campaign, he now affects a distant and aloof manner toward his supporters—elect one of their number, Jordan, to be the recipient of a symbolic fifty-dollar bribe. "Is not something just for Jordan," Harbans is told. "You could say is a sort of thank-you present for everybody in Elvira. . . . Can't just come to a place and collect people good good vote and walk away. Don't look nice." As Harbans counts out the fifty dollars, his Jaguar is set afire and explodes.

The Suffrage of Elvira received little attention in the United States, nor is it now considered an important work in comparison with Naipaul's later fiction. All three of Naipaul's early books continue to be overshadowed by his masterpiece, *A House for Mr Biswas* (1961). Naipaul has said that his first three books are apprentice work, and, although they share an admirable stylistic proficiency, they are more important in consideration

of the work they anticipate than on their own merit. In them Naipaul experiments with the possibilities of plot, character, and setting, and works out his bitterness toward the restrictiveness of Trinidadian life so that he can return to it objectively.

After making his study of shallow but successful men and their ambitions, Naipaul turned his attention, in *A House for Mr Biswas*, toward the consideration of an unsuccessful man and the importance of his unremarkable ambition to own a house. "The original idea was simple . . . to tell the story of a man like my father, and . . . to tell the story of the life as the story of the simple possessions by which the man is surrounded at his death. In the writing the book changed. It became the story of a man's search for a house and all that the possession of one's own home implies. . . . The novel, once it had ceased to be an idea and had begun to exist as a novel, called up its own truth."

Naipaul added this statement about the development of his novel to a new edition in 1983. In his foreword he recalls the anxiety and the elation of writing the book. The period of four years between his graduation from University College and beginning work on *A House for Mr Biswas* in 1958 had been an active one for Naipaul. He had written three books, become a free-lance editor and writer for the BBC, married Patricia Ann Hale in 1955, changed his place of residence twice, and begun, in 1957, to review fiction for the *New Statesman*. Naipaul began "writing toward" the novel late in 1957 and completed it in 1961.

Mr. Biswas inauspiciously enters the world late one evening in his grandmother's house. "Six fingered, and born in the wrong way. . . . Whatever you do, this boy will eat up his own mother and father," says the midwife who delivers him. The midwife's prophecy proves true. Mr. Biswas's father, Raghu, drowns while diving to rescue Mr. Biswas, who Raghu mistakenly thinks has fallen into a pool. His mother, Bipti, is forced to sell her house by neighbors who threaten her for the money they think Raghu has buried in the yard.

No longer able to support or house her family, Bipti sends her children away to live with relatives. While his brothers Prasad and Pratap and his sister Dehuti begin lives of servitude, Mr. Biswas is enrolled by his Aunt Tara in school and is later given as an apprentice to the pundit Jairam. After Mr. Biswas profanes Jairam's sacred oleander tree with night soil, Jairam releases him from the apprenticeship. Once again made homeless by people more powerful than he, Mr. Biswas begins to associate ownership of a house with power and security. The strong, he reasons, have a place to go; the weak do not. His position of weakness humiliates him but plants the seed of ambition.

Mr. Biswas returns briefly to his aunt's house to collect his few possessions and goes into the world to make his way as a sign writer. A job at the Tulsi family store in Arwacas leads to his introduction to Shama, the youngest Tulsi daughter, and results in the marriage that changes his life. Mr. Biswas quickly falls into disagreement with the Tulsis; he refuses to do what the family expects of him, though he willingly takes advantage of the amenities it offers. Shama does not appreciate his rebellion; Mr. Biswas resents the responsibilities of marriage and fatherhood. Estranged from his wife and family, he spends his next years roaming the Tulsis' holdings. During his lonely drift, Mr. Biswas returns for comfort to the idea of his own house, a place of which he is master.

His first attempt to build a house leads to a nervous breakdown when the pressures to complete it become too great. Rescued by the Tulsis, he convalesces at their home, Hanuman House, for the first time thankful for its sanctuary. Soon after his recovery Mr. Biswas resolves to go to Port of Spain, where he intends to live with his sister Dehuti until he has found a job. His only skill is sign writing, but he has a strong desire to be a newspaper writer. One day he marches boldly into the office of the *Trinidad Sentinel* to demand a job as a reporter. The editor, Mr. Burnett, asks him to paint some signs—one of which reads "No Hands Wanted"—in the hope of discouraging him.

Finally Mr. Burnett offers Mr. Biswas a one-month trial without pay, with the understanding that when Mr. Biswas "frightens" his editor with a truly macabre and sensational story he will be given a salary. The story Mr. Biswas submits wins him the status of top reporter for the paper:

> Within twenty-four hours Mr. Biswas was notorious, the *Sentinel*, reviled on every hand, momentarily increased its circulation, and Mr. Burnett was jubilant.
>
> He said, "You have even chilled me."
>
> The story, the leading one on page three, read:

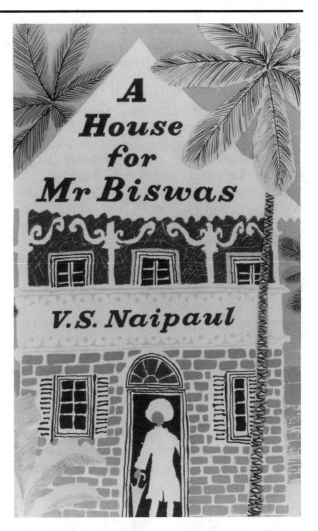

Dust jacket for the American edition of Naipaul's favorite of his novels

DADDY COMES HOME IN A COFFIN
U.S. Explorer's Last Journey
ON ICE
by M. Biswas

Somewhere in America in a neat little red-roofed cottage four children ask their mother every day, "Mummy, when is Daddy coming home?"

Less than a year ago Daddy—George Elmer Edman, the celebrated traveller and explorer—left home to explore the Amazon.

Well. I have news for you, kiddies.

Daddy is on his way home.

Yesterday he passed through Trinidad. In a coffin.

His notoriety and salary give him the necessary status to return to Hanuman House and reclaim his family. Mrs. Tulsi invites him to live with her in

Port of Spain while her son Owad prepares for his college entrance examinations. The strain of rebellion against the family eases, and Mr. Biswas enjoys a brief period of peace that allows him to develop a close relationship with Shama and his children, especially with his son Anand. The happiness is short-lived, however: Mr. Burnett is fired; new, conservative management takes control of the paper; Mr. Biswas is demoted from news writing to funeral coverage. World War II, with rationing, shortages, and salary reductions, brings further disruption.

The run of bad luck and hardship continues when Mr. Biswas accompanies his wife to a communal plantation Mrs. Tulsi has purchased. Here he attempts to raise a second house but fails. Defeated again, Mr. Biswas returns with the Tulsis to the misery of the now-communal Port of Spain house, strengthened in his resolve to escape.

When Owad returns from England a loud and selfish socialist, his abuse of Mr. Biswas and his family causes the final break with the Tulsis. After a particularly violent scene, Mr. Biswas acts on impulse; he borrows three thousand dollars to supplement his own meager savings and—without first considering his needs or consulting his family—buys the first house that is cleverly presented to him:

> The very day the house was bought they began to see flaws in it. The staircase was dangerous; the upper floor sagged; there was no back door; most of the windows didn't close; one door could not be opened; the celotex panels under the eaves had fallen out and left gaps between which bats could enter the attic. They discussed these things as calmly as they could and took care not to express their disappointment openly. And it was astonishing how quickly they had accommodated themselves to every peculiarity and awkwardness of the house. And once that had happened their eyes ceased to be critical, and the house became simply their house.

Soon after Mr. Biswas moves into the house, he suffers a heart attack that prevents him from working for several months. Worry about repayment of the loan causes his condition to worsen, and a second attack makes him an invalid. Before he dies, Mr. Biswas considers the enormity of his debt and the great gift of that debt, the house: "How terrible it would have been, at this time, to be without it: to have died among the Tulsis, amid the squalor of that large, disinte-grating and indifferent family; to have left Shama and the children among them, in one room; worse, to have lived without even attempting to lay claim to one's own portion of the earth; to have lived and died as one had been born, unnecessary and unaccommodated."

With sympathy and clarity, Naipaul gave his simple plot a depth of honesty and universality that won him acclaim as a major novelist. His themes—the sense of homelessness, the frustrations and humiliations of weakness, the price of dreams—are presented with humor and irony and without bitterness. Naipaul characterizes Mr. Biswas as a simple man overwhelmed at the end of his life by the achievement of a simple dream. His success is great, for, without aid or encouragement, Mr. Biswas has taken control of his life and given his family haven against the buffetings and vagaries of a world indifferent to the weak.

Reviewers admired the work. The reviewer for the *New York Herald Tribune Books* commented that "Naipaul has a wry and an engaging sense of humor, as well as a delicate understanding of sadness and futility and a profound but unobtrusive sense of the tragi-comedy of ordinary living. He is particularly sensitive to the subtle changes which enduring relationships undergo beneath their surface continuity, particularly within a family." Louis Chapin, writing for the *Christian Science Monitor*, noted that Naipaul's style was "explicit, keen for irony, though with a realism that involves some scatological detail."

After he had finished writing *A House for Mr Biswas*, Naipaul began a seven-month, expense-paid tour of the West Indies at the invitation of the Trinidad government. From the journal of his observations in Trinidad, Suriname, British Guiana, and Jamaica, he wrote *The Middle Passage* (1962), a consideration of postcolonial decline. "Middle passage" was the name slave traders gave the slave-carrying voyages between Africa and the Caribbean. Naipaul used the phrase to describe the effect of three colonial cultures—British, Dutch, and French—upon the recent history of the Caribbean. These three nations established slave trades and slave-labor-based economies in their Caribbean colonies, which they abandoned when agitation, unrest, and distance made their administration impossible. This abandonment, says Naipaul, has been the cause of economic and political difficulty in the Caribbean.

Naipaul had returned to England briefly late in 1961 to write *The Middle Passage*. After its completion he left for a year-long tour of India. While in India he wrote his fourth novel, *Mr Stone and the Knights Companion* (1963), which was awarded the Hawthornden Prize in 1964. His first novel set in England, the book considers the impulse to create and the transforming quality of creation.

Mr. Stone, nearing retirement at age sixty-eight, begins to have disturbing intimations of death which disrupt the placid flow of his life. Reacting impulsively against the idea of his mortality, Mr. Stone marries and, while honeymooning in Cornwall, discovers the cause of his uneasiness. Having lunch at an inn, he and his wife encounter an old man whose retirement has robbed him of his reason to live.

Shaken, Mr. Stone returns home, where he conceives the plan for the Knights Companion, a program to ease with activity and camaraderie the loneliness and spiritual decline caused by retirement. He submits his proposal to Excal, his employer, and it is quickly accepted. Mr. Whymper, a young Research and Development man, turns the proposal into a public-relations and personnel-management coup by substituting extended service in the company for retirement benefits. Whymper's betrayal of Mr. Stone's original intention convinces Mr. Stone that his idea has no value. Concluding that "nothing that came out of the heart, nothing that was pure ought to be exposed," that "all he had done, and even the anguish he was feeling now was a betrayal of that good emotion" he had felt while working in his study to prepare his plan, Mr. Stone rejects the urge to create as disruptive and resigns himself to his approaching retirement.

Reviews of the book were mixed, but Naipaul was being given closer and more respectful reading since the success of *A House for Mr Biswas*, and reviewers appreciated his effort to gain a wider audience by writing about an English character. Naipaul had complained in his 1958 essay "London" that he felt he would have to write about sex, race, or a British or American character before he could hope to gain attention for his work, though he added that to write about sex would embarrass him, that race was too complex an issue, and that the introduction of a British character was "good business, but bad art." Compounding the difficulty of writing an English novel was the difference in temperament between the English and the Caribbeans. Wrote Naipaul, "in a warm country life is conducted out of doors. . . . In England everything goes on behind closed doors."

Naipaul did not understand the closed-door style of conducting business well enough to draw it accurately in *Mr Stone and the Knights Companion*. Walter Allen, in the *New York Review of Books*, noted that the book was "a very odd work that, despite its patent distinction, fails to satisfy. . . . What comes out . . . is the statement of a general truth rather than the vivid apprehension of a particular truth that sets up the shock of recognition in the reader."

Mr. Stone's rejection of the impulse to create marked his exhaustion with his project. Naipaul, at the time he was writing the book, was himself undergoing an exhausting ordeal of rejection. His tour of India, planned as a spiritual pilgrimage to the land of his family's heritage, proved to be a test of endurance that profoundly changed his view of himself and of the world. Naipaul's interest in India had been genealogical and sociological. His grandfather had come from India to Trinidad as an indentured laborer. By returning to India, Naipaul hoped to learn how well Indian sensibilities had survived in the rural Hindu communities of his home. He had rejected the provincial and religious values of his native Trinidad for England but had found no comfortable place for himself in English life or letters, other than his exotic value. India promised affirmation that he belonged to an older, richer culture than the colonial one that had failed to satisfy his needs.

He found instead that he could accept nothing Indian or Hindu. The poverty and squalor horrified him. The caste system, enforced by Hindu tenets of spiritual detachment and acceptance of fate, outraged him. India has not progressed, cannot progress, said Naipaul, because it limits itself too severely by absurd, outdated boundaries of tradition and religion that constrict intellectual growth. Throughout the account of his trip, *An Area of Darkness* (1964), Naipaul repeated his observation angrily, bitterly, and—after a visit to his grandfather's village, where he repudiated his kinship with India—wearily. Naipaul returned to Great Britain near the end of 1963; the trip to India, he concluded, "ought not to have been made; it had broken my life in two."

Naipaul had reached a pivotal point in his career. He had been traveling for nearly three years and had returned to England briefly while he wrote the accounts of his journeys. In London, where he had never truly felt he belonged, he came to the discomfiting realization that he was a former colonial cast adrift. Though critics considered his novels of Trinidad too exotic for the common taste, he had no genuine feeling for the English character. India had made such an overwhelmingly negative impression on him that he could not set his fiction there. What, then, was to be the subject of his writing? He decided once again to travel and, in 1965, left for Uganda, where he wrote *The Mimic Men* (1967), his first novel on the theme that now dominates his fiction and journalism—the rootlessness and debasing mimicry of the former colonial in a world of decaying values.

Naipaul wrote *The Mimic Men* in the style of a memoir. Ralph Singh, a Caribbean politician in exile, retires to the quiet of his hotel room to record his career. Convinced at the beginning that he can complete his memoir in a few weeks, Singh spends over four months in the writing but manages to find some order in his tumultuous past. He recalls his early days as a restless Caribbean scholarship student in London, where he met Sandra, an English girl whose rejection of her family's class and values had made her feel alien and alone. They had felt the common bond of their alienation and, at Sandra's suggestion, had married. After the wedding they had returned to Isabella, a fictional island modeled on Trinidad.

Singh next considers the history of his childhood and learns that, as a child, he had been "sunk in the taint of fantasy." From his reading in the history of Aryan migrations, he had created an image of himself as the leader of a warrior horde sweeping on horseback across the plains and snowy steppes of central Asia. This image solaced him against the shame of his father's notoriety as Gurudeva, the charismatic leader of a short-lived political movement which espoused a Hindu pastoral way of life. Though his status as the son of Gurudeva had greatly embarrassed him in his youth, Singh later benefited from it when he entered politics.

Back on Isabella, Singh had made a fortune in real-estate speculation, built a Roman-style house, and become disaffected from the society of the island's affluent aliens. Estrangement and divorce from Sandra had followed, and Singh soon afterward became involved in politics. He notes in his memoir that his life seems to have been an uninterrupted flow of events preparing him for this last great adventure.

Singh's political career had been brief. By playing upon the same cause that his father had championed—an end to the sense of shame at personal defeat and powerlessness—Singh helped elect a Negro schoolmate to the office of minister. But Singh's wealth and Asian heritage had made him suspect to his mostly black colleagues, and, when a crisis arose, they sacrificed him. Dispatched to Great Britain to negotiate a treaty for the nationalization of Isabella's bauxite mines, Singh learned that his party had sent him to be the scapegoat for a failed campaign promise. While he dallied in England with the daughter of a lord, the party circulated rumors that he had taken bribes. Singh returned to Isabella long enough to be expelled from the country with his luggage and a small fraction of his fortune.

The Mimic Men has two themes—the frustration of the former colonial, who feels he can only mimic the example of an established culture, and the power of art to transform disorder into order. Singh discovers he can face the pain and confusion of his life by understanding the recurring patterns that characterize it. A prizewinning triumph for Naipaul—the work received the W. H. Smith Award in 1968—*The Mimic Men* impressed many critics. "Mr. Naipaul sees both the futility and the comedy in the lives he portrays. The comedy is subtle, often in the manner of Joyce Cary or Evelyn Waugh, and carefully concealed in a complex fabric of minute observation and of polished expression," wrote Arthur Curley in *Library Journal*.

The *Times Literary Supplement* reviewer called the book "commonwealth literature" and noted that it "discusses, evokes and exemplifies the situation of the former dependencies with such vigour and intensity that the vague, sometimes patronizing description is given a fresh dignity. . . ." Naipaul's reputation as a mature and important commentator on the drift of the modern world was now firmly established.

Naipaul gathered his early short stories and a screen story into the collection *A Flag on the Island* in 1967. The title story was his first attempt to write for the screen, and it was unsuccessful. Set on a nameless island in the Caribbean, "A Flag on the Island" refines the theme of colonial mimicry.

Frank, the American narrator stranded on the island by the approach of Hurricane Irene, recalls that during World War II American soldiers stationed there "brought the tropics to the island." Frank recalls that he had imported his

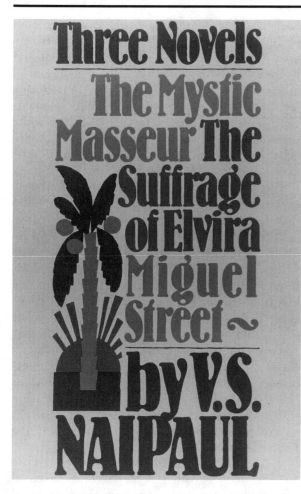

Dust jacket for the American collection of Naipaul's first three books, including the first publication in the United States of The Suffrage of Elvira

own illicit ideal of free enterprise to a small neighborhood whose residents had quickly turned their own quaintness into lucrative business. Feeling guilty over his responsibility in teaching the natives his American skill for turning a profit and at the same time ending the simple happiness of their lives, Frank becomes obsessed with his idea that the hurricane will destroy the island and restore it to the peace of earlier days.

Naipaul's history of Trinidad, *The Loss of El Dorado* (1969), is based on rare histories of the region and the Venezuelan Boundary Arbitration Papers in the British Museum. Focusing on two incidents from Trinidad's history—the island's use by the Spanish as the launching point for gold-hunting expeditions into South America, and the torture of a slave girl by an English governor of the island—Naipaul presents his argument that Trinidad has never recovered from the rottenness of its past and that the founding principles of greed and cruelty still operate behind the gai-

ety of its colorful tourist posters. The book is written in the style of a narrative and focuses on the motivation and meaning of actions taken by the Spanish and English in their administration of Trinidad as a colony.

Naipaul was awarded the Booker Prize in 1971 for his next work of fiction, widely celebrated as his most brilliant work since *A House for Mr Biswas*. *In a Free State* (1971) is made up of two stories and the title novella set between two episodes from Naipaul's travel journals. This work treats exclusively the problems of people "in a free state" who pay for their freedom with alienation, loneliness, and a loss of identity.

Santosh, in the story "One Out Of Many," is alarmed to learn that his employer has taken a diplomatic post in Washington, D.C. Although he is uncertain that his job as personal cook will be as highly regarded in Washington as it is in Bombay, Santosh is certain that if he remains in India he will lose not only his job but his cherished sense of identity. Forsaking Bombay, he convinces his master to take him to the United States. In Washington he learns that he is one among many and that his greatest fear has come to pass; gaining his freedom comes at the cost of his idea of himself: "All that my freedom has brought me is the knowledge that I have a face and have a body, that I must feed this body and clothe this body for a certain number of years. Then it will be over."

"Tell Me Who To Kill," the story of a man who has traded the provincial limitations of his Caribbean home for the uncertainties of London life, has none of the poignant humor of "One Out Of Many." On his brother's wedding day, as he dines with the family of the English bride, he considers the dreams and disappointments of his life that have made him a bitter, ruined man.

"In a Free State," set in Africa, paints an ugly portrait of the expatriate civil servant Bobby, whose homosexuality had set him apart in London and led to a nervous breakdown. Sent to Africa for therapy, Bobby claims that the combination of service to Africa and the adventure of living in a different culture has made him a better man. When a civil war breaks out, Bobby is forced to flee across country to the safety of the consular compound with Linda, the wife of a diplomat. As he berates Linda for her reasons for coming to Africa, it becomes evident that his own motives are less than pure. He exploits Africans and Africa to assuage his guilt and confusion at being outcast because of his homosexuality. Adventure and sexual gratification are his true goals, and he feels that Africa owes him these things in payment for his service. Other expatriates encountered on the trip to the compound seem to have the same selfish notion that service entitles them to abuse Africans with impunity. Bobby's exploitation and abuse are repaid near the end of the story, just as he nears the safety of the compound, when African soldiers savagely beat him.

The prologue and epilogue to *In a Free State*, taken from journal accounts of two different trips to Egypt, serve to draw the stories together. The prologue records a trip to Cairo by ship, aboard which Naipaul witnessed the persecution of a graceless old English tramp by his Lebanese, Egyptian, and German bunkmates. The epilogue considers several episodes of a journey to Luxor from Milan. In both cities Naipaul encountered a Red Chinese acrobatic troupe whose presence soothed the anger and sense of futility he had experienced in his dealings with the older civilizations of Italy and Egypt.

In a Free State was followed by *"The Overcrowded Barracoon"* (1972), a selection of Naipaul's essays and journalism written between 1958 and 1972. The overcrowded barracoon, or temporary slave-holding barracks, of the title is the former French colony of Mauritius, where overpopulation, growing unemployment, and a weak agricultural economy have created a bleak and potentially dangerous political situation for the governments of the island and of France. Other articles survey the political climate of the smaller Caribbean islands, such as Antigua, Grenada, and Saint Kitts. Naipaul also included impressions of his visit to the United States, his early consideration of his place in English letters, and previously uncollected articles about India.

Naipaul's novel *Guerrillas* (1975) is based on ugly actual events he had reported in the article "Michael X and the Black Power Killings in Trinidad," published in 1973. In the novel Jimmy Ahmed, a Black Power revolutionary, Roche, a white South African activist, and Jane, a white, middle-aged woman caught up in the excitement of political intrigue, become involved in an unsavory relationship of personal gratification and power play. None seems genuinely interested in the revolution Jimmy has started. As an epigraph to the novel, Naipaul quotes from the writing of Jimmy Ahmed: "When everybody wants to fight there's nothing to fight for. Everybody wants to fight his own little war, everybody is a guerrilla."

Each character fights his battle at the expense of his professed ideal, but Jane pays the ultimate price for Jimmy's self-aggrandizement and Roche's paralyzing indecision. To regain control of his disintegrating commune, Jimmy reasserts his claim to revolutionary power and demands sacrifices to the cause. Because she is a white woman, and because Roche is considered an enemy, Jane's sexual involvement with both men makes her a convenient victim.

Naipaul wrote in his preface to *"The Return of Eva Perón"* with *"The Killings in Trinidad"* (1980) that the essays collected there "bridged a creative gap: from the end of 1970 to the end of 1973 no novel offered itself to me." *Guerrillas*, though well written and well made, hardly seems to have offered itself to him. By basing his work on actual events instead of memories of personal experience, as he had done in the past, Naipaul wrote what could be called a historical novel. This may account for the sterility of his presentation. Naipaul's narrative is clinical, disengaged; he expresses neither sympathy nor contempt for his characters and makes it clear that he does not wish to be associated with them in any way. His neutral prose expressed only the absurdity of the historical lesson.

The suspension of India's constitution in 1976 brought Naipaul back for a second consideration of that country the same year. The series of essays he wrote while there was collected under the title *India: A Wounded Civilization* and published in 1977. In his foreword Naipaul explained why his series has such a strong personal focus: "India is for me a difficult country. It isn't my home and cannot be my home; and yet I cannot reject it or be indifferent to it; I cannot travel only for the sights. . . . An inquiry about India . . . has to be an inquiry about attitudes; it has to be an inquiry about the civilization itself." Naipaul concluded that, because in himself there survived "phantasmal memories of old India which . . . outline a whole vanished world," the starting point of his inquiry must be himself.

Naipaul had not forgotten the lesson of his 1962-1963 tour. In *India: A Wounded Civilization* he further elaborated upon his conclusion that the Indian traditions of caste and Hindu belief are impeding progress there when he described Indian nationalism as a return to archaism. "The sentimental conviction that India is eternal and forever revives," Naipaul contended, serves as the basis for the continuing survival of the caste system, which Indian intellectuals associate with the glories of their history. By returning to the traditions of the past, they feel, India can regain the glory of early days. Naipaul viewed this idea as the greatest failure of the Indian intellectual, for promoting a return to archaic values encourages an indifference not only to failure but to success as well.

This work aroused more controversy than Naipaul's first report, which was not as bitterly condemnatory. Many reviewers questioned the validity of his arguments and the bleakness of his outlook. L. A. Gordon, writing in *Nation*, found Naipaul's "dismissals of Indian efforts . . . much too comprehensive" and cautioned that Naipaul's "view of India is part of a larger pessimistic vision of the human condition today." Shernaz Mollinger called the work "a perceptive, humane, and moral book" after noting that Naipaul's anger seemed "the only possible honorable attitude—one certainly more moral and far healthier than either the Western observer's usual ironic detachment or the Indian's placid acceptance of the continuing human horror that constitutes his country."

An essay he wrote in 1975, "A New King for the Congo: Mobutu and the Nihilism of Africa," formed the basis for Naipaul's novel *A Bend in the River* (1979), currently favored by critics as his best book. It is set in the town of Kisangani, which is modeled on Zaire, and represents the political upheaval of Central Africa. Salim, an East Indian Muslim, comes to Kisangani to open a store he has bought. In the space of the ten years he lives there, Salim watches the rise of the new Africa, personified in Ferdinand, who is taken from the bush, educated at the college called the Domain, and sent to the capital to participate in the building of a modern Africa.

Salim had arrived in the town not long after it had been razed by postrevolutionary violence. All reminders that European imperialists had previously built there had been pulled down, and the bleak little town of Kisangani had been erected on the ruin. Salim's outlook on the success of the current government is pessimistic, and he hordes ivory should flight become necessary. At the same time, he begins an affair with the Belgian wife of a professor at the Domain. Forced to flee Kisangani when an impending visit by the president, modeled on Mobutu Sese Seko, panics the incompetent officials whose lives it threatens, Salim makes his escape on a steamboat.

The reviewer in *Choice* wrote that the book "may be the most accurate available single account of what life feels like in parts of Central Africa." Irving Howe noted in the *New York Times Book Review* that *A Bend in the River* was "a much better and deeper novel" than *Guerrillas*—though it lacked the excitement of that novel—because Naipaul had "mastered the gift of creating an aura of psychic and moral tension." Other reviewers praised Naipaul as "one of the best writers now at work" and called the book "a classic dark satire," the effort of a "playful, serious mind at work on the grim stuff of modern life."

Two of the four essays collected in *"The Return of Eva Perón"* formed the bases of Naipaul's two latest novels. "The Return of Eva Perón" is a series of articles written between 1972 and 1977 when Naipaul several times toured South America. The publisher's note adequately summarizes Naipaul's view of Argentine society: "a sterile, second-hand society vandalized by inflation, corruption, and the illusion of being European, where an expensively embalmed Eva Perón is trotted out to glamorize the 'new Perónism.'" In the concluding essay of the collection, "Conrad's Darkness," Naipaul discusses the writer's purpose. He notes that "the novel as a form no longer carries conviction," that "experimentation, not aimed at the real difficulties, has corrupted response." Naipaul feels that the real difficulty for a writer is to make his fiction work, to create from his imagination and experience books that awaken "the sense of true wonder."

In 1979 Naipaul began a seven-month tour of Asia to visit the Islamic states of Pakistan, Malaysia, and Indonesia. Out of this trip came *Among the Believers: An Islamic Journey* (1981). Anecdotal and perceptive, full of sharply drawn characters and rich physical detail, *Among the Believers* nevertheless lacks the sympathy, humor, or the desire to understand different viewpoints that characterized Naipaul's earlier travel writing. His view of Islam as the religion of fanatics who substitute crude faith for reason, who destroy the benefits of Western civilization as satanic only to replace them with their own barbaric code, colors his judgment of everyone he meets and every project he visits. From the opening pages, when he expresses his unhappiness with the man who was to drive him to Qom, Naipaul's dislike and distrust grow.

Reviewers were critical of Naipaul's tone. Fred Halliday noted in *Nation* the "skepticism, which, as in his books about India, frames and sours often acute observation." Halliday added that Naipaul's pessimism caused him to miss "the role that Islam plays not just in the fantasies of intellectuals but in the ideological consolidation of Third World states. . . . Naipaul underplays or perhaps misses the forms of foreign domination to which the Islamic revival is a deeply felt, if catastrophic, response." R. R. Harris, writing for *Saturday Review*, observed that "Naipaul is . . . a comic writer. When he keeps ironic distance, he tells wonderful, subtle stories that explain why people act the way they do. But when his sense of humor wanes, his bitterness, his impatience, his feeling of superiority become embarrassingly obvious. And this leads to quick sweeping judgments." However, Naipaul's views on Islam may have won him favor in Israel. In April 1983 he was awarded the Jerusalem Prize.

Finding the Centre (1984) contains two personal narratives that have as their subject "the process of writing" and "seek in different ways to admit the reader to that process." Naipaul's "Prologue to an Autobiography" recounts his beginnings as a writer; "The Crocodiles of Yamoussoukro" is an account of his 1982 visit to the Ivory Coast, an African nation that had enjoyed a stable government for more than twenty years. "The Crocodiles of Yamoussoukro" also tells something about how and why Naipaul travels.

Naipaul undertook his trip to the Ivory Coast primarily to study an African political and economic system that had succeeded for nearly twenty years under black rule, and to enjoy the glamour of France, its mother country, in Africa. These professed reasons soon became secondary as Naipaul became fascinated with manifestations of African belief in the spirit world: the nighttime of power when the spirit leaves the body to accomplish all things; the totemic crocodiles of President Houphouët-Boigny, to which sacrifice is made for the assurance of power; the spirit-exorcising Celestial Christians, who saved the house of a schoolteacher from burning; the language of ancestral drums which are the seat of tribal power. Naipaul found in this spiritual belief a completeness that he had never before thought existed in Africa and that he could relate to his knowledge of Trinidad's slave culture. His tone of good-humored fascination and openness to ideas he had previously rejected allowed him greater ease with natives and expatriates than he had previously shown and was a marked improvement over the prejudice and impatience of his Islamic tour. His bleak view that the Ivory Coast would, sometime in the future, go the same bloody way that other African nations have gone

was not urgently stated and did not overshadow the upbeat spirit of his narrative. Some reviewers noted the change of tone as a mellowing of spirit and ascribed it to either weariness or age—Naipaul turned fifty in 1982.

"Prologue to an Autobiography" is, writes Naipaul, "what its title says. It is not an autobiography, a story of a life or deeds done. It is an account of something less easily seized: my literary beginnings and the imaginative promptings of my many-sided background." Naipaul cast the work in six sections, the first re-creating the wretchedness and uncertainty he felt during the writing of his first important story. Included in other sections are a consideration of Naipaul's debt to his father for the desire to become a writer, a report of Naipaul's 1977 visit to the distant relative who inspired the story of Bogart, an investigation of Seepersad Naipaul's breakdown and the part his wife's family played in the humiliation that ended his newswriting career, and a brief sketch of his father's early years in Trinidad. This work is informed by a spirit of wonder that a writer could be made from a many-sided and seemingly unfavorable cultural background.

With "Prologue to an Autobiography" Naipaul had reached a point in his career at which he could deal with the personal concerns that had influenced much of his life—the essay, in fact, can be considered a short, meditative introduction to his next book. *The Enigma of Arrival* (1987) is a novel in five sections recounting the career of a Trinidad-born author of East Indian extraction who, at age eighteen, departs the island for an education in England. One section sketches the twenty-year journey of an arduous career, beginning with the author's arrival in London wanting only to become a writer and concluding with his intellectual and emotional collapse following the failure of a particularly difficult book. The other four sections detail the writer's recovery of stability and health in the Wiltshire countryside of England.

"The Journey," the section which elaborates material from "Prologue to an Autobiography," is the most satisfying of the five. The author's presentation of details from his early career re-creates admirably the ferment of ambition and pride that drove him to collapse. Although Naipaul argues that *The Enigma of Arrival* is fiction, he is easily recognizable, to anyone familiar with the essentials of his life, as the distressed and wearied narrator. Less satisfying is the account of ten years on the grounds of a decayed English manor home which comprises the novel's other four sections. Numbingly repetitive in his descriptions of the landscape and its effect upon him, the narrator crosses and recrosses territory that he gradually comes to realize is as disordered as his native land. While the frenzied disorder of Trinidad and the narrator's frantic efforts to escape it had unsettled his life, the complacent decay of the English countryside, with its history and empire crumbling back into the soil that nurtured it, restores his equilibrium.

Reviewers were generally favorable, with all commenting on the autobiographical aspects of the work. Many marveled at the engrossing power of Naipaul's prose. Alan Brien, in a review for *New Statesman*, said that Naipaul's "style is nigglingly precise.... he picks up words like an antiquary collecting shards, turning them over and over to let every angle catch the light." He noted, however, that, due to the extreme care with which Naipaul considered his surroundings, "*The Enigma of Arrival* is one of those books . . . which irritates, tires and confuses while also exciting, informing and satisfying. The defects are almost as important as the excellences because what is valuable here is the inside story of the development of an exceptional writer."

Derek Walcott, in his long, meditative review of the book for *New Republic*, noted that "To detail the plot of this non-autobiography/non-novel would be to consider it by the very terms it avoids. If nothing happens in it, or, rather, if what happens takes place across a fence, or on the far side of a field, that is in fact how life itself is . . . our own egocentricity absorbs other people's tragedies as interruptions or irritations. *The Enigma of Arrival* is mercilessly honest in its self-centeredness, in its seasonal or eruptive sadnesses. It is as true as life, in the terrible sense that nothing really concerns us."

Frank Kermode cautioned, in the *New York Times Book Review*, that "a prodigious talent might be damaged by too much solemn scrutiny" but reminded readers that "if you believe an author has real stature you really have to trust him, to believe that he chose to do it this way, after long meditation, because this was the shape that was needed if the writing of the experience was to be itself a valid experience. Mr. Naipaul has done enough over the past 30 years to earn that trust."

In 1986 Naipaul was awarded the Ingersoll Foundation's T. S. Eliot Award. Additionally in 1986 Naipaul abruptly and without explanation

dropped his English publisher of twenty-nine years, André Deutsch. Naipaul enjoyed another first with this book—bestsellerdom. He became widely known in the United States thanks to the popularity of *The Enigma of Arrival*, and, with publication of *A Turn in the South* (1989), interest in his other works greatly increased.

A Turn in the South recounts Naipaul's five-month journey through seven states in the American South to investigate race, roots, and religion in a region strikingly similar to his Trinidad homeland in its history of slavery and defeat. Naipaul was most deeply impressed by the large part religion contributes to the southern sense of rootedness and devoted many of his pages to discussion of the various types of faith that bind people to the idea of home. Naipaul visited Charleston, South Carolina, to get the white perspective on slavery and current race relations. In Alabama he spent time at Tuskegee Institute and examined the empathy his father had felt for Booker T. Washington and his struggle to found a school for the advancement of his race. In Nashville, Tennessee, Naipaul discussed the meaning and import of country music with various songwriters and commentators on the subject. In Jackson, Mississippi, a fellow named Campbell gave Naipaul a lengthy, lyrical character analysis of the redneck. Naipaul was fascinated by this southern character type and decided he liked rednecks for their spirited independence and cavalier style.

In his review of the book for *Atlantic Monthly*, Nicolas Lemann noted that Naipaul's writing is "clear and beautiful, and he has a great eye for nuance. He lacks the traditional reporter's skills.... But he extracts what seems to be the maximum possible insight from every encounter.... Many years of intense travel and reading have given him the ability to put everything in a larger context." Eugene Genovese, considering Naipaul's book in the larger context of southern history in his review for *New Republic*, said that Naipaul had contributed "mightily to our understanding of a deep and religiously grounded community, or congeries of communities, that doggedly holds to God, the family, law and order . . . and to explosive resentment against outside interference in its affairs."

Although Naipaul had said that *A Turn in the South* would be his last travel book, almost immediately after he had submitted the book to his publisher he commenced research on the next, departing for his third trip to India, to be amid the racial and political upheavals currently galvanizing the subcontinent. He traveled widely there for nearly a year. *India: A Million Mutinies Now* (1990) is Naipaul's lengthiest and most sympathetic study of his ancestral homeland. The assertions of caste, religious sectarianism, and racial separatism among various factions have fractured India. Naipaul expresses deep satisfaction that, for perhaps the first time, the Indian sense of the past has worked to stir pride and create a desire for change rather than acquiescence to the way things are. India has awakened to the glories of its past, he concludes, and has thus seen a way to realize the potential of its future.

Reviewers were pleased that Naipaul seemed, at last, to have made his peace with India. Citing the injured and angry tone of his first two works about India as indicative of Naipaul's uncertainty about the place in the development of his East Indian heritage, many reviewers admired the mature and more objective viewpoint Naipaul was able to assume in this work. James Buchan, in the *Spectator*, said that Naipaul's "greatest gift is his talent for understanding how a person's view of the world enlarges and narrows, how time and the movement of generations change families. The best passages in this book describe places . . . where we would see just teeming people but Naipaul sees communities struggling to escape or accommodate change." Bhikhu Parekh, in *New Statesman*, said that Naipaul "brings out both the contradictions of modern Indian life and the way they are glossed over or lived with. Approaching India with all five senses at full alert . . . and gently letting a critical and affectionate intelligence guide and coordinate them, he probes opaque individuals, situations, relations, places and movements with characteristic penetration and intensity. No student of modern India can afford to ignore this book." Naipaul gained wider recognition in the United States for his work following publication of *The Enigma of Arrival*, with critics expressing greatest admiration for *A House for Mr Biswas*, *A Bend in the River*, and *Among the Believers*. Edward Hoagland, in his review of *Finding the Centre*, remarked that this is because Naipaul's "previously dependable flaying of the third world nations he visited has made him popular with sectors of the American intellectual community who do not ordinarily pay much attention to contemporary novelists, and he has developed here the odd celebrity of an Erskine Caldwell in Russia: brilliant local portraiture being touted for pur-

poses of disparagement as an accurate picture of a whole continent." However fashionable Naipaul's bitterness toward Islam or the bleakness of his vision of the Third World's future may be in the United States, or however unpopular in the rest of the world, fashion is neither the purpose nor the concern of his art. His opinions are those of a curious, intelligent, apolitical outsider who cannot and will not be deluded. Hoagland notes that Naipaul often "thinks through his companions' opinions more precisely than they themselves have done," that he is "both merciless and emphatic as he watches." Naipaul travels and writes to find the center of motivation—of nations and of himself. If observation proves that bitterness and bleakness of opinion seem warranted, that is what he expresses, as clearly and concisely as he knows how.

Since 1961, when he first began to travel, Naipaul's range of interest has broadened but his worldview has grown bleaker; the troubled Third World nations he has visited have taxed his sensibilities and, perhaps, worn him out with anger and frustration that the Western civilization he loves has not benefited but beleaguered these nations. He has said many times that he has become an intelligent writer rather than an emotional one because he wishes to protect himself from the violence of his reaction to what he has seen. The characters he has created in later novels, such as Roche in *Guerrillas* and Salim in *A Bend in the River*, share a weariness, a pessimism, a confusion that limits the range of their response to the tumult of their worlds. Both seem capable only of preparing for the fall of doom and waiting for their slim chance to escape ruin. And though they escape, they surrender vitality to caution and settle into restricted, joyless lives.

Naipaul's fiction after 1961 has almost inevitably become less humorous, and he regrets this. In his foreword to the 1983 edition of *A House for Mr Biswas*, a work that contains, he says, "some of my funniest writing," Naipaul admits that he has "no higher literary ambition than to write a piece of comedy that might complement or match this early book." The humor of his books prior to 1961—an emotional comment on the ironies and difficulties of his early life on Trinidad—has a vitality that allows his characters a wider, more accommodating response to hardship.

Finding the Centre and *The Enigma of Arrival* reveal humor, compassion, open-hearted sympathy, and open-minded interest that have long been absent from Naipaul's writing. He seems willing to believe that childhood on Trinidad may have helped, more than hindered, him in his ambition to be a writer, that life there gave him the special vision that characterizes his writing. He seems ready, after years of bleak pessimism, to write comically again. And crossing the bar of middle age has encouraged him to look back not nostalgically but thoughtfully on the influences of his past: "To write was to learn. Beginning a book, I always felt I was in possession of all the facts about myself; at the end I was always surprised." Though the surprise has not always been a pleasant one for him, it has always made worthwhile the hard half of a writer's job, the discovery of himself.

Bibliography:

Kelvin Jarvis, *V. S. Naipaul: A Selective Bibliography with Annotations, 1957-1987* (Metuchen, N.J.: Scarecrow Press, 1989).

References:

Michael Gilkes, *The West Indian Novel* (Boston: G. K. Hall, 1981), pp. 91-102;

Robert Hamner, *Critical Perspectives on V. S. Naipaul* (Washington, D.C.: Three Continents Press, 1977);

Hamner, *V. S. Naipaul* (New York: Twayne, 1973);

Bruce King, "V. S. Naipaul," in *West Indian Literature*, edited by King (Hamden, Conn.: Archon Books, 1979), pp. 161-178;

Kerry McSweeny, "V. S. Naipaul: Clear-sightedness and Sensibility," in his *Four Contemporary Novelists* (Kingston & Montreal: McGill-Queen's University Press, 1983), pp. 151-195;

Karl Miller, "V. S. Naipaul and the New Order: A View of *The Mimic Men*," in *Critics on Caribbean Literature*, edited by Edward Baugh (New York: St. Martin's Press, 1978), pp. 75-83;

Modern Fiction Studies, 30 (Autumn 1984), special Naipaul issue;

Robert K. Morris, *Paradoxes of Order: Some Perspectives on the Fiction of V. S. Naipaul* (Columbia: University of Missouri Press, 1975);

David Omerod, " 'Unaccommodated Man': Naipaul's B. Wordsworth and Biswas," in *Critics on Caribbean Literature*, edited by Baugh (New York: St. Martin's Press, 1978), pp. 87-92;

Kenneth Ramchand, "A House for Mr Biswas," in his *An Introduction to the Study of West Indian Literature* (Kingston: Thomas Nelson & Sons, Ltd., 1976);

Michael Thorpe, *V. S. Naipaul* (Essex: Longman Group, Ltd., 1976);

William Walsh, *V. S. Naipaul* (Edinburgh: Oliver & Boyd, 1973);

Landeg White, *V. S. Naipaul: A Critical Introduction* (London: Macmillan, 1975).

Edna O'Brien
(15 December 1932 -)

This entry was written by Patricia Boyle Haberstroh (La Salle College) for
DLB 14: British Novelists Since 1960: Part Two.

BOOKS: *The Country Girls* (London: Hutchinson, 1960; New York: Knopf, 1960);

The Lonely Girl (London: Cape, 1962; New York: Random House, 1962); republished as *Girl with Green Eyes* (London: Penguin, 1964);

Girls in their Married Bliss (London: Cape, 1964; New York: Simon & Schuster, 1968);

August Is a Wicked Month (London: Cape, 1965; New York: Simon & Schuster, 1965);

Casualties of Peace (London: Cape, 1966; New York: Simon & Schuster, 1967);

The Love Object (London: Cape, 1968; New York: Knopf, 1969);

A Pagan Place (London: Weidenfeld & Nicolson, 1970; New York: Knopf, 1970);

Zee & Co.: A Novel (London: Weidenfeld & Nicolson, 1971);

Night (London: Weidenfeld & Nicolson, 1972; New York: Knopf, 1973);

A Pagan Place: A Play (London: Faber & Faber, 1973);

A Scandalous Woman and Other Stories (London: Weidenfeld & Nicolson, 1974; New York: Harcourt Brace Jovanovich, 1974);

Mother Ireland, text by O'Brien, photographs by Fergus Bourke (London: Weidenfeld & Nicolson, 1976; New York: Harcourt Brace Jovanovich, 1976);

Johnny I Hardly Knew You (London: Weidenfeld & Nicolson, 1977); republished as *I Hardly Knew You* (Garden City, N.Y.: Doubleday, 1978);

Arabian Days, text by O'Brien, photographs by Gerard Klijan (London & New York: Quartet Books, 1977);

Seven Novels and Other Short Stories (London: Collins, 1978);

Mrs. Reinhardt and Other Stories (London: Weidenfeld & Nicolson, 1978); republished as *A Rose in the Heart* (Garden City, N.Y.: Doubleday, 1979);

Virginia (London: Hogarth Press, 1981; revised,

Edna O'Brien (photograph by Mark Gerson)

San Diego: Harcourt Brace Jovanovich, 1985);

The Dazzle (London: Stodder & Houghton, 1981);

Returning (London: Weidenfeld & Nicolson, 1982);

The Rescue (London: Stodder & Houghton, 1983);

A Fanatic Heart (London: Weidenfeld & Nicolson, 1984; New York: Farrar Straus Giroux, 1984);

Tales for the Telling (London: Pavilion, 1986; New York: Atheneum, 1986);

298

The Country Girls Trilogy and Epilogue (New York: Farrar Straus Giroux, 1986; London: Cape, 1987);

The High Road (London: Weidenfeld & Nicolson, 1988; New York: Farrar Straus Giroux, 1988);

On the Bone (Warwick: Greville Press, 1989);

Lantern Slides (London: Weidenfeld & Nicolson, 1990; New York: Farrar Straus Giroux, 1990);

Time and Tide (New York: Farrar Straus Giroux, 1992).

PLAY PRODUCTIONS: *A Cheap Bunch of Nice Flowers*, London, New Arts Theatre, 20 November 1962;

A Pagan Place, London, Royal Court Theatre, 2 November 1972;

Virginia, Stratford, Ontario, Stratford Shakespeare Festival, July 1980.

MOTION PICTURES: *Girl with Green Eyes*, adapted from O'Brien's *The Lonely Girl*, Woodfall Production, 1964;

Time Lost and Time Remembered, by O'Brien and Desmond Davis, adapted from O'Brien's short story "A Woman at the Seaside," Rank, 1966;

Three into Two Won't Go, adapted from the novel by Andrea Newman, Universal, 1969;

X Y and Zee, adapted from *Zee & Co.*, Columbia, 1971.

OTHER: *A Cheap Bunch of Nice Flowers*, in *Plays of the Year*, volume 26, edited by J. C. Trewin (New York: Ungar, 1963);

Some Irish Loving: A Selection, edited by O'Brien (London: Weidenfeld & Nicolson, 1979; New York: Harper & Row, 1979).

SELECTED PERIODICAL PUBLICATIONS—
UNCOLLECTED: "Dear Mr. Joyce," *Audience*, 1 (July-August 1971): 75-77;

"Joyce & Nora," *Harper's*, 261 (September 1980): 60-64.

As a contemporary novelist Edna O'Brien is in the unique position of appealing to two audiences: she has attracted the attention of a high-brow literary establishment and of a popular audience that eagerly awaits each new novel. Her short stories have appeared frequently in the *New Yorker*, but she has also been published in *Ladies' Home Journal, Redbook*, and *Cosmopolitan*.

Among literary critics, opinion on O'Brien's fiction is divided. Reviewed by John Updike, V. S. Naipaul, and Anthony Burgess, among others, her work has drawn judgments ranging from charges that she writes "meretricious trash" or "Gothic malarkey" to comments on her "extraordinary effectiveness and power."

This broad range of audience and opinion arises both from O'Brien's subject matter and from her attitude toward her work. In a 1970 interview with Barbara Bannon, O'Brien stated that she was "very much against literature as such but for the written word with color and life and air in it." Certainly there is color and life in her work. By 1969 five of her novels, branded obscene and pornographic, had been banned in her native Ireland. These novels, and the ones to follow, often brutally and realistically chart a course of affairs where her heroines' emotional and sexual frustrations sometimes lead them into casual sex and liaisons with married men, young priests, and other women. What Stanley Kauffman calls her "lyrics of the loins" created a stir in some quarters, a full-blown scandal in others. How a nice, Irish Catholic convent girl could write so explicitly about sex and so often about despair and disappointment intrigued many critics and readers. The Irish censors, who in banning had promoted many other twentieth-century literary figures, turned their full force against Ireland's latest exile.

The confessional nature of much of O'Brien's prose has likewise led to speculation that little distance separates her work from her life. When asked by Ludovic Kennedy in 1976 how close her stories were to her own life, O'Brien answered: "They're quite close, but they're not as close as they seem. If you write in the first person, which I often do, and if you have a slightly confessional voice—you know, rather than the epistle voice—it looks like that.... I think writing, especially semi-autobiographical writing, is the life you might have liked to have had." Talking with Nell Dunn eleven years earlier, O'Brien had also stressed how "close to fantasy writing is" and had suggested that she herself had "pursued pain and humiliation" and emerged to write about it.

Every work Edna O'Brien has written has focused on women, from her first novel, *The Country Girls* (1960), to *Virginia*, a play adapted from the diaries of Virginia Woolf and produced at the Stratford (Ontario) Shakespeare Festival in 1980 and in London at the Haymarket Theatre in 1981. Year after year O'Brien has drawn portraits of frustrated women dependent on men, struggling to emerge from the trap that society has set for them and into which they have walked almost willingly, though sometimes unconsciously or indifferently. The prototypical O'Brien fictional family emerges in her novels: irresponsible, drunken, Irish father; martyred, submissive mother; cold, detached, cruel husband; lonely, frightened wife; and children about to be sucked into this ongoing cycle. Focusing on the predominant themes of love and sex, O'Brien has explored how these have affected and conditioned the relationships of parents and children, husbands and wives, men and women.

In most of her fiction O'Brien deliberately highlights the sexual drives and attitudes of her heroines. These women, especially Irish women indoctrinated at an early age to the sinfulness of sex, explore many responses in their struggles to come to terms with their sexual selves. Taught by mothers to submit to men and warned by their church to remain chaste, they soon find themselves rejected by lovers and humiliated by husbands. Consequently, they move through tangled lives, often courting a deliberate wantonness while still searching for Prince Charming, the man with whom they can live happily ever after. That such happiness is impossible echoes through every page of O'Brien's work.

Like sex, love for O'Brien's heroines is a craving. The quest for someone to love is revealed in family interactions: in the child's search for a loving father or father substitute; in the young woman's ambiguous feelings toward a mother whose love she wants but whose legacy she rejects; and in parents, especially mothers, clinging to their children despite inevitable breaches, seeking in them an antidote to the unhappiness of their adult worlds. These women want to be mothers, but they reject the rigid domestic role defined for them; they seek not only lovers and husbands, but love, and are continually disappointed. O'Brien's blend of lyrical realism, most often rendered through a female narrator, defines a sensibility, a tone, an attitude distinctly female.

Edna O'Brien was born 15 December 1932, one of four children of Michael and Lena Cleary O'Brien, in Taumgraney, county Clare, in the rural west of Ireland. In *Mother Ireland* (1976) she describes her years growing up in "a town in a townland that bordered on other townlands of equal indistinctiveness." Her memories include

her picture of a "sad irresponsible father" and a sacrificial mother. Not until later, she remarks, did she see them as characters in the drama enacted not only in her home but also in the village, and later in what she calls "the treacherous world" beyond county Clare. In her recollections of Taumgraney she remembers the men as cruel and cross, the women as tender and loving. O'Brien has spoken frequently of the village reading habits: women handing round books of romance, and three popular classics—*Gone With the Wind* (1936), *Rebecca* (1938), and *How Green Was My Valley* (1939)—circulated page by page throughout the village, providing escape from a place the novelist describes as "fervid, enclosed and catastrophic." Taumgraney was so enclosed that O'Brien's earliest dreams revolved around romantic fantasies of growing up, marrying the family workman, and settling comfortably into farm life.

Her education, "medieval" by her own accounts, began at the National School in Scariff, which she attended from 1936 to 1941. O'Brien filled her school days with excursions into the glories of the Irish past and her notebooks with "made-up people." At age twelve she continued her schooling at the Convent of Mercy at Loughrea, county Galway, where, trying to live in a self-created state of religious ecstasy, she spent some of her time dreaming up "superb acts of mortification" and the rest committing sins "by the hour." She revealed to Ludovic Kennedy that Jesus Christ, Dracula, and Heathcliff were the loves of her early life. O'Brien tells a prophetic story of being chosen for the coveted role of Our Lady of Fatima in a school play and of falling off the butter boxes she was standing on during the production, much to her own mortification and the nuns' anger. At this point, O'Brien claims, her visions of the Blessed Virgin began to wane, only to be replaced by new fantasies, among them a desire to become a film star.

In 1946 she left county Clare and arrived in Dublin with a suitcase bound with twine and a "head full of fancy." Settling in one of Dublin's poorer districts, she worked in a chemist shop by day and attended pharmaceutical lectures at night. In her first days in Dublin, O'Brien discovered a copy of *Introducing James Joyce* and was amazed that for the first time she had found a book that was exactly like her own life. During this time, "I could not decide," O'Brien reminisces, "whether to become a scholar or an adventuress." For a while she tried both, balancing the "nourishment of reading" with the delights of cinemas and pubs. Encouraged by Paedar O'Donnell, O'Brien grew more serious about writing and submitted her first pieces to the *Irish Press* in 1948.

In 1952, defying family and friends, O'Brien eloped with Ernest Gebler, another writer, and soon moved back to the country, to the mountains of county Wicklow. Her two sons, Carlos and Sacha, were born in 1952 and 1954. This marriage seems to have been doomed from the beginning; O'Brien claims she married in response to "a need for and dread of authority" in a "spirit of expiation and submissiveness." The marriage was dissolved in 1964.

O'Brien's move to London in 1959 with her two sons can be seen as another step in her quarrel with an Ireland she felt had warped her with fear and guilt and as a new stage in the continuing odyssey of seeking the person she wanted to be. While she was working as a manuscript reader in London, two publishers offered her a small sum of money to write a novel. *The Country Girls*, published in 1960 and still considered by many to be her best novel, was written in less than three weeks. This novel forms a trilogy with two that followed: *The Lonely Girl* (1962) and *Girls in their Married Bliss* (1964). By 1965 Ireland's country girl found herself the focus of attention in London literary circles.

The trilogy, which begins in a convent school and ends in London, certainly has autobiographical overtones. O'Brien's vivid descriptions in *Mother Ireland* of her life in the convent school, and later in Dublin, leave little doubt that many of the details and incidents in these novels derive from her personal experiences. With the two voices in this trilogy—the brazen, slightly loony Baba, wise (or so she thinks) to the ways of the world and the wiles of men, and the quieter, naive Kate, bullied by circumstances and especially by Baba—O'Brien establishes the two women who continue to appear in her fiction. Embarrassed by her family's poverty, Kate teams up with Baba, daughter of the village veterinarian, in a series of tragicomic adventures in search of sex and a romantic husband. As the trilogy opens, Kate's happiness at winning a scholarship to the convent diminishes after her mother, having left Kate's father and abandoned Kate to Baba's family, drowns in an accident. Alienated from a father whose drunkenness and cruelty have been the source of a good deal of childhood pain and worry, Kate is drawn to both Mr. Gentleman, a rich Dublin solicitor who visits his house in the village each weekend, and to Mr. Brennan, Baba's father, who protects Kate from her father's violence.

Dismissed from school after Baba writes a dirty comment about a nun and a priest on the back of a holy picture, Kate and Baba take off for Dublin, much as O'Brien herself had done, "the country girls brazening the big city." Soon settled in a boardinghouse, they set off on an orgy of smoking, dancing, pubs, and parties in the company of middle-aged men because, as Baba says, "young men have no bloody money." But their adventures come to a halt when Baba contracts tuberculosis. The novel ends with Kate suddenly realizing she has forgotten the anniversary of her mother's death, just as Mr. Gentleman deserts her under the cloud of his wife's nervous breakdown and threats from Kate's father.

The Country Girls sets the tone and theme for the other books in the trilogy. The loss of the mother, the family conflicts and strife, the series of desertions and disappointments in love, and Baba's ridiculing Kate's naiveté and poverty but dragging her along with the promise that soon they both will meet wonderful men establish the pattern for the other two novels.

The Lonely Girl, with Kate as narrator, continues to juxtapose the country girls. It opens with Baba (now recovered from illness) crashing a winetasting reception, pretending to be a representative from the magazine *Woman's Night*, and Kate standing beside her, mortified in the rubber boots she has to wear because she has stupidly left her shoes on the bus. Kate's introduction to Eugene Gaillard, a documentary filmmaker, quickly pulls her out of the tedious routine of the grocery shop, where she works, into a love affair. Soon, however, Kate discovers that Eugene has a wife and child, and later her father arrives to drag her back to the scorn of her Irish village and a priest who condemns her for walking the path of moral damnation. Kate escapes back to her lover, but the distance between them grows as Eugene begins to ridicule her peasant origins and Kate discovers the gulf between a man "of reason and brain" and a woman desperately desiring to be loved. Eventually Kate returns to Baba and her former lodgings just as Baba is off to England proclaiming, "Soho, that's where I'll see life." At the end of this novel both country girls are on a boat bound for England, Kate overwhelmed by her disappointment and loss, and Baba carrying pills ("in case we puke") and trying to figure out how to steal some towels. When they settle in England, Baba working in a big hotel, Kate in a delicatessen, Kate looks toward the future: "When I'm able to talk I imagine that I won't be so alone. . . ."

In the last novel of the trilogy, *Girls in their Married Bliss*, O'Brien alternates the voice of Baba with a third-person narrator for the final phase in the lives of the country girls. Speaking of her marriage to Frank, Baba explains: "I knew that I'd end up with him; he being rich and a slob and the sort of man who would buy you seasick tablets before you travelled." She ridicules her ignorant and foolish husband and confesses, without any sense of guilt, "Normally I'm praying he'll fall off a scaffold." Another narrator describes Kate's crumbling marriage, her gradual loss of her child, and her husband, who chooses another woman to replace her.

Baba and Kate are soon involved with other men, but these adventures lead again to tragedy. Baba meets the drummer Harvey, who boasts that he can make love to twenty-five women a night, and who insists, in one of the most hilarious scenes in the novel, on drumming her into an erotic frenzy. However, Harvey, a typical O'Brien male character, jilts Baba, leaving her pregnant. Meanwhile, on the verge of a breakdown, Kate finally reveals to her psychiatrist that she now sees her mother as a self-appointed martyr and blackmailer. Kate's own role as mother diminishes until, at the end of the novel, Eugene takes her son to Fiji. To a solicitor who asks why she married, Kate replies helplessly: "It seemed to be what I wanted." At the end of the novel, Kate, sterilized to avoid the risk of more children, plans to move back with Baba. Baba, ironically cornered in the end by "niceness, weakness, and dependence," sees Kate as "someone of whom too much had been cut away."

In the country girls trilogy O'Brien has used some of the experiences of her Irish past to construct a fictional world of women destroyed by their dependence on men. Perhaps the most successful character O'Brien has ever created, and certainly the most humorous, Baba seems to have the best chance for survival in this world: she lies her way in and out of situations with the craziest of stories, steals from the refrigerators of men she sleeps with, and asks for very little: "I don't expect parents to fit you out with anything other than a birth certificate, and an occasional pair of new shoes." Of her marriage to Frank, Baba says: "I don't hate him, I don't love him, I put up with him and he puts up with me." But

Dust jacket for the American edition of O'Brien's 1962 novel, the second in her autobiographical trilogy

these compromises ultimately defeat Baba; she ends up with a drunken husband, hosting dinner parties for his friends, but still believing that she and Kate can have "each other, chats, their moments of recklessness, the plans that they'd both stopped believing in long ago." And Kate, one of those "serious people," in Baba's eyes so "goddam servile I could have killed her," finds herself trapped by lack of money and power at the moment when "reality caught up with the nightmare."

Of the three novels *The Country Girls* received the most praise. In the *New Statesman* (July 1960), V. S. Naipaul attributed the novel's success to the fact that O'Brien is a natural writer: "The true tragedy lies in the sense of time passing, of waste, decay, waiting, relationships that come to nothing. Yet Miss O'Brien never says so. . . . She simply offers her characters, and they come to us living." Sean McMahon, writing in *Eire-Ireland*, agreed, suggesting that *The Country Girls* established O'Brien as an important Irish writer and *The Lonely Girl* "affirmed this reputation." McMahon criticized *Girls in their Married Bliss*, however, finding it to be "startlingly disappointing" because of its increasingly more strident "note of ironic disillusion."

After the notoriety of *The Country Girls*, Edna O'Brien settled in London, continued to write novels and short stories, and began producing screenplays as well. Between 1964 and 1970 three of her novels, *August is a Wicked Month* (1965), *Casualties of Peace* (1966), and *A Pagan Place* (1970), were published, the last winning the Yorkshire Post Book Award for finest fiction of the year. *Girl with Green Eyes* (1964), adapted from her novel *The Lonely Girl*; *Time Lost and Time Remembered* (1966), written with Desmond Davis and based on O'Brien's short story "A Woman at the Seaside, "; and *Three into Two Won't Go* (1969), a screenplay O'Brien adapted from Andrea Newman's novel, became popular films. *The Love Object*, a collection of eight stories (five originally published in the *New Yorker*), appeared in 1968, continuing the O'Brien narrative of frustrated and disappointed women.

Missing from the novels written during these years is the humor that enlivens *The Country Girls*. Although Kate's naiveté reappears in several other characters, the wisecracking voice of young Baba disappears. The failure of O'Brien's own marriage, as well as her personal experiences rejecting the traditional roles of woman and wife that she had been brought up to believe in, undoubtedly influenced the novels she wrote at this time. Grace Eckley sees *August Is a Wicked Month* as a novel that marks a transition between the quests of O'Brien's earlier heroines for fulfillment through marriage and those of her later heroines, who realize that this sort of fulfillment is impossible.

August Is a Wicked Month, possibly the least successful of O'Brien's novels, focuses on the confusion of a divorced woman trying to redefine her role as mother, rid herself of wifehood, and search for a new definition of herself as a woman. Ellen, a nurse from a rural Irish village, has married, then separated, leaving church and home, and now fends for herself. The novel describes her short vacation to the Mediterranean, where, caught between her intense desire for physical pleasure and the residual guilt of her Catholic upbringing, she soon finds herself involved with either masochistic or impotent men. Punctuating the scenes of decadence are her recollec-

tions of moments with her young son, which continue to haunt her. However, Ellen "had been brought up to believe in punishment," and by the end of the novel she must pay for her sins when her son is killed in a camping accident with his father. In the final scene, much like Kate Brady in *Girls in their Married Bliss*, the heroine waits, neither happy nor unhappy, for the coming of autumn.

August Is a Wicked Month reflects O'Brien's growing interest in fictional technique, as symbolism replaces the realistic narrative of *The Country Girls*. In the symbolic structure of this novel the sun becomes "the opponent of dreams," and Ellen's intense pursuit of both sun and sex becomes a purging in the August heat. The obvious and heavy-handed symbolism, however, develops a heroine too vulnerable to be believed, and critics generally responded unfavorably. Ultimately *August Is a Wicked Month* suffers from what Lotus Snow called "its self-pitying rancour."

In 1966 O'Brien produced her next novel, *Casualties of Peace*, which centers on the relationship between Willa, a virgin "though tampered with," and Patsy, unhappily married to Tom and about to leave him for another man. Searching for peace after a terrifying marriage to Herod, Willa seeks security with Tom and Patsy; since they came, she feels "her life had a new order, a solid peace." But in O'Brien's world peace never lasts. Through a bizarre series of circumstances involving Auro, Willa's lover, Tom kills Willa, mistaking her for Patsy. The novel, which begins with Willa's dream of being "slit in multiple pieces" by two strange men, closes with all the casualties of peace scattered about: Willa, dead; Tom, imprisoned; and Patsy, alone. In this novel O'Brien has moved from the decadence of *August Is a Wicked Month* to masochistic violence, and the result is disappointing. As some critics have noted, the plot, contrived around a borrowed coat, cannot quite carry the thematic burden O'Brien imposes on it.

By 1970 O'Brien had lived in London for eleven years, but, like Joyce before her, she eventually turned to her Irish childhood to re-create in fiction moments from the past. "I believe," she has said, "that memory and the welter of memory, packed into a single lonely and bereft moment, is the strongest ally a person can have. The further I went away from the past, the more clearly I returned inwardly. . . ." *A Pagan Place*, published in 1970, is set in the rural west of Ireland. Talking to David Heycock after the novel was published, O'Brien explained that she wrote *A Pagan Place* because she wanted to get into the "kingdom of children": "I wanted to get the minute to minute essence of what it is when you're very young, when you're both meticulously aware of everything that's going on around you and totally uncritical."

The novel develops from a series of juxtapositions. The village's pagan past continually intrudes upon its Catholic present, where the poverty and sterility of daily life are charged with the superstitious lore that permeates the place, and repressed sexuality emerges in sinful and hidden sexual encounters. The minute details of the characters and life of the village show O'Brien at her best. The minor characters, such as the nationalistic teacher Miss Davitt, who goes mad right before the children's eyes, and Hilda, the neighbor who tries to speak to her dead husband even though "she hadn't spoken a civil word" to him when he was alive, are particularly effective. O'Brien's details, such as the description of the bedroom wallpaper that had been put on upside down, reveal her talent for suggestive imagery.

In *A Pagan Place* a young girl's family is thrown into a crisis when they discover that Emma, her older sister, is pregnant. The protagonist, shaken by her family's reactions and in the midst of her own sexual awakening, is lured into her first sexual experience by a priest who afterward quickly rejects her. To atone for her sin she joins an order of nuns dedicated to saving the world. In the final scene, aware that the family's knowledge of her involvement with the priest has severed her from them, the young girl prepares to leave home, hoping her mother will emerge to say goodbye. Disappointed, she hears only her mother's cry, the "howl" that will haunt her for her entire life.

The novel, constructed as a stream of memories, draws on the symbolic and ironic connotations of the word *pagan* to suggest that the Irish villagers, in their guilt, fear, and repression, make sins of the natural pleasures that most attract them and so create a split between what they believe and what they feel. This split ultimately leads to loneliness and cruelty, to mothers who teach their daughters that "love is a form of dope," and to the ironic and wasted sacrifice of the young girl choosing a marriage to God so that she can bring to distant pagans the happiness Christ merited for them.

Discussing her use of the second person, O'Brien explains, "I felt that in every person

there are two selves: I suppose they would be called the ego and the alter ego. And then there's almost a kind of negative state where things happen to you and you're not really realizing that they're happening. . . ." The narrator of this novel sounds very much as if she is talking to a younger self, having achieved a mature perspective on the experiences and people of her childhood. Combined with the symbolic implications of setting in *A Pagan Place*, this technique illustrates O'Brien's continuing experiments with form.

The narrative recollection of *A Pagan Place* turns into a Molly Bloom-type interior monologue in O'Brien's next novel, *Night* (1972). Mary Hooligan, adult counterpart of young Baba, settles into a four-poster bed with "satinized headboard" and begins to think about her past. Memories of her mother and her childhood home in the village of Coose; of men, the "cretins, pilgrims and scholars" she has known and loved; and of "high teas, serge suits, binding attachments" crowd the slowly moving minutes of the night. Left as caretaker of a vacationing couple's home, Mary appropriates the master bedroom after being haunted in another room by visions of her mother, who, like Hamlet's ghost, continues to reappear. The master bedroom is a temporary resting place for Mary's chaotic soul. Claiming she wants to be alone, she still admits to being on the lookout for pals, "pen pals and pub pals." Mary's life spills out as she recollects the many men and women with whom she has seen nights through, some for consolation, some for sexual fulfillment. Saddened by her growing separation from her son, she looks back with horror on her marriage to Dr. Flaggler, not, she admits, a blessed union. As dawn arrives, Mary, though solving nothing, feels refreshed, as one does after a long convalescence. She gladly quits the house and resolves to "live a little" before "the all-embracing darkness descends." Getting through the night, for Mary Hooligan, is a qualified kind of triumph.

In *Night*, which John Updike called a "brilliant and beautiful book," all past O'Brien heroines merge. A woman, hurt by a disastrous marriage to a cruel man and wise to the tricks of the world, desperately craves the love of her child, of her lost mother, of any man or woman who will have her. But at the same time Mary doubts that love is possible: "You have separateness thrust upon you," she says at the end of the novel. Though Mary Hooligan moves toward what she calls "some other shore," bolstering herself with the fragments of residual hope, her overwhelming loneliness pervades every page.

Although O'Brien did not publish another novel until 1977, in the five-year period between *Night* and *Johnny I Hardly Knew You* (1977) she continued to publish short stories, primarily in the *New Yorker*. Her collection *A Scandalous Woman and Other Stories* appeared in 1974.

In interviews in 1976 and 1977, O'Brien described her dual role as novelist and mother. Divorced at this time for more than twelve years, she was financially independent, with her sons university students at Cambridge and York. While she claimed, in talking to Ludovic Kennedy, that bringing up children by herself had been "glorious" because she had no one to argue with over "clothes and schools," O'Brien acknowledged that living alone often caused one to be extremely removed from people. "I feel," she told Susan Heller Anderson, "that I have been too often used and abused, and angry with myself for allowing it." O'Brien suggested at this time that, although she enjoyed the advantages of London, the city could dry up people. In London people don't tell stories, she claimed, while Ireland is full of stories and curiosity. Despite fifteen years in London, O'Brien still saw herself as a gypsy.

The autobiographical *Mother Ireland* (1976), a blend of myth, history, geography, and personal memories, with photographs by Fergus Bourke, records a pilgrimage back to Ireland. Filled with details of the day-to-day life of the Irish people, *Mother Ireland* reflects O'Brien's ambivalence and pinpoints the ironic juxtapositions she has always seen at the heart of Irish culture. Describing the hill of Tara, the seat of the ancient kings of Ireland, O'Brien notes that Tara is now an "unassuming place." "Six miles away," she writes, "is a holiday camp where girls in plastic hair rollers parade up and down the small toy-like concrete paths looking for Mister Right and ironically enough finding only distraught fathers hauling their children in and out of a Mickey Mouse Show." Though nonfiction, *Mother Ireland*, with its central metaphor of a woman raped by various enemies, displays the same energy and detail as *The Country Girls*. O'Brien's sharp and disillusioned eye picks up the contrast between the natural beauty of the land and what she calls the "intellectual morass." Readers and critics agree that *Mother Ireland* is not only an exile's autobiographical essay on the land to which she inevitably returns but also one of O'Brien's best pieces.

Johnny I Hardly Knew You, a novel published in 1977, does not enjoy the same reputation. O'Brien creates a first-person narrator who explains, on the day before her trial begins, why she has smothered her son's young friend, with whom she was involved in an affair. As Nora attempts to sort things out, the men in her life—her son, father, husband, lovers—blend into one another to become the male demon who must be slain by the wronged female. Mad Nora wants others to believe that the killing is not a crime, but an aberration caused by men, "the stampeders of our dreams." Obvious Freudian overtones, including Nora's prophetic nightmares and the suggestion that the "terrors that rise up from below . . . will have to be met," carry the narrative along. Like *The Country Girls*, *Johnny I Hardly Knew You* was written in three weeks, but most critics agree that it lacks the originality of the first novel, borders on melodrama, and presents a woman with whom we cannot sympathize. Anatole Broyard, who praises many of O'Brien's other novels, sums up: "I hardly knew him either and I see no reason to regret his demise."

Mrs. Reinhardt and Other Stories, a collection published in 1978, has been enthusiastically received. Benedict Kiely rates these as some of O'Brien's best stories, and Patricia Highsmith, in the *Times Literary Supplement*, nominated the collection as one of the best books to appear in that year. Although the settings vary and the characters come from different classes and backgrounds, these stories, like those in her earlier collections, highlight frustrated heroines such as Miss Hawkins, the lonely fifty-five-year-old woman who takes up with a twenty-one-year-old transient male, or Hilda, one of "The Small Town Lovers" who ends up as the latest "casualty of peace." But O'Brien's other heroines in *Mrs. Reinhardt* do not as readily succumb; sometimes they show a tendency to resist temptation. In "Ways," for example, Nell, attracted to Jane's husband, retreats out of respect for the rights of her friend. Some of these women discover a qualified kind of peace: Mrs. Reinhardt, jilted by her husband, is reunited with him at the end of the story, "at least for the duration of a windy night." After that? "And by morning who knows? Who knows anything anyhow." In "Clara," O'Brien creates a unique male narrator, but some readers, used to the familiar O'Brien female voice, might echo Victoria Glendinning's judgment: "I never believed in him for a moment."

Mrs. Reinhardt and Other Stories demonstrates a slight shift in the direction of O'Brien's fiction. In his review in the *Times Literary Supplement*, Frank Tuohy notes that "a certain decorousness" seems to have set in that is attributable perhaps to the "chastening influence of the editors of the *New Yorker*." As important as this decorousness, however, could be the peace that a few of the heroines temporarily achieve, especially in relation to men. Edna O'Brien's greatest achievement, her delineation of a female psyche, has also created a limitation: her male characters are often one-dimensional figures who serve as little more than backdrops for her heroines' loneliness, frustration, and disappointment. Hints, as far back as Mary Hooligan in *Night*, suggest that O'Brien wants her women not only to survive, but also to grow, to be independent and even—perhaps—content. A few of the women in *Mrs. Reinhardt* are.

In *Returning* (1982), a collection of stories (several of which had been published in the *New Yorker*), O'Brien again focuses exclusively on the Irish village life dramatized in her earliest fiction. The stories are filtered through an enlightened narrator (all but one is told in the first person) whose memories of her childhood in Ireland reveal the inescapable links to a past she cannot shake. These stories re-create the characters and terrain of *The Country Girls* trilogy and recall the narration of memories in *A Pagan Place* and *Night*. The idiosyncrasies of village life—the town "dummies" and "maddies," the young girl craving love from an absent mother ("My Mother's Mother") or a favorite nun ("Sister Imelda"), and the frustrated women flirting with the town bachelors or the parish curate—are rendered in that typical O'Brien style that captures the essence of village life in the seemingly insignificant details of daily struggles.

The central theme of returning is carried through all of the stories, not only by narrators reminiscing about childhood experiences, but also by characters such as Mabel in "Savages," who went off to Australia and saved for ten years to return to Ireland, only to realize that her coming back has been a mistake. The women who stay are frustrated, sometimes unstable and isolated, but the exiles are often no better off. As the narrator of "The Doll" explains, she has deserted the village for the city, but she now finds herself dangling between two worlds: "I am far from those I am with, and far from those I have left."

Death is a recurring theme in this collection. O'Brien counterpoises Irish burial rituals with the irony of characters who avoid a real confrontation with death because, as the girl in "My Mother's Mother" says, death was "some weird journey you made alone and unbefriended." The narrator of "Ghosts," one of the best stories in the collection, suggests, however, that the dead are preserved in memory. After describing three women from her past life, she finally realizes: "I still can't imagine any of them dead. They live on, they are fixed in that far off region called childhood where nothing ever dies, not even oneself." The interplay between two selves—with the limited perspective of the younger child who often knows something is wrong but does not quite understand what is happening, contrasted with the enlightened perspective of the older narrator—contributes to the success of several of these stories. The ambiguity of these narrators' attitudes toward their memories, some obviously based on O'Brien's own experiences, suggests the relevance of a passage from *Mother Ireland*: "It is true that a country encapsulates our childhood and those lanes, byres, fields, flowers, insects, suns, moons and stars are forever re-occuring and tantalizing one with a possibility of a golden key which would lead beyond birth to the roots of one's lineage. Irish? In truth I would not want to be anything else. It is a state of mind as well as an actual country." As *Returning* demonstrates, that "state of mind" continues to provide material for O'Brien's fiction.

Time and Tide (1992) concerns another "country girl," Nell Steadman, who believes "self-immolation [is] everything." According to a *Publishers Weekly* review, "The plot recounts the end of her marriage to a cool-headed tyrant, the paths of her two sons to adulthood, her pursuit of a career as a book editor in London and her ill-fated further erotic adventures. But such details don't speak to the heart of O'Brien's abiding preoccupations: the barbarism of home and family, and the deathly cast of all loving."

Even Edna O'Brien's strongest supporters admit that she does not always write well, that some of her fiction is "trite" and "second rate." Although she has moved stylistically from what Grace Eckley calls the "simple barren naivete" of *The Country Girls*, through the heightened lyricism of *Night* and *Johnny I Hardly Knew You*, to the sophisticated, realistic narrators of her more recent stories, she has always had a unique talent for exposing the minute and telling detail, for capturing the nuances of everyday life. The authenticity of her female voices makes Edna O'Brien a novelist to be reckoned with.

Interviews:

Nell Dunn, ed., *Talking to Women* (London: MacGibbon & Kee, 1965), pp. 69-107;

David Heycock, "Edna O'Brien Talks to David Heycock about Her New Novel *A Pagan Place*," *Listener*, 83 (7 May 1970): 616-617;

Joseph McCulloch, "Dialogue with Edna O'Brien," *Under Bow Bells: Dialogues with Joseph McCulloch* (London: Sheldon Press, 1974), pp. 23-29;

Ludovic Kennedy, "Three Loves of Childhood, Irish Thoughts by Edna O'Brien," *Listener*, 95 (3 June 1976): 701-702.

References:

Susan Heller Anderson, "Writing, A Kind of Illness for Edna O'Brien," *New York Times*, 11 October 1977, p. 33;

Barbara Bannon, "Authors and Editors," *Publishers Weekly*, 197 (25 May 1970): 21-22;

Grace Eckley, *Edna O'Brien* (Lewisburg, Pa.: Bucknell University Press, 1964);

Sean McMahon, "A Sex by Themselves: An Interim Report on the Novels of Edna O'Brien," *Eire-Ireland*, 12 (Spring 1977): 79-87;

Review of *Time and Tide, Publishers Weekly*, 24 February 1992, p. 41;

Lotus Snow, "'That Trenchant Childhood Route': Quest in Edna O'Brien's Novels," *Eire-Ireland*, 14 (Spring 1979): 74-83.

Joe Orton

(1 January 1933 - 9 August 1967)

This entry was updated by M. D. Allen (University of Wisconsin Center—Fox Valley) from his entry in DLB 13: British Dramatists Since World War II: Part Two.

BOOKS: *Entertaining Mr. Sloane* (London: Hamish Hamilton, 1964; New York: Grove, 1965);

Loot (London: Methuen, 1967; New York: Grove, 1967);

Crimes of Passion (London: Methuen, 1967)—includes *The Ruffian on the Stair* (revised version) and *The Erpingham Camp*;

What the Butler Saw (London: Methuen, 1969; New York: French, 1970);

Funeral Games and The Good and Faithful Servant (London: Methuen, 1970);

Head to Toe (London: Anthony Blond, 1971);

Orton: The Complete Plays (London: Eyre Methuen, 1976; New York: Grove, 1977);

Up Against It: A Screenplay for the Beatles (London: Eyre Methuen, 1979);

The Orton Diaries: Including the Correspondence of Edna Welthorpe and Others, edited by John Lahr (London: Methuen, 1986; New York: Harper & Row, 1986).

PLAY PRODUCTIONS: *Entertaining Mr. Sloane*, London, New Arts Theatre, 6 May 1964 (transferred to Wyndham's Theatre, 29 June 1964; to Queen's Theatre, 5 October 1964); New York, Lyceum Theater, 12 October 1965, 13 [performances];

Loot, Cambridge, Arts Theatre, 1 February 1965; London, Jeannette Cochrane Theatre, 27 September 1966; New York, Biltmore Theater, 18 March 1968, 22;

The Ruffian on the Stair, London, Royal Court Theatre, 21 August 1966, 1; produced again with *The Erpingham Camp*, in *Crimes of Passion*, London, Royal Court Theatre, 6 June 1967; New York, Astor Place Theater, 26 October 1969, 9;

The Good and Faithful Servant, London, King's Head Theatre, 17 March 1967;

The Erpingham Camp, produced with *The Ruffian on the Stair*, in *Crimes of Passion*, London, Royal Court Theatre, 6 June 1967, 12; New

Joe Orton

York, Astor Place Theater, 26 October 1969, 9;

What the Butler Saw, London, Queen's Theatre, 5 March 1969; New York, McAlpin Rooftop Theater, 4 May 1970, 224.

TELEVISION: *The Erpingham Camp*, Rediffusion Television, 27 June 1966;

The Good and Faithful Servant, Rediffusion Television, 6 April 1967;

Funeral Games, Yorkshire Television, 25 August 1968.

RADIO: *The Ruffian on the Stair*, BBC, 31 August 1964.

OTHER: *The Ruffian on the Stair*, in *New Radio Drama* (London: BBC, 1966);
"Until She Screams," in *Oh! Calcutta!*, edited by Kenneth Tynan (New York: Grove, 1969).

Between 1963 and his death in 1967 Joe Orton wrote three important and four lesser plays. In the tolerant theatrical climate of the 1960s, he persuaded audiences that homosexuality, incest, and violence could be shown on the stage and even be found uproariously funny. He communicated so successfully his vision of the world that we recognize the word *Ortonesque* as implying a peculiar mixture of the violent, the formal, and the amusing. The development of Orton's talent was brutally cut short by his murder. It was a death that helped create a minor legend and made more difficult the claim that his drama has nothing to do with the world outside the theater's walls.

John Kingsley Orton was born and lived the first eighteen years of his life in Leicester in conditions of dreary material adequacy but emotional and intellectual impoverishment. His father, William Orton, was a gardener for the city, and his mother, Elsie Orton, worked as a machinist. Because of recurring asthma attacks that kept him home for long periods Orton failed to qualify for grammar school and would thus have received at a secondary modern school an education considered suitable to the less academically gifted. But his prestige-conscious mother sent him to a local private school, Clark's College, because she was apparently under the impression that its curriculum was more academic than it actually was. Orton later worked at despised dead-end jobs and invested his evenings and his hopes for excitement and escape in local amateur dramatic circles. One entry in his adolescent diary conveys the authentic note of self-recognition and ambition: "Last night sitting in the empty theatre watching the electricians flashing lights on and off, the empty stage waiting for rehearsal to begin, I suddenly knew that my ambition is and has always been to act and act. To be connected with the stage in some way, with the magic of the Theatre and everything it means. I know now I shall *always* want to act and I can no more sit in an office all my life than fly. I know this sounds sentimental and soppy but it is all perfectly true." Orton did manage to gain some local acting experience before winning a Leicester Educational Committee grant to study at the Royal Academy of Dramatic Art (RADA). He traveled to London in May 1951

and spent most of the rest of his life there until his death at the hands of Kenneth Halliwell, his flat mate and lover, sixteen years later.

From June 1951 until Orton's death, the story of his life—and, at first, of his writing—is largely the story of his relationship with Halliwell. The two were fellow students at RADA and set up house together when their acting careers failed to prosper (Orton spent two years at RADA then four unenthusiastic months at the Ipswich Repertory Theatre). They wrote unpublishable novels in collaboration, while at first living on an inheritance of Halliwell's at the rate of five pounds a week and later working half of each year. In 1957, after the rejection of a jointly written novel, Orton began submitting his own work. But, five years later, both Halliwell and Orton came into literary limelight of a sort for the "borrowing" and defacing of library books: a picture of a gibbon's head was carefully stuck in the middle of that of a rose on the cover of the *Collins Guide to Roses*; mildly obscene blurbs were typed on the inside covers of Dorothy Sayers's detective novels. Halliwell and Orton were sentenced to six months in prison for what amounted to Orton's first mischievous attack on middle-class cultural proprieties. Later, Orton would claim the experience of prison as an artistically beneficial one: "I tried writing before I went into the nick . . . but it was no good. Being in the nick . . . brought detachment to my writing. I wasn't involved anymore and it suddenly worked."

The Ruffian on the Stair was broadcast by the BBC on 31 August 1964 but was subsequently revised before it reached the stage two years later. The plot of the radio script shows the influence of early Pinter. Although both versions are set in a room invaded by a stranger, the actions and motives of the characters are more clearly cut in the stage version. Mike, a small-time crook, has killed someone in a road accident. The dead man's brother, Wilson, invades the home of Mike and his girlfriend, Joyce, and eventually tricks Mike into shooting him. Mike has not only removed the obligation of living from the bereft Wilson but has also provided him with the revenge he desired, for Mike must now explain himself to the police.

Entertaining Mr. Sloane, which opened at the New Arts Theatre in May 1964, was already a success when *The Ruffian on the Stair* was broadcast. The eponymous central character, an attractive young lout, arranges an easy life for himself by

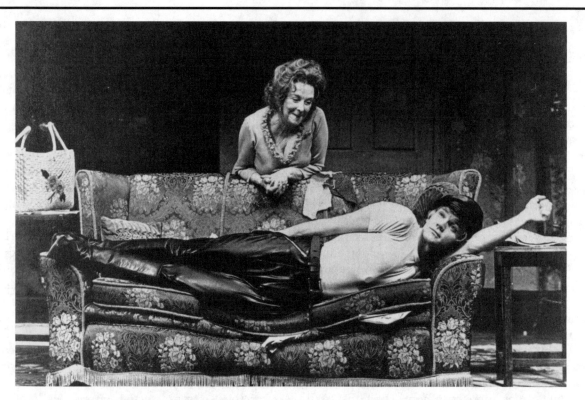

Beryl Reid and Malcolm McDowell in the first production of Entertaining Mr. Sloane

playing off against each other his amorous land-lady, Kath, and her bisexual brother, Ed. But their father, Kemp, realizes that Sloane has killed a man and threatens to incriminate him. Sloane murders Kemp, and then finds himself ma-nipulated—by blackmail—in his turn, and be-comes the object of sexual sharing. Kath and Ed attempt actively to entertain Sloane until the mur-der, after which he must entertain them.

Entertaining Mr. Sloane, wrote John Russell Taylor, is "the first solid, well-managed commer-cial play which belonged, specifically and unmis-takably, to the post-Osborne era." Sloane does not spend time lamenting the loss of big, brave causes: some critics see his philosophy—selfish, amoral pragmatism—as characterizing the decade in which the play was written. The play deals with the gap between the masks we wear to de-ceive society and ourselves and the flesh behind them, between our professions and our true mo-tives. Ed's defense of "principles" makes the point most tellingly and hilariously: "Why am I in-terested in your welfare? . . . Why do thinking men everywhere show young boys the strait and narrow? Flash cheque-books when delinquency is mentioned? Support the Scout-movement? Princi-ples, boy, bleeding principles."

The play deals too with the barriers we hide behind in an effort to spare ourselves a disturb-ing apprehension of life. Ed's cliché-ridden fanta-sies of the executive good life and Kath's novelettish accounts of her past and cheap-romance perceptions of her present are both somewhat precariously maintained; but they do provide comfort. It is not only individuals, how-ever, who have lost contact with absolutes of truth and falsehood, right and wrong. Sloane has absorbed would-be sociological explanations of de-linquency and other evils ("I'm an orphan"), and Ed is not sure if hanging is still the punishment for murder ("I get confused by the changes in the law"). With the addition of Orton's unfailing awareness of social pretension and false gentility, *Entertaining Mr. Sloane* can be viewed as a percep-tive and consistently witty report on the state of the nation in the early 1960s. Terence Rattigan ap-proved of the play, commenting favorably on its construction, and invested three thousand pounds in its transfer to the West End. *Entertain-ing Mr. Sloane* aroused both critical outrage and de-light, with Orton adding contributions on both sides in letters written under various pseud-onyms.

If *Entertaining Mr. Sloane* did well, then *Loot* (1965), Orton's next major play, eventually did bet-

Program cover and title page for the London Traverse production of Loot, *which restored deletions ordered by the Lord Chamberlain's Office from the first production*

ter, being voted by the *Evening Standard* the best play of 1966 and also winning the *Plays and Players* award. Nevertheless, the original touring version failed, partly due to misconceived direction and casting. The problem, Orton realized, was that any stylization or "camp" treatment of his script went at odds with the zaniness of the farce. "The play is not written naturalistically," he wrote about *The Ruffian on the Stair* with the failure of *Loot* on his mind, "but it must be directed and acted with absolute realism.... No attempt in fact to match the author's extravagance of dialogue with extravagance of direction."

Loot is a farcical parody of the detective drama, but its detective, instead of being, in W. H. Auden's words, "either the official representative of the ethical or the exceptional individual who is in a state of grace," is a bully who takes a bribe to protect the guilty and will arrange for McLeavy, the only innocent man in the play, to meet an "accidental" death. Truscott of Scotland Yard—a corruptible policeman out to "solve" a bank robbery and line his pockets—is a

splendid creation. He is partly a lampoon of Sherlock Holmes and his ilk. "When I shook your hand I felt a roughness on one of your wedding rings," he tells Fay, the scheming nurse who has killed her first and subsequent husbands and now hopes to profit from marriage to the recently widowed McLeavy. "A roughness I associate with powder burns and salt. The two together spell a gun and sea air. When found on a wedding ring only one solution is possible." He is partly, in typical Ortonesque inversion, a representative of a corrupt and greedy society.

In the play, McLeavy's son, Hal, and his friend, Dennis, hide the loot from their bank robbery in Hal's mother's coffin. This leads to the use of the corpse as a comic property as Orton seduces the audience into laughter at the outraging of conventional attitudes toward death: Mrs. McLeavy's corpse is stood upside down in a wardrobe, undressed behind a screen, and her teeth and glass eye are "passed around like nuts at Christmas." Farce was latent in some scenes of *Entertaining Mr. Sloane*; in *Loot* it is gloriously

Stanley Baxter, Ralph Richardson, and Coral Browne in the first production of What the Butler Saw

achieved. Moreover, in *Loot* Orton fully developed the technique of having the characters who are actively involved in situations of violence, murder, and unrestrained sexual ambition express themselves in language that is a mixture of the contemporary informal and the elegant, polished, and epigrammatic ("My mate Dennis has done you. He speaks of it with relish.")—often, as in the cases of Fay and Truscott, with a preponderance of the latter.

In Orton's work poetic justice never occurs, and every aspect of bourgeois life is treated with studied irreverence and a gift for parody, which proves Orton to be among the most deceptively literate—and literary—of farceurs. "You can't do this [to me]," McLeavy appeals to Truscott as he—the only innocent in the play—is led off to

prison. "I've always been a law-abiding citizen. The police are for the protection of ordinary people." "I don't know where you pick up these slogans, sir," says the police inspector. "You must read them on hoardings [billboards]."

Orton wrote three more plays which are considered, like *The Ruffian on the Stair*, to be minor works. *The Good and Faithful Servant*, written in 1964, was staged in March 1967, and was televised the next month. The play is of some interest because it is Orton's vision of the road not taken. He was set apart from family and job—most people's destiny—by self-chosen poverty (then by considerable wealth), by the very nature of his talent, and by his homosexuality. He regarded with horror what he saw as industrial society's contempt for the individual and the way

The Queen's Theatre

LICENSED BY THE LORD CHAMBERLAIN TO PRINCE LITTLER
MANAGER - WYBERT R. ALLEN
BOX OFFICE (CHARLES GOFFREY) OPEN 10 a m -8 p m REG 1196

Prices of Admission:
Stalls 35/-, 25/-, 17/6. Dress Circle 35 -, 30/-, 20/-, Upper Circle 15/-, 10 6.

Lewenstein-Delfont Productions Ltd. and H. M. Tennent Ltd.

present

RALPH RICHARDSON

CORAL BROWNE

and

STANLEY BAXTER

JULIA FOSTER

PETER BAYLISS　　HAYWARD MORSE

in

WHAT THE BUTLER SAW

A Comedy by JOE ORTON

"Surely we're all mad people, and they whom we think are, are not."
The Revenger's Tragedy

Directed by ROBERT CHETWYN

Designed by Hutchinson Scott

Coral Browne's dresses by Pierre Balmain - Paris

Lighting by Joe Davis

First performance at this Theatre Wednesday 5th March 1969

WHAT THE BUTLER SAW

by Joe Orton

Characters in order of appearance

Geraldine Barclay	JULIA FOSTER
Dr. Prentice	STANLEY BAXTER
Mrs. Prentice	CORAL BROWNE
Nicholas Beckett	HAYWARD MORSE
Dr. Rance	RALPH RICHARDSON
Sergeant Match	PETER BAYLISS

Directed by ROBERT CHETWYN

Designed by HUTCHINSON SCOTT

Lighting by JOE DAVIS

ACT I

A room in a private clinic in the country
Time — morning

INTERVAL

ACT II

The same, one minute later

Program title page, cast list, and synopsis of scenes for the first production of Orton's last play

in which its servants surrender responsibility for their own lives. In *The Good and Faithful Servant* Buchanan has given a lifetime of conscientious work to his company and lost an arm in its service. However, his timid faith in authority is destroyed in the course of the play; he realizes that he has wasted his life, achieved nothing, is not even remembered at the Bright Hours club for retired employees. Yet, more depressingly, his grandson Ray is in the process of being trapped by the need for a weekly wage packet. *The Erpingham Camp*, written in 1965, was produced in an early version the next year by Rediffusion Television and presented, in the double bill *Crimes of Passion*, with *The Ruffian on the Stair* in 1967. It is adapted from Euripides' *Bacchae*, with Erpingham himself as the self-ignorant man destroyed by frenzy. *Funeral Games*, written in 1966 and televised in 1968, is the least satisfactory of Orton's plays, religion being the main target. These minor works have not received the same ac-

claim as the three plays upon which Orton's reputation rests.

Orton's masterpiece, *What the Butler Saw*, was written in 1967, the last year of his life, but was not produced until two years later. Dr. Prentice, the owner of a private psychiatric clinic, attempts to seduce a girl who applies to be his secretary, and his subsequent efforts to conceal his attempt begin a punishing series of mistaken identities made even more confusing by transvestism. The girl is finally revealed as his long-lost daughter and the twin sister of the page boy who is blackmailing Mrs. Prentice. Dr. Rance blithely imposes absurd psychiatric explanations on the chaos around him, and gathers material for a " 'documentary-type' novelette" that is to make his fortune. The plot is ingeniously neat and absurd, a parody of the farce plot. (One character asks, "Why are there so many doors? Was the house designed by a lunatic?") The function of farce, says Eric Bentley, is to permit us the outrage but spare us its consequences. The outrages in *What the Butler Saw* include incest, violence, and the castration of the father figure, Sir Winston Churchill. Indulgence in drugs and alcohol, as well as the inability of the characters to rely on their usual dress and roles, helps guarantee a chaos that is both liberating and terrifying. And the Orton who once said that a playwright should use the language of his age, and use every bit of it, here mocks psychiatric interpretations of life and newspaper confessions and reports. The final Euripidean ending, in which Sergeant Match in a leopard-spotted dress descends from the skylight, carries with it the implication that "All is forgiven," as Orton himself realized.

What the Butler Saw was greeted on its opening night with cries of "Filth!" Ralph Richardson, playing Dr. Rance, was told by a member of the audience to "Give back your knighthood!" Furthermore, the critics blamed the play for mistakes in its production. But since Lindsay Anderson's revival in 1975 the play's reputation has been secure. John Lahr, Orton's best-known critic, describes "momentum building masterfully," a "brilliant traffic plan [creating] tumult," and "the brilliant play of language" in *What the Butler Saw.*

Halliwell had meanwhile achieved nothing as a writer. Finding his personal and artistic sterility and Orton's success impossible to live with, on 9 August 1967 he smashed in Orton's head with a hammer and then took twenty-two Nembutals, ending his own life.

Orton's reputation today is as high as it was in 1967. He is generally acknowledged as a unique anarchic talent whose works, progressing from the comedy of manners to the framework of farce, are subversive of any person or group of people who manifest what he called "this enormous wish to explain everything." Orton is an enemy of authority, routine, and sexual compartmentalization and gleefully insists on man's animal nature. His message is not unfashionable. Now the subject of serious scholarly scrutiny, even his minor writings are published and discussed.

Interviews:

"The Biter Bit," *Plays and Players*, 11 (August 1964): 16;

Giles Gordon, "Joe Orton," *Transatlantic Review*, 24 (Spring 1967): 93-100.

Bibliography:

Kimball King, *Twenty Modern British Playwrights: A Bibliography, 1956 to 1976* (New York & London: Garland, 1977), pp. 77-83.

Biographies:

John Lahr, *Prick Up Your Ears: The Biography of Joe Orton* (London: Allen Lane, 1978);

C. W. E. Bigsby, *Joe Orton* (London & New York: Methuen, 1982);

Maurice Charney, *Joe Orton* (London: Macmillan, 1984; New York: Grove, 1984).

References:

Maurice Charney, "Orton's *Loot* as 'Quotidian Farce': The Intersection of Clack Comedy and Daily Life," *Modern Drama*, 24 (December 1981): 514-524;

Manfred Draudt, "Comic, Tragic, or Absurd? On Some Parallels Between the Farces of Joe Orton and Seventeenth-Century Tragedy," *English Studies*, 59 (1978): 202-217;

Martin Esslin, "Joe Orton: The Comedy of (Ill) Manners," in *Contemporary English Drama*, edited, with a preface, by C. W. E. Bigsby (New York: Holmes & Meier, 1981), pp. 95-107;

Keath Fraser, "Joe Orton: His Brief Career," *Modern Drama*, 14 (1971): 414-419;

Frank S. Galassi, "The Absurd Theatre of Joe Orton and N. F. Simpson," Ph.D. dissertation, New York University, 1971;

William Hutchings, "Joe Orton's Jacobean Assimilations in *What the Butler Saw*," in *Farce*, edited by James Redmond (Cambridge: Cambridge University Press, 1988), pp. 227-235;

Frank Marcus, "Comedy or Farce?," *London Magazine*, 6 (February 1967): 73-77;

Leslie Smith, "Democratic Lunacy: The Comedies of Joe Orton," *Adam: International Review*, 394-396 (1976): 73-92;

John Russell Taylor, *The Second Wave: New British Drama for the Seventies* (New York: Hill & Wang, 1971), pp. 125-140.

Harold Pinter
(10 October 1930 -   )

This entry was updated by Stephen Grecco (Pennsylvania State University) from his entry in
DLB 13: British Dramatists Since World War II: Part Two.

SELECTED BOOKS: *The Birthday Party* (London: Encore, 1959);

The Birthday Party and Other Plays (London: Methuen, 1960); republished as *The Birthday Party and The Room* (New York: Grove, 1961) —includes *The Birthday Party, The Room,* and *The Dumb Waiter;*

The Caretaker (London: Methuen, 1960);

The Caretaker and The Dumb Waiter (New York: Grove, 1961);

A Night Out (London: French, 1961);

A Slight Ache and Other Plays (London: Methuen, 1961)—includes *A Slight Ache, A Night Out, The Dwarfs, Trouble in the Works, The Black and White, Request Stop, Last to Go,* and *Applicant;*

Three Plays: A Slight Ache, The Collection, The Dwarfs (New York: Grove, 1962);

The Collection and The Lover (London: Methuen, 1963);

The Dwarfs and Eight Revue Sketches (New York: Dramatists Play Service, 1965)—includes *The Dwarfs, Trouble in the Works, The Black and White, Request Stop, Last to Go, Applicant, Interview, That's All,* and *That's Your Trouble;*

The Homecoming (London: Methuen, 1965; New York: Grove, 1967);

Tea Party (London: Methuen, 1965; New York: Grove, 1966);

Tea Party and Other Plays (London: Methuen, 1967) —includes *Tea Party, The Basement,* and *Night School;*

The Lover, Tea Party, The Basement (New York: Grove, 1967);

Poems (London: Enitharmon, 1968);

A Night Out, Night School, Revue Sketches (New York: Grove, 1968);

Mac (London: Pendragon Press, 1968);

Landscape (London: Pendragon Press, 1968);

Landscape and Silence (London: Methuen, 1969; New York: Grove, 1970)—includes *Landscape, Silence,* and *Night;*

Five Screenplays (London: Methuen, 1971; New York: Grove, 1973)—includes *Accident, The*

Harold Pinter, 1960 (photograph by Mark Gerson)

Go-Between, The Pumpkin Eater, The Quiller Memorandum, and *The Servant;*

Old Times (London: Methuen, 1971; New York: Grove, 1973);

No Man's Land (London: Eyre Methuen, 1975; New York: Eyre Methuen, 1975);

The Proust Screenplay (New York: Grove, 1978; London: Eyre Methuen/Chatto & Windus, 1978);

Poems and Prose 1949-1977 (New York: Grove, 1978; London: Eyre Methuen, 1978);

Betrayal (London: Eyre Methuen, 1978; New York: Grove, 1979);

The Hothouse (New York: Grove, 1980);

Family Voices (New York: Grove, 1981);

The French Lieutenant's Woman: A Screenplay (New York: Little, Brown, 1981);

Other Places (New York: Grove Weidenfeld, 1983) —includes *A Kind of Alaska, Victoria Station,* and *Family Voices*;

One for the Road (New York: Grove Weidenfeld, 1986);

Mountain Language (New York: Grove Weidenfeld, 1990);

The Dwarfs (New York: Grove Weidenfeld, 1990).

Editions and Collections: *Complete Works*, volumes 1-4 (New York: Grove, 1977-1981);

Collected Poems and Prose (London: Methuen, 1986);

Complete Works, 4 volumes (New York: Grove Weidenfeld, 1990).

PLAY PRODUCTIONS: *The Room*, Bristol, Bristol University Memorial Building, 15 May 1957; produced with *The Dumb Waiter*, London, Hampstead Theatre Club (transferred 8 March 1960 to Royal Court Theatre) 21 January 1960; produced with *A Slight Ache*, New York, Writers Stage Theatre, 9 December 1964, 343 [performances];

The Birthday Party, Cambridge, Arts Theatre, 28 April 1958; Hammersmith, Lyric Theatre, 19 May 1958; New York, Booth Theatre, 3 October 1967, 343;

The Dumb Waiter, translated into German by Willy H. Thiem, Frankfurt-am-Main, Germany, 28 February 1959; produced with *The Room*, London, Hampstead Theatre Club (transferred 8 March 1960 to Royal Court Theatre), 21 January 1960; produced with *The Collection*, New York, Cherry Lane Theatre, 26 November 1962, 578;

A Slight Ache, London, BBC Radio Third Programme, 2 July 1959; London, Arts Theatre Club, 18 January 1961; produced with *The Room*, New York, Writers Stage Theatre, 9 December 1964, 343;

Trouble in the Works and *The Black and White*, in *One to Another* (revue), Hammersmith, Lyric Theatre, 15 July 1959; London, Apollo Theatre, 19 August 1959;

Request Stop, Last to Go, Special Offer, Getting Acquainted, in *Pieces of Eight* (revue), London, Apollo Theatre, 23 September 1959;

A Night Out, London, BBC Third Programme, 1 March 1960; London, Comedy Theatre, 2 October 1961;

The Caretaker, London, Arts Theatre Club (transferred 30 May 1960 to Duchess Theatre), 27 April 1960, 444; New York, Lyceum Theatre, 4 October 1961, 165;

The Dwarfs, London, BBC Third Programme, 2 December 1960; produced with *The Lover*, London, Arts Theatre Club, 18 September 1963; produced with *The Dumb Waiter*, New York, Abbey Theatre, 3 May 1974, 11;

The Collection, London, Associated Rediffusion Television, 11 May 1961; London, Aldwych Theatre, 18 June 1962; produced with *The Dumb Waiter*, New York, Cherry Lane Theatre, 26 November 1962, 578;

The Lover, London, Associated Rediffusion Television, 28 March 1963; produced with *The Dwarfs*, London, Arts Theatre Club, 18 September 1963; New York, Cherry Lane Theatre, 4 January 1964, 89;

The Homecoming, Cardiff, New Theatre, 22 March 1965; London, Aldwych Theatre, 3 June 1965; New York, Music Box Theatre, 5 January 1967, 324;

Tea Party, London, BBC Television, 25 March 1965; produced with *The Basement*, New York, Eastside Playhouse, 15 October 1968, 176;

The Basement, London, BBC Television, 20 February 1967; produced with *The Tea Party*, New York, Eastside Playhouse, 15 October 1968, 176;

Night, in *We Who Are About To . . .* , London, Hampstead Theatre Club, 6 February 1969; produced again in *Mixed Doubles: An Entertainment on Marriage* (revised version of *We Who Are About To . . .*), London, Comedy Theatre, 9 April 1969;

Landscape and *Silence*, London, Aldwych Theatre, 2 July 1969; New York, Forum Theatre, 2 April 1970, 53;

Old Times, London, Aldwych Theatre, 1 June 1971; New York, Billy Rose Theatre, 16 November 1971, 119;

No Man's Land, London, National Theatre at the Old Vic, 23 April 1975;

Betrayal, London, National Theatre, 15 November 1978; New York, 1980;

The Hothouse, London, Hampstead Theatre Club, 1 May 1980; New York, 1982;

Family Voices, London, BBC Radio Third Programme, 22 January 1981; London, National Theatre, 13 February 1981;

A Kind of Alaska and Victoria Station, London, National Theatre, 14 October 1982;

One for the Road, Hammersmith, Lyric Theatre, 13 March 1984;

Mountain Language, London, National Theatre, 20 October 1988.

MOTION PICTURES: *The Servant*, Springbok-Elstree, 1963;

The Guest, adapted from *The Caretaker*, Janus, 1964;

The Pumpkin Eater, Rank, 1964;

The Quiller Memorandum, Twentieth Century-Fox, 1967;

Accident, Cinema V, 1967;

The Birthday Party, Continental, 1968;

The Go-Between, World Film Services, 1971;

The Homecoming, American Film Theatre, 1971;

The Last Tycoon, Paramount, 1975;

The French Lieutenant's Woman, United Artists, 1981;

Betrayal, Horizon Films, 1982;

Turtle Diary, United British Artists/Brittanic Productions, 1986;

Reunion, Castle Hill, 1989;

The Handmaid's Tale, Cinecom, 1990;

The Comfort of Strangers, Skouras Pictures, 1990.

TELEVISION: *Night School*, Associated Rediffusion Television, 1960;

The Collection, Associated Rediffusion Television, 1961;

The Lover, Associated Rediffusion Television, 1963;

Tea Party, BBC, 1965;

The Basement, BBC, 1967;

Monologue, BBC, 1973;

Langrishe, Go Down, BBC, 1978;

The Hothouse, BBC, 1982;

One for the Road, BBC, 1985;

Dumb Waiter, BBC, 1985;

The Room, ABC, 1987;

The Heat of the Day, Granada, 1989.

RADIO: *A Slight Ache*, BBC Third Programme, 1959;

A Night Out, BBC Third Programme, 1960;

The Dwarfs, BBC Third Programme, 1960;

That's Your Trouble, BBC Third Programme, 1964;

That's All, BBC Third Programme, 1964;

Applicant, BBC Third Programme, 1964;

Interview, BBC Third Programme, 1964;

Dialogue for Three, BBC Third Programme, 1964;

Landscape, BBC Third Programme, 1968;

Family Voices, BBC Third Programme, 1981;

A Kind of Alaska, World Service, 1990.

OTHER: *New Poems 1967*, edited by Pinter and others (London: Hutchinson, 1968);

One Hundred Poems by 100 Poets, Selected by Pinter, Geoffrey Godbert, and Anthony Astbury (New York: Grove Weidenfeld, 1987).

Harold Pinter, Britain's most significant playwright since Bernard Shaw, was born in Hackney, a small working-class section just beyond the borders of London's East End. He grew up in a modest brick house on Thistlewaite Road, near Clapton Pond, in an area that had "some big, run-down Victorian houses, and soap factories with a terrible smell, and a lot of railway yards. And shops." His immediate forebears were Sephardic Jews from Portugal, who first settled in Hungary before coming to England around the turn of the century. Pinter believes his surname is the Anglicized version of the Spanish or Portuguese *Pinto*, *da Pinto*, or *da Pinta*. His first nom de plume was Harold Pinta, which he used on his first publications, two of his poems published in *Poetry London* in 1950.

Pinter's father, Hyman (Jack) Pinter, was a ladies' tailor who worked twelve-hour days making clothes in his shop, but he eventually lost the business and went to work for someone else. Pinter's mother, Frances Mann Pinter, he says, "was a marvelous cook, as she still is." At the outbreak of the war in 1939 Pinter and a group of other boys were evacuated to a castle in Cornwall, where he claims he became a "morose little boy" and returned home after a year or so.

From 1941 to 1947 Pinter attended the Hackney Downs Grammar School, acting in school productions (he played Macbeth and Romeo) and writing essays and poetry. He recalled that the school was "pretty awful," but he had kind words for his English master, Joseph Brearley, "a very brilliant man" with an obsession for the theater who directed him in the Shakespeare roles. It was during this period that Pinter directly experienced the war that was threatening to envelop England. "There were times when I would open our back door and find our garden in flames. Our house never burned, but we had to evacuate several times." On leaving grammar school, he applied for and received a grant to study acting at the Royal Academy of Dramatic Art. After two unhappy terms, though, he left "of my own free will; I didn't care for it very much." Finding the at-

Harold Pinter

mosphere and the other students too sophisticated, he escaped by faking a nervous breakdown and, unknown to his parents, roamed around for months while continuing to draw his grant.

In 1948 Pinter declared himself a conscientious objector: "I was aware of the suffering and the horror of war, and by no means was I going to subscribe to keep it going. I said no." He appeared before two tribunals, both of which refused his request for C.O. status. Shortly afterward he received his call-up papers for the army, but persisted in his determination not to be drafted. Expecting to go to prison, he was instead fined thirty pounds by a magistrate, a sum paid by his parents.

Pinter's aversion to war is understandable if not inevitable, for in addition to having a large Jewish population, London's East End had an active ultra-right-wing movement, headed by Sir Oswald Mosley, the notorious Fascist. Said Pinter: "If you went by, or happened to be passing, a Fascist street meeting and looked in any way antagonistic . . . they'd interpret your very being, especially if you had books under your arms, as evi-

dence of your being a Communist. There was a good deal of violence there, in those days."

During his extended *Wanderjahr*, he continued to write poems and in 1949 composed the first fragment of his dramatic dialogue, "Kullus" (published in 1968 in his *Poems*). The next year he obtained work as an actor in small parts for the BBC Home Service radio programs, and early in 1951 he moved up a notch as a professional actor by performing the part of Abergavenny in the BBC Third Programme production of *Henry VIII*. At this point he decided to sample student life again and resumed his training as an actor at the Central School of Speech and Drama.

That summer "Harold Pinta" had another poem published in *Poetry London* and Harold Pinter answered an advertisement in the *Stage* for a Shakespearean actor. To his surprise he was hired and obtained his first acting engagement in the legitimate theater. For the next eighteen months he toured Ireland in the company of the veteran actor-manager Anew McMaster, whom Pinter warmly remembers in his brief memoir, *Mac* (1968).

After the tour Pinter returned to London and soon appeared in Donald Wolfit's 1953 classical season at the King's Theatre in Hammersmith, where he met the actress Vivien Merchant. In 1954 Pinter assumed the stage name David Baron and began acting in provincial repertory theaters, where he once again encountered Vivien Merchant when they played leads opposite each other at Bournemouth in 1956. They were married that year and continued to tour obscure seaside resorts and small local theaters until she became pregnant, at which time they returned to London to find a more permanent place to live and work. The Pinters' first home was a basement room in a shabby part of town in a building where Pinter worked as a caretaker to pay their rent. After their son, Daniel, was born on 29 January 1958, they borrowed some money to move to a better part of London, but both had to return to full-time acting to make ends meet.

In 1957 a friend of Pinter's telephoned to ask if he would write a play for production by the drama department at Bristol University six days later. Never having written a play before, Pinter immediately said no, but he quickly changed his mind and began a drama based on an image of two men he had seen in a small room at a London party. He finished it in four days, working in the afternoons between morning rehearsals of

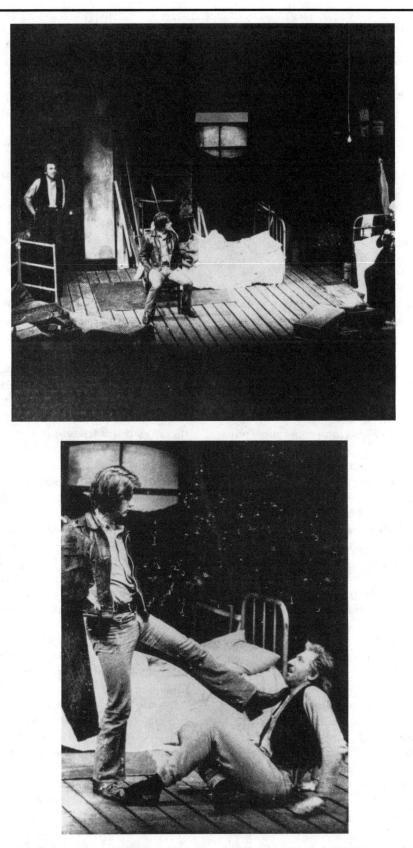

Scenes from a 1972 London production of The Caretaker: *(top) Leonard Rossiter, John Hurt, and Jeremy Kemp;*
(bottom) John Hurt and Leonard Rossiter

one play and evening performances of another, a remarkable feat when one considers that Pinter's previous writing consisted of a few published poems and an unfinished biographical novel.

First performed in a converted squash court in Bristol University's Memorial Building, *The Room* was so successful that a new production was entered in the *Sunday Times* student drama festival in December. The paper's drama critic Harold Hobson, who was one of the judges and not expected to review any of the plays, was so impressed that he wrote a favorable notice for *The Room*.

Set in a room of a large house that has been converted to an apartment building, Pinter's first play opens with a sixty-year-old woman, Rose, serving a hot meal to Bert prior to his going out to drive a delivery truck on an icy winter day. While serving the food, Rose continually compares the cold, dark, dangerous world outside with the warmth and safety of their cozy little domicile. Here is what became Pinter's basic dramatic setting: a room with a door leading to a hostile and intrusive world. The play's first intruder is an old man, Mr. Kidd, who seems to be the landlord. Kidd makes numerous and somewhat obscure references to the basement, and after a while he leaves; so does the silent Bert. Now alone, Rose opens the door to empty the garbage can and discovers a young couple looking for a room to rent. The husband tells her that "the man in the basement" said number seven was available. Rose, whose room is number seven, violently denies that it is going to become vacant, and the visitors leave. Presently a blind Negro enters. He calls himself Riley, and, in spite of being blind, he "looks about the room," notes that it is large and claims he wants to "see" Rose. Suddenly he calls her by a different name, Sal. At this point Bert comes back from his trip and, for the first time, begins to speak. Without warning, Bert turns to the Negro, throws him out of the armchair in which he has been sitting, and kicks his head against the gas stove until he lies still, presumably dead. Rose clutches her eyes and repeatedly screams "I can't see." There is a blackout and the curtain comes down.

The Room is in many ways a remarkable first play. The plot is simple without being simplistic; the dialogue, with its rambling syntax and tautologies, is both realistic and poetic; and the characters, mysterious and allusive as they often are, are nonetheless flesh and blood creatures who are rendered in psychologically accurate terms.

Only the character of Riley is problematic, something the playwright himself today admits when he remarks that Riley behaves "too differently" from the other characters.

Hobson's review of *The Room* attracted the attention of a young London producer, Michael Codron, who wrote to Pinter asking about any other plays he might have written. Pinter replied by submitting the two further plays he had completed: *The Birthday Party* (then called "The Party") and *The Dumb Waiter*. Codron expressed interest in the former and decided to produce it.

The Birthday Party begins with breakfast at the run-down boardinghouse of Meg and Petey Boles, who have only one guest at the moment, a neurotic middle-aged man named Stanley, who seems to be a concert pianist on the run. Later, while Stanley is out, two strangers arrive and it is obvious from their conversation that they have been looking for him all over town. When Meg joins them in the living room, she lets slip that it is his birthday. One of the strangers, Goldberg, insists they have a party in Stanley's honor.

The second act is devoted to Stanley's party— and to his psychological destruction by his two pursuers, who interrogate him in a litany of serious and ridiculous charges. The third act opens again with breakfast and serves as an epilogue showing the results of Stanley's ordeal. Out of a desire not to upset her and fearful of what the intruders might do to him and his wife, Petey keeps Meg in the dark about the psychological tortures that Goldberg and his partner McCann have inflicted upon Stanley during the night. Petey makes an attempt to save his boarder, but on being invited to join the threesome he retreats, and the men take Stanley away to "Monty" for "treatment."

Unfortunately, Pinter's first play to be professionally produced closed after a week's run. The reviews of opening night (28 April 1958) were unfavorable, but a few days later in the *Sunday Times* Hobson took a stand that might have saved the play had the review come earlier: "Now I am well aware that Mr. Pinter's play received extremely bad notices last Tuesday morning. . . . Deliberately, I am willing to risk whatever reputation I have as a judge of plays by saying that . . . Mr. Pinter, on the evidence of this work, possesses the most original, disturbing and arresting talent in theatrical London." Milton Shulman of the *Evening Standard* was far less generous, but his judgment was much more representative: "Sitting through *The Birthday party* . . . is like trying to solve a crossword puzzle where every vertical clue is designed to put you off the horizontal. It will be best enjoyed by those who believe that obscurity is its own reward."

Because of the complexity of the work, interpretations abound; curiously enough, most of them seem relevant. Martin Esslin sees the work as a metaphor for the process of growing up: Stanley is reluctant to leave the nest that motherly Meg has built for him, but he is finally forced out by Goldberg, the father figure of the play. Bernard F. Dukore presents another picture, that of Stanley as the artist, representing humanity, all of which is reduced to conformity. He suggests that Goldberg and McCann are two henchmen of society, who bring pressure to bear on Stanley, and Dukore points out that they are symbolically appropriate because they represent the two traditional religions of Western civilization, Judaism and Catholicism.

Although Pinter's reputation as a playwright in 1959 was far from established, he continued to receive valuable critical attention both at home and abroad. As evidence of his growing stature, his third play, *The Dumb Waiter*, had its world premiere in German at Frankfurt-am-Main in February 1959. However, it was not until the English production a year later (on a double bill with *The Room*) at the Hampstead Theatre Club that the play came into its own. Anticipating the kind of response that contributed to the failure of *The Birthday Party*, Pinter attempted to disarm his more skeptical critics by providing a program note that has now come to represent one of his more definitive statements concerning his work: "The desire for verification is understandable, but cannot be always satisfied. There are no hard distinctions between what is real and what is unreal, nor between what is true and what is false. The thing is not necessarily either true or false; it can be both true and false. The assumption that to verify what has happened and what is happening presents few problems, I take to be inaccurate. A character on the stage who can present no convincing argument or information as to his past experiences, his present behavior or his aspirations, nor give a comprehensive analysis of his motives is as legitimate and as worthy of attention as one who, alarmingly, can do all these things. The more acute the experience the less articulate its expression."

The Dumb Waiter concerns two working-class Cockneys who spend a morning in a basement bedroom in Birmingham waiting for instructions.

To pass the time they talk about football, read newspapers, and argue about the various idioms associated with lighting a gas stove. As in his other works, Pinter is content to lean back and let his characters chat rather than to plant clues to get the plot going. The men, Gus and Ben, know comparatively little about the organization they are working for, and it is only incidentally that we come to learn that they are in the business of murdering people.

We soon discover that this basement was a restaurant kitchen at one time, for without warning a dumbwaiter at the back suddenly begins to work. When the serving hatch descends completely, the gunmen find an order for a meal—which they fill with the little food they have with them. The orders continue coming, and their willingness to obey them without question is both frightening and amusing. After Gus goes off to the lavatory, Ben gets an additional order: to shoot the next person to come in through the outside door. When Gus enters through that door, Ben faces him, gun in hand. The curtain comes down before we have a chance to see Ben pull the trigger, a coup de theatre that adds a chilling coda to a play that has earlier seemed like a minor and more comic version of Samuel Beckett's *Waiting for Godot* (1953).

The play, which was favorably reviewed, marks an important step forward in Pinter's style; here he suggests that the mysterious forces dictating the characters' actions and behavior are in reality expressions of their subconscious motivations. Pinter's ability to create a drama that is seemingly both realistic and expressionistic provided further testimony to his considerable promise as a playwright.

As a measure of his acceptance as a playwright of real merit, Pinter was commissioned by the BBC to write a radio drama for its Third Programme. He wrote a piece called "Something in Common," but the play was not produced and rather mysteriously disappeared from the Pinter canon. The BBC then commissioned another sixty-minute play, and he soon produced *A Slight Ache* (1959), the first of his many plays written for radio or television and subsequently adapted for the stage. The work begins a new phase in his career, marking the end of a period of relative obscurity. Up to mid 1959 his plays, though heralded in certain critical circles, had made little impact on the public at large. *A Slight Ache* is also the first of his plays based on a middle-class

Gabrielle Drake, Barry Foster, and Donald Pleasence in a scene from a 1970 London production of Tea Party

idiom and the first in which the action is not confined to a single room.

The setting of *A Slight Ache* is an elegant country house, with a garden, inhabited by a middle-class couple, Edward and Flora, who have more than their share of pretensions. They are discovered sitting at the breakfast table, engaged in a trivial but tense conversation that shows considerable friction between them. As in the three earlier plays, there is the threat of an intruder, in this case an old man with a tray, who is selling matches near the back entrance to their garden. Edward's attempts to draw the matchseller into a conversation reveal the anxiety behind his sophisticated facade. From his remarks we learn that Edward is a snob, is selfish, and has very little love for Flora, whose own questions to the matchseller intimate a deep need for sexual fulfillment. Edward, who has "a slight ache" in his eyes, wonders if the matchseller also has difficulty seeing. Gradually he breaks down and falls

to the floor complaining about the germ he caught in his eyes. As Edward grows weaker the old man becomes stronger, until finally Edward and the matchseller change positions, Flora herself hanging the tray around her husband's neck. As in his other plays, Pinter uses sight imagery as a poetic motif having to do with mental or physical disintegration. Those afflicted often experience epiphanies revealing new truths and long-suppressed fears. For instance, Edward realizes his early premonition has been proved correct: an outsider can destroy the comfortable world that the individual erects and desperately tries to protect with social and verbal stratagems.

After menacing his audiences for two years, Pinter in mid 1959, at the suggestion of Disley Jones, a friend who was producing a musical revue, turned his hand to pure comedy (or as pure as his comedy was ever to get) and wrote some humorous sketches. *Trouble in the Works* and *The Black and White* were used in the Disley Jones

revue, *One to Another* (1959), while *Request Stop,
Last to Go, Special Offer*, and *Getting Acquainted*
were placed in *Pieces of Eight*, a popular revue produced in London later that year. Although most
of them are little more than finger exercises, all
of them present in some small ways the characteristic concerns of his major plays.

Trouble in the Works takes place in a factory
and brings together two men representing management and labor. Mr. Wills, a personnel officer, tells his boss, Mr. Fibbs, that the workers are
viciously turning against the products his factory
turns out, items such as "hemi unibal spherical
rod ends" and "high speed taper shank spiral
flute reamers." Pinter is playing a game with language, using pseudotechnical jargon to illustrate
the difficulty of communication. According to
the playwright, who narrated *Pinter People*, an ani-
mated television production of some of the
sketches, the exchange grew out of his experiences on a job he held in a factory service department for half a day.

In *The Black and White* two homeless women
pass their evenings in a milk bar, discussing all-
night buses. It is a study of simple, lonely lives
that is saved from bleakness by humorously realistic dialogue and a genuine affection and warmth
that the writer lavishes on his characters, the prototypes of whom Pinter observed in real life.

Pinter refused to have two of the sketches
from *Pieces of Eight* published because he considered them too slight. *Getting Acquainted*, a farcical
piece having to do with civil defense, is presumably lost. *Special Offer* is a very short monologue
by a BBC secretary who is at her office desk and
talking about an incident that happened to her
in the ladies room at Swan and Edgar, a once-
stylish London department store. An old woman
approached her while she was sitting in a stall
and put a card into her hand announcing "MEN
FOR SALE." The secretary appears to be
shocked by the incident, but her apparent indignation may only be a cover for the sexual excitement she is experiencing.

In *Request Stop* a woman with xenophobic tendencies abuses a man in a bus queue after asking
him for directions to Shepherds Bush. Having
been born "just around the corner," the woman
obviously spends her days accusing people who
happen to look non-British of indecent acts and remarks. She seeks witnesses, but the others ignore
her and run after a passing bus. Presently another man walks up to the bus stop and the
whole ritual begins again, the woman now ostensi-

bly seeking information about a bus to Marble
Arch. In *Last to Go*, a barman and an old newspaper seller at a coffee stall aimlessly chat about
newspapers and a man named George, whom neither seems to know well. The conversation of the
two men seems to represent a ritualistic act in
which the content of their discussion is minor.

Five comedy sketches, *That's Your Trouble,
That's All, Applicant, Interview*, and *Dialogue for
Three*, were produced in 1964 by the BBC Radio
Third Programme. *That's Your Trouble* involves
two men in a park observing a third man offstage carrying a sandwich board. Desperate for
things to say and do, they argue heatedly about
whether the board is giving the man a headache
or a backache. Their conversation becomes increasingly illogical and childish as both men studiously avoid the obvious choice of asking the
sandwichman himself.

Applicant is a fragment from *The Hothouse*,
Pinter's "discarded" play written in 1958 but not
produced until 1980. A comic treatment of sadism and man-hating, the sketch shows a young
man appropriately named Lamb entering an office for a job interview. Almost immediately he is
subjected to various tests to determine his "psychological suitability" for the job by a woman named
Piffs, who attaches electrodes to his palms and earphones to his head. Lamb, who initially had been
eager, cheerful, and enthusiastic, is psychologically slaughtered by this "essence of efficiency."
The playlet would be morbid were it not for the
distance provided by the cartoonlike characters.

Interview may be the slightest of the sketches. A pornographic bookseller with the unsub-
tle name of Mr. Jakes is being interviewed about
his business during the pre-Christmas rush. Business is bad, he tells his questioner, because very
few people send pornographic books as "Xmas"
presents. When asked what sort of people frequent his shop, Jakes talks about compiling dossi-
ers on his customers, who are all the same,
"every single one of them. COMMUNISTS."

Like *The Black and White*, *That's All* examines
the monotony and the loneliness of the lives of
two old women, here Mrs. A. and Mrs. B., who discuss the reasons why a friend who used to visit
Mrs. A. on Wednesdays now usually comes on
Thursdays. As in *Last to Go*, it is the ritualistic nature of their discourse rather than the substance
of what they say that is important.

Dialogue for Three is really a dialogue for
two, since one character, 2nd Man, gets only one
line, "The snow has turned to slush" (taken, inci-

Barry Foster and Donald Pleasence in a scene from a 1970 London production of The Basement

dentally, from *The Hothouse*). The remainder of the lines are given to the 1st Man, who tells improbable adventure stories, and to the Woman, who speaks mostly about masculinity and femininity. The sketch implies the solipsistic nature of most people's lives.

Ten years after completing these comic sketches, Pinter in 1969 wrote another for a program of miniature plays by various playwrights about marriage, *We Who Are About To . . .*, which was later revised as *Mixed Doubles: An Entertainment On Marriage*. Pinter's contribution, *Night*, is a serious piece in which a husband and wife recall their first meeting. Although only in their forties, they have difficulty remembering the exact incidents of that fateful night. She says they met at a party, he says on a bridge. It may be, as she later suggests, that he is talking about another woman, or possibly they are both remembering other people. The verification theme, simply and poignantly rendered, emerges in the play.

A Night Out was originally written in 1959 for radio and was first produced by BBC Radio in 1960. Almost immediately afterwards it was adapted and broadcast in a television version. It later became a stage play and thus far has proved to be popular, particularly with amateur groups. The play is the first of Pinter's works that is entirely realistic, and perhaps because of this is generally regarded as one of his lesser pieces. The story is a cliché of psychological realism: a domineering mother is in conflict with her weak-willed, passive son who attempts to escape from her grasp. Albert is a twenty-eight-year-old insurance clerk preparing to go to an office party. The news surprises and disappoints his mother, for this is the first time that he has attempted to sever the umbilical cord. In an effort to keep him from going, Mrs. Stokes makes numerous emotional appeals, including references to his dead father and grandmother, all designed to generate guilt and anxiety.

Albert, however, does go, after first meeting two male friends at a coffee stall, where he is maliciously teased about being a mama's boy. The final scene shows his return home, where he is welcomed by Mrs. Stokes as if nothing had happened. As the play ends, the audience is left wondering whether Albert's ability to dominate the prostitute he met during his night out will enable him to achieve dominance over his mother, who sits in a chair close to him, stroking his hand as the curtain comes down.

Aside from the minor ambiguity of the ending, *A Night Out* is completely straightforward in its intentions and meaning. One reason for this lack of subtlety may have been Pinter's awareness of the size and nature of radio and television audiences. Structurally, the play is designed episodically, with quick cuts and rapid scene changes, typical of works created for more fluid media. But the play's explicitness often borders on condescension, as if the writer felt he had to talk down to a mass audience. Many of the play's points about mother-son relationships, prostitutes, secretaries, and the like, are precariously close to parlor psychology and college-level Freud.

Pinter's next play, *The Caretaker* (1960), was his first major success in the theater. It is also one of postwar Britain's most important plays and, along with *The Homecoming*, perhaps his most significant contribution to the drama thus far. In describing how it came to be written, Pinter said: "I went into a room and saw one person standing up and one person sitting down, and a few weeks later I wrote *The Room*. I went into another room and saw two people sitting down, and a few years later I wrote *The Birthday Party*. I looked through a door into a third room, and saw two people standing up and I wrote *The Caretaker*." The response, tongue-and-cheek though it may sound, very likely is an accurate description of the play's origins. When pressed for a fuller definition of the work, Pinter merely replied that it was about a caretaker and two brothers.

Certainly on the narrative level he is right. *The Caretaker* begins with Aston, the older brother, bringing home a man who calls himself Davies, an opinionated, prejudiced old tramp whom Aston rescued from a fight. Although Davies is unpleasant in the extreme—his general grubbiness and hatred of Poles, Greeks, blacks, and other minorities are off-putting if not downright offensive—Aston rather kindly offers Davies a place to sleep for the night. It is only later that we learn that Aston's gentleness derives in part from his having had electric-shock treatments in a mental home two years before.

Sensing a chance to exploit his host, Davies presents himself as a hard-luck creature who is in desperate need of a home, but he emerges as a man who has tricked the world into providing a liv-

ing for him, a fact which Mick, the younger brother and real owner of the house, senses during his extended encounter with the tramp in the second act. Mick gratuitously reminisces about his past and comments that the old man reminds him "of my uncle's brother." He then cross-examines Davies both brutally and politely, frightening and confusing the tramp. Later, after Aston has offered him a position as caretaker of the house, Davies attempts to ingratiate himself with Mick by flattering him and deriding his brother. When Davies calls Aston "nutty," Mick becomes furious and dismisses him from the job. The tramp then tries futilely to reconcile himself with Aston, and the play ends with Davies talking disjointedly about going to Sidcup, a London suburb, to claim his identity papers.

The Caretaker has been discussed by critics more fully than any other Pinter work. No two seem to agree on a particular interpretation, though most explanations contain a good deal of merit because what they offer is at least partly true. Esslin sees a strong Beckett influence; the way in which the characters of the two brothers complement each other suggests that Mick and Aston (like Didi and Gogo in *Waiting for Godot*) are aspects of the same personality, Mick representing the worldy, Aston the deeply emotional. He also views them as archetypes "of the conflict between two young men and an old one, of the battle between the sons and the father."

William Baker and Stephen Tabachnick call Davies "the first truly realistic bum in the history of literature" and credit this character with the literary and theatrical success of the play. Ronald Hayman, differing from most of his fellow critics, views the play as a partial failure, due primarily to what he regards as Pinter's heavy-handedness in explaining present behavior in terms of past history. Specifically he objects to the detailed psychoanalyzing of Aston, whose somewhat mysterious behavior is clarified in a most un-Pinteresque manner by the character himself. The play was made into a major motion picture, *The Guest* (1964), and it is interesting to note that in the film version Pinter asked that the setting be located in his old neighborhood near Hackney Downs.

Next came *Night School*, "The worst thing I have written," according to Pinter, who felt so dissatisfied with this television play that he would not include this version of it in any of the volumes of his plays and refused to permit further performances. The playwright rewrote the work

Royal Shakespeare Company in

THE HOMECOMING

by Harold Pinter

Teddy	Michael Bryant
Lenny	Ian Holm
Ruth	Vivien Merchant
Sam	John Normington
Joey	Terence Rigby
Max	Paul Rogers

The play takes place in an old house
in north London.

Act I　　　　　　　　　　Evening

Interval

Act II　　　　　　　　　　Afternoon

Directed by Peter Hall
Designed by John Bury

(THE HOMECOMING is presented by arrangement with
Roger L. Stevens)

Olivier Cigarettes by Benson and Hedges. King Six cigars by
J R Freeman and Son. Wardrobe care by Persil. Starch and
shoecare by the Kiwi Polish Co. Ltd. Hoovermatic Washing
Machine, Steam and Dry Irons used in the Wardrobe supplied
by Hoover Ltd. Typewriter by British Olivetti Ltd.

THE HOMECOMING

This is the world premiere of Harold Pinter's first full-length
play since THE CARETAKER (which won the Evening
Standard drama award for the best play of 1960, the Page
One award of the Newspaper Guild of New York, and was
recently filmed). Pinter was born in London in 1930 and
before becoming a playwright worked as a professional
actor. He wrote his first play THE ROOM in 1957 and
completed THE DUMB WAITER and THE BIRTHDAY
PARTY in the same year. In 1962 he co-directed with
Peter Hall his own play THE COLLECTION for the Royal
Shakespeare Company at the Aldwych, where he also directed a production of THE BIRTHDAY PARTY for the company
last summer. Pinter won the Italia Prize for his television
play THE LOVER which was also seen at the Arts Theatre.
He has also written the screenplay for the films THE
SERVANT and THE PUMPKIN EATER. This week his latest
play TEA-PARTY is on BBC Television. It will also be
shown in eleven other Eurovision countries.

ROYAL SHAKESPEARE COMPANY

The Royal Shakespeare Company are divided between Stratford-upon-Avon
and London playing concurrently at two theatres. For as well as their
continuous repertoire of new and classic plays at the London theatre, they
give the annual April-to-November Shakespeare season at Stratford.

POLICY

The Royal Shakespeare Company believe that the Elizabethan theatre —
and especially Shakespeare — offers a dramatic richness unequalled in any
other epoch or language.

The aim of the RSC is to express this richness so that it is immediate to
modern audiences. Such an aim must have certain instruments.
One is a company, built round a core of actors under long term contract,
playing constantly together, and so able to explore a modern Shakespeare
style. Another is a London repertoire of mainly non-Shakespearean plays
in which the actors can respond to all the influences of modern and classic
drama and use these influences in their Shakespeare repertoire at Stratford.

The company also give experimental seasons where they attempt to
recapture something of the Elizabethan fullness of expression by challenging
accepted forms of production, acting and writing, and they develop in
private in their studio the agility and freedom that Shakespeare's plays
demand.

Cast list, synopsis of scenes, and program notes for the first London production of Pinter's third full-length play,
inspired by the experiences of a boyhood friend

in 1966, as a radio drama, consenting the following year to its publication. Of the first version Pinter said, "I realized that in one short television
play of mine there were characteristics that implied I was slipping into a formula. . . . The
words and ideas had become automatic, redundant. That was the red light for me. . . ." Indeed,
themes and techniques of earlier plays are recapitulated with disturbing familiarity. The dialogue
is consciously Pinteresque, with its deliberate re-
petitiveness and its definite rhythm, and once
again the basic conflict is a battle for possession
of a room. In the radio play, a petty criminal
named Walter returns home from prison to discover that his two maiden aunts have rented his
room to an attractive young woman, ostensibly a
schoolteacher, who goes to night school three

times a week to study languages. Hurt and defen-
sive, he secretly rummages through her possessions and finds a photograph that convinces him
she is less innocent than she appears. Frightened
and presumably ashamed that Walter is aware of
her "other side," she secretly moves out, leaving
behind a genteel farewell note to the aunts. Walter thus gets what he wanted, his room, but in
the bargain he loses what may be the only chance
he will ever have to find a loving partner. Despite the improvement in the play when it was
adapted for radio, most critics still sympathize
with Pinter's original assessment, agreeing that it
is superficial compared with his previous works.
Night School merits our attention because it begins to explore a question that becomes paramount in Pinter's later plays: Can an honest relationship be founded on a lie?

Both audiences and drama and academic critics agree that *The Dwarfs* is Pinter's most difficult play, and some claim that it is not a play at all. Taken from his unpublished novel of the same name, which he worked on from 1950 to 1959, the piece is basically a series of fragmentary and sometimes incoherent conversations among three friends in their thirties: Len, Mark, and Pete. The play was originally written for radio and was broadcast in 1960; it was later adapted for the stage and produced in 1963. *The Dwarfs* stems from one of Pinter's early major efforts as a writer and therefore shows us some of the themes Pinter later developed in his other plays.

The work begins with a scene in which Len and Pete are eating and drinking in Mark's apartment, complaining about the food and their absent friend. Like Pinter in the 1950s, Mark is an actor and frequently away from his home because of professional engagements outside London. Little is known about Pete, but it appears that Len has a job as a porter at one of London's main train stations. The main character, through whose eyes we view most of the action, Len imagines himself being pursued by "dwarfs," tiny, dirty creatures who offer him scraps of food. Not unlike Aston in *The Caretaker*, Len seems to be undergoing a mental breakdown. There is no plot to speak of and practically no action. There is, however, a conflict between Mark and Pete concerning their inability to help their disordered friend. All three men are mutually dependent—and mutually distrustful. Len is eventually hospitalized, an experience that proves beneficial because the dwarfs are preparing to leave him, and at the very end of the play they apparently do. As Len says in his closing monologue, "Now all is bare. All is clean. All is scrubbed. There is a lawn. There is a shrub. There is a flower."

The three have gone through a therapeutic rite of passage marking a transition between one stage of growth to the next. They have found out, if only for the moment, who they are. They have also made some necessary psychological and emotional adjustments that will permit them to become better functioning members of society rather than the misfits they consciously and unconsciously viewed themselves as being.

It has been noted by more than a few critics that homosexuality is a theme in many of Pinter's works. Certainly the closeness of the three men in *The Dwarfs* implies that they may be homosexuals. Homosexuality in Pinter's next play, *The Collection* (1961), is much more obvious and a great deal more central to the main action. Harry Kane, a wealthy middle-aged dress designer, lives with Bill Lloyd, another designer, twenty years his junior. Although Pinter never states so directly, their behavior suggests that Harry and Bill are sexually intimate, though not necessarily emotionally involved.

Their relationship is upset one day by James Horne, a neighbor whom they have not met before, who runs a dress shop with Stella, his wife. Stella has apparently told Horne that she had an affair with Bill in Leeds while both were attending a convention there the week before. He accuses the young man of following his wife to her room and then taking advantage of her in her loneliness. Bill initially denies the allegations but seems fascinated by the charges, which may not be as baseless as they originally seemed. When James claims that Bill was sitting next to his wife on her bed when he, James, phoned, Bill immediately corrects him: "Not sitting. Lying."

The following scenes illustrate the domestic tension between the two couples. It is revealed that Harry and Bill are together only because of the older man's largess and that Stella and James mean practically nothing to each other, their marriage having gone stale well before Stella's chance encounter with Bill in a hotel elevator. Pinter seems to be saying that truth becomes what each person makes of it. Is Stella's story true? The business of verification turns into a highly serious but rather amusing game for the four principals, three of whom—the men—are both frustrated and titillated by the ambiguities involved in the conflicting versions of the truth. The play ends with James returning home to attempt once more to get a satisfactory answer from Stella, although his infatuation with Bill leads us to believe that he would probably not want one, precluding as it would further opportunities to meet with the young man. The lives of both couples will never again be the same now that they have been energized by suspicion and the threat of violence stemming from an incident that may or may not have happened. Pinter makes no judgment about the nature of the behavior he depicts in *The Collection*. A lesser playwright might have created the impression that his characters were suffering from various neuroses, but Pinter's people are as normal as the audiences who observe them, which is to say as perplexed and as amused as most individuals are when forcefully confronted with the question of truth and reality.

The Lover (1963) is frequently produced with *The Collection*, for thematically the two plays have much in common, particularly the examination of fantasy and wish fulfillment in marriage. Richard and Sarah are a young, sophisticated couple who would not be out of place in a Noel Coward comedy. Though they are outwardly "respectable," the first line of the play suggests that they are anything but pillars of society: Richard says amiably, "Is your lover coming today?" He is, replies Sarah, and from the remaining conversation of the first scene it becomes clear that the arrangement they speak about is for them neither shocking nor disturbing.

Later, after the husband leaves, the doorbell rings, leading the audience to believe that the wife's lover is about to arrive. In a good-natured swipe at more traditional dramaturgy and the expectations of part of his audience, Pinter brings on the milkman, whose only functions are to offer Sarah some cream, which she refuses, and to offer the audience a Freudian in-joke.

The lover enters shortly after the milkman exits. It is Richard, dressed casually and going by the name of Max. Sarah greets him warmly and immediately they begin to perform an elaborate erotic ritual. While Pinter is detailing the need for variety in relationships, he is also examining the multifaceted human personality, which operates on many disparate and conflicting levels. Man is both a social and instinctive being, and it is the conflict between these two states that in large measure accounts for his dynamism. The play ends several scenes later with the possibility that the characters' fantasy world is becoming more real than the world from which they are attempting to escape.

Tea Party was first a short story and a television play before it became a play for the stage. Pinter wrote the story in 1963 and read it on the BBC Third Programme in 1964. The following year it was published in *Playboy* magazine. Pinter was not entirely happy with the television (1965) and stage (1968) versions, claiming "the story is more successful." The dramatized versions have been much expanded, but the story lines of all three are more or less identical.

Tea Party deals with the downfall of Disson, a successful businessman whose firm is England's largest producer of toilets and bidets. A self-made man painfully aware of his plebeian background, he is about to enter into a second marriage. His fiancée, Diana, is an upper-class wo-

man who represents to him high social status and respectability. Throughout the action, which takes place over a period of one year and culminates in a tea party celebrating the first anniversary of his marriage, Disson experiences difficulty with his vision. Once a highly disciplined and fanatically reasonable man, he futilely tries to cope with a rapidly changing life-style by acquiescing to the entreaties and demands of his new wife and her brother, who may in fact be her lover. When Disson suddenly begins seeing two balls instead of one during a Ping-Pong game with Diana's brother, it becomes evident that he is gradually going mad. Much of the play's action takes place in the mind of the protagonist, the absurdity of the language and situations merely being projections of Disson's disordered consciousness. If Disson were a man of greater stature and seriousness and if the play were less outwardly comic, *Tea Party* might well approach the tragic. Like Oedipus, he is a man who believes deeply in the power of reason. He is also like Oedipus in that he is an intensely emotional and basically irrational individual who, like all tragic heroes, must share the responsibility for his fall, and in effect does so by willfully blinding himself at the very end of the play.

In 1963 Grove Press asked Pinter to contribute a screenplay for a composite film entitled "Project I: Three Original Motion Picture Scripts by Samuel Beckett, Eugene Ionesco, Harold Pinter." With the exception of Beckett's work, *Film*, directed by Alan Schneider in 1964, the project never materialized. Pinter did, however, complete a screenplay which he called "The Compartment," based in part on "The Examination," a short story he had written in 1958, and the prose poem *Kullus* begun in 1949 when Pinter was nineteen. The screenplay was eventually transformed into a television play, which was broadcast on the BBC in 1967 under its new title, *The Basement*. The following year it was given its world premiere as a stage play (on a double bill with *Tea Party*) in an off-Broadway theater in New York City.

The outline of the play is simple. Tim Law is visited one winter evening by a former roommate, Charles Stott, and Stott's young girlfriend, Jane. After a relatively brief chat about old times, Charles and Jane climb into Law's bed and begin making love. Amidst long sighs and gasps by Jane, Law reads from an illustrated Persian love manual. In a series of short scenes that take place over a period of several years, the characters play

Michael Bryant, Terence Rigby, and Ian Holme in a scene from the first London production of The Homecoming
(photograph by Zoë Dominic)

sexually oriented power games with each other. Much of the play is concerned with Stott's appropriating Law's apartment for himself and Law's edging out Stott in order to become Jane's lover. The play ends exactly as it has begun, except this time Law and Jane come to what is now Stott's apartment to begin the cycle anew.

Like many of Pinter's plays, *The Basement* starts off realistically enough, but the fact that Jane casually undresses before a complete stranger and begins to make love to her boyfriend in that stranger's company tells us that we are not witnessing a realistic story. All of what transpires in *The Basement* may be nothing more than Law's increasing dependence on wish fulfillment. Obviously lonely and desirous of company, he could be merely preparing himself for that eventuality by rehearsing in his mind the incidents that might legitimately arise from such a visit. Pinter seems to be saying that man is constantly shifting

back and forth between the extremes of fact and fantasy, a process guaranteed to perpetuate anxiety and frustration, but one that provides the unpredictability and variety needed to animate what would otherwise be a static and life-denying existence.

The Homecoming (1965) is Pinter's third full-length play and by general consensus his best and most important. Certainly it is his most honored, particularly in the United States, where it won Broadway's Tony Award, the New York Drama Critics Circle Award, and the Whitbread Anglo-American Award. Its longevity seems assured in part by the excellent 1971 film version (screenplay by Pinter) which gave audiences a second chance to ponder and appreciate one of the most challenging and entertaining dramas of postwar Britain.

The narrative of *The Homecoming* was inspired by a boyhood friend from Hackney who

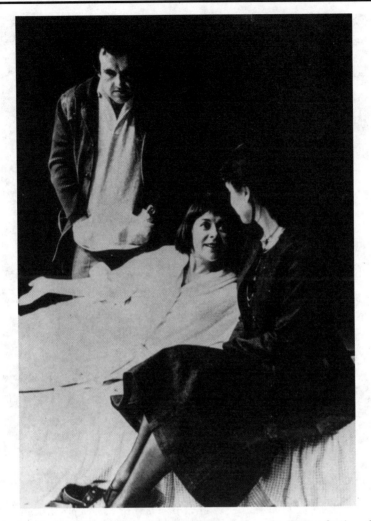

Colin Blakely, Dorothy Tutin, and Vivien Merchant in a scene from the first production of Old Times

went to Canada to teach and get married secretly before returning home to surprise his family with his new bride. In the play the eldest and brightest of three sons, Teddy, a philosophy professor at an American university, returns to visit his family in the north of London. Accompanied by Ruth, a woman he alleges to be his wife, Teddy talks about their six years in America, their three children, and a just-completed trip to Venice. His father, Max, a retired butcher who shares the house with his two remaining sons, Lenny and Joey, and Max's brother, Sam, is less than pleased by his unexpected return. Seeing Ruth but not yet knowing exactly who she is, Max refers to her as a dirty tart and a stinking pox-ridden slut. "I've never had a whore under this roof before," he tells Teddy. "Ever since your mother died."

The ambiguous reference to his dead wife helps to explain Max's initial hostility toward Ruth, for although it is never clearly stated in the play, the four remaining family members are or were or will be pimps. Claiming to have been a butcher like his father, Max has very likely traded in another kind of flesh—human. Sam strongly suggests that Max's wife, Jessie, was a call girl, and that Max approved of and fostered the arrangement. At the end of the play Teddy returns to his teaching job in America, and his wife stays behind to help support her husband's family by becoming a prostitute. That she so readily accepts their offer can be explained by numerous allusions to what could have been her own sordid past: "I was a model for the body," she tells the family. "A photographic model for the body." At the very end Teddy indirectly encourages Ruth to change her mind, but she does not and says to her departing husband, "Don't become a stranger." Alone now with her new family, Ruth relaxes in her chair while the father and sons hover about her seeking favors and affection. What makes the scene even more grotesque is the presence of Sam, lying on the floor nearby after suffering what seems to have been a terminal stroke.

In spite of the shockingly casual and matter-of-fact way Pinter treats illness, sex, prostitution, and sadism in this work, *The Homecoming* is a genuinely amusing play, abounding with sudden surprises and filled with theatrical effectiveness. Most reviewers were cautious in their appraisal, having been too quick in the past to condemn what later turned out to be well in advance of its time. Academic critics, on the other hand, were well nigh ecstatic, particularly Esslin, who called the work "a poetic image of a basic human situation [which] can also stand up to the most meticulous examination as a piece of realistic theatre." He believes that the play reexamines the major themes of *King Lear* and *Oedipus Rex*: "the desolation of old age and the sons' desire for the sexual conquest of the mother." John Russell Taylor thinks the work is about "the battle between intellect and instinct, between thought and action"; Teddy, the thinker of the family, is pitted against a savage and irrational family whose only saving grace is its vitality. Austin E. Quigley in *The Pinter Problem* observes that the play "explores relationships in a family context, but it is in no way limited to the kinds of stereotypical relationships that prominent psychological, sociological, and anthropological theories have made widely known." The play continues to engender critical commentary and discussion, and given its highly complex and allusive nature, it will no doubt do so for some time to come.

Landscape and *Silence* represent a significant departure for Pinter. Together running less than two hours, these short works show the playwright shifting his attention almost exclusively from the physical world to the mental world of his characters. Pinter has said that after *The Homecoming* he "couldn't any longer stay in the room with this bunch of people who opened doors and came in and went out. *Landscape* and *Silence* are in a very different form. There isn't any menace at all." He also believed at this time that he could never write another full-length play. "My plays are getting shorter," he said in a London *Times* interview. "Words are so tender. One-act plays are all I seem to be able to write at the moment."

Landscape was written for the stage but Pinter withdrew it from production when the stage censor in 1968, the last year before the office was

abolished, insisted that Pinter remove a four-letter word from the text. When he refused, the play received its first performance on BBC radio, a medium not subject to the Lord Chamberlain's powers. The following year it was produced on the stage in a double bill with *Silence*.

Landscape runs only thirty minutes and has only two characters, Duff and Beth, a married middle-aged couple who sit in opposite corners of a kitchen in a country house. There is no dialogue between them, even though they talk at length. In essence, the play alternates between their two monologues. Duff talks of Beth as "you" but does not address her directly. She talks about someone called her "man" and the experiences she has had with him on a beach, yet it is never altogether clear if she is reminiscing about Duff or someone who might have been a secret lover. Both characters display traditional human and sexual concerns: she dreams of experiencing intercourse and conceiving a baby, he muses about playing with children and avoiding the rain.

Although *Silence* was not planned as a sequel to *Landscape*, it has come to be regarded as its natural companion piece. "It was one of those happy things that rarely happen with me," said Pinter. "I always feel after completing something that I'll never write again, but then came *Silence*." Short as it is, the play took longer to write than any of his full-length works. *Silence* goes even further than *Landscape* in diminishing the importance of scenery, which is now largely created by words spoken by two men—Rumsey, who is forty, and Bates, in his mid thirties—and a young woman in her twenties, Ellen. Each of the characters has an area with a chair in it, and for all practical purposes they live apart from each other. Like *Landscape*, *Silence* consists of crosscut monologues. The lyricism of the play is intense and often penetrable only by emotional means rather than by rational means. Especially in this work, Pinter is reveling in the musicality of words; each letter and syllable is counterpointed with those frequent Pinter pauses to create the fluid world of a musical composition.

The play is an attempt to tell a story simultaneously from three different points of view and three different points in time. Rumsey, Ellen's first lover, eventually leaves her and advises her to find a younger man. She meets Bates, lives with him, but continues to love Rumsey. Their relationship becomes strained and they grow apart. Thus the play is a musical picture of three isolated and unhappy people using words and silences to help fill the void.

By the time *Old Times* premiered at the Aldwych Theatre in June 1971), Pinter was one of the world's most famous living playwrights. Articles and books about his plays continued to be published at a furious rate since the late 1950s. Most of them were now laudatory, full of praise for what had earlier been derided or dismissed by drama and academic critics. Still, there was a lingering suspicion that his dramaturgy was persistently problematic for most theatergoers and reviewers. While *New York Times* drama critic Clive Barnes called the Broadway production of *Old Times* "A joyous, wonderful play that people will talk about as long as we have theatre" and compared it in technique if not in stature to the works of Joyce and Proust, he betrayed an ambivalence symptomatic of current criticism of Pinter's works. "Pinter's ideas," he continued, "leap madly like March hares in desperate need of April."

The characters in *Old Times* are three: Deeley and his wife, Kate, and Anna, Kate's friend and former roommate whom she has not seen in twenty years. The action opens in a converted farmhouse one night in autumn as Deeley and Kate await the arrival of Anna, who, it is obliquely suggested, may have had a lesbian affair with Kate and is now trying to recapitulate their past relationship. During the course of the evening husband, wife, and friend reminisce about their youth, comparing memories and stories that both corroborate and contradict the events and relationships under discussion. Kate tells Deeley that Anna used to steal her underwear, but later Anna tells him that Kate continually offered her these personal items. Deeley is patently suspicious and jealous of his wife's friend, and Anna might be said to feel the same toward Deeley, for the two are engaged in a battle for possession of Kate's mind and body. While Kate is taking a bath, Anna and Deeley talk about how she might properly dry herself. Both want to "dry" and "powder" her in ways that are unambiguously sexual. Finally, Deeley asserts himself. "Listen. I'll tell you what. I'll do it.... After all, I am her husband." He nonetheless has difficulty removing Anna completely from the picture ("But you can supervise the whole thing. And give me some hot tips while you're at it"), and he could be suggesting a ménage à trois.

Each character in *Old Times* reconstructs the past selectively and uses it to substantiate or negate the other characters' perceptions about the present. That Pinter chose to present this idea in a sexually charged atmosphere further demonstrates his earlier notion that the sex drive and man's propensity for illusion may well share a similar source.

Monologue is a twenty-minute monologue that BBC Television produced in 1973. A slight piece, it bears some resemblance to *Old Times* in that it deals with a third party attempting to enter into an intimate relationship. The play examines two male friends and a woman, although the only character who appears onstage is one man who is a friend of the married couple. He sits in a chair throughout and speaks to the empty chair next to him. At the play's outset he is openly friendly and witty: "Fancy a game [of Ping-Pong]? How would you like a categorical thrashing? I'm willing to accept any challenge, any stakes, any gauntlet you'd care to fling down. What have you done with your gauntlets, by the way?" At the end of the play the speaker's friendliness and affection give way to his loneliness and resentment. "I feel for you," he tells the absent husband. "Even if you feel nothing . . . for me." He insists that they are friends and reveals that they were and possibly still are rivals for the wife's affections: "She loved my soul. It was my soul she loved." But, despite this assertion, it is clear she did not love his soul and that the husband no longer feels anything for him, something he himself has acknowledged. He insists, however, that he feels free, not rejected. His final words, though, betray his lingering attachment to the couple: "I love your children."

No Man's Land proved a disappointment to some critics and many Pinter fans when it premiered in 1975. Some felt that the play succeeded largely because of the excellent cast headed by Ralph Richardson and John Gielgud. *No Man's Land* is a veritable catalogue of a number of previous Pinter plays and themes, as Dukore points out in his study of Pinter's tragicomedy. Like *The Caretaker*, it has a derelict who tries and fails to establish himself in the home of a would-be benefactor; it repeats a major Pinter theme, the unreliability of memory; as in earlier plays there are hints of homosexuality; and its characters are similar to those in *The Homecoming* when they maliciously taunt each other while presenting a front of affability. Perhaps because of this heavy self-indebtedness, the play does not appear to be an assured and convincing work.

The action of the play is set in the living room of a large house in northwest London on a

Ralph Richardson in a scene from the first production of No Man's Land

summer night. Hirst, an elderly, wealthy writer, probably an alcoholic, invites Spooner, a seedy stranger, into his home for a drink. Spooner is a talker and reveals himself and his circumstances in a way designed to ingratiate himself with his host. "You need a friend," he tells Hirst. "I offer myself to you as a friend." Soon Spooner and Hirst engage in hurtful conversations about the past, or what they would like to believe or have others believe is the past. Their dialogue about their presumed lives becomes overtly cruel, until the entrance of Foster and Briggs, slightly younger men who are part of the Hirst household. That they stand between Spooner and Hirst is an unmistakable sign to both audience and guest about their function. The servants in this household appear to be the real masters.

Undaunted, Spooner still tries to gain a more permanent foothold by asking Hirst to take him on as secretary and to displace Foster. But the three residents soon close ranks against the outsider, who is to be expelled. Hirst is thus estranged from Spooner, whose continuing pres-

ence as a companion might have made a positive difference in his life. Spooner is the alternative considered but not taken, a thought which both men acknowledge. Says Spooner: "You are in no man's land. Which never moves, which never changes, which never grows older, but which remains forever icy and silent." There is a silence before Hirst concludes the play with "I'll drink to that."

In addition to being a playwright and actor, Pinter is also a screenwriter and stage director of some note. His interest in film dates back to his membership in the Hackney Downs School Literary and Debating Society, where he once gave a speech on "Realism and Post-Realism in the French Cinema." Since 1962 he has written twelve screenplays and has developed a reputation in film circles as a master screenwriter. All of the filmscripts have been adaptations, including three based on his own dramas, *The Birthday Party*, *The Caretaker* (adapted as *The Guest*), and *The Homecoming*, which is more a filmed reproduction of the stage play rather than a truly cinematic work.

Most of Pinter's films have been critically acclaimed and have given him enough financial security to allow him to write his dramatic works at a more thoughtful pace. Noteworthy among the films based on the writing of others are three films directed by Joseph Losey, a man connected with many of Pinter's film projects: *The Servant* (1963), from Robin Maugham's 1948 novel of the same name; *Accident* (1967), from a 1965 novel by Nicholas Mosley; and *The Go-Between* (1971), based on L. P. Hartley's 1953 novel. Similar in style to Pinter's work to begin with, all three books have been thoroughly "Pinterized" with that special humor, dialogue, and situation that is typical in his plays. More recently, he wrote the screenplay for the 1981 film version of John Fowles's novel, *The French Lieutenant's Woman*. Pinter's finest work for film, "The Proust Screenplay," based on Marcel Proust's *A la Recherche du Temps Perdu* and considered by some to be a major literary work in its own right, has yet to find funding for production.

Pinter's directorial efforts have been equally well received. In 1967 he directed Robert Shaw's *The Man in the Glass Booth* in London and again on Broadway a year later. More recently he has directed James Joyce's *Exiles* (1970), the 1971 production of Simon Gray's *Butley* (he also directed the film version), and Gray's *Otherwise Engaged* (1975) and *Close of Play* (1981). One of his more surprising engagements as a director was the National Theatre's production of Noel Coward's *Blithe Spirit* in 1976, surprising because of Coward's reputation as a dramatic lightweight. Two years later, when the National Theatre produced Pinter's *Betrayal* (1978), his choice of a Coward play seemed more logical, for *Betrayal*, far more than any other Pinter work, shows his indebtedness to Coward, particularly in the areas of narrative and language.

Betrayal employs an unusual conceit: the play begins in the present, in this case, spring 1977, and progressively moves into the past, ending finally in the winter of 1968. This journey into the past is meant to reveal in reverse fashion the conduct and origin of an extramarital affair between Emma and Jerry, her husband's best man at their wedding. The affair itself seems to have been rather ordinary, the only real twist being that Emma, unknown to Jerry, informed Robert of the affair in 1973.

The play contains a fair share of wit and intrigue, reminiscent of Coward, but remarkably little else. Emma and Jerry are flat, basically uninter-

esting characters whose private lives are ordinary to the point of dullness. "Pinter's least Pinteresque play" was the cry most often heard. And yet it proved to be popular in no small measure because of Pinter's own extramarital affair with Lady Antonia Fraser, the historian and biographer who left her husband of twenty-one years, Sir Hugh Fraser, a member of Parliament, and their six children, to live with the playwright. On the eve of his fiftieth birthday, Pinter and Lady Antonia were married in London, just a few weeks after his divorce from Vivien Merchant became final. *Betrayal*, many believed, was patently and deliberately autobiographical. Pinter denied any such intention, but audiences were still skeptical and continued to be delighted by the thought that they were being made obliquely privy to inside information about one of London's most talked about scandals.

One of Pinter's most recent plays is actually one of his earliest. "I wrote *The Hothouse* in the winter of 1958," he said in a program note for the premiere production of the play at London's Hampstead Theatre Club in May 1980. "I put it aside for further deliberation and made no attempt to have it produced at the time. I then went on to write *The Caretaker*. In 1979 I re-read *The Hothouse* and decided it was worth presenting on the stage. I made a few cuts but no changes."

The action of the play is set in an institution, very likely a government-run mental home, although its nature is never fully made known to the audience. The staff members are the only people who appear onstage, and the patients are known by numbers. The characters are grotesques, unusual for a Pinter work, with names like Hogg, Lush, Peck, Lamb, and Cutts. The director of the home, an ex-army man named Roote, and his immediate subordinate, Gibbs, are both having affairs with Miss Cutts. Most of their time is spent investigating two mysterious events: the death of patient 6457 and the birth of a child to patient 6459. Suspicion is centered on the newest member of the staff, Lamb (seen earlier in the revue sketch *Applicant*), who, despite his innocent-sounding name, is subjected to sadistic experiments.

In the end Gibbs, one of the newer members, reports to a bureaucrat in Whitehall that the remainder of the staff has been killed by the patients in an orgy of bloodshed. Blame for the death of the patient then falls on Roote, but Gibbs might also be guilty. He might also be the one responsible for the massacre, but his role is left ambiguous, presumably by intention. The play ends with the forgotten Lamb in a soundproof room "sitting in the chair, earphones and electrodes attached, quite still."

In 1966 Pinter told Lawrence Bensky why he originally discarded the play: "The characters were so purely cardboard. I was intentionally—for the only time, I think—trying to make a point, an explicit point, that these were nasty people and I disapproved of them. And therefore they didn't begin to live." Obviously, Pinter had a change of heart since he made those comments, and most Pinter fans were glad he did. Said reviewer Blake Morrison in the *Times Literary Supplement*: "However subtly edited by late Pinter, *The Hothouse* remains early Pinter. . . . But early Pinter, even bottom-drawer Pinter, is worth the mature, top drawer work of just about anyone else around, and *The Hothouse* more than justifies its retrieval."

Pinter's *Family Voices* is a thirty-five-minute drama for three voices, those of a widowed mother, her young son, and briefly at the end, her dead husband. Similar in style to *Silence* and in substance to *A Night Out*, it was first performed in early 1981 on BBC Radio and immediately afterward was added to the repertory of the National Theatre as a dramatized reading, during which the two principal actors, Peggy Ashcroft and Michael Kitchen, sat in cane chairs before a lighted backdrop.

Family Voices begins with the mother apparently reading aloud her letters to her adolescent son, now sharing a home with a family by the name of Withers (who bring to mind the clan of *The Homecoming*). Her initial remark is pleasant enough: "I miss you." But her comments become increasingly hostile: "If you are alive, you are a monster." A short distance away the young man "responds" by telling himself exciting and somewhat lurid stories about the Withers family and puzzling over their relationships to one another. From what he says it is clear that there is a great deal of sexual activity in his new home. "Oh, Mother," he cries to the absent character at one point. "Little did I ever dream I could know such happiness." The play ends with Voice 3 (the father) saying, "I have so much to say to you. But I am quite dead. What I have to say to you will never be said." The play thus appears to be largely about the young man's discovery and acceptance of those dark Dionysian impulses that were suppressed and repressed when he lived at home with his real family.

Since 1981 Pinter has written only four brief one-act plays, none of them—with the possible exception of *A Kind of Alaska* (1982)—comparable in stature to his previous works. *Victoria Station* (1982), a duologue on a car radio between a lost and seemingly confused London taxi driver and his controller, is meant to be eerily amusing but winds up being merely silly. *A Kind of Alaska* is far more substantial. A poetic treatment of a middle-aged woman's brief recovery from a thirty-year-long coma induced by sleeping sickness, it is unique in that it is Pinter's only stage play inspired by another writer's work, *Awakenings* (1973), by physician Oliver Sacks, a nonfiction study of the effects of the drug L-Dopa on a group of comatose patients.

In spite of the fact that *Drama* magazine named *One for the Road* as its 1984 Play of the Year, some critics feel the piece represents a serious falling off in Pinter's artistry and an unwelcome move into political propaganda. set in an unnamed totalitarian state, *One for the Road* is a portrait of political horror in which an interrogator tortures a prisoner and his wife and eventually kills their little son. Reflecting on the origins of the play, Pinter said he met at a party two "extremely attractive and intelligent" young Turkish women whose indifference to a political trial going on in their country enraged him. "Instead of strangling them," he said, "I came back immediately, sat down and, it's true, out of rage started to write *One for the Road*."

Pinter traveled to Turkey in 1985 to investigate personally the Turkish record on human rights, and out of that visit came his most recent drama, *Mountain Language*. With a running time of only twenty-five minutes, it was given a major production at London's National Theatre in 1988. Likewise set in an unnamed country—but suggestive of Turkey and its government's alleged brutal treatment of the Kurds—*Mountain Language* consists of four scenes detailing the physical and psychological savaging of political prisoners whose only discernible offense is their desire to speak their native language. In the final scene an old woman, when finally permitted to speak the forbidden tongue, is rendered mute by the violence done to her and her clan.

At this point in his career, Pinter appears more at home in the film medium. Thus far he has written fifteen screenplays, five since 1982, all based on his plays or the works of others. He has been adapting two novels for the screen:

Franz Kafka's *The Trial* (1937), and Kazuo Ishiguro's *The Remains of the Day* (1989).

Despite a falling off in some of his later plays, Pinter remains one of the world's most respected and widely produced writers for the contemporary stage. Probably more than any other dramatist writing in English this century, he has challenged and changed expectations of what dramatic language, action, and character should be. His unique blending of absurdist and realist techniques continues to fascinate and inform audiences in a way seldom witnessed in the history of the theater. It may not be too much to say that Pinter is one of the true theatrical voices of his age.

Interviews:
Lawrence Bensky, "Harold Pinter: An Interview," *Paris Review*, 10 (Fall 1966): 13-37; republished in *Writers at Work: The Paris Review Interviews*, third series (New York: Viking, 1967), pp. 347-368;

"Two People in a Room; Playwriting," *New Yorker* (25 February 1967): 34-36;

Mel Gussow, "A Conversation [Pause] with Harold Pinter," *New York Times Magazine*, 5 December 1971, pp. 42-43, 126-136;

Nicholas Hern, "A Play and Its Politics," in *One for the Road* (New York: Grove Weidenfeld, 1986);

Anna Ford, "Radical Departures," *The Listener*, 27 October 1988;

Michel Ciment, "Visually Speaking," *Film Comment*, 25 (May/June 1989): 20-22.

Bibliographies:
David S. Palmer, "A Harold Pinter Checklist," *Twentieth Century Literature*, 16 (1970): 287-296;

Herman T. Schroll, *Harold Pinter: A Study of His Reputation (1958-1969) and a Checklist* (Metuchen, N.J.: Scarecrow Press, 1971);

Steven H. Gale, "Harold Pinter: An Annotated Bibliography 1957-1971," *Bulletin of Bibliography*, 29 (1972): 46-56;

Rudiger Imhof, *Pinter: A Bibliography*, Theatre Facts Supplement, Bibliography Series 1 (London & Los Angeles: TQ Publications, 1975);

Kimball King, *Twenty Modern British Playwrights: A Bibliography, 1956 to 1976* (New York & London: Garland, 1977);

Francis Gillen and Gale, eds., *The Pinter Review* (Tampa: University of Tampa Press, 1987-   ).

References:
William Baker and Stephen Ely Tabachnick, *Harold Pinter* (New York: Harper & Row, 1973);

Harold Bloom, ed., *Harold Pinter: Modern Critical Views* (New York: Chelsea House, 1987);

Alan Bold, *Harold Pinter: You Never Heard Such Silence* (London: Vision, 1984);

Elin Diamond, *Pinter's Comic Play* (London & Toronto: Associated University Presses, 1985);

Bernard F. Dukore, *Harold Pinter* (New York: Macmillan, 1982);

Dukore, *Where Laughter Stops* (Columbia & London: University of Missouri Press, 1976);

Martin Esslin, *The Peopled Wound: The Works of Harold Pinter* (Garden City, N.Y.: Doubleday, 1970);

Steven H. Gale, *Butter's Going Up* (Durham, N.C.: Duke University Press, 1977);

Ronald Hayman, *Harold Pinter* (New York: Ungar, 1973);

Arnold P. Hinchliffe, *Harold Pinter* (New York: Twayne, 1967);

Joanne Klein, *The Pinter Screenplays* (Columbus: Ohio State University Press, 1985);

Austin E. Quigley, *The Pinter Problem* (Princeton: Princeton University Press, 1975);

Elizabeth Sakellerridou, *Pinter's Female Portraits* (London: Macmillan, 1988);

John Russell Taylor, *The Angry Theatre* (New York: Hill & Wang, 1969);

David T. Thompson, *The Player's Playwright* (London: Macmillan, 1985).

Peter Shaffer

(15 May 1926 -   )

This entry was written by Warren Sylvester Smith (Pennsylvania State University) for
DLB 13: British Dramatists Since World War II: Part Two.

BOOKS: *The Woman in the Wardrobe*, by Peter
Shaffer and Anthony Shaffer, as Peter Antony (London: Evans, 1951);

How Doth the Little Crocodile?, by Peter Shaffer
and Anthony Shaffer, as Peter Antony (London: Evans, 1952); as Peter Shaffer and
Anthony Shaffer (New York: Macmillan,
1957);

Withered Murder, by Peter Shaffer and Anthony Shaffer (London: Gollancz, 1955; New
York: Macmillan, 1956);

Five Finger Exercise (London: Hamish Hamilton,
1958; New York: Harcourt Brace, 1959);

The Private Ear and The Public Eye (London:
Hamish Hamilton, 1962; New York: Stein &
Day, 1964);

The Royal Hunt of the Sun (London & New York:
French, 1964; London: Hamish Hamilton,
1964; New York: Stein & Day, 1965);

Black Comedy (London: French, 1967);

The White Liars (London: French, 1967);

Black Comedy; including White Lies (New York:
Stein & Day, 1967);

The White Liars, Black Comedy (London: Hamilton,
1968);

Equus (London: Deutsch, 1973);

Equus and Shrivings (New York: Atheneum,
1974);

Amadeus (London: Deutsch, 1980);

The Collected Plays of Peter Shaffer (New York:
Crown, 1982);

Lettice and Lovage (London: Deutsch, 1988; New
York: Harper & Row, 1990; revised, New
York: French, 1990);

Whom Do I Have the Honour of Addressing? (London: Deutsch, 1990).

PLAY PRODUCTIONS: *Five Finger Exercise*, London, Comedy Theatre, 16 July 1958, 608
[performances]; New York, Music Box Theatre, 2 December 1959, 337;

The Private Ear and *The Public Eye*, London,
Globe Theatre, 10 May 1962, 548; New

Peter Shaffer

York, Morosco Theatre, 9 October 1963,
163;

The Merry Roosters Panto, by Shaffer and Theatre
Workshop, London, 1963;

The Royal Hunt of the Sun, Chichester, Festival Theatre, 7 July 1964; London, Old Vic (National Theatre), 8 December 1964; New
York, ANTA Theatre, 26 October 1965,
261;

Black Comedy, Chichester, Festival Theatre, 27
July 1965; London, Old Vic (National Theatre), 8 March 1966; New York, Ethel Barrymore Theatre, 12 February 1967, 337;

White Lies, New York, Ethel Barrymore Theatre, 12 February 1967, 337; revised as *The White Liars*, Hammersmith, Lyric Theatre, 21 February 1968, 93;

A Warning Game, New York, 1967;

It's About Cinderella, London, 1969;

The Battle of Shrivings, Hammersmith, Lyric Theatre, 5 February 1970, 73;

Equus, London, Old Vic (National Theatre), 26 July 1973; New York, Plymouth Theatre, 24 October 1974, 1,209;

Amadeus, London, Olivier Theatre (National Theatre), 2 November 1979; New York, Broadhurst Theatre, 17 December 1980, 1,181.

MOTION PICTURES: *Follow Me!*, Universal/Hal B. Wallis, 1971;

Equus, United Artists/Winkest, 1977;

Amadeus, Orion, 1984.

TELEVISION: *The Salt Land*, ITV, 1955;

The Balance of Terror, BBC, 1957.

RADIO: *The Prodigal Father*, BBC, 1955.

SELECTED PERIODICAL PUBLICATIONS—
UNCOLLECTED: "Labels Aren't for Playwrights," *Theatre Arts*, 44 (February 1960): 20-23;

"Cannibal Theatre," *Atlantic*, 206 (October 1960): 48-50;

"Rituals at the G and S Club," *Time and Tide*, 43 (4 January 1962): 28;

"Gilbert's Insubstantial World," *Time and Tide*, 43 (5 April 1962): 25;

"Liszt's Embryonic Inventions: Faust Symphony," *Time and Tide*, 43 (12 April 1962): 24;

"The Pity Was Distilled: War Requiem," *Time and Tide*, 43 (7 June 1962): 23-24;

"Artaud for Artaud's Sake," a discussion by Shaffer, Peter Hall, Peter Brook, and Michel Saint-Denis, *Encore*, 11 (May-June 1964): 20-31;

"What We Owe Britten," *Sunday Times*, 18 November 1973, p. 35.

With less than a dozen major productions since his emergence on the London scene in 1958, Peter Shaffer can hardly be called one of England's more prolific playwrights. But he may well be one of the most enduring and consistently workmanlike dramatists of a generation that includes John Osborne, Harold Pinter, Arnold Wesker, and John Arden, all born within six years of one another. (Shaffer is actually the eldest of the group.) Almost all of Shaffer's plays have been commercial successes, and most of them have engendered vigorous—often conflicting—critical response. More significant in any overall estimation is that he has so far managed to escape the categorizing labels attached to his contemporaries. After his first success, *Five Finger Exercise* (1958), he warned those who praised him for bringing theater back to the realistic environment of the living room: "I want to do many different kinds of theatre." Each play since has been something of a stylistic surprise.

Twins Peter Levin and Anthony Shaffer were born to Jack and Reka Fredman Shaffer in Liverpool. Anthony is also a novelist and playwright, best know for his play *Sleuth* (1970). Nevertheless, Anthony, who has pursued law, advertising, and television, has not treated the stage as his principal vocation. In their mid twenties the brothers collaborated on the writing of three mystery novels, using at first the combination pseudonym Peter Antony.

Peter attended St. Paul's School in London, from which he was graduated in 1944. He then served as a conscript coal miner until 1947, when he entered Trinity College, Cambridge. After he received his B.A. degree in 1950, he felt the need to set out on his own and, without any prospect of employment, went to New York City. He later looked back on this period as two and a half years of "exile"—an "unreal period," he says. "I'm not proud of my life in those days." While in New York he worked at Doubleday Book Shop and in the acquisitions department of the New York Public Library. Later, as a successful dramatist he entered into an ardent love affair with New York City and in 1980 made it his home, but those early years were not pleasantly memorable ones.

After his return to London in 1954, while working for the music publishers Boosey and Hawkes, he completed a television script about the then-new state of Israel, *The Salt Land*, which was produced in 1955. This was followed by a radio play, *The Prodigal Father*, broadcast by the BBC in the same year, and another television script, *The Balance of Terror* (1957). Thus modestly launched, Shaffer settled down to a writing career. Despite his later dramatic successes, he has never made any attempt to become a public figure. He lives quietly and stays out of the news except as regards his work.

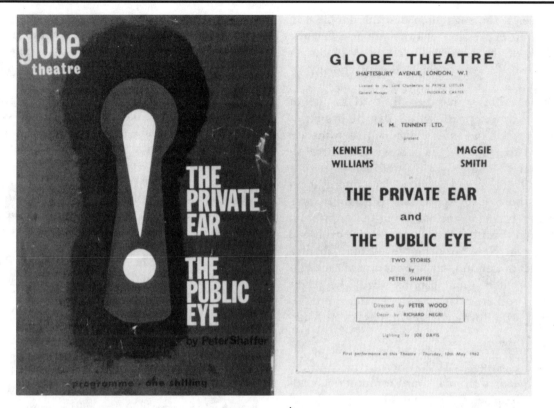

Program cover and title page for the first production of Shaffer's pair of one-act plays

Shaffer says he is "fascinated by the endless ambiguity of the human situation, of the conflict between two different kinds of right." His dramatizations of such conflict often have mythological connotations. Shaffer seems to be speaking for psychologist Carl Jung (whom he has called "one of the greatest minds of the twentieth century") when he says that "the cells of one's brain contain endless archetypal images that stretch back beyond the Stone Age." Particularly in his later plays these archetypal images are presented with high theatricality, making use of the ancient elements of chant, dance, music, colorful costumes, and masks. Shaffer believes that the theater should be "an ecstatic and alarming experience," but that it should also contain "spaces of tranquility and lyricism." It is not surprising, then, to learn that Shaffer is highly sophisticated in his knowledge of music and that he served as music critic for *Time and Tide* from 1961 through 1962.

Much significance—perhaps too much—has been attached to the Shaffer brothers' twinship. Jules Glenn, a specialist in the psychology of twinship, has pursued this theme through many articles, including "Anthony and Peter Shaffer's Plays: The Influence of Twinship on Creativity," published in *American Imago* in 1974. He finds in the work of both brothers all the characteristics that he has observed in his study of twins: intense rivalry with libidinal attachment; lifelong identification with the other twin; the sense of being an incomplete person; the desire for revenge and the wish to make things even. These elements, he observes, are present in the conflicts between the principal characters in the Shaffers' plays: between Andrew and Milo in Anthony Shaffer's *Sleuth*, between Pizarro and Atahuallpa in Peter Shaffer's *The Royal Hunt of the Sun* (1964), and between Alan Strang and Dr. Dysart in *Equus* (1973). Glenn could now add the conflict between Antonio Salieri and Wolfgang Amadeus Mozart in *Amadeus* (1979).

Glenn's evidence is less persuasive when one recalls that this same twinlike ambivalence is present throughout the whole of drama. It is notable, for instance, between Othello and Iago and between the Devil and Don Juan, though neither William Shakespeare nor George Bernard Shaw was a twin. Most of the best playwrights have possessed the ability to create pairs of characters who are dramatic foils for one another. This is not to deny that the close relationship between the Shaffer brothers has influenced their lives and their works but merely to remark that, to a layman at least, the suggestion that the double *u* in *Equus* is an expression of two *you*'s and that the two eyes of the horses blinded by Alan Strang signify two *I*'s is stretching the psychology of twinship a bit far.

Peter Shaffer has had little to say about being a twin except to remark that he has never been aware of the intense rivalry that twins are supposed to feel, that he and Anthony have always gotten along extremely well, and that they are very different and not in the least interchangeable. Anthony loves sports and is a family man. Peter is a bachelor and moves in quite different circles than Anthony. Before Peter established residence in New York, they lived only about a mile apart in London, saw a great deal of each other, and visited their parents regularly. Their younger brother, Brian, "really the clever one," is an artist who formerly taught physics at Cambridge.

Five Finger Exercise launched Shaffer on his playwriting career in 1958, when he received the *Evening Standard* Drama Award for most outstanding British playwright. Though very well received—winning the New York Drama Critics Circle Award for best foreign play in 1960—*Five Finger Exercise* betrayed little evidence of the scope of his theatrical imagination. Structurally it is a "textbook" play in the most traditional sense. It takes place in a single setting representing several rooms in an English middle-class home. After an expository after-breakfast scene and a lapse of two months, the main action is compressed within "Saturday night after dinner" to "Sunday night after dinner." The play opens with a "basic situation": the Harrington family with their continuing tensions under tenuous control. An "exciting force" disturbs the equilibrium: the German tutor Walter Langer, hired to teach the young teenager Pamela. A series of crises ensues, all involving Walter with some member of the Harrington family; and finally, in a last-scene climax, the head of the household, Stanley, confronts Walter with the accusation of making love to his wife—an accusation that is at least technically false—and threatens to take action that will deport Walter back to Germany. Walter, in despair, attempts suicide. In the wake of the near catastrophe each of the Harringtons tries to reassemble the pieces of their lives for a fresh start. It is not a very comfortable denouement, but it does represent a new basic situation, permanently altered from the opening one.

Critics praised the play as constructed with great skill, but its favorable reception is the more remarkable in that it appeared at a time when the theater was in revolt against the well-made play and more serious critical attention was being given to the absurdists and the angry postwar neonaturalists. The old-fashioned formal surface of *Five Finger Exercise* proves, however, to be deceptive. Psychologically the play is as much an expression of the postwar Western world as Osborne's *Look Back in Anger* (1956) is. It has the same challenge to conventional family values and the same frustration—though not quite the same sentimental despair—as Osborne's revolutionary work.

What Shaffer has done is to invent a theatrical crucible in which the nuclear British family (father, mother, son, daughter) is forced, in the manner of Henrik Ibsen, to face the truth about itself. The experience is harrowing and shatters all the pretensions of familial devotion and closeness in which the family members had wrapped themselves. The parallel with Ibsen's *The Wild Duck* (1884) is, in fact, hardly avoidable. Walter's relationship with Clive (the son) is similar to that of the messianic Gregers with Hialmar in the Ibsen play. In both cases the outsider wants to help solve personal problems and creates instead a situation that the insiders cannot handle. There is a difference in that Walter in the end cannot remain aloof from the mess he has unwittingly helped to make, as Gregers at least pretends to do.

As in *The Wild Duck*, too, it is difficult to identify the protagonist. Probably the playwright's original intention was that it should be Clive. But each of the four family members gets a turn at self-revelation, as Walter himself does—it is a five-finger exercise—and each can claim moments of sympathy from the audience. These revelations often come in the form of long speeches in which the speaker may seem to be soliloquizing. Shaffer has been criticized for breaking with his realistic format at these points, but the actor is never alone on the stage during these outpourings and has always the option of treating them as a supreme effort to communicate his innermost thoughts and feelings to some other person onstage.

Although Walter's role is reminiscent of Gregers's, it is more difficult to dislike him than to dislike Gregers. Walter is in flight from a terrible family situation of his own—unregenerate Nazi parents, a father who proudly served his

Robert Stephens in a scene from the first production of The Royal Hunt of the Sun *(photograph by Chris Arthur)*

führer at Auschwitz. At first Walter insists that his parents are dead, but he confesses the truth to Clive in an effort to establish a more candid relationship with him. Because he needs this surrogate family so badly, Walter treats the Harringtons with great warmth and charm. But they misunderstand his gratitude and misinterpret his motives. Mother, daughter, and son are physically attracted to him and are secretly jealous of one another. Each of them is unaware of the emotional web in which they are all being entangled and of how vulnerable they have become.

The Harringtons have been married for twenty years. They are mismated and have tried unsuccessfully to transfer their affections to their children. Clive, at nineteen, is not the masculine, aggressive son Stanley would have been comfortable with, and Pamela is a fourteen-year-old tomboy who has created a private world of her own. Even when the conversation in this household is about the most ordinary comings and goings,

there is a subtext of bitterness and frustration. This is particularly painful to Clive, who is on the edge of adulthood but has not yet acquired the armor of cynicism.

The entrance of a personable, even fascinating, outsider into this tense little world reorients all the magnetic lines of force. There is at once a fierce competition for Walter's affection and approval. And Walter, though fluent in English, is still unfamiliar with middle-class English culture and deceives himself in his desperate need to find in this family a microcosm of a more fulfilling world than the one from which he has fled. Obviously he cannot satisfy all the passions his presence has aroused, and inevitably he becomes the fall guy. He scrupulously treats Pamela as his young pupil, though she would prefer a more romantic relationship—at least that of a loving big brother and confidant. Her mother, Louise, is not bold enough to think of seducing the young man, but she would be pleased to be thought of as a possible mistress. Instead he confesses to her his need for a mother. He makes the fatal mistake of trying to help Clive in his relationship with his father, when Clive would want Walter's arms around him. In the backlash of their disappointments Louise decides that Walter is having a bad effect on Pamela, and Clive uses Walter to punish his father by reporting an affectionate little scene between Walter and Louise as a full-fledged love affair.

The savagery of Stanley's attack on Walter is predictable. When Walter realizes what his presence has done to this family and perhaps realizes, too, that his own feelings have not always been entirely platonic, the young self-exiled German is driven to destroy himself. His last-minute rescue from the gas-filled room is merely the author's attempt to avoid too melodramatic a final curtain. Walter, as a compassionate force for good, has been destroyed, and so has the family that had taken him in. There remains the slight hope that a new and more honest relationship will arise out of the tragedy, but the chances do not seem good. They rest on Clive's final prayer over the prostrate Walter: "The courage. For all of us. Oh, God—give it."

Beyond the sheer dramatic effectiveness of the play, what makes it especially disturbing—and universal—is the realization that the Harringtons represent no more of a misalliance than most families. How many families could withstand so insistent and well-meaning a challenge as Walter brought to the Harringtons? The challenge is not merely to a family, but to the entire value system that is inherent in contemporary family life. If such a family cannot survive having its emotional relationships so exposed, can the family, the viewer is forced to ask, continue as a viable unit in contemporary Western civilization? Shaffer is not a social dramatist in any highly self-conscious sense. His plays are specifically about individuals. Yet his characters are conceived as part of a social fabric, and they are destined by their actions, by their behavior, to form a commentary—not an answer, not even necessarily a criticism—on the society to which they belong, and this commentary may, as in the case of *Five Finger Exercise*, have unsettling implications.

It was another four years before London again became aware of Shaffer. A major work, very different from *Five Finger Exercise*, was evolving, but in the meantime, in 1962, a pair of one-act plays, *The Private Ear* and *The Public Eye*, were produced in the West End. They were in no way revolutionary, but they were entertaining, and

they did reasonably well commercially on both sides of the Atlantic. (Shaffer is one of only a few playwrights who have had box-office success with the one-act format.)

The Private Ear, like *Five Finger Exercise*, is, at first glance, a fairly pat situation: the extrovert helps the introvert to build up enough courage to invite a young lady to his apartment and even stays to make dinner for the couple. The young lady, naturally enough, falls for the extroverted friend. Although this basic plot has been used often, Shaffer once remarked in an interview, "There are many tunes yet to be written in C-major." His handling of the situation justifies the observation.

Shaffer's shy young man, Bob, is a stereo buff whose inner life is constantly nourished by music. He spends his days filing invoices and feels himself utterly incapable of rising in the competitive business world. He is completely enervated by his job and comes to life only when he comes home to feed classical records to Behemoth, his personified record player. His friend Ted, full of vitality, loves his job and has the tastes of a healthy philistine. The contrast is immediately established when Bob's high-fidelity Mozart is shattered by Tom's "blaring little transistor." Doreen, whom Bob has met at a concert, turns out, alas, to be as philistine as Ted—someone had given her the concert ticket, and she did not want to see it wasted. But as Bob does not yet know this, he views the evening as "the one big chance" to break out of his private world, to listen with something other than his private ear. The result, therefore, is a personal tragedy for Bob, even though the tone of the play is somewhere between comedy and farce.

Shaffer's development as a playwright is demonstrated in his frank use at two points in the play of expressionistic devices. To cover the lapse in time—the duration of the dinner—the three diners "freeze," and a condensed version of the dialogue is heard from a prerecorded tape. The conversation seems to be entirely between Ted and Doreen, speeded up at times to "a high-pitched gabble." This is apparently the way the evening sounds to Bob's private ear.

Ted has promised Bob that he would leave the two of them alone, and immediately after dinner he tactfully withdraws—but not before making it implicitly clear to Doreen that he would welcome a future contact with her. The moment has now arrived for Bob, but it is obvious that he is not up to it. He seeks help from Behemoth. He puts on the Love Duet from Giacomo Puccini's opera *Madame Butterfly* (1904). For six minutes without dialogue, aided by the music, Bob tries to become the passionate lover. His gauche attempts at seduction are in hilarious incongruity with the sublimity of the music. Doreen is at first mildly cooperative, then nonplussed, and finally rebellious. At the climax of the Love Duet she slaps his face. Bob's worst fears of his own ineptitude are confirmed. When Doreen, more embarrassed than infuriated, leaves, Bob resignedly gives her Ted's phone number.

The dinner scene and the love scene, both making use of recorded sound, reflect Bob's inner emotional state. They signal the playwright's emerging confidence in handling the tools of theatricality, his daring to leave the time-tested world of *Five Finger Exercise* and explore, even if somewhat tentatively, other modes of theatrical expression.

There is no such evidence in the play's companion piece, *The Public Eye*, which, though charming as a story, is less effective as theater. An accountant who has grown rather stuffy and self-important mistrusts his young wife, who has taken to wandering off by herself around London. He hires a detective to observe her. But the original detective is replaced by a nervous little Greek, Cristoforou, who is certainly not the stereotypical television detective. Among other peculiarities, he cannot control his appetite for sweets, especially when he is a bit excited, and so carries a confection-filled paper bag with him as standard equipment. The young Belinda has no lover. She is simply trying to escape the boring monotony of a marriage in which there are no longer any surprises. As Cristoforou follows her at a discreet distance, a secret communication grows between them. They never speak to each other, and the wife is not aware of the detective's mission, but the pursuit takes on an exciting and romantic flavor. It becomes the strange task of this unconventional private eye to convince his employer that his wife is a thoroughly engaging person in her own right and that trying to remake her into his own image is what is really destroying their marriage. His method of accomplishing this is to trade roles with the husband. At the end, the accountant silently trails his wife through the streets and parks and cinemas of London, while the detective sits at the husband's desk, answering questions about taxes and eating a grapefruit.

Derek Jacobi and Albert Finney in the first production of Black Comedy *(photograph by Angus McBean)*

The characters are delightfully conceived and sharply drawn, and the play is a cameo of marital relations. But because the play takes place entirely in the accountant's office (on a Saturday morning, when the office is not open for business), it becomes a mere series of confrontations. The audience cannot watch the detective—and finally Belinda's husband—follow her on the streets and is finally left with the unsatisfying sense that much of the play has taken place somewhere else. It would seem, therefore, that *The Public Eye* would be better adapted for film, but in fact the actual film made from the play under the title of *Follow Me!* (1971) was not well received.

The Public Eye was an attempt to escape the confines of time and space imposed by a realistic concept. It was becoming apparent that Shaffer's view of the world had come to require a freer, more flexible form of dramaturgy. This he found in the conception of *The Royal Hunt of the Sun*, which made its appearance in 1964. Here the audience witnesses the action—or some symbolic representation of it—on a formal stage and in a style that is part Elizabethan, part Brechtian. The play moves easily through four years of conquest, from Spain to Panama to the ancient empire of the Incas.

But the ability to move through space and time is only a part of the freedom Shaffer has achieved in his bold new theatrical approach. It allows him also a wider emotional latitude. His use of crowds and crowd noises, of music, of carefully controlled light, and of visual symbols adds up to a powerful statement about nobility and greed. He includes choreographed passages of mime, such as that of the Great Massacre, where symbolically thousands of Indians are treacherously slain. For such a scene to be effective, the playwright must trust the director and the players. In this respect Shaffer has been most fortunate in having the collaboration of John Dexter as director for this and two of his later plays. Since the experience of *The Royal Hunt of the Sun*, Shaffer's most distinguished growth as a dramatist has continued to occur outside the strictures of the conventional realistic play.

Old Martin, who serves as narrator, tells the audience at the beginning: "This story is about ruin. Ruin and gold." All the characters, both Spanish and Indian, priests, laymen, and pagans, are debased in this vicious conquest of an innocent people. But especially the ruin is of the two larger-than-life figures: the old Spanish captain, Francisco Pizarro, ruthless, cynical, illiterate, but somehow greatly human; and the young god-king of the Incas, Atahuallpa, beautiful in body, magnanimous in spirit, but also ruthless and illiterate—a man who killed his brother to seize the throne. In this sense the play is an Aristotelian tragedy, for it enacts the downfall of great

men. It is Aristotelian, too, in its single-minded pursuit of the main action.

But there is a thoroughly un-Aristotelian quality that runs through all of Shaffer's work: an ambiguity in identifying the protagonist. The audience's sympathies are morally with Atahuallpa. He is the victim of the Spanish invasion and of Pizarro's broken word. He retains his nobility to the final slaughter. It is Pizzaro and his lust for gold, however, that cause the play to happen, and it is Pizzaro who, by sheer force of character, keeps his unruly and incongruous band of adventurers in some semblance of a disciplined army. So it may be argued that the corrupt one, like Macbeth, must be technically called the protagonist.

With *The Royal Hunt of the Sun*, Shaffer proves to be a twentieth-century playwright interested in human psychology and not simply an accomplished dramatizer of a distant piece of history. Some critics feel that since the Pizarro of history was a brutish, unintelligent mercenary and Atahuallpa, as far as is known, a traitor and usurper, Shaffer has therefore falsified his materials. However, it is not the business of a dramatist to be a historian in any literal sense, but rather to convince the audience for a couple of hours that history might well have been this way and that the characters might really have thought and felt as their stage counterparts do. In *The Royal Hunt of the Sun*, the audience is made to believe that while the god-king is held in captivity, the two absolute rulers explore one another and develop something more than mutual respect. They come to love one another. Atahuallpa, as a god, has had no prior opportunity to associate with equals. He is quick to perceive that Pizarro is not a conformist Christian like his followers. Atahuallpa tells him, "You do not believe [the Holy Men]. Their God is not in your face." For his part Pizarro finds what he has never experienced in other company—laughter and a kind of joy. To their mutual delight they discover that they are both bastards. Atahuallpa sings and dances for him and even persuades Pizarro to attempt a clumsy dance in return. They become as father and son.

The relationship is doomed. When the gold that Atahuallpa has promised has been amassed and it is time for Pizarro to keep his part of the bargain and set the god-king free, the proud monarch makes no secret of his intentions. His first decree will be to kill all the Spaniards in revenge for the mass killing of the Incas. He will spare only his new-found friend. Pizarro is thus faced

Derek Jacobi, Maggie Smith, and Albert Finney in the first production of Black Comedy *(photograph by Angus McBean)*

with the tragic choice: the destruction of his men and his mission, or the destruction of his "son." He has no choice, really, for the Spaniards, eager to divide the gold and be gone, take matters into their own hands. In a climactic scene in which the rituals of the Incas are played in counterpoint with the rituals of the Christians, the god-king is tied to a stake and garroted. The body is then thrown at the feet of Pizarro, and the crowds depart.

Atahuallpa's followers had no doubt that their god would rise to new life with the rising sun. The viewer is witness therefore not only to the despoliation of their land but also to their spiritual disillusion and despair when the first rays of the sun reveal an ordinary corpse. Perhaps Pizarro, too, expected, or at least hoped for, the resurrection of his "son." Critic Harold Hobson emphasizes the implied parallel with the Christian Resurrection and finds Pizarro's search a search for God. Renee Winegarten also finds Shaffer "haunted by the idea of God," though opposed to both church and synagogue, and believing that the capacity of organized religion is greater

for harm than for good. These observers are justified in sensing Pizarro's restlessness as a longing to fill the spiritual void left by his rejection of the Christian dogma of his time. But in the end, Shaffer is no more a theologian than he is a historian. The tragedy is a personal one. There are few scenes in modern drama as moving as that of the broken Spanish commander trying to sing a song that Atahuallpa had taught him: "It's over, lad, I'm coming after you. . . . We'll be put into the same earth, father and son in our own land."

In *The Royal Hunt of the Sun*, Shaffer paints on a large ground, like one of the huge sixteenth- or seventeenth-century murals that show battles or coronations or paradise. The conflict, though it centers on the two men, is also a conflict between two ways of life and of thought. The Incas, as ruled by Atahuallpa, represented an almost perfect economic and social system. Everyone had a parcel of land. Marriages were arranged. Workers retired at the age of fifty. Children and the elderly were compassionately cared for. Their religion was a simple worship of their king, who was also their god. The Spaniards found them contented rather than happy. Since they had never known want, they had no feeling of gratitude. They knew nothing of either hope or despair. They had no need for competition, and so knew nothing of the thrill of victory.

On the other hand, the values of the Spaniards were very like our own. The invaders came for gold. They rivaled one another for prestige and profit. Their religion promised them forgiveness of their sins within a rigid orthodoxy that also permitted them to slaughter the pagan Incas and despoil the Indians' land in the name of their Christian king and church. The Spaniards may be regarded as more primitive than we are, but they are recognizably Westerners as we know them. They disagreed and fought among themselves, but under strong leadership a small band of them, reckless of life and well armed, destroyed an entire civilization.

The Royal Hunt of the Sun is a surprising dramatic accomplishment for which the audiences of Shaffer's earlier plays were not prepared. Most of the regular reviewers, too, were caught off guard by so unusual an event as *The Royal Hunt of the Sun* and reported it as high theater, colorful staging, an exciting rendition of history. Those who tried to probe its deeper significance found everything from a rejection of the Resurrection of Christ to pretentious emptiness concealed beneath impressive production values. "Without spectacular theatricality," Robert Brustein concluded, "the play amounts to very little." However, Alan Downer found in the play an experience of "total theatre" comparable to Peter Weiss's *Marat/Sade* (1964). Winegarten saw also the influence of Antonin Artaud, who had once planned a play about the conquest of Mexico. Artaud's theater is one of ritual, dance, music, and imagery. There is something, too, of Artaud's theater of cruelty in *The Royal Hunt of the Sun*. But Shaffer would not subordinate his text wholly to the mise-en-scène as Artaud would, nor would he abandon psychology in favor of pure sensation.

The words of the play, however, sometimes fail to achieve the magnitude of the characters or to match the scope of the events. J. C. Trewin of the *London Illustrated News* would have welcomed some of the great resonance of Christopher Marlowe or at least some of the underlying rhythms of T. S. Eliot's *Murder in the Cathedral* (1935). Winegarten comments that the language, in its attempt "to avoid both fustian and slang . . . lacks the lion's stamp." This lack is more apparent on the printed page than in the theater, where the story moves with sensational force.

It was now apparent that Shaffer had to be seriously considered as one of that long line of British dramatists who treated the platform with actors on it as a unique form of high art. But before returning to the dramatization of more profound human relationships, he took time to sharpen his techniques on a couple of lighter pieces. First produced on Broadway in 1967, *White Lies* is a brief one-act in which a phony baroness-clairvoyant attempts to introduce a bit of truth into the lives of two young clients—a pop singer and his manager, who are both in love with the same girl. The young men are at least as phony as Sophie, the "baroness." The pop singer, Tom, pretends to have come from an impoverished background to hold the sympathy of his working-class audiences, whereas he is really the well-educated son of wealthy parents. The manager, Frank, tries to bribe Sophie to advise the singer to give up the girl, in order, as he says, to preserve the group and to save both the girl and the boy from being hurt. But it turns out that his motives are considerably less generous. The play is a deft unweaving of a web of hypocrisy.

White Lies was meant to fill out the bill with *Black Comedy* when the latter moved from London to New York in 1967. Obviously unsatisfied with it, Shaffer rewrote it as *The White Liars* for its London production the following year. In the revision "The White Liars" becomes the name of Frank's musical group, and the offstage situation is made tighter, more precise. The main change, however, is the addition of taped voices that reveal what is happening inside Sophie's head. It is no surprise to learn that Sophie lies even to herself. For instance, speaking of her father, she soliloquizes, "A noble man. You never realized what aristocracy could mean until you met my Father." But on tape: "Pennies in his bowler hat. Mustache always wet with beer! Disgusting!" Though *The White Liars* is far more revealing than *White Lies*, either version seems more of a dramatic device than a real drama.

The companion piece, *Black Comedy* (1965), is a masterpiece of gimmickry that somehow succeeds as a valid play. It, too, is a one-act, not quite long enough to be considered full-length. (In Chichester and London it was paired with August Strindberg's *Miss Julie* [1888]; later with Osborne's adaptation of Lope de Vega's *A Bond Honored* [1966].) Revived in London after its New

York success, it played with *The White Liars* in 1968 at the Lyric Theatre. *Black Comedy* rests on the device, which Shaffer apparently borrowed from the Chinese, of the actors' pretending to be in complete darkness when, in fact, they are brightly lighted and visible to the audience. Shaffer carried the idea one step further: stage darkness equals light; stage light equals darkness. Fortunately for the audience a fuse blows almost immediately after the play begins in darkness and is not replaced until the end. The audience can therefore see the play, while the actors can see hardly anything. Except for moments when a match or lighter is ignited or when an electric torch is eventually produced (all of these cause a slight dimming of the lights), the audience sees the characters groping in the darkness. Shaffer exploits the gimmick to its limits—and perhaps beyond. It is farce par excellence.

An impoverished sculptor, Brindsley Miller, tries to impress his fiancée's military father as well as a millionaire art collector by "borrowing" the antique furniture from his neighbor's flat across the hall, intending to take it back before the fussy neighbor returns. In the darkness an ex-girlfriend shows up, only too willing to complicate the evening. The prissy spinster from upstairs descends and mistakes the gin for lemonade (enjoying it and getting thoroughly plastered). Predictably the neighbor from across the hall shows up ahead of schedule, and Brindsley tries to supervise the surreptitious return of the stolen furniture before the electrician arrives to repair the fuse. When the electrician arrives, he is mistaken for the art collector and enjoys the unusual deference with which he is treated. Through all this hilarity the play manages to chronicle the complete disintegration of Brindsley Miller. Even the prospective father-in-law, stupid and pompous as he is, is forced to see through Brindsley's deceptions; and the actual art dealer, when he finally comes on the scene, literally falls through the floor.

Brindsley is, the viewer gathers, neither a very fine sculptor nor a very exemplary person. His fall is not awesome. However, if the destruction of Pizarro and Atahuallpa is tragic in the Aristotelian sense, the collapse of Brindsley Miller is equally classic as comedy; that is, the play is "an imitation of bad characters, yet [comedy] does not imitate them according to every vice, but the ridiculous only."

After Shaffer had successfully managed two such different tours de force as *The Royal Hunt of*

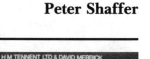

Handbill for the first production of Shaffer's 1970 play, an examination of pacifism

the Sun and *Black Comedy*, both he and his public suffered a considerable letdown when his next major work, *The Battle of Shrivings*, did not attract favorable notices. It was written in 1969 and produced in London early in 1970. It was never staged in New York, and the play, as produced in London, never appeared in print. The following year Shaffer completely rewrote it, and the new version, which has not been produced, was published as *Shrivings* in 1974.

In the late 1960s Shaffer spent much of his time in New York and became emotionally involved in the American trauma of Vietnam. The play, though set in England rather than the United States, is about pacifism and rebellious youth, issues about which Shaffer seems to have had such intense—and confused—feelings that the play, even in its revised form, became more a public soul-searching than a dramatized narrative. It is nevertheless a revealing document. In his note in the published version he says he "wanted the electricity to be sparked almost exclusively from the spoken words" and confesses that the main encounter in the play "sprang out of a division of feeling in myself." In any case the characters remain spokesmen for their beliefs (or lack of belief) rather than vital personalities who could attract or interest the audience.

Shrivings is the estate of Sir Gideon Petrie, an elderly English pacifist. Sir Gideon has turned the estate, whose name suggests an obvious place of confession, into a retreat "for kids on their way someplace." But only four inhabitants are present during the weekend of the play: the world-renowned pacifist himself, a young American girl who is his secretary and disciple, an eminent visiting poet who is a former student of Petrie's, and the poet's son, who has more or less taken up residence there. (In the original play Sir Gideon's wife was also in the cast.)

The play poses a searing challenge by the poet, Mark, a compulsive alcoholic cynic, to the rational idealism of the pacifist and the young girl. Every pacifist, on or off stage, is sure to be asked, "How far would you go before resorting to violence? Would you allow yourself to be crucified? Would you allow your loved ones to be tortured? raped?" And the pacifist, if he is honest, must answer, "I won't know until I have met the test." The "battle" at Shrivings is a conscious attempt on Mark's part to move Sir Gideon to violence. If Mark fails, he has promised to return to the humanistic philosophy of his former mentor. To achieve his end Mark blatantly plays on sexual drives and parental jealousy. He manages to be thoroughly obnoxious. Before the weekend is out he provokes Sir Gideon to slap the face of the American girl.

Regardless of what the playwright meant to imply by this action, certainly it does not disprove the validity of Sir Gideon's Gandhian position. The situation is too artificial, too much a game. Mark's seduction of the young girl (with whom his own son is in love) may be symbolic, but it is not, in context, credible. The play is really a series of symbolic acts supported by much discussion. Some of the acts are dramatic, such as the game set up by Mark where he has himself tied to a chair for "torture" and arranges three apples as "buttons" to be pushed to regulate the severity of the inflicted torment. The game recalls the artificial ritual of the "trinity" in Eliot's *The Cocktail Party* (1949). For a few moments the play comes alive.

But the symbolism is not enough to hold the play together. The viewer senses that the suffering of the author is genuine but that the suffer-

ing of his characters is contrived. Shaffer's method of making drama is to invent a crucible in which two characters, very different in background and point of view, but with the same deep emotional substratum, confront one another. When the method is successful, as with Pizarro and Atahuallpa, the confrontation builds to a dramatic climax that imparts to the playgoer a richer apprehension of the human mystery. The clash between Sir Gideon and Mark leaves the audience merely disturbed, confused, and disheartened.

The method works, however, in *Equus* (1973), both theatrically and philosophically. The confrontation here is between a child psychiatrist and his teenage patient. As in prior cases, there would seem at first to be few similarities between the two. But as the play unfolds it is revealed that both have destructive impulses. The boy's have been explicit. The psychiatrist's show up in dreams. Both have debilitating inhibitions. Both have substituted mythology for formal religion. The psychiatrist has gone back to that of ancient Greece. The boy has devised a mythology of his own. Jules Glenn properly observes that by the end of the play it is difficult to distinguish who is the psychiatrist and who the patient.

As in *The Royal Hunt of the Sun*, the stage again moves beyond realistic restrictions to become a vast theatrical space. Only here, instead of encompassing years and continents, it probes deep into the mind and memory of a seventeen-year-old boy.

The boy, Alan Strang, has done a dreadful thing. He has savagely stabbed out the eyes of six beautiful horses in a stable where he worked as a groom. Shaffer heard of such an actual case from a friend: a boy from the north of England had blinded twenty-six horses. He was the son of strict, religious parents. He was seduced on the floor of the stable under the eyes of the horses, and in his disturbed mind he feared they would reveal the act to his parents. Beyond this basic situation the story is totally Shaffer's invention. It took about two years for the play to take theatrical form. Shaffer heard, apparently, only the barest details of the incident and resisted learning anything more. What he wanted to preserve of the initial impact was "the play's central mystery, the erotic ritual of the boy and the horse . . . the reckless midnight gallop through the mist."

At the beginning of the play, the court has found the boy mentally ill, and a compassionate magistrate has persuaded authorities to place

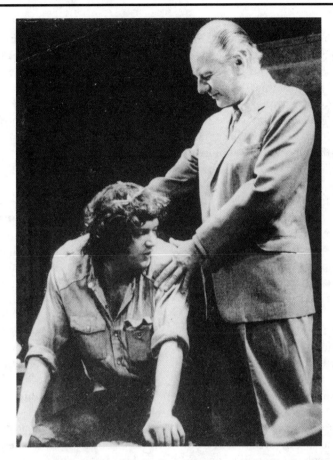

Martin Shaw and John Gielgud in the first production of The Battle of Shrivings

him in a mental hospital for treatment with Dr. Martin Dysart, a character with whom Shaffer seems to identify as closely as he did with the pacifist Sir Gideon of *The Battle of Shrivings,* but whom he manages to keep in effective dramatic focus. By means of shifting atmospheric lighting, the audience's attention shifts freely from the doctor's office to the events in Alan's past as, under treatment, he becomes willing to unlock them and face them. The horses are played by actors wearing stylized masks and elevated metal hooves. To the boy they have become gods, and their bearing, movement, and sounds take on a mythical quality that strikes a resonance in Dysart's own inner life. He, too, has turned to the gods and heroes of a mythological past for comfort and meaning. Moreover, the horse, from ancient Greece through the visions of Pablo Picasso, has been closely linked with man's idealized image of himself.

As Alan permits the layers of his psyche, one by one, to be exposed, the audience learns that there was religious turbulence in his lower-class home—a struggle between a devout mother and an agnostic father. At one point Alan has replaced the picture of a suffering Jesus on his bedroom wall with a picture of horses. He has had learning difficulties and is all but illiterate, but he gets a part-time job in a stable and takes off on secret midnight rides that become a sexual-religious experience. A stable girl, Jill, tries to introduce him to normal sexual intercourse, but even with the horses shut out of sight, he finds himself unable to function. His humiliation and guilt are so overwhelming that, after Jill has left, he attacks the horses' eyes with a hoof pick.

These are the events that Dysart skillfully manages to get Alan to recall, partly by narration and partly through actual reenactment. Once these truths are known, it is assumed that the psychiatrist can bring the boy at least part of the way back to "normalcy" (though psychiatrists in the real world do not agree that such an outcome is likely). Alan's progression toward "normalcy" is, in any case, how one would expect the events of the play to develop. But here the play takes an unusual turn and makes a bid for greatness. For Dysart finds that the treatment has affected not only the boy—the dark caverns of his own psyche are also lighted by the boy's experiences. His own middle-class existence and his cold, unsatisfactory marriage suddenly seem pallid in the reflection of Alan's fierce and primitive passion. Nothing in the doctor's life can compare with the mystical, orgiastic midnight rides on the horse, Nugget. For Dysart, an amateur classicist, the Jungian resonances with the Greek myths are inescapable. He comes actually to envy his patient and must force himself, against painful reluctance, to proceed with the treatment. Through Alan he is given to know what few people ever comprehend clearly—the emotional price they pay for civilization.

Though this development emerges as a surprise, the thread is introduced into the play quite early when Dysart expresses his dissatisfaction with normalcy to Hester Salomon, the magistrate who first refers Alan to Dysart. It is the view of R. D. Laing, the psychiatrist who, beyond Jung, has most influenced Shaffer, that modern psychiatry is used, perhaps unconsciously, to bring deviant personalities back into the establishment.

What happens to Dysart is not too different from what happens to Pizarro in his confrontation with the god-king, and, less obviously, to Sir Gideon Petrie with the dissolute poet. The mythical, uncivilized forces that we assume have been safely tamed by reason and by conformance to acceptable cultural patterns respond to the genuine primitive model with such violence as to shatter our conception of ourselves as civilized beings. The revelation destroyed Pizarro, broke through the gentle pacifist mold of Sir Gideon, and leaves Dysart in a state of Promethean suffering: "There is now, in my mouth, this sharp chain. And it never comes out."

Like Dysart, Shaffer is himself something of a classicist. In a February 1975 *Vogue* interview, he emphasizes the fact that in *Equus* the psychiatrist has no choice but to do what he does. Civilization cannot tolerate unbridled violence. He is in the same trap that closed upon Oedipus and Antigone. Yet in doing what he must do he is conscious that he will probably eviscerate the source of Alan's ecstasy, the really beautiful part of his emotional life.

Shaffer, in the process of writing the play, consulted at least one eminent child psychologist and wished to give a credible picture of one kind of psychiatric treatment. Inevitably his picture did not satisfy the entire profession. Some of the complaints were merely carping. But in an article in *Psychology Today*, Oscar Grusky expressed concern that the general public would gain the impression that the play's assumptions about psychiatry are universally accepted, when in fact they are far from proved. He warns that bizarre behavior does not necessarily derive from sexual repression, that there is no known "method" of rearing children that can guarantee acceptable personality development, and, especially, that psychiatry rarely "cures" emotional disorders. The reliving of repressed memories (abreaction), which furnishes the climactic scene in *Equus*, is not, he says, a proved therapeutic technique.

Possibly the warning is useful, for theatergoers should be reminded that the theater's purpose is not to present the science of psychiatry or Peruvian history or eighteenth-century musicology with textbook accuracy, but to excite audiences with fresh views of human relationships. Beyond the context of the play, Shaffer is generally critical of psychiatry. He regards it as a substitute religion (mostly American), and too often a convenient excuse for not being responsible for one's own life. But in *Equus* it becomes a device of exceptional dramatic power.

The more theatrical devices of the play may not all be credited to the author. Robert Brustein had underscored Shaffer's dependence on his theatrical colleagues when he noted that the New York production of *The Royal Hunt of the Sun* lacked the precision of the London production and became consequently a less compelling play. Again in *Equus* the imaginative John Dexter was at least partially responsible for the style of the horses' masks and hooves and was quick to perceive the power of the metallic sounds against the floor. Dexter also decided to have all the actors remain visible onstage when they were not involved in the action, seating them at the edge of the lighted area. In addition he made the conventional proscenium stage into something of an arena by placing some of the audience behind the action, giving the lighted area the semblance of a clinic where surgical operations are performed under the eyes of medical students. It was Dexter's inspiration, too, to play the seduction scene in the nude. The sheer sensationalism of this decision is undeniable; but it also led to the moving gesture of Dysart's covering the exhausted boy with a blanket and to the mental image of Alan lying there naked—physically as well as psychologically—during the psychiatrist's peroration to the audience. These are not mere directorial embellishments. They are in the nature

Equus
by Peter Shaffer

Martin Dysart	Colin Blakely
Nurse	Jennifer Piercey
Hesther Saloman	Louie Ramsay
Alan Strang	Gerry Sundquist
Frank Strang	Glyn Owen
Dora Strang	Jane Wenham
Horseman	Rupert Frazer
Harry Dalton	Peter Schofield
Jill Mason	Petra Markham
and	
	Philip Compton
	Tony Goodall
	Marc Harrison
	Deborah Makepeace
	Robin Marchal
	Harry Meacher
	Alasdair Ramsay
	Gillian Webb
	Jeremy Woolston

From 14 June Marc Harrison's role will be played by Andrew Dunford

Director	John Dexter
Designer	John Napier
Music	Marc Wilkinson
Lighting	Andy Phillips
Staff Director	Alan Brown
Movement	Sue Lefton
Production Manager	Richard Bullimore
Company and Stage Manager	Tom Redman
Deputy Stage Manager	Mark ap Robert
Assistant Stage Manager	Catherine Bailey
Sound	Ric Green

The main action takes place in Rokeby Psychiatric Hospital in southern England. The time is the present

There is one interval of 15 minutes

First performance of this production the Old Vic 26 July 1973, returned to the repertoire 21 August 1974; first performance in the West End Albery Theatre 20 April 1976

Head of Horse; Picasso

One might compare the relations of the ego to the id with that between a rider and his horse. The horse provides the locomotor energy and the rider has the prerogative of determining the goal and of guiding the movements of his powerful mount towards it. But all too often in the relations between the ego and the id we find a picture of the less ideal situation in which the rider is obliged to guide his horse in the direction in which it itself wants to go.

- Sigmund Freud

Cast list and credits for the 1976 National Theatre production of Shaffer's award-winning play, which ran for 1,209 performances on Broadway

of dramatic extensions to Shaffer's play. They were developed during the initial rehearsal period and have become established in the printed stage directions. It may be argued that these are interpretive devices only, and the play could survive without them, but how successful *Equus* would have been without Dexter's creative additions is impossible to know. Following its National Theatre production, *Equus* opened in October 1974 in New York, where it ran for more than one thousand performances. It received the New York Drama Critics Circle Award and an Antoinette Perry (Tony) Award, both in 1975.

As in the case of *The Royal Hunt of the Sun*, the critical comments on *Equus* were varied and often confused. Perhaps it is one of the attributes of a truly exceptional work that the critics will not know what to make of it. Almost all acknowledged that it was powerfully moving. *Time* called it Freudian exorcism—a kind of psychological detective thriller. It was apparent to most that the

play operated on a series of levels and that it was linked to the ancient myths. The Manchester *Guardian* reviewer Christopher Ford was especially fascinated with the imagery of the horse: "Equus has such lithe magnificence, at once so warm and alive, so naked and virile." The *New York Times* reviewer Clive Barnes, at a first viewing in London, found a subtext of "conformity's lack of ecstasy" and felt himself haunted by the play. Critic Walter Kerr wrote that *Equus* was "the closest I have seen a contemporary play come—it comes powerfully close—to reanimating the spirit of mystery that makes the stage a place of breathless discovery."

In a foreword to his next play, *Amadeus* (1980), Shaffer has acknowledged his debt to the directors he has worked with (Dexter, John Gielgud, Peter Wood, Peter Hall). "Many of my plays have been intentionally gestural and spectacular in effect," he writes. The published versions are in many ways descriptions of their first productions. He is careful to state, however, "that it is no part of my desire to imprison the play in one particular presentation; still less to encourage the automatic borrowing of an original director's ideas by future interpreters."

Shaffer fans—and by this time there was a sizable throng of them—had to wait until late 1979 for *Amadeus*, which was named best play of the year by *Plays and Players*. This play, though produced by the National Theatre, did not have the help of John Dexter. There were those who thought they missed his presence, despite the fact that the new play was directed by one of Britain's most adventurous directors, Peter Hall, who had also directed *The Battle of Shrivings*.

The setting designed by John Bury for the London production resembles those of *The Royal Hunt of the Sun* and *Equus* in that it provides a neutral acting space that can represent a variety of locations. It is a bit more self-conscious of its flexibility, backed by a proscenium opening through which is seen, as a "light box," the elaborate rococo images of eighteenth-century Vienna.

Some of the storytelling devices of *Amadeus* have also become more formalized and self-conscious. The play opens in 1823 with an aged Antonio Salieri, who frames the story of his fateful vendetta against Wolfgang Amadeus Mozart as a recall. The play proper is thus in the nature of a deathbed confession. We return to the old man's bedroom at the middle of the play and at the end. The playwright also employs two "venticelli" ("little winds") who function in the Oriental tradition as carriers of information and gossip without ever becoming identified as characters in the play. Frequently Salieri addresses the audience directly, sometimes in an aside while the other characters "freeze" or the music is momentarily silenced. Since this is the story of two composers, and since the playwright himself is a knowledgeable music critic, the music assumes the importance of an additional character in the play. It is, in fact, the music that passes through Mozart that makes him, for Salieri, the vessel of God.

Some commentators like to call these devices "Brechtian," but they are more in the spirit of the early expressionists than of Bertolt Brecht. That is to say, their purpose is not merely to explain, or to remind the audience that they are looking in from the outside, but to let the audience share the inner thoughts and feelings of the characters. The theatricality is meant to aid, not deter, emotional involvement. The artifice, however, sometimes becomes so complicated and slick that it may momentarily get in its own way.

Shaffer once again presents a story of two men of widely differing temperaments linked by a common spiritual bond. The audience is more likely to identify with Salieri than with Mozart, first because it is difficult to identify with a genius, and second because the young Mozart, as Shaffer presents him, is hopelessly immature, self-centered, and spoiled. He shocks Salieri (and the audience) by his outrageous behavior and by his obsession with scatological language. One senses that even the playwright was never comfortable with this strange but intriguing phenomenon. Unfortunately Mozart needs the support of Salieri, the official court composer for the emperor Joseph II, to succeed in Vienna. Unfortunately, too, Salieri is the only member of Joseph's inner circle who can perceive immediately and intuitively the rapture and the depth of the young rival's music.

As a youth Salieri had made a pact with God: "*Signore*, let me be a composer! Grant me sufficient fame to enjoy it. In return I will live with virtue. I will strive to better the lot of my fellows. And I will honor you with much music all the days of my life." By 1781 it appeared that both God and he had kept their parts of the bargain. Then Salieri heard a Mozart adagio of such sublime pain and such sublime fulfillment that he was forced to cry out: "*What?! What is this? Tell me, Signore!* . . . It seemed to me that I had heard a voice of God—and that it issued from a creature whose own voice I had also heard—and it was the voice of an obscene child."

Mozart, the intruder, seems destined for failure on every count. His marriage is stormy. He cannot keep pupils. He insults the only people who might possibly help him. He sinks ever deeper into debt. The great flood of music he composes between 1781 and 1791—to be regarded as an unparalleled treasure by all of Western civilization—is received with little enthusiasm and less remuneration. Apparently Salieri has little to fear from this unprepossessing ex-prodigy. But Salieri alone is not deceived. He recognizes God's love (*Ama-deus*) pouring through Mozart's music as it has never entered his. He becomes convinced that the God with whom he bargained is now mocking him. And he declares war—a war of pride that he knows in the end he must lose. He cannot destroy those God-given sounds. He must be satisfied with destroying, simply, Mozart. This he does while posing, like Iago, as his only

A scene from the 1974 production of Equus *(photograph by Zoë Dominic)*

friend. A quiet word to the emperor here and there keeps students and commissions away from Mozart, tempers any enthusiasm that his music might engender, and reduces his allowance as chamber composer to a pittance.

Finally, in a macabre plot, Salieri sends his gaunt servant, dressed as an emissary of Death, to commission from Mozart a requiem. Mozart accepts the commission, believing it to be for his own funeral. The spectral figure continues to haunt him. When the servant refuses to continue the masquerade, the court composer himself dons the disguise and makes the final call on his distraught victim. When he sees firsthand the pitiable figure that Mozart has become, Salieri is so distressed that he rips off his mask and exposes himself. The revelation is almost a deathblow. Stupefied, Mozart can only ask, "Why?" Salieri replies: "(Simply: opening his arms wide): 'Eccomi!— il tuo assassino! . . . For you I go to Hell.' "

Mozart's actual death a month later is attributed to various causes including typhus, kidney failure, and syphilis. But Salieri in his old age insists that he poisoned the young composer. His confession is literally false, virtually true. The irony of the situation persists to the end. No one believes his confession, and he botches an attempt at suicide. Salieri knew himself to be the Champion of Mediocrity. He could not live with that knowledge. He wished only to be "exhausted by an Absolute. . . . If I cannot be Mozart, I do not wish to be anything."

Shaffer has confessed that he is a compulsive revisionist. For the Washington, D.C., opening of *Amadeus* (November 1980) he changed up to 10 percent of the play, not, as he said, to make a new play out of it, "but to make it more and more itself." The basic story was not altered, but motivations were enriched and sharpened. In July 1981 the "American version" returned to Lon-

Dermat Crowley, Paul Scofield, and Donald Gee in the first production of Amadeus *(photograph by Nobby Clark)*

don for a run at Her Majesty's Theatre. The *Sunday Times*, which had not approved of the first version, also called the new one "tripe." But by this time *Amadeus* was playing in Vienna, Warsaw, Berlin, Munich, the Hague, Brussels, and Oslo.

The serious critics find *Amadeus* flawed, but they also find it overwhelming theater. Even Martin Esslin in his condescending review for *Plays and Players* admits to its "bold and profound interest" and its "epic scale." Walter Kerr thinks the flaw is inherent in the story line: "No matter how betrayed or jealous or secretly humiliated [Salieri] may feel, it is impossible to believe that he should wish to destroy music that so moves him." But this is rather like objecting to the "pound of flesh" plot in *The Merchant of Venice*. Who can complain when it has produced both Shylock and Portia? In any case, it may be argued that Kerr has misread Shaffer's motivation. Salieri is not trying to get rid of Mozart's music. He knows that would be impossible. He is revenging himself on an ironic God with whom he had made a youthful bargain. God has literally kept the bargain—he has made Salieri a famous and respected court composer—all that Salieri had asked. But God has now mocked him by sending this obnoxious genius to convince him of his own mediocrity. His own self-image and his place before posterity have been shattered. Bargains made with

God are as unpredictable as those made with the devil. *Amadeus* is, as some critics have observed, the Faust legend stood on its head. But Salieri, like Faust and John Milton's Satan, is a proud man, and he will revenge himself on the humiliating agent through whom God's music flows, even at the price of his own damnation.

Amadeus continues a theme that began at least as far back as *The Royal Hunt of the Sun*. Salieri's God, like Pizarro's and Alan Strang's, is simplistic, primitive, anthropomorphic. But the search for meaning that lies behind these primal images is a search for some spiritual meaning in Peter Shaffer's—and our own—incomprehensible world.

Shaffer adapted *Amadeus* for the screen in 1984, and the film won critical praise and eight Academy Awards, including Best Picture and Best Screenplay. Shaffer's most recent theatrical piece, *Lettice and Lovage*, proved a triumph for both its author and its star, Maggie Smith, who appeared in the London (1987) and New York (1989) productions.

The play concerns a tour guide assigned to the most boring castle in England, Fustian House. When she begins to embellish the history of the place, she is dismissed, although it turns out her supervisor shares her sensibilities. The supervisor and her former employee ultimately strike up a friendship, then vocalize and proselytize against modern architecture. *New York Daily News* drama critic Howard Kissel observed, "*Lettice and Lovage* is a more solid edifice than it first appears. The delights of Shaffer's conceits, of course, were magnified by the performances."

Both in his exploration of human nature and in his idea of theater, Shaffer has shown adventurous growth since *Five Finger Exercise*. The postwar theater has been inundated by dramas of little people whose energies are absorbed by sordid adulteries or by alienation from the job or the family—a procession punctuated by lavish musicals filled with desperate cheerfulness. Audiences and critics alike have come to await Shaffer's plays as a kind of antidote. His characters have some of the stature associated with the great dramas of the past. They wrestle with the gods—such gods as are left to them—and if they despair, it is because they cannot comprehend the mysterious power that has conferred grace on Atahuallpa, that has made a glorious madman of Alan Strang, that has lavished a talent on the undeserving Mozart that could not be earned by the deserving Salieri. These are struggles of scope, and even though the wrestlers are vanquished, they become, as a Maxwell Anderson character said, "emperors of the endless dark, even in seeking."

The lesser struggles—for philistine success, for a comfortable life and a pleasant mate—are for comedy and farce. It may be that Shaffer has other "black comedies" to give us. But his most encouraging development so far is toward the themes that are classically tragic and toward the use of stage space that is more presentational than representational.

Critics have accused Shaffer of trying to be profound beyond his own comprehension; of leaning too heavily on theatrical devices; of oververbalizing; or of simply lacking the poetic talent needed for his larger-than-life conceptions. This last criticism is the most frequent and probably the most justified. But none of these imputed failings has inhibited the lines at the box office or deterred serious theatergoers from expressing gratitude for the revitalization Shaffer has brought to contemporary drama.

Interviews:

"Peter Shaffer Interviewed by Barry Pree," *Transatlantic Review*, 14 (Autumn 1963): 62-66;

John Russell Taylor, "Shaffer and the Incas," *Plays and Players*, 12 (April 1964);

"Philip Oakes Talks to Peter Shaffer," *Sunday Times*, 29 July 1973;

Christopher Ford, "High Horse," *Guardian*, 6 August 1973, p. 8;

"Equus: Playwright Peter Shaffer Interprets its Ritual," *Vogue*, 165 (February 1975): 136, 192;

Joseph McLellan, "Myth, Murder and Mozart," *Washington Post*, 9 November 1980.

References:

Robert Brustein, "Peru in New York," *The Third Theatre* (London: Cape, 1969), pp. 114-117;

Tom Buckley, "Write Me, Said the Play to Peter Shaffer," *New York Times Magazine*, 13 April 1975, pp. 20-21;

Alan Downer, "Total Theatre and Partial Drama: Notes on the New York Theatre, 1965-1966," *Quarterly Journal of Speech*, 52 (October 1966): 225-236;

Martin Esslin, Review of *Amadeus*, *Plays and Players*, 27 (November 1979): 20;

Jules Glenn, "Anthony and Peter Shaffer's Plays: The Influence of Twinship on Creativity," *American Imago*, 31 (Fall 1974): 270-292;

Glenn, "Twins in Disguise: A Psychoanalytic Essay on *Sleuth* and *The Royal Hunt of the Sun*," *Psychoanalytic Quarterly*, 43 (April 1974): 288-302;

Oscar Grusky, "Equestrian Follies," *Psychology Today*, 11 (October 1977): 21-22;

Ronald Hayman, "Like a Woman They Keep Going Back To," *Drama*, 98 (Autumn 1970): 57-64;

Walter Kerr, "Waiting for an Ingenious Twist that Never Comes," Review of *Amadeus*, *New York Times*, 4 January 1981, p. 3;

Wayne P. Lawson, "The Dramatic Hunt: A Critical Evaluation of Peter Shaffer's Plays," Ph. D dissertation, Ohio State University, 1974;

Allan Lewis, *The Contemporary Theatre*, revised edition (New York: Crown, 1971);

Frederick Lumley, *New Trends in 20th Century Drama* (New York: Oxford University Press, 1972);

Benedict Nightingale, "Some Immortal Business," *New Statesman* (13 February 1970): 227;

John Russell Taylor, "Peter Shaffer," in his *Anger and After* (London: Eyre Methuen, 1962), pp. 227-230;

Taylor, *Peter Shaffer* (Harlow: Longman, 1974);

Tobi Tobias, "Playing Without Words," *Dance Magazine*, 49 (May 1975): 48-50;

J. C. Trewin, "In the Grand Manner," Review of *Amadeus, London Illustrated News*, 268 (January 1980): 73;

Irving Wardle, "*Amadeus*," *Times* (London), 3 July 1981, p. 11;

Wil Webb, "Committed to Nothing but the Theatre," *Guardian*, 27 August 1959, p. 4;

Renee Winegarten, "The Anglo-Jewish Dramatist in Search of His Soul," *Midstream*, 12 (October 1966): 40-52.

Alan Sillitoe
(4 March 1928 -   )

This entry was written by Catherine Smith for
DLB 14: British Novelists Since 1960: Part Two.

BOOKS: *Without Beer or Bread* (Dulwich Village, U.K.: Outposts Publications, 1957);

Saturday Night and Sunday Morning (London: W. H. Allen, 1958; New York: Knopf, 1959);

The Loneliness of the Long-Distance Runner (London: W. H. Allen, 1959; New York: Knopf, 1960);

The General (London: W. H. Allen, 1960; New York: Knopf, 1961);

The Rats and Other Poems (London: W. H. Allen, 1960);

Key to the Door (London: W. H. Allen, 1961; New York: Knopf, 1962);

The Ragman's Daughter and Other Stories (London: W. H. Allen, 1963; New York: Knopf, 1964);

Road to Volgograd (London: W. H. Allen, 1964; New York: Knopf, 1964);

A Falling Out of Love and Other Poems (London: W. H. Allen, 1964);

The Death of William Posters (London: W. H. Allen, 1965; New York: Knopf, 1965);

A Tree on Fire (London: Macmillan, 1967; Garden City, N.Y.: Doubleday, 1968);

The City Adventures of Marmalade Jim (London: Macmillan, 1967);

Shaman and Other Poems (London: Turret, 1968);

Love in the Environs of Vorenezh and Other Poems (London: Macmillan, 1968; Garden City, N.Y.: Doubleday, 1969);

Guzman, Go Home, and Other Stories (London: Macmillan, 1968; Garden City, N.Y.: Doubleday, 1969);

Alan Sillitoe (photograph by Jerry Bauer)

All Citizens Are Soldiers, adapted by Sillitoe and Ruth Fainlight from Lope de Vega's play (London: Macmillan, 1969; Chester Springs, Pa.: Dufour, 1969);

A Start in Life (London: W. H. Allen, 1970; New York: Scribners, 1970);

Poems, by Sillitoe, Fainlight, and Ted Hughes (London: Rainbow Press, 1971);

Travels in Nihilon (London: W. H. Allen, 1971; New York: Scribners, 1972);

Raw Material (London: W. H. Allen, 1972; New York: Scribners, 1973; revised, 1978);

Men, Women and Children (London & New York: W. H. Allen, 1973; New York: Scribners, 1974);

Barbarians and Other Poems (London: Turret, 1973);

Storm: New Poems (London: W. H. Allen, 1974);

The Flame of Life (London & New York: W. H. Allen, 1974);

Mountains and Caverns (London: W. H. Allen, 1975);

The Widower's Son (London: W. H. Allen, 1976; New York: Harper & Row, 1977);

Big John and the Stars (London: Robson Books, 1977);

Three Plays (London: W. H. Allen, 1978);

The Incredible Fencing Fleas (London: Robson Books, 1978);

Snow on the North Side of Lucifer (London: W. H. Allen, 1979);

The Storyteller (London: W. H. Allen, 1979; New York: Simon & Schuster, 1980);

The Second Chance and Other Stories (New York: Simon & Schuster, 1980; London: Cape, 1981);

Her Victory (London: Granada, 1982; New York: Watts, 1982);

The Lost Flying Boat (London: Granada, 1983; Boston: Little, Brown, 1983);

Sun Before Departure (London: Granada, 1984);

Down from the Hill (London: Granada, 1984);

Life Goes On (London: Granada, 1985);

Tides and Stone Walls (London: Grafton, 1986);

Every Day of the Week (London: W. H. Allen, 1987);

Out of the Whirlpool (London: Hutchinson, 1987; New York: Harper & Row, 1988);

The Far Side of the Street (London: W. H. Allen, 1988);

The Open Door (London: Grafton, 1989);

Last Loves (London: Grafton, 1990);

Leonard's War (London: HarperCollins, 1991).

PLAY PRODUCTIONS: *All Citizens Are Soldiers*, adapted by Sillitoe and Ruth Fainlight from Lope de Vega's play, Stratford-upon-Avon, 20 June 1967;

This Foreign Field, London, Roundhouse, March 1970;

The Interview, St. Martins-in-the-Fields, 16 September 1976; London, Almost Free Theatre, March 1978.

MOTION PICTURES: *Saturday Night and Sunday Morning*, screenplay by Sillitoe, Continental, 1960;

The Loneliness of the Long-Distance Runner, screenplay by Sillitoe, Continental, 1962;

The Ragman's Daughter, screenplay by Sillitoe, Penelope, 1972.

TELEVISION: *Pit Strike*, BBC, September 1977.

OTHER: Introduction to *Saturday Night and Sunday Morning* (London: Longmans, Green, 1968);

Introduction to *A Sillitoe Selection*, selected and edited by Michael Marland (London: Longmans, Green, 1968).

SELECTED PERIODICAL PUBLICATIONS—
UNCOLLECTED: "Both Sides of the Street," *Times Literary Supplement*, 8 July 1960, p. 435;

"Novel or Play?," *Twentieth Century*, 169 (February 1961): 206-211;

"Drilling and Burring," *Spectator* (3 January 1964): 11-12;

"Poor People," *Anarchy*, 38 (April 1964): 124-128;

"The Wild Horse," *Twentieth Century*, 173 (Winter 1964-1965): 90-92;

"My Israel," *New Statesman*, 20 December 1974, pp. 890-892;

"Writing and Publishing," *London Review of Books*, 14 (April 1982): 8-10.

Alan Sillitoe had no plans for becoming a writer; writing seemed a most unlikely, even "inconceivable" career for a factory worker raised in the industrial town of Nottingham, England. Despite, or perhaps because of, his working-class origins, Sillitoe became a writer whose first two works assured him of a place in English letters. The prize-winning author of poetry, plays, screenplays, short stories, and novels, Sillitoe has capitalized on his background in ways few writers equal. Though actual settings vary, Nottingham is never too far distant in his writing.

Uncertainty born of poverty characterized Sillitoe's earliest years in Nottingham. Born 4 March 1928 to Christopher and Sylvina Burton Sillitoe, Alan Sillitoe watched his father, an unskilled laborer, struggle with unemployment during the financially precarious 1930s. Lack of money sometimes meant government assistance in the form of hot meals for Sillitoe and his four siblings and caused frequent moves over rent disputes for the entire family during Sillitoe's early childhood.

School provided a kind of stability in the constant flux of Sillitoe's volatile home life. By age eight he had become a dedicated student with a wide range of interests, particularly topography, which has remained a lifelong hobby and has figured in several of his novels and stories. Despite two attempts, Sillitoe failed the difficult eleven-plus examination, forcing him to abandon plans for grammar school and higher education. He instead spent the next three years in a local school eagerly reading all sorts of adventure stories by authors ranging from Sir Walter Scott to Sir Arthur Conan Doyle. This reading often supplied needed plots for the stories Sillitoe told to entertain his siblings. In 1942 his formal education ended in typical working-class fashion.

At age fourteen Sillitoe quit school and found a job doing piecework at the Raleigh Bicycle factory. After three months, a dispute over wages led to the end of this job and to the beginning of a new one in a plywood factory. Sillitoe found this work boring, and after eighteen months he became a capstan lathe operator at a small engineering firm where he remained until his military service began in 1946. As Sillitoe points out, his interests were those of any Nottingham youth: visiting local pubs, enjoying women, having money for the first time in his life, and spending it as fast as he made it. Factory work soon dulled what creativity he had begun to develop. Escape from such deadening work and the promise of travel made him a willing volunteer for the RAF. Though he was accepted for pilot's training, the end of war with Japan eliminated the need for more air personnel, and Sillitoe began training as a wireless operator.

Stationed in Malaya for the next two years, Sillitoe had ample time for reading. In addition to the adventure stories he had favored as a child, he read Robert Noonan's *The Ragged Trousered Philanthropists* (1914), which explores working-class existence in Edwardian England. Sillitoe admired Noonan's work because it was one of the few novels that treated working-class characters as people rather than as caricatures. While Noonan's work influenced Sillitoe's writing

in a general fashion, his Malaysian duty later shaped specific scenes in his third novel.

After his tour of duty in the RAF, Sillitoe returned to England in 1948 for his discharge. Routine medical tests revealed that he had contracted tuberculosis while abroad. Consequently, he spent the next sixteen months in an air force hospital where the enforced isolation prompted another period of reading. Sillitoe's reading this time, beginning with the Greek and Latin classics in translation, represented a deliberate effort to educate himself. Simultaneously, as he began reading books, he began trying to write them. The next ten years represent what Sillitoe terms an apprenticeship spent writing novels that were pastiches of all the authors who most influenced him, from Fyodor Dostoyevski and D. H. Lawrence to Henry Fielding and Joseph Conrad. As Sillitoe worked through these influences, he said, he learned to write "clear English." Some of his early stories reappear, though revised and reworked, in later fiction, such as *The General* (1960), his second novel. Shortly before his release from the hospital in December 1949, Sillitoe wrote his first novel and received his first rejection slip. Not discouraged, he remained firm in his commitment to writing.

Sillitoe spent the following year living in Nottingham and writing short stories and another novel. In 1951 he retired to his aunt's cottage in Kent, where he met Ruth Fainlight, an American-born poet living with her husband in nearby Hastings. For six months, with Ruth Fainlight's help and encouragement, Sillitoe concentrated on writing poetry. In January 1952 they left together for France. They remained away from England for six years, living first in France and later in Spain. With his limited RAF pension and National Health allowance as the primary sources of income, Sillitoe still managed to write steadily during this period, even writing on book jackets when paper proved too expensive.

While abroad he met Robert Graves, and in 1954, following Graves's suggestion that he write about Nottingham, Sillitoe began work on *Saturday Night and Sunday Morning*. Having already written short stories set in Nottingham, he started with these brief works and combined them into a picaresque novel. *Saturday Night and Sunday Morning* was finally completed to his satisfaction in 1957. One year and five rejection slips later, the novel was published in 1958, after Sillitoe and Ruth Fainlight had returned to England. The immediate positive response to the novel astounded everyone, including its writer. Assuring the novel of success, the Authors' Club in London awarded Sillitoe its Silver Quill for most promising first novel of 1958.

Praised for its verisimilitude in depicting working-class life, this account of Arthur Seaton, a lathe operator in a Nottingham bicycle factory, follows his progress toward marriage. The novel immediately establishes some favorite Sillitoe themes: the social injustice inherent in working-class life, the "jungle" of social classes, the mindlessness and monotony of the only work accessible to the lower classes, and the "us versus them" mentality of workers pitted against establishment, whether in the person of politician, policeman, or foreman. Arthur's affairs with two sisters, both married, result in the pregnancy and subsequent abortion of one and Arthur's defeat by the husband of the other. The end of the novel finds Arthur at once rebelling against society and conforming to some of its expectations by preparing to marry. Sillitoe does not consider the novel autobiographical because Arthur represents a compilation of many personalities, including about 10 percent of Sillitoe's own, tempered by memories and imagination. An immediate popular success, *Saturday Night and Sunday Morning* remains a favorite of later critics as well as early reviewers.

With his improved prospects, Sillitoe and Ruth Fainlight moved to London and settled in an inexpensive flat where he completed a collection of short stories, *The Loneliness of the Long-Distance Runner* (1959). Advances from publishers allowed Sillitoe to lease a cottage in Whitwell, Hertfordshire, where he readied his second novel, *The General*, for publication and continued work on *Key to the Door* (1961). Two events especially distinguished 1959 for Sillitoe: his marriage to Ruth Fainlight in November and the publication of *The Loneliness of the Long-Distance Runner*. The critical and commercial success of Sillitoe's second work coupled with that of his first signaled the end of his writing apprenticeship.

In 1960 *The Loneliness of the Long-Distance Runner* won for Sillitoe the Hawthornden Prize, awarded each year for the best imaginative writing by a writer under forty. This remarkable volume contains some of Sillitoe's finest short stories, in which he writes about survivors and the hardships they confront. Several of the stories focus on youths in Nottingham as Sillitoe explores a child's fascination with suicide in "Saturday Afternoon" or follows the Goose Fair adven-

tures of two boys who steal one last ride in "Noah's Ark." In the final story of the collection Sillitoe describes childish war games led by a childlike adult, Frankie Buller, later subjected to shock treatment by an indifferent society more interested in control than compassion. All the stories emphasize the sense of futility shrouding every aspect of working-class existence, but the title story offers the harshest indictment of the upper classes. In this story, Smith, an unrepentant youth sentenced to a borstal, or reformatory, for theft, deliberately loses a long-distance race and its attendant trophy, which the borstal director wants him to win for the prestige of the reformatory. Because self-esteem does not come easily for Smith, he refuses to risk its loss by winning a race for the director, much as a trained horse might. Though the protagonist's deliberate and obvious losing of the race complicates the remainder of his sentence, he regrets neither his action nor its consequences, and concludes that "in-laws" and "out-laws" can never see eye to eye. This story explores the resentment the lower classes feel for any of the innumerable ways government and, by extension, society dehumanize them. With few reservations critics welcomed Sillitoe's second work and eagerly awaited his third.

The General proved a disappointment to reviewers, who quickly dismissed it. Though some criticized it as a hasty effort written to cash in on the success of Sillitoe's earlier two works, *The General* was actually written over a long period of time. It developed from a story Sillitoe first wrote in 1949 and later revised while living in Majorca in 1953, and during the next seven years it went through several more thorough revisions. A fable about war, art, and the nature of man, *The General* chronicles the actions and reactions of an anonymous protagonist, the General, commander of the somewhat barbaric Gorshek forces, and of Evart, conductor of a symphony orchestra that, on its way to the front lines to entertain troops, is captured by Gorshek forces. While awaiting instructions about the orchestra's fate, the General and Evart debate the relative merits of war and pacifism. When the high command's computers demand the musicians' deaths, the General, at high personal cost, arranges for their escape. His decision, influenced in part by the orchestra's moving performance, introduces freedom of choice into the novel's central debate as the General selects integrity over blind obedience and so assures himself of certain disgrace and punishment. His insistence that the orchestra members carry weapons spells a type of defeat for the pacifist Evart as well. Either ignored or condemned by critics, *The General* was made into a film, which also failed to win an audience.

The Rats and Other Poems, also published in 1960, includes the long title poem and thirty-three short lyrics from *Without Beer or Bread* (1957), a small collection of poems published in a limited paperback edition. For the most part undistinguished, the volume did introduce a favorite Sillitoe theme: individual rebellion against the collected pressures of government and other bureaucracies. Though Sillitoe considers himself first a poet, then a novelist, critics regard his fiction much more highly. Interestingly, however, the passage in *Saturday Night and Sunday Morning* that most critics single out for praise was originally a long poem. Sillitoe spent the rest of 1960 preparing the screenplay for the film version of *Saturday Night and Sunday Morning*. The film, starring Albert Finney, proved both a critical and a commercial success.

After a five-month holiday in Tangier, Sillitoe returned in 1961 to London where he rented a flat and began revising *Key to the Door* while he worked on another screenplay, this time for *The Loneliness of the Long-Distance Runner*. As with Sillitoe's first novel, this story translated well into film. Both critics and public responded with quick enthusiasm to the motion picture, which starred Tom Courtenay and Sir Michael Redgrave. *Key to the Door* was published in October 1961 to a generally tentative critical reaction, which stemmed from reservations about Sillitoe's often overworked style and his heavy-handed attempts to inject his political philosophy into the novel. Most critics recognized the merit of the novel's first two sections, which recount the Nottingham childhood of Brian Seaton, older brother of Sillitoe's first protagonist. In contrast, the account of Brian's military service in Malaya, detailed in the novel's last two parts, provoked harsh criticism for its insufficiently prepared-for climax in which Brian refuses to kill one of the Communist rebels fighting the British. Sillitoe fails to convince the reader that Brian is willing to die for a system of which he is only superficially aware. The author's naive use of political propaganda coupled with the lack of a definite structure weakens a novel that contains some of his most vivid writing. Uneven but worthwhile, *Key to the Door* evidences a preoccupation with politics that colors Sillitoe's succeeding works.

Dust jacket for the American edition of Sillitoe's 1961 novel, a sequel to Saturday Night and Sunday Morning

Shortly after his son's birth in March 1962 and six months after the publication of *Key to the Door*, Sillitoe uprooted his entire family for a year and traveled to Tangier and later throughout Morocco. Here he began his next novel and wrote some of the short stories included in *The Ragman's Daughter and Other Stories* (1963). This volume met with generally favorable, if not enthusiastic, reviews. Although most critics praised the stories' technical skill, reviewers regarded as myopic and oversimplified Sillitoe's view that society is comprised solely of oppressed workers and oppressing bureaucracies. Most of the stories urge rebellion against the establishment in any form, and while many of the protagonists cheat their employers more for enjoyment than from necessity, several characters are reduced to scavenging through trash heaps in order to survive. In this volume the emphasis on violent rebellion replaces the thorough character development and psychological analysis of the earlier stories. Though resistance to authority colored much of his writing by 1963, politics became even more dominant in later work. Sillitoe's unhappiness with the British system increased after he had an opportunity to observe Communist life.

After his return to England in 1963, Sillitoe received an invitation from the Soviet Writers' Union to visit the USSR, where he spent a month. Later in the year he traveled for four weeks in Czechoslovakia and catalogued his observations in *Road to Volgograd*, which was published in 1964. An individual, highly personal account of his travels, the work reveals much about Sillitoe's own tastes, such as his interest in geography and military strategy and his love of cartography and topography. Distinctly uncritical of Soviet politics, *Road to Volgograd* offers a new perspective on Sillitoe's dissatisfaction with England in general, not just with the handicaps imposed on its workers.

David Brett's stage adaptation of *Saturday Night and Sunday Morning* opened and quickly closed in Nottingham in spring 1964. A 1966 London production was equally unsuccessful. In its transition to the stage the picaresque structure of the novel became episodic drama, which was not enhanced by interruptions of pop music. A new volume of poetry, *A Falling Out of Love and Other Poems*, also appeared in 1964. Though the poems in this volume showed much discipline and craft, none provoked an enthusiastic critical response. Late in 1964 Sillitoe resettled his family in Spain and for the next four years divided his time between his homes there and in England. Despite commuting, he managed to finish *The Death of William Posters* (1965), the first novel of his Frank Dawley trilogy. In this novel Sillitoe takes his argument against social injustice beyond Nottingham.

The protagonist, Frank Dawley, is both older and more ready to rebel than either of the Seaton brothers. While *Saturday Night and Sunday Morning* ends with Arthur's convincing himself that marriage should be his next step and *Key to the Door* ends with Brian's returning to a marriage interrupted by military service, *The Death of William Posters* begins with Dawley's deserting wife, children, and job in order to find freedom and a sense of identity. Dawley creates an imaginary figure, William Posters—a name suggested by the signs Dawley sees everywhere: "Bill Post-

ers Will Be Prosecuted"—who comes to symbolize the underdog workman apparently hounded by authorities. Dawley's relationship with his first lover ends when his commitment to causes becomes more important than his commitment to individuals. The protagonist's alliances with an eccentric painter, a new lover, and an American revolutionary lead to his enlistment in the Algerian rebellion against France. As Dawley begins his new life as a revolutionary, his old symbol of the oppressed workman, William Posters, dies. Difficulties in style and weaknesses in the conception of Sillitoe's hero prompted critical reservations. The second novel of the trilogy fared little better.

A Tree on Fire (1967) continues the story of Frank Dawley's own revolution. In this novel Dawley's lover, Myra, and their son return to England and share a home with Albert Handley, the painter who earlier befriended Dawley. The scene then shifts back to Dawley and the desert fighting, which incorporates the most basic of working-class biases—the "us versus them" dichotomy. After attacking with the rebels, Dawley is sick for ten days, and deciding he would be more useful in England raising money for the insurgents' cause, he returns and joins his lover and child at Handley's home. A successful painter but also a confirmed revolutionary, Handley enlists Dawley in his efforts to establish a utopian community, which becomes the subject of the third novel. While reviewers commended Sillitoe's rendering of battle scenes, they criticized his style in other passages. As his characters receded before his theme of violent rebellion, his art degenerated into propaganda.

Though begun in 1967, the final novel of the trilogy, *The Flame of Life*, was not published until 1974, and the delay proved devastating. In this novel Dawley, Handley, and various members of their families keep trying to establish a utopian community while disrupting the English society around them. Yet their own bickering continually interrupts and delays their revolutionary plots to correct social injustices. Little action, less direction, and too much purposeless theorizing coupled with such stylistic excesses as overlush prose and self-conscious imagery make this novel Sillitoe's weakest. Critics generally agreed *The Flame of Life* added little to Sillitoe's reputation.

In 1966, after the publication of the first novel in his trilogy and while working on the second one, Sillitoe collaborated with his wife in adapting for the British stage Lope de Vega's play *All Citizens Are Soldiers*. In 1967 a group of young actors staged the play, but it closed after only a few performances. While his play was opening and closing, Sillitoe traveled again to Russia. This time, however, he was openly critical of restraints on Soviet writers. Upon his return in fall 1967, he collected his family, and they all wintered in Majorca in a house loaned by Robert Graves. During this period Sillitoe finished some short stories as he worked on another play, *This Foreign Field*, and readied for publication another volume of poetry, *Love in the Environs of Vorenezh* (1968). Late in 1968 Sillitoe again journeyed to the Soviet Union but was increasingly disenchanted with Soviet treatment of minorities.

Sillitoe's third collection of short stories, *Guzman, Go Home, and Other Stories*, was published at the end of 1968. About the circumstances and pressures that force people together or apart, these stories concern survivors, as Sillitoe's stories often do. In "Revenge," as marital love turns bitter, the protagonist survives both his wife's blundering murder attempt and the contemptuous indifference of his psychiatrists. "Canals" examines the effect of the past on the present in rendering certain things at once familiar and alien. In the title story Sillitoe returns to the theme of his second novel, the interdependence of art and politics, as Guzman, a German war criminal, tries to justify his life to himself as well as to a young English painter. Sillitoe creates sympathy for Guzman by making fun of him. Though the themes are familiar, the writer treats them with a skill and assurance critics applauded. For one reviewer Sillitoe's technique even invited comparison with that of Charles Dickens.

Sillitoe spent most of 1969 in England writing various short stories and a long, picaresque novel, *A Start in Life* (1970), in which he experimented with such traditional comic forms as satire, irony, farce, and parody as he followed in the tradition of Fielding, an author he had long admired. The protagonist, Michael Cullen, flees his Nottingham background, his pregnant girlfriend, and the dubious circumstances surrounding his dismissal for unethical real-estate dealings. Escaping to London, he has a series of adventures that eventually land him in prison. At the end of the novel, Cullen retires to the country, ostensibly to lead a respectable life. Generally receptive to *A Start in Life*, critics appreciated the writer's humor and his skill in manipulating traditional literary forms.

Sillitoe spent part of 1970 working on a utopian fantasy, and in March 1970 the same company that had staged *All Citizens Are Soldiers* produced *This Foreign Field*, but it too closed after only a few performances. Sillitoe spent most of this year finishing the screenplay for *The Ragman's Daughter*, which premiered in 1972. The film, starring Victoria Tennant, met with mixed reviews and received little promotion. Though Sillitoe was pleased with the film, it did not enjoy the success of his first two screenplays.

Sillitoe's refusal to complete a census form resulted in a fine in 1971 after seven months of legal maneuvering. He spent the summer of 1971 traveling on the Continent with his family. He also joined with his wife and his friend Ted Hughes to produce *Poems*, a handsome, signed, limited edition of three hundred copies. Sillitoe's fantasy *Travels in Nihilon* appeared in the fall of this year.

Exploring the possibilities of life in a totally nihilistic state, *Travels in Nihilon* met critical reserve and public indifference. The novel follows five travelers to Nihilon where citizens value cheating and violence, scorn honor and loyalty, and deliberately create chaos and disaster. The five travelers join an insurrection against the established government but ultimately realize that the rebels are as corrupt as the government they want to overthrow. The farce and satire of some of the adventures do not compensate for the weak multiple perspectives imposed on the novel by five protagonists. Though *Travels in Nihilon* sparked little enthusiasm, Sillitoe's *Raw Material* aroused great interest when it was published in 1972.

Both novel and memoir, biography and autobiography, *Raw Material* attempts to explain how someone of Sillitoe's background becomes a writer. According to its author, *Raw Material* attempts to trace through the "raw material" of his grandparents' lives the events and circumstances that shaped his decision to become a novelist. In part 1 he alternates sections of philosophical speculation, primarily about the relativity of truth, with accounts of family history, in particular biographical details about his grandfather Burton, so that he can examine the interrelationship of a writer and the raw material of his own life. Much of part 2 concerns World War I as Sillitoe interweaves carefully researched facts, relatives' memories about the war, and his own theories about the misuse of power by government and other bureaucracies. The last chapters include anecdotes about more recent family history between commentaries on writing. The book works best when Sillitoe explores his familial relationships. The indirect, oblique analysis of the fiction-making process in these passages succeeds much more than the direct philosophical speculations of the commentaries. Somewhat uneven, the work offers valuable insights about Sillitoe, who considers it one of his most important works. To his gratification, a slightly revised edition was published in 1978.

Later in 1972, at Stephen Spender's invitation, Sillitoe wrote a paper on D. H. Lawrence, "Lawrence's District," which was later included in *Mountains and Caverns* (1975), a collection of Sillitoe's essays. After the undistinguished release of the film version of *The Ragman's Daughter*, the writer moved his family back to London, ending three years in the Kent countryside. The following year he produced his fourth collection of short stories, *Men, Women and Children*, which was well received, in part because it included "Mimic," one of Sillitoe's most memorable stories.

The stories in this collection may share a Nottingham setting, but they focus on limitations arising from character rather than from environment, and geography has little to do with self-image. Only one of the stories, "Pit Strike," indicts, in the usual Sillitoe manner, a society that encourages repressive, unjust conditions. The other stories focus on individuals and the ways they cope with circumstances, not yield to them. The most important story, one of Sillitoe's finest, is "Mimic," about a man who tries to cope with life by imitating it. His relationships with people exhausted, the protagonist is reduced to the impossible task of mimicking nature. His unsuccessful efforts drive him mad, but in the second half of the story he comes to recognize the dangers of self-delusion inherent in mimicry and rids his mind of its collected phantoms. Well received by critics, the stories in this collection represent a technical sophistication even more pronounced in Sillitoe's latest novels.

Always protesting the repression of minorities, Sillitoe has never hesitated to express his markedly pro-Zionist views, which prompted a 1974 invitation by the Israeli Foreign Office to spend ten days in Israel. He subsequently had published two brief articles in a geographical journal as well as an article in the *New Statesman* that detailed his enthusiasm for Israel. Later in 1974 Sillitoe's love of geography led to a series of lectures at the University of Nebraska. One of these lectures, "Maps," is included in *Mountains and Cav-*

erns. During this same year Sillitoe also reiterated his criticism of Soviet repression. Concern for the repressed also marks the poems in *Storm: New Poems* (1974), a volume that includes Sillitoe's verse from *Poems* as well as short lyrics published in two earlier small-press editions, *Shaman and Other Poems* (1968) and *Barbarians and Other Poems* (1973). As a group, the poems reveal Sillitoe's improved control and increasingly skillful technique.

For the next two years Sillitoe produced little besides *Mountains and Caverns*, which included an account of his early years as well as essays and speeches written since 1963. He remained active in humanitarian causes, often attending conferences, such as the one sponsored by UNESCO to discuss the cultural aspects of Arab-Israeli relations. In November 1975 Sillitoe was elected a fellow of the Royal Geographical Society, an especially gratifying honor for him. Early in 1976 at a conference in Brussels, he harshly criticized Soviet treatment of Jews, the subject of a short play, *The Interview*, which was performed in September 1976.

While revising an early story for children prior to its publication as a book, Sillitoe researched the life of a career army officer for his next novel. This book, *The Widower's Son*, published in the fall of 1976 to general acclaim, examines the life of William Scorton, raised by his widowed father, a retired professional soldier dedicated to molding his son in his own image. Conditioned from an early age to perceive life in military terms, first as a young cadet at gunnery school and later as a colonel in the royal artillery, William never comes to terms with his background. He can resolve neither the immediate conflicts with his father, who secretly considers his son better off as a noncommissioned officer, nor his later conflicts with his wife, a brigadier's daughter who can never quite overcome the differences in their backgrounds. Over his wife's objections, William resigns his commission to discover much about life that the army failed to teach him. William's initiation destroys his marriage. Sillitoe's elaborate, extended metaphor of marriage as war details the collapse of William's relationship with his wife. His subsequent mental breakdown culminates in an attempted suicide from which he emerges with the beginnings of a self-awareness denied him in his army career and in his relationships with both wife and father. Beginning in midlife a new career as a teacher, William prepares to face life on his own terms, no longer colored by the orders and desires of others. In this novel Sillitoe does more than catalogue the problems caused by working-class origins; he focuses on the inner agonies of one individual.

In 1977 Sillitoe produced *Big John and the Stars*, a well-received story for children, and later that year "Pit Strike" from *Men, Women and Children* was dramatized successfully on BBC television. The 1978 *Three Plays* collected *This Foreign Field*, retitled *The Slot Machine*; *The Interview*, an expanded and revised version that was performed in March 1978 in London; and *Pit Strike*. During the summer of 1977 Sillitoe and his family spent two months at the invitation of the mayor of Jerusalem at the Mishkenot Sha'anamin, a retreat for celebrated artists. Though Sillitoe recorded his impressions in a daily journal, an account of his experiences has yet to be published. After the publication of *The Incredible Fencing Fleas* (1978), another story for children, Sillitoe released his ninth volume of poetry, *Snow on the North Side of Lucifer* (1979). More important, in fall 1979 Sillitoe produced his tenth, and most ambitious, novel, *The Storyteller*.

The Storyteller chronicles the progress into madness of Ernest Cotgrave, who begins storytelling to escape the violence threatened by the school bully and ends committed to a mental institution following a suicide attempt that renders him mute. Cotgrave retreats into schizophrenia as his life becomes so intertwined with those of his characters that he can no longer distinguish reality from illusion. Peopling his tales with persons and events from his own life, he is finally so overwhelmed by the multiple personalities that the only response possible to his lover's rejection is attempted suicide. Because he is a mute, Cotgrave's complex oral existence is reduced to "block capitals" on "bits of paper."

Multiple personalities characterize writers for Sillitoe, who pictures the writer as empty before he peoples his mind with his fictional creations. In *The Storyteller*, Sillitoe deliberately blurs distinctions between fantasy and reality, as intricate interior monologues become, without warning, perorations before audiences both appreciative and hostile. Though some overextended metaphors and awkward sentence patterns persist, the word-echoes and refrains, the expert interweaving of inner thoughts and public performances, and the sophisticated treatment of what Sillitoe terms the "same old identity situation" mark *The Storyteller* as one of his finest novels.

Sillitoe again explores the problem of identity in his sixth collection of short stories, *The Second Chance and Other Stories* (1980). Critical reaction was for the most part favorable, with different reviewers praising different stories. However, "A Scream of Toys," "The Sniper," and the title story were singled out by most. Sillitoe's concern with acting, masks, and mimicry, which dominated *The Storyteller*, figures most clearly in "The Second Chance," a story about a larcenous young man inextricably caught up in his own masquerade of playing the dead son to an elderly couple. Living a lie becomes a leitmotif that echoes throughout the volume.

Sillitoe defies critical attempts to pigeonhole him. Critics labeled him an "angry young man" early in his career, before he had even read much by such writers as John Osborne and John Braine. Also rejecting the label of working-class novelist, Sillitoe prefers to be thought of as simply a novelist. For him Arthur Seaton is first an individual, then a representative of the working class. In his later novels Sillitoe tempers his concern for social injustice, which dominates the early fiction, with a closer examination of the individual victims of such injustices. As the externalized battles between the working class and the establishment become the internal conflicts within a single character, Sillitoe continues to draw on his Nottingham origins. The images of imprisonment, factory, borstal, and conscription in earlier books yield to more subtle metaphors of schizophrenia, suicide, and madness. Not willing to settle for the place *Saturday Night and Sunday Morning* earned him in English letters, Alan Sillitoe continues to explore the writer's limits with volumes of children's literature, poetry, drama, short stories, and increasingly complex novels.

Interviews:

"Silver Quill for New Novelist: Mr. Alan Sillitoe Looks Forward to Wider Travels," *Times* (London), 23 April 1959, p. 9;

"Alan Sillitoe," *Times* (London), 6 February 1964, p. 15;

Igor Hajek, "Morning Coffee with Sillitoe," *Nation*, 27 January 1969, pp. 122-124;

Bolivar Le Franc, "Sillitoe at Forty," *Books and Bookmen*, 14 (June 1969): 21-22, 24;

P. H. S., "Very Alive," *Times* (London), 21 July 1969, p. 4;

Brendan Hennessy, "Alan Sillitoe," *Transatlantic Review*, 41 (Winter-Spring 1972): 108-113;

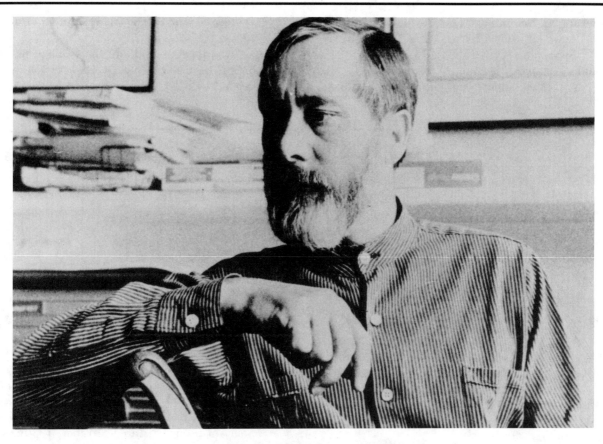

Alan Sillitoe (photograph by David Sillitoe)

Barry Norman, "Alan Sillitoe Avoids the Complacency Trap," *Times* (London), 26 October 1972, p. 12;

M. Lefranc, "Alan Sillitoe: An Interview," *Etudes Anglaises*, 26 (January-March 1973): 35-48;

Josef-Hermann Sauter, "Interview mit Alan Sillitoe," *Weimarer Beitrage*, 19 (1973): 44-59;

John Halperin, "Interview with Alan Sillitoe," *Modern Fiction Studies*, 25 (Summer 1979): 175-189.

Bibliography:

David E. Gerard, *Alan Sillitoe: A Bibliography* (London: Mansell / Westport, Conn.: Meckler, 1988).

References:

Stanley S. Atherton, *Alan Sillitoe: A Critical Assessment* (London: W. H. Allen, 1979);

James Gindin, "Alan Sillitoe's Jungle," *Texas Studies in Literature and Language*, 4 (Spring 1962): 35-48;

John Dennis Hurrell, "Alan Sillitoe and the Serious Novel," *Critique*, 4 (Fall-Winter 1960-1961): 3-16;

Frederick P. W. McDowell, "Self and Society: Alan Sillitoe's *Key to the Door*," *Critique*, 6 (Spring 1963): 116-123;

Anna Ryan Nardella, "The Existential Dilemmas of Alan Sillitoe's Working-Class Heroes," *Studies in the Novel*, 5 (Winter 1973): 469-482;

Marie Peel, "The loneliness of Alan Sillitoe," *Books and Bookmen*, 19 (December 1973): 42-46;

Allen Richard Penner, *Alan Sillitoe* (New York: Twayne, 1972);

Eugene F. Quirk, "Social Class as Audience: Sillitoe's Story and Screenplay," *Literature-Film Quarterly*, 9 (1981): 161-171;

Janet Buck Rollins, "Novel into Film: *The Loneliness of the Long-Distance Runner*," *Literature-Film Quarterly*, 9 (1981): 172-188;

D. M. Roskies, "Alan Sillitoe's Anti-Pastoral," *Journal of Narrative Technique*, 10, no. 3 (1980): 170-185;

Roskies, " 'I'd Rather Be Like I Am': Character, Style, and the Language of Class in Sillitoe's Narratives," *Neophilogus*, 65, no. 2 (1981): 308-319;

Michael K. Simmons, "The 'In-Laws' and 'Out-Laws' of Alan Sillitoe," *Ball State University Forum*, 14 (Winter 1973): 76-79;

Hugh B. Staples, "*Saturday Night and Sunday Morning*: Alan Sillitoe and the White Goddess,"

Modern Fiction Studies, 10 (Summer 1964): 171-181;

Ramsay Wood, "Alan Sillitoe: The Image Shedding the Author," *Four Quarters*, 21 (November 1971): 3-10.

Tom Stoppard

(3 July 1937 -   )

This entry was written by Anne Wright (Hatfield Polytechnic) for
DLB 13: British Dramatists Since World War II: Part Two.

See also the Stoppard entry in DLB Yearbook: 1985.

BOOKS: *Lord Malquist and Mr. Moon: A Novel* (London: Blond, 1966; New York: Knopf, 1968);

Rosencrantz and Guildenstern are Dead (London: Faber & Faber, 1967; New York: Grove, 1967);

Enter a Free Man (London: Faber & Faber, 1968; New York: Grove, 1969);

The Real Inspector Hound (London: Faber & Faber, 1968; New York: Grove, 1969);

Tango, adapted by Tom Stoppard from the play by Slawomir Mrozek, translated by Nicholas Bethell (London: Cape, 1968);

If You're Glad I'll be Frank: a play for radio (London: Faber & Faber, 1969);

Albert's Bridge: A Play (London: Faber & Faber, 1969);

Albert's Bridge and If You're Glad I'll be Frank (London: Faber & Faber, 1969);

After Magritte (London: Faber & Faber, 1971; New York: Grove, 1972);

Jumpers (London: Faber & Faber, 1972; New York: Grove, 1972);

Artist Descending a Staircase and Where Are They Now? Two plays for radio (London: Faber & Faber, 1973);

Travesties (London: Faber & Faber, 1975; New York: Grove, 1975);

Every Good Boy Deserves Favour: a play for actors and orchestra and Professional Foul: a play for television (London: Faber & Faber, 1978);

The Fifteen-minute Hamlet (London: French, 1978);

Night and Day (London: Faber & Faber, 1978; revised, 1979);

Dogg's Hamlet, Cahoot's Macbeth (London: Inter-Action Imprint, 1979; London: Faber & Faber, 1979);

Undiscovered Country (Das Weite Land), by Arthur Schnitzler, in an English version by Tom Stoppard (London: Faber & Faber, 1980);

On the Razzle, Adapted from Einen Jux will er sich machen by Johann Nestroy (London: Faber & Faber, 1981);

The Real Thing (London: Faber & Faber, 1982);

The Dog It Was That Died and Other Plays (London: Faber & Faber, 1983);

Squaring the Circle (London: Faber & Faber, 1984; Boston: Faber & Faber, 1985);

Rough Crossing (London: Faber & Faber, 1985);

Hapgood (London & New York: French, 1988);

In the Native State (London: Faber & Faber, 1991);

The Boundary (London & New York: French, 1991).

PLAY PRODUCTIONS: *A Walk on the Water*, Hamburg, 1964; revised as *Enter a Free Man*, London, St. Martin's Theatre, 28 March 1968; New York, St. Clements Theatre, 17 December 1974;

The Gamblers, Bristol, University of Bristol, 1965;

Tango, adapted by Stoppard from Nicholas Bethell's translation of Slawomir Mrozek's play, London, Aldwych Theatre, 25 May 1966;

Rosencrantz and Guildenstern are Dead, Edinburgh, Cranston Street Hall, 24 August 1966; complete version, London, Old Vic Theatre, 11

photograph by Mark Gerson

April 1967; New York, Alvin Theatre, 16 October 1967, 421 [performances];

The Real Inspector Hound, London, Criterion Theatre, 17 June 1968; produced with *After Magritte*, New York, Theatre Four, 23 April 1972, 465; London, Shaw Theatre, 6 November 1972;

Albert's Bridge, produced with *If You're Glad I'll be Frank*, Edinburgh, St. Mary's Hall, 29 August 1969; London, Kings Head Lunchtime Theatre, 18 October 1976;

If You're Glad I'll be Frank, produced with *Albert's Bridge*, Edinburgh, St. Mary's Hall, 29 August 1969;

After Magritte, London, Green Banana Restaurant, 9 April 1970; produced with *The Real Inspector Hound*, New York, Theatre Four,

23 April 1972, 465; London, Shaw Theatre, 6 November 1972;

Dogg's Our Pet, London, Almost Free Theatre, 7 December 1971;

Jumpers, London, Old Vic Theatre (National Theatre), 2 February 1972; Washington, D.C., Kennedy Center, 18 February 1974; New York, Billy Rose Theatre, 22 April 1974, 46;

The House of Bernarda Alba, adapted by Stoppard from Federico García Lorca's play, translated by Katie Kendall, London, Greenwich Theatre, 22 March 1973;

Travesties, New York, Aldwych Theatre, 10 June 1974; London, Ethel Barrymore Theater, 1975, 155;

Dirty Linen and New-Found-Land, London, Almost Free Theatre, 6 April 1976; London, Arts

Theatre, 16 June 1976; New York, John Golden Theatre, 11 January 1977, 159;

Every Good Boy Deserves Favour, music by Andre Previn, London, Festival Hall, 1 July 1977;

Night and Day, London, Phoenix Theatre, 8 November 1978;

Dogg's Hamlet, Cahoot's Macbeth, Warwick, University of Warwick Arts Centre, 21 May 1979; London, Collegiate Theatre, 30 July 1979;

Undiscovered Country, adapted from John Harrison's translation of Arthur Schnitzler's *Das Weite Land*, London, Olivier Theatre (National Theatre), 20 June 1979;

On the Razzle, adapted from Johann Nestroy's *Einen Jux will er sich machen*, London, Lyttelton Theatre (National Theatre), 18 September 1981;

The Real Thing, London, Strand Theatre, 16 November 1982; New York, Plymouth Theater, 5 January 1984.

MOTION PICTURES: *The Romantic Englishwoman*, screenplay by Stoppard and Thomas Wiseman, New World Pictures, 1975;

Despair, adapted from Vladimir Nabokov's novel, screenplay by Stoppard, Peter Martheshamer, 1979;

The Human Factor, adapted from Graham Greene's novel, screenplay by Stoppard, Otto Preminger, 1979; Otto Preminger, 1979;

Rosencrantz and Guildenstern Are Dead, screenplay by Stoppard, Thirteen WNET/Cinecom, 1991.

TELEVISION: *A Walk on the Water*, ITV, November 1963; revised as *The Preservation of George Riley*, BBC, 1964;

A Separate Peace, BBC, 22 August 1966;

Teeth, BBC, 7 February 1967;

Another Moon Called Earth, BBC, 28 June 1967;

Neutral Ground, Thames Television, 11 December 1968;

The Engagement, revised version of *The Dissolution of Dominic Boot*, NBC, 8 March 1970;

One Pair of Eyes, BBC, 1972;

Eleventh House, by Stoppard and Clive Exton, BBC, 1975;

Three Men in a Boat, adapted from Jerome K. Jerome's novel, BBC, 1975;

The Boundary, by Stoppard and Clive Exton, BBC, 1975;

Professional Foul, BBC, 21 September 1977;

Squaring the Circle, TVS, May 1984.

RADIO: *The Dissolution of Dominic Boot*, BBC Radio 4, 1964;

"M" is for Moon and Other Things, BBC Radio 4, 1964;

A Walk on the Water, BBC, 1965;

If You're Glad I'll be Frank, BBC, 1966;

Albert's Bridge, BBC, 13 July 1967;

Where Are They Now?, BBC, 18 January 1970;

Artist Descending a Staircase, BBC, 14 November 1972;

The Dog It Was That Died, BBC Radio 3, 9 December 1982.

OTHER: "Reunion," "Life, Times: Fragments," "The Story," in *Introduction 2: Stories by New Writers* (London: Faber & Faber, 1964);

A Separate Peace, in *Playbill 2*, edited by Alan Durband (London: Hutchinson, 1969);

Dogg's Our Pet, in *Six of the Best* (London: Inter-Action Imprint, 1976).

SELECTED PERIODICAL PUBLICATIONS—
UNCOLLECTED: "The Positive Maybe," *Author*, 78 (Spring 1967): 17-19;

"Something to Declare," *Sunday Times*, 25 February 1968, p. 47;

"The Engagement," *New York Times*, 8 March 1970, Sect. II, p. 17;

Commentary, on Ted Hughes's *Orghast*, *Times Literary Supplement*, 1 October 1971, p. 1,174;

"Yes We Have No Banana," *Guardian*, 10 December 1971, p. 10;

"Playwrights and Professors," *Times Literary Supplement*, 13 October 1973, p. 1,219;

"The Face at the Window," *Sunday Times*, 27 February 1977.

Tom Stoppard, a leading figure of the British theater since the mid 1960s, ranks as a dramatist of brilliant and original comic genius. His first major success established him as a master of philosophical farce, combining dazzling theatricality and wit with a profound exploration of metaphysical concerns. His output through three decades has been extensive and varied, including original plays for radio and television, screenplays for television and film, adaptations and translations of works by European dramatists, several short stories, and a novel. His work for the stage comprises many short pieces and relatively few full-length plays. However, the interest generated by the éclat of his theatrical debut has been maintained, and successive plays have been heralded as major events by both audiences and critics. He is now a playwright of international reputation in Europe and the United States. Stoppard is emphatically a professional writer, with a primary interest in stagecraft: each new play is designed specifically for a small fringe company, a commercial West End production, or for performance at the National Theatre in London. His popularity extends to both the intellectual avantgarde and the ordinary theatergoer. Since the 1960s his work has developed in other areas, from absurdist or surrealist comedy to political and even polemical drama. Toward the end of the 1970s the plays became less experimental in method and more overtly serious in tone, although with a return to pure farce in some productions. His career to date confirms his importance, not merely as a theatrical phenomenon, but as a major contemporary playwright.

Born Tomas Straussler in Zlin, Czechoslovakia, Stoppard is the younger son of Eugene and Martha Straussler. His father, a doctor with the shoe manufacturing firm Bata, was moved by the company to Singapore shortly before World War II. When his wife and family were evacuated to India, Eugene Straussler remained in Singapore and was killed after the Japanese invasion in 1941. In India the family lived in Darjeeling, where Martha was, for a time, manager of the Bata shoe shop and where Tom received his early schooling. In 1946 Martha married Maj. Kenneth Stoppard, then serving with the British army in India. On returning to England with his new family, Kenneth Stoppard worked in the machine-tool business. The Stoppards lived in several English counties before moving, around 1950, to Bristol in the southwest, which was to become a particular focus for Tom as he grew up. He went to the Dolphin School, a preparatory school in Nottinghamshire, and subsequently to Pocklington School in Yorkshire. In 1954, when he was seventeen, Stoppard left school and started work with a Bristol newspaper, the *Western Daily Press*, moving in 1958 to the *Bristol Evening World*. In these early years as a journalist Stoppard wrote articles that ranged from news reports, features, and gossip columns to film and theater reviews. It was not long, however, before his interest swung positively in the direction of the theater: in 1960 he turned to free-lance journalism and embarked on writing his first play.

Stoppard's Czech nationality and his early childhood spent in central Europe add autobiographical force to the concern for human rights expressed in his explicitly political plays and perhaps to his fondness for adapting the work of European dramatists. Similarly, his youthful career in journalism was to provide material for stories and plays. There is, however, less direct biographical input than a more general preoccupation with the role of the artist—or the journalist—in society and with the social purpose of art. Indeed, Stoppard is more interested in ideas than in characterization, and his plays explore topics such as the nature of perception, art, illusion and reality, the relativity of meaning, and the problematic status of truth. Recurring themes include chance, choice, freedom, identity, memory, time, and death. The purpose of existence is questioned in a dramatic universe without moral absolutes, whose relativity removes the security of a single governing perspective. The concerns of the later plays, however, are ethical rather than epistemological or existential, and overall Stoppard adopts a broadly humanist stance, endorsing moral responsibility as well as individual freedom. Nevertheless, the claims of artistic irresponsibility and Wildean aestheticism are also implicitly recognized in the baroque style and exuberance of a playwright who exploits theater as sheer entertainment.

Stoppard's theater is eclectic, parodic, and creatively derivative. In several plays he uses another text, such as William Shakespeare's *Hamlet* (circa 1600) or Oscar Wilde's *The Importance of Being Earnest* (1895), as a dramatic framework or point of intersection, and Stoppard delights in parodying authors, subgenres, and styles. Influences on his work, in addition to Shakespeare and Wilde, include the drama of Samuel Beckett, Eugène Ionesco, and N. F. Simpson and the painting of René Magritte, and his plays can often be called absurdist or surrealist. There are also links with the poetry and fiction of T. S. Eliot, James Joyce, and Beckett, in a theatrical equivalent of the themes and techniques of modernism. He is a skilled craftsman, handling with great dexterity and precision plots of extreme ingenuity and intricacy. The plays are steeped in theatrical convention and stock comic situations, with mistaken identity, verbal misunderstandings, innuendo, and farcical incongruity. Jokes, visual as well as verbal, are fundamental to his plays: puns are translated into structural terms, and an entire play may be an extended metaphor. Jokes, puns,

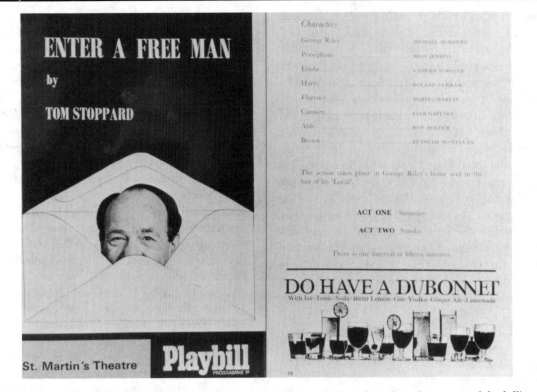

Program cover and cast list for the first stage production of Stoppard's first play, about the unsuccessful rebellion
of an impractical inventor

and language games emphasize the linguistic dimension of his dramatic world, after the philosopher Ludwig Wittgenstein as well as Beckett. But there is a sense, verging on the metaphysical, in which the pun, with its dual perspective, is a vague apprehension of cosmic congruence as well as comic incongruity: in Stoppard's work the frivolous and the serious are fused.

Stoppard frequently revises and rewrites his plays in rehearsal, or even reuses material, either within a play or from one piece to another. A single joke may provide the idea for a subsequent play. This process of reworking, like Stoppard's use of the plays of other artists, does not indicate paucity of inspiration: at its best, it is a progressive enrichment and concentration of the material. The reworking of material, especially in adapting a play for another medium, can be traced back to the beginning of his career as a playwright.

Stoppard's first play, *A Walk on the Water*, was written in the second half of 1960, while he was living in Bristol. He offered it to the Bristol Old Vic theater company, which referred him to the agent Kenneth Ewing. Ewing, who bought the play, has remained Stoppard's agent. Tennent Productions took an option on *A Walk on*

the Water but did not proceed to a production. The play was later bought by Rediffusion ITV and transmitted in November 1963. In 1964 it was staged in Hamburg, and in 1965 Stoppard adapted the play for broadcasting on BBC Radio. It eventually reached the London stage in 1968 as *Enter a Free Man*.

The central character of *Enter a Free Man* is an impractical inventor, George Riley, dependent for emotional support on his wife, Persephone, and for financial support on his daughter, Linda. George regularly announces he is leaving home; however, he never gets farther than the pub in either attempt during the play. On the second attempt, he is planning to run away with Florence. At the end of the play he is back at home. Linda, whose frustrations and aspirations parallel those of her father, also makes an abortive attempt to elope with her boyfriend. Arranged side-by-side on the stage are two settings: the living room of George's home and his local public house. In act 1 George enters the pub to announce his latest invention, a reusable envelope with gum on both sides of the flap. In the course of this and the succeeding act, the invention is found to be unworkable; George's imagined business partnership with the younger and sharper Harry collapses;

and his "assignation" with Harry's girlfriend, Florence, proves illusory. As the play ends, it begins to rain, and George's invention of "indoor rain," a self-watering system for plants, is found to work after all—but there is no way of turning it off. Stoppard referred to *Enter a Free Man* as "Flowering Death of a Salesman," and it depends heavily on both Robert Bolt's *Flowering Cherry* (1957) and Arthur Miller's *Death of a Salesman* (1949); there are also echoes of Henrik Ibsen. The play is not wholly successful: moments of emotional intensity are awkwardly handled and do not offer compensatory wit. But here in embryo are the themes of choice, freedom, and identity, and the play deals with constraints on the life of a small man. The long speech in act 1 in which George articulates the dreary routine of his existence is one of the most convincing sequences. George strives to choose and create his world: the use of two distinct playing areas—which would become characteristic of Stoppard—imaginatively reinforces this theme, as George moves from the home in which he feels he does not exist into the pub that for him is the realization of his aspirations.

After leaving the *Bristol Evening World* in 1960, Stoppard continued with free-lance journalism, writing critical articles and, under a pseudonym, two weekly columns. In 1963 he was drama critic for the magazine *Scene* and saw 132 plays in a period of seven months. In the same year he was commissioned by the publisher Anthony Blond to write a novel, *Lord Malquist and Mr. Moon*, which was later published in 1966. He also wrote short stories, three of which—"Reunion," "Life, Times: Fragments," and "The Story"—were published by Faber and Faber the next year in a collection of stories by new and promising writers. The three stories are more overtly autobiographical, and less consistently comic, than Stoppard's later work. "Reunion," which shows the influence of Eliot's early poems, concerns the reconciliation of a husband and wife. The other stories deal with journalism. In "Life, Times: Fragments" a journalist applies unsuccessfully for a job on the *Evening Standard*, and one of the main scenes of the story is his interview with the editor. There is a wide range of references to the work of other writers, from Stendhal to Ernest Hemingway. "The Story" concerns a journalist who feeds the story of a local teacher's indecent assault of a young girl to the national press, with the result that the teacher commits suicide. The ethics of journalism, and the interaction between

news story and event, would reappear in the play *Night and Day* (1978).

Working for *Scene* magazine had brought Stoppard to London, where he lived in one room and made little money. By the time *A Walk on the Water* was bought for television, he was beginning to earn a living as a professional playwright. Over the next few years he obtained commissions that gave him varied experience in writing for radio and television as well as for the theater. In 1964 he wrote five episodes of the long-running radio serial *The Dales*, and in 1965 he was writing regular weekly episodes of a serial, *A Student's Diary*, for transmission in Arabic translation to the Middle East. Also in 1964 he was commissioned to write two plays for BBC Radio 4, each occupying a transmission slot of fifteen minutes. The action of *The Dissolution of Dominic Boot* (1964) centers on a taxi ride taken by Dominic and his ambitious and demanding fiancée Vivian and on Dominic's efforts to raise money for the fare after he has dropped Vivian off. As he rides around trying to raise money, the fare continues to rise, and he ends up selling his clothes and losing both his job and his fiancée. Within this framework the play loops back to earlier incidents. Stoppard subsequently extended this short play in a version for television, *The Engagement*, which ran for fifty minutes and was transmitted in the United States by NBC on 8 March 1970. The plot is identical, but the action is filled out with scenes in Dominic's office and a jeweler's shop and with several new episodes.

The second radio play, *"M" is for Moon and Other Things* (1964), was worked up from a story that Faber and Faber had not wanted to include in their anthology. It is a slight piece but with some resonance in Stoppard's later work. Alfred and Constance, a middle-aged and middle-class couple, are reading at home: he a newspaper, she a mail-order encyclopedia. Their conversation is interwoven with self-absorbed monologue, and despite their emotional isolation, there is comic interplay and coincidence in their respective thought sequences. When Alfred turns on the television he finds that the thriller *Dial M for Murder* (1954) is just finishing, and the news that follows is of the death of Marilyn Monroe. By coincidence, Constance has reached the letter "M" in her encyclopedia.

In May 1964 Stoppard went to Berlin as a guest of the Ford Foundation to take part in a colloquium of young playwrights. During his five months in Berlin he wrote a Shakespearean pas-

Program cover and title page for the first production of Stoppard's spoof on theater critics and detective plays

tiche, "Rosencrantz and Guildenstern Meet King Lear." The idea for this one-act verse play—which would later take shape as *Rosencrantz and Guildenstern are Dead* (1966)—came from his agent, Kenneth Ewing. When Stoppard rewrote the play, he eliminated Lear, translated his own verse into prose, moved the setting to Elsinore, and focused more on the action of *Hamlet*. In the middle of 1965 the Royal Shakespeare Company bought an option on the new script, but the play had still not received a production twelve months later. Meanwhile, Stoppard had written the two-act play *The Gamblers* (1965), which he described as "Waiting for Godot in the Condemned Cell." The action is a reversal of roles between a condemned prisoner and his jailer. In the first act the jailer joins the prisoner in his cell; in the second he takes his place at the gallows. The prisoner used to be the jailer, before he joined the revolutionaries. If the revolution had succeeded, he would now be a hero, and the present jailer, who used to be the public hangman, would have been in prison. At the close of the play the prisoner wears the mask of the executioner, and the jailer wears the hood of the condemned man. The crowd will not be able to distinguish between the ex-revolutionary and the ex-hangman. *The Gam-*

blers, which Stoppard regarded as his first original play, was performed by the drama department of the University of Bristol in 1965.

If You're Glad I'll be Frank, broadcast in 1966, was commissioned by the BBC for a series of radio plays, *Strange Occupations*, about bizarre and nonexistent jobs. The play was subsequently staged in a double bill with *Albert's Bridge* in 1969. Its main joke is that the voice of TIM the speaking clock (then dialed by a letter coding on the telephone) is not a mechanical recording but belongs to a real woman. Frank, a bus driver, recognizes the voice as that of his long-lost wife, Gladys, and attempts to find and free her. Meanwhile, Gladys's thoughts and feelings are expressed alongside her official, precise TIM utterances. Frank eventually breaks through obstructive bureaucracy, only to be convinced by the first lord of the Post Office that TIM is, after all, a machine. After he leaves, Gladys is heard on the verge of hysteria: she is finally persuaded once more to submerge her identity and individuality in the role of the speaking clock. This short play skillfully uses the medium of radio to interweave dialogue and unspoken thought, and the style ranges from the colloquial to a near-verse reminiscent of the later poetry and plays of Eliot.

The comedy recalls the absurd drama of Ionesco and Simpson, but with an underlying serious concern with the nature of time and with the suppression of freedom within a mechanistic system. Gladys is one of several figures in Stoppard's plays who, in willing or unwilling isolation from everyday social relationships, see life from a perspective that reduces all human activity to insignificance.

The theme of withdrawal to a private world recurs in the television play *A Separate Peace*, transmitted on 22 August 1966. John Brown, a middle-aged man in perfect health, checks himself in as a resident in a nursing home. His ambiguous status as a healthy patient is disruptive, and he is driven back into the world when relatives attempt to visit him. Stoppard's preoccupation with isolation and retreat shows the influence of Beckett's early fiction, especially *More Pricks Than Kicks* (1934) and *Murphy* (1938).

In May 1966 the Royal Shakespeare Company staged Stoppard's adaptation of Polish playwright Slawomir Mrozek's play *Tango*. The Warsaw opening of *Tango* in 1965 had been an explosive event in Polish theatrical history, for the play brilliantly combined political protest with comic invention. However, it was with *Rosencrantz and Guildenstern are Dead* that Stoppard emerged into the theatrical spotlight. A philosophical farce pervaded by existential anxiety, the play was first performed by the Oxford Theatre Group as part of the fringe of the Edinburgh Festival on 24 August 1966. Kenneth Tynan read the favorable reviews and accepted the script for the National Theatre. It opened at the Old Vic in London on 11 April 1967 to almost universal acclaim. For the *Observer* it was "the most brilliant debut of the sixties"; Harold Hobson, in the *Sunday Times*, thought it "the most important event in the British professional theatre of the last nine years." In 1967 Stoppard won the *Evening Standard* Drama Award for most promising playwright and the John Whiting Award. The following autumn the play opened in New York and later received an Antoinette Perry (Tony) Award and the New York Drama Critics Circle Award. Revivals, translations, and further productions followed, making this work the most firmly established play in Stoppard's repertoire. It has received much academic attention from critics and philosophers, some of whom have suspected a meretricious brilliance in its dramatic and philosophical eclecticism. Others have seen in Stoppard's use of parody and montage a distinc-

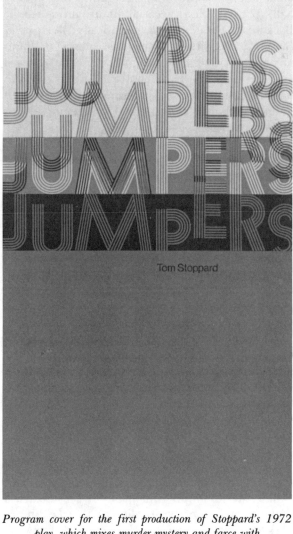

Program cover for the first production of Stoppard's 1972 play, which mixes murder mystery and farce with philosophical inquiry

tive comic method that is fundamentally serious but precludes endorsement of any single or particular philosophy or viewpoint.

Rosencrantz and Guildenstern are Dead explicitly operates in the dramatic margins of *Hamlet*, in a creative interaction with Shakespeare's text. In focusing on Shakespeare's minor characters Stoppard does not fill out their lives but rather extends their thinness. Between their exits and entrances the attendant lords lead a marginal existence, virtually without identity (although Stoppard provides a "character note" for each, partly for convenience). Relevant parts of *Hamlet* are incorporated intact, with further allusion—often by dumb show—to other scenes in which Rosencrantz and Guildenstern are offstage. Effective use is made of stylistic counterpoint of

Shakespeare's poetry and rhetoric with the colloquial idiom of the linguistic games and music-hall patter. The second main influence is Beckettian theater, and specifically *Waiting for Godot* (1953), with its analogous figures of Vladimir and Estragon. Drawing on both Shakespeare and Beckett, Stoppard continues their exploration of the meaning of existence and of such themes as chance, choice, freedom, memory, identity, and death.

The play opens with Rosencrantz and Guildenstern on the road to Elsinore, tossing coins to pass the time. The game introduces themes of chance, probability, and inevitability. Aware that they are circumscribed by a script—they dimly recall a summons at dawn—they are anxious to identify their roles but are unable to comprehend the situation or take an initiative. Their encounter with the Player and the Tragedians, also on their way to the castle, introduces a persistent theme of the play, that of the implications of theatricality and its relation to reality. Act 1 leads up to their first encounter with Hamlet; act 2 encompasses the main intrigue of the lords' attempt to investigate Hamlet's behavior on behalf of Claudius, and it makes substantial verbatim use of Shakespeare's text. Act 3 is a dramatic elaboration or fantasia on the reports given by Shakespeare's Hamlet of the journey to England. This act is increasingly concerned with the theme of death, again, with punning reference to the stage deaths of the players. Rosencrantz and Guildenstern simply disappear by a theatrical trick: they cannot really die, as their existence goes no further than the containing framework of *Hamlet*. The action finally merges with the end of *Hamlet*, with the Tragedians acting Shakespeare's characters.

Stoppard's novel, *Lord Malquist and Mr. Moon*, was published in August 1966, in the same week as the Edinburgh premiere of *Rosencrantz and Guildenstern are Dead*. The novel combines serious speculation with extravagant comedy and is highly self-conscious in both narrative method and style, with persistent paradox and wordplay. Indeed the central character, Lord Malquist, by his own admission, embodies style as a refuge from chaos. Malquist is a Wildean figure, and the novel owes much to admiring parody of Wildean techniques. Mr. Moon, hired as a secretary and companion by Lord Malquist, is a less secure and more tormented character, worried by what he takes to be his wife's infidelity. Moon carries a bomb around in his pocket, a device that

adds suspense to the plot. After a series of improbable coincidences, Moon is killed in a case of mistaken identity. Riding in a coach, he is taken for Lord Malquist. The novel also contains a butler named Birdboot, who, with the naming and character of Mr. Moon, points to later plays, in particular *The Real Inspector Hound* (1968). The plot of *Lord Malquist and Mr. Moon* also prefigures to some extent the situation of *Jumpers* (1972).

In 1967 Stoppard wrote further plays for television and radio. *Teeth*, a thirty-minute television play broadcast on 7 February 1967 by the BBC, takes place in a dentist's office. The dentist Harry Dunn finds that he has his wife's lover in his dental chair for a checkup and exploits the situation to investigate the affair. He finally takes revenge on George by staining his teeth green and by seducing George's wife, who is Harry's receptionist. *Another Moon Called Earth*, televised by the BBC on 28 June 1967, is intermediate between *Lord Malquist and Mr. Moon* and *Jumpers*. All three works share the situation of an ambiguous adultery, where the circumstantial evidence is plausibly explained away by the wife. The triangle of George Moore, his wife, Dotty, and Sir Archie Jumper in *Jumpers* is prefigured in the characters of Penelope, Bone (a historian working on a world history), and the "doctor" Albert in *Another Moon Called Earth*. As in *Jumpers*, suspicions of an affair are confirmed, but not unequivocally proved, by circumstances. This play also anticipates *Jumpers* in its reference to the landing of a "lunanaut" on the moon. The event represents a radical shift of perspective for Penelope, disturbing her previous assumptions as to the moral shape of the universe. Like *Jumpers*, *Another Moon Called Earth* contains a "murder," as Miss Pinkerton, Penelope's former nurse, "falls" from a window and Penelope claims to have pushed her.

Albert's Bridge, a sixty-minute radio play broadcast in July 1967, is Stoppard's finest work in this medium. Once more the central joke is that of a bizarre occupation. Albert, a philosophy graduate, accepts the solitary and Sisyphean job of continually repainting the Clufton Bay Suspension Bridge. He thereby angers his father, chairman of a large industrial concern, and gradually isolates himself from his wife. But for Albert the repetitive routine realizes a positive vision: he sees the bridge as akin to a work of art and delights in the perfection of its mathematical proportions and engineering design. Albert's ideal existence is doubly threatened. His peace is broken by a would-be suicide, Frazer, who finds the

Diana Rigg in a scene from the first production of Jumpers

noise and chaos of society unbearable. He has climbed the bridge in order to jump off but is calmed by the perspective it provides, reducing the clutter of humanity to a neat pattern far below. So he climbs down again into the noise, and the process repeats itself. The second threat comes from the committee of local officials responsible for maintenance of the bridge, and especially Fitch, who is keen to optimize the repainting by using only one painter and new, long-lasting paint. (The problem is that while Albert paints one end, the paint on the other end is rapidly deteriorating.) Fitch's solution is to send in a massed army of painters to finish the job in one day: under their weight, the bridge collapses, destroying Albert's ideal and fulfilling Frazer's apocalyptic predictions. In *Albert's Bridge*, Stoppard again creates a dual space—this time in sound—which suggests alternative realities, as the prosaic discussions of the Bridge Committee are interspersed with poetic monologue expressing Albert's vision. Here the shifting perspectives are

spatial, in contrast to the temporal relativity of *If You're Glad I'll be Frank*. Albert is dwarfed by the bridge, but from its height the human world appears diminutive. The play creates a dramatic experience at once abstract and mathematical and yet intensely, if paradoxically, visual and concrete, which exploits and transcends the aural medium to operate as a metaphor for the human condition. *Albert's Bridge* won the Prix Italia in 1968. The following year the play was performed in a stage version at the Edinburgh Festival, where it shared a double bill with *If You're Glad I'll be Frank*.

The Real Inspector Hound, first performed in 1968, was Stoppard's first play for the stage since *Rosencrantz and Guildenstern are Dead*. In a double bill with *After Magritte*, *The Real Inspector Hound* was staged four years later in New York and London. Although some reviewers felt sensitive about its being a satire on critics and avoided being critical for that reason, overall they saw it as a spoof and good entertainment. It is a play outside a play, with a Pirandellian concern with the nature of theatricality and reality. In act 1 Moon and Birdboot, two theater critics, are seated in an "audience" onstage watching a conventional whodunit that they are to review. In act 2 they move into the action of the thriller: when the phone rings onstage, the call is for Birdboot, who takes over the role of Simon in the inner play and is shot. Moon is accused of murder; and the corpse that has lain onstage throughout turns out to be that of Higgs, the senior critic. The real Inspector Hound is identified as Magnus, alias Puckeridge, the junior critic and rival, who shoots Moon. The confusion with names is deliberate, resulting from Stoppard's technique of muddling the roles and identities of various characters. This farcical denouement enacts the wish fulfillment of the hierarchy of frustrated critics, even though according to Stoppard the plotting was a "risk operation" not worked out beforehand but developed as he wrote.

The idea for *The Real Inspector Hound* came to Stoppard while he was still in Bristol, after writing *The Gamblers*, in which an exchange of roles also has a fatal outcome. The nomenclature of Moon and Birdboot also dates to this time. Stoppard saw the film *The Left Handed Gun* (1958), starring Paul Newman, in which a character called Moon is killed by the hero. At one point in the film there is a striking coincidence of visual image and language, when a drunken crowd shoots at the reflection of the moon in the water in a horse trough and Newman shouts out "Moon." Stoppard was then sketching out a "sort of goonshow version" of *The Real Inspector Hound* and was attracted by the name Moon. He used the name several times for rather similar characters, and its connotations are reflected in recurrent lunar imagery of various kinds (for example, in Albert's crooned lyrics on his bridge). The name also became paired with Birdboot and Boot. When Stoppard was working for *Scene*, he adopted the pseudonym of William Boot, which is the name of an innocent but incompetent journalist in Evelyn Waugh's novel *Scoop* (1938). Despite Stoppard's disclaimers of mere convenience in the choice and collocation of these names, they accrue a thematic relevance and resonance in successive plays, written over the subsequent decade. The author admitted that the lunar landing constituted for him the destruction of an entire mythology and set of imagery to express human aspirations and emotions.

Neutral Ground, a spy thriller, was commissioned by Thames Television for a series based on classical myths and was transmitted on 11 December 1968. It is a reworking of Sophocles' *Philoctetes*. Stoppard's Philo is an aging ex-secret agent suspected of being a double agent. The British agent Charles Acheson is assigned to bring Philo back to England, under cover of pretending to help him return to his country, now Russian-occupied territory. When the disillusioned Acheson reveals his duplicity, Philo urges him to stay on neutral ground in the country adjacent to Austria. Philo eventually "saves" Acheson by leaving for England. The main interest of this play, which was written in the year of the Soviet invasion of Czechoslovakia, lies in its anticipation of the issues of *Professional Foul* (1977). Both plays involve an ethical dilemma for a central figure placed in a difficult and compromising political situation that is further complicated by personal doubts and emotions.

In *After Magritte*, a one-act play first performed for a lunchtime theater club in April 1970 and later staged in 1972 in a double bill with *The Real Inspector Hound*, the point of reference is not another playwright but the surrealist artist René Magritte. Like Magritte's paintings, Stoppard's surrealist comedy combines exact surface verisimilitude with surprising and incongruous juxtaposition of character and incident. The narratives within the play—variant scenarios of a single incident—are perhaps analogous to Magritte's technique of painting-within-painting. *After Magritte* opens and closes with two extraordinary tableaux, visual riddles that are explicable only in their dramatic context. The main action involves the solving of another riddle. Harris, Thelma, and Mother have returned from a Magritte exhibition and are quarreling over a mysterious figure they saw fleetingly in the street that morning. Their respective descriptions of the man are bizarre in themselves and very different from each other: a one-legged footballer; an old blind man in pajamas with a tortoise under his arm; and a convict playing hopscotch and carrying a handbag and a cricket bat. The problem is further complicated by the entry of Inspector Foot, investigating a suspected robbery associated with the unknown man. The "mystery" is solved when it transpires that the man was Foot himself, who rushed out wearing pajamas and with shaving foam on his face, clutching his wife's bag, in order to put money in a parking meter. The play is a process of demystification, reaching toward a rational explanation. Nevertheless, the alternative interpretations underline the relativity of experience and the difficulty of determining the truth. The surreal is an improbable montage that invites a readjustment of concepts of reality. *After Magritte* is one of several plays written by Stoppard in the early 1970s, which, in the course of reconstructing an event, examine the refraction of objective reality in individual perception and memory.

Where Are They Now?, a short play especially commissioned for Schools Radio and broadcast on 18 January 1970, is particularly concerned with memory. The play moves between an Old Boys' reunion dinner in 1969 and a school dinner in 1945 recalled in a series of flashbacks. The time shifts reveal both change and continuity: the boys are middle-aged men, but retain their childhood slang and social code. The cruelty of their school days is softened by memory, but one of them, Gale, is spurred into a realization of the conformist pressures exerted by the British public school system. That system is evoked by the old master Dobson and by the authoritarian voice of the headmaster. The play oscillates between nostalgia, satire, and protest, and its overall stance is uncertain. At the end, one of the "Old Boys," Jenkins, discovers as the school song is sung that he is at the wrong school's reunion.

In 1965 Stoppard had married Jose Ingle, with whom he had two sons. The marriage was dissolved in 1972, and that same year Stoppard married Miriam Moore-Robinson. She trained as a medical doctor in London and Durham and later became managing director of a pharmaceutical firm. She has written books on popular medicine dealing with child care and family health and makes frequent television appearances. The couple has two sons and lives in Iver, Buckinghamshire.

Jumpers, dedicated to Miriam Stoppard, was first staged by the National Theatre at the Old Vic in February 1972 and won the *Evening Standard* Drama Award for best play of the year. The play, in "two acts and a coda," is a montage of themes and techniques, by turns a whodunit, a farce of marital infidelity, and a philosophical inquiry. In theme and method it draws on several of Stoppard's previous plays and his novel. George Moore, a university professor of moral philosophy, is preparing a lecture on the existence of God and the validity of moral absolutes, to be delivered at the annual symposium. His wife, Dotty, a former musical-comedy actress, is apparently having an affair with Sir Archibald Jumper, vice-chancellor and chairman of the philosophy department. The context of the play is the victory of a Radical-Liberal coalition and the landing on the moon of two astronauts, only one of whom can survive. Act 1 begins with an election party held by Dotty, at which Duncan McFee, professor of logic, is shot while taking part in an acrobatics display. Dotty becomes a suspect because she appears at the moment the murder takes place. The murder investigation is led by Inspector Bones, a fan of Dotty's, who is charmed by her and who is bought off by Archie's offering him a chair in philosophy. The play ends with the murder unsolved, both the adultery and the existence of God unproved, one of the astronauts killed by the other, and another gymnast—the Archbishop of Canterbury—shot.

Jumpers is structured around running gags and is a dense fabric of pun and wordplay. The "jumpers" are analytic philosophers, with a pun on intellectual gymnastics; the behavior of Archie Jumper adds connotations of ambitious expediency. The "short, blunt human pyramid" of acrobats was suggested by a line in *Rosencrantz and Guildenstern are Dead*. Verbal and visual puns are also central to the charades that George and Dotty play intermittently throughout. George's pet hare and tortoise, which he uses to demonstrate a philosophical argument, provide another running gag: its comic climax comes when George discovers he has killed the hare and in his distress steps back onto the tortoise. Further jokes deal with the punning, puzzling nature of appearance: the blood, which may belong to McFee or the jugged hare; and the circumstantial evidence of adultery, strong but inconclusive. Jumper, as Dotty's psychiatrist, spends much time in her bedroom, removing his clothes to "examine" her. The coda, which presents the symposium in dream form, is a witty mélange of styles, using Joycean logical disquisition for Jumper, song lyrics for Dotty, and a parody of philosophical discourse for George—with a gesture to Beckett in Archie's closing speech. The modernist montage of the coda reinforces the play's multiple perspectives. *Jumpers* takes philosophy as its main focus—along with entertainment—but it propounds no specific arguments. Jumper's cynical metaphysical position is contrasted with the idealist humanism of George. The arguments that George employs have been dismissed by some philosophers as dated or superficial; but A. J. Ayer

Michael Hordern in a scene from the first production of Jumpers *(photograph by Zoë Dominic)*

came closest to a realization of the force of the dramatic context in which these arguments operate when he noted that George, at least, was humane. Both George and Dotty are forlorn survivors of a lost moral universe. Dotty retired from musical comedy when the imagery of her songs was rendered meaningless by the moon landing. George anxiously and unsuccessfully searches for moral absolutes and is conscience-stricken over killing his pets. Indeed the deaths of a goldfish, a hare, and a tortoise involve a farcical but genuine bereavement and loss. Loss and alienation pervade this bleak picture of modern life, focused on a vulnerable and isolated couple: the dazzling comedy of *Jumpers* masks (and in part expresses) a hollow center. The play was generally well received by critics, who noted its intellectual agility and deep moral sense, although some reviewers seemed to mistrust its theatrical pyrotechnics. It was revived in the National Theatre's repertory in 1976.

Stoppard's exploitation of the whodunit continued in the short radio play *Artist Descending a Staircase*, commissioned by the BBC for a Euro-pean exchange program and broadcast by the BBC on 14 November 1972. Within the play a tape recording whose sequence of sounds can be variously interpreted is repeatedly played. At first, the artists Beauchamp and Martello "hear" their friend Donner greeting one of them, who then knocks him down the staircase: they dispute the killer's identity. At the end of the play, Beauchamp swats a fly while the tape is played once again. The sound of the stage action matches the sound on the tape, suggesting Donner's swatting a fly and falling downstairs accidentally. This aural riddle contrasts with the visual riddles of *After Magritte*; but the play reconstructs another scenario, a case of mistaken identity—also with a fatal outcome—that hinges on visual ambiguity. The friendship of the three modernist artists and their relationship with Sophie are dramatized in a series of flashbacks. Sophie had fallen in love with one of the artists because she admired one of his paintings, but she never met him. She later became blind and could identify which one only by recalling the painting, which is apparently by Beauchamp. He later rejected her, and she killed herself. Donner, who still loves her, discovers fifty years later that the painting, which was susceptible to contradictory visual interpretation, may have been mistakenly identified as Beauchamp's. Both riddles thus involve subjectivity of perception and meaning, in relation to time and memory (Donner and Beauchamp quarrel as to what "really" happened). The themes are reinforced structurally: the action is symmetrically arranged in eleven sequences, going back to 1914 in the middle sequence, and proceeding again to the present. *Artist Descending a Staircase* anticipates *Travesties* (1974), not only in its direct reference to dadaist Tristan Tzara and Lenin in Zurich in 1915, but more generally in the focus on a specific moment of artistic ferment and historical crisis—modernism and World War I—that raises issues of the purpose and significance of art.

Travesties, first staged in June 1974, takes as its starting point the fact that Lenin, James Joyce, and Tzara all lived in Zurich during World War I. It posits a common meeting ground—the Zurich Public Library—and juxtaposes their respective politics and aesthetics—revolutionary Marxism, modernism, and dadaism. The play draws on critical events in the lives of each: the writing of *Ulysses* (1922), the formulation of the precepts of Dada, and Lenin's journey from Switzerland through Germany in a sealed train to aid the Russian Revolution. These events impinge on the more immediate and local focus, which also has some basis in fact. Henry Carr, a minor consular official, was cast as Algernon Moncrieff in a production of *The Importance of Being Earnest* mounted by a company called the English Players, whose business manager was James Joyce. From the meager facts available about Carr—including his subsequent litigation with Joyce over alleged nonpayment—Stoppard developed the central character of his play: an elderly gentleman still living in Zurich, married to the girl he met in the library when Lenin worked there, and recalling his meetings with Joyce and Tzara. Stoppard also seized the dramatic opportunity offered by the historical connection to create a Wildean pastiche, in a specific interplay with the action of *The Importance of Being Earnest*. Farcical complications arise from misunderstandings and mistaken identity: the names of Gwendolen and Cecily are used for the female leads; and the characters of Carr and Tzara act out "for real" their parts in the play-within-the-play, Carr as Algernon Moncrieff, Tzara as John Worthing, and the few authentic Wildean lines used as ironic counterpoint to the action. More fundamentally, the Wildean 1890s aestheticism, reproduced in the Europe of 1918, underpins the debate of *Travesties* about the purpose and significance of art. Moreover, *Travesties* is a virtuoso piece, a "travesty" of the style of each of its masters, including Joycean narrative and dadaist verse as well as Wildean wit. The parody extends to the discourse appropriate to Lenin, as the play incorporates lectures and polemical sequences. The opening scene, with its montage of private languages, acts as a prelude to the play's concern with language and language barriers: Lenin and his wife are talking in Russian; Joyce and Tzara each dictate their esoteric writings. The stylistic parody is multilayered: the denouement, in which the true identity of Tzara, apparently engaged to both Gwendolen and Cecily, is revealed, intersects with the plot of Wilde but uses the idiom of a popular song of the period, "Mr. Gallagher and Mr. Shean."

Travesties is not a flawless play: the Lenin plot is hampered by an overregard for accuracy of historical detail, in contrast with the imaginative license of the treatment of Joyce. Perhaps the least successful sequence is Cecily's lengthy lecture at the start of act 2, which provides historical and political background to Lenin's part in the revolution. Stoppard felt this failed theatrically, and the published play recommends heavy cutting at this point. However, the lecture is not merely too long: it violates the dominant mode in which the action operates. The play uses a containing consciousness in the figure of old Carr, and its flashbacks are refracted through his memory, using what Stoppard calls "time slips," in which sequences are repeated with variations that indicate the subjective status of past events. One projected title for the play was "Prism": history is experienced through the prism of Carr's memory, which refracts events passing through it. The theme of memory is resonant enough, but it forms only one strand of an ambitious and complex play. Nevertheless, *Travesties*, which won the *Evening Standard* Drama Award for best comedy of the year in 1974 and a Tony Award in 1976, is recognized as among Stoppard's finest work, not least by the playwright himself. Stoppard finds that despite its patchiness, *Travesties* contains some things that he considers he will never better. On the whole, he felt that *Travesties* was as good as he could get at putting together serious statement and witty expression. Importantly, the

Beth Morris and John Wood in the first production of Travesties

play also registers a change of direction toward the ethical and the political, which is more fully articulated in later plays. In an interview just after he had completed this play, Stoppard discussed the issue of the political aspect of art and admitted to a concern with moral justice but a lack of political commitment. Art is important "because it provides the moral matrix, the moral sensibility, from which we make our judgments about the world." The responsibility of the artist, the philosopher, or the journalist would prove to be a persistent preoccupation.

Responsibility in politics and journalism is the focus of the lightweight farce *Dirty Linen and New-Found-Land*, which Stoppard wrote to celebrate the British naturalization of the American Ed Berman, founder of the Inter-Action community arts project. The play, which presents *New-Found-Land* as an interlude in the middle of *Dirty Linen*, was first performed at the Inter-Action Almost Free Theatre on 6 April 1976, the date of Berman's naturalization. *Dirty Linen* is set in the House of Commons of the British Parliament: a select committee of members of Parliament has been set up to report on moral standards among politicians, to counter scandalous press reports. The "dirty linen" of the title is the hypocritical private lives of the politicians, with a pun on the fancy knickers worn by the glamorous typist Maddie. All the members of the committee are sexually involved with Maddie, but she does not share their sense of guilt. On Maddie's recommendation, the committee concludes that politicians have the right to lead their lives without persecution by the press. This stereotyped dumb blond shows more sense than all of them. Using the same set as *Dirty Linen*, *New-Found-Land* is an interlude in which Berman's application for naturalization is being considered by the home secretary and his assistant. The assistant dreams of going to the United States, in a rapturous travelogue that describes the cultural delights from coast to coast. When this interlude merges with the action of *Dirty Linen*, the audience discovers that the home secretary is also associated with Maddie, whereupon both the naturalization and the report are hastily concluded. The play transferred to the small Arts Theatre, where it proved a great commercial success, with a run lasting five years. During 1976 Stoppard wrote another piece for Inter-Action, a fifteen-minute version of *Hamlet*.

Stoppard was moving further toward political drama with the music-play *Every Good Boy Deserves Favour*, produced in 1977. Stoppard had written *Every Good Boy Deserves Favour* when, in 1974, Andre Previn, principal conductor of the London Symphony Orchestra, had commissioned him to write a play for performance in a concert hall by actors and an orchestra. By 1976 Stoppard was actively interested in human rights and the plight of Russian dissidents. In April he met Victor Fainberg, arrested in August 1968 during a peaceful protest against the invasion of Czechoslovakia and held for five years as insane in a Soviet prison hospital. Stoppard also supported the campaign for the release of Vladimir Bukovsky, detained following his denunciation of Soviet abuse of psychiatry. Bukovsky was exiled to the West in December 1976, and in June 1977 Stoppard met him in London, when *Every Good Boy Deserves Favour* was in rehearsal. The play is set in a prison hospital where two men are detained. One is a political dissident; the other suffers from the delusion that he has an orchestra. The orchestra on stage is integrated into the action: it provides the music for Ivanov's fantasies, and one of its violinists is also the "doctor" (a lackey of the asylum authorities) in charge of the prisoner-patients. Both detainees are eventually released, in a neat verbal trick hinging on the fact that they have the same name, Alexander Ivanov. The political content of the play is a blend of polemic and satire, with a tendency toward sentimentality in the treatment of the dissident's son Sasha. There is also a trace, in the figure of the deluded musician, of the theme of art, illusion, and reality. The orchestra exists only in the artist's imagination: this recalls the private visions of Albert and Gladys, and—in the equivalence of Ivanov to the imprisoned dissident—the repressive forces that threaten those visions. *Every Good Boy Deserves Favour* was performed in the Festival Hall, London, in July 1977, to a score by Previn. It was enthusiastically received: the critic Bernard Levin found it a profoundly moral play; Irving Wardle, in the *Times*, praised its firm moral viewpoint.

An emphasis on the moral implications of political issues also informs *Professional Foul*, Stoppard's first full-length play for BBC Television, transmitted on 21 September 1977. The central figure, a professor of ethics, is shocked by events away from philosophical speculation and political neutrality into direct action. Stoppard wished to write a play that would mark 1977 as Amnesty International's "Prisoner of Conscience Year." In February 1977 he visited Moscow and Leningrad with the assistant director of the British section of Amnesty International and met Russians concerned with human rights, including the wife of the dissident Yuri Orlov. Stoppard then learned of the arrest in Prague of the playwright Vaclav Havel. These events gave him the inspiration for *Professional Foul*, which was written quickly in the spring of 1977. During rehearsals Stoppard visited Prague for the first time since childhood.

The play opens with Anderson, a Cambridge professor of ethics, on a plane bound for an international conference in Prague, where he is to deliver a lecture. The conference coincides with a football match between England and Czechoslovakia, which Anderson is anxious to attend. However, his posture of liberal detachment is challenged when a former student, Hollar, a Czechoslovak who is now a dissident in his own country, asks Anderson to smuggle out a politically contentious thesis on the ethics of the state. Anderson visits Hollar's flat after he has been arrested and is enraged by the behavior of government officials. His sympathies are further engaged when he meets Hollar's wife and child, and he pledges his assistance. He replaces his prepared lecture on "Ethical Fact in Ethical Fiction" with a speech on human rights, which is hastily and deftly suppressed. However, he succeeds in smuggling out the thesis, hidden in the luggage of an unwitting colleague.

Professional Foul is primarily a moral play, despite its political focus. Moreover, its treatment of academic philosophy is similar to that in *Jumpers*, and there is an analogy with the earlier pun on the intellectual acrobatics of analytic philosophy in the comic juxtaposition of footballers and philosophers. The fundamentally serious pun rebounds on the ethics of strategies and tactics involved in philosophy and politics as well as the game of football. *Professional Foul* skillfully employs the medium of television, combining narrative tension, comic incident, and moral inquiry, and it was well received. It confirmed Stoppard's movement toward a more conventional and conservative method, and the absence of theatrical and verbal flamboyance is compensated by subtlety and thoughtfulness. Its anxiety over the moral and social purpose of artistic and intellectual activity is a continuation from the themes of Stoppard's earliest plays. His next full-length stage play, *Night and Day*, in its focus on the ethics of journalism, explicitly returns to issues deriving from his early career.

Night and Day, a play in two acts, is set in the fictitious African state of Kimbawe, a former British colony where a rebellion against the dictatorial president forms the background to the action. By the end of the play, the anticipated war of secession has broken out. However, the political context is secondary to the concern with journalism and the freedom of the press: "Information is light." The competitive world of journalism, the pressures exerted both by capitalist ownership and trade-union militancy, and the irresponsibility of the mass media in fueling real conflict are among the topics discussed in the course of the play. *Night and Day* is a play of ideas, in the context of violent action. The main characters are Guthrie, a photographer, and Wagner, a reporter, who both work for a fictitious national paper, the *Sunday Globe*, and Jacob Milne, a young reporter who has recently opposed a trade-union closed shop on his local newspaper in Grimsby, and has lost his job, caught between unions and management. When the play starts, Milne has obtained a major scoop from inside rebel lines. Increasingly his enthusiasm and idealism are set against the ruthless pragmatism of the other journalists. Moreover, the innocent Milne cannot comprehend the deals set up between the Englishman Geoffrey Carson, in whose house the action takes place, President Mageeba, and the rebel leader Shimbu. A meeting is planned in Carson's house to enable negotiations to take place between Mageeba and Shimbu: Milne, who is anxious to return to rebel territory, is used to carry the message to Shimbu but is killed before he reaches his destination. Wagner obtains an interview with the president, but ironically his scoop will not be printed: it is subject to the ban that he had enforced to "black" Milne's copy. At the close Guthrie, inspired and distressed by Milne's virtual martyrdom, remains in the war-torn country, but Wagner leaves. Woven into the play is the subplot concerning Carson's wife, Ruth, who had a brief affair with Wagner in London and who is now attracted to Milne.

Ruth's consciousness governs the action, as did old Carr's in *Travesties*, and there are several dream and fantasy sequences. The opening of the play is a prelude to the violence of the remainder, as Guthrie's nightmare of being shot merges with the noise of the landing of Carson's helicopter.

Night and Day was first performed at the Phoenix Theatre on 8 November 1978. It received generally favorable reviews and had a successful run in London's West End, winning the *Evening Standard* Drama Award. However, to some critics the play showed Stoppard in a less creative and innovative light, if not in actual decline. Certainly *Night and Day* is, in a sense, a mature reworking of familiar and recurrent themes and techniques, and it is not without flaws. The representation of Ruth's perspective by means of unrealistic disjunctures relies heavily on the skill of director and actors; the same may be said of moments of emotional intensity such as the reception of the news of Milne's death by Guthrie. But this is a taut drama, dealing intelligently and with a degree of moral passion with a range of difficult issues. Moreover, despite its clear plea for freedom of speech and action, the play does not oversimplify the issues: *Night and Day* presents a genuine dramatic debate that confronts divergent and often contradictory attitudes.

As the comma dividing *Dogg's Hamlet, Cahoot's Macbeth* indicates, these are two distinct plays with common elements, put together to form a full-length program. *Dogg's Hamlet* is a conflation of *Dogg's Our Pet* (1971) and *The 15 Minute Dogg's Troupe Hamlet*. *Dogg's Our Pet*—the title is an anagram of Dogg's Troupe, Professor Dogg being a pseudonym of Ed Berman—is based on language games, using a central image from Wittgenstein's *Philosophical Investigations* (1953). A man engaged in building a platform from planks, blocks, bricks, cubes, and slabs of wood shouts out instructions to his workmate. In the private language established by the play, each word he yells arbitrarily denotes one of the physical items, such as "Here!" for "plank." The point is that language constructs, rather than passively records, reality. The builder is building blocks of words; the "building blocks" of language punningly merge with the construction of the platform, which, when completed, carries the message "DOGGES TROUPE THE END." The occasion of the play was the opening of Inter-Action's Almost Free Theatre in 1971. *Dogg's Hamlet* reworks this material, adding to it *The 15 Minute*

Dogg's Troupe Hamlet written for Inter-Action in 1976. The conflation draws together two restricted languages encoding a self-contained linguistic world: the artificial language of *Dogg's Our Pet* and the idiom of Shakespearean tragedy. At the end, *Hamlet* is collapsed into a three-minute version, with a yet further reduced encore.

Cahoot's Macbeth is dedicated to the Czech playwright Pavel Kohout, whom Stoppard had met during his visit to Prague in 1977. Sometime later Kohout wrote telling Stoppard of an alternative theater, the Living Theatre, which would present a version of *Macbeth* adapted by Kohout. Stoppard's play, inspired by this event, presents a reduced version of *Macbeth* in a living room. The performance is interrupted by an Inspector and the players being threatened with official action. At the end, one of the characters from *Dogg's Hamlet* enters, to merge the two plays and increase the linguistic confusion. *Dogg's Hamlet, Cahoot's Macbeth* returns to the linguistic games of Stoppard's early plays (up to the time when *Dogg's Our Pet* was written) combined with the later theme of the struggle for individual freedom within a totalitarian regime. The plays were performed in May 1979 at the University of Warwick and transferred in July to the Collegiate Theatre in London.

Stoppard's two next plays are adaptations of works by European dramatists. In June 1979 *Undiscovered Country*, a version of *Das Weite Land* (1911) by Arthur Schnitzler, opened at the Olivier Theatre of the National Theatre in London. The literal translation was provided by John Harrison (English is Stoppard's first and only fluent language). The play, which is relatively unknown in England, is set in turn-of-the-century Viennese society and concerns the sexual intrigues and liaisons among a group of wealthy families. The central figure, Friedrich Hofreiter, has a series of mistresses and emerges as a callous husband and lover. Ironically, he regards the infidelity of his wife, Genia, as a serious point of honor and at the end of the play kills her young lover, Otto von Aigner, in a duel. The play opens with another death—Korsakow, a gifted pianist, has killed himself because Genia would not become his mistress. After Korsakow's death, Hofreiter leaves Genia and takes a group of friends for a walking holiday in the mountains. There he has an affair with a young girl engaged to be married, whom he subsequently rejects. He also puts at risk the lives of his companions in a difficult climb, which had killed one of his friends years be-

fore. Meanwhile Genia, in reaction against Korsakow's suicide and her husband's departure, forms a liaison with von Aigner. To Hofreiter the events constitute confrontations with the virility of youth; but his triumph in the duel and his conquest of the young girl are equivocal victories. Youth is tragically wasted, and Hofreiter passes on toward old age and death. The play, which is in five acts, is reminiscent of Ibsen in its tight construction, its sense of doom and of past guilt working itself out in the present, and its themes of repression and fulfillment. Overall the feeling is of fear, anxiety, and corruption, as the action darkens toward violence and premature death. For all its Viennese glitter, this is a pessimistic view of the human condition. The "uncharted country," as von Aigner explains, is human behavior in all its variety and contradiction: the undiscovered country of the soul.

In February 1980 Stoppard delivered the Clark Lectures at Cambridge. At that time he was not working on a new play, and nothing appeared until he completed another adaptation in the middle of 1981. *On the Razzle* was first performed in London at the Lyttelton Theatre of the National Theatre on 18 September 1981. With this play, Stoppard returned to farce. *On the Razzle* is a version of Johann Nestroy's *Einen Jux will er sich machen*, first performed in 1842. The popular Viennese dramatist based his play on an English farce, *A Day Well Spent* (1835), by John Oxenford, and there have been several subsequent versions, including *The Merchant of Yonkers* (1938) and its revised version, *The Matchmaker* (1954), both by Thornton Wilder, and the musical *Hello, Dolly!* (1964), adapted by Michael Stewart from Wilder's plays. Nestroy wrote in the Viennese comic tradition, descended from the commedia dell'arte, to which he added sharp social comment. He used the Vienna argot, which was not just a German dialect but a language compounded of various European influences. Additionally, Nestroy was preoccupied with verbal ingenuity, using puns and innuendo with extreme subtlety. Indeed, his work has been thought to be untranslatable; but Stoppard abandoned early any objective of providing a close rendition. His version is less sharp in its social comment but is theatrically and linguistically exuberant.

The intricate farcical plot concerns the adventures of Weinberl and Christopher, assistants to the master grocer Herr Zangler, when their employer leaves them in charge of the shop for a single day while he attends a procession in Vienna and entertains his fiancée. The two go "on the razzle" in Vienna, in a once-in-a-lifetime illicit spree. Complications arise when they encounter Zangler in the city: these amount to a farcical climax. At the end they return to the routine of their jobs, having stepped one rung up the hierarchy of servant and master after Weinberl hires a boy off the street and, in a slight way, becomes a master. The plot and situations of *On the Razzle* are unimportant, except for the significance of the "razzle" as the realization of the assistants' private and idealized vision of life in Vienna, which recalls the subjective visions in Stoppard's earlier work. The main focus of the play is its unbroken sequence of jokes: here is the verbal dazzle of the early Stoppard, as each word is squeezed for its maximum comic mileage. The central figure, Zangler, is provided with a running gag in his constant malapropisms and parapraxes, laboriously assisted by the other characters in his search for the correct word or phrase. The large cast is grouped into pairs, recalling the routines of stand-up comics and music-hall patter: the grocer and his new servant; the fiancée and her female friend; the young lovers; and the two assistants, senior and junior. In the National Theatre production the junior assistant, Christopher, was played by a woman, in the Viennese tradition.

With its emphasis on farcical stage business and continuous jokes, the success of *On the Razzle* depends heavily on comic timing. In this use of the text of another playwright as framework for a play, Stoppard to an extent takes as his focus comedy itself, going beyond even the verbal joke into the unscripted area of comic theater. Significantly, the unscripted prelude of the first production was a dumb show of farcical stage business in the grocer's shop, and the production also included further unscripted sequences of intricate and fast comic movement.

An immediate success, *On the Razzle* was welcomed by critics, who noted, however, its sheer indulgence in comedy for its own sake. Robert Cushman, in the *Observer*, wrote that "from political farce and philosophical farce Mr. Stoppard has turned to writing farcical farce" and compared the script with *The Importance of Being Earnest* as the funniest in the English language. This claim may be an exaggeration, but the comparison with Wilde is apt. Stoppard is again in the self-contained world of art-for-art's-sake. *On the Razzle* amply bears out his repeated assertion that he is a professional, a craftsman for the theater, whose primary objective is to entertain.

A sampling of critical opinion on *The Real Thing* (1982) reveals both a deep distrust and admiration of Stoppard's success. Gerald Weales in *Commentary* remarked that "despite the witty lines, the play is essentially sentimental, which may be why it is so popular, and it ends on a lightly, lubriciously happy note that seems benignly fake to me." Catharine Hughes in *America* faulted the playwright for his "smug cleverness" while acknowledging his "ingenious manipulation of theatrical conventions and his adroit mastery of apt literary allusion." Elliott Sirkin in the *Nation* recognized Stoppard as a "subtle, astute, complicated writer," but he attacked the New York production of *The Real Thing* for overemphasizing its old-fashioned aspects in a refined style reminiscent of Noël Coward and Philip Barry. On the other hand, Robert E. Lauder in *America* and Hersh Zeifman in *Modern Drama*, viewing Stoppard carefully in the context of his whole career, discovered, in Lauder's words, "a significant development in the vision of one of the most stimulating and thought-provoking of our contemporary playwrights." Zeifman, who provides the most thorough analysis of the play to date, found that Stoppard rigorously follows through with the major theme of this stage work: "we thus find ourselves at the end invariably questioning, among a host of other 'realities,' the precise nature of love—as Stoppard, of course, intended."

The Real Thing is divided into twelve scenes, the first of which engages in a familiar Stoppardian ploy of presenting a play within a play. The difference in this instance is that the audience is not aware that the first scene is, in effect, a fake until the second scene reveals that Max and Charlotte have been on stage performing part of her husband Henry's play, *House of Cards*. Right from the beginning, then, the playwright challenges the audience to sort out what is real and what is feigned. Judging by the reviews and the reactions of a New York audience, it comes as something of shock to realize that Max and Charlotte are actors, even though in retrospect the artificiality of their dialogue is apparent. Gradually their "real" lives come to resemble their stage roles, but the point is that the theatricality of human lives is as "real" as anything else about the nature of their existence. This is not to say that there is no difference between theater and everyday life, but how one tells the difference is what *The Real Thing* is all about. Henry, for example, is manipulative as both a playwright and a husband deceiving his wife, Charlotte, by having an affair with Max's wife, Annie. But it is only after the initial scene of *House of Cards* that Henry, and the audience, begins to learn how to discriminate between dialogue in a play and dialogue in real life. As Charlotte predicts, Henry will not be so witty or so polished as his cuckolded character in *House of Cards* when Henry learns that he has been deceived.

The following dialogue from scene 2 illustrates how Henry and Charlotte cannot talk without making their conversation into a commentary on their lives and on Henry's art:

HENRY: How was last night, by the way?

CHARLOTTE: I had to fake it again.

HENRY: Very witty woman, my present wife. Actually I was talking about my play.

CHARLOTTE: Actually, so was I.

Husband and wife are doing this scene for Max's benefit. Naturally these theatrical characters will be especially adept at fudging the distinctions between real and imagined life, but their dialogue is not simply characterizing them; it also reveals how people portray themselves in front of others on stage and off. Real life, in other words, is also staged and scripted; and theatrical life also has its own standards of realism and authenticity. In scene 2 neither Charlotte nor Max knows that Henry is having an affair with Annie, who makes her first entrance a short time later, an entrance that has been calculated to give her some time with Henry while seeming to be joining her husband Max on a social visit.

Annie actually is the character who would most like to drop the pretense of theatricality, for she urges Henry to escape from the false scene he has created and would like to prolong until, as she puts it, "you'll know it wasn't the real thing." She wants Henry to take some responsibility for his feelings instead of shamming principles such as "I don't steal other men's wives." For this is exactly what he is doing, and she bluntly tells him off: *"Sod* you." Her straightforwardness is in sharp contrast to Henry's histrionic and stylized manner. Even when he is joking and covering his tracks, he is also foreshadowing, like a good playwright, his lack of commitment to his "present wife."

Almost like one of Stoppard's critics, Annie tries to get Henry to commit himself. She is playful, but she is also serious, and she wants a frank

demonstration of his feelings. The flat speech, the declarative style, are a challenge to him:

HENRY: I love you.

ANNIE: Touch me then. They'll come in or they won't. Take a chance. Kiss me.

HENRY: For Christ's sake.

ANNIE: Quick one on the carpet then.

HENRY: You're crackers.

ANNIE: I'm not interested in your mind.

HENRY: Yes, you are.

ANNIE: No, I'm not, I lied to you.

Words will take Henry a long way, but they will not suffice for Annie. When Max discovers her infidelity in scene 3, she does not finesse her motivations as Henry would. She tells Max that she loves Henry and he loves her. "That's that, isn't it. I'm sorry it's awful. But it's better really. All that lying." Max would prefer to pretend that Annie does not love Henry and would prefer to be let down easily, but Annie will not play such a scene for him.

The Real Thing is Stoppard's most autobiographical play. He is not Henry, to be sure, but Henry is certainly representative of one of Stoppard's guises as a literary man exuberantly living off of his style who is suspected of not having "real" convictions. At the same time, however, Annie is hardly a satisfactory antidote to the equivocating stylist. She can be tactless and cruel, and she values content over style so highly that she is put in the ridiculous position of supporting Brodie, an oafish young man involved in protesting against nuclear weapons in Britain.

Brodie writes an awkward, amateurish play that Annie badgers Henry to fix. Henry is appalled at both Brodie's style and his opinions. He is even more revolted by Brodie's idea that politics has an objective reality like a coffee mug that can be handled straightforwardly and without the necessary ambiguity and humility of a supple style. Politics, justice, and patriotism have no reality "separate from our perceptions of them," Henry tells Annie. His argument cannot be fairly summarized because it depends so heavily on his own style, a style that implies there is no such thing as just a bald statement of the facts. The relationship between Henry and Annie, for example, is not as simple as the words Annie uses with Max: "I love him. . . . Yes, I do. And he loves me." The play progresses by breaking down her neat formula so that she will have to make exceptions to it—make room for Billie, an actor who plays Brodie in Brodie's atrocious play. Henry, in fact, is the one who wants to be loved without qualifications or exceptions, and he is the one who espouses a simpleminded view of fidelity that Annie has to reject in a style not nearly so rigid as the one she employed in the early scenes when her life seemed much tidier. Indeed, she rivals Henry's facility in finding verbal equivalents of her complicated feelings about Billie: "He sort of got in under the radar. Acting daft on a train. Next thing I'm looking round for him, makes the day feel better, it's like love or something: no—love, absolutely, how can I say it wasn't? You weren't replaced, or even replaceable. But I. . . ." The involved syntax, the questioning and qualification of her feelings, and the way she now elaborately punctuates her experience in scene 11 suggest the theatrical bent of this wife and actress. Love means, in one of its manifestations, "acting daft." Love is, in fact, theatrical but also real; it is a complex emotion that cannot be encompassed in the monosyllabic style Annie favored when speaking with Max.

The accommodation Henry and Annie eventually reach at the end of *The Real Thing* is a melding of content and style, a melding that has also taken place in Stoppard's writing of the play. The husband and wife seem very much like "the real thing" in their gradual and loving recognition of each other's similarities and differences. The playwright has found a credible way of getting them to talk like each other, to adopt each other's style. In doing so, he has also slyly supported his own reliance on language for its dialectic grasp of reality. His characters have convictions; Stoppard has convictions, but the convictions shift with time and place and are dependent on the context in which they get expressed.

Take Max as a final example of the playwright's reply to his critics. In scene 1 he is thoroughly convincing as a cool and witty Noël Cowardian husband who has been deceived by his wife; the same Max—that is the man and actor who has Annie as his wife—is movingly broken by the evidence of adultery: Henry's bloodied handkerchief in Annie's automobile:

> It looks filthy. It's dried filthy.
> You're filthy.

> You filthy cow.
> You rotten filthy—

Max starts to cry; he drops his genuine but still histrionic actor's reaction, is immobilized by deep feeling, and says to Annie in a barely audible voice: "It's not true, is it?" The audience can tell where the acting, the style, leaves off and the crude content begins, but it can also respond to how closely connected theater and life are to each other in Stoppard's art. The playwright received the New York Drama Critics Circle Award for *The Real Thing*, along with a Tony Award for Best New Play of 1983-1984.

Stoppard's reputation continues to be enhanced in both theatrical and academic circles. Students of modern drama inevitably encounter the playwright's works, and his repertoire remains popular among college, community, and regional theaters. In 1989 a theatrical version of his *Artist Descending a Staircase* was produced at the Helen Hayes Theater in New York. The play prompted *New York Daily News* drama critic Howard Kissel to remark that "the evening afforded the pleasure of Stoppard's customarily brilliant language."

Interviews:

Keith Harper, "The Devious Road to Waterloo," *Guardian*, 7 April 1967, p. 7;

Dan Sullivan, "Young British Playwright Here for Rehearsals of 'Rosencrantz,'" *New York Times*, 29 August 1967, p. 27;

Kathleen Halton, "Young British Playwright Here for Rehearsal," *Vogue* (15 October 1967): 112;

John Gale, "Writing's My 43rd Priority," *Observer*, 17 December 1967, p. 4;

Giles Gordon, "Tom Stoppard," *Transatlantic Review*, no. 29 (Summer 1968): 17-25;

Mel Gussow, "'Jumpers' Author is Verbal Gymnast," *New York Times*, 23 April 1972, p. 36;

Barry Norman, "Tom Stoppard and the Contentment of Insecurity," *Times* (London), 11 November 1972;

Janet Watts, "Interview with Tom Stoppard," *Guardian*, 21 March 1973;

Michael Leech, "The Translators: Tom Stoppard," *Plays and Players*, 20 (April 1973): pp. 36-37;

"Ambushes for the Audience: Towards a High Comedy of Ideas," *Theatre Quarterly*, 4 (May-July 1974);

Mark Amory, "The Joke's the Thing," *Observer Magazine*, 9 June 1974;

A. C. H. Smith, "Tom Stoppard," *Flourish*, Royal Shakespeare Company Club News-sheet, no. 1, 1974;

"Pauline Young Talks to Our Leading Dramatist: London 16 January 1980," *Madog Arts Magazine* (Spring 1981);

Nancy S. Hardin, "An Interview with Tom Stoppard," *Contemporary Literature*, 22 (1981): 153-166;

Mel Gussow, "The Real Tom Stoppard," *New York Times Magazine*, January 1984, pp. 18-23.

Bibliographies:

"Theatre Checklist No. 2: Tom Stoppard," *Theatrefacts*, no. 2 (May-July 1974);

Kimball King, *Twenty Modern British Playwrights: A Bibliography, 1956 to 1976* (New York & London: Garland, 1977);

David Bratt, *Tom Stoppard: A Reference Guide* (Boston: G. K. Hall, 1982).

References:

Michael Anderson, "The Unnatural Scene: Plays about Plays," *New Theatre Magazine*, 8 (Spring 1968): 28-31;

Walter D. Asmus, "Rosencrantz and Guildenstern are Dead," *Shakespeare-Jahrbuch*, 106 (1970): 118-131;

A. J. Ayer, "Love among the Logical Positivists," *Sunday Times*, 9 April 1972;

William Babula, "The Play-Life Metaphor in Shakespeare and Stoppard," *Modern Drama*, 15 (Winter 1972): 279-281;

Clive Barker, "Contemporary Shakespearean Parody in British Theatre," *Shakespeare-Jahrbuch*, 105 (1969): 104-120;

Jonathan Bennett, "Philosophy and Mr. Stoppard," *Philosophy*, 50 (January 1975): 5-18;

Norman Berlin, "Rosencrantz and Guildenstern are Dead: Theater of Criticism," *Modern Drama*, 16 (December 1973): 269-277;

C. W. E. Bigsby, *Tom Stoppard*, Writers and their Work series (Harlow: Longman, 1976);

Tim Brassell, *Tom Stoppard: An Assessment* (London: Macmillan, 1985);

Robert Brustein, *The Third Theatre* (New York: Knopf, 1969);

Victor L. Cahn, *Beyond Absurdity: The Plays of Tom Stoppard* (London & Rutherford, N.J.: Fairleigh Dickinson University Press, 1979);

Anthony Callan, "Stoppard's Godot: Some French Influences on Postwar English Drama," *New Theatre Magazine* (Winter 1969): 22-30;

Douglas Colby, *As the Curtain Rises: On Contemporary British Drama 1966-76* (London & Rutherford, N.J.: Fairleigh Dickinson University Press, 1978);

Richard Corballis, *Stoppard: The Mystery and the Clockwork* (New York: Methuen, 1984);

Joan Fitzpatrick Dean, *Tom Stoppard: Comedy As a Moral Matrix* (Columbia: University of Missouri Press, 1981);

Richard Ellmann, "The Zealots of Zurich," *Times Literary Supplement*, 12 July 1974;

Lucina Paquet Gabbard, *The Stoppard Plays* (Troy, N.Y.: Whitson, 1982);

C. O. Gardner, "Correspondence: *Rosencrantz and Guildenstern are Dead*," *Theoria*, 34 (1970): 83;

C. J. Ginakaris, "Absurdism Altered: *Rosencrantz and Guildenstern are Dead*," *Drama Survey*, 7 (1969): 52-58;

Jim Hunter, *Tom Stoppard's Plays* (New York: Grove, 1982);

Clive James, "Count Zero Splits the Infinite," *Encounter*, 45 (November 1975);

Andrew K. Kennedy, "Tom Stoppard's Dissident Comedies," *Modern Drama*, 25 (1982): 469-476;

Robert E. Lauder, "Tom Stoppard's Mystery and Metaphysics," *America*, 11 May 1985, pp. 393-394;

R. H. Lee, "The Circle and Its Tangent," *Theoria*, 33 (1969): 37-43;

Felicia Hardison Londre, *Tom Stoppard* (New York: Ungar, 1981);

A. Mansat, "Rosencrantz et Guildenstern sont Morts," *Les Langues Modernes*, 64 (1970): 396-400;

Roger Scruton, "The Real Stoppard," *Encounter*, 60 (1983): 44-47;

Elliot Sirkin, "Theater," *Nation*, 238 (1984): 200-201;

John Russell Taylor, *Anger and After* (London: Methuen, 1969);

Taylor, *The Second Wave* (London: Methuen, 1971);

Kenneth Tynan, *Show People* (London: Weidenfeld & Nicolson, 1980);

Gerald Weales, "Playwright's Dilemma," *Commonweal*, 111 (1984): 404-405;

John Weightman, "A Metaphysical Comedy," *Encounter*, 38 (April 1972): 44-46;

Weightman, "Mini-Hamlets in Limbo," *Encounter*, 29 (July 1967): 38-40;

Thomas R. Whitaker, *Tom Stoppard* (New York: Grove, 1983);

Hersh Zeifman, "Comedy of Ambush: Tom Stoppard's *The Real Thing*," *Modern Drama*, 26 (1983): 139-149;

Zeifman, "Tomfoolery: Stoppard's Theatrical Puns," *Yearbook of English Studies* (1979): 204-220.

D. M. Thomas
(27 January 1935 -   )

This entry was updated by Karen Dorn from her entry in
DLB 40: Poets of Great Britain and Ireland Since 1960: Part Two.

See also the Thomas article in DLB Yearbook: 1982.

SELECTED BOOKS: *Penguin Modern Poets 11*, by Thomas, D. M. Black, and Peter Redgrove (Harmondsworth: Penguin, 1968);

Two Voices (London: Cape Goliard, 1968; New York: Viking, 1968);

Logan Stone (London: Cape Goliard, 1971; New York: Viking, 1971);

The Shaft (Gillingham, Kent: Arx, 1973);

Love and Other Deaths: Poems (London: Elek, 1975);

The Rock (Knotting: Sceptre Press, 1975);

The Honeymoon Voyage (London: Secker & Warburg, 1978);

The Flute-Player (New York: Dutton, 1978; London: Gollancz, 1979);

The Devil and the Floral Dance (London: Robson, 1978);

Birthstone (London: Gollancz, 1980; New York: Viking, 1984);

Dreaming in Bronze (London: Secker & Warburg, 1981);

The White Hotel (London: Gollancz, 1981; New York: Viking, 1981);

News from the Front, by Thomas and Sylvia Kantaris (Todmorden: Ark, 1983);

Ararat (London: Gollancz, 1983; New York: Viking, 1983);

Selected Poems (London: Secker & Warburg, 1983; New York: Viking, 1983);

Swallow (London: Gollancz, 1984; New York: Viking, 1984);

D. M. Thomas (photograph © Jerry Bauer)

Sphinx (London: Gollancz, 1986);

Summit (London: Gollancz, 1987);

Memories and Hallucinations (London: Gollancz, 1988);

Lying Together (London: Gollancz, 1990);

Flying into Love (London: Bloomsbury, 1992).

OTHER: Introduction to *Work in Progress*, by Peter Redgrove (London: Poet & Printer, 1968);

The Granite Kingdom, Poems of Cornwall: An Anthology, edited by Thomas (Truro: Bradford Barton, 1970);

Poetry in Crosslight, edited by Thomas (London: Longman, 1975);

Anna Akhmatova, *Requiem and Poem without a Hero*, translated by Thomas (Athens: Ohio University Press, 1976; London: Elek, 1976);

John Harris, *Songs from the Earth*, edited by Thomas (Padstow: Lodenek, 1977);

Akhmatova, *Way of All the Earth*, translated by Thomas (London: Secker & Warburg, 1979);

"On Literary Celebrity," *New York Times Magazine*, 13 June 1982, pp. 24-38;

Aleksandr Pushkin, *The Bronze Horseman and Other Poems*, translated by Thomas (London: Secker & Warburg, 1982; New York: Viking, 1982);

Yevgeny Yevtushenko, *A Dove in Santiago*, translated by Thomas (London: Secker & Warburg, 1982; New York: Atheneum, 1982);

Akhmatova, *You Will Hear Thunder*, translated by Thomas (London: Secker & Warburg, 1985).

D. M. Thomas is widely known for his novel *The White Hotel*, which quickly rose to the top of the best-seller lists after its American publication in the spring of 1981. Yet, he is also an accomplished poet. In his poetry, as well as in his novels, he has developed a style that is a powerful evocation of the imaginative life.

A native of Carnkai, near Redruth, Cornwall, Donald Michael Thomas grew up in what he considered a "distinctive landscape with a spirit," and as part of a Methodist chapel-going family with a strong interest in America. An ancestor had lived briefly in New York, and Thomas's parents, Harold Redvers and Amy Thomas, had spent ten years in California, where his father, a plasterer, had built a house. The Cornish seacoast and abandoned tin mines of Thomas's childhood have been transformed into what he calls the "inner landscape" of his writing.

When he was fourteen, Thomas went with his parents to Australia, where his recently married older sister, Lois, was living. They remained there for two years, during which time Thomas attended University High School in Melbourne.

During his two years of compulsory national service—at a time in the early 1950s when Winston Churchill was concerned about the shortage of Russian-speaking interrogators in the event of a third world war—Thomas underwent a course in Russian. Though he did not do well at the final examination—he was passed for low-level interrogation after further study—his knowledge of Russian developed into a consuming interest in Russian literature. He has published three highly regarded translations of the poetry of Anna Akhmatova—*Requiem and Poem without a Hero* (1976), *Way of All the Earth* (1979), and *You Will Hear Thunder* (1985)—and his translations of Aleksandr Pushkin's *The Bronze Horseman* and Yevgeny Yevtushenko's *A Dove in Santiago* appeared in 1982. A portrait of Akhmatova, painted in the Russian realist style of the 1920s, hangs in his study in Hereford, near the Welsh border.

Thomas studied English at New College, Oxford, where he gained a first-class undergraduate degree in 1958 and an M.A. in 1961. He later said his favorite poets at that time were William Butler Yeats, Robert Frost, and Emily Dickinson—and it was at Oxford that he began his own career as a poet. Quite by chance on an afternoon walk he came upon the scene of an accident: the white face of a girl covered with a red coat was the compelling image that led to his first poem. Though the poem was never published, he showed it to his tutor, John Bayley, who predicted that Thomas would be a late developer. His recent career has seemed a fulfillment of that prediction, for after a decade of writing poetry he has written nine novels. He still regards himself as a poet who also writes novels, and many readers have admired the complex web of images that gives each novel its distinctively poetic tone and structure. Indeed, Thomas's initial experience in Oxford—the image of the girl—illustrates the importance of the germinal image in his more recent work. He has said that he can "only get to grips with a novel when there is some kind of *symbol* at work. . . . I'm not really interested in exploring motivation. I need an image that is capable of expanding, and then individual words, enriched by association with that central image."

Thomas has been married twice and has three children. For fifteen years he taught English at Hereford College of Education and was head of the English department at the time the college was closed in 1978.

As a young writer Thomas admired the "imaginative vision" of science fiction, and *Penguin Modern Poets 11* (1968) includes a selection of his early poems based on the science-fiction myths of Ray Bradbury, Arthur C. Clarke, Tom Godwin, Damon Knight, and James H. Schmitz. Thomas soon abandoned the conventions of science-fiction writing, which he thought did not allow for the "concreteness" he wanted in his poetry.

His later volumes of poems include experimental pieces built up from a phantasmagoria of details and images drawn from contemporary life. The title poem in *Two Voices* (1968) combines prose and poetry, science fiction, and scenes from travels in the American Southwest. He is interested in the interplay between dreams and waking, of inner consciousness and the outer world. The various voices and levels of diction create a kaleidoscope of images, but in the concluding poem of *Two Voices*, "Requiem for Aberfan," Thomas achieves a similar effect through a new simplicity. "Requiem for Aberfan" is a sequence of ten poems on the deaths of 116 children and 28 adults that occurred when a landslide overwhelmed the school in the coal-mining village of Aberfan. Using contemporary accounts from a book by Tony Austin and a BBC television documentary, especially the reports of siblings' dreams and parents' reactions to the tragedy, Thomas juxtaposes his poems to the original prose passages to suggest the living presence of the dead.

In *Logan Stone* (1971) Thomas continued to experiment with juxtapositions of literary styles and images. The most ambitious poem in the volume, "Computer 70: Dreams and Love Poems," combines prose and verse to portray a couple's sexual life amid the shaping images of fantasy, dreams, and the television screen: Chappaquiddick, the Boston strangler, the moon landing, the assassination of President John F. Kennedy, and atrocities reported from the war in Vietnam. Even the simplest sections are heavily embellished:

Ophelia in your party dress
  the automobile's skirts of steel,

heavy with their drink,
have pulled you to an unmelodious
and evil lay.

Thomas has described his early poetry as "over-elaborate" and "too intellectual, too cerebral." The compression of viewpoints and images in "Two Voices" and "Computer 70" had no successor in his subsequent volumes of poetry, and he may be said to have found a new mode of expression in his narrative prose. During his last years at Hereford College he began work on his first novel, *Birthstone* (1980; the second novel to be published). Drawing upon local Cornish characters and Thomas's fascination with America, the novel depicts the adventures of an American couple—mother and son—who return to Cornwall with a Welsh guide in search of their ancestry. The construction of the plot began as a game with a Welsh friend, who exchanged episodes with Thomas as a way of keeping in touch. They chose Cornwall as the setting and decided that the woman guide would be Welsh. Thomas was intrigued with the Cornish stone Men-an-Tol and suggested that they start "with someone crawling through that. And as you obviously have to have more than one person in a novel, we developed three main characters—the American couple and the woman. At that stage I didn't know the character was going to be a split personality." The characters grow older and younger as the magical stone takes its effect. The varied sexual activity was regarded by some readers as pornographic and led one reviewer, Alan Hollinghurst, to describe the novel as "immensely unlikable."

In contrast with the method of composition in which essential elements are discovered en route, Thomas's poetry began increasingly to spring from a central controlling image. An autobiographical sequence, *The Shaft* (1973), took its main image from the reopening of the Cornish tin mines by international combines. Thomas saw the shaft in the poem "as one and many, like the persona: who is variously a foreign mining engineer, myself, my father, dead miners related to me."

The next two volumes of poetry, *Love and Other Deaths: Poems* (1975) and *The Honeymoon Voyage* (1978), employ a variety of poetic forms to explore two themes that increasingly dominate Thomas's work—the theme of death and loss and the theme of sexual attraction in its erotic and destructive aspects. In *Love and Other Deaths*,

"Lilith-prints" is a sexual-creation sequence in which all historical development is imagined as stemming from the sexual activity of Lilith, Eve's apocryphal rival, and the volume includes a series of erotic poems written in response to the ancient Chinese book of divination, *I Ching*. "Sonoran Poems" explores the bond between brutality and lust through the kidnapping of a diplomat by extremists. The poems of death and loss are the most impressive: "Cecie," about the death of a beloved maiden aunt, "Rest-Home: Visiting Hour," about his dying father, "The Journey" and "Rubble," about his frail and dying mother, are all poems of steady tone and well-observed detail.

Thomas returns to these themes in *The Honeymoon Voyage* with "Diary of a Myth-Boy," based on a Brazilian tribal myth, "Ninemaidens," inspired by a Cornish stone circle, and "Weddings," after Catullus LXII. His most accomplished poem is the title poem, on the death of his mother. For readers of his earlier poetry, the detail is familiar: the Cornish coast, the seas and harsh storms, his parents' journey to California, family photographs. These details are transformed by the central image of the voyage, at once a journey to death ("We have felt lost before, / I tell your mother as the dead / Ship's engines nose through the silent / Mist . . ."), and a reliving of a honeymoon trip to America. The final stanza—the persona is the poet's dead father—is a resolution of the images of harsh climate and stormy journey:

> Trust me, I tell her, for
> The last time I returned I led
> You, little more than a child when
> We parted, to a city
> So wonderful it took away your speech . . .
> And she trusts me, while her grief spills
> Naturally with the honeymoon snow.

Readers who have followed Thomas's development as a poet—the increasingly controlled poetic form and simpler evocative images—see in his work as a translator of Anna Akhmatova the galvanizing experience for his own writing. *Requiem and Poem without a Hero* (1976) was published while he was still teaching at Hereford College. By that time the future of the college was in jeopardy because of a series of political decisions that had led first to the expansion and then the closing of the institution. Following the closing Thomas returned to Oxford to do research in the problems of verse translation. His second

translation of Akhmatova's poetry, *Way of All the Earth*, was published in 1979. In his introduction he draws attention to her fidelity to "the clear, familiar, material world," and he sees in his earlier translation, *Requiem*" her response to the Stalinist terror, not a relentless piling-on of detail, as in Solzhenitsyn's *Gulag Archipelago*, but rather an intensity of understatement: the life of one woman standing in the endless queue outside a Leningrad prison." According to Thomas, Akhmatova "achieves universality, through an exquisiteness of style that is at the same time anonymous and transparent. . . ."

Anna Akhmatova's life and poetry have become the inspiration for Thomas's own work. The image of her alone in her bare room in Leningrad is the model for the character Elena in *The Flute-Player* (1978), whom Hollinghurst called "an angelic whore of artistic inspiration, a symbol of the unexpressible instinct towards art." From her bare room she keeps alive a generation of persecuted artists in the midst of a chaotic totalitarian city. Thomas has described the novel as a "microcosm of the twentieth century but also in another way of all centuries—writers throughout the centuries and indeed women throughout time." *The Flute-Player*, written virtually in one draft, was conceived in response to a fantasy competition conducted by Gollancz Press. Thomas won the Gollancz Prize in 1978, though he considers the novel not an escape from reality, as in science fiction, but an escape into reality (the fantasy label was not included on the American edition). That same year Thomas was given the Cholmondeley Award for Poetry. In 1980 *Birthstone*, the first novel he wrote, was published, and he was awarded an Arts Council award for Literature. He was still relatively unknown until the publication in 1981 of *The White Hotel*, an immensely moving and powerful novel that, in Margaret Drabble's words, completely changed the habit of novel writing.

The critical reception of *The White Hotel* was extraordinary. First published by Gollancz in England in January 1981, the novel received cautious and contradictory reviews. (The *Spectator* announced the appearance of a major author while the *New Statesman* decried the book as a muddle of pornography and violence.) Later, in March 1981, Viking Press brought out the American edition, and, in reaction to the tremendous American response, Penguin published a paperback edition in England that went straight to the top of the best-seller lists, won the Cheltenham Prize,

Dust jacket for Thomas's 1983 selection of poems written over a span of twenty years. In his preface he explains that "all my poems take issue with love and death."

and narrowly missed the Booker Prize for Fiction in 1981. On the strength of the book's critical reception, Thomas was invited as a visiting lecturer to American University in Washington, D.C., early in 1982. After little more than a week he resigned and returned to England to escape from what he has described as the confining image of the "successor author." He returned briefly in the spring for a promotion tour.

The story of *The White Hotel* is revealed through a variety of literary forms: letters of correspondence, poetry, analytical prose, and prose narrative. The themes of love and death in Thomas's earlier poetry reappear in the story of Lisa Erdman, a Viennese soprano who undergoes psychoanalysis with Sigmund Freud as a treatment for hysteria. There are six sections of the novel, prefaced by an imaginary correspondence between Freud and his colleagues about an erotic poem written by a female patient, Lisa, whose case history Freud plans to write. The first section, the poem itself, which describes the sexual fantasies of the patient during a stay at a white hotel, is followed by a prose-narrative account of

the same fantasy. Then in what is regarded as the strongest section of the novel, an imaginative reconstruction of a real case history based on Freud's actual studies of Fräulein Anna O. and "Dora," Thomas's character Freud analyzes the autoerotic paradise of the poem. In the fourth section Lisa has recovered and resumed her career, remarrying and moving to Kiev with her Russian husband, also a singer, whose first wife Lisa had understudied. After her husband's disappearance in the Stalinist purges, Lisa and her stepson are murdered in Babi Yar, in a brutal parody of her earlier symptoms of hysteria. In the final section, a dream coda, Lisa is reunited with her friends and family in the new paradise of Palestine. Thomas was interested by the suggestion of one reviewer that *The White Hotel* was a paradigm of Thomas's own career as a poet, and Thomas recalled that he was "aware that in some ways the changes of style were some kind of mental development—the very primitive thing with the poetry, then the expansion of it in the prose, analytical, and so on. Becoming more and more realistic, until the last episode which then drifts away into a kind of mysticism."

Thomas's imaginative treatment of contemporary issues—female sexuality, psychoanalysis, and the Holocaust—led to the enthusiastic reception of the novel in America. Readers have been fascinated by the construction of the book, which began, according to Thomas, with a poem about Freud and Carl Jung, "Vienna. Zürich. Constance," written five years earlier (and included in *The Honeymoon Voyage*). In the poem a young man and woman, aspects of Freud and Jung, travel on different trains for a rendezvous, though they never actually meet. Thomas then wrote "The Woman to Sigmund Freud," which he incorporated in the poem of *The White Hotel*, but not until he read Anatoli Kuznetsov's *Babi Yar* (1967) did he realize that the poems were the beginning of a novel that would end in Babi Yar. The psychological element of the story came from Thomas's observation that Freud's Jewish patients had symptoms that Freud traced to their childhood experience, "whereas in fact it could just as easily have been an awareness of the terror that was approaching. . . . That seemed to be a very exciting idea to work on. . . ."

The White Hotel has led in turn to new poems. Thomas's *Dreaming in Bronze* (1981) includes "Peter Kürten to the Witnesses," based on the German murderer who appears as a character in the novel; "The Wolf-Man," about one of Freud's best-known case histories; and a sequence of letters in verse, imagined to have been exchanged between Freud and three colleagues, in which their inner compulsions leading to the suicide of one colleague are given definition through the imagery of wild animals. "Two Women, Made by the Selfsame Hand" is a narrative poem about a couple tempted by two different figurines in a crafts shop—an erotic nymph and a madonna and child. The nature of their relationship, according to Thomas, is reflected in their different tastes.

Thomas's *Selected Poems* was published in 1983, as was his fourth novel, *Ararat*. The image of the sacred mountain on the border between the East and the West embodies Thomas's interest in the division between the outer world and the life of the imagination. *Ararat* was the first of a series of novels collectively called *Russian Nights*. For some readers *Ararat* was a reply to the inaccurate charges of plagiarism directed at *The White Hotel*. The narrator, a Soviet poet, entertains his mistress with an extemporaneous tale based on the theme of Mount Ararat, where memory and invention build up a pattern of wordplay.

Thomas builds on this device in subsequent novels of the series through characters who are expert in the art of improvisation, a traditionally popular Italian form of entertainment. In *Swallow* (1984) the framing plot concerns a Finnish olympiad of twelve finalists, expert improvisationalists. The mistress in *Ararat* reappears as the chief contender, and punning and wordplay become the driving force of the narrative. *Sphinx* (1986) was followed by *Summit* (1987), a parody of a summit meeting in Geneva between a President O'Reilly and Comrade G. and their wives. The plot is simpler than that of other novels in the series, and the dialogue and caricatures are in the tradition of satire invoked by the jacket illustration of puppets from the British television series "Spitting Image." In the words of the *Financial Times* reviewer, Ronald Reagan has been "an incomparable gift to satirists; D. M. Thomas has made a splendid creation, an amiable knucklehead who laughs like a drain at the jokes in *Reader's Digest*."

With *Lying Together* (1990), the final novel of *Russian Nights*, Thomas returns to the multiple plotting and improvised fantasies of the earlier novels. An international conference of writers is being held at a Hyde Park hotel, the scene also of a conference of undertakers. A semifictional version of Thomas himself appears together with Russian and European characters from previous novels who claim to have written them all. To relieve the boredom of the conference, the friends give improvisations based on the theme of the title "lying together" in a series of creations and analyses of the relationship of a Russian couple. The layers of reality are mixed with *Psychological Correspondences*, a series of letters between the German neuropsychiatrist Richard von Krafft-Ebing and a masochistic maidservant, a structure that Thomas had used with such effect in *The White Hotel*.

Thomas's novels have provoked a range of responses, from readers who feel they are a "rudderless and portentous odyssey of improvisation" to those who admire what Thomas calls "a mixture of the surreal and the magical." He does not place his work within the realistic tradition of the English novel with its powerful evocation of character and motivation, of action and consequence. Rosemary Dinnage suggests another tradition: "The principle of surrealistic collage and pastiche has been accepted for decades in painting and the cinema, but in the novel in English there are few precedents." She adds that Thomas says he has no style of his own; again in contemporary poetry, the adoption of other voices, and the development of a nucleus from another writer's work or life, have been successful and accepted devices."

Thomas's love and knowledge of Russian literature have been recurring themes in his career, but the pre-*glasnost* Russia that inspired *Russian Nights* has become a part of history. In an interview for *Topical Books* in 1990 that appeared at the publication of *Lying Together*, Thomas says, "I would find it very difficult to write about Russia now. It's no longer Dante's *Inferno*—it has lost its mythic quality, but fortunately I can always find infernos in myself!" His autobiography, *Memories and Hallucinations* (1988), contains many clues to these infernos and illuminates the early poetry of Cornwall and his parents as much as it does his later novels.

In all his work, dreams have played a major role. Thomas has also described his use of dreams in composition: "By thinking about the problems at night you often wake up with possible answers. You somehow usher your work into the realms of sleep and dreams so it then becomes part of it." When he had completed the first draft of his controversial new novel, *Flying into Love* (1992), a fantasy about the private life of President Kennedy, he had a dream that suggested to him that "my obsession with Kennedy was related to my grief over my father's death, which happened around the same period in 1963. . . . My father had not died alone. He died with people who loved him, and it suddenly struck me that this was very like what I'd heard about Kennedy. He didn't like to fall asleep alone. . . ." Thomas saw a correspondence in his dream between the myth of Camelot, which in the 1960 Broadway musical version inspired Kennedy's supporters, and a familiar Cornish castle that is linked to the tradition of King Arthur. Readers familiar with Thomas's interests will remember the 1982 BBC radio talk in which he recalled Boris Pasternak's remark in *Doctor Zhivago*

(1957) that the artist is always meditating on death and thus always creating new life.

Interviews:

David Wingrove, "Different Voices," *London Magazine*, new series 21 (February 1982): 27-43;

Belinda Seward, "D. M. Thomas," *Topical Books* (Autumn 1990): 32-33.

References:

A. Alvarez, Review of *The White Hotel*, *New York Review of Books*, 28 (19 November 1981): 16;

Patrick Skene Catling, Review of *Swallow*, *Spectator* (London), 30 June 1984, p. 24;

Leslie Chamberlain, Review of *Summit*, *Times Literary Supplement*, 26 June 1987, p. 698;

Rosemary Dinnage, Review of *Memories and Hallucinations*, *Times Literary Supplement*, 1 July 1988, p. 728;

Tim Dooley, "The Suffering Objects of Desire," *Times Literary Supplement*, 22 January 1982, p. 90;

Ann Duchêne, Review of *The White Hotel*, *Times Literary Supplement*, 16 January 1981, p. 50;

Maureen Freely, "Don's Party Tricks," *New Statesman and Society*, 22 June 1990, p. 49;

Paul Gray, "Beyond Pleasure and Pain," *Time*, 117 (16 March 1981): 88;

Alan Hollinghurst [On the poems and novels of the author of *The White Hotel*], *London Review of Books* (3 December 1981): 14;

Andro Linklater, "Borrow a Drama and Add Sex," *Spectator* (London), 8 February 1992, p. 28;

Penny Perrick, "Unspontaneous Improvisation," *Sunday Times*, 17 June 1990;

Sam Pickering, Review of *Memories and Hallucinations*, *Sewanee Review*, 97 (April 1989): 297;

Peter Prescott, "The Selling of a Novel," *Newsweek*, 99 (15 March 1982): 70;

Norman Shrapnel, "Serious Money in the Eternal City," *Guardian*, 28 June 1990;

Galen Strawson, Review of *Swallow*, *Times Literary Supplement*, 29 June 1984, p. 717;

John Updike, Review of *The Flute-Player*, *New York Review of Books*, 28 (14 December 1981): 203.

R. S. Thomas

(28 March 1913 -   )

This entry was updated by W. J. Keith (University of Toronto) from his entry in
DLB 27: Poets of Great Britain and Ireland, 1945-1960.

BOOKS: *The Stones of the Field* (Carmarthen: Druid Press, 1946);

An Acre of Land (Newtown: Montgomeryshire Printing Company, 1952);

The Minister (Newtown: Montgomeryshire, 1953);

Song at the Year's Turning: Poems 1942-1954 (London: Hart-Davis, 1955);

Poetry for Supper (London: Hart-Davis, 1958; Chester Springs, Pa.: Dufour, 1961);

Tares (London: Hart-Davis, 1961; Chester Springs, Pa.: Dufour, 1961);

Penguin Modern Poets 1, by Thomas, Lawrence Durrell, and Elizabeth Jennings (Harmondsworth: Penguin, 1961);

The Bread of Truth (London: Hart-Davis, 1963; Chester Springs, Pa.: Dufour, 1963);

Words and the Poet, W. D. Thomas Memorial Lecture (Cardiff: University of Wales Press, 1964);

Pietà (London: Hart-Davis, 1966);

Not That He Brought Flowers (London: Hart-Davis, 1968);

The Mountains, text by Thomas, illustrations by John Piper (New York: Chilmark, 1968);

H'm (London: Macmillan, 1972; New York: St. Martin's Press, 1972);

Young and Old (London: Chatto & Windus, 1972);

Selected Poems 1946-1968 (London: Hart-Davis, MacGibbon, 1973; New York: St. Martin's Press, 1974);

What is a Welshman? (Landybie, Carmarthenshire: Christopher Davies, 1974);

Laboratories of the Spirit (London: Macmillan, 1975; Boston: Godine, 1976);

The Way of It, text by Thomas, illustrations by Barry Hirst (Sunderland: Ceolfrith Press, 1977);

Frequencies (London: Macmillan, 1978);

Between Here and Now (London: Macmillan, 1981);

Later Poems: A Selection (London: Macmillan, 1983);

Selected Prose, edited by Sandra Ahstey (Bridgend, Mid Glamorgan: Poetry Wales Press, 1983);

Destinations, illustrations by Paul Nash (Shipston-on-Stour, Warwick: Celandine Press, 1985);

Ingrowing Thoughts (Bridgend, Mid Glamorgan: Poetry Wales Press, 1985);

Experimenting with an Amen (London: Macmillan, 1986);

Welsh Airs (Bridgend, Mid Glamorgan: Poetry Wales Press, 1987);

The Echoes Return Slow (London: Macmillan, 1988).

OTHER: *The Batsford Book of Country Verse*, edited by Thomas (London: Batsford, 1961);

The Penguin Book of Religious Verse, edited by Thomas (Harmondsworth: Penguin, 1963);

Selected Poems of Edward Thomas, edited by Thomas (London: Faber & Faber, 1964);

A Choice of George Herbert's Verse, edited by Thomas (London: Faber & Faber, 1967);

A Choice of Wordsworth's Verse, edited by Thomas (London: Faber & Faber, 1971).

When Rupert Hart-Davis agreed to publish *Song at the Year's Turning* (1955), R. S. Thomas's collection of all his previous poems that he wished to preserve, it was decided that a well-known poetic figure should be asked to draw attention to the volume, and the services of John Betjeman were enlisted. In his dignified and sensitive introduction Betjeman remarked that "the 'name' which has the honour to introduce this fine poet to a larger public will be forgotten long before that of R. S. Thomas." Betjeman, who later became poet laureate (as well as Sir John), may have been excessively modest; nonetheless, R. S. Thomas, at that time barely known outside his native Wales, is now recognized as a prominent voice in British poetry of the second half of the twentieth century. Since David Jones's death in 1974, indeed, he has strong claims to be considered the most important contemporary Anglo-Welsh poet.

Born in Cardiff in 1913 ("begotten in a drab town," as he writes in *The Bread of Truth* [1963]), Ronald Stuart Thomas was educated at Holyhead Grammar School in Anglesey and obtained a B.A. in classics at the University College of North Wales (Bangor) in 1935. After studying theology at St. Michael's College, Llandaff, he was ordained as a deacon in 1936 and as a priest of the Anglican church in the following year. Since then he has served at Chirk, Denbighshire (1936-1940), and in mainly rural parishes, notably at Manafon, Montgomeryshire (1942-1954), Eglwsfach, Cardiganshire (1954-1967), and Aberdaron, originally in Caernarvonshire and now in Gwynedd (1967-1978). He retired in 1978 but still lives locally. He is married to a painter, Mildred Eldridge, and they have one son. His biography, if we ignore his poetic distinction, has been uneventful, and his succession of livings represents a continuing withdrawal to the wilder, more desolate and thinly populated parts of his country. Manafon is a parish made up of "starved pastures" in the central Welsh hill country, Eglwsfach is close to the sea, near the estuary of the river Dovey, while Aberdaron is at the extreme tip of the Lleyn Peninsula in north Wales, one of the most isolated spots in the land.

Song at the Year's Turning, which caused quite a stir on its first appearance in 1955, is subtitled *Poems 1942-1954*, and it is interesting to note that the years in question correspond exactly to the span of his residence at Manafon. But although this volume introduced his work to readers outside Wales, it was in a sense a retrospective collection. His first book, *The Stones of the Field*, privately printed in 1946, had been followed by *An Acre of Land* in 1952 and *The Minister*, a radio play performed on the Welsh BBC a year later. In *Song at the Year's Turning*, Thomas included selections from the first two books, the complete but revised text of *The Minister*, and some more recent poems.

There are four aspects of R. S. Thomas that immediately become noticeable in his poetry: the priest, the poet, the Welshman, the countryman. It is the last that perhaps strikes the reader of his early work most forcibly, though this element in his makeup becomes less conspicuous as his poetic career proceeds. Like Edward Thomas, a fellow Welshman whom he has always admired and a selection of whose poems he edited in 1964, he is one of the urban born who has chosen to live in a rural environment, but his introduction to life in Manafon must nonetheless have been a rude shock. Throughout his life Thomas has been attracted to the poetry of William Wordsworth (again, he demonstrated his admiration by editing *A Choice of Wordsworth's Verse* in 1971), but the harsh landscape in which he found himself in 1942 was very different from the gentle beauties of the Lake District, and the countrymen he met there bore little resemblance to the likes of Michael or Margaret or the leech gatherer.

In Thomas's first volume, *The Stones of the Field*, we are introduced to Iago Prytherch, the laborer about whom Thomas was to write many poems in subsequent volumes. The poet has explained that "A Peasant" was written "after visiting a 1,000 feet up farm in Manafon where I saw a labourer docking swedes in the cold, grey air of a Manafon afternoon," but the poem is not about the joys of living close to the soil. Prytherch is anything but prepossessing on a first encounter. "Just an ordinary man of the bald Welsh hills," he is given "a half-witted grin," his clothes are "sour with years of sweat / And animal contact," and the poet admits: "There is something frightening in the vacancy of his mind." Neither landscape nor countryman is idealized.

Although in another poem Thomas praises "The land's patience and a tree's / Knotted endurance," and although he makes an effort to find admirable qualities in the people who inhabit this countryside, we detect from the start a tension between the poet-priest and his congregation.

Part of this tension is, of course, derived from the religious makeup of his parish. Many of the inhabitants were Methodist by persuasion, and most of the others paid at best a token lip service to the Anglican church. Thomas is enraged not so much at their religious heterodoxy as at their neglect of all spiritual values. While he can understand the materialism of a people that perforce lives barely above subsistence level, he finds it difficult to reconcile this understanding with what must at this time (though it is hardly a characteristic we normally associate with him) have been his religious idealism. In what is in many respects the most directly personal of his poems, "A Priest to his People," he offers a combination of testament and confession that gives vent to his impatience while at the same time it tries to acknowledge the potential heroism of their harsh lives. We can see his anger at their refusal to respond to his ardor—"I whose invective would spurt like a flame of fire / To be quenched always in the coldness of your stare." But he is also anxious to detect a different kind of spiritual satisfaction in their lives, and he tries desperately to recognize "The *artistry* of your dwelling on the bare hill" (italics added). The poem is moving for the personal urgency it communicates, but it is notable also as an example of an intensely local poem that gains universal applicability. Like J. M. Synge, like William Shakespeare in *King Lear*, Thomas can present human life stripped to its basic elements and thereby offer a poignant portrait of "unaccommodated man."

Thomas may be said to pay his debt to these people who "affront, bewilder, yet compel [his] gaze" in one of his few long poems, "The Airy Tomb." Here he presents, sympathetically yet firmly, the day-to-day life of another ordinary man from the bare Welsh hills. Tomos is seen first as an unwilling schoolboy who at the end of his official education "could write and spell / No more than the clouds could"; he returns to help his father on the "gaunt wilderness" of his hill farm and finds the work "play after the dull school." But his father dies, then his mother, and Tomos continues on the farm at the only labor he understands. He lives a hermit-like existence, alone, unmarried because he has learned nothing of love:

> the one language he knew
> Was the shrill scream in the dark, the shadow
> within the shadow,
> The glimmer of flesh, deadly as mistletoe.

Not understood by his neighbors, and so disliked by them, he ekes out a hard existence and meets a hard death, as solitary as his life which, for all its deprivation, was in a strange sense free:

> and a fortnight gone
> Was the shy soul from the festering flesh and
> bone
> When they found him there, entombed in the
> lucid weather.

Tomas was entombed (the word makes one think fleetingly of Christ), but there are perhaps worse prisons than "the lucid weather." This eloquently moving poem ends, then, on a complex irony.

Thomas has been unsparingly critical of his early verse. He omitted almost half of the poems in *The Stones of the Field* from *Song at the Year's Turning*, and only three survive in *Selected Poems 1946-1968* (1973). In "To a Young Poet" (in *The Bread of Truth*) the older Thomas observes:

> You will take seriously those first affairs
> With young poems, but no attachments
> Formed then but come to shame you.

This poem was written at a time when Thomas's poetry was in the process of changing course, and he may well have found the verbal richness of his previous verse increasingly inappropriate. Nonetheless, he displays a remarkable poetic technique in his early poems, upon which the spare effectiveness of his later work also depends. What one first notices is the characteristic intonations of a particular speaking voice manifest in an especially strong accentual beat. An early example is the opening of "Song":

> We, who are men, how shall we know
> Earth's ecstasy, who feels the plough
> Probing her womb,
> And after, the sweet gestation
> And the year's care for her condition?

The attractive jaggedness is caused by the way the verse moves not from poetic foot to poetic foot, as in more conventional prosody, but from one emphatically stressed syllable to the next.

The rhythmic balance within the opening line, the alliterating stresses (faintly suggesting the measures of Anglo-Saxon), the deliberate half-rhymes—all these, characteristic of Thomas—are secondary to the rhetorical force of the accents. So far as his early verse is concerned, these characteristics were to be his poetic trademark.

Another feature of the early poetry, to be severely qualified later, is what Calvin Bedient has described as his "magnificent talent for metaphor" in which Thomas "perhaps excels all English poets since Hopkins." This metaphorical display often manifests itself through adjectives, and it is worth noting at this point that Thomas pays considerable attention to the use of adjectives in English poetry in his W. D. Thomas Memorial Lecture *Words and the Poet* (1964). There he observes: "I consider adjectives to be the mark of the poet as observer, and verbs of the poet as participator." In his early poetry Thomas is most often an observer, and it would not be difficult to add examples from his own verse ("the curious stars," "the night's unscaleable boughs," "the sun-dusted moor") to Thomas's list in that address. More specifically, a metaphorical identification is established between man and the land that he inhabits. Examples abound in the early verse. The human body in general is addressed as "Lean acre of ground that the years master / Though fenced cunningly from wind and cold," and in the particular body of an old man he detects

> the bare boughs of bone,
> The trellised thicket, where the heart, that
>   robin
> Greets with a song the seasons of the blood.

The later Thomas has seemingly renounced this kind of linguistic exuberance, but we recognize it as a luxuriant celebration of language ("words and the poet"), the mastery of which makes the spare directness of subsequent work all the more impressive.

An Acre of Land, introduced by an epigraph in Welsh from the sixteenth-century poet Siôn Tudur, is noticeably more nationalistic in emphasis, with titles such as "The Welsh Hill Country," "Wales," "Song for Gwydion" (a Welsh mythological hero after whom Thomas named his son), "Cynddylan on a Tractor," "Welsh History," "Welsh Landscape." Nationalism is also manifest in erudite references to Welsh legend and story as well as in a dramatic monologue, "The Tree," put into the mouth of Owain Glyn Dŵr. The pre-

dominant tone in the volume is, however, complex. Traces of idealism still remain. "Memories" shows an immediate change of heart towards Prytherch, who is now addressed as "my friend," and Thomas continues:

> I will sing
> The land's praises, making articulate
> Your strong feelings, your thoughts of no
>   date,
> Your secret learning, innocent of books.

But Thomas will later find little to praise in the state of the land. The Welsh references suggest a positive concentration on tradition and heritage; yet Thomas is at the same time aware of the contemporary erosion of that heritage. "Welsh History" embodies this uneasy tension:

> We were a people bred on legends,
> Warming our hands at the red past.
> . . . .
> We were a people, and are so yet.
> When we have finished quarrelling for crumbs
> Under the table, or gnawing the bones
> Of a dead culture, we will arise,
> Armed, but not in the old way.

This mixture of determination and distaste, of muted hopes and dour suggestions of despair, becomes characteristic. In "Welsh Landscape," Thomas argues that there is no present and no future in Wales, "There is only the past": and the Welsh themselves are seen as "an impotent people, / Sick with inbreeding, / Worrying the carcase of an old song."

Thomas seems split between reverence for the old traditions and realization of the need for a new start. A similar tension is to be found in his attitude to the hill people themselves. He can see both the urgency for improvement in material conditions and at the same time the heavy price that will have to be paid for such improvement. The opening of "Cynddylan on a Tractor" is central:

> Ah, you should see Cynddylan on a tractor.
> Gone the old look that yoked him to the soil;
> He's a new man now, part of the machine.

The tone seems positive—indeed, this is the closest one is likely to come in Thomas's verse to the rhythms of approval. No one is likely to yearn nostalgically for the days when a peasant was "yoked . . . to the soil," and "a new man now" has religious as well as material connotations. But "part of the machine" sounds ominous, and "machine" is, in fact, a word that becomes increasingly important in Thomas's poetry, whether used in local, sociopolitical, or even cosmological contexts. The main lines of Thomas's position are by now clear. The relative merits of past and present and the gloomy prospects for the future despite superficial (because merely technological) improvements are all debated and become focal concerns in later volumes.

It is curious to note how rare in these early books are unequivocally religious poems. What we do find, however (perhaps surprisingly in a poet otherwise so preoccupied with rural subjects), is an increasingly intellectual, even philosophical emphasis. As he notes in "Soil," "the hedge defines / The mind's limits," and the comparison between physical and mental landscapes becomes a recurrent device hereafter. One of the features of Thomas's verse that readers gradually come to recognize is the way in which he establishes various key words and concepts at different stages in his poetic development and employs them again and again. As he notes in *Words and the Poet*, "there is probably something symptomatic in words that tend to recur in a poet's work." They come close, indeed, to fulfilling the function of leitmotivs. Like "machine," "mind" is certainly a key word in this volume; together they form the perimeters of his subject matter and express the dichotomies that generate much of his best poetry.

The Minister, which followed hard upon *An Acre of Land*, is an effective play for voices embodying the basic attitudes that Thomas had already expressed elsewhere. It is set in "The marginal land where flesh meets spirit / Only on Sundays," and we can see here the interchangeability of inner and outer landscapes with particular clarity. Furthermore, the insistence that, although the valley may be regarded as an open book, "the green tale / Told in its pages is not true" measures the extent to which Thomas's rural vision has transcended the limits of Romantic Wordsworthianism. The central figure, Rev. Elias Morgan, B.A., is the minister of a dissenting chapel, but his physical and emotional situation is almost identical with Thomas's own. He is a pathetic, poignant figure, never accepted by his flock, never able to raise them from their harsh lives and often insensitive ways. An accepted truce uncomfortably close to hypocritical acquiescence develops. In Morgan's words, "I knew and pretended I didn't / And they knew that I knew and

pretended I didn't." And at the close, in sentiments that echo the earlier "A Priest to his People," Thomas, under the cover of the narrator, attacks

Protestantism—the adroit castrator
Of art; the bitter negation
Of song and dance and the heart's innocent
    joy—
You have botched our flesh and left us only
    the soul's
Terrible impotence in a warm world.

As Roland Mathias has pointed out, the attack here (probably an unfair one) is not on Puritanism but on Protestantism, which makes the remark as much a reflection on Thomas's creed as on that of the Methodist minister. One detects here, and more generally just beneath the surface of Thomas's writings at this time, the evidence of a considerable inner crisis, which affects the tone of his earlier poetry and provides a starting point for the extraordinary intellectual and theological odyssey that manifests itself later.

The remaining poems in *Song at the Year's Turning*, first appearing in that volume, round off the collection and develop some earlier themes. There are more poems about Prytherch, allusions to the "bland philosophy of nature," and further confrontations between the natural world and the human mind. References to Plato, Samuel Taylor Coleridge, and Percy Bysshe Shelley emphasize Thomas's intellectual interests—and, perhaps, his intellectual loneliness. There are, too, a number of poems about God—often an aged, seemingly indifferent God—that anticipate later preoccupations.

At first sight *Poetry for Supper* (1958), following up the success of *Song at the Year's Turning* and dedicated to his publisher, Rupert Hart-Davis, and his sponsor, John Betjeman, seems to offer the same mixture as before. But the atmosphere is decidedly bleaker. Thomas is now especially concerned with the urbanization of Wales—stemming, of course, from England—and the flood of vulgarization that it has brought in its wake. Cynddylan on his tractor is here complemented by "Olwen in nylons." The other side of this particular coin is the depopulation of rural Wales (about which Thomas had written an early prose article) as the male work force is forced or cajoled into the industrialized cities. Thomas protests not merely the break in a traditional pattern of life but the acceptance of an imposed and alien English "culture" on the part of a Welsh population that has lost contact with its own roots. One of the speakers in "Border Blues," the opening poem, is placidly content with an excursion to the English pantomime at Shrewsbury ("It was 'The Babes' this year, all about nature") while another satisfies himself by whistling "tunes / From the world's dancehalls." Thomas as Jeremiah scourging his degraded contemporary countrymen is especially prominent here.

Also prominent is Thomas's increasing concern with the artistic role and problems of the poet—all part of a general turning inward. While there are more poems about Iago Prytherch, who continues to be treated sympathetically, Thomas is all the more aware of the fact that, as a poet, he is himself an intellectual among those who are conscious of no need for intellectualism. "Green Categories" begins: "You never heard of Kant, did you, Prytherch?" And the title poem, which takes the form of a dialogue between "two old poets" discussing their art over beer at an inn, ends not with any adjudication between their viewpoints (basically they represent the age-old rivalry between the respective claims of nature and artifice) but with the awareness that they are both out of place, outmoded, in a noisy environment "glib with prose." Other titles, "Temptation of a Poet," "Death of a Poet," are evidence of Thomas's discovery that his art can be its own subject, and this realization goes along with an uneasy suspicion that his previous material, with its emphasis on traditional ways of life and the values that are being lost, bound him to an excessively easy romanticism. In the first of the poems mentioned, the temptation in question is "to go back," and in the second a dying poet is imagined to have "preferred / The easier rhythms of the heart / To the mind's scansion." Despite the distanced effect ("a poet"), it is difficult not to believe that Thomas has his own poetry in mind; certainly the direction indicated is that which his poetry was about to take.

In *Tares* (1961) the prevalent tone becomes darker still. The balance of the universe has shifted; Thomas can talk no more of "the old triumph / Of nature over the brief violence / Of man." Technology has now rendered such statements not only obsolete but untrue. He can see, even if Prytherch to whom he is speaking cannot, the "cold brain of the machine / That will destroy you and your race." While he never idealizes the harsh life that the traditional peasant was forced to live in the past, Thomas compares it unfavorably with his present lot as

        a servant hired to flog
The life out of the slow soil
Or come obediently as a dog

To the pound's whistle.

And as the situation of the countryman has changed, so has the countryside itself. "I have seen land emptied of Godhead," he writes, implying not (it needs to be stressed) that God is dead—Thomas would have no patience with such clichés—but that he is displaced, unrecognized, denied.

While the same basic preoccupations established in the earlier volumes are here repeated, an interesting new formal development becomes noticeable. No less than ten of the thirty-six poems that compose this book may be classified as either regular or irregular sonnets. Although nowhere is its employment as conspicuous as in *Tares*, a survey of his whole canon reveals that Thomas has a particular and (in terms of the period in which he writes) an unusual interest in the form. It doubtless relates to the didactic preoccupations to which he has readily admitted on more than one occasion. As he notes in *Words and the Poet*, "there is always lurking at the back of my poetry a kind of moralistic or propagandist intention," and the sonnet form as a concise but convenient unit for the expression of a single thought appears well suited to his particular vision. Needless to say, there is no question of Thomas's slavishly imitating what has already been achieved within the sonnet convention. Occasionally his poems follow the regular rules, but more often they are either unrhymed or half-rhymed, and in later books the lines may be basically tetrameter rather than pentameter. The division between octave and sestet, however, is generally maintained. Above all, the sense of unity of thought, of a meditation worked out comfortably and appropriately within the gentle confines of the form (Wordsworth's "scanty plot of ground"), makes these poems sonnetlike for all their superficial deviations from the strict rules.

His next three volumes, *The Bread of Truth*, *Pietà* (1966), and *Not That He Brought Flowers* (1968), must be considered transitional. Although the verse is as accomplished and as eloquent as ever, *The Bread of Truth* shows little extension of range and only a limited development. For the most part, the same preoccupations recur. Wales is once again the subject for a kind of savage elegy, its green grass "not ours" because visitors are "buying us up" ("Looking at Sheep"). In "Strangers" Thomas speaks for an embittered, unfriendly native community addressing those who are intruding into their land: "We don't like your white cottage. / We don't like the way you live." The old Wales seems to be passing once and for all into a now neglected history. But this is only a somewhat more sardonic version of an earlier strain. One cannot help wondering whether his determination, expressed as early as *An Acre of Land*, to "keep to the one furrow" has now become a liability rather than a virtue. Thomas's tendency to repeat himself in theme and approach (the recurring man/land analogy, for example) suggests that his distinctive style is in danger of degenerating into a forecastable mannerism. Although by contrast with *Song at the Year's Turning* these songs can be seen as starker, barer in language and thought, they also seem less impressive, less authoritative. The passionate directness of the earlier poems has given way to a mordant bitterness that, if encountered without the prior will to admire, may appear not far removed from a sour if stoical version of the stiff upper lip. Within the context of Thomas's development as a maturing poet, *The Bread of Truth* lacks—at least at first sight—the excitement of fresh growth.

Nonetheless, with the aid of hindsight it is possible to see evidence here of a significant shift in Thomas's technique that will eventually be found appropriate for the new concerns articulated in his later work. In poems such as the sonnet "This" we find all the stylistic qualities that had flowered in *Song at the Year's Turning*:

> I thought, you see, that on some still night,
> When stars were shrill over his farm,
> And he and I kept ourselves warm
> By an old fire, whose bars were bright
> With real heat, the truth might ripen
> Between us naturally as the fruit
> Of his wild hedges or as the roots,
> Swedes or mangels, he grew then.

That is the R. S. Thomas we have come to expect, and many—indeed most—of the poems here share the same accentual qualities. But a few achieve a very different effect, as the opening lines of "Becoming" illustrate:

> Not for long.
> After the dark
> The dawning.
> After the first light

> The sun.
> After the calm the wind,
> Creasing the water.

Here the spareness of diction that had been increasingly characteristic of Thomas's verse is taken to its extreme. Bedrock directness and simplicity replace verbal luxuriance and emphatic rhythms. And alongside this development we may discern the final stage of a related process. In *Song at the Year's Turning* more than sixty percent of the poems employ rhyme. This percentage declines steadily through *Poetry for Supper* and *Tares* until in *The Bread of Truth* it is barely more than ten percent ("This" belongs to the small minority). Henceforward, rhyme in the strict sense of the word all but disappears, though he continues to employ the occasional internal or dissonantal rhyme within basically unrhymed poems and retains an effect which Robert Duncan has called "rhymes of image" and might also be called conceptual rhyme ("out/in," "book/pages," "birds/flowers"). It is not unreasonable, then, to see *The Bread of Truth* as a pivotal volume between early and late Thomas.

Pietà also faces both ways. The opening poem, "Rhodri," is yet another critical portrait of the modern, deracinated Welshman:

> He has six shirts
> For the week-end and a pocketful
> Of notes. Don't mention roots
> To Rhodri.

But "Because," which follows immediately, sounds a new note:

> The youth enters
> The brothel, and the girl enters
> The nunnery, and a bell tolls.
> Viruses invade the blood.

Moreover, the very title of *Pietà* anticipates the religious preoccupation of Thomas's later poems, even if it suggests a traditionalism that is the reverse of Thomas's spiritual attitude. Thomas has edited *The Penguin Book of Religious Verse* (1963) and *A Choice of George Herbert's Verse* (1967) and is clearly acquainted with the meditational poetry of his predecessors, but his own religious poems face up to the realities of a secular world where faith is difficult and sanctioned conceptions of the holy and the divine no longer seem satisfactory. One of the finest poems in *Pietà* is entitled "In Church," where Thomas characteristically offers the unexpected. The poem is set not during but after a service. "Is this," Thomas asks, "where God hides / From my searching?" Thomas's God is most likely to be found in silence, solitude, and darkness. As priest, he is not a man with an impregnable and bracing faith but rather one who finds religious meaning in doubt, absence, and even betrayal. The poem ends on a note of dour splendor:

> There is no sound
> In the darkness but the sound of a man
> Breathing, testing his faith
> On emptiness, nailing his questions
> One by one to an untenanted cross.

In the last two lines we note a revival of Thomas's earlier metaphorical and adjectival gifts, but they are here subsumed into a new meditational eloquence.

The last of the transitional volumes is *Not That He Brought Flowers*. Here are more poems about Wales (though Prytherch is absent) and a few—not representing Thomas at his best—written as the result of trips to Spain and Scandinavia. And once again there is a series of often effective but at the same time troubling poems ("After the Lecture," "Kneeling") about religious observation and faith or the lack of it. "The meaning," we are told in "Kneeling," "is in the waiting," and we realize with something of a shock that Thomas has moved out of the orbit of Wordsworth and the Romantics into that of Samuel Beckett. And "A Grave Unvisited" ("Soren's grave / In Copenhagen"), recalling a poem entitled simply "Kierkegaard" in *Pietà*, provides a clue to the special, brooding, daunting atmosphere of Thomas's personal Christianity.

His next book of poetry, the curiously titled *H'm* (1972), is to Thomas's later style what *Song at the Year's Turning* is to the earlier. It has a consistency of tone, style, content, and attitude that had not existed in the immediately preceding volumes. *H'm* is unified by a series of poems scattered artfully through the book that offer, as it were, alternative versions of Genesis. Half a dozen such poems, varied in approach and viewpoint—sometimes God is speaking, sometimes Adam—provide the dominant atmosphere, while others involve God, or Thomas's search for God, or present human experience within the context of a religious if often dour presentation of the universe. But the Genesis poems establish the peculiar distinction of the book. In "Once," the opening poem, Adam recalls his first coming to

consciousness, his first awareness of Eve, and the manner in which (although no Fall is adumbrated within this particular version of the myth), they "went forth to meet the Machine." In "Cain" God anoints himself "In readiness for the journey / To the doomed tree you were at work upon." And in "Soliloquy," in which God speaks to himself, a series of creations and destructions are remembered ("I have blundered / Before; the glaciers erased / My error") and we catch a fleeting glimpse, to be explored in later books, of a God who is not only totally misunderstood by his worshippers but who manifests himself through the "nature" not of Romantic Wordsworthians but of twentieth-century scientists:

> Within the churches
> You built me you genuflected
> To the machine. Where will it
> Take you from the invisible
> Viruses, the personnel
> Of the darkness that do my will?

Whether the poems offer the narrative of original myth or the somber meditations of Thomas or Thomas's God, they are unified stylistically or by a beautifully controlled language that is devoid of ornamentation, never rises above the most economical and basic statement, yet at the same time never falls into monotony. The renunciation of his earlier delight in the possibilities of language doubtless connects with his withdrawal from the materialist rat race of the twentieth century, his renunciation of human interchange (beyond his pastoral service to a small parish of simple folk forgotten by the world who understand neither his philosophy nor his anguish) in order to fulfill his lonely vigil, his personal and unimpeded quest for God. His language is as bleak as the countryside in which he lives, as gaunt as his own character, as uncompromising as the God he serves.

Subsequent volumes—*Laboratories of the Spirit* (1975), *The Way of It* (on which he collaborated with the artist Barry Hirst, 1977), and *Frequencies* (1978)—make further exploration of the material treated so consummately in *H'm*. They are not so rigorously focused as *H'm*, and there are occasional returns to the worlds of the Welshman and the countryman that seemed to have been left behind. Again we see the studied repetition of certain key words. "God" and "machine" here exist at the ends of Thomas's spectrum, and the extremes meet appropriately when reference is made in "Perhaps" (*Frequencies*) to "the machinery of God." In between, other significant words are "absence," "prayer" (and its cognates), "waiting," "darkness," "silence," and (the title of two poems, one in *Laboratories of the Spirit*, one in *Frequencies*) "emerging." The opening of the one in *Laboratories of the Spirit* provides an excellent example of the way Thomas can achieve originality while juggling his leitmotivs:

> Not as in the old days I pray,
> God. My life is not what it was.
> Yours, too, accepts the presence of
> the machine?

Moreover, the acknowledgement of change, whether for good or ill, at least relieves the burden of a deadening sameness. Although Thomas's private sentiments appear bleak ("The quality of life is deteriorating everywhere," he told Byron Rogers in an interview), his poetic self—which contains his intellectual, religious self—occasionally hints at redeeming positives. He has become increasingly fascinated with what he considers as the manifestations of God in science. As early as 1966, in "A Frame for Poetry," he had noted that science "has many branches, some of them perhaps poetic in themselves." In "Emerging" he speaks with a seemingly rejuvenated awe: "I begin to recognize / you anew, God of form and number." The "laboratory of the spirit" is the tall city of the scientific future rather than "that snake-haunted / garden" of the mythic past. And it is worth remembering that his continual searching for new ways to probe the problem of how to come to terms with God is itself positive. He differs from Thomas Hardy (whose poems about God—or It—are often brought to mind by Thomas's) in that the divine existence is never called into question; God's ways are acknowledged as inexplicable, given the state of the world, but he is never doubted. For Thomas, indeed, God is almost identifiable with "emerging."

The predominantly gray tone of his later verse is, however, regularly qualified by poems that seem hardly affirmative, perhaps, but at least not depressing. The title of one poem in *H'm* is "Via Negativa," but there are other ways possible. "The Bright Field" (*Laboratories of the Spirit*) is important because it suggests that Thomas's early Wordsworthianism, though tempered by hard experience, is never wholly renounced:

> I have seen the sun break through
> to illuminate a small field

> for a while, and gone my way
> and forgotten it. But that was the pearl
> of great price. . . .

The biblical allusion to Matthew 13:46 is used to describe a natural experience whose effect on Thomas was very like one of Wordsworth's "spots of time." Later in the poem (another unrhymed sonnet) Thomas insists that life is neither a hurrying into the future nor a retreat back into the past but "the turning / aside like Moses to the miracle / of the lit bush." The poem offers evidence of an eternal now, and thus connects with Thomas's statement quoted in the 1972 special issue of *Poetry Wales*: Eternity, he remarked, "is all around us and at any given moment we can pass into it." The simple, natural image of the sun shining upon a field reminds us that, although Thomas hardly ever celebrates natural beauty in his later poetry, it is always present, a revelation that can both satisfy and sustain.

It suggests also that the early and later phases of Thomas's poetic career may not, in fact, be radically different in emphasis. Later commentators on Thomas have tended to underestimate the rural element in his work. Jeremy Hooker, for instance, in the course of a sensitive review of *H'm* in the same issue of *Poetry Wales*, wrote: "Of all the books so far this one offers the least excuse for encapsulating his work in the image still common in England and Wales, of the bleak nature poet taking his stand on the primal sanities of rural Wales. But perhaps that half-truth really is a straw man by now." The remark is valid enough for *H'm* itself, but subsequent volumes qualify the qualification. In the same number Thomas described himself as "a nature mystic" and went on to assert: "Poetry is religion, religion is poetry." Such remarks imply that his various roles as poet, priest, countryman, Welshman are all subordinate parts of a larger unity.

In *Words and the Poet*, written at a time when his earlier "nature poetry" was in the process of giving way to (or blending into) his later religious meditations, Thomas offered a statement on the problem that remains crucial: "The common environment of the majority is an urban-industrial one. The political audience of a poet is one of town dwellers, who are mainly out of touch, if not of sympathy with nature. Their contact with it is modified by the machine. . . . And this is a problem which all poets must face. I don't believe for a moment the superiority of urban to country life. . . . But the fact remains that a very different kind of life is being lived by a majority of the people in this country now, and that most of the everyday objects of their world have new, often technical names. A vast amount of new knowledge is accumulating, with its accompanying vocabulary. One of the great questions facing the poet is: Can significant poetry be made with these new words and terms?" One can see how the later poems were in a sense written as a response to this same challenge. The imagery of nature is played down (not played out) because Thomas needs, like a clergyman preaching an effective sermon, to find an appropriate vocabulary for his contemporaries. God remains the god behind and within nature, but nature itself is offered as "a self-regulating machine / of blood and faeces" ("Rough," *Laboratories of the Spirit*). Yet God also writes "in invisible handwriting the instructions / the genes follow" ("At It," *Frequencies*) and is described as an unseen power "whose sphere is the cell / and the electron" ("Adjustments," *Frequencies*). The vocabulary has changed, but the basic conception of the relation of God to the things of this world has not. And Thomas continues to scatter poems within his books that illustrate the continuity. "The Moor," in *Pietà*, may be taken as a supreme instance. The moorland is "like a church" to him, but a church in which no prayers need be said. An account of another profoundly Wordsworthian experience, the poem shows an achieved unity between creature and creator, between personal and eternal, between the inner mind and the external world. Within the natural silence is revelation:

> What God was there made himself felt,
> Not listened to, in clean colours
> That brought a moistening of the eye,
> In movement of the wind over grass.

God, nature, and the enrapt poet are, for an eternal moment, one.

With the publication of *Frequencies*, it seemed as if the pattern of Thomas's poetic work were clear. But, like his God and the countryside he loves, he is full of surprises, and *Between Here and Now* (1981), while containing a section of "other poems" in which he continues searching the world, the universe, and his own mind for the God who may (or must) hide there, promises to initiate an exciting new phase. The first part, "Impressions," is made up of poems written as commentaries on a number of paintings in the

Louvre, and they appear side by side with black-and-white reproductions of the paintings in question. Each poem accurately transposes the mood of a painting into words, and we can frequently hear the attitudes prominent in his earlier work. So "MONET: The Gare Saint-Lazure" begins:

> The engines
>   are ready to start
> but why travel
>   where they are aimed
> at?

And in "PISSARRO: Landscape at Chaponval" he observes:

> It would be good to live
> in this village with time
> stationary.

Many of the poems both discuss and evoke the beauty of the natural world as it is expressed within the paintings, but art becomes the prime subject for meditation: "Art is recuperation / from time" and "Art is a sacrament / in itself." These are, for Thomas, remarkably placid poems, revealing a poise and assurance that makes this volume his most impressive since *H'm*. It reads as the harvest of his earlier collaborations with John Piper and Barry Hirst, but here poem and painting are fully integrated into a new artistic unity. It is also the harvest of the more positive hints and moments scattered in his later work. But in no way do these poems constitute a withdrawal.

"I keep searching for meaning," he insists, and the search is renewed in his later publications during the 1980s. *Later Poems* (1983) includes a selection from the books published since 1972 and forty-three new poems as crisp as anything he has written. *Destinations* (1985), with its illustrations by Paul Nash, and *Ingrowing Thoughts* (1985), containing poems stimulated by twentieth-century artists, further extend the artistic inquiries that became central in *Between Here and Now*. *Experimenting with an Amen* (1986) is a substantial collection of new poems in the vein of *Laboratories of the Spirit* and *Frequencies*, while in *The Echoes Return Slow* (1988) Thomas breaks new ground. Here prose paragraphs of an autobiographical (albeit distanced and stylized) character are interspersed with haunting, enigmatic, introspective poems that also experiment with an amen by casting up the spiritual accounts of a lifetime. His poetic debate with God and the universe continues in the same terms and is even extended. "Our art is our meaning," he observes in "Sonata" (*Later Poems*); over the past half century R. S. Thomas's art has persistently revealed its meaning and displayed a single-minded personal discipline unrivaled in contemporary British poetry.

References:

A. M. Allchin, " 'Generous as Bread': A Study of the Poetry of R. S. Thomas," *New Blackfriars*, 51 (June 1970): 274-280;

Sandra Anstey, ed., *Critical Writings on R. S. Thomas* (Bridgend, Mid Glamorgan: Poetry Wales Press, 1982);

Calvin Bedient, "R. S. Thomas," in his *Eight Contemporary Poets* (London: Oxford University Press, 1974), pp. 51-68;

A. E. Dyson, "The Poetry of R. S. Thomas," *Critical Quarterly*, 20 (Summer 1978): 5-31;

Dyson, *Yeats, Eliot, and R. S. Thomas: Riding the Echo* (London: Macmillan, 1981);

J. D. Hainsworth, "Extremes in Poetry: R. S. Thomas and Ted Hughes," *English*, 14 (Autumn 1963): 222-230;

Belinda Humfrey, "The Gap in the Hedge: R. S. Thomas's Emblem Poetry," *Anglo-Welsh Review*, 26 (Spring 1977): 49-57;

W. J. Keith, "The Georgians and After," in his *The Poetry of Nature* (Toronto: University of Toronto Press, 1980), pp. 186-195;

James F. Knapp, "The Poetry of R. S. Thomas, *Twentieth Century Literature*, 17 (January 1971): 1-9;

Little Review, special Thomas issue, 13/14 (1980);

Colin Meir, "The Poetry of R. S. Thomas," in *British Poetry Since 1970*, edited by Peter Jones and Michael Schmidt (Manchester: Carcanet Press, 1980), pp. 1-13;

W. Moelwyn Merchant, *R. S. Thomas* (Cardiff: University of Wales Press, 1979);

Merchant, "R. S. Thomas," *Critical Quarterly*, 2 (Winter 1960): 341-351;

Linden Peach, "R. S. Thomas: Dylan's Successor?," in his *The Prose Writings of Dylan Thomas* (London: Macmillan, 1988), pp. 106-129;

D. Z. Phillips, *R. S. Thomas: Poet of the Hidden God: Meaning and Mediation in the Poetry of R. S. Thomas* (London: Macmillan, 1986);

Poetry Wales, special Thomas issue, 7 (Spring 1972);

Poetry Wales, special issue on Thomas's later poetry, 14 (Spring 1979);

Byron Rogers, "The Enigma of Aberdaron," *Sunday Telegraph Magazine*, 7 November 1975, pp. 25-29;

R. George Thomas, "The Poetry of R. S. Thomas," *Review of English Literature*, 3 (October 1962): 85-95;

Thomas, *R. S. Thomas*, with *Andrew Young*, by Leonard Clark, Writers and Their Work, no. 166 (London: Longmans, Green, 1964), pp. 27-43;

J. P. Ward, *The Poetry of R. S. Thomas* (Bridgend, Mid Glamorgan: Poetry Wales Press, 1987).

John Wain

(14 March 1925 -   )

This entry was written by Augustus M. Kolich (Pennsylvania State University) for
DLB 15: British Novelists, 1930-1959: Part Two.

See also the Wain entry in DLB 27: Poets of Great Britain and Ireland, 1945-1960.

BOOKS: *Mixed Feelings* (Reading, Berkshire: Reading University School of Art, 1951);

Hurry on Down (London: Secker & Warburg, 1953); republished as *Born in Captivity* (New York: Knopf, 1954);

Living in the Present (London: Secker & Warburg, 1955; New York: Putnam's, 1960);

A Word Carved on a Sill (London: Routledge, 1956; New York: St. Martin's Press, 1956);

Preliminary Essays (London: Macmillan, 1957; New York: St. Martin's Press, 1957);

The Contenders (London: Macmillan, 1958; New York: St. Martin's Press, 1958);

A Travelling Woman (London: Macmillan, 1959; New York: St. Martin's Press, 1959);

Gerard Manley Hopkins: An Idiom of Desperation (London: Oxford University Press, 1959; Darby, Pa.: Folcroft Editions, 1974);

Nuncle and Other Stories (London: Macmillan, 1960; New York: St. Martin's Press, 1961);

A Song about Major Eatherly (Iowa City: Quara Press, 1960);

Weep Before God: Poems (London: Macmillan, 1961; New York: St. Martin's Press, 1961);

Strike the Father Dead (London: Macmillan, 1962; New York: St. Martin's Press, 1962);

Sprightly Running: Part of an Autobiography (London: Macmillan, 1962; New York: St. Martin's Press, 1963);

Essays on Literature and Ideas (London: Macmillan, 1963; New York: St. Martin's Press, 1963);

The Living World of Shakespeare: A Playgoer's Guide (London: Macmillan, 1964; New York: St. Martin's Press, 1964);

The Young Visitors (London: Macmillan, 1965; New York: Viking, 1965);

Wildtrack: A Poem (London: Macmillan, 1965; New York: Viking, 1965);

The Young Visitors (London: Macmillan, 1965; New York: Viking, 1965);

Death of the Hind Legs and Other Stories (London: Macmillan, 1966; New York: Viking, 1966);

Arnold Bennett (New York: Columbia University Press, 1967);

The Smaller Sky (London: Macmillan, 1967);

Letters to Five Artists (London: Macmillan, 1969; New York: Viking, 1970);

A Winter in the Hills (London: Macmillan, 1970; New York: Viking, 1970);

The Life Guard (London: Macmillan, 1971);

The Shape of Feng (London: Covent Garden Press, 1972);

A House for the Truth: Critical Essays (London: Macmillan, 1972; New York: Viking, 1973);

Samuel Johnson (London: Macmillan, 1974; New York: Viking, 1975);

Feng (London: Macmillan, 1975; New York: Viking, 1975);

A John Wain Selection, edited by Geoffrey Halson (London: Longman, 1977);

Professing Poetry (London: Macmillan, 1977; abridged edition, New York: Viking, 1978);

The Pardoner's Tale (London: Macmillan, 1978; New York: Viking, 1979);

King Caliban and Other Stories (London: Macmillan, 1978);

Poems: 1949-1979 (London: Macmillan, 1982);

Young Shoulders (London: Macmillan, 1982);

Mid-week Period Return: Home Thoughts of a Native (Stratford-upon-Avon: Celandine Press, 1982);

Frank (Oxford: AmberLane Press, 1984);

Dear Shadows (London: Murray, 1986);

Open Country (London: Hutchinson, 1987);

Where the Rivers Meet (London: Hutchinson, 1988);

Comedies (London: Hutchinson, 1990).

OTHER: *Contemporary Reviews of Romantic Poetry*, edited by Wain (London: Harrap, 1953; New York: Barnes & Noble, 1953);

Interpretations: Essays on Twelve English Poems, edited by Wain (London: Routledge, 1955; New York: Hillary House, 1957);

John Wain

International Literary Annual, volume 1, edited by Wain (London: Calder, 1959; New York: Criterion, 1959);

International Literary Annual, volume 2, edited by Wain (London: Calder, 1960; New York: Criterion, 1960);

Fanny Burney's Diary, edited by Wain (London: Folio Society, 1960);

Anthology of Modern Poetry, edited by Wain (London: Hutchinson, 1963);

Selected Shorter Poems of Thomas Hardy, edited by Wain (London: Macmillan, 1966; New York: St. Martin's Press, 1966);

Thomas Hardy, *The Dynasts*, edited by Wain (London: Macmillan, 1966; New York: St. Martin's Press, 1966);

Selected Shorter Stories of Thomas Hardy, edited by Wain (London: Macmillan, 1966; New York: St. Martin's Press, 1966);

Shakespeare: Macbeth, A Casebook, edited by Wain (London: Macmillan, 1968);

Shakespeare: Othello, A Casebook, edited by Wain (London & Boston: Routledge, 1973);

Lives of the English Poets: A Selection, edited by Wain (London: Dent, 1975; New York: Dutton, 1975);

Johnson on Johnson: A Selection of the Personal and Autobiographical Writings of Samuel Johnson, edited by Wain (London: Dent, 1976; New York: Dutton, 1976);

An Edmund Wilson Celebration, edited by Wain (Oxford: Phaidon Press, 1978);

The Seafarer, translated from the Anglo-Saxon by Wain (Warwick: Grenville Press, 1980);

Everyman's Book of English Verse, edited by Wain (London: Dent, 1981).

A writer of novels, short stories, poetry, and criticism, John Barrington Wain was born in Stoke-on-Trent, Staffordshire, to a dentist, Arnold A. Wain, and his wife, Anne. After attending high school in Newcastle-under-Lyme, John Wain went on to St. John's College, Oxford, where he received a B.A. in 1946. Staying on as Fereday Fellow at Oxford (1946-1949), Wain was granted an M.A. in 1950 and has been an instructor at his alma mater. Wain's first marriage, to Marianne

JOHN WAIN, a graduate of St. John's College, Oxford, taught for a time at Reading University and at Oxford. He is a leading member of the outspoken and articulate group of young British writers. His book of poems *A Word Carved on a Sill*, and his recently published novel, *The Contenders*, won critical acclaim on both sides of the Atlantic. In 1957, he visited the United States on behalf of the *Observer*, to conduct a series of interviews with American men of letters, and in 1958 he received the Somerset Maugham Award, for travel abroad. He is presently living in the United States and will visit Yugoslavia and Greece later this year.

Dust jacket for Wain's 1959 novel about an intricate web of infidelity among five people

Urmstrom in 1947, ended in 1956, and he married Eirian James in 1960. He has three children.

In his autobiography, *Sprightly Running* (1962), Wain recounts several childhood episodes of fear and anxiety involving boys who terrorized him. The stories sound real enough, painful enough, and familiar enough, but more than this, they help explain what may be Wain's central, thematic preoccupation in his writing: the survival of the individual with dignity and purpose in a world that is always conspiring to bully and dominate. Wain describes, with some remorse and shame, the "combination of protective colouring, lackeying, and sheer evasiveness" that he had to assume in order to avoid the terrible punishments of rougher boys, and he concludes that these lessons in "manhood" left their mark on him: "my childhood taught me very effectively to understand the nature of totalitarianism. I felt able to enter imaginatively into the world of any modern dictatorship. . . . But the atmosphere of treacheries and loyalties, the same feeling that power, the naked lust to dominate, is the mainspring of life." If "naked lust to dominate" forms the instinctual "mainspring of life," then the individual must either adapt to and be seduced into

a meaningless conformity by the pressures from society and his own obedient superego, or he may fight and be driven into conflicts that will probably prove to be dangerous and destructive. Wain's heroes usually fight, and this is why, early in the 1950s, Wain was branded one of the "angry young men" of English letters, along with John Braine and Kingsley Amis. Although Wain never liked the title, or any reductive title for that matter, anger and defiance seem to be just descriptions for the satirical, social attacks to which Wain seems so committed. His reputation as a literary maverick was enhanced in 1953 when he introduced new writers, such as Philip Larkin and Kingsley Amis, in a BBC production called "First Reading."

In Wain's criticism of contemporary English society, his target is clearly the totalitarian consciousness that has as its object the manipulation and domination of the small child in all of us— that part of our self-concept that naturally sees through folly and pretense and always expects to be left uncontrolled and free. Hence, Wain's fiction is above all morally pledged to a set of values that aim at offending the status quo, when it seems either silly, absurd, or oppressive, and

Dust jacket for the American edition of Wain's 1970 novel about a philologist who becomes embroiled in the working-class conflicts of a small Welsh town

championing commonsense individualism, whenever it can be championed in a world of anti-heroes.

At the same time, Wain is not a political ideologue, and his great dislike for the "Beat industry" of the 1950s reflects his conservative intellectual tendencies. Finding poets such as Allen Ginsberg to be New Left "ad men" for the "journalistic machine," Wain has continually attacked didactic or politically motivated literature that tries to create a cause or define a social movement. The meshing of journalism and contemporary fiction is for him an abhorrence that has worked to undermine the universality of literary significance; for Wain, neither fiction nor poetry can be too tightly tied to transient political problems if these genres are to flourish perennially. In his essay "Forms in Contemporary Literature," Wain outlines his ideal novelist: "The pure novelist, to come back to our thread, writes fiction that is intended to be taken as fiction; its relevance to actual life is not less, but more, than that of documentary fiction, since its engagement with experience is at a much deeper level. Both author and reader step back from the limelight; the relation-

ship between them is no longer a matter of simple give-and-take; this is life, and they are sharing in the experience of contemplating it." The magic of literature itself must be revered, and in Wain's canon of literary propriety there is no room for the celebrity author who wants the "limelight" on himself rather than the excellence of his art. Wain seems to long for the time in literary history when "the fast-talking, self-boosting fake" was scorned, for an age, such as Samuel Johnson's, when there existed "a literary conscience; to gain a reputation that passed in current London, it was at least necessary to do *something*" (Wain's italics). In a complicated way, Wain praises the existence of universities, as Saul Bellow does in America, because they provide "the pure novelist" a place where he can go about the business of establishing the truth about humanity, undisturbed and unbothered by the demands of a public market. As an Oxford don, Wain feels free to live out the dream of many of his heroes, never to surrender to the prevailing cultural trends that threaten to subvert individual liberty.

Wain's iconoclasm is thus derived from a privately felt moral sense of self-determination, a con-

John Wain (photograph by Mark Gerson)

cept that he hopes can be shared by a community of equals, scholars and artists, working toward "the establishment of a hierarchy of quality." But part of the problem of establishing any hierarchy is first establishing standards for judgment that can be agreed upon by equals. Obviously, Wain ascribes to F. R. Leavis's notion of the Great Tradition and to the idea that in the best literature "certain human potentialities are nobly celebrated." And a prerequisite for this celebration is Leavis's belief that good men of honor and reason, morally cultivated by a proper upbringing and education, can come to a shared consensus on both the meaning and value of literature: "Literary criticism is the discussion, between equals, of works of literature, with a view to establishing common ground on which judgments of value can be based."

One imagines that Wain has always wanted to be a critical equal to such men as his mentor, William Empson, about whom Wain writes: "He has never used his critical powers to attack any great writer. On the contrary, every work he has discussed has been effectually upgraded by his treatment, even where he makes no overt judgment of value. The reader has been left with an en-

hanced feeling for its beauty and significance." In his preface to *Essays on Literature and Ideas* (1963), Wain continues on this tack of professing faith in reverential readings of the masters by describing his own critical aspirations and satisfactions with the words of another of his critical heroes, John Middleton Murry, who praised the "mystery" of reading great literature and feeling the "moment when, as though unconsciously and out of my control, the deeper rhythm of a poet's work, the rise and fall of the great moods which determined what he was and what he wrote, enter into me also." The basis of Wain's critical judgments thus resides in his devotion to the idea that the study of the best literature that has been written can provide the criteria for the best judgments. Although he is not a theorist advocating a specific approach to literature, Wain does seem adamantly committed to the mystery of literary truths that can advance the universal human experience; he is an iconoclast who is uncompromising in his dedication to the belief that in a world where "destruction and disintegration" are the norm, only the artist's creative language can clear the ruins and establish a foundation for heroic individualism.

This stress on individual sensibility and heroism is the mainstay of Wain's fiction. Many of his stories concern the plight of the social misanthrope, usually a well-educated but disillusioned young man, who must struggle against his parents and friends and their demands that he conform to the recognizable standards of social behavior. Charles Lumley in *Hurry on Down* (1953) is running away from "the strait-jacket of his upbringing," always fearful that he might become "a parasite on the world he detested." Nevertheless, Lumley must make moral sacrifices, even while attempting to break the mold of the class-conscious British society, and his efforts as hero (or antihero) often end in disaster and irony. *Hurry on Down* established Wain's reputation as a member of the "angry decade," as he came to be identified with his hero. Walter Allen writes that this novel made Wain "the satirist of this period of social change. . . ."

The theme of disillusioned hero was to remain a trademark of Wain's fiction. Jeremy Coleman in *Strike the Father Dead* (1962) becomes a jazz pianist in defiance of a father he hates, the professor of classics who embodies the generation of cultural expectations and values that Jeremy must angrily ignore. In the process of breaking away from the confines of economic

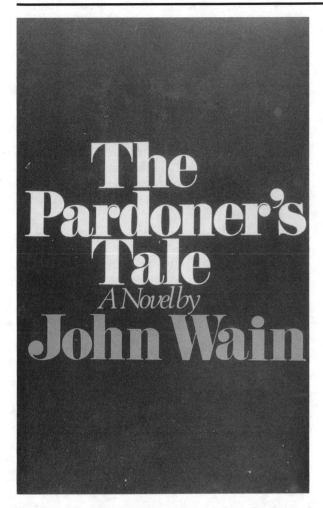

Dust jacket for Wain's 1980 novel, which fuses the stories of two men whose lives are altered by chance meetings with enthralling women

and social success and the seductive powers of competitive capitalism, Wain's heroes still must face the unsettling business of reordering their lives outside the conventional set plans that either religion or business might offer. They still must satisfy the basic needs not only for food, shelter, and love, but for personal fulfillment as well. Very often, though, they seem lost and unable to cope with the shifting emotional currents generated by those toward whom they feel drawn. Although in most of Wain's novels love seems to offer the only answer to the problem of cultural alienation, his women often appear to be incomprehensible and unattainable for Wain's heroes. In *The Pardoner's Tale* (1978), Giles Hermitage, a successful novelist, is spiritually shattered when his wife leaves him for another man. As a result, Giles writes a novel trying to create a vision of his perfect woman in a fictional romance, only to meet such a woman, Dinah, in actual life and even-

tually to lose her also to another man. Giles is humiliated and defeated when he realizes that he has frightened Dinah away by projecting his imagined fantasies of perfection on her; the only thing they seem to have in common is sex, which, like alcohol, provides escape but no deliverance from the problems of life.

Perhaps the most typical of Wain's novels in terms of themes and characters is *A Winter in the Hills* (1970). Roger Furnivall, a philologist, and by extension a member of the effete intellectual class, decides to move to North Wales to study Welsh, only to be enmeshed in a local struggle of small bus owners in conflict with the brutal forces of capitalistic exploitation. Dic Sharp, the capitalist bully and villain, is trying to buy out all the one-man bus companies in the district so that he can establish a monopoly in that service. Only one bus owner, Gareth, is left unbought, and Roger signs on as an unpaid fare collector in order to champion the cause. At first the educated and well-bred Roger is not accepted by the working-class Welsh, who naturally see him as the ineffectual outsider who is not good for much—a situation that nearly all of Wain's heroes face. But slowly they warm to him when they understand the extent of his commitment. Dic Sharp sends his henchmen to brutalize Roger, first by throwing red paint at his front door, then by loosening a wheel on his car (causing an accident that nearly kills him and that he cannot afford), and finally by beating him up. The problem for Sharp is that if he cannot add Gareth's bus to his collection, the larger transit company to which he plans to sell the local monopoly will default on the agreement altogether. So when Sharp finally gives up, as all bullies supposedly do at the first sign of real opposition, he sells all the buses back to their original owners, and the struggle for individual rights and freedom is won unequivocally.

In the end, truth and beauty do seem to have their rewards in Wain's novels, but what prevents these stories from falling into melodrama is Wain's careful handling of character and humor. For instance, Roger Furnivall is a man of obvious limitations, but he remains realistically admirable to the reader who comes to judge him in total, the good man in search of the morally just action that will produce the best in himself and his world. But mixed with this notion is the sense that "life is tragic, because humanity is made up of contradictions," and so Wain's characters grow all the more believable and empathetic as a result of their "contradictions."

Wain describes the condition of many of his heroes by describing himself in his autobiography: "As for me, I have long recognized myself as a participator. I am the sort of person who rushes headlong at life, collides with it, and gets hurt. But the hurt of staying away, the dull ache of standing by and seeing life go past without you, is worse than the shock of participation. Let me be where the action is thickest, whatever the cost! Not that I enjoy getting hurt. If I knew of any armour, I would buckle it on. But the only armour I know of, and it is not a very stout one, is a basic stoicism that prevents one from crying out too petulantly against one's fate." As a teacher, scholar, critic, biographer, poet, and novelist, Wain seems well established as a leading "participator" in contemporary British literature.

Bibliography:

Dale Salwak, *John Braine and John Wain: A Reference Guide* (Boston: G. K. Hall, 1980).

References:

Walter Allen, "War and Post War: British," in his *Tradition and Dream: The English and American Novel from the Twenties to Our Time* (London: Phoenix House, 1964);

Anthony Burgess, "A Sort of Rebels," in his *The Novel Now: A Guide to Contemporary Fiction* (New York: Norton, 1967);

G. S. Fraser, *The Modern Writer and His World* (Baltimore: Penguin, 1964);

David Gerard, *My Work as a Novelist: John Wain* (Cardiff, Wales: Drake Educational Associates, 1978);

James J. Gindin, *Postwar British Fiction: New Accents and Attitudes* (Berkeley & Los Angeles: University of California Press, 1962);

Dale Salwak, *John Wain* (Boston: G. K. Hall, 1981).

Fay Weldon

(22 September 1931 -   )

This entry was written by Harriet Blodgett (University of California, Davis) for
DLB 14: British Novelists Since 1960: Part Two.

BOOKS: *The Fat Woman's Joke* (London: Mac-
Gibbon & Kee, 1967); republished as . . .
And the Wife Ran Away (New York: McKay,
1968);

Down Among the Women (London: Heinemann,
1971; New York: St. Martin's Press, 1972);

Words of Advice [play] (London & New York:
French, 1974);

Female Friends (London: Heinemann, 1975; New
York: St. Martin's Press, 1975);

Remember Me (London: Hodder & Stoughton,
1976; New York: Random House, 1976);

Words of Advice [novel] (New York: Random
House, 1977); republished as *Little Sisters*
(London: Hodder & Stoughton, 1978);

Praxis (London: Hodder & Stoughton, 1978;
New York: Summit, 1978);

Puffball (London: Hodder & Stoughton, 1980;
New York: Summit, 1980);

Watching Me, Watching You (London: Hodder
& Stoughton, 1981; New York: Summit,
1981);

The President's Child (London: Hodder & Stoughton, 1982; Garden City, N.Y.: Doubleday,
1983);

The Life and Loves of a She-Devil (London: Hodder
& Stoughton, 1983; New York: Pantheon,
1984);

Letters to Alice on First Reading Jane Austen (London: Joseph, 1984; New York: Taplinger,
1985);

Rebecca West (London & New York: Viking,
1985);

The Shrapnel Academy (London: Hodder &
Stoughton, 1986; New York: Viking, 1987);

The Rules of Life (London: Hutchinson, 1987;
New York: Harper & Row, 1987);

The Hearts and Lives of Men (London: Heinemann, 1987; New York: Viking, 1988);

The Heart of the Country (London: Hutchinson,
1987; New York: Viking, 1988);

Leader of the Band (London: Hodder & Stoughton, 1988; New York: Viking, 1989);

Sacred Cows (London: Chatto & Windus, 1989);

Fay Weldon (photograph by Jerry Bauer)

The Cloning of Joanna May (London: Collins,
1989; New York: Viking, 1990);

Darcy's Utopia (London: Collins, 1990; New York:
Viking, 1991);

Moon Over Minneapolis, or, Why She Couldn't Stay
(London: Collins, 1991); published as *Moon
Over Minneapolis* (New York: Penguin,
1992);

Life Force (New York: Viking, 1992);

Growing Rich (London & New York: Harper-
Collins, 1992).

PLAY PRODUCTIONS: *Permanence* (in *Mixed Doubles: An Entertainment on Marriage*), London, Comedy Theatre, 9 April 1969;

Words of Advice, Richmond (England), Orange Tree Theatre, 1 March 1974;

Friends, Richmond, Orange Tree Theatre, April 1975;

Moving House, Farnham, Redgrave Theatre, 9 June 1976;

Mr. Director, Richmond, Orange Tree Theatre, 24 March 1978;

Action Replay, Birmingham Repertory Studio Theatre, 22 February 1979;

I Love My Love, Exeter, Northcott Theatre, February 1981;

After the Prize, New York, Phoenix Theater, November 1981; produced as *Woodworm*, Melbourne, Australia, Playbox Theatre, March 1983.

TELEVISION: *The Fat Woman's Tale*, Granada, 1966;

Wife in a Blond Wig, BBC, 1966;

Office Party, Thames, 1970;

"On Trial" (episode of *Upstairs, Downstairs*), London Weekend Television, 1971;

Hands, BBC, 1972;

Poor Baby, ATV, 1975;

The Terrible Tale of Timothy Bagshott, BBC, 1975;

Aunt Tatty, adaptation of the Elizabeth Bowen short story, BBC, 1975;

Married Love, BBC, 1977;

Pride and Prejudice, adaptation of the Jane Austen novel, BBC, 1980;

"Watching Me, Watching You" (episode of *Leap in the Dark*), BBC, 1980;

Life for Christine, Granada, 1980;

Little Miss Perkins, London Weekend Television, 1982;

Loving Women, Granada, 1983;

The Wife's Revenge, BBC, 1983;

The Life and Loves of a She-Devil, BBC, 1986;

The Cloning of Joanna May, Granada, 1991.

RADIO: *Spider*, BBC-3, 1972;

Housebreaker, BBC-3, 1973;

Mr. Fox and Mr. First, BBC-3, 1974;

The Doctor's Wife, BBC-4, 1975;

Polaris, ABC, 1977;

"Weekend" (episode of *Just Before Midnight*), BBC-4, 1979;

All the Bells of Paradise, BBC-4, 1979.

Fay Weldon, who is also a successful stage, radio, and television playwright, established her reputation as a novelist by writing tart, intelligent, and often comic fictions about the lives and natures of women. A satirist with a sharp sense of the ridiculous, adept at wry humor and witty prose, she has the feminist urge to improve women's attitudes toward themselves and their sisters and an imagination fertile in finding unusual embodiments for her independent attitudes and unsentimental values.

Born in the village of Alvechurch in Worcestershire, Weldon was to continue a family tradition with her writing. Her father, Frank Thornton Birkinshaw, was a physician, but her mother, Margaret Jepson Birkinshaw, published two light novels in the 1930s under her maiden name. Weldon's grandfather Edgar Jepson, a turn-of-the-century editor of *Vanity Fair*, was a prolific writer of best-seller romances of adventure until the 1930s; her uncle, Selwyn Jepson, wrote mystery-thriller novels and films, as well as radio and television plays, until the 1970s. During early childhood Weldon emigrated to New Zealand with her parents, where she later attended Girls' High School in Christchurch. From the time she was six, when her parents were divorced, she lived with her mother and sister, seeing her father only during summer holidays—a circumstance reflected in her books in the preponderance of daughters reared by mothers alone. Upon her mother's receiving a small legacy, just sufficient for fare, Weldon returned to England, at age fourteen, to live in London: by her account, a period of "hardship and deprivation" in her life. It was also an intensification of living in a household of women, now with her grandmother as well as her mother and sister, besides attending a convent school, Hampstead High School in London—all of which made her feel that "the world was composed of women." She later theorized that experiencing so female a milieu since childhood had made her forever independent of the need for male approbation, hence able to write more openly and honestly. Her environment no doubt also contributed to the diminished role men play in her books. In 1949 she entered St. Andrews University in Scotland, on a scholarship, and by 1952 had earned her M.A. in economics and psychology.

By 1955 she had borne her first son, Nicholas, and was to know the hardship of supporting him by herself. The unwed mother would also be a recurrent figure in her novels. Weldon has said, "I am all of them [my characters] to some degree," in that she has herself known the frustrations, helplessness, feelings of compromise and desperation she has depicted in them. But even more specifically, she has pointed out that one unwed mother, twenty-year-old Scarlet of her novel *Down Among the Women* (1971), is partly "a portrait of me when I was younger, a mess . . . totally and completely," and that like Scarlet she too had a bout with psychoanalysis (though during her own thirties). Other of her experiences would become her characters' too. By the 1950s Weldon had already tried writing novels, but in desultory fashion and only resulting in rejection slips for them. With no particular professional ambitions as yet, in another period of "odd jobs and hard times," she drifted first into writing propaganda for the Foreign Office, then into doing market research and answering problem letters for the London *Daily Mirror*, and, finally, into composing advertising copy. She worked her way up to more prestigious firms and continued in advertising until the 1970s. Meanwhile, she remained close to her family. When her sister died of cancer in 1969, leaving three children, Weldon assisted her mother in rearing them.

In 1960 she had married Ronald Weldon, a London antique dealer, to whom she would bear three sons (Daniel, in 1963; Thomas, in 1970; and Samuel, in 1977). The Weldons settled in Primrose Hill, a conventional North London suburb where they would live for some fifteen years. Weldon successfully combined domesticity with her ever-expanding writing career, which really began only in the mid 1960s. Her marriage, she felt, had finally given a focus to a life "messed up hopelessly until I met my husband." Ever the woman to make her own decisions about feminist issues, she would later refuse to wear a wedding ring, regarding such banding as a symbolic insult to women; but she would delight in the title "Mrs.," declare herself in many ways conventionally female, and refuse to subscribe to the notion that it would be a better world for women without men. Without them, she would much later insist, "one misses the richness of life . . . the vibes that men radiate . . . make them essential." So conventional did she seem as devoted wife and mother, despite her career, that she was invited to participate in a David Frost debate in 1971, on the assumption that she would mock the radical agitators who were currently in the English news for denouncing the Miss World contest as a flesh market. Instead she disrupted the program by

hailing their efforts. Even had the Frost researchers troubled to read her first—and feminist—novel, already published by then, before inviting her to speak, they could not have predicted her stand. In another characteristic anecdote, while working in the 1970s on a program about rape that brought her in contact with some of the women's movement's more ardent spokeswomen, she decided that they were "without doubt very dedicated women," who, had they been men, would "all have been rapists."

Already one of the most successful advertising copywriters in England, by the late 1960s Weldon was also well advanced in her career as script (and later scenario) writer and playwright. Her one-act *Permanence* was part of a multiact play on the theme of married life, *Mixed Doubles*, which included other such distinguished contributors as Harold Pinter and was produced in London at the Comedy Theatre in 1969. There would later be seven other one-acts, and longer plays as well. And there would be radio plays, such as *Spider* (1972), which won the Writer's Guild Award for Best Radio Play in 1973; and *Polaris* (1977), which won the Giles Cooper Award for Best Radio Play in 1978. For the BBC and English commercial networks, she would write more than fifty television plays (plus films) on a wide range of subjects; for American television, a film on migrant workers. In 1971 and 1972 she wrote two episodes for the *Upstairs, Downstairs* series, the first of which, "On Trial," won the SFTA Award for Best Series. Her five-part dramatization of *Pride and Prejudice* (1980) has been praised for its fidelity to Jane Austen's manner and perceptions.

Television writing proved to be Weldon's entry into fiction. Her first novel, the seriocomic *Fat Woman's Joke* (1967), was originally written as a television play (*The Fat Woman's Tale*, Granada, 1966) and then extended into a novel. But it is a skillful, if minor, work whose humor critics admired and which introduces some of Weldon's typical themes and methods. Middle-aged, tubby Esther (who will triumph without losing a pound) has left her paunchy husband, Alan, in the aftermath of their ill-advised crash diet to regain something of their youthful selves. While he continues to philander with his slim, young secretary Susan, Esther retreats to a dingy basement apartment, where she gorges herself and testily parades her marital woes before the younger friend, Phyllis, who has sought her out. Although Esther's mother, eighteen-year-old son, and Susan also visit this ironic Job to urge her back to her husband, Esther assents only after he enters his plea too. Meanwhile, she has had somewhat of a rebirth of personality while vegetating underground, imaged by the sprouting of a potted plant—Weldon often reinforces themes with symbolic objects and names, traditional analogies and myths. Esther's too omniscient reminiscence of the past month is told for her by a narrator, and dialogue, as always in Weldon's novels, preponderates. The narrator rather awkwardly interleaves in Esther's tale a separate account of the love lives of Susan's roommate and Susan, who finally prefers the son to his father.

Stout and aging in a world where youthful looks count, Esther conveys Weldon's fervent resentment of the devaluation of woman to a brainless, sexual object, a pretty and docile doll. Phyllis readily betrays her absent friend to sleep with Alan and be praised for fitting that category because she finds her self-respect (like most women) only in men's desire for her; like husband-stalking Susan, she has no sense of loyalty to women. Weldon in her novels will not tolerate such lack of sisterhood. Esther, whose sexuality has waned and in whom a more valid basis for self-respect is struggling to emerge, has seen (like Weldon) that it is a "fearful thing to be a woman in a man's world accepting masculine values" when "their opinion of womankind is . . . conditioned by fear, resentment and natural feelings of inferiority." But acknowledging women's woes while denying the right to self-indulgence over them is the distinguishing trait of a Weldon novel. Weldon will have no basking in self-pity, as Esther tries to do, or putting all the blame on men; women share in ruining lives, including their own. The domestic squabbles of Esther and Alan are designed to expose both sides of the story. Whether Esther, like the reader, recognizes all the ways in which she has denied Alan's needs, trammeled her energies, and reduced her marriage to gourmet meals is not entirely clear; later Weldon heroines will be more explicit about their blameworthiness. What Esther does recognize clearly is that she needs her marriage—one of "those human organizations that stand between us and chaos." The marriages Weldon depicts are usually, if not invariably, failures in communion of spirit even when they occasionally succeed as sexual outlets, but Weldon does not scorn marriage in her novels. Life is so imperfect, we need whatever defenses against chaos we

can find. Her heroines are to find a variety of them.

When she wrote *The Fat Woman's Joke*, Weldon claimed to have no knowledge of a women's movement. By the time of her more elaborately structured second novel, the satiric yet compassionate *Down Among the Women*, she evidently did. A meditation on contemporary womanhood and an illustration of it, through glimpses into the lives of the semi-autobiographical Scarlet, her family, and her four girlfriends, this book is told at the beginning and end and occasionally in between by a first-person, reminiscent narrator, who elsewhere lapses into third person. The "I" is Scarlet's friend Jocelyn, who serves as a persona for Weldon (and has been given her Foreign Office experience). *Down Among the Women* takes its title from the refrain starting most of the chapters, which is the theme song of devastating introductory passages of commentary on the female condition. Enlivened by pointed jokes, anecdotes, and cross-patter as well—Weldon is always uninhibited about the form of the novel—these illusion-breaking, but clever, chapter introductions convey her feministic themes more effectively than her narrative, where the main story of Scarlet and her family is encumbered by Scarlet's too sketchily portrayed friends. We meet them and Scarlet's stepmother, Susan, still "down among the girls," rather than the women, and yet to learn that the great enemy is not just men, but existence, which tends to chaos and cancer. They are "down" because they are the preliberation females of the 1950s, still subjugated to subordinate roles and general inconsequence. But "down" is also both a lament for women, who have only a "brief dance in the sun" before going "down into the darkness" of domestic stupor, and a tart reprimand to them for living "at floor level" and looking upward only "to dust the tops of the windows. We have only ourselves to blame." However, the narrator optimistically (if ironically) envisions a brave new woman evolving, and Weldon shows such evolution working its way through three generations of Scarlet's family.

Most impressive is Scarlet's mother—feisty, middle-aged Wanda—an ex-communist and a feminist before her time, who was independent enough to leave her artist-husband, Kim, (during Scarlet's childhood) for prostituting his talent, even if it meant poverty. Wanda explicitly pities, rather than hates, men, like the narrator, who finds the male creature "not so much wicked as

Dust jacket for Weldon's 1975 novel about the web of relationships in which three women are entangled

frail" and depicts him accordingly. Kim, to Scarlet's distress (she wants her father for herself), marries her peer Susan, whom pregnant Scarlet, to comic effect, bilks of her lying-in quarters. Reared by Wanda to believe in sexual freedom, untidy Scarlet, to Wanda's chagrin, produces a bastard daughter, Byzantia, and, still in search of a father (though now more for Byzantia), marries an impotent old man, whom she later divorces. Scarlet and her friends constitute the youth of the 1950s discovering rebellion against the strictures of the past, if not against their need of men. Not so Byzantia, who becomes the nihilistic young woman developed by the 1960s, a self-assured radical intent on tearing down "the old order" of women by the 1970s. Byzantia cannot fancy seeing success in terms of men, the "symptom . . . of a fearful disease from which you all suffered," not that she can name the disease. Weldon finds glib Byzantia frightening in her single-mindedness. Freedom is not so simple as Byzantia assumes—inspiration for Weldon's next book. Critics admired this novel for its witty lines and richly varied comic effects. Since they also thought it discerning and clever in its version of the female condition, they began hailing Weldon as a valuable addition to the feminist cadre.

In 1974 Weldon saw the one-act *Words of Advice*, her second play on marital life, performed and the next year published her substantial, better-focused third novel, *Female Friends*, the story of fortyish Chloe and her longtime friends, Marjorie and Grace. This novel is told sometimes from Chloe's first-person point of view, more often from a narrator's third-person one, or in the form of terse, play-script dialogue. The narrator and Chloe often merge, but whereas the narrator always conveys Weldon's attitudes, Chloe only develops assent to them. Covering only two days in the present, when Chloe resolves her marital crisis, *Female Friends* simultaneously recaptures a more eventful past (individual and joint) that began for the three women in Ulden in 1940. The three friends may have exasperated and backbitten each other since then, but they have also "clung together for comfort." Although "our loyalties are to men, not to each other," and therefore sisterhood may be hard to come by (as minor relationships in the novel show), these three friends attest to the possibility of the female community that forms out of distress and to which men are inconsequential. That all three have slept with artist Patrick Bates, Grace and Chloe even having borne his children, scarcely ripples their friendship. Having gravitated together because they sensed each other's emotional needs as children, they remain each other's mutual support as adults; and Weldon urges even more such alliances. Her friends quite rightly urge Chloe to leave her contemptuous, bullying husband, Oliver, a hack film writer, but she reassures herself that she is better off than the childless spinster Marjorie and hedonistic divorcée Grace and clings to her demeaning marriage.

Actually, Chloe is worse off. Weldon flatters neither her egotistical male figures here, nor their friendships: temporary camaraderie for bouts of drinking and sex or alliances for self-profit. At the heyday of their marriage, Oliver loves Chloe "as much as he loves himself—and what more than this can any woman ask of any man?" Since Weldon calls attention to names, the reader may notice that Oliver Rodure easily rearranges into Oliver Ordure and Patrick Bates (who drives his wife Midge to suicide) into Patrick Beast. Chloe, however, reverberates as the name of Demeter, goddess of the young green crops—Chloe is rearing not only her own two children, but the three offspring of Midge's and Grace's failed lives. Having already cost Chloe her college degree and jealously stopped publication of her first novel, Oliver now caps his liaison with their au pair by inviting Chloe to participate too, in order to accuse her of lesbianism. Yet Weldon remains careful about allotting blame. Chloe's friends have explicitly been responsible for men's deaths, and Chloe herself pushed Francoise into Oliver's bed—most important: Chloe knows that she lets Oliver exploit her and domineer.

The central thematic issue of women's control over their lives—"women live by necessity, not choice"—is taken up by Chloe. Weldon grants the powerful reality that women are shackled by fears and dependencies forged by maternal indoctrination. Chloe may chafe at maternal training in patient acceptance of suffering "for the children's sake" and female subordination (her widowed mother, Gwyneth, a barmaid, and Grace's mother, Esther, an Ulden housewife, are exemplary martyrs). But Chloe has been so well conditioned that she subscribes to such ways nonetheless. The powerless, Weldon also sees, lose their nerve; after a deprived childhood and a submissive adulthood, Chloe dares not challenge fate: to her, asking for trouble. It also remains true that women are at the mercy of physical nature: their active hormones, their cancer-prone reproductive systems. And incalculable chance, or fate beyond individual control, creates its own level of necessity. The train on which Chloe and Marjorie first met stopped in Ulden by mistake; its cargo of evacuee children (such as Marjorie) was intended for elsewhere. However, Weldon insists that women must eschew the spineless habit of giving fate the credit or (as is Chloe's habit) the blame for their lives, since fate merely creates opportunities, not the directions they will take. Women are responsible for what happens to them, not in blame now, but in obligation to self-respect; they must assert choice over necessity. Gwyneth counseled "understand, forgive, endure"—but "what kind of lesson is that for daughters?"

Chloe finally leaves Oliver. With five children to rear, she is not free, but she is freed of her husband's and her mother's negative influence; she has attained freedom of choice, which

state Weldon wisely accounts victory enough. The blessing Chloe retains from Gwyneth and Esther is another defense against chaos: love of children and a sense of "maternal warmth. . . . It seeps down through the generations, fertilising the ground, preparing it for more kindnesses." With good reason *Female Friends* was very favorably reviewed, earning particular praise for its terse prose, controlled tone, and avoidance of feminist tendentiousness in favor of believable, sharply realized characters and situations. As one reviewer said, the "real triumph of *Female Friends* is the gritty replication of the gross texture of everyday life, placed in perspective and made universal."

In summer 1976 the Weldon family moved to a substantial country house near Shepton Mallet, Somerset. The move was to prove more agreeable to Ronald Weldon, whose business flourished in Somerset, than to Fay, who would discover that she sorely missed her own friends and the London ambience. In 1976 Weldon's play *Moving House* was produced, and she started what were to be some four years of work on her adaptation of *Pride and Prejudice*. She also published another novel, whose moral values perhaps reflect Austen's influence. In any case, the strength of the mother-child bond, prominent in *Female Friends*, recurs as a motivation for the uncanny events of this skillful fourth novel, *Remember Me*, on human identity and the roles that shape it.

The unhappy ghost of Jarvis's first wife—middle-aged Madeleine, killed in an auto crash early in the book—refuses to rest until her teenage daughter, Hilary, is out of the clutches of her unloving stepmother, Lily. (Madeleine haunts the more kindly Margot until she undertakes to mother Hilary.) Lily herself finally decides that "To have a husband is nothing. To be a wife is nothing. Sex is an idle pastime. To be a mother is all that counts"—sentiments not necessarily Weldon's, but a fair rendition of many women's sense of identity, and not without Weldon's approval. If Madeleine's ghostly presence precipitates an identity crisis for mean-spirited Lily, proud to be an architect's wife when she was once just a New Zealand butcher's daughter, more centrally it shatters and restores middle-aged Margot, the doctor's wife, whose ego is quivering for appreciation outside her roles as devoted wife and mother. Weldon sensibly has no quarrel with such feminine roles; her quarrel is only with letting roles become absolutes. Her narrator (now clearly distanced from the characters and prone to evaluating them) deliberately presents the characters and repeatedly has the characters see themselves in terms of their roles in relation to others, even young Hilary, who identifies herself as "daughter of a dead mother, child of a lost father . . . [and] Lily's obligation." We know ourselves and are shaped by roles, past and present. But we must be wary of letting a role replace a self, distinct from any role it enters on. Although Madeleine so resents being "stripped of my identity" as Jarvis's lawful wife that her life is corroded, she will recognize (too late) that she must change and be just "myself. Neither daughter nor wife, but myself." We have, moreover, Weldon reminds us, our moral identity to consider.

The incredible return of a ghost is rendered highly probable through a novel filled with mundane domestic details rather than sensational incidents. (The precise observation of daily life includes a new fictional device: line-by-numbered-line analyses of the obfuscations with which family conversations disguise actual motives.) Furthermore, the pervasive theme "we are all part of one another" does much to explain Madeleine's continued presence. A psychic link with the dead, forged by guilt, might well let them prey on our minds. Margot knows that sixteen years ago she slept once with Jarvis, even if he, most insultingly, has forgotten the incident. During the course of the action, Margot acknowledges her long-suppressed awareness that her son, Laurence, is the fruit of that brief encounter and therefore should be reared with Hilary as her brother. More importantly, in a further development of oneness, she also acknowledges her guilt before Madeleine, whom she once "wronged": Madeleine was part of her in being "my sister, after all."

But even sisterhood is not the summit of oneness. Weldon insists, as never before, not only that "All things have meaning," but that we all participate in a "greater humanity," a family of humankind whose days are numbered and should be more kindly spent toward one another: the parting advice of Madeleine's spirit to "my sisters . . . and my brothers too." Emotionally matured by her experiences, Margot reaffirms her domestic roles, eased by having faced not only her own sufferings but "the damage that I did" to more than sisters. Even Lily rediscovers her long-stifled humanity, and Jarvis manages some penitence for his past philandering. As a satirist, Weldon still does not spare her characters exposure of their pretensions, hypocrisies, and self-

indulgences, but she is less willing to turn an epigram at their expense now, and this novel lacks anyone approaching a villain. Even Renee (a minor character) is portrayed more sympathetically than is Weldon's wont with lesbians. Greater charity is not just a plea in this novel, but a practice. The responses of reviewers, of mixed minds about this book, were captured by the *Times Literary Supplement* reviewer, who concluded her list of objections with the admission that she found herself reading it "with an avidity way beyond the call of duty." The most frequent criticism was of authorial intrusions, primer-style question-and-answer dialogue, and role typing. But it was balanced by praise for solid construction, shrewdness, and authenticity.

Weldon discarded mellowing of attitude and domestication of fantasy for her next novel, *Little Sisters*, published in England in 1978. (It appeared in America in 1977 as *Words of Advice*, a title reused from her earlier, but unconnected, play.) This fifth fiction, with its thinly developed characters, improbably exaggerated situations, and abrupt reversals, is a satiric, modern fairy tale, not a realistic novel. It mocks the shoddy parvenus and aspirants to wealth and glamour of the 1970s and the illusion-ridden, sensation-seeking folk of the 1960s, when the enemy was "forced back by peace and love and a little help from hallucinogens." Cautioning against the glittering promises of wealth and luck in fairy tales, Weldon subverts them with wicked wit, but she uses the psychological wisdom and moral certainty they embody to develop her maturation theme, coupled here with a characteristically Weldon plea for greater sisterhood.

The principal learners who fall from innocence into experience are the hefty, nineteen-year-old maiden Elsa, social-climbing mistress of middle-aged Victor, the antique dealer who is her "prince among men"; and Gemma, both wicked witch and wise old crone. Bastard daughter of an errant mother and now the beautiful, but hysterically paralyzed, wife of an elderly millionaire, Hamish, Gemma has had Victor bring Elsa for a weekend at her nouveau-riche castle outside London because she is scheming for Elsa to conceive a child for her by Hamish and is prepared to keep her locked in the tower until she does.

Within this frame story, Gemma tells Elsa a monitory tale—in both first and third person, occupying half the novel—of her own initiation to worldly wisdom in London ten years earlier.

Gemma's subjectively distorted account is modeled on the brothers Grimm tale of the cannibalistic robber bridegroom—a cautionary tale for women and most unflattering to men, though Gemma turns it against women, who are blind in their faith, in their own sexuality, and in their romantic delusions; and Weldon turns it against Gemma, who does not see her own lack of sisterhood.

Gemma's beloved boss, Leon (lion) Fox, designer of erotic jewelry, proved to be not the Prince Charming she saw, but a predatory bisexual aesthete, "wounding, piercing with his you-know-what." Gemma cared neither about the ugly woman he murdered, after cutting off her ring finger, nor about rivalry with her friend Marion, since "girlfriends must fall when boyfriends push. That's one of the laws of nature." As Gemma tells it, Leon raped her and cut off her finger bearing two of his rings, and she became paralyzed by a fall; actually, she lost her finger in an elevator door and her mobility when she married Hamish. If Gemma's tale, as a character remarks, sounds overly "phallic," mad Leon did dismember his male lover, an event long preying on Gemma's psyche. More significantly, Gemma has chosen a fantasy that projects male fear of the destructive female, as much as female fear of the threatening male. She is herself both a male and a female menace. Gemma (the jewel) of the two rings, diamond and ruby, is repeatedly called Snow White and Rose Red, in allusion to the two devoted "little sisters" of fairy-tale fame, and having gone so far as to express a redemptive impulse to help another woman, she suddenly transcends herself and sets Elsa free to "run for me and all of us"; whereupon, Gemma once again can walk.

Since Victor has already returned to his wife and daughter (who have had their own incredible sexual escapades) and a visiting lesbian has been routed, normalcy of a sort has been restored to this stylized fictional world. Reviewers rightly were not favorably impressed, finding the book cliché-ridden in language and situation, unconvincing as reality (except for minor characters), and ineffectual as fantasy. However inaccurate, the puzzled decision of the *Time* reviewer that it "hasn't an idea in its head" pointed up the novel's failure to integrate a profusion of ideas on sexual and familial relations, psychological injuries, social pretensions, and cultural fads.

In 1978 Weldon not only had *Mr. Director*, her play on scientism in the welfare state, pro-

duced, but also published her ambitious sixth novel, *Praxis*, nominated for the prestigious Booker Prize. A grimmer book than her preceding ones, it was written under more trying circumstances. While living in Somerset and writing it, Weldon feared she might die of a current pregnancy, complicated by placenta praevia (misattached placenta). Although intellectually certain that she would carry safely, she was emotionally far less secure and thought of *Praxis* as her last testament.

The narrator quickly explains the strange name of the title character as meaning "turning point, culmination, action; orgasm; some said the Goddess herself"; whereas her sister Hypatia's name comes from "a learned woman; stoned to death by an irate crowd for teaching mathematics when she should have stayed modestly at home." The outlandish names their Jewish father, Ben, gave them, "out of a culture so far gone as to be meaningless," are changed by their Christian mother, Lucy, into the more prosaic Patricia and Hilda. Yet the spirit of the goddess persists. Pat-Praxis Duveen (divine), an entirely individualized character, is also an ironic, great goddess declined into modern woman, but with her cult resurgent in the women's movement's own Eleusinian mysteries. Hilda-Hypatia, the thinker, is her own woman, as an ambitious and half-mad intellectual who uses her mind to protect herself from reality and becomes a successful, antifeminist career woman. But she is also implicitly a distorting aspect of Praxis's nature. She has stood Praxis, the doer, on her head "metaphorically, often enough, until I doubted the truth of my own perceptions."

The symbolic suggestiveness enriches the themes of women's need to regain a sense of female importance and cohesiveness ("It does not take a man to make a woman cry") and the courage to act by conviction instead of sheltering behind men, respectability, and nature: truths of whose importance the women's movement convinces Praxis. Blind Nature remains the great enemy, decayer of female flesh and perverter of values; "Nature our Friend is an argument used, quite understandably, by men," Nature being "no more than our disposition, as laid down by evolutionary forces, in order to best procreate the species."

Praxis's story, told in retrospect, begins in Brighton with her traumatic childhood in the 1920s and ends in London in the present, spanning a period of change in some women's, if not men's, attitudes toward womanhood. Ben beats Lucy and abandons her to madness and institutionalization. Praxis's unwashed college boyfriend Willie exploits her to gain his degree at the expense of hers (as in *Female Friends*), but then Praxis doubts her self-worth and still assumes that catching a man is the goal of life. Yet she outgrows being Willie's servant and then suburban doll-wife to Philip, abandons him and her prim children to snatch her girlfriend's man, and when finally herself betrayed in turn, becomes a zealous convert to, even a heroine of, the women's movement. Nonetheless, like narrator Jocelyn of *Down Among the Women*, she retains reservations about the New Young Woman: "Heartless, soulless, mindless—free!" True, a careless young Amazon has painfully bruised Praxis's foot, but Weldon still feels that hard experience has given her older women a humanity their more privileged descendants lack. The women's movement educates her but proves no panacea for Praxis, who has yet to come to personal terms with her sense of a meaningless life.

The novel alternates between Praxis's first- and third-person accounts, the latter being the voice of her writing personality, on whose veracity she sometimes comments. Like most Weldon narrators, Praxis inclines toward Weldon's recurrent sentiments and characteristic voice: deft ironic understatement and wry appraisals. She has also shared Weldon's copywriting experience. Writing her story while confined to her room with injuries and imprisoned in despair and self-doubt, Praxis has been recently released from two years in jail for smothering the mongoloid infant of her foster-daughter (an opportunity for Weldon to explore right-to-life attitudes). Playing Oedipus, the swollen-footed woman (who once slept with her own father) is searching out the truth of her past, looking for "the root of my pain and yours" to see whether it is inherent in existence or something foisted on women. (It is both and more.) Recollection proves to be a cathartic act of vision that finally frees her from her isolation and returns her to faith "in some kind of force which turns the wheels of action and reaction, and gives meaning and purpose to our lives." But reaffirmation comes only after Praxis (a true Weldon heroine) has fully accepted responsibility for the course of her life and can say, "I did it all myself" when asked, "What have they done to you?" at the hospital. If we cannot change circumstances, we can modify our attitudes and consequent behavior, and Praxis, who

has courted pain throughout her life, by now sees her share in exacerbating her ordeals.

Praxis is one of Weldon's best novels to date, with a fully realized female character who succeeds in unifying a crowded plot and cast. The control of tone—and in Praxis's past, of atmosphere—is impressive. Social comedy is subdued, largely embedded in minor characters; earnestness prevails. Although there was some objection to occasional obscurities and simplifications and needless extension of Praxis into Anywoman, reviewers admired this book. They praised its energetic narration, polished style, and "personal and idiosyncratic" version of woman's plight, happy that Praxis had "all the exasperating contradictions of a real woman."

In 1979 *Action Replay*, Weldon's drama on sexual incompatibility and warfare, was produced, and in 1980 her seventh novel, *Puffball*, was published. It reflects her dangerous pregnancy in Somerset (as does her 1978 short story "Angel, All Innocence"). But it was completed when she had already removed herself and her children to a terraced house in Kentish Town, North London, in summer 1979. Now living not far from the neighborhood where she had grown up, she would henceforth commute on weekends to Somerset. That country life had palled on her is evident enough in her novel, though there the pregnant wife remains the country mouse whom the husband visits on weekends. *Puffball* shares with *Remember Me* and with Weldon's 1977 radio play about nuclear submarine crews, *Polaris*, which incorporates telepathy and thought transference, Weldon's fascination with the weird. As she had done, her characters live in the shadow of numinous Glastonbury Tor, a region in the occult tradition and, to Weldon, imbued with an elemental power whose energy people may try to harness to their own ends, as does her villain Mabs with manipulative malice. The novel takes its title from a recurrent image: the swelling mushroom that usually resembles a pregnant abdomen, but sometimes the human brain, and therefore is an apt symbol for the book's central conflict between mind and biological mechanism. Satire is muted, and the story entirely positive.

Twenty-eight-year-old Liffey, who persuades her advertising agency husband to move to an isolated Somerset cottage by agreeing to the pregnancy she has always feared, becomes, at first, unsuspecting prey of witchlike neighbor Mabs, whose powerful concoctions give Mabs's husband, Tucker, entry into Liffey's bed, then threaten her pregnancy and life—occasions for much suspense. But the baby (it is Richard's) is safely born, despite placenta praevia, and Richard, who has philandered away his weekdays in London and deserted his wife for infidelity, returns and is accepted back for the child's sake. Not only has a healthy baby been born, but, as a result of pregnancy, marital disillusionments, financial problems, and local ordeals, a more mature and expansive Liffey has been reborn. Even Richard, who rejected the adult responsibilities of fatherhood and fidelity, shows signs of growth, accepting what he assumes is Tucker's child rather than lose Liffey. (Before allowing publication of this book, Weldon rewrote her male characters so that they would not be ciphers.)

The simple story proceeds chronologically through fifteen months of present time, told by an omniscient narrator clearly distanced from characters who are no more complex than the formal structure. Complexity belongs instead to the thematic structure. Although Nature here is no longer the decayer of female bodies but the creator of new life, biological and spiritual, a major theme is still the tyranny of the biological functions that control our bodies, of the chemistry that dictates so much of our behavior. Weldon's Darwinian definition of Nature remains unchanged—"the chance summation of evolutionary events"—and so blind is Nature that her narrator would like to see its very name toppled to its "Nature" so that we will stop confusing it with God. "Nature works by waste. . . . Auntie Evolution, Mother Nature—bitches both!" fumes the narrator. Nonetheless, Weldon effects a reconciliation with the burden of subjection to natural process.

It requires the right kind of woman. Not chthonic, lunar Mabs, who revels in pregnancy as a tranquilizer and abuses her children once born, sends Tucker to Liffey out of general nastiness, then attacks her out of jealousy because she herself apparently cannot conceive again. (As soon as Mabs does conceive, she becomes harmless.) The mere breeder betrays her human nature. The vernal and sun goddess Liffey, appropriately named for her feminine fertility of both body and spirit (even if Weldon was not consciously thinking of James Joyce's *Finnegans Wake*, 1939), is the necessary woman. She, like her child, reflects another natural possibility, "a lifeforce, a determination in the individual of the species, as distinct from the group, not to . . . be wasted." Capable of fulfilling her nature as the

human being Nature chanced to evolve, Liffey discovers the desire to feel herself "part of nature's process: to subdue the individual to some greater whole." Nor does Weldon mock her; like Praxis, Liffey has found a meaningful "force." That life is more than body chemistry is amply evident from Weldon's ironic use of extended, clinically precise descriptions of physiological processes, from menarche through ejaculation and conception to parturition: the "inside" story accompanying outer events.

Puzzled by this book, missing the comic writer, and sensing a softening of attitude, reviewers objected above all to such an "intrusion" of physiological data. But they failed to see the integral role and narrative value of the factual passages, which give *Puffball* a resonance its slim story otherwise lacks. If the impersonal functioning of a Nature beyond our control is manifest in Weldon's biology lectures, so too is Nature's orderliness and purposefulness, in contrast to the confusions and dishonesties in the outer events of the narrative. Nor can Weldon resist some explicit praise for Nature's works in the form of highly specialized cells "enabling their owner to read, and write, and reason in a way entirely surplus to its survival." Nature proves something at which to marvel too, an attitude that may be irrelevant to Nature's mechanical processes but is pertinent to our existence and Weldon's fiction. She consistently says that by our attitudes we control the quality of our lives; mind has its way of mastering matter as well as fate—let women take heed.

The critics who wondered if *Puffball* showed a writer in transition, preparing to abandon the newer woman for an older feminine myth, probably overlooked the high valuation Weldon places on motherhood throughout her fiction, where it rivals sisterhood, self-responsibility, and self-determination as her positive standards for women. Always inspired by indignation at female suffering, Weldon has never been a feminist party liner, but rather a sometime affiliate, reserving the right to decide for herself what matters in female lives. It saves her from glibness and tendentiousness and allows her to depict different kinds of women persuasively, though it is true that her characters tend to be, or become, agents for her own perceptions. Her independence of mind manifests itself increasingly in her fiction, along with more polished technique and (except for *Little Sisters*) mellowing of tone: less reliance on satiric barbs and comic effects, more on thoughtfulness. Her inventiveness is unfailing; al-

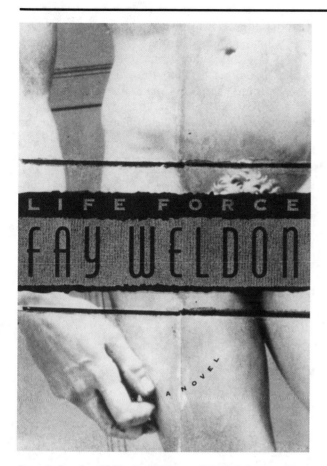

Dust jacket for Weldon's 1992 novel, which one reviewer called "a sock-in-the-eye look at the male need to share their genetic code and the consequence to compliant females, a bearing of the fruit"

though her books may repeat themes and, in minor ways, situations, each is a fresh act of imagination, not only unlike its predecessors, but unusual in itself. *Watching Me, Watching You* (1981), a collection of all her short stories up to that point, was followed in 1982 by *The President's Child*. A novel that has been described as a "feminist thriller," it presents a woman who advances from the Australian outback, to Washington high life (of the less reputable sort), to a home and career in London—only to have political intrigue and murderous conspiracy suddenly intrude on her private life.

Weldon continues to produce novels at a steady clip, usually one a year. Her *Life and Loves of a She-Devil* (1983) has become one of her most popular works to date, owing in part to television and film adaptations. The novel concerns an unattractive woman, Ruth, who loses her husband to a beautiful romance novelist. In the course of the plot, Ruth exacts her revenge on the two philanderers and gets an extensive plastic-surgery make-

over to become an exact duplicate of the romance novelist.

Sybil Steinberg, writing in *Publishers Weekly*, called *She-Devil* a "biting satire of the war between the sexes, indicting not only the male establishment's standards of beauty and feminine worthiness, but also women's own willingness . . . to subscribe to these standards." *New York Times* reviewer Michiko Kakutani noted that Ruth's "final act—having extensive plastic surgery that makes her irresistible to men—actually seems like a capitulation to the male values she says she despises." Weldon commented on the contradictions in the novel: "The first half of the book is an exercise in feminist thought. . . . It's the feminist manifesto really: a woman must be free, independent, and rich. But I found myself asking, What then? . . . I think women are discovering that liberation isn't enough. The companionship of women is not enough. The other side of their nature is unfulfilled."

Life Force (1992) involves a lothario, Leslie Beck, who has dabbled with the female friends of Nora, who works at a sinking realty firm. Absent for twenty years, Beck pops up after the death of his second wife, and Nora begins writing her autobiography, in which she recalls her friends' dalliances with him. *Moon Over Minneapolis*, a new collection of short stories by Weldon, appeared in Great Britain in 1991, and in the United States in 1992. Weldon adapted *The Cloning of Joanna May* (1989) for Granada Television in 1991; the program aired in the United States on the Arts and Entertainment network in February 1992.

Weldon has a large popular following both in Britain and the United States, and her novels are abundantly reviewed. Though sometimes faulted for bias and shallow characterization (especially of men), they have been admired for their astringent and terse prose, vitality, originality, authenticity, and moral conviction. Fellow novelist John Braine has called Weldon a "natural novelist"; Anita Brookner in the London *Times Literary Supplement* in 1980 reappraised all of Weldon's fiction to estimate her as "one of the most astute and distinctive women writing fiction today."

Interviews:
Melvin Maddocks, "Mothers and Masochists," *Time*, 101 (26 February 1973): 91;
John Heilpern, "Facts of Female Life," *London Observer Magazine* (18 February 1979): 36-37;

Angela Neustatter, "Earth Mother Truths," *Manchester Guardian Daily*, 20 February 1979, p. 24;

Elisabeth Dunn, "Among the Women," *London Telegraph Sunday Magazine*, 16 December 1979, pp. 55, 58, 61, 64;

Pauline Peters, "The Fay Behind Puffball," *London Sunday Times*, 17 February 1980, p. 36.

References:

Martin Amis, "Prose Is the Leading Lady," *New York Times Book Review*, (2 October 1977: pp. 13, 52;

Claudia Smith Brinson, "Weldon's Shots Never Cheap, Always Funny," *The State* (Columbia, S.C.), 26 January 1992, p. F6;

Anita Brookner, "The Return of the Earth Mother," *Times Literary Supplement* (London), 22 February 1980, p. 202;

Agate Nesaule Krouse, "Feminism and Art in Fay Weldon's Novels," *Critique*, 22, no. 2 (1978): 5-20;

Anthea Zeman, *Presumptuous Girls: Women and Their World in the Serious Woman's Novel* (London: Weidenfeld & Nicolson, 1977), pp. 64-65.

Arnold Wesker

(24 May 1932 -   )

This entry was updated by T. F. Evans (University of London) from his entry in
DLB 13: British Dramatists Since World War II: Part Two.

BOOKS: *Roots* (Harmondsworth: Penguin, 1959);

I'm Talking about Jerusalem (Harmondsworth: Penguin, 1960);

The Wesker Trilogy (London: Cape, 1960; New York: Random House, 1961)—includes *Chicken Soup with Barley*, *Roots*, and *I'm Talking about Jerusalem*;

Labour and the Arts (Oxford: Gemini, 1960);

The Modern Playwright (Oxford: Gemini, 1960);

Chicken Soup with Barley (London: Evans, 1961);

The Kitchen (London: Cape, 1961; New York: Random House, 1962);

Chips with Everything (London: Cape, 1962; New York: Random House, 1963);

Their Very Own and Golden City (London: Cape, 1966);

The Four Seasons (London: Cape, 1966);

The Friends (London: Cape, 1970);

Fears of Fragmentation (London: Cape, 1970);

Six Sundays in January (London: Cape, 1971);

The Old Ones (London: Cape, 1973);

Love Letters on Blue Paper: Three Stories (London: Cape, 1974; New York: Harper & Row, 1975);

Say Goodbye—You May Never See Them Again: Scenes from Two East-End Backgrounds, paintings by John Allin and text by Wesker (London: Cape, 1974);

The Journalists (London: Writers and Readers Publishing Cooperative, 1975);

The Plays of Arnold Wesker, 2 volumes (New York: Harper & Row, 1976)—includes *The Kitchen*, *Chicken Soup with Barley*, *Roots*, *I'm Talking about Jerusalem*, *Chips with Everything*, *The Four Seasons*, *Their Very Own and Golden City*, *Menace*, *The Friends*, and *The Old Ones*;

Words as Definitions of Experience (London: Writers and Readers Publishing Cooperative, 1976);

Journey into Journalism: A Very Personal Account in Four Parts (London: Writers and Readers Publishing Cooperative, 1977);

Fatlips: A Story for Children (London: Writers and Readers Publishing Cooperative, 1978; New York: Harper & Row, 1978);

Said the Old Man to the Young Man: Three Stories (London: Cape, 1978);

Chips with Everything, The Friends, The Old Ones, Love Letters on Blue Paper [play] (Harmondsworth: Penguin, 1980);

The Journalists, The Wedding Feast, The Merchant (Harmondsworth: Penguin, 1980);

Caritas (London: Cape, 1981);

photograph by Mark Gerson

Distinctions (London: Cape, 1985);
Collected Plays, 6 volumes (London: Penguin / New York: Viking, 1989-1990).

PLAY PRODUCTIONS: *Chicken Soup with Barley*, Coventry, Belgrade Theatre, 7 July 1958; London, Royal Court Theatre, 14 July 1958;
Roots, Coventry, Belgrade Theatre, 25 May 1959; London, Royal Court Theatre, 30 June 1959 (transferred 30 July 1959 to Duke of York's Theatre); New York, Mayfair Theatre, 6 March 1961, 72 [performances];
The Kitchen, London, Royal Court Theatre, 16 September 1959; expanded version, London,

Royal Court Theatre, 27 June 1961; New York, New Theatre Workshop, 9 May 1966, 3; New York, New 81st St. Theatre, 13 June 1966, 137;
I'm Talking about Jerusalem, Coventry, Belgrade Theatre, 4 April 1960; London, Royal Court Theatre, 27 July 1960;
Chips with Everything, London, Royal Court Theatre, 27 April 1962; New York, Plymouth Theatre, 1 October 1963, 151;
The Nottingham Captain, libretto by Wesker, Wellingborough, Centre 42 Festival, 11 September 1962;
Their Very Own and Golden City, Spa, Belgium National Theatre, 13 August 1965; London, Royal Court Theatre, 19 May 1966;

The Four Seasons, Coventry, Belgrade Theatre, August 1965; London, Saville Theatre, 21 September 1965; New York, Theatre Four, 14 March 1968, 6;

The Friends, Stockholm, Stadtsteater, 23 January 1970; London, Round House, 19 May 1970;

The Old Ones, London, Royal Court Theatre, 8 August 1972; New York, Theatre at the Lambs Club, 6 December 1974;

The Wedding Feast, based on Fyodor Dostoyevski's "An Unpleasant Predicament," Stockholm, Stadtsteater, 8 May 1974; revised version, Leeds, Leeds Playhouse, 20 January 1977;

The Journalists, Highgate, Jackson's Lane Community Centre, 13 July 1975; Coventry, Criterion Theatre, 27 March 1977;

Love Letters on Blue Paper, London, BBC Television, January 1976; Syracuse, New York, Syracuse Stage, 14 October 1977; London, Cottesloe Theatre (National Theatre), 15 February 1978;

The Merchant, based on William Shakespeare's *The Merchant of Venice*, Stockholm, Royal Dramatenteater, 8 October 1976; New York, Plymouth Theatre, 15 November 1977; Birmingham, Birmingham Repertory Theatre, 12 October 1978;

Caritas, London, Cottesloe Theatre, 7 October 1981;

Four Portraits, Tokyo, Mitzukoshi Theatre, 2 July 1982;

One More Ride on the Merry-Go-Round, Leicester, Phoenix Theatre, 25 April 1988.

Arnold Wesker was born in Stepney in the East End of London. His father, Joseph Wesker, was a tailor of Russian-Jewish extraction, and his mother, Leah Perlmutter Wesker, was Hungarian. Stepney is in a poor part of the city, and Wesker's mother helped to augment the family income by doing odd jobs as a kitchen worker. Wesker has said that he enjoyed the life of the East End. The family's poverty did not worry him, and he found a sense of warmth in the community. His parents quarreled, but there were street games with friends, and, as he grew up, he realized that the social feeling in the family (aunts and a grandmother lived next door) and the sense of concern for political matters helped to make up for the worries caused by his parents' squabbling. There was no religious life in his home, but he developed a strong consciousness of his Jewish origins and the feeling that the Jews formed a unit in a hostile world. His parents inculcated in him a gentleness of temperament and an opposition to violence.

Wesker began school at elementary schools in Stepney and the neighboring borough of Hackney, but, when World War II began in 1939, he was evacuated to the country and spent some time in the west of England and Wales. After returning to his parents' home in 1943, he went to Upton House School in Hackney, where, in addition to the usual subjects for a student of his age, he was taught bookkeeping, shorthand, and typing. He left school in 1948, and between then and 1950 he worked at a series of different and unrelated occupations, including apprentice to a firm that made reproductions of antique furniture, carpenter's mate, and bookseller's assistant. One of the bookshops in which he worked was in Fleet Street, the newspaper-publishing area of central London. In 1950 he entered the Royal Air Force, where he served for nearly two years. His service career was not distinguished, but he later put his RAF experiences to good use in his writing.

After leaving the RAF, he went to work as an assistant in another bookshop and then as a plumber's mate. London had ceased to attract him as it had in the past, and he moved with a young woman friend to live with his married sister and her husband in Norfolk, where he worked at various jobs, such as seed sorter and farm laborer. After his friend decided that she would prefer to marry a local farmer, Wesker went to the city of Norwich, where he worked as a kitchen porter for about eighteen months, before returning to London and becoming a trainee pastry cook at the Hungaria Restaurant on Lower Regent Street, in the affluent West End of London. In London he met his future wife, Doreen (Dusty) Bicker, and decided to make a career in the restaurant business. When he tired of London and went to Paris, Dusty accompanied him and took work as an au pair girl while he worked in Le Rallye restaurant for about six months. By that time he had wearied of work as a pastry cook and realized that he had always wanted to be a student. The money he had saved while working in the Paris restaurant was enough to pay for a six-month course at the London School of Film Technique, which he attended in 1955-1956. During the period since he had left the RAF, he had begun to write plays and short stories, and he now considered becoming a writer of film scripts and a director, but he found the course at the London School of Film

Technique useless. At the school, however, he met Lindsay Anderson, now well known as a producer and director, and Anderson's encouragement and interest helped Wesker to continue writing. Writing brought in little money at first, and he now thinks that he must have been living off Dusty, who was working in the food shop Sainsbury's. His first completed play, *The Kitchen*, was entered in a play competition run by the *Observer* in 1956, but it received no notice and was subsequently rejected by theater managers.

Chicken Soup with Barley, which was to become the first play in *The Wesker Trilogy*, was the first of Wesker's works to be staged. The Arts Council had decided to make special awards to commemorate the fiftieth anniversary of the opening of the Gaiety Theatre in Manchester and Miss A. E. F. Horniman's repertory seasons there. Any repertory company producing a new play was eligible. The Royal Court Theatre in London was already considering *Chicken Soup with Barley*, and they decided to send the play to the Belgrade Theatre at Coventry with a guarantee that, if it were produced there, it could have a week's run at the Royal Court immediately after. The play opened in Coventry on 7 July 1958 and transferred for the week at the Royal Court on 14 July. George Devine of the Royal Court had now become interested in Wesker's work and nominated him for an Arts Council award. The receipt of this award allowed Wesker and Dusty Bicker to marry in November 1958. *Roots*, the second play in the trilogy, was presented at the Belgrade in May 1959; it was transferred to the Royal Court in June and then to the Duke of York's Theatre in the heart of the West End theater area in July. Because of the success of *Chicken Soup with Barley*, *The Kitchen* was produced at the Royal Court in September 1959. Finally, *I'm Talking about Jerusalem*, the third play in *The Wesker Trilogy*, was presented at the Belgrade in April 1960. The entire trilogy was produced at the Royal Court in June and July 1960. Wesker had now arrived as a playwright. The royalties began to come in regularly, and he settled down to the last of his many occupations, that of professional writer.

The Kitchen and the trilogy may be considered as the first important section of Wesker's work as a dramatist. With these four plays, he forced himself to the center of attention at a time when there was a strong tide running in the direction of plays about "real" people in "real" life. It was never clear what was meant by "reality," but

the general inference seemed to be that dramatists should turn their attentions to the way in which the mass of people lived instead of writing about the activities of a comparatively small section of the leisured middle or upper classes. From the 1950s onward many of the plays put on by such a deliberately experimental and socially progressive theater as the Royal Court concentrated on the details of everyday life. This type of play came to be called, partly in definition, but mostly in contempt, the "kitchen-sink" drama. (The fact that those who used the phrase were hard put to think of a single play in which a kitchen sink appeared did not affect the implications of the term.) Wesker's *The Kitchen* satisfied all definitions of the kitchen-sink play: it was concerned with work, with working people, and with Wesker's own life. It was not the type of play that a matinee audience would flock to; it was, by the same token, a play that would certainly have been avoided by Terence Rattigan's mythical Aunt Edna, the playgoer on the lookout for an "entertaining" play that would give her a couple of hours of pleasant relaxation without anything that would either remind her of the uncomfortable side of the life outside the theater or invite her to think about anything that could be called a "social problem."

Writing in the *New Statesman* on 12 September 1969, A. Alvarez said firmly: "This seems to me, without any qualifications at all, the best play of the decade. Since the war a great deal of second-rate work has got by because its authors were Clever Young Men, Angry Young Men, or simply Young Men. Writers have been pleading their age as women condemned to the gallows used to plead their belly. *The Kitchen* needs no excuses; it is a first-rate dramatic achievement in its own right and by any standards."

The Kitchen is set in the kitchen of a large restaurant called the Tivoli. There is no curtain because, as the stage directions declare, "The kitchen is always there." Wesker, in an introduction and notes for the producer, explains the play and his purpose in writing it: "All kitchens, especially during service, go insane. There is the rush, there are the petty quarrels, grumbles, false prides, and snobbery. Kitchen staff instinctively hate dining room staff, and all of them hate the customer. He is the personal enemy. The world might have been a stage for Shakespeare, but to me it is a kitchen, where people come and go and cannot stay long enough to understand each other, and friendships, loves, and

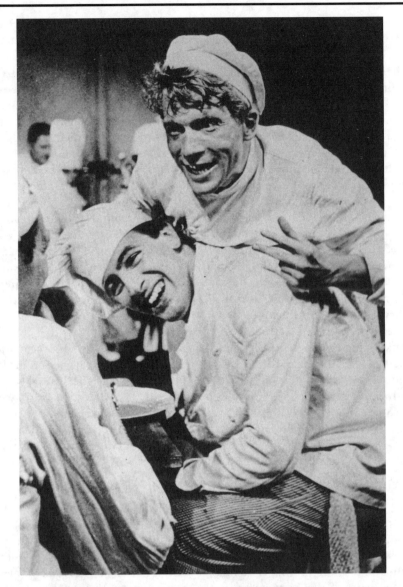

Robert Stephens and Wolf Parr in the 1961 Royal Court Theatre production of The Kitchen

enmities are forgotten as quickly as they are made." In addition to the introduction and notes on the play as a whole, there are also lengthy notes on the individual members of the large cast "in order of stations" and further details on the actions of the cooks. The play is obviously born out of the author's carefully observed and no less carefully recalled experience of his own work in kitchens. With such a large cast and its loose construction and development, the play may at first seem clumsy and shambling, but Wesker has skillfully orchestrated the play to illustrate the rhythm of the normal working day and the emotional states of the characters.

The play begins when the night porter wakes up, sees that it is seven o'clock in the morn-

ing, and lights the ovens, the center of the kitchen's existence. The action starts slowly with the characters carrying on apparently desultory conversations about their work, each other (with special attention to the shortcomings of their fellow workers), and, of course, the boss. Gradually, the demands of the work take control. The cooks prepare the dishes; the waitresses begin to arrive, to shout their orders, and to pick up the dishes as they are ready. The speed at which they all have to work approaches frenzy. Kevin, a young Irish newcomer who finds himself rushing around, cries: "Jesus, is this a bloody madhouse or something? You all gone mad?"

After the rush of the lunch service, there is a period of comparative peace in the afternoon, presented in an interlude during which the ovens are on at only half their full force. Kevin, still in his role as onlooker, feels caught in the insanity of it all and says that he is finished, suggesting that his colleagues can serve him for supper. A young Cypriot kitchen porter, Dimitri, attempts to convince him that his complaints are unnecessary: "This stinking kitchen is like the world—you know what I mean? It's too fast to know what happens. People come and people go, big excitement, big noise. . . . What for? In the end who do you know? You make a friend, you going to be all your life his friend, but when you go from here—pshtt! you forget! Why you grumble about this one kitchen?" Later in the interlude, a pastry cook, Paul, says that he agrees with Dimitri. Maintaining that "the world is filled with kitchens—and when it's filled with kitchens you get pigs," he tells a story of his neighbor, a bus driver. During a bus driver's strike, he had encouraged his neighbor to remain on strike no matter what the difficulty. Sometime later, during a demonstration in favor of peace, a cause to which Paul is sympathetic, the marchers have held up the buses in the streets. The bus driver, despite the solidarity Paul has shown during his own political action, says he would like to have dropped a bomb on the demonstrators because they were preventing the traffic from flowing freely.

The interlude ends, and everyone returns for the evening work. Gradually the tempo increases once again. In the second half of the play, some of the personal themes sketched in fairly lightly in the first part are developed sympathetically against the background of the developing tension. The German cook, in charge of the fried fish, becomes the central character of the play. After one of the waitresses, with whom he is engaged in a sexual relationship, tells him that she cannot leave her husband for him, the combination of personal frustration and the tension of his work drives him to an act of violence. With a chopper, he cuts through the gas lead, and the great ovens hiss to a halt. There is a scuffle in which fellow workers try to restrain the frenzied cook, but he breaks away and a tremendous crash is heard from the dining room as he sweeps piles of crockery to the ground. His hands are cut and bleeding when he is brought back into the kitchen, and an ambulance is telephoned. The boss, Marango, brings the play to its end with an appeal: "Why does everybody sabotage me, Frank? I give work, I pay well, yes? They eat what they want, don't they? I don't

know what more to give a man. He works, he eats, I give him money. This is life, isn't it? I haven't made a mistake, have I? I live in the right world, don't I? (to Peter) And you've stopped the world. A shnip! A boy! You've stopped it. Well why? Maybe you can tell me something I don't know—just tell me. I want to learn something. (to Frank) Is there something I don't know? (Peter rises and in pain moves off. . . . Marango cries at him) BLOODY FOOL! (Rushes round to him) What more do you want? What is there more, tell me?" The bewildered boss's last question is one which Wesker poses in later plays and, indeed, in other contexts apart from the stage.

The Kitchen had a great impact on the theatrical world. Kenneth Tynan, an influential figure in the theater of the 1950s and 1960s, said that the play "achieves something that few playwrights have ever attempted; it dramatises work, the daily collision of man with economic necessity, the repetitive toil that consumes that large portion of human life which is not devoted to living," and he called the "climactic lunch-hour frenzy" at the end of the first act "the fullest theatrical expression I have ever seen of the laws of supply and demand." Admiration was also expressed by a critic who did not share Tynan's sympathy for Wesker's socialism. Wesker's fellow dramatist John Whiting, at the time a drama critic for the *London Magazine*, thought the play "a fine piece of work." He noted that Wesker had rejected any conventional ideas of structure, yet he found that the work in which the characters were engaged became part of the drama in a way that was aesthetically impressive and satisfying. It is important to keep in mind Wesker's stage directions "that at no time is food ever used. . . . Therefore the waitresses will carry empty dishes and the cooks will mime their cooking." Realizing that Wesker wanted his audience to see the play on one level as allegory, Whiting nevertheless concluded that the allegory became lost "because the people in the play are so interesting in their attitude towards work, so very often moving in their acceptance of life that any more formal or philosophical reason they may have for behaving as they do is lost in their fascination as *people*." By this time Wesker was coming to feel that "art is beginning to have no meaning for me—it is not enough," but Whiting urged him to concentrate on his art and to ignore such feelings, claiming that "Like all socialists," Wesker was "obsessed by material things." Whiting urged Wesker to resist the temptation to be a moralist and concentrate on the kind of art which he found in *The Kitchen*.

Whiting's view of Wesker as a moralist is probably more correct than Tynan's Marxist interpretation. The boss's bewilderment at the end of the play could be explained as a symbolic representation of the gap between employer and employees, but the speech does not seem that criticism of the entire basis of capitalist society that Tynan wished it and similar utterances to be. As for the art, Tynan is right in saying that there is a weakness in the play because "it gets nowhere; instead of ending, it stops; and this in turn is due to the fact that its central character is too vague and amorphous to provide a solid point d'appui." Wesker's own feelings of vague dissatisfaction with the play point to the efforts that he was to make later to integrate his art with the purposes of society itself.

Just as *The Kitchen* was firmly planted in his own experience, so Wesker's next work, the trilogy, dug deep into his own life also. While the three plays first appeared separately, they were conceived as parts of a whole; this unity was clear when they were finally presented together in the repertory of the Royal Court in summer 1960. The plays cover a span of twenty-three years, from October 1936 to October 1959. In the first few lines of *Chicken Soup with Barley* there are references to a political demonstration, and the final scene of *I'm Talking about Jerusalem* begins with the reading of the results of the general election. The plays are thus concerned, directly or indirectly, with political developments, which are woven into a story of the life of a Jewish East End family, clearly based on Wesker's own. The interweaving is not always entirely successful, but Wesker has made an ambitious and impressive attempt to write about the times through which he lived and to do it in a way that brings out the political significances of the period and the impact of politics on his family's life.

The demonstration at the beginning of *Chicken Soup with Barley* is being organized to counter the proposed march of Mosley's Fascists through the East End. The Communist party, with strong support from other sections of the East End community, especially, for obvious reasons, the large Jewish population, is taking the lead in organizing the demonstration. The family, in whose house the play opens, is that of Harry and Sarah Kahn. Sarah is much more committed to the demonstration than is her husband, and this difference forms one of the dominating

Lobby poster for the 1967 Royal Court Theatre production of the second play in Wesker's trilogy about an East End Jewish family

strands in the plays. Another strand, one of the lessons that Wesker is seeking to teach, is expressed in an exchange of dialogue between Sarah and Hymie, a neighbor, about Harry's sister, Cissie, a trade-union organizer:

SARAH: I hate her!

HYMIE: Don't be a silly girl. Cissie is a good trade union organizer.

SARAH: She's a cow! Not a bit of warmth, not a bit! What's the good of being a Socialist if you're not warm?

HYMIE: But Cissie has *never* liked Harry.

SARAH: Not a bit of warmth. Everything cold and calculated. People like that can't teach love and brotherhood.

PRINCE: Love comes later, Sarah.

SARAH: Love comes now. You have to start with love. How can you talk about socialism otherwise?

A little later Sarah and Harry quarrel violently. Not only does Harry run off to his mother when there is anything that he is unable to face at home, but he steals money from his wife's handbag. Sarah's rage is such that Harry declares that she has gone mad, and he rushes out in alarm. This quarrel is significant, but the first act presents the Kahn family and their friends and neighbors in a mood of optimism, having helped to prevent the Fascist march and, as another neighbor puts it, having "won one of the biggest fights in working-class history." They realize that a bigger fight, a European war, cannot be far away, but they feel for the time being that they have triumphed.

The second act is in June 1946, after the war; from then on, everything goes downhill. In the first act, there was optimism because the characters had a cause in which they believed. They had something to fight for, and there seemed to be a chance of their winning. Now, they are by no means certain about the values and faith which gave sense and purpose to their lives a decade before, and there are arguments and squabbles about the political situation and the corresponding personal difficulties which are thought to rise from it. Sarah's daughter, Ada, is bitter at the long absence of her husband, Dave, who, after serving in the Spanish civil war, fought for the British in World War II and is still waiting to be demobilized from the army. Ronnie, Ada's brother, is the only one, apart from Sarah, who retains his political ardor, which is shown in his readiness to deliver leaflets and to take part in demonstrations. The others question and argue, are unimpressed by the Labour government, and even call into doubt the Communist party itself. Ronnie tries to encourage Ada by telling her that Dave will not, as he puts it, desert humanity. Ada sneers.

> RONNIE: Listen to her! With a Labour majority in the House? And two of our own Party members? It's only just beginning.
> ADA: It's always only just beginning for the Party. Every defeat is victory and every victory is the beginning.

Harry has had a stroke, and by the last act he has had another stroke, which has paralyzed him and made him unfit for work. At the end of the play, in December 1956, Ronnie returns from abroad. He, too, is now disillusioned and bitter. He has worked in a kitchen and hated it; it has taught him that "the notion of earning an honest penny

is all my eye." People do not work for a lifetime in hope and confidence of a serene and happy old age; they are terrified at the thought of growing old. Moreover, Ronnie has been terribly shocked and disillusioned by the events in Hungary that year, with the Russians' suppression of the popular uprising. In another quarrel scene, he tells his mother that the family has disintegrated and that her ideals have exploded. She is "a pathological case"; she is "still a Communist!" Sarah defies him by reasserting her faith at a time when she thinks it is more needed than ever, and, moreover, she asserts her love and her belief in love, illustrating her point by telling him what happened when she was pregnant and Ada was ill with diphtheria. Harry was, as usual, useless, not there to take Ada to a hospital: "It was Mrs. Bernstein who saved her—you remember Mrs. Bernstein? No, of course not, she died before you were born. It was Mrs. Bernstein's soup. Ada still has that taste in her mouth—chicken soup with barley. She says it is a friendly taste—ask her. That saved her." Ronnie is unimpressed, and his mother pleads with him. The last words of the play are shouted after him as he starts to leave the room: "You'll die, you'll die—if you don't care you'll die. Ronnie, if you don't care you'll die."

In a valuable study of Wesker's work, Glenda Leeming and Simon Trussler offer an ingenious, if somewhat oversubtle, comparison of *Chicken Soup with Barley* with Henrik Ibsen's *Ghosts* (1881), pointing out that "Both sons return in stricken resentment to their homes, and both mothers hear those sons reject the ideals they have taught them. Oswald Alving's father has bequeathed his son a physical corruption stemming from self-indulgence, which, seesaw-like, tips liberal Oswald into an invalid's rapaciously self-indulgent hedonism: whilst Harry Kahn by the end of Wesker's play has transmitted his moral enervation, though not yet his bodily paralysis, to his son Ronnie." It seems unlikely that Wesker consciously modeled his play on one by Ibsen, a playwright who carefully veiled his political statements, if any, in equivocation verging on the obscure or, at least, enigmatic. In *Chicken Soup with Barley*, there is little doubt where Wesker's sympathies lie. He is concerned with problems of practical implementation of political ideals, a problem which worried Ibsen, if at all, in an entirely different way. Moreover, the strength of the conflict between mother and son in *Ghosts* resides principally in such essential facts as the concealment

Patsy Byrne and Joan Plowright in the first production of Roots *(photograph by Zoë Dominic)*

and secrecy that have cloaked the true relationship between Mrs. Alving and her husband. Ibsen's method of revealing the true interpretation of the past as part of the action of the play in the present gives the play an excitement and tension that cannot be matched by *Chicken Soup with Barley*, where Harry's inadequacy is obvious early. Similarly, while the story of the play is one of gradual disillusionment, the lines on which the principal characters are likely to move are fairly clear from the start. The excitement of revelation is thus absent.

The second play of the trilogy, *Roots*, had probably the most favorable reception of all when it was first presented in May 1959, but at that time few critics related this play to *Chicken Soup with Barley*. No character from the earlier play appears in *Roots*, although one, Ronnie Kahn, is frequently mentioned and, in effect, plays an important part. Yet it is clear that Wesker is continuing to work out the problems that worried him in *Chicken Soup with Barley*, and, despite the fresh company of characters, the play is still the Kahn family's story seen from a different but not distant angle. The scene has moved from the East End of London to the rural county

of Norfolk. A young girl, Beatie Bryant, who has been working in London, returns to her home and family in an isolated part of the county. For about three years she has been Ronnie Kahn's mistress. She tells her parents that she and Ronnie are to marry and that he is coming to Norfolk in two weeks time to meet them. Ronnie has clearly been shaping her mind in a way that has opened a gap between Beatie and her family. Often condescending and smug, Beatie passes on to her relations all the lessons that Ronnie has taught her, almost making herself intolerable in the process. At the end of the play Ronnie sends Beatie a letter telling her that he does not think their friendship should continue: "My ideas about handing on a new kind of life to people are quite useless and romantic if I'm really honest. Perhaps I am asking too much of you. If I were a healthy human being it might have been alright but most of us intellectuals are pretty sick and neurotic—as you have often observed—and we couldn't build a world even if we were given the reins of government—not yet any rate." Beatie is desolate, but while her family feels some sympathy, they have other emotions as well. Her mother explains that for a fortnight her daughter has been telling her what to do and what not to do. Now it seems that there is still a great deal that she does not understand, and for all her new learning and newly acquired knowledge, she is not greatly superior to the members of her family who have stayed in Norfolk.

This reaction provokes Beatie to an outburst about people like her self-satisfied family. She declares that the workers do not count, not because she or anyone else does not believe in them or value them highly enough but because they do not believe in or value themselves. Beatie explains that the writers and the artists do not create for the workers because workers make no effort to understand their creations. On the other hand, "the slop singers and the pop writers and the film makers" and other providers for mass audiences know that the workers have money, so they give the workers what they want: "If they want slop songs and film idols, we'll give 'em that then. If they want words of one syllable, we'll give 'em that then. If they want the third rate . . . We'll give 'em THAT then. Anything's good enough for them 'cos they don't ask for no more! The whole stinkin' commercial world insults us and we don't care a damn. Well, Ronnie's right—it's our own bloody fault. We want the third rate—we got it! We got it! We got it! We . . . ," she stops short. She realizes that, for the first time, she is expressing her own ideas. She is quoting Ronnie no more. At last, something has happened. She cries: "God in heaven, RONNIE! It does work, it's happening to me. I can feel it's happened, I'm beginning, on my own two feet—I'm beginning. . . ." There is triumph in Beatie's discovery of herself, but the stage direction with which the printed version of the play comes to an end is depressing nonetheless in its comment on the other characters: "The murmur of the family sitting down to eat grows as BEATIE'S last cry is heard. Whatever she will do they will continue to live as before and the CURTAIN FALLS as BEATIE stands alone—articulate at last."

Some people, chiefly in Norfolk, were outraged at Wesker's picture of country folk. A writer in the May-June 1960 issue of *Encore*, however, pointed out that, while some had called the play "A travesty of Norfolk village life" and insisted that "Norfolk people are not like that," there might be some truth in Beatie's strictures. At the time Wesker was writing *Roots*, Norfolk had no great reputation for support of the arts, and the county appeared indifferent to the depre-

dations being wrought upon its countryside by military and other interests.

The play was, on the whole, extraordinarily well received. When it was presented at the Royal Court in June 1959, Walter Allen wrote at the end of an appreciative notice in the *New Statesman* that "This is by far the best and most faithful play about British working-class life that has appeared for a long time." Kenneth Tynan, not surprisingly, was enthusiastic, proclaiming that Wesker "has managed to build an intensely moving play out of the raw materials of old-fashioned kitchen comedy, if not of outright farce" and adding that, like Anton Chekhov, Wesker has set his comic details "in a context of such tangible reality that sympathy banishes belly-laughs." He also sees political significance in Beatie's "cry of self-discovery" at the end of "the most affecting last act in contemporary English drama," saying, "It would be wrong to describe *Roots* as a Socialist play, but if anyone were to tell me that a Tory had written it I should be mightily amazed." Bernard Levin, who did not share Tynan's political views, wrote in almost as favorable terms, approaching the play more strictly as drama than as social or political comment. Finding Wesker's ear for dialogue acute and complimenting him on the rhythms in the speech of his people, he added, "His anger is shot through with humour and understanding, vibrant with compassion and respect. He has made a striking contribution to man's understanding of man, and he has at the same time made a striking contribution to the English stage." Levin's comments appeared in an introduction to the Penguin edition of *Roots*, the publication of which as a single thin volume was perhaps an indication of the amount of interest Wesker's play aroused.

During the years since it was first produced, *Roots*, if not quite winning the approval that it gained at first, has continued to impress some critics. The initial success of the play may have been the result of the striking performance of the powerful actress Joan Plowright, who created the part of Beatie. Yet she may have given the impression of a girl who was bound to succeed whatever happened to her. In later revivals younger and less experienced actresses have been able to give a greater sense of growing and development in the character during the course of the play. From another direction, novelist Kingsley Amis is among those who have not admired the play. He wrote in 1962 that he could not believe "that the semi-rural existence we are shown in *Roots* need

Keith Johnstone, Bill Gaskill, Miriam Brickman, Pauline Melville, Anthony Page, and Derek Goldby protesting the jailing of Wesker, Robert Bolt, and others for their attempts to organize resistance to nuclear armament

be as thin and uneventful as this, nor that protest (or declamation) about it need be so meagrely motivated and so insubstantial as Beatie's."

It may have been inevitable that, when the third play, *I'm Talking about Jerusalem*, was presented at the Belgrade, Coventry, in April 1960 and then performed as part of the trilogy at the Royal Court in July 1960, there should have been some feelings of anticlimax. The play is set in Norfolk, as was *Roots*, but this play focuses on the Kahn family once again and includes none of the characters from *Roots*. The date is September 1956. Ronnie is helping Ada and Dave move into their new home. At the start, he is standing on a box, pretending to conduct Ludwig van Beethoven's Ninth Symphony, which is heard from a portable radio. Ronnie's concern with culture is thus carried on from the references to it in the closing scene of *Roots*. Ada and Dave are escaping from the city, where Dave has found work in a factory dull and degrading. He plans to work for an employer for a time and then set himself up in business as a carpenter after a year. They have a visit from an old wartime friend of Dave's, Libby Dobson, who is disillu-

sioned and explains: "I've tried it, Dave—listen to me and go home—I've tried it and failed. Socialism? I didn't sell out that easily. You've gone back to William Morris, but I went back to old Robert Owen." He has tried to set up a cooperative with fellow workers but it has failed. Immediately (and too soon to be believable) Dave meets his own failure. His employer, Colonel Dewhurst, calls to say that he has discovered Dave's theft of two rolls of linoleum. Dave makes feeble excuses, but his guilt is clear, and he is dismissed. Ada is bitter and snarls at him: "By Christ, Dave—your ideals have got some pretty big leaks in places haven't they?" Dave starts his own business as a carpenter, and the remaining scenes trace his gradual failure, in inverse correlation with the growth of his family. News is brought from outside that Harry is now in an asylum, and Ronnie, who shares the general mood of disillusionment, talks about the failure of his friendship with Beatie. There is a dying fall in the closing scenes of the play, and the report on the radio of the Conservative's general-election victory in 1959, the third in a row, connects private and public events. The implication is clear. The experiment has failed.

All the hopes at the beginning of *Chicken Soup with Barley* have proved to have been built on nothing substantial, and the play implies there is no future in any attempt to build a new society on the ideal of human brotherhood. Individuals may succeed in limited aims, as Beatie succeeds in standing on her own feet, but the outlook for society itself is bleak. Ronnie Kahn, who is hardly nearer the central action than he is in *Roots*, nevertheless sums up the frustration by telling his mother what went wrong. Sarah, to the end, retains some feeling that all is not lost, that, in spite of everything, some progress has been made. She reminds the others that "we won the last war didn't we" and "We put a Labour Party in power."

> RONNIE: (with irony) Oh, yes, that's right! We put a Labour Party in power. Glory! Hurrah! It wasn't such a useless war after all, was it, Mother? But what did the bleeders do, eh? They sang the Red Flag in Parliament and then started building atom bombs. Lunatics! Raving lunatics! And a whole generation of us laid down our arms and retreated into ourselves, a whole generation! But you two [Ada and Dave]. I don't understand what happened to you two, I used to watch you and boast about you. Well, thank God, I thought, it works! But look at us now, now it's all of us.

The play ends with echoes of the closing scene of *Chicken Soup with Barley*. When Sarah calls Ronnie a fool for crying, he cups his hands and yells to the sky with bitterness and venom: "We—must—be—bloody—mad—to—cry!"

Wesker's ambitious trilogy was received by some critics not simply as a theatrical masterpiece but as an affirmation of personal and social values, of which society was in serious need. Mervyn Jones titled his eulogistic article in the September-October 1960 issue of *Encore* "Arnold Wesker's Epic." After praising the plays for their artistic value and literary qualities and insisting that they gained enormously by being played together as a trilogy, Jones found their message in Sarah's attitude throughout the first and the last plays and quoted from a speech by Esther, Ronnie and Ada's aunt, in the final scene of *I'm Talking about Jerusalem*: "My mother loved her children. You know how I know? The way she used to cook our food. With songs." Yet this message does not go beyond the presumably universally accepted values of the mother caring for her children, and only by a strained analogy does it relate to the mission of the dramatist in his relationship with society.

Wesker was, however, deeply concerned with his function in relation to society. In "Let Battle Commence!," an article for the November-December 1956 issue of *Encore*, he had declared that he wanted to teach by writing "my plays not only for the class of people who acknowledge plays to be a legitimate form of expression, but for those to whom the phrase 'form of expression' may mean nothing whatsoever. It is the bus driver, the housewife, the miner and the Teddy Boy to whom I should like to address myself." He stressed the need to write plays that would have an effect on society, that would, to some extent, catch the tide of progressive ideas that he thought was then in full flood. Yet, it was not clear what the "new movement" had produced and where it was going. The great problem was to find financial support, and he looked in the direction of the trade unions. The purpose of the unions, as he understood it, was to protect the interests of their members, but, he asked, "what can be the virtues of protecting the interests of people who are apathetic to living because no one involves them in living?" Although there were some who could, with no difficulty, think of other things more worth working for than attempting to interest the working man in the arts, there was a certain amount of spoken and written support. At the Trades Union Congress on the Isle of Man in September 1969, the congress passed a resolution on the motion of the Association of Cine and Television Technicians. This resolution, Resolution 42, declared that the congress recognized the importance of the arts in the life of the community and noted the trade unions' small amount of participation in the direct promotion of artistic enterprises, "including those of value to its beliefs and principles." It went on to request that the central council make a special examination of the problem and make proposals to a future congress. An organization with the title Centre 42 was created to implement the aims and purposes of the resolution. It aimed to "destroy the mystique and snobbery associated with the arts," to decentralize the theater, and to renounce the identification of the arts with commercial interests. The positive results of this ambitious and worthy enterprise were not great. Wesker launched himself into this campaign, writing privately and publicly to those whom he thought might be, or should be, interested. Typical was an open letter to the then secretary of the

Colin Farrell, John Bull, and John Kelland in the first production of Chips With Everything

Trades Union Congress, George Woodcock. With the arresting title "Vision! Vision! Mr Woodcock!," it appeared in the 30 July 1960 issue of the *New Statesman*. He said that it did not matter if the present generation did not support the cause. There would be other generations, but "The future costs money! We want a society built on the assumption that man is beautiful. It doesn't matter whether he is or not. On that assumption, there is always the chance that he will be. Vision, vision, vision, Mr Woodcock."

Wesker was appointed director of Centre 42 in 1961, and for the best part of a decade these activities were the center of his life. Yet he had time and energy for other social and political concerns as well, and in that same year he was found guilty and served a month in prison for offenses he had committed in connection with a protest staged by the Campaign for Nuclear Disarmament. As early as the first months of 1963, Geoffrey Reeves, writing in *Encore*, called Centre 42 by the unflattering title "The biggest Aunt Sally of them all." There had been a series of theater and arts festivals in Wellingborough, Notting-

ham, Leicester, Birmingham, Bristol, and Hayes, Middlesex, but despite great goodwill and generous local support by individuals, financial and other difficulties had proved enormous. It was almost impossible to find satisfactory halls; the trade unions and local trade councils had little interest; organization of events was insufficient. Reeves concluded that something more was needed than the simple effort to let everyone know that good art was available. It would be necessary to make people feel that the whole thing was vital to their lives. The article ended with the words "*Vive* Wesker!" Wesker had contributed to the festivals the libretto for *The Nottingham Captain*, which was described as "a moral for narrator, voices and orchestra." Set in the early nineteenth century, it is a simple tale of three workmen, arrested, tried, condemned to death, and executed for taking part in a Luddite insurrection against poverty and oppression. Their leader, Jeremiah Brandreth, is known as "the Nottingham Captain."

Wesker, who did not give up the struggle on behalf of Centre 42 until 1970, tried hard to

Sebastian Shaw and Ian McKellen in the first London production of Their Very Own and Golden City *(photograph by Zoë Dominic)*

keep the movement alive, but his disappointments and frustrations are described in a book of short essays, *Fears of Fragmentation* (1970). One of the culminating disappointments was the failure to raise enough money to obtain an old railway locomotive shed, the Roundhouse, Chalk Farm, and to renovate it as an arts center. A writer for the *Times Literary Supplement* concluded that "the Roundhouse is shunned by the real left," and it was described by a journal called *Radical Arts*, which was apparently written by and for the type of people that Centre 42 was trying to attract, as "that disastrous junk-heap of good intentions."

The experiences of the Centre 42 experiment left a mark on Wesker the dramatist as well as on Wesker the man. In the meantime, he had had a big success with *Chips with Everything*, which he had started to write at the beginning of the Centre 42 activities. First produced at the Royal Court in April 1962, it was transferred to the Vaudeville Theatre in June, and in October 1963 it was presented on Broadway. *Chips with Everything* is the story of Pip Thompson, who joins the Royal Air Force at the time of compulsory service in the years following World War II. He is very much of the middle classes compared with the working-class recruits in whose midst he finds himself, but, even though his father is a former general who is now a banker, he shows no interest in the possibility of becoming an officer himself. The officers know of his family background, and the focus of the play is their attempt to persuade Pip to abandon his revolutionary and anti-authoritarian attitudes and to conform by accepting commissioned rank.

Underlying the entire play is Wesker's contention that the RAF and, by implication, the society of which it is both reflection and part, is based on principles of hierarchy and that the individual, no matter how well intentioned or revolutionary in spirit, is powerless against those principles and in the end will conform, as Pip does. He does not do so without a struggle, but his motives are not easy to understand clearly. In a scene near the beginning of the play, he and fellow airmen are in the Naafi (the lower ranks' refreshment room and recreation center), discussing their attitudes to life and society. Pip, who has explained his own social position and his unwillingness to become an officer, is asked whether he minds being a snob. He replies in a long speech about a visit he once made to a café in the East End, where he "drank a cup of tea from a thick, white, cracked cup and I ate a piece of tasteless currant cake." Noting the unattractive appearance of the café and the dirty face of an old workingman who came into the café and sat beside him, Pip could not quite understand why he should have been so surprised at the appearance of the place and its occupants: "And then I saw the menu, stained with tea and beautifully written by a foreign hand, and on top it said—God I hated that old man—it said 'Chips with everything.' Chips with every damn thing. You breed babies and you eat chips with everything." Pip is a rebel against his upbringing and his class, and this attitude of rebellion leads him to refuse to accept the place that his class reserves for him. At the same time, this speech seems to imply that he has a deep revulsion for the class with which he ought to feel himself an ally.

There are two important episodes that illustrate Pip's opposition to authority. In an early scene, at a Christmas Eve party in the Naafi, the officers try to create an atmosphere of jollity among the men, but their attempts are hypocritical and condescending. The Wing Commander suggests that the men should contribute to the entertainment themselves. One of the airmen recites a poem by Burns, "This ae night," not at all the kind of thing for which the Wing Commander had asked. There is silence, and once more the Wing Commander tries to raise spirits by calling for something more cheerful, something by Elvis Presley. Pip makes a suggestion to the guitar player who, after first reluctance, complies, and gradually all the airmen join in the old peasant revolt song "The Cutty Wren," a concerted gesture of defiance to authority, as represented by the officers. In another episode Pip organizes and directs a group that steals cases of Coca Cola from a wire compound. He tells the other young airmen that there are no risks in the enterprise, which is "efficient, precise, but humane. They happen to be the only qualities for absolute power. That's what we want—absolute success but without a price." The theft is carried out just as he envisages, in a scene almost entirely without words. At the end, a stage direction says, "This scene can be, and has to be, silent, precise, breathtaking, and finally very funny."

The success of *Chips with Everything* in the theater owed much to the ingenuity of the production and the skill of the acting. The two scenes of rebellion were theatrically alive and effective, and the play appears to be saying something of great value about the nature of authority in society, but it is by no means clear exactly what Wesker is trying to say. Of course, he is showing the strength of tradition, of the old conservative order against which socialists such as he will have to fight hard. At the same time, however, he seems to be suggesting that the conservatives will nevertheless win. The play is finally too didactic and loses ultimate dramatic credibility as a result. There has been much discussion of this problem in the various critical comments and analyses of the play.

Wesker himself has been very frank about his intentions and his methods. In an interview with Ronald Hayman included in Hayman's study of Wesker, Wesker explains that when he was in the air force, he wrote a long letter to a friend or a relative every day and asked that the letters be kept. Eventually he assembled all the letters in chronological order and created a novel from them. The different scenes in the play approximate the chapters in the novel. In the same

interview, he goes on to speculate about the composition of any work of art, contending that the act of re-creating experience which results in art happens in two steps: first, "the organization of experience" and then "the transformation of experience." Applying this theory to *Chips with Everything* may account for the way in which the play is based obviously on the author's own experiences and yet, at several crucial places, has the ring of unreality about it.

Some critics have seen traces of Bertolt Brecht in Wesker's work at this time. (The Berliner Ensemble, Brecht's company, had visited London in 1956 and achieved remarkable success. His theories of dramatic method were widely discussed, and the effect of Brecht was to be seen plainly in work of the early 1960s.) Brecht's beliefs that it was essential to remind the audience that the play was a play, not an imitation of reality, and that the play must have a clear didactic purpose, while, at the same time, details of stage presentation were to be as scrupulously close to photographic reality as possible, may well have appealed to Wesker. Thus, some speeches are probably true to life as might be reasonably expected on the stage while there is considerable contrivance in other significant episodes.

Stanley Weintraub, in his essay "Wesker's Mint" (*London Review*, Winter 1966), notices that much in Wesker's play resembles T. E. Lawrence's account of his life in the Royal Air Force in *The Mint* (1955): "the ramifications of both works cross the frontier from uniquely 'English' productions about endemic class guilt to go, perhaps more profoundly than each writer knew, into the psychology of all hierarchical organizations, of the leader and the led. As events continue to dictate the retention of substantial standing armies, staffed often by officers who are (technically, at least) gentlemen, and men who would rather be elsewhere, *Chips* will continue to have a peculiar force, one perhaps beyond its absolute literary or dramatic qualities."

The reactions of some critics to the original production testify to the lack of clarity in Wesker's didactic purpose. Kenneth Tynan called *Chips with Everything* "a gauntlet of a play" flung down on the stage of the Royal Court Theatre and said that it revealed the class system in action. He found some of the play difficult to accept but, while questioning the resolution at the end, thought the dramatic knot "magnificently tied" and said that he would not quickly forget

Arnold Wesker (photograph by Gro Jarta)

the rebuke by the military Establishment to the man who defied it. In conclusion, he said that: "Mr. Wesker implies what might have been, and there are few theatrical gifts more basic than that." In the *New Statesman*, Roger Gellert called Pip "a public school version of Ronnie Kahn," whose personal relationships with the other airmen are well depicted and work "both humanly and dramatically, which the missionary scenes uncomfortably don't." He goes on to say that "the proselytizing tendency is Wesker's biggest pitfall as a dramatist." A fellow Royal Court dramatist, Nigel Dennis, referred to the play's "rather degrading and silly title" but went on to call it "one of the noblest tributes to the English fighting man since *Henry V* and *In Which We Serve*," an achievement that cannot have been in the forefront of Wesker's mind.

Other critics were much blunter in their lack of enthusiasm for the play. Those who started from an initial hostility to Wesker's leftwing aspirations rejected his view of the hierarchical class structure of British society as hopelessly out of date and on this basis demolished the infer-

ences and conclusions that Wesker drew from that theory. The critic in the *London Magazine*, Frank McGuiness, called the play "the most arrogant, misconceived, simple minded piece of proselytizing burlesque that it has ever been my misfortune to grip the edge of my seat through."

Wesker wrote two more plays in the 1960s, and both failed in the theater. Unfortunately, Wesker the social and political campaigner, the dreamer who tried to combine the visions of a Percy Bysshe Shelley with the practical sense of a William Morris, sometimes failed to see the danger of confusing, as Shaw once put it, one's emotions with a public movement. *Their Very Own and Golden City*, which he started in January 1963 and which went through as many as nine drafts before it received its first production in 1965, was presented at the Royal Court Theatre in May 1966. It is a strange hodgepodge of a play in which characteristically vague Wesker idealism is found side by side with sentimental presentation of personal relations, and there is, here and there, a solid chunk of more or less faithfully recorded history, such as verbatim passages from debates at Labour party conferences. The play also experiments with dramatic form, thus showing that the Brechtian developments in *Chips with Everything* were not a mere temporary aberration but indicated a desire to move away from the realism of *The Kitchen* and the trilogy. *Their Very Own and Golden City* is published with an epigraph taken from a lecture on socialism, given by William Morris in 1886. Morris saw the trade unions as having gotten so much control over workers that they had "an authoritative ordering of the whole tenor of their lives, what they shall eat, drink, wear, what houses they shall have, books or newspapers rather, they shall read, down to the very days on which they shall take their holidays like a drove of cattle driven out from the stable to graze." The play's two acts are divided into twenty-nine scenes, with the first scene set in the interior of Durham cathedral, 1926. In the published version there is a note for the producer and actor to the effect that the cathedral scenes could cause the play to fail if they are played heavily: "Innocence, gaiety and a touch of lunacy is their atmosphere." An exchange of dialogue in the first minutes may show what Wesker intends. A young man, Andrew Cobham, the central character, looks at the majesty of the cathedral and declares: "Give me wings and I'll build you a city." A young woman, Jessie, enters:

> ANDY: For one man, Jessie, a cathedral is built for one man.
> JESSIE: Do you talk to yourself ?
> ANDY: Every man should have a cathedral in his back garden.
> JESSIE: I've never heard you talk to yourself.
> ANDY: Look at the way that roof soars.
> JESSIE: Talk to yourself and you'll go mad.
> ANDY: Doesn't it make you love yourself ?
> JESSIE: "Those whom the gods wish to destroy they first turn mad."
> ANDY: When a man loves himself he loves the world. Listen. (Music swells). I reckon the gods touch composers with a fever every night. I bet Bach got to heaven before Shakespeare. Look. (Sunlight strikes through the coloured glass). Jessie, if you'll marry me I'll build you a house that soars—like this cathedral. And you, you'll give me six beautiful children, and they'll soar, mad, like that roof there. How's that?
> JESSIE: The gods'll destroy you, that's for sure.
> ANDY: Today, Jessie, I know, I know. I know everything I want to do with my life.

From this opening the play proceeds by a series of what Wesker calls "flash-forwards," as opposed to flashbacks. Glenda Leeming and Simon Trussler see in the progress of Andrew Cobham something that is akin to the career of Solness in Ibsen's *The Master Builder* (1892). Solness begins by building churches, moves to building homes for human beings, and finishes (and is finished by) building dwellings that have a churchlike quality. Andrew Cobham takes a shorter course that is at the same time more ambitious. After first dreaming of building a cathedral, his goal is to build a group of golden cities. Only one city is built, and the total result, as often in Wesker, is Cobham's disappointment and frustration. The obstacles he meets on the way are recognizable reminders of the fate of left-wing movements.

Latham, an old trade-union leader clearly based on the former Labour leader George Lansbury, makes a highly idealistic speech (taken from Lansbury's actual words at a party conference) that ends with the words "I want to say this, defeat doesn't matter. In the long run, all defeat is temporary. It doesn't matter about present generations, but future ones always want to look back and know that someone was around acting on their beliefs." He declares himself ready to die for his beliefs if it should be necessary. In the debate at the party conference where Lansbury made this idealistic utterance, Ernest Bevin defeated him. In the play, Andy Cobham is Bevin to Latham's Lansbury, saying, "if you want Jake Latham to become a saint then let me make it easier for you by lighting the faggots for his martyrdom." The act ends with Cobham's return to the cathedral, where he assumes once again a "mood of prophecy and catechism" and cries that the people will be proud. " 'Build us cities,' they'll say, they'll command. 'Build us cities of light.' "

Wesker told Hayman that he was trying by means of the flash-forward "to keep us in a present in which there is still hope," and he wished it to be understood that there was nothing of fantasy about the flash-forwards; they were reality. He went on to say that: "what the play is about is the spirit of the City, the relationships people have with each other which I see through the relationships people have with their work. Whether they're owning it or not. You know, the spirit of cooperation. This has failed and that's what's important and I spend much more time lamenting that than having them pat themselves on the back because they've built a beautiful city." Wesker seems to have put into this play much of his own experi-

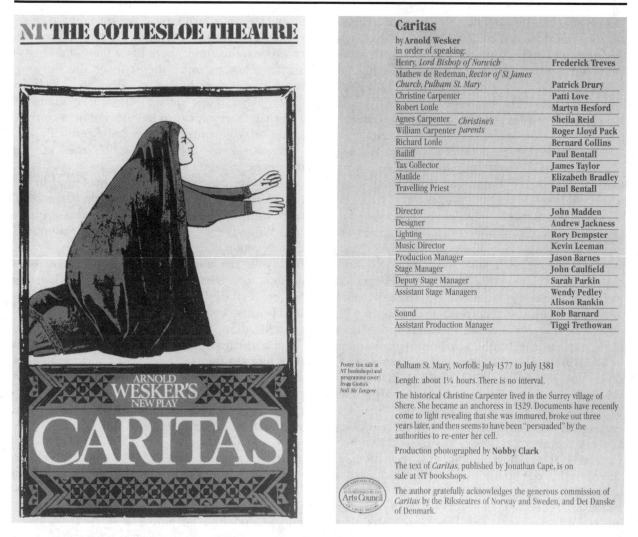

NT THE COTTESLOE THEATRE

ARNOLD WESKER'S NEW PLAY

CARITAS

Caritas

by **Arnold Wesker**

in order of speaking:

Henry, *Lord Bishop of Norwich*	**Frederick Treves**
Mathew de Redeman, *Rector of St James Church, Pulham St. Mary*	**Patrick Drury**
Christine Carpenter	**Patti Love**
Robert Lonle	**Martyn Hesford**
Agnes Carpenter *Christine's*	**Sheila Reid**
William Carpenter *parents*	**Roger Lloyd Pack**
Richard Lonle	**Bernard Collins**
Bailiff	**Paul Bentall**
Tax Collector	**James Taylor**
Matilde	**Elizabeth Bradley**
Travelling Priest	**Paul Bentall**
Director	**John Madden**
Designer	**Andrew Jackness**
Lighting	**Rory Dempster**
Music Director	**Kevin Leeman**
Production Manager	**Jason Barnes**
Stage Manager	**John Caulfield**
Deputy Stage Manager	**Sarah Parkin**
Assistant Stage Managers	**Wendy Pedley**
	Alison Rankin
Sound	**Rob Barnard**
Assistant Production Manager	**Tiggi Trethowan**

Poster (on sale at NT bookshops) and programme cover: from Giotto's *Noli Me Tangere*

Pulham St. Mary, Norfolk: July 1377 to July 1381

Length: about 1¼ hours. There is no interval.

The historical Christine Carpenter lived in the Surrey village of Shere. She became an anchoress in 1329. Documents have recently come to light revealing that she was immured, broke out three years later, and then seems to have been "persuaded" by the authorities to re-enter her cell.

Production photographed by **Nobby Clark**

The text of *Caritas*, published by Jonathan Cape, is on sale at NT bookshops.

The author gratefully acknowledges the generous commission of *Caritas* by the Riksteatres of Norway and Sweden, and Det Danske of Denmark.

Program cover, cast list, and production note for Wesker's 1980 play, his second to be produced by the National Theatre

ence and feelings about the Centre 42 struggles. The play is, yet again, a flawed piece, and admiration for the author's motives was matched by sympathy for his inability to find an adequate and convincing means of portraying in dramatic form the aspirations and ambitions that he obviously felt.

It was surprising that the play which he began to write after he had made his first drafts of *Their Very Own and Golden City* and which he finished before it was so different. *The Four Seasons* is not only unlike *Their Very Own and Golden City* but unlike all that Wesker had written before. Begun in May 1964 and finished in 1965, *The Four Seasons* was first staged at the Belgrade, Coventry, in August 1965. It transferred to the Saville Theatre in the West End of London in September 1965. In this play Wesker set himself to write an allegory of love. There are only two char-

acters, Adam and Beatrice, the names seemingly chosen to suggest that the subject of the play is man and his beloved. The hint was hardly needed. It is clear from the beginning that, even if Adam and Beatrice are, in some ways, related to Ronnie Kahn and Beatie Bryant, they are worlds away from the East End and Norfolk in space and time. *The Four Seasons* sets out to present the experience of love, uncluttered by the usual appurtenances of story, families, and a recognizable contemporary setting.

As the curtain goes up, two people, whom the stage directions describe as between thirty and thirty-five, are entering a deserted house. They have their belongings with them and are obviously setting up home together. It gradually emerges that they are both escaping from previous unions. He has had a wife; she looks back on failures with a husband and a lover. The play passes at a gentle pace, as the seasons change and the two discuss their love. While he is asleep, she decorates him from head to foot with bluebells and declares, leaping up and shouting, "I HAVE A GOLDEN EAGLE FOR A LOVER!" There are also tiffs and even quarrels. At one stage, Adam decides to make apple strudel, an important and even sacramental act. In the published play Wesker says, "actors learn to fence—why not to cook?" and ends the notes by saying that "advice should be sought from a high-class pastry-cook."

Ronald Bryden, reviewing a preview in Golders Green, a London suburb with a large German and Jewish population, for the *New Statesman* (17 September 1965), was pleased to note that Adam's making apple strudel was greeted with "justifiable applause." He praised this action as a piece of theater that could be compared with other visual and nonverbal incidents in Wesker's plays, such as the frantic activities of the waiters in *The Kitchen* and the coke-stealing operation in *Chips with Everything*, but he added that it was "also the evening's first and only touch of reality." He asked why Wesker, whose particular talents lay in other directions, should have chosen to write a study of an abstract, idealized, and universalized love affair, calling *The Four Seasons* "highfalutin, essentially non-verbal kitsch." In a later notice, he suggested that it would be best to forget *The Four Seasons* and to wait for the first English production of *Their Very Own and Golden City*.

The Friends (1970), Wesker's first play of the 1970s, is less pretentious than either *Their Very Own and Golden City* or *The Four Seasons*. Nevertheless, it seems that once again Wesker is trying to say something for which he has not the essential equipment. If, in *The Four Seasons*, he was trying to write poetic prose on the subject of love, he is trying this time to write poetic prose on the subject of death. Wisely, he has not sought to express his ideas in such a vague and imprecise way as in *The Four Seasons*.

In *The Friends* the central character, Esther, is dying of leukemia. The friends are all associated in various ways with the business of interior decorating. They are thus concerned with aesthetic values, and, because they are all, in one way or another, "intellectuals," the conversation takes in many aspects of life—and death. Because there are seven characters as compared with two, the play seems to present less disembodied speculation than *The Four Seasons*. Although *The Friends*

is not free from such typical Wesker faults as overwriting and diffuseness when he has nothing direct to say, the atmosphere has a faint and satisfying Chekhovian tone; the style of the opening scene is clearly modeled on Chekhov's style in such a play as *Three Sisters* (1901) where often several characters appear to be carrying on a conversation at cross purposes and only gradually can some sense of orchestration of the various themes be appreciated.

Wesker has nothing new or profound to say on the subject of death itself, but the characters' consciousness of the passage of the years is effective. While their object in life is the creation and dissemination of beautiful things and the idea of beauty in the abstract, they have only to look around to realize that success in this is hard to achieve. Esther speaks for all of them: "Some people of course know that when they're old they'll become tired and ready to go; or else they grow to despise themselves so much for not being what they thought they were that they become anxious and eager to fade out. Not me, though. Just not me. I can't tell you how much I cherish everything. I know there's a lot that's obscene and ugly but it's never been too oppressive, I've always had the capacity not to be oppressed. . . . Every year the world finds something new to offer me: another man makes music or carves an impossible shape out of the rocks or sings us a poem. Someone is always rising up, taking wing, and behind him he pulls the rest of us; and I want to be there, for every movement, every sound. Why should I want to die away from all that?" In the middle of the play, Esther dies, and the second act consists of reactions to the fact of her death.

Macey, the fifty-five-year-old manager of the main shop in the interior decorator's business, speaks in condemnation of the "swinging" attitude of a few years previously: "Esther was the only healthy one of the lot of you. Just let the press get pictures of you all now. That'd be a scoop. 'The Trend-makers'! Huh! The habit of discontent was all your lot ever created. . . . You never thought you'd grow old or die. Even the politicians and the poets were frightened of you, you screamed so loudly about your squalid backgrounds." Macey also addresses the question of whether "the people" can appreciate art: "if bourgeois values were only decadent and working-class values were only beautiful, then what were you complaining about in the first place? One minute you claim the need for revolution because inequality has left the people ignorant and the next minute you claim you want to do nothing but what the people want. But why should you want to do that which an ignorant people want? What kind of logic is that?" A young girl, Simone, responds that a work of art is still a work of art even if it is the product of an unjust society. She declares that she stands for "liberty and love and the sharing between all men of the good things this good earth and man's ingenuity can give," and in the last moments of the play, she calls Esther's desire to live a sign of affirmation.

While Benedict Nightingale may have been right when he said in the *New Statesman* (29 May 1970) that it was possible to admire Wesker's ideas without being sure that he had made them arresting and exciting in dialogue and physical action, it is also possible to praise Wesker for showing readiness to try new approaches. Wesker, with the disappointments of Centre 42 behind him and some failures among his recent plays, was in a barren land with no clear idea in which direction to turn. It might be remembered also that the wilderness can be a place for constructive meditation. *The Friends* may be an example of the play of meditation rather than of action.

A later play, *Love Letters on Blue Paper*, is similar in theme to *The Friends*. Originating as a short story published in 1974, *Love Letters on Blue Paper* was then adapted for television before being made into a stageplay, which was first produced in Syracuse, New York, on 14 October 1977. Its British premiere was at the small Cottesloe Theatre of the National Theatre on 15 February 1978. The play, slighter than *The Friends*, has as its central figure Victor, a retired Yorkshire trade-union official who is dying of cancer. The other main characters are Victor's wife, Sonia, and a friend and confidant, Maurice, who seeks to comfort Victor. In the end, however, Victor is the stronger character, and Maurice is overcome by grief.

Possibly because the play was not conceived for the stage originally, Wesker makes use of a somewhat clumsy device. During the play, recordings of Sonia's letters to Victor, written at various times during their life together, are played over loudspeakers that have been placed around the theater. Wesker intended that this device should "give the effect of Sonia's voice speaking gently to each member of the audience," but it seems a sad example of modern technology being used for its own sake. The atmosphere of *Love Letters*

on Blue Paper is more intimate and personal than that of *The Friends*. There are moments of tenderness and moments of mawkish sentiment. The play does little more, perhaps, than give Wesker another opportunity to assert his beliefs in love and art, and, through the mouths of Victor and a young trade-union interviewer (who appears onstage only briefly), to express a firm contempt for the trade-union leaders who have adopted the capitalist values and way of life that they profess to oppose and despise, and, what is worse, for which they seem to have won the approbation of their supporters for this development.

During the 1970s Wesker continued to write plays with unabated energy, but none of them achieved any great success, although his work was gradually being recognized more favorably in non-English-speaking countries such as Sweden, Norway, Germany, and Spain. *The Old Ones*, which was presented at the Royal Court on 8 August 1972, was produced in Munich the following year, and a workshop production was well received off-Broadway in New York in 1974. This play, which captures much of the warmth, the humor, and the cadences of speech of Wesker's earlier East End plays, is defined by Wesker as "essentially about defiant old age." There is little overt political or social comment, but the attitudes of the characters, the great majority of them elderly and Jewish, reflect a lifetime of struggle. Wesker seems to be seeking what is fundamental in life, but, admirable as his efforts may be, they tend to rob the play of any solid dramatic qualities.

The Wedding Feast, which was first seen in Stockholm at the Stadtsteater in May 1974, was extensively revised for its first British presentation at the Leeds Playhouse on 20 January 1977. Based on "An Unpleasant Predicament," a short story by Fyodor Dostoyevski, *The Wedding Feast* focuses on Louis Litvanov, a shoe manufacturer in Norwich who adopts a kindly, paternalistic policy toward his employees. Because he has always acceded to his staff's requests for benefits, he believes that he has built up a happy as well as a successful working group, but when he attends the wedding party of one of his staff, he finds that, fundamentally, he is considered not a friend but an employer. Less sentimental than many Wesker plays, *The Wedding Feast* has an almost explicit Marxist moral: there is a gulf between employer and workers that cannot be bridged, however clearly the employer bears his own peasant origins in mind and however kindly he behaves. A true relationship can only exist when there is true cooperation, which must spring from a real sharing of power and profits.

The next Wesker play to be produced is also an adaptation. *The Merchant*, a new version of Shakespeare's *The Merchant of Venice*, had its first performance at the Royal Dramatenteater in Stockholm on 8 October 1976, its first production in English at the Plymouth Theatre in New York on 15 November 1977, and its British premiere at the Birmingham Repertory Theatre on 12 October 1978. Each of the productions was of a different version of the play, suggesting that Wesker had some difficulty in finding what exactly it was that he had to say. The published text, presumably the one with which he is most satisfied, emphasizes that Portia is a "new woman" and that Shylock is prepared to respect the law, even though his books, together with all his other goods, must be forfeited at the end of the trial. Insisting that "I do not want the law departed from, not one letter departed from," he decides, "Perhaps now is the time to make that journey to Jerusalem. Join those other old men on the quayside, waiting to make a pilgrimage, to be buried there—ach! What do I care! My heart will not follow me, wherever it is. My appetites are dying, dear friend, for anything in this world. I am so tired of men." Shylock's frustration and bitterness are contrasted by Portia's hopes for the future: "I'll fill my house with poets and philosophers, and politicians who are poets and philosophers. Bassanio will come to know his place, accept it, or leave it. I am to be reckoned with, you know, not merely dutiful. Although, something in me has died struggling to grow up." Wesker's own mood is expressed by Portia.

One of Wesker's most recent works, *The Journalists*, returns to the style of *The Kitchen* as it tries to reproduce in dramatic form the actual rhythms of men and women at work. To obtain the necessary experience and background material, Wesker was allowed to spend about two months studying at close quarters all the departments of the *Sunday Times*. The play, for which a term such as *stage documentary* might be more accurate, is described in a publisher's note as "a fictional, dramatic account of the workings of a present-day Sunday newspaper." In his own introduction, Wesker declares: "*The Kitchen* is not about cooking, it's about man and his relationship to work. *The Journalists* is not about journalism, it is about the poisonous human need to cut better men down to our size, from which need

we all suffer in varying degrees. To identify and isolate this need is important because it corrupts such necessary or serious human activities as government, love, revolution or journalism." While the play is a long and shapeless piece, the series of scenes does contribute to a vivid impression of the gradual crescendo in the production of a weekly newspaper, from the leisurely preparation of the features and articles that can be written in advance to the speedy composition of the final pages, which have to be up-to-the-minute. *The Journalists* was given a reading by professional actors in suburban London on 13 July 1975. It has since been produced as a radio play in France and as a television play in Yugoslavia. The first stage production of the play was by amateurs at the Criterion Theatre in Coventry on 27 March 1977, and it received a workshop production in June 1979 at the Back Alley Theatre in Burbank, California.

Wesker's work has been honored worldwide. In 1964 *Their Very Own and Golden City* was awarded the Italian Premio Marzotto drama prize, and in 1973 *The Kitchen* won a Critic's Gold Medal Award in Spain. Wesker received another award in Spain in 1979, when *Chicken Soup with Barley* was awarded "El Espectador y La Critica" prize for the best foreign play performed by the National Theatre in Madrid. During the 1970s the sales of *The Wesker Trilogy* passed half a million, and Wesker has written a film version of the trilogy, for which a producer has not yet been found. As chairman of the British Centre of the International Theatre Institute and president of the Permanent Committee of Playwrights set up under the central office of the institute, Wesker concerns himself closely with the interests of the drama and dramatists, but he has not turned away from his own creative work. In January 1980 the Rikstheaters (touring theaters) of Norway and Sweden and Det Danske of Denmark gave Wesker a commission of about nine thousand pounds for *Caritas*, which is about a young anchoress in the fourteenth century. The play was produced at the Cottesloe Theatre in London in October 1981.

During the 1980s, while Wesker did not write anything to compare with the more important of his earlier works, he was far from idle. He wrote full-length plays, several plays for radio and television, and a few to be performed in schools, as well as a community play "for a cast of hundreds." In addition, he wrote a group of one-woman plays in which he experimented with work for one performer. He emphasized that these are plays, not mere monologues, and drew an analogy with musical pieces for the solo instrument. Few of his recent plays have been presented in the commercial theater. Yet his work has become widely known and popular in other media. Many of his plays, the short as well as the longer, have been presented on radio and television in France, Germany, Sweden, Denmark, and Japan, as well as in English-speaking countries.

It may be surprising that Wesker produced no work in the 1980s with the strong political note that was dominant in such earlier plays as the *Trilogy* and *Chips with Everything*. During that period, reaction against the aggressive conservatism of the Margaret Thatcher regime stimulated playwrights such as David Hare, Howard Brenton, David Edgar, and Caryl Churchill to write in expressed or implied political terms critical of the values of the government in which they have seen predominantly greedy and selfish motives. It would not have been strange if Wesker had been found in this company, but he has appeared to have been going through a fallow period.

Wesker asserted in 1959 that he did not write *Chicken Soup with Barley* simply because he wanted to amuse people with "working-class types" but because he had a personal vision. In one of his unpublished lectures some years later (referred to in *Wesker on File*, edited by Glenda Leeming, 1985), he declared that he was "of the school which begins with experience rather than ideas." By this time he had established himself, and Leeming and Trussler comment in *The Plays of Arnold Wesker: An Assessment* (1971) that "alike as dramatist and humanist, in concern for local colour and universal truth, he is an Ibsen of our times—not least in determining to write as the times require, not as they or even his own inclinations entirely dictate."

It may seem farfetched to liken Wesker to Ibsen, except insofar as no twentieth-century playwright can fail to be influenced by Ibsen to some extent, particularly if one is keenly sensitive to societal developments. Some critics, swayed perhaps by an inability to come to terms with Wesker's left-wing political stance, have praised his skill as a writer while regretting that this has been impaired by the strength of his political opinions. The same could be said of any writer on political themes if the critic did not happen to agree with him. What is important is whether the writer has

found the most effective way of presenting his vision, political or otherwise, in dramatic form. If Wesker finds the best way in which to body forth the experience and the passionate convictions that have grown from that experience, it will worry only the most bigoted of critics that he is writing from a view of life and society that differs from theirs. In an interview with Ronald Hayman (1970), Wesker says that in the theater "we want to be able to feel that here is a man carving some shape out of his experience." If Wesker has failed to reach the achievements of which, at his best, he has seemed capable, it is because he has not found the right shape and not merely because of the particular direction of his political convictions.

To some extent, Wesker may have lacked the detachment that, in T. S. Eliot's formulation, should separate the man who suffers from the man who creates. If this obstacle is overcome, those who admire Wesker most will still think that his response to modern problems and his command of twentieth-century speech rhythms will bring him even greater success.

References:

Kingsley Amis, "Not Talking about Jerusalem," in his *What Became of Jane Austen? and Other Questions* (London: Cape, 1970; London & New York: Penguin, 1981);

John Russell Brown, *Theatre Language: A Study of Arden, Osborne, Pinter and Wesker* (London: Allen Lane, 1972), pp. 159-189;

J. Chiari, *Landmarks of Contemporary Drama* (London: Jenkins, 1965), pp. 115-118;

Bamber Gascoigne, *Twentieth Century Drama* (London: Hutchinson, 1962), pp. 176-208;

Ronald Hayman, *Arnold Wesker* (London: Heinemann, 1970);

Glenda Leeming, ed., *Wesker on File* (London & New York: Methuen, 1985);

Leeming and Simon Trussler, *The Plays of Arnold Wesker: An Assessment* (London: Gollancz, 1971);

Allardyce Nicoll, *English Drama: A Modern Viewpoint* (London: Harrap, 1968), pp. 126-149;

Harold U. Ribalow, *Arnold Wesker* (New York: Twayne, 1966);

John Russell Taylor, *Anger and After* (London: Methuen, 1962), pp. 143-158;

Kenneth Tynan, *Tynan Right and Left* (London: Longmans, Green, 1967; New York: Atheneum, 1967).

Cumulative Index to
Volumes 1-8

Cumulative Index

This index includes proper names (people, places, and works) mentioned in the texts of entries for Volumes 1-8 of the *Concise Dictionary of British Literary Biography*. The primary checklists, which appear at the beginning of each entry, are not included in this index. Also omitted are the names London and Dublin, because they appear so frequently.

A.B.C. Murders, The (Christie), VI: 78, 79, 82

A. E. H.: Some Poems, Some Letters, And A Personal Memoir (L. Housman), V: 220

A la recherche du temps perdu (Proust), II: 500; VII: 20, 330; VIII: 278, 334

À Rebours (Huysmans), V: 345, 348

Aaron, Jane, III: 305, 309, 310, 311

"Aaron" (Herbert), I: 143

Aaron's Rod (Lawrence), VI: 166, 259, 260

ABBA ABBA (Burgess), VIII: 26, 30

Abbess of Crewe, The (Spark), VII: 345

Abbey, Richard, III: 247, 248, 249, 262

Abbey School, III: 8

Abbot, The (Scott), III: 331

Abbott, Charles, VI: 451

Abbott, Claude Colleer, II: 48

Abelard, Pierre, II: 341

Abenteuer G.m.B.H., Die (film), VI: 80

Abercrombie, Lascelles, VI: 36, 39; VII: 372

Aberdaron, Gwynedd, Wales, VIII: 396

Aberdeen, Scotland, III: 98; VIII: 73

Aberdeen University, II: 250, 252, 429; V: 278

Abîmes, Les (Clouët), IV: 390

Abinger Hammer, Surrey, England, VI: 146, 148, 149

Abinger Harvest (Forster), VI: 147, 148

Abington, Frances, II: 412

Abolition of Man, The (C. S. Lewis), VII: 183, 187

About the House (Auden), VI: 27

Absalom and Achitophel (Dryden), II: 122, 130, 133, 134, 135, 137, 138, 254, 276

Absent Man, The (Smollett), II: 434

"Absent-minded Beggar, The" (Kipling), V: 249

"Absentee, The" (Edgeworth), III: 327

"Abt Vogler" (R. Browning), IV: 104

Abuses of Conscience, The (Sterne), II: 476

Académie Française, II: 237

Academy (periodical), IV: 334, 350; V: 23, 48, 66, 185; VI: 59, 60, 276

Academy and Literature (see *Academy*), VI: 60

Academy Antique School, IV: 342

Accademia della Crusca, II: 237, 238

Acceptance World, The (Powell), VII: 256, 263, 367

Accident (film), VIII: 334

Accidental Man, An (Murdoch), VIII: 271, 278

Account of Corsica, An (Boswell), II: 32, 33, 40

Account of the Casualty Department, An (Bridges), V: 33

Account of the Growth of Popery, An (Marvell), II: 263, 277

Account of the Seminary that will be opened on Monday the Fourth Day of August, at Epsom in Surrey, for the Instruction of Twelve Pupils in the Greek, Latin, French, and English Languages (Godwin), III: 233

Achilles in Scyros (Bridges), V: 39, 41

Ackerly, J. R., VI: 142, 148, 151

Ackroyd, Tabitha, IV: 32

Acland, Henry, IV: 380

"Acre of Grass, An" (Yeats), V: 404

Acre of Land, An (R. S. Thomas), VIII: 396, 398, 399, 401

Across the Plains, with Other Memories and Essays (Stevenson), V: 297

Act of Creation, The (Koestler), VII: 176, 177

Act Without Words I (Beckett), VII: 30

Acte sans paroles I (Beckett), VII: 30

Action Replay (Weldon), VIII: 421

Acton, Harold, VI: 382, 389

Acton, John Emerich Edward Dalberg-Acton, first Baron, IV: 226

"Ad Mariam" (G. M. Hopkins), V: 210

"Ad Patrem" (Milton), II: 284

"Ad Regem Carolum Parodia" (Marvell), II: 262

Adam, Pearl, VII: 287

Adam and Eve Sleeping (Blake), III: 59

Adam Bede (G. Eliot), IV: 184, 193, 194, 195, 197, 198, 200, 201, 207; V: 172, 217

Adam in Moonshine (Priestley), VI: 323, 326

"Adam's Curse" (Yeats), V: 369, 395

Adams, Henry, IV: 389; V: 242

Adams, Maude, V: 7, 9

Adams, Percy G., II: 514

Adams, Phoebe, VII: 344

Adams, Polly, VI: 92, 94

Adams, Reverend William, II: 38, 40

Adderley, Sir Charles, IV: 16

Addison, Charlotte, II: 25

Addison, Charlotte Myddleton Rich, II: 25, 26

Addison, Joseph, II: 3-28, 160, 166, 189, 207, 228, 241, 254, 313, 337, 342, 343, 348, 360, 362, 457, 462, 464, 465, 466, 470, 471, 472, 508, 531; III: 8, 235, 298, 305, 326, 327; IV: 23, 165, 238, 451, 460; VI: 56

Addison, Lancelot, II: 6

"Address to the Deil" (Burns), III: 77

Address to the People on the Death of Princess Charlotte, An (P. Shelley), III: 365

Address to the Public, An (Richardson), II: 393

Address to the Swindon Branch of the Workers' Educational Association (Bridges), V: 48

"Address to the Tooth-Ache" (Burns), III: 88

Address, to the Irish People, An (P. Shelley), III: 359

"Addressed to the Same [Haydon]" (Keats), III: 256

Ade, George, VI: 426

Adelphi (periodical), VII: 371

"Adjustments" (R. S. Thomas), VIII: 404

Gore-Booth, Constance, Countess Markiewicz, V: 377
Gorges, Arthur, I: 379
Goring-on-Thames, England, V: 349
Gorky, Maxim, VI: 412, 417, 418; VIII: 147
Gorsas, Antoine Joseph, III: 411
Gort, Ireland, V: 365, 367, 369
Goslar, Germany, III: 415
Gospel of the Brothers Barnabas, The (Shaw), VI: 361
Gosse, Sir Edmund, III: 269, 286; IV: 233, 337, 339, 385, 388, 389, 396, 400, 425; V: 72, 156, 179, 180, 237, 242, 297, 373; VI: 60
Gosson, Stephen, I: 347
Gottschalk, Laura Riding (see Jackson, Laura Riding)
Gould, F. Carruthers, V: 282
Gould, Sir Henry, II: 155, 167, 172
Gould, Nat, VIII: 109
Gould, Stephen Jay, III: 305
Goulden, Mark, VII: 371
Goulding, Edmund, VI: 427
Gounod, Charles-François, I: 257
Gourmont, Remy de, V: 346
Gower, George, I: 373
Gower, John, I: 58, 66, 286, 323
Gownsman (periodical), IV: 432, 433
Goya, Francisco, VII: 325
Gozzoli, Benozzo, IV: 343
"Grace" (Joyce), VI: 212, 214
"Grace" (Sterne), II: 498
Grace Abounding to the Chief of Sinners (Bunyan), II: 56, 57, 58, 59, 60
Grace Before Ploughing: Fragments of Autobiography (Masefield), V: 279
Graham, John W., VI: 447
Graham, William, IV: 352
Graham of Claverhouse, John, IV: 245, 247
Grahame, Kenneth, IV: 115
"Grammar Lecture" (Beaumont), I: 22
Grammar of General Geography (Goldsmith), IV: 33
Grand Babylon Hotel, The (Bennett), V: 23, 28
Grand Hotel (Baum), V: 28, 29
"Grand Oul' Dame Brittania, The" (O'Casey), VI: 287, 288
"Grandame, The" (C. Lamb), III: 289
Granite and Rainbow (Woolf), VI: 447
Grant, Duncan, VI: 127, 435, 437, 439
Grant Richards (publishing house), V: 263
Granta (periodical), VIII: 129
Grantchester, England, VI: 40
Graphic (periodical), IV: 479, 485, 489; V: 184

Grasmere, England, III: 189, 206, 207, 208, 211, 213, 294, 420, 421, 433
Grass Is Singing, The (Lessing), VIII: 230, 231, 232
Grasse, France, VI: 416
"Gratitude to the Unknown Instructors" (Yeats), V: 383
Grattan, Henry, V: 390, 392
"Grauballe Man, The" (Heaney), VIII: 153
Grave, The (R. Blair), III: 64
"Grave of the Hundred Head, The" (Kipling), V: 238
"Grave Unvisited, A" (R. S. Thomas), VIII: 402
"Grave-Digger, The" (M. Hopkins), V: 197
Graves, Alfred Perceval, VI: 160
Graves, Amalie von Ranke, VI: 160, 161
Graves, Beryl Hodge, VI: 184
Graves, Caroline, IV: 138
Graves, Catherine, VI: 169
Graves, David, VI: 169, 176
Graves, Jenny, VI: 169
Graves, Juan, VI: 176
Graves, Lawrence, VII: 345
Graves, Lizzie, IV: 138
Graves, Lucia, VI: 176
Graves, Robert, VI: 36, 155-185, 308, 311, 440; VII: 136, 160, 362; VIII: 130, 262, 358, 362
Graves, Sam, VI: 169
Graves, Thomas, VI: 176
Graves, William, VI: 176
Graveyard by the Sea, The (Valery), VIII: 280
Gray, Dorothy Antrobus, II: 209
Gray, Paul, VII: 32
Gray, Philip, II: 209
Gray, Samuel, II: 24
Gray, Simon, VII: 252
Gray, Simon, VIII: 334
Gray, Thomas, II: 32, 187, 209-223, 254; III: 8, 51, 77, 89, 100, 168, 170, 182, 409; IV: 24; V: 48, 175; VIII: 135
Gray's Inn, London, I: 7, 22, 50
Great Adventure, The (Bennett), V: 26
Great Boer War, The (Doyle), V: 137
Great Contemporaries (Churchill), V: 80, 81
Great Divorce, The (C. S. Lewis), VII: 184, 186
Great Expectations (Dickens), IV: 153, 171, 176, 178, 203; VI: 431; VIII: 91, 279
Great Favourite; or, The Duke of Lerna (Dryden), II: 127
Great Fawley, Berkshire, England, V: 187

Great Gatsby, The (Fitzgerald), VI: 227
Great Hampden, Buckinghamshire, England, V: 266, 267, 268, 269
"Great Hunger, The" (Heaney), VIII: 145
"Great Lover, The" (Brooke), VI: 39
Great Missenden, Buckinghamshire, England, VIII: 214
Great Shadow, The (Doyle), V: 132
"Great spirits now on earth are sojourning" (Keats), III: 262
Great Trade Route (Ford), VI: 121
Great Tradition, The (Leavis), II: 500; IV: 184; VII: 321
Great War and Modern Memory, The (Fussell), VI: 165
"Great Wheel, The" (Yeats), V: 396
Greater Hampstead, England, V: 272
"Great-Grandmother, The" (Graves), VI: 173
Greaves, John, IV: 163
Grecian History, from the Earliest State to the Death of Alexander the Great (Goldsmith),II: 205
Greek Anthology, The I: 150
"Greek Interpreter, The" (Doyle), V: 135
Greek Myths, The (Graves), VI: 159
Greek Studies (Pater), IV: 336
Green, Benny, VI: 97
Green, Eleanor, V: 24
Green, Jane, II: 405
Green, Jullian, V: 24
Green Carnation, The (Hichens), V: 351
"Green Categories" (R. S. Thomas), VIII: 400
Green Chartreuse (periodical), VI: 159
Green Crow, The (O'Casey), VI: 296, 301
Green Flag and Other Stories of War and Sport, The (Doyle), V: 135
Green Helmet and Other Poems, The (Yeats), V: 371
Green Man, The (Amis), VII: 11, 13
Green Mansions (Hudson), V: 166
Greenberg, Herbert, VI: 32
Greene, Benjamin, II: 302
Greene, Charles Henry, VII: 136
Greene, Graham, III: 285; IV: 180; V: 85; VII: 395; VII: 97, 132-158, 264, 333; VIII: 37, 42, 212, 215, 216, 265
Greene, Guy, VIII: 90
Greene, Marion R., VII: 136
Greene, Richard, I: 254
Greene, Robert, I: 93, 261, 267, 284, 324, 412
Greene, Vivien Dayrell-Browning, VII: 139
Greene's Groatsworth of Wit (Greene), I: 261, 267
"Greensleeves" (anon.), VIII: 49

Cumulative Index of Author Entries for Concise Dictionary of British Literary Biography

Cumulative Index
of Author Entries

ISBN 0-8103-7988-0

90000>

EAN

9 780810 379886